Financial and M t Information

Sheffield Hallam University

CUSTOM
CENGAGE Learning

Australia • Brazil • Japan • Korea • Mexico • Singapore • Spain • United Kingdom • United States

CUSTOM
CENGAGE Learning

Financial and Management Information 3e, Custom Edition
Oz, Jones and Gowthorpe

Publishing Director: Linden Harris

Custom Solutions Manager: Jeni Evans

Custom Editor: Isabel Florence

Production Editor – Custom Lead: Alison Cooke

Production Controller: Eyvett Davis

British Library Cataloguing-in-Publication Data
A catalogue record for this book is available from the British Library.

ISBN: 978-1-4080-7222-6

Cengage Learning EMEA
Cheriton House, North Way, Andover, Hampshire, SP10 5BE, United Kingdom

Cengage Learning products are represented in Canada by Nelson Education Ltd.

For your lifelong learning solutions, visit
www.cengage.co.uk

Purchase your next print book, e-book or e-chapter at
www.cengagebrain.com

MIX
Paper from responsible sources
FSC www.fsc.org FSC® C013056

Printed in in the United Kingdom by TJ International
1 2 3 4 5 6 7 8 9 10 – 14 13 12

Acknowledgements

The content of this text has been adapted from the following product(s):

Business Accounting and Finance, 3e
Gowthorpe (9781408018378)

Management Information Systems,
Oz and Jones (9781844807581)

Full copyright details and acknowledgements will appear in the aforementioned publications.

Table of Contents

BETTER BITES

'Maybe we should start our own business.' As soon as Paul said it, his two friends put down their coffee and stared at him. Paul Clermont, Sarah Odell and Christina Healy were second-year hotel and restaurant management degree students and they were looking over the business and travel news and lamenting the sluggish job outlook in their chosen field. They had always joked about starting a business together, but this time Paul was serious. With few prospects in the job advertisements, the three friends were worried that travel and entertainment wouldn't pick up by the time they graduated. They'd begun their job searches in the autumn but weren't interested in the available positions. So, like many other young people, they considered heading out on their own and becoming entrepreneurs.

'Well, you know that I've always wanted to open a restaurant eventually, Paul,' said Sarah. 'I love being a chef. But aren't we getting ahead of ourselves? How could we get enough cash together to rent a place and staff it? Rental space is really expensive locally and we don't have the funds to pay anyone right now. We still have student loans to pay off when we graduate.'

'What about a pushcart in the university concourse?' suggested Christina. 'We could start small and take turns manning it ourselves. That'd keep our labour costs and store rental low. Besides, you're always complaining about the greasy food at that burger place, Sarah. We could offer better alternatives to burgers and fries. The student concourse has been improved recently with new benches and tables, too. It'd be a perfect spot to open a small lunch business. All we would need is permission from the University Director of Services.'

PHOTO SOURCE: © PYMCA/ALAMY

'We'd still need a business plan to get a loan for start-up,' Paul advised. He was excited about organizing a new firm, but knew they needed a detailed plan. 'We have to think everything through carefully and show people that we know what we're doing, or we'll never get off the ground.'

Sarah laughed. 'You're good with facts and figures,' she said to Paul. 'Must be the business and finance modules you took. With my restaurant management background, I'd love to develop the new menu. That's the fun, creative part of this for me. Christina, you have so many contacts through your student union experience. That could come in handy down the road, don't you think?'

'Looks like we each have some strengths that could help us get started,' observed Christina. 'So, what do you think? Shall we try it?'

The three friends stood up and raised their coffee cups in a formal toast to the new business – Better Bites.

Assessing business needs

When Paul, Sarah and Christina agreed to start their business, they had no clear idea of the amount of work involved. They each had certain skills to contribute – innate skills and skills they had polished in their modules – and they were excited about becoming entrepreneurs. But as they continued to meet to sketch out their plans, they quickly realized they'd need to collect quite a lot of information and allocate responsibilities:

- They needed facts and figures on the local lunch business to draft a business plan.
- They needed to negotiate an agreement with the university to set up their cart and rent the cart itself.
- They needed to ensure that they met health and safety regulations.
- They needed to plan a menu and price items and then track which offerings generated the most revenue.
- They needed to advertise their business and print menus.
- They needed a system to record food inventory, plastic serving utensils, paper wraps and serviettes – both costs and quantities.

Keeping track of so much information could be a headache, but computer systems would provide part of the solution. The three friends had grown up using computers in their classes, surfing the Web for fun and sending emails and instant messages to their families to keep in touch. But this was different. For the first time they were seeing computers as a critical tool for their success. Computer systems could track and store information they collected, help them calculate financial information, create forms and documents and even assist in future planning and forecasting. The entrepreneurs knew they needed to become proficient in information systems so that they could concentrate on their real business – running the lunch cart and attracting customers. They were determined not to take shortcuts and if information systems could help them, they would use them.

Formulating a plan

Paul Clermont had gained some restaurant experience through his family. His uncle owned a small French restaurant in the city that was open for lunch and dinner. Paul thought his uncle might be persuaded to allow the three entrepreneurs to use the kitchen early in the morning to prepare their cold sandwiches – for a small fee. So the three met with Paul's uncle, Philippe, and convinced him that they were serious about their business and would not interfere with his; he was adamant that they had to leave the kitchen spotless and be out of the way by 10.00 each morning. They also agreed on a rental fee to compensate Philippe for use of his facilities.

Sarah and Christina had participated in the University's Future Chefs lunch programme, in which cooking and nutrition students prepared and served hot lunches to paying staff members – to simulate a restaurant experience. Sarah loved selecting main dishes and their accompaniments and hoped some day to become a chef. Christina liked the organizational aspects of planning and wanted to concentrate on management.

Sarah began thinking about Better Bites' menu. She thought that limiting their food to cold sandwiches, drinks and side dishes simplified food preparation and storage – they would only need to keep items cold, not cook them on the spot. She discussed the menu with Paul and Christina and decided that wraps and small side dishes would work well for the cart – they weren't too bulky and would be healthy, lighter alternatives to burgers or pizza, which were sold nearby. Sarah also had heard about a computer application that could track and print calorie and nutritional information; that program would be useful for their menu later.

Christina, with her student union experience, had attended University Council meetings where she had heard of the Business Start-up Scheme. Local venture capitalists would consider loaning funds for small, student-lead enterprises.

Writing a business plan

Once Paul, Sarah and Christina had their initial plans set, they turned to the task of writing a business plan. They knew a business plan would be the key to obtaining the seed capital from the University Business Start-up Scheme. The plan would be scrutinized in every detail to be sure that the three students were worth the risk and were reliable. A good plan would also need to catch the interest of the lender – to generate excitement so that it would stand out from the other loan applicants. So, they began work, fleshing out the sections of the plan to provide an overview of their business.

The Executive Summary provided a general synopsis of who the three entrepreneurs were, what business they planned to start, when they planned to start their operations, why they were qualified to own the business, why there was a need for it and where they planned to place their lunch cart. It also explained their enduring interest in the restaurant industry and their eagerness to bring their ideas to life in the new business.

The Introduction stated the general concept of the business, its purpose and general objectives and gave an overview of the lunch business in the area. They also included general information on their own backgrounds – education, experience and training.

The Marketing section outlined the target market, the business's main competitors and plans for advertising, pricing, food and supply procurement and preparation and location of the pushcart. They also included information and statistics on the growing trend towards more healthy alternatives to fast food and the lack of healthy, organic lunch options near campus. Finally, they mentioned their autumn start-up date, the start of the academic year and how they would then take into account the leaner times during the vacation period. Christina ensured that the fact that the university intended to move towards two-year degrees with teaching over the summer was mentioned in this section.

The Financial section detailed equipment and kitchen rental fees, the pushcart leasing fee, and initial food and supply purchase costs. The partners explained their plan to staff the cart themselves and so avoid additional labour costs. They included a budget forecast, the estimated total lunch business market in the area and the percentage they thought they could capture with their new business, the need for start-up capital and a plan for spending the funds.

The curriculum vitae (CV) section completed the plan, listing all three partners' backgrounds, experiences and references.

Ruth Phillipson from the Business Start-up Scheme reviewed their plan and was impressed with the work the three had done. She met with Paul, Sarah and Christina and discussed their completed business plan. She told them she thought they had provided critical information overall, but she requested more details on foot traffic counts at the student concourse and nearby lunch business competitors to be sure the cart could generate enough customers to be profitable. Also, she asked for more specifics on pricing details versus the competition and the point at which the three projected to break even on their business and begin earning a profit. Those details would help Ruth determine whether the business was a good risk and when the loan would be paid off.

Paul, Sarah and Christina did additional research and recorded the details in the revised plan. Then they provided Ruth with this additional information. Their hard work paid off. The loan was approved – they were in business! The three partners were excited but realized they needed to get started immediately to open their business in only four short months.

Business challenges

In the next three chapters, you will learn what Paul, Sarah and Christina need to know to get started: how to harness information technology to help build and grow their lunch business.

- In Chapter 1, 'Business Information Systems: An Overview', you will learn what your role in information technology might be, which types of information systems you would need whether you are running a large or small business and what information you need, in what form you need it, where you might find it and how to process it. You will also learn what computer-based information tools you need to build a business and some of the major ethical and societal concerns about acquiring, using, storing and reporting potentially sensitive information.
- In Chapter 2, 'Strategic Uses of Information Systems', you will learn how to use information strategically, how to initiate strategic moves and how to deal with competitive challenges.
- In Chapter 3, 'Business Functions and Supply Chains', you will learn how you might best use information technology to help manage a business, whether you need to order inventory and track sales, generate financial statements, or automate payroll systems. You will also learn how all the various business information systems work together.

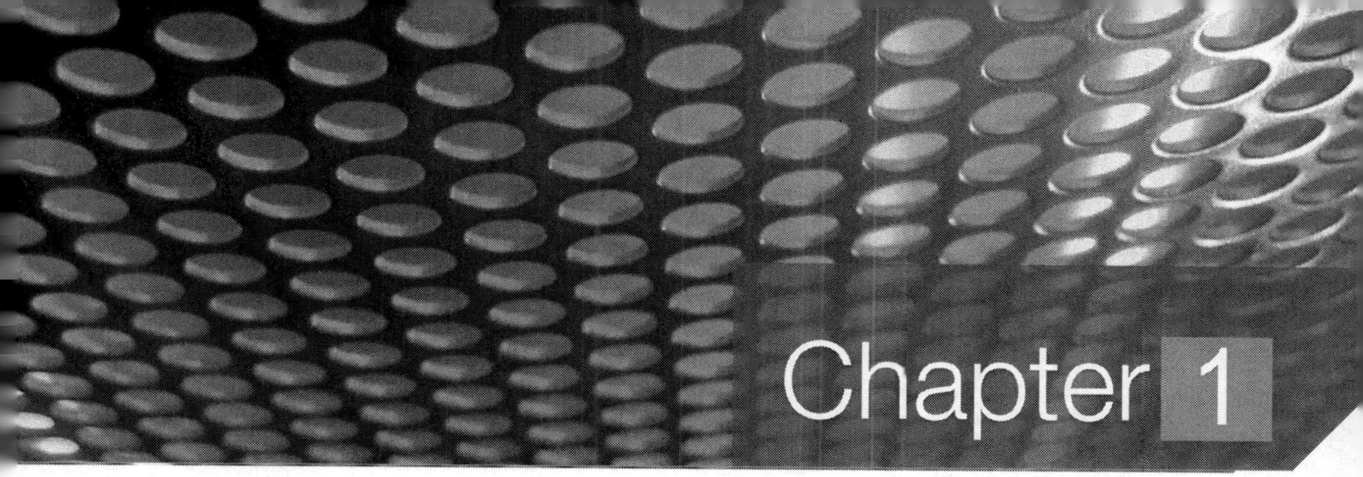

Chapter 1

Business information systems: an overview

LEARNING OBJECTIVES

Information systems pervade almost every aspect of our lives. Whether you are withdrawing money from a bank's ATM or surfing the World Wide Web, hardly a day goes by without our feeding data into, or using information generated by, an information system. In business especially, computer-based information systems generate most of the information we use. These systems have become essential to successful business operations.

When you finish this chapter, you will be able to:

Explain why information systems are essential to business.

Describe how computers process data into useful information for problem-solving and decision-making.

Identify the functions of different types of information systems in business.

Describe careers in information technology.

Identify major ethical and societal concerns created by widespread use of information technology.

BETTER BITES

BUSINESS SYSTEMS AND INFORMATION

Paul Clermont, Sarah Odell and Christina Healy couldn't believe what they had accomplished in the five months since they obtained their small-business loan for their lunch pushcart business, Better Bites. They'd made so many decisions and solved so many problems, it was hard to keep track of them all.

Solving problems and making decisions

Paul rented a pushcart to place in the middle of the student concourse. Christina investigated a new PC, software and printer and the partners selected a desktop system that would fill their current computing needs and still allow for growth. Paul and Sarah worked on the food service side of the business. Paul's uncle, Philippe, had referred them to a food wholesaler who gave them a small discount because he could deliver Better Bites' supplies directly to Paul's uncle's restaurant.

Sarah developed her own recipes for wraps that would offer healthier alternatives to the cheeseburgers and pizza offered locally. She, Christina and Paul arose at dawn three weeks before opening to do practice runs in the kitchen and work out a smooth production process. By the fourth practice run, they thought they had a good system – the wraps and side orders were prepared and packaged for storage in the cart. Best of all, they were out of Philippe Clermont's kitchen by the 10.00 deadline.

Generating business information

Christina and Paul worked up a simple printed menu for the cart and used the calorie-counting application to generate nutrition information for their customers. Key advantages of their food were the freshness of their ingredients and their health-conscious menu, so they made sure the menu highlighted those features. They set prices a bit higher than the burger and pizza places down the street because their ingredients were completely fresh – without preservatives or additives.

Christina designed and arranged for advertisements to run in the university newspaper, both the paper and Web versions, two weeks before they opened for business. She also prepared simple flyers to hand out on campus.

Paul set up Better Bites' computer programs: a word-processing program to create basic business stationery and forms; a spreadsheet to record and track sales and profits; and a database to manage food inventory and supplies.

Managing data

After the business had been operating for a month, sales started to pick up. Whoever was staffing the pushcart wrote out a receipt for all items in an order and placed the receipt in a small plastic folder to be entered into the business's computer later. But as the lunch customers multiplied, Better Bites' owners realized that they were falling behind on their paperwork for the business. It was becoming inefficient to handwrite the many sales receipts and later record them into the spreadsheets.

As the backlog in sales receipts grew, Paul had to spend more and more time on weekends inputting sales data so that they could order supplies from the wholesaler on Mondays. He also was bogged down at the end of the month, when he prepared Better Bites' loan and rental payments and expenses.

Gathering useful information from customers

Sarah noticed that some of the items on the lunch menu sold better than others – the chicken pesto salad was a big hit, but the roast beef sold less

PHOTO SOURCE: © CHRISTINE BALDERAS

well – and she was surprised by the many requests for additional side dishes. And they needed to consider adding some seasonal menu items to keep the customers coming back. Paul, Sarah and Chris needed to consider the costs and profits of adding or dropping menu items, or re-pricing items. Also, several times the partners had had to place emergency calls to restock depleted ingredients and supplies. They had to find a better way to track all the data and forecast their needs so that they wouldn't run short of items or throw away unused ingredients. Dissatisfied customers meant lost sales and fewer profits. So, they thought that they could generate some reports on customer-ordering preferences.

The purpose of information systems

People require information for many reasons and in varied ways. For instance, you probably seek information for entertainment and enlightenment by viewing television, watching films, browsing the Internet, listening to the radio and reading newspapers, magazines and books. In business, however, people and organizations seek and use information specifically to make sound decisions and to solve problems – two closely related practices that form the foundation of every successful company.

What is a problem? A *problem* is any undesirable situation. When you are stuck in the middle of nowhere with a flat tyre, you have a problem. If you know that some customers do not pay their debts on time, but you don't know who or how much they owe, you have a problem. You can solve both problems with the aid of information. In the first case, you can call a breakdown and recovery company, which might use a computerized tracking system to send the breakdown van closest to your location; in the second case, simple accounting software can help.

An organization or individual that finds more than one way to solve a problem or a dilemma must make a *decision*. The problem '2 + 2 = ?' does not require decision-making because it has only one solution. However, as a manager, you might face a dilemma such as 'Which is the best way to promote the company's new car?' There are many potential ways to promote the new car – television advertising, radio advertising, newspaper advertising, Web advertising, car shows, direct mail, or any combination of these methods. This dilemma calls for decision-making.

Both problem-solving and decision-making require information. Gathering the right information efficiently, storing it so that it can be used and manipulated as necessary and using it to help an organization achieve its business goals – all topics covered in this book – are the keys to success in business today. The purpose of information systems is to support these activities. As a future professional, you need to understand and apply these information fundamentals to succeed.

Data, information and information systems

We use the words 'data', 'information' and 'system' almost daily. Understanding what these terms mean, both generally and in the business context, is necessary if you are to use information effectively in your career.

Data vs. information

data Facts about people, other subjects and events. These may be manipulated and processed to produce information.

The terms 'data' and 'information' do not mean the same thing. The word **data** is derived from the Latin *datum*, literally a given or fact, which might take the form

Industry SNAPSHOT

A paperless society?

The Information Age was supposed to reduce the amount of paper that offices use. The emergence of the Web was supposed to reduce paper use even further. As can be seen from the graph in Figure 1.1 this is certainly not the case. About 95 per cent of the world's information is still printed or written on paper. Environmentalists are interested in such figures because a growing percentage of this paper becomes waste.

Electronic storage of data and the electronic display and distribution of information are not a substitute for paper-based media; a business just wants more information to improve business decisions.

Figure 1.1 Co-existence of media

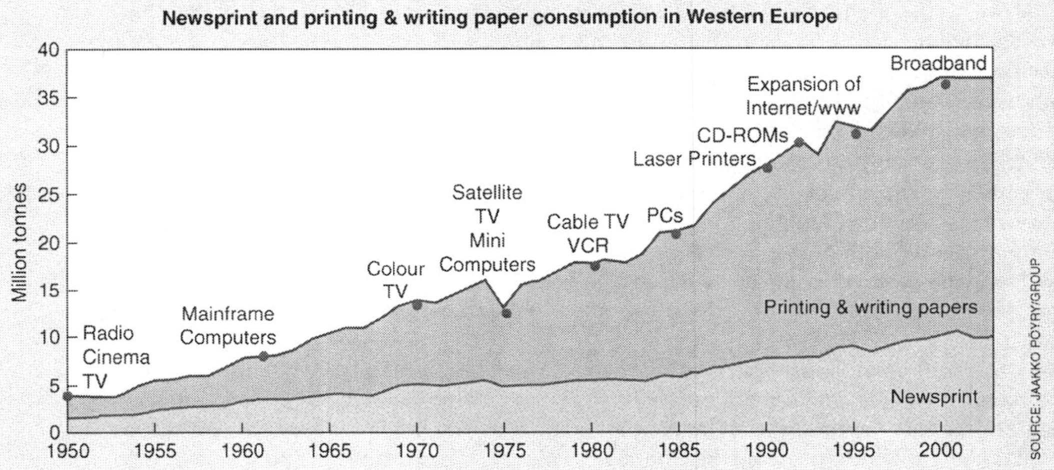

information The product of processing data so that they can be used in a context by human beings.

of a number, a statement, or a picture. Data are the raw material in the production of information. **Information**, on the other hand, is facts or conclusions that have meaning within a context. Raw data are rarely meaningful or useful as information. To become information, data are manipulated through tabulation, addition, subtraction, division, or any other operation that leads to greater understanding of a situation.

Data manipulation

Here's a simple example that demonstrates the difference between data and information. Assume that you work for a car manufacturer. Last year, the company introduced a new vehicle to the market. Because management realizes that keeping a loyal customer base requires continuously improving products and services, it periodically surveys large samples of buyers. It sends out questionnaires that include 30 questions in several categories, including demographic data (such as gender, age and annual income); complaints about different performance areas (such as ease of handling, braking and the quality of the sound system); features that satisfy buyers most; and courtesy of the dealer's personnel.

Reading through all this data would be extremely time-consuming and not very helpful. However, if the data are manipulated, they might provide highly useful information. For example, by categorizing complaints by topic and totalling the number of complaints for each type of complaint and each car model, the company might be able to pinpoint a car's weaknesses. The company then can pass the resulting information along to the appropriate engineering or manufacturing unit.

Also, the company might already have sufficient data on dealers who sold cars to the customers surveyed, the car models they sold and the financing method for each purchase. But with the survey results, the company can generate new information to improve its marketing. For instance, by calculating the average age and income of current buyers and categorizing them by the car they purchased, marketing executives can better target advertising to groups most likely to purchase each car. If the majority of buyers of a particular type of car do not ask for financing, the company might wish to drop this service option for that car and divert more loan money to finance purchases of other cars. In this way, the company generates useful information from data.

Generating information

In the examples just cited, calculating totals and averages of different complaints or purchasers' ages reveals trends associated with customers. These calculations are processes. A **process** is any manipulation of data, usually with the goal of producing information. Hence, while data are raw materials, information is output. Just as raw materials are processed in manufacturing to create useful end-products, so raw data are processed in information systems to create useful information (see Figure 1.2). Some processes, however, produce yet another set of data.

process Any manipulation of data, usually with the goal of producing information.

Sometimes, data in one context are considered information in another context. For example, if an organization needs to know the age of every person attending a concert, then a list of that data is actually information. But if that same organization wants to know the average price of tickets each age group purchases, the list of ages is only data, which the organization must process to generate information.

Figure 1.2 Input–process–output

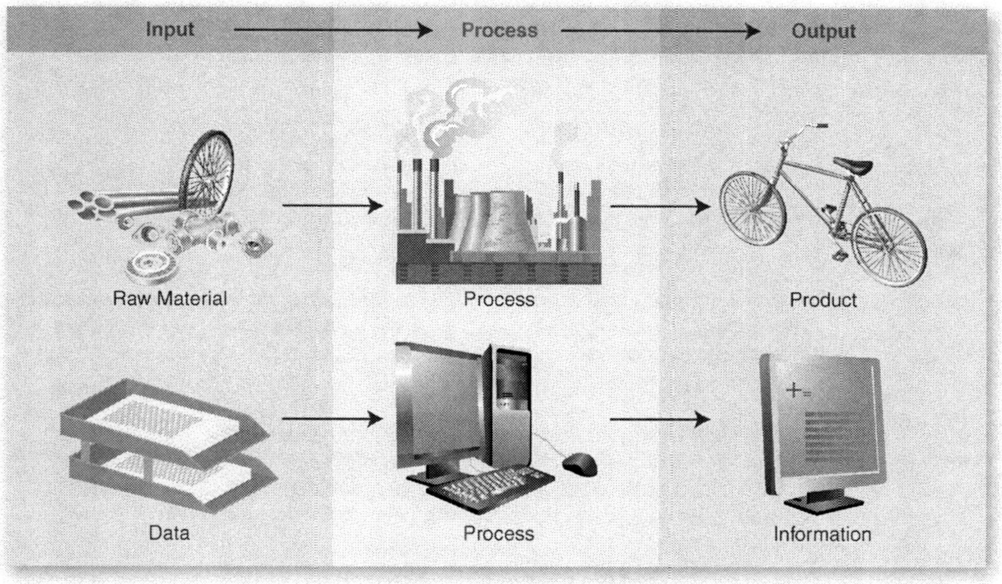

Information in context

Information is an extremely important resource for both individuals and organizations, but not all information is useful. Consider the following story. Two people touring in a hot-air balloon encountered unexpected wind that soon blew them off course. When they managed to lower their balloon, they shouted to a farmer on the ground, 'Where are we?' The farmer answered, 'You are right above a cornfield!' The balloonists looked at each other and one groaned, 'Some information! Highly accurate and totally useless!' To be useful, information must be relevant, complete, accurate and current. And in business, information must also be obtained economically, that is, cost-effectively. Figure 1.3 lists characteristics of useful information.

system An array of components that work together to achieve a common goal or multiple goals.

What is a system?

Simply put, a **system** is an array of components that work together to achieve a common goal, or multiple goals, by accepting input, processing it and producing output in an organized manner. Consider the following examples:

- A sound system consists of many electronic and mechanical parts, such as a laser head, an amplifier, an equalizer and so on. This system uses input in the form of electrical power and sound recorded on a medium such as a CD or DVD and processes the input to reproduce music and other sounds. The components work together to achieve this goal.

Figure 1.3 Characteristics of useful information

Relevant 	Information must pertain to the problem at hand. For example, the total number of years of education might not be relevant to a person's qualifications for a new job. Relevant information might be that the person has so many years of education in mechanical engineering and so many years of experience. The information must also be presented in a way that helps a person understand it in a specific context.
Complete 	Partial information is often worse than no information. For example, marketing data about household incomes might lead to bad decisions if not accompanied by vital information on the consumption habits of the targeted population.
Accurate 	Erroneous information might lead to disastrous decisions. For example, an inaccurate record of a patient's reaction to penicillin might lead a doctor to harm the patient while believing that she is helping him.
Current 	Decisions are often based on the latest information available, but what was a fact yesterday might no longer be one today. For example, a short-term Investment decision to purchase a stock today based on yesterday's stock prices might be a costly mistake if the stock's price has risen in the interim.
Economical €	In a business setting, the cost of obtaining information must be considered as one cost element involved in any decision. For example, demand for a new product must be researched to reduce risk of marketing failure, but if market research is too expensive, the cost of obtaining the information might diminish profit from sales.

- Consider the times you have heard the phrase 'to beat the system'. Here, the term 'system' refers to an organization of human beings – a government agency, a commercial company, or any other bureaucracy. Organizations, too, are systems; they consist of components – people organized into departments and divisions – that work together to achieve common goals.

Systems and subsystems Not every system has a single goal. Often, a system consists of several **subsystems** – components of a larger system – with subgoals, all contributing to meeting the main goal. Subsystems can receive input from, and transfer output to, other systems or subsystems.

subsystem A component of a larger system.

Consider the different departments of a manufacturing business. The marketing department promotes sales of the organization's products; the engineering department designs new products and improves existing ones; the finance department plans a clear budget and arranges for every unused penny to earn interest by the end of the day. Each department is a subsystem with its own goal, which is a sub-goal of a larger system (the company), whose goal is to maximize profit.

Now consider the goals of a manufacturing organization's information system, which stores and processes operational data and produces information about all aspects of company operations. The purpose of its inventory control subsystem is to let managers know what quantities of which items are available; the purpose of its production control subsystem is to track the status of manufactured parts; and the assembly control subsystem presents the bill of material (a list of all parts that make up a product) and the status of assembled products. The entire system's goal is to help deliver finished goods at the lowest possible cost within the shortest possible time.

Figure 1.4 shows an example of a system found in every business: an accounting system. An accounting system consists of several subsystems: accounts payable records information about money that the organization owes to other organizations and individuals; accounts receivable records sums owed to the organization and by whom; a general ledger records current transactions; and a reporting mechanism generates reports reflecting the company's

Figure 1.4 Several subsystems make up this corporate accounting system

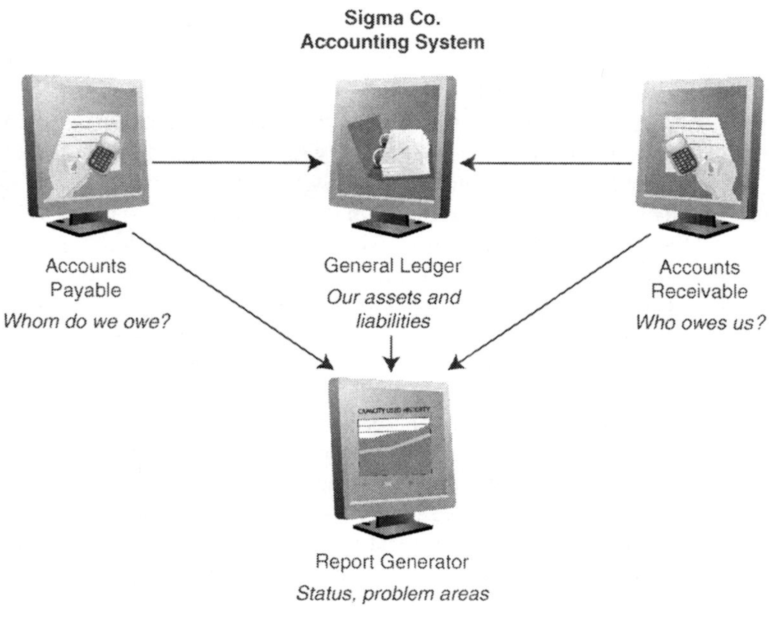

financial status. Each subsystem has a well-defined goal. Together, the subsystems make up the organization's accounting system.

Of course this is a simplistic view of the world. Goals are not always so well defined, human factors come into the equation when developing solutions, and different stakeholders in the whole system (customers, suppliers, operational staff, managers) have different interpretations of the problems that need to be solved. In the early 1980s Peter Checkland published research papers and books that put forward the idea of 'soft systems methodology' which recognized that conventional systems engineering is based on the solving of well defined problems and that most management problems are not as clear cut. His process of a continuous learning cycle in the development of systems was well received and underpins much of modern system thinking.

closed system A system that stands alone, with no connection to another system.

open system A system that interfaces and interacts with other systems.

Closed vs. open systems Systems are closed or open, depending on the nature of the information flow in the system. A **closed system** stands alone, with no connection to another system: nothing flows in from another system, nothing flows out to another system. For example, a small cheque-producing system that prints cheques when an employee enters data through a keyboard is a closed system. The system might be isolated for security purposes. An **open system** interfaces and interacts with other systems. For example, an accounting system that records accounts receivable, accounts payable and cash flow is open if it receives its payroll figures from the payroll system. Subsystems, by definition, are always open, because as components of a bigger system, they must receive information from and give information to other subsystems. Increasingly, companies are implementing open information systems that can be linked to other systems owned by business partners such as suppliers and clients.

information system (IS) A computer-based set of hardware, software and telecommunications components, supported by people and procedures, to process data and turn it into useful information.

Information systems With an understanding of the words 'information' and 'system', the definition of an information system is almost intuitive: an **information system (IS)** consists of all the components that work together to process data and produce information. Almost all business information systems consist of many subsystems with subgoals, all contributing to the organization's main goal.

Information and managers

Thinking of an organization in terms of its sub-organizations or subsystems – called systems thinking – is a powerful management approach because it creates a framework for both excellent problem-solving and excellent decision-making. To solve problems, managers need to isolate them, which they do by recognizing the subsystems in which the problems occur and solving the problems within those subsystems' constraints and strengths.

Systems thinking can also help keep managers focused on the overall goals and operations of a business. It encourages them to consider the entire system, not only their specific subsystem, when solving problems and making decisions. A satisfactory solution for one subsystem might be inadequate for the business as a whole. For example, when the sales department creates a website to take online customer orders, it automates a formerly labour-intensive activity of the sales subsystem. This saves cost. With systems thinking, improving the sales process could also improve other company processes. Without systems thinking, managers from other departments aren't involved in the decision, so they don't benefit. In the case of the sales department, if other managers are involved in planning for automated online ordering, they could suggest that sales data recorded on the **database** – a large collection of electronic records – connected to the Web also be accessible to other departments, such as distribution and manufacturing. The distribution department could use the records to expedite

database A collection of shared, interrelated records, usually in more than one file. An approach to data management that facilitates data entry, update and manipulation.

packaging and delivery, thanks to the information that appears on a computer monitor rather than a piece of paper. The manufacturing units could use the order records for planning resources such as labourers and inventory. Figuratively, by applying systems thinking, effective managers view their areas of responsibility as puzzle pieces. Each piece is important and should fit well with adjacent pieces, but the entire picture should always be kept in view.

One of an information system's most important contributions to the sound workings of an organization is the automation of information exchange among subsystems (such as departments and divisions). Consider the earlier example: customer orders taken via a website by the sales department could be automatically routed to the manufacturing and distribution units and processed by their own information systems for their specific purposes. In fact, such information exchanges make up a major portion of all interactions among business subsystems.

The **information map** of a modern business – that is, the description of data and information flow within an organization – shows a network of information subsystems that exchange information with each other and with the world outside the system. In an ideal organization, no human would need to retrieve information from one IS and transfer it to another. The organization would capture only new raw data, usually from its operations or from outside the organization. Then, data captured at any point in the system would automatically become available to any other subsystem that needs it. Thus, systems thinking is served well by **information technology (IT)**, a term that refers to all technologies that collectively facilitate construction and maintenance of information systems. Systems thinking is the basic reasoning behind equipping organizations with enterprise software applications. Enterprise software applications are systems that serve many parts of the organization by minimizing the need for human data entry and

information map The description of data and information flow within an organization.

information technology (IT) Refers to all technologies that collectively facilitate construction and maintenance of information systems.

Why you should...
be well versed in information systems

You might be surprised at how much information technology (IT) knowledge your prospective employer will expect of you when you are interviewed for your next job, even if the position you seek is not in the IT area. Today's corporations look for IT-savvy professionals and with good reason. Information is the lifeblood of any organization, commercial or nonprofit; it is essential to sound problem-solving and decision-making, upon which business success is built. In fact, the main factor limiting the services and information that computers can provide within an organization is the budget.

Because of rapid changes in technology, information systems, unlike many other business components, are quickly changing in form and content. A computer considered fast and powerful today will be an outdated machine in 18–24 months. In 12–24 months, a better program will surpass one that is considered innovative right now. The dynamic nature of information technology is like a moving target. A professional who does not stay informed is of diminishing value to an organization. All knowledge workers, professionals, scientists, managers and others who create new information and knowledge in their work, must be familiar with IT.

Managers must at all times maintain a clear picture of their organizations and the outside business environment. They must know what resources are available to them and to their competitors. Information technology provides excellent tools for collecting, storing and presenting facts. But to be truly effective, those facts must be manipulated into useful information that indicates the best allocation of various resources, including personnel, time, money, equipment and other assets. Regardless of the operations being managed, information systems (ISs) are important tools. Successful professionals must know which ISs are available to their organizations and what ISs might be developed in the future.

Industry **SNAPSHOT**

Looking for more skilled graduates

Sandra Smith, IS director at Toshiba UK, says companies and technology leaders take it as an absolute given that graduates will come to the workplace equipped with basic IT skills, including the ability to use word processing, spreadsheet and presentation tools. But most companies need that little bit extra.

'Businesses need graduates to have an appreciation and enthusiasm for how IT enables the modern business world, such as the Internet, email, mobile communications and databases. But unless they're going to work in IT, I don't think it's necessary that graduates are particularly expert with the details of the technology', she says.

'It's more important that graduates are aware of the possibilities of technology and know how to research and present their findings. I'm not sure it's an IT skill – but problem-solving, mental energy, planning and lateral thinking always seem to be in short supply. You can't put good systems in without them, that's for sure.'

SOURCE: http://www.vnunet.com/computing/analysis/2138557/skills-imperative-graduates

Companies like Toshiba look for more than just basic IT skills in today's graduates.

PHOTO SOURCE: © CARO/ALAMY

ensuring timely, useful information for the organization's entire supply chain, including taking customer orders, receiving raw materials, manufacturing and shipping, and billing and collection. In the service sector, companies often use document management systems, enabling workers from many departments to add information and signatures to a document from request to approval, or from draft to a final document. You will learn about these systems throughout this book.

The benefits of human–computer synergy

It is important to remember that computers can only carry out instructions that humans give them. Computers can process data accurately at far greater speeds than people can, yet they are limited in many respects – most importantly, they lack common sense. However, combining the strengths of these machines with human strengths creates synergy.

Some people call synergy the '2 + 2 = 5' rule. **Synergy** (from the Greek 'work together') occurs when combined resources produce output that exceeds the sum of the outputs of the same resources employed separately. A computer works quickly and accurately; humans work relatively slowly and make mistakes. A computer cannot make independent decisions, however, or formulate steps for solving problems, unless programmed to do so by humans. Even with sophisticated artificial intelligence, which enables the computer to learn and implement what it learns, the initial programming must be done by humans. Thus, a human–computer combination allows the results of human thought to be translated into efficient processing of large amounts of data. For example, when you use a Web search engine to find

synergy From Greek 'to work together.' The attainment of output, when two factors work together, that is greater or better than the sum of their products when they work separately.

Figure 1.5 Qualities of humans and computers that contribute to synergy

Humans	Computers

Think	Calculate and perform programmed logical operations extremely rapidly
Have common sense	Store and retrieve data and information extremely rapidly
Can make decisions	Perform complex logical and arithmetical functions accurately
Can instruct the computer what to do	Execute long, tedious operations
Can learn new methods and techniques	Perform routine tasks less expensively than humans
Can accumulate expertise	Are adaptable (can be programmed and reprogrammed)

articles about a topic, you, the human, enter a keyword or a series of keywords. By clicking the Search button you shift control to a computer program that quickly finds the articles for you. A human programmed a computer to perform an extremely fast search in a huge database of Web links; another human entered keywords and triggered the program; and the computer performed the matching of keywords with the links at a speed that is way beyond the capability of any human. The result is an efficient search that takes only seconds, which no human would be able to complete in a lifetime. Figure 1.5 presents qualities of humans and computers that result in synergy. It is important to notice not only the potential benefits of synergy, but also what computers should not be expected to do independently.

Information systems in organizations

In an organization, an information system consists of data, hardware, software, telecommunications, people and procedures as summarized in Table 1.1. An information system has become synonymous with a computer-based information system, a system with a computer at its centre to which peripheral equipment is connected. That is how this term is used in this book. In a computer-based information system, computers collect, store and process data into information, according to instructions people provide via computer programs.

Several trends have made the use of information systems (ISs) very important in business:

- The power of computers has grown tremendously while their prices have dropped.
- The variety and ingenuity of computer programs have increased.
- Quick and reliable communication lines and access to the Internet and the Web have become widely available and affordable.

Table 1.1 Components of an information system

Data	Input that the system takes to produce information
Hardware	A computer and its peripheral equipment: input, output and storage devices; hardware also includes data communication equipment
Software	Sets of instructions that tell the computer how to take data in, how to process it, how to display information and how to store data and information
Telecommunications	Hardware and software that facilitate fast transmission and reception of text, pictures, sound and animation in the form of electronic data
People	Information systems professionals and users who analyse organizational information needs, design and construct information systems, write computer programs, operate the hardware and maintain software
Procedures	Rules for achieving optimal and secure operations in data processing; procedures include priorities in dispensing software applications and security measures

- The fast growth of the Internet has opened opportunities and encouraged competition in global markets.
- An increasing ratio of the global workforce is computer literate.

In this environment, organizations quickly lag behind if they do not use information systems and skills to meet their goals. Moreover, they must continuously upgrade hardware, software and the skills of their employees to stay competitive.

The four stages of processing

All information systems operate in the same basic fashion whether they include a computer or not. However, the computer provides a convenient means to execute the four main operations of an information system:

- Entering data into the IS **(input)**.
- Changing and manipulating the data in the IS **(data processing)**.
- Getting information out of the IS **(output)**.
- Storing data and information **(storage)**.

A computer-based IS also uses a logical process to decide which data to capture and how to process them. This process will be discussed later.

input Raw data entered into a computer for processing.

transaction A business event. In an IS context, the record of a business event.

transaction processing system (TPS) Any system that records transactions.

Input The first step in producing information is collecting and introducing data, known as **input**, into the IS. Most data an organization uses as input to its IS are generated and collected within the organization. These data result from transactions undertaken in the course of business. A **transaction** is a business event: a sale, a purchase, the hiring of a new employee and the like. These transactions can be recorded on paper and later entered into a computer system, directly recorded through terminals of a **transaction processing system (TPS)**, such as a till, or captured online when someone transacts through the Web. A TPS is any system that records transactions. Often, the same system also processes the transactions,

Ethical and Societal ISSUES

The not-so-bright side

New technology almost always improves lives. But new technology often also has undesirable effects. This was true of the labour-saving machines that prompted the industrial revolution (introducing 16-hour workdays and child labour under harsh conditions) and it is also true about information technology. Think of the bliss of IT: it makes our work more productive because a few keystrokes on a computer keyboard prompt the computer to calculate and print what would otherwise take many human hours. It educates us via technologies such as multimedia classes delivered online. It opens new economic opportunities such as trading with overseas consumers via the Internet. It makes the world smaller by letting people work and socialize together over great distances via networks such as the Web. It democratizes the business community by making important business tools affordable to both rich and start-up companies. And it puts at our fingertips information on practically every imaginable subject. So, what's the dark side? There are quite a few dark sides, which we will discuss in the following chapters. Here is a sample of the main issues and the questions they raise.

Consumer privacy The ability to inexpensively and quickly collect, maintain, manipulate and transfer data enables every individual and organization to collect millions of personal records. When visiting a commercial website, chances are the site installs a little file, a 'cookie', on your computer's hard disk. This file helps track every click you make on that site, so companies specializing in consumer profiling can learn your shopping and buying habits. When you collect a prescription, the chemist collects details about you. Before you send a warranty card for a newly purchased product, you are asked to answer some questions that have nothing to do with the warranty but much to do with your lifestyle. All these data are channelled into large databases for commercial exploitation. Your control of such data is minimal. While consumers, patients and employees might consent to the collection of information on one aspect of their lives by one party and on another aspect by another party, the combination of such information might reveal more than they would like. For example, a firm can easily and inexpensively purchase *your* data from a chemist and several consumer goods companies, combine the data into larger records and practically prepare a dossier about you: your name, age and gender; your shopping habits; the medicines you take (and through this information, the diseases you might have); the political party to which you contributed; and so on.

Civil rights advocates argue that IT has created a Big Brother society where anyone can be observed. US business leaders oppose European-style legislation to curb collection and dissemination of private data because this limits target marketing and other economic activities. Business leaders ask, 'How can we target our products to consumers who are most likely to want them if we have no information about those consumers?' Are you willing to give up some of your privacy to help companies better market to you products and services you might be interested in? Do you accept the manipulation and selling of your personal data?

Employee privacy IT helps employers monitor their employees, not only via the ubiquitous video camera, but also through the personal computers they use. Employers feel it is their right to monitor keystrokes, email traffic, the websites employees visit and the whereabouts of people whose wages they pay while on the job. So, while IT increases productivity, it might violate privacy and create stress. Which is more important: your employer's right to electronically monitor you, or your privacy and mental well-being?

Freedom of speech The Web opens opportunities for many activities that people consider undesirable, such as the broadcast of violent and pornographic images and the dissemination of illegally copied digitized work. Almost anyone can become a publisher. If someone posts slurs about your ethnic group on a website, do you want the government to step in and ban such postings? And if one government legislates, can it impose its law on a network that crosses many national borders?

The problem is not only at international level. Playground bullying has now gone hi-tech. 'Bullies are increasingly using the Internet to terrorise teenagers outside of school, a survey suggests. More than 10 per cent of UK teenagers said they had been bullied online, while 24 per cent knew a victim, the MSN/YouGov survey found.'

Online annoyances Email is so popular because it allows easy and inexpensive transfer of ideas and creative work within seconds. However, more and more of us find our email boxes clogged with unsolicited messages, popularly called spam. Spam now makes up about 80 per cent of all email. Do you accept this? And if you own a new small business and want to advertise via email (because it is the least expensive advertising method), wouldn't you want the freedom to do so? While surfing the Web you encounter pop-up windows and pop-under windows. Your computer contracts spyware. Sometimes special software hijacks your browser and automatically takes you to a commercial site that you do not care for. Are these annoyances legitimate, or should they be stopped by legislation?

IT professionalism IT specialists play an increasing role in the lives of individuals and the operations of organizations. The information systems they develop and maintain affect our physical and financial well-being tremendously. Are IT specialists professionals? If they are, why don't they comply with a mandatory code of ethics as other professionals (such as doctors and lawyers) do? There are professional bodies, such as the British Computer Society, the Council of European Professional Informatics Societies and the Computer Society South Africa, with their clearly defined codes of conduct and good practice, but membership is not mandatory for anyone undertaking, for example, the development of a financial accounting system.

We will discuss these and other ethical and social issues throughout this book. As you will see, these issues are not easy to resolve. The purpose of these discussions is to make you aware of issues and provoke your thoughts. Remember that the purpose of education is not only to develop skilled professionals, but also to remind professionals of the impact of their work on the welfare of other people and to make professionals socially responsible.

SOURCE: http://news.bbc.co.uk/1/hi/technology/4805760.stm

summarizing and routing information to other systems; therefore, these systems are transaction *processing* systems, not just transaction *recording* systems.

Input devices (devices used to enter data into an IS) include the keyboard (currently the most widely used), infrared devices that sense bar codes, voice recognition systems and touch screens. Chapter 4, 'Business Hardware and Software', describes these and other means to input data. The trend has been to shorten the time and ease the effort of input by using devices that allow visual or auditory data entry.

data processing The operation of manipulating data to produce information.

Processing The computer's greatest contribution to ISs is efficient data processing, which is essential to a robust IS. The computer's speed and accuracy let organizations process millions of pieces of data in several seconds. For example, managers of a national retail chain can receive up-to-date information on inventory levels of every item the chain carries and order accordingly; in the past, obtaining such information would take days. These astronomic gains in the speed and affordability of computing have made information the essential ingredient for an organization's success.

output The result of processing data by the computer; usually, information.

Output Output is the information an IS produces and displays in the format most useful to an organization. The most widely used output device is the video display, or video monitor, which displays output visually. Another common output device is the printer, used to print hard copies of information on paper. However, computers can communicate output through speakers in the form of music or speech

Industry SNAPSHOT

Do it yourself – save labour (perhaps), please the customer (definitely)

Over the past few years there has been an increase in the number of supermarkets offering self-checkout systems. One of the market leaders is NCR Fastlane. A study commissioned by National Cash Registers (NCR) reported that 33 per cent of customers would choose one retailer over another if it offered self-checkout. From other studies it can be seen that such systems return greater user satisfaction. In addition to this there are possibilities for some savings on checkout staff, although experience has shown that these savings are not as high as they might be because there must be some staff on hand to deal with customer difficulties and to prevent theft. On this last point, the technology can help in that the latest systems compare the expected weight of the item (obtained from the bar code) with the actual weight of the item placed on the conveyor belt.

When self-checkout systems were first introduced, it was expected that the target market would be young professionals, comfortable with using new technology. However, experience has shown that older people like the fact that they can go through their shopping at their own pace, checking prices as they go. Also those people who have had to drag their children round the store find it useful to occupy them in helping out at the checkout point. There are signs that the similar systems have scope for use in different retail outlets. For example, Vodafone has recently launched the Quickphone kiosk, a machine for vending mobile phones.

SOURCE: 'Learning from the Supermarkets', Bill Waterson, UK Head of Retail, Fujitsu Services and 'Self-Checkout Systems: Creating Value Across the Retail Store', Kelly Matthews and Meredith Whalen, IDC White Paper, October 2004

A customer using a self-checkout system at a Tesco supermarket.

PHOTO SOURCE: © DAVID WILLIAMS/ALAMY

and also can transmit it to another computer or electronic device in computer-coded form, for later interpretation.

Storage One of the greatest benefits of using IT is the ability to maintain the storage of vast amounts of data and information. Technically, storing a library of millions of volumes on optical discs is not inconceivable. In fact, some universities are moving to do just that.

storage The operation of storing data and information in an information system.

Computer equipment for information systems

Figure 1.6 illustrates the five basic components of the computer system within an IS:

- Input devices introduce data into the IS.
- The computer processes data through the IS.
- Output devices display information.
- Storage devices store data and information.
- Networking devices and communications lines transfer data and information over long distances.

Figure 1.6 Input, process, output, storage and networking devices

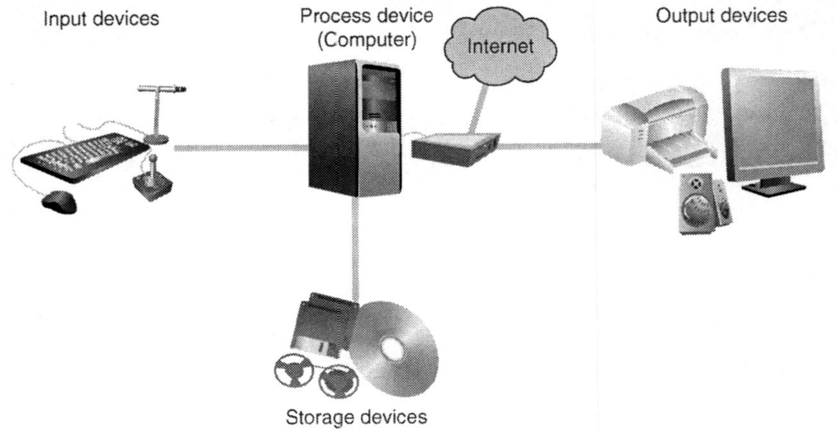

telecommunications Communications over a long distance, as opposed to communication within a computer, or between adjacent hardware pieces.

In addition to communication that takes place between computer components, communication occurs between computers over great distances (called telecommunications). Communications technology lets users access data and other electronic resources of many computers, all connected in a network. This way, a computer's power might be augmented with the power of an entire network.

From recording transactions to providing expertise: types of information systems

There are many different types of information systems – for different types of organizations, for different functions within organizations, for different business needs and at different management levels of an organization. Business enterprises differ in their objectives, structures, interests and approaches. However, ISs can be generally categorized according to the level of a system's complexity and the type of functions it serves. ISs in business range from the basic transaction processing system that records events such as sales to sophisticated expert systems, such as computer programs that provide advice and reduce the need for the expensive services of a human expert. In recent years the capabilities of these applications have been combined and merged. It is less and less likely that you will find any of the following applications as stand-alone systems with a single capability. Managers and other professionals plan, control and make decisions. As long as a system supports one or more of these activities, it may be referred to as a management information system (MIS).

management information system (MIS) A computer-based information system used for planning, control, decision-making or problem-solving.

Transaction processing systems

Transaction processing systems (TPSs) are the most widely used information systems. The predominant function of TPSs is to record data collected at the boundaries of organizations, in other words, at the point where the organization transacts business with other parties. TPSs include tills, which record sales; automatic teller machines (ATMs), which record cash withdrawals, deposits and transfers; and purchase order systems, which record purchases. A typical example would be the purchase of petrol at a pump, using a credit card. The purchase is recorded by the petrol company and later at the credit card processing bank. After these data are collected, the IS either automatically processes the data immediately or stores them for later access on demand.

Supply chain management systems

The term 'supply chain' refers to the sequence of activities involved in producing a product or service. In industries that produce goods, the activities include marketing, purchasing raw materials, manufacturing and assembly, packing and shipping, billing, collection and after-the-sale services. In service industries, the sequence might include marketing, document management and monitoring customer portfolios. Information systems that support these activities and are linked to become one large IS providing information on any stage of a business process are called **supply chain management (SCM) systems**.

supply chain management (SCM) The coordination of purchasing, manufacturing, shipping and billing operations, often supported by an enterprise resource planning system.

Often, such systems are called **enterprise resource planning (ERP) systems**, because the information they provide supports planning of shipping resources such as personnel, funds, raw materials and vehicles. However, ERP is a misnomer for the systems, because they mainly serve managers in monitoring and modifying business processes as they occur and not only for planning. The term 'supply chain', too, is somewhat misleading. Business processes do not always take the form of a sequence. There are processes that take place in parallel. This is true in manufacturing, where two or three teams work on different parts of a product and in services, where two or three different people peruse a document online and add their input to it within a certain period of time rather than sequentially. In the production of goods and services, some modules of SCM systems provide support to the major processes. These components include human resources (HR) information systems and cost accounting systems.

enterprise resource planning (ERP) system An information system that supports different activities for different departments, assisting executives with planning and running different interdependent functions.

SCM systems are the result of systems thinking and support systems thinking. They eliminate the need to reenter data that have already been captured somewhere else in the organization. An SCM is an **enterprise application** because the systems that support each business process are connected to each other to form one large IS. Technically, anyone with access to the system can know the status of every part of an order the business received: whether the raw materials have been purchased, which sub-assemblies are ready, how many units of the finished product have been shipped and how much money has been billed or collected for this order. HR managers can tell which workers are involved in any of the processes of the order. Accountants can use their module of the system to know how much money has been spent on this order and what the breakdown of the cost is into labour, materials and overhead expenditures.

enterprise application An application that fulfils a number of functions together, such as inventory planning, purchasing, payment and billing.

Customer relationship management systems

Customer relationship management (CRM) systems help manage an organization's relationships with its customers. The term refers to a large variety of information systems, from simple ones that help maintain customer records to sophisticated ones that dynamically analyse and detect buying patterns and predict when a specific customer is about to switch to a competitor. Many CRM systems are used by service representatives in combination with a telephone. When a customer telephones, the representative can view the entire history of the customer's relationship with the company: anything that the customer has purchased, deliveries made, unfulfilled orders and other information that can help resolve a problem or help the customer find the goods or service he or she is seeking. The main goals of CRM systems are to increase the quality of

customer relationship management (CRM) A set of applications designed to gather and analyse information about customers.

customer service, reduce the amount of labour involved in serving customers and learn as much as possible about the preferences of individual customers.

CRM systems are often linked to Web applications that track online shopping and process online transactions. Using sophisticated applications, a company can learn what makes a customer baulk just before submitting an online order, or what a customer prefers to see displayed on Web pages. Online retailers such as Amazon.co.uk, and Lastminute.com use applications that construct different Web pages for different customers, even when they search on the same keywords. The pages are constructed to optimally suit the individual customer's interests as inferred from previous visits and purchases. CRM systems provide important data that can be accumulated in large databases and processed into business intelligence.

business intelligence (BI) Information gleaned from large amounts of data, usually a data warehouse or online databases; a BI system discovers not-yet-known patterns, trends and other useful information that can help improve the organization's performance.

data warehouse A huge collection of historical data that can be processed to support management decision-making.

Business intelligence systems

ISs whose purpose is to glean from raw data relationships and trends that might help organizations compete better are called **business intelligence (BI)** systems. Usually, these applications consist of sophisticated statistical models, sometimes general and sometimes tailored for an industry or an organization. The applications access large pools of data, usually historical transaction records stored in large databases called **data warehouses**. With proper analysis models, BI systems might discover peculiar buying patterns of consumers, such as combinations of products purchased by a certain demographic group or on certain days; products that are sold at greater cycles than others; reasons for customer's churns, that is, customers leaving a service provider for a competitor; and other valuable business intelligence that helps managers quickly decide to change a strategy.

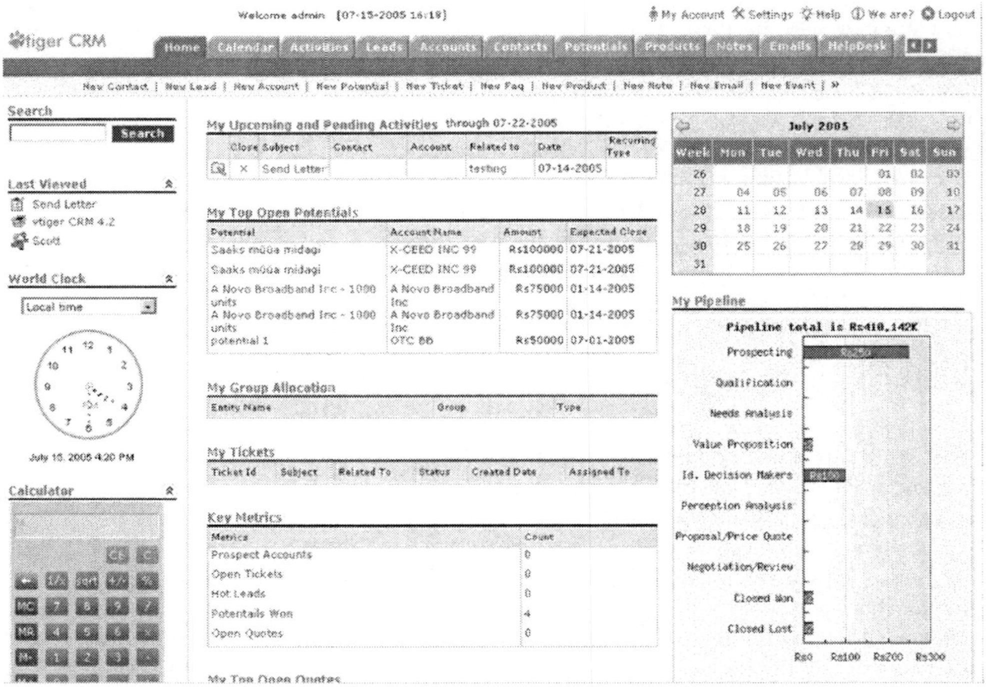

Vtiger CRM is an example of an Open Source CRM product designed mainly for small and medium businesses.

PHOTO SOURCE: VTIGER SYSTEMS INDIA PRIVATE LIMITED

Industry SNAPSHOT

CRM at DHL

DHL, wholly owned by Deutsche Post World Net, is the leading global delivery network dealing with overland express, air freight and international express delivery. It has approximately 285,000 employees who are dedicated to servicing 120,000 destinations in 220 countries. The company prides itself on its dedicated staff and is unusual in the logistics business in that two-thirds of its world-wide offices are owned by the company whereas most of its competitors make significant use of third parties. This means that DHL staff can help to achieve better transit time, efficient billing, easy tracking and so on. All of these can be considered to be part of customer relations, and to this end DHL make use of a CRM system called salesforce.com. This gives a holistic view of customers across the globe, enabling staff to give customers up-to-date information about the service that they are receiving from DHL, to resolve queries and problems, to enhance the service given to customers and so on.

The use of salesforce.com as the CRM platform involved a number of significant factors including

- the delivery of intensive staff training – If the company was to get maximum benefit from the system then the users (customer relations staff) needed to know how to use it properly.
- the importing of data from other sales systems – It would have been a shame to lose all the valuable data gathered over the previous years concerning customer profiles.
- integration with DHL Global Mail's other systems – The CRM system is just one of many IT systems within the company. It is vital that it interacts with these to ensure effective and efficient use of data in the whole of the organization.

The system aims to provide each customer with support via a single point of contact for all service-related issues. As Steve Garnett, SVP and general manager EMEA at salesforce.com says, 'an integrated approach to CRM worldwide and a single, 360 degree view of the customer regardless of geographic location was urgently required. This investment will undoubtedly support DHL Global Mail's long-term strategic goal to be the number one mail supplier on a worldwide level.'

SOURCE: www.crmintoline.com/crm-articles/crm-dhl.htm and http://www.salesforce.com/company/news-press/press-releases/2005/03/05030*.jsp

DHL's IT service centre in Prague, which manages and supports the IT infrastructure within DHL Europe from a single state-of-the-art headquarters.

PHOTO SOURCE: DEUTSCHE POST AG

Decision support and expert systems

Professionals often need to select one course of action from many alternatives. Because they have neither the time nor the resources to study and absorb long, detailed reports of data and information, organizations often build information systems specifically designed to help make decisions. These systems are called decision support systems (DSSs). While DSSs rely on models and formulae to produce concise tables or a single number that determines a decision, expert systems (ESs) rely on artificial intelligence techniques to support knowledge-intensive decision-making processes.

decision support system (DSS) Information system that aids managers in making decisions based on built-in models. DSSs comprise three modules: data management, model management and dialog management. DSSs may be an integral part of a larger application, such as an ERP system.

Decision support systems help find the optimal course of action and answer 'What if?' questions. 'What if we purchase raw materials overseas?' 'What if we merge our warehouses?' 'What if we double our shifts and cut our staff?' These questions seek answers such as, 'This is how this action will impact our revenue,

expert system (ES) A computer program that mimics the decision process of a human expert in providing a solution to a problem. Current expert systems deal with problems and diagnostics in narrow domains. An ES consists of a knowledge base, an inference engine and a dialog management module.

or our market share, or our costs.' DSSs are programmed to process raw data, make comparisons and generate information to help professionals glean the best alternatives for financial investment, marketing strategy, credit approval and the like. However, it is important to understand that a DSS is only a decision aid, not an absolute alternative to human decision-making.

Many environments are not sufficiently structured to let an IS use data to provide the one best answer. For instance, stock portfolio management takes place in a highly uncertain environment. No single method exists to determine which securities portfolio is best, that is, which one will yield the highest return. Medical care is another unstructured environment. There might be many methods of diagnosing a patient's illness on the basis of his or her symptoms. Indeed, a patient with a particular set of symptoms might receive as many different diagnoses as the number of doctors he or she visits.

Using ESs saves a company the high cost of employing human experts. After gathering expertise from experts and building a program, the program can be distributed and used repeatedly. The expertise resides in the program in the form of a knowledge base consisting of facts and relationships among the facts. You learn about DSS and ES in detail in Chapter 10.

geographic information system (GIS) Information system that exhibits information visually on a computer monitor with local, regional, national or international maps, so that the information can easily be related to locations or routes on the map. GISs are used, for example, in the planning of transportation and product distribution, or the examination of government resources distributed over an area.

Geographic information systems

In some cases, the information that decision-makers need is related to a map. In such cases, special ISs called **geographic information systems (GISs)** can be used to tie data to physical locations. A GIS application accesses a database that contains data about a neighbourhood, city, county, country or even the entire world. By representing data on a map in different graphical forms, a user is able to understand promptly a situation taking place in that part of the world and act upon it. Examples of such information include population levels, the number of police officers deployed, probabilities of finding minerals, transportation routes and vehicle allocation for transportation or distribution systems. Thus, when a supermarket chain considers locations for expansion, executives look at a map that reflects not only geographic attributes but also demographic information such as population growth by age and income groups. GISs are often used to manage daily operations but also in planning and decision-making. They also have been used to provide service via the Web, such as helping residents find locations of different services on a city map or plan travel routes. Some GISs that support operations use information from global positioning system (GPS) satellites, especially to show the current location of a vehicle or person on a map or to provide directions.

Information systems in business functions

ISs serve various purposes throughout an organization in what are known as functional business areas – in-house services that support an organization's main business. Functional business areas include, but are not limited to, accounting, finance, marketing and human resources. As mentioned before, in a growing number of organizations these systems are modules of a larger enterprise system, an SCM or ERP system. Chapter 3, 'Business Functions and Supply Chains', discusses business functions and their systems in detail.

Accounting

CD TASK

In accounting, information systems help record business transactions, produce periodic financial statements and create reports required by law, such as balance sheets and profit-and-loss statements. ISs also help create reports that might not be required by law, but that help managers understand changes in an organization's finances. Accounting ISs contain controls to ascertain adherence to standards, such as double entry.

Finance

While accounting systems focus on recording and reporting financial changes and states, the purpose of financial systems is to facilitate financial planning and business transactions. In finance, information systems help organize budgets, manage cash flow, analyse investments and make decisions that could reduce interest payments and increase revenues from financial transactions.

Marketing

CD TASK

Marketing's purpose is to pinpoint the people and organizations most likely to purchase what the organization sells and to promote the appropriate products and services to those people and organizations. For instance, marketing information systems help analyse demand for various products in different regions and population groups in order to more accurately market the right product to the right consumers. Marketing ISs provide information that helps management decide how many sales representatives to assign to specific products in specific geographical areas. The systems identify trends in the demand for the company's products and services. They also help answer such questions as, 'How can an advertising campaign affect our profit?' The Web has created excellent opportunities both to collect marketing data and to promote products and services by displaying information about them. That is why organizations conduct so much of their marketing efforts through ISs linked to the Web.

Geographic information systems help associate information with locations and regions.

Human resources

Human resource (HR) management systems mainly help in record-keeping and employee evaluation. Every organization must maintain accurate employee records. Human resource management systems maintain such records, including employees' pictures, employee marital status and tax information and other data that other systems such as payroll might use.

Performance evaluation systems provide essential checklists that managers can use to assess their subordinates. These systems also offer a scoring utility to quantify workers' strengths and weaknesses.

HR management systems have evolved to serve many purposes: recruiting, selection, placement, benefits analysis, online benefits information for employees to access through an intranet, requirement projections (how many employees with certain skills will be required in so many months?) and other services.

CD TASK

Web-empowered enterprises

The most exciting intersection of IT and business in recent years is networked commerce – buying and selling goods and services via a telecommunications network – or as it is popularly called, e-commerce. The development of the Web and the opening of the Internet to commercial activities spawned a huge surge in business-to-business and business-to-consumer electronic trade. Now, every individual and small business can afford to use a network for business: the Internet.

e-commerce Business activity that is electronically executed between parties, such as between two businesses or between a business and a consumer.

The Internet is a vast network of computers connected across the globe that can share both information and processing. The Web is capable of displaying text, graphics, sounds and moving images. It has enticed thousands of businesses to become involved in commercial, social and educational initiatives. Almost every brick-and-mortar business has extended its operations to the Web. Chapter 7, 'The Web-Enabled Enterprise', discusses Web technologies and how they are used in business activities. Because of its great impact on the use of information technology, the Web's impact on the use of information systems is discussed throughout the book.

Careers in information systems

The IT industry is made up of people in a wide variety of activities, but there has been a blurring of the edges between IT professionals and business professionals. It is worthwhile having a general idea of the subdivision of IT-specific jobs but everyone associated with the business will have a need for IT skills if 'only' as a user of IT systems. More organizations are realizing that there is scope for 'power-users' who are able to adapt and develop IT applications in order to gain the maximum advantage from the information that the business possesses.

Seventy-eight different IT jobs have been defined by the UK government-backed Skills Framework for the Information Age (SFIA). The range of jobs is divided into six broad categories, namely

- Strategy and planning, e.g. business systems strategy, technical strategy
- Development, e.g. systems development, implementation
- Business change, e.g. business change management
- Service provision, e.g. operations, user support
- Procurement and management support, e.g. supply management, resource management
- Ancillary skills, e.g. education and training, sales.

Industry SNAPSHOT

E-Christmas boom

The volume of online sales continues to grow year on year and a good metric is the amount of Christmas shopping carried out online. British consumers spent GB £7.66 billion online in the ten-week run-up to Christmas 2006, a 54 per cent increase on the 2005 figure. Germany had an increase in Internet traffic generally of 63 per cent in the first week of December while the French retail giant PPR saw a growth of Internet traffic of 73 per cent. Outside Europe, things are looking up for South African online shopping, with a massive 837 per cent increase from 2004 to 2006. Airline ticket purchases made up the majority of this increase, but flowers and groceries also showed significant increases of 113 per cent and 20 per cent respectively.

SOURCE: Interactive Media in Retail Group Index, 'Internet Retail Sales Leading Europe's Christmas Season', The *WWW.theaplahmarketer.com*, 6 December 2006 and 'MWEB online Christmas Shopping Up By 800 per cent in two years', ICTWorld, 24 January 2007

Consumer spending online continues to rise.

PHOTO SOURCE: © MARK GODDARD

The British Computer Society (www.bcs.org) has many case studies of real people employed in the industry categorized using the SFIA definitions. The job titles below are only indicative – an employer in an advertisement can call the job anything they like. It is the job description that is important. Salaries are also very variable. A useful site checking the current situation of IT salaries in the UK can be found at http://www.computingcareers.co.uk/it-salary-checker/. A similar annual survey for South Africa can be found at http://www.itweb.co.za/surveys/salary/2007/.

Systems developer

The term *programmer* may also be used but the more generic term *systems developer* is now more widely used. This recognizes the fact that much of what modern programmers do is higher-level programming, that is using pre-existing building blocks of code to create the desired application. That is not to say the job is any less skillful, just more efficient. Why should a programmer spend time writing a routine to sort a set of records into alphabetical order when someone has already written this function? The systems developer simply calls up the routine and then spends useful time on the specific processing of that set of records. Similar arguments can be made for elements of the user interface. There are predefined routines to produce, for example, a calendar on the screen so that the user can pick a date for their train ticket. Once again, the predefined piece of code can be called up and then the programmer can concentrate on the next part of the transaction, checking the database for availability.

systems analyst An IT professional who analyses business problems and recommends technological solutions.

Systems analyst

Many IT professionals start their careers as programmers, or *programmer/analysts* and then are promoted to **systems analysts**, positions that require a broad range of skills. A programmer/analyst is partly involved in the analysis of business needs and ISs, but the greater part of the job involves setting up business applications. A systems analyst is involved in designing new ISs and in updating and maintaining existing ISs. A big part of this job includes developing alternative system plans based on (1) analysing system requirements provided by user input, (2) documenting development efforts and system features and (3) providing adequate specifications for programmers.

To succeed, systems analysts must possess excellent communication skills to translate users' descriptions of business processes into system concepts. They must understand a wide range of business processes and ways in which IT can be applied to support them. Since analysts often deal with systems that serve more than one organizational unit, they must also understand organizational politics and be shrewd negotiators.

Most importantly, systems analysts must always keep in mind that they are agents of change and that most people resist change. Unlike many other occupations, theirs often involves the creation of new systems or the modification of existing ones. Because new or modified systems often affect human activities and organizational cultures, systems analysts must be able to convince both line workers and managers that change will benefit them. Thus, these IS professionals must possess good persuasive and presentation skills.

Job DESCRIPTION

Systems analyst

Analyses, documents and proposes solutions for large and/or complex business areas and prepares functional specifications. Assists in the preparation of user and system test plans.

Duties and responsibilities

- Collecting, understanding and transmitting the business requirements for the project, and translating these into functional specifications and detailed test plans.
- Analyse and document business processes.
- Document workflows and results of business analysis and obtain sign-off from client on the specifications.
- Provide the link between the customer, development team and any third party regarding software functionality, throughout the development lifecycle.
- Design and execute the test scenarios and test scripts.
- Day-to-day management of change requests in relation to the project plans to ensure agreed deadlines are met.
- Weekly reports to be produced for the project manager showing progress against outstanding milestones, status, resource requirements, issues, risks and dependencies.

Skills/attributes required

- Demonstrable evidence of analysing and documenting complex business processes.
- Demonstrable experience writing requirements specifications for information systems.
- A proven track record in software development.
- End-to-end experience of the project lifecycle.
- Proven experience interacting directly with end users.
- Results orientated with good communication and interpersonal skills.

SOURCE: © CV Screen Ltd

Senior systems analysts often advance to become project leaders. In this capacity, they are put in charge of several analysts and programmers. They seek and allocate resources, such as personnel, hardware and software, which are used in the development process, and they use project management methods to plan activities, determine milestones and control use of resources.

Database administrator

database administrator (DBA) The individual in charge of building and maintaining organizational databases.

The **database administrator (DBA)** is responsible for the databases and data warehouses of an organization – a very sensitive and powerful position. Since access to information often connotes power, this person must be astute not only technologically but politically as well. He or she must evaluate requests for access to data from managers to determine who has a real 'need to know'. The DBA is responsible for developing or acquiring database applications and must carefully consider how data will be used. In addition, the DBA must adhere to government and corporate regulations to protect the privacy of customers and employees.

A growing number of organizations link their databases to the Web for use by employees, business partners and customers. Attacks on corporate databases by hackers and computer viruses have made the DBA's job more difficult. In addition to optimizing databases and developing data management applications, this person must oversee the planning and implementation of sophisticated security measures to block unauthorized access but at the same

Job DESCRIPTION

Oracle database administrator

Responsible for supporting the Oracle databases and ensuring their performance, availability and security.

Duties and responsibilities

- Responsible for ensuring availability and performance of the databases that support the system.
- Work with the team to ensure that the associated hardware resources allocated to the databases are adequate and to ensure high availability and optimum performance.
- Proactively monitor the database systems to ensure secure services with minimum downtime.
- Responsible for providing trend analysis to the service management team to enable them to make informed decisions regarding resource management.
- Responsible for problem escalation to Oracle development team and third parties as appropriate.
- Responsible for improvement and maintenance of the databases to include rollout and upgrades.
- Responsible for implementation and release of database changes as submitted by the development team.

Skills/attributes required

- Proven Oracle database administration experience.
- Experience of managing multiple RDBMS on large systems.
- Experience of working in a team that delivers a high-availability service.
- Practical experience in monitoring and tuning a database to provide a high-availability service.
- Experience of other database systems, preferably SQL Server.
- Practical experience in managing the internal and external MS SQL database security.
- Oracle Certification, preferably OCP.

SOURCE: © CV Screen Ltd

time to allow easy and timely access to authorized users. The DBA is also highly involved in the implementation of SCM systems, because they access corporate databases.

Data administrator

Many organizations have realized that they need to look at data from a strategic point of view. A data administrator (DA) needs to understand the data that the company owns or has access to and the ability to consider this valuable resource in relation to the needs of senior management in the organization. If the DA does not instigate the development of new systems aimed at giving the company a competitive edge, he or she will certainly be charged with ensuring that these developments take place.

network administrator The individual who is responsible for the acquisition, implementation, management, maintenance and troubleshooting of computer networks throughout the organization.

Network administrator

Among the many IT areas, the one that has seen the most exciting developments in recent years is networks and telecommunications. Not surprisingly, this area has also seen the greatest increase in corporate allocation of IT resources in many organizations. The emergence of new technologies, such as Voice over Internet Protocol and Wi-Fi, which are discussed in Chapter 5, is expected to sustain this trend for some years, allowing specialized professionals to be in great demand and to command high salaries.

The **network administrator** is responsible for acquiring, implementing, managing, maintaining and troubleshooting networks throughout the organization and the links with the

Job DESCRIPTION

Network administrator

Responsible for the operation and administration of the company's internal networks, servers, email and network security systems and for the development of the company website and database.

Duties and responsibilities

- Administration and maintenance of company's internal systems.
- Configuration and set-up of all new server systems required internally for the company's activities.
- Firewall administration and overall responsibility for company IT security.
- Administration of email servers for company-wide email.
- Providing telephone and desktop support to internal users.
- Forecasting any needed improvements, budgeting for and implementing any changes.

Skills/attributes required

- Good working knowledge of the following operating systems: Windows 2000 Server, Windows 2003 Server, Exchange, Citrix.
- Strong working knowledge of major networking components, network operating systems and basic computer hardware components.
- Hands-on knowledge of the procedures used in the installation, modification, maintenance and repair of IT hardware and software.

SOURCE: © CV Screen Ltd

outside world. He or she is also often involved in selecting and implementing network security measures such as firewalls and access codes.

Webmaster

CD TASK

The rapid spread of the Web, intranets and extranets has increased the responsibility and stature of the organizational Webmaster. A **Webmaster** is responsible for creating and maintaining the organization's website and its intranet and extranet pages. Webmasters are increasingly involved in creatively deciding how to represent the organization on the Web. These decisions involve elements of marketing and graphic design. Since many organizations use the Web for commerce, Webmasters must also be well versed in Web transaction software, payment-processing

Webmaster The person who is in charge of constructing and maintaining the organization's website.

Job DESCRIPTION

Webmaster

The Webmaster implements web pages, maintains content and oversees day-to-day management of the company website, and assures quality and filing integrity of web pages.

Duties and responsibilities

- Responsible for the design of company web pages, including graphics, animation and functionality.
- Develop web page infrastructure and application related to pages with more advanced graphics and features.
- Monitor web server and site technical performance.
- Implement search engine optimization strategies.
- Promote client websites online to increase prominence within their web community where possible.
- Management of Pay Per Click (PPC) campaigns to achieve optimum ROI (return on investment) for individual active search terms for each of the major search engines.
- Work closely with the Operations Director to set and ensure marketing campaigns achieve budgeted commercial targets.
- Circulate efficient and accurate reporting, detailing results of each web marketing campaign and possible improvement.
- Advise Director on the improvement, results, competition and new directions in technology to assist with marketing of the brand.
- Maximize online affiliate opportunities and revenue generation for the brand (with possibility of widening affiliate advertising schemes).
- Ensure regular communication and email contact with affiliates and act as main point of contact.
- Source and manage new revenue-generating online marketing opportunities.

Skills/attributes required

- Proven website management experience.
- You will have strong web design skills which will include the ability to edit HTML and JavaScript skills.
- A thorough knowledge of search engine optimization (SEO) techniques.
- Experience of running and evaluating online marketing campaigns, which will include the management of Pay Per Click (PPC) campaigns.
- A flexible attitude with proven experience of working in a small team.
- Excellent communication skills and attention to detail.

SOURCE: © CV Screen Ltd

software and security software. The demand for Webmasters is expected to grow as long as corporate use of the Web continues to grow.

chief security officer (CSO) Also called chief information security officer (CISO), the highest-ranking officer in charge of planning and implementing information security measures in the organization, such as access codes and backup procedures.

Chief security officer

Because of the growing threat to information security, many organizations have created the position of **chief security officer (CSO)**, or chief information security officer (CISO). In most organizations the person in this position reports to the chief information officer (CIO) (see next section), but in some the two executives report to the same person, usually the chief executive officer (CEO). The rationale is that security should be a business issue, not an IT issue. A major challenge for CSOs is the misperception of other executives that IT security is an inhibitor rather than an enabler to operations.

Job DESCRIPTION

Chief technology officer

Plans, directs, manages and oversees the activities and operations of the IT department; administers the IT budget, staff and physical facilities of the department.

Duties and responsibilities

- Develop information technology strategy in support of the company's mission and core objectives.
- Direct, control and motivate the staff of the information technology department.
- Develop an annual business plan and operating budget for the department and monitor the implementation of these to ensure that the financial targets are met.
- Negotiate service level agreements with both internal and external customers and service providers and monitor service delivery to ensure the agreed targets and standards are met.
- Accountable for the management, mentoring and career development of all IT staff.
- Define and seek approval for the level of IT resources required to meet these goals and prioritizes and schedules major projects.
- Direct the preparation and implementation of policies, procedures and standards relating to information and telecommunications systems.
- Responsible for researching and evaluating new technologies.
- Direct, attend and participate in staff meetings and related activities; attend workshops to keep up to date with information technology issues.

Skills/attributes required

- Proven senior IT management experience.
- A proven track record of driving and defining complex IT strategy.
- Budgetary experience of £3 million or more.
- Exceptional communication skills are essential in order to explain complex IT concepts to non-technical colleagues.
- Experience of managing multiple IT disciplines, e.g. software development, technical support, systems architecture and so on.
- A broad understanding of computer systems, applications and operating systems.
- Educated to degree level in computer science or related field.
- In-depth experience of negotiating with and managing third parties.

SOURCE: © CV Screen Ltd.

Chief information officer and chief technology officer

The fact that a corporation has a position titled chief information officer (CIO) reflects the importance that the company places on ISs as a strategic resource. The CIO, who is responsible for all aspects of an organization's ISs, is often, but not always, a corporate vice president. Some companies prefer to call this position chief technology officer (CTO). However, you might find organizations where there are both a CIO and a CTO and one reports to the other. There is no universal agreement on what the responsibility of each should be. Yet, in most cases when you encounter both positions in one organization, the CTO reports to the CIO.

A person who holds the position of CIO must have both technical understanding of current and developing information technologies and business knowledge. As Figure 1.7 shows, the CIO plays an important role in integrating the IS strategic plan into the organization's overall strategic plan. He or she must not only keep abreast of technical developments but also have a keen understanding of how different technologies can improve business processes or aid in the creation of new products and services.

chief information officer (CIO) The highest-ranking IS officer in the organization, usually a vice president, who oversees the planning, development and implementation of IS and serves as leader to all IS professionals in the organization.

chief technology officer (CTO) A high-level corporate officer who is in charge of all information technology needs of the organization. Sometimes the CTO reports to the chief information officer, but in some companies this person practically serves as the CIO.

Figure 1.7 Traits of a successful CIO

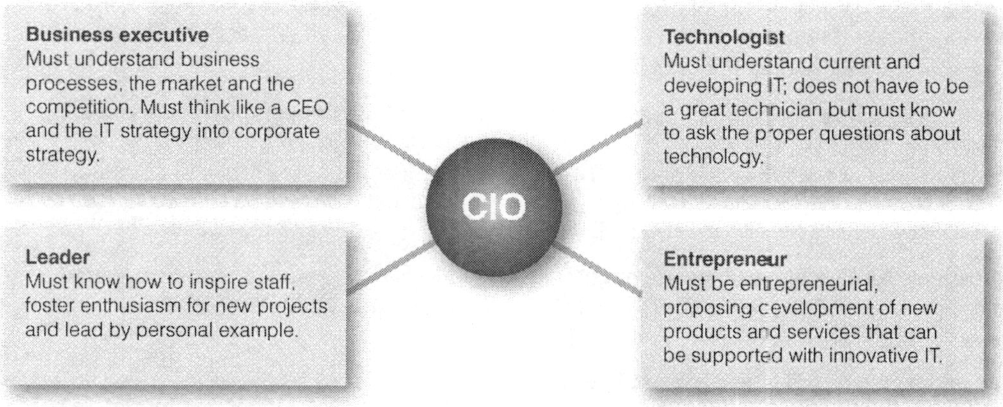

SUMMARY

Computer-based information systems pervade almost every aspect of our lives. Their ability to help solve problems and make decisions makes them indispensable in business and management. Computer-based information systems take data as raw material, process the data and produce information as output. While data sometimes can be useful as they are, they usually must be manipulated to produce information, facts, statistics and other items useful for reporting and decision-making.

A system is a set of components that work together to achieve a common goal. An information system (IS) consists of several components: hardware (the computer and its peripheral equipment), software (programs that run the computer), data, people and procedures. The components' common goal is to produce the best information from available data.

Often, a system performs a limited task that produces an end result, which must be combined with other products from other systems to reach an ultimate goal. Such a system is called a subsystem. Several subsystems might make up a system. Sometimes, systems are also classified as closed or open. A stand-alone system that has no contact with other systems is called a closed system. A system that interfaces with other systems is an open system.

Data processing has four basic stages. In the input stage, data are collected and entered into the computer. The computer then performs the next stage, data processing, which is the manipulation of data into information using mathematical, statistical and other tools. The subsequent stage, output, displays or presents the information. We often also want to maintain data and information for later use. This activity is called storage.

Any information system that helps in management may be referred to as a management information system (MIS). MISs use recorded transactions and other data to produce information for problem-solving and decision-making.

There are several different types of information systems. They include transaction processing systems (TPSs), supply chain management (SCM) systems, customer relationship management (CRM) systems, business intelligence (BI) systems, decision support systems (DSSs) and expert systems (ESs) and geographic information systems (GISs). Often, some or all of these systems are linked to each other or to other information systems.

Enterprise application systems, such as SCM or ERP systems, are information systems that tie together the different functional areas of a business, such as order entry, inventory management, accounting and finance and manufacturing. Such systems allow businesses to operate more efficiently by avoiding reentry and duplication of information. The systems can provide an up-to-the-minute picture of inventory, work in progress and the status of an order to be fulfilled.

ISs are used in many business functions, most commonly accounting, finance, marketing and human resources. These systems aid in the daily operations of organizations by maintaining proper accounting information and producing reports, assisting in managing cash and investments, helping marketing professionals find the most likely buyers for their products and services and keeping accurate employee records and assisting with their performance evaluations.

The job prospects for IT professionals are bright. Among the typical careers in this field are systems analyst, database administrator, network administrator, Webmaster, chief security officer, chief information officer and chief technology officer.

IT has many advantages, but it also has created societal concerns. Issues such as privacy, free speech on the Web, spam and web annoyances are viewed by many people as serious ethical issues. And while IT professionals increasingly affect our lives through the systems they develop and maintain, they are not required to adhere to any code of ethics as other professionals are. These and related issues are discussed throughout the book.

BETTER BITES

BETTER BITES REVISITED

Now that Chapter 1 has helped you understand how business uses data, information and information systems, let's revisit Better Bites. Paul, Sarah and Christina are trying to improve their lunch business. How would you cope with their challenges?

What would you do?

1. Paul has been bogged down entering sales receipts into the business's computer programs at the end of the week. He has also been swamped at the end of the month, when he generates reports on overall sales and expenses. He needs a better system. What would you do to increase the efficiency of the business transactions? Examine the business's inputs, processing and outputs. Formulate a method to streamline the business transactions. What type of reports does Paul need?
2. Sarah noticed the varying sales of some menu items. What information about sales does she need to order the optimum amount of each ingredient and the labour spent on food preparation?
3. Currently, Better Bites does not collect information about the items that are ordered together by an individual customer. Do you think that information would be helpful to the owners? How might they generate and use such information?
4. Are SCM or CRM applicable to Better Bites? If so, which one is more important to Better Bites at the beginning of their business? Explain.

New perspectives

1. What business opportunities can Better Bites generate from the following changes in the food industry?
   - The British government recently adopted new standards for organic food labelling. Consumers now can determine exactly how a product has been produced from the label it carries. Food producers and retailers can apply for certification from the Food Standards Agency. You have advised the team to apply for certification, which means they would have to label each wrapped meal. Advise them how a personal computer could help with this task.
   - The food wholesaler the business uses is setting up a website to allow its customers to order supplies online. How would this change Better Bites' current operations? List both benefits and drawbacks.
2. The City Council has approached Better Bites to provide food snacks at the city's organized events for bank holidays. Advise Paul, Sarah and Christina: what information do they need to decide whether to accept this offer? Do they currently have this information from the data they have collected? If they decide to accept this offer, what information will tell them whether they made the right decision?

Review questions

1. What does the word 'processing' in data processing mean?
2. Give three examples in which raw data also serve as useful information.
3. Give three business examples (not mentioned in the text) of data that must be processed to provide useful information.
4. Give three examples of subsystems not operating in the context of IT. Why are these subsystems and not systems?

5 How do TPSs and DSSs differ?
6 What is a problem? Give an example of a business problem and discuss how a computer-based information system could solve it.
7 What is synergy? How is synergy accomplished when a person uses a computer?
8 'An information system consists of hardware and software.' Why is this statement inadequate?
9 When does one need to make a decision?
10 How can a DSS help make decisions?
11 Note the word 'support' in decision support systems. Why are these applications not called decision-*making* systems?
12 Who is considered a knowledge worker? Will you have a career as a knowledge worker? Explain.
13 What is the most prevalent type of information system? Why is this type of IS so ubiquitous?
14 TPSs are usually used at the boundaries of the organization. What are boundaries in this context? Give three examples of boundaries.
15 Among IT professionals, the greatest demand is for network administrators and analysts Why?

Discussion questions

1 No longer the domain of technical personnel, information systems are the business of every professional. Why?
2 Assume that computers can recognize voices easily and detect their users' exact meaning when talking. Will the necessity for written language be reduced to zero? Why or why not?
3 Information systems cannot solve some business problems. Give three examples and explain why technology cannot help.
4 An increasing number of knowledge workers must know how to use information systems. Why?
5 Often, computer illiteracy is likened to reading illiteracy. Is this realistic? Is computer illiteracy as severe a handicap as reading illiteracy?
6 Think of two examples of fully web-based businesses. What made the Web so attractive for these entrepreneurs?
7 We will soon stop talking of e-commerce and simply speak of commerce. Why?
8 'Help wanted' advertisements do not use the term 'computer specialists'; rather, they use the term 'information system professionals' or 'information technology professionals'. Why?
9 How do traditional commerce and web-based commerce differ?
10 What changed the average citizen's life more, the industrial revolution or the information revolution? How and why?
11 Information technology might bring people together, but it also isolates them. Explain the latter claim and give an example.
12 Give two examples of phenomena that are a social concern because of information technology. Explain.
13 What irritates you about the Web? What would you do to minimize this irritation?
14 Do you foresee an IT-related societal or ethical concern that is not a current concern? Explain.
15 If you chose a career in IT apart from CIO or CTO, which position would you choose and why?

Tutorial activities

1 Recall what you did yesterday from the moment you got up until the moment you went to bed. How many times did you use a computer or receive data or information from someone who used a computer? (Do not forget ATMs, tills, automated kiosks, etc.) Consider the inputs, processing and outputs associated with each interaction and write a two-page essay on society's dependency on computers.
2 Contact a business organization and ask permission to observe a business process. Pinpoint the segments in the process that a computer-based information system could aid. Write a report detailing your observations and suggestions.

3 Observe activities in a supermarket: shoppers looking down aisles for specific products; queues forming at the tills; workers sticking new prices to items on the shelves. Prepare a list of shoppers' and workers' activities that could be carried out with less use of human time and more accuracy if they were aided by IT. Explain how you would change those activities.

4 Scientists are researching a contagious disease. They found that, on average, each person who is infected transmits the disease to three other people within one year. Currently, there are 3,000 infected people in the country. Use Excel or another spreadsheet application to find out (1) how many people will contract the disease each year over the next decade and (2) how many infected people will there be each year if no medication is administered. (Do not worry: there is a medication for this disease.) 'Currently' means in the first year of your calculation. Calculate for the next nine years. Explain why this is a modelling problem. What is your model in the spreadsheet?

5 Use a CV template in your word-processing program to type your CV. If you don't have a lot of direct work experience, remember to include all types of work, whether it's babysitting, mowing the lawn, or whatever.

6 Use your word-processing application to prepare a list: what information that you currently receive through other means could you receive through your computer? The list should include text, images, audio and animated information. Would you prefer to receive this information on the computer or as you do now?

7 Form a team with two other students. Each team member should play the role of a vice president in charge of a business function: human resources, accounting, marketing, finance and so on. Each vice president should enumerate information he or she needs to perform his or her function. Now list information that two or more of the functions must share and data produced by one function that another function uses.

8 Team up with another two students. Brainstorm and try to think of a new business opportunity that you would like to pursue in which you will not need IT. You should be able to convince the rest of the class that IT cannot improve the operations of this business.

Companion CD questions

1 Use Excel to create a simple financial spreadsheet for Better Bites' business plan.

2 Use presentation software to create a presentation in support of Better Bites' application to the bank for a business loan.

Video questions

1 The video segment mentions Jef Raskin. Who was he? What were some of his inventions? What are his theories about design?

2 Do you agree with Buxton's contention that devices should be designed by humanists rather than engineers? Why or why not?

From ideas to application

REAL CASES

Case study 1.1

IT strategy as part of business strategy

BY ALAN HOGARTH

The information systems function, after years of being seen as a prime candidate for outsourcing, is now once again viewed as an essential and core department in most large organizations. The main reason for this change of view is the need for information systems (IS) or information technology (IT) strategy to be part of an organization's wider business strategy. Due to the global nature of business it is now essential that organizations plan their IT strategy in conjunction with their business strategy. One organization which has recognized the importance of this approach is Unilever.

The consumer goods giant – producer of such brands as Sunsilk, Dove, Bertolli and Lipton – recently had to take a careful look at its strategy due to the first profit warning in the corporation's history. Global Chief Information Officer (CIO) of Unilever, Neil Cameron, says that, 'Having achieved that [strategy revision] and consolidated the organization, for 2006 the agenda [was] execution.' The company's plan was to cut 700 million euros from costs through streamlining and simplification of their systems by 2007 in a strategy titled 'One Unilever'.

According to Cameron, in Europe Unilever used to operate two systems: one for their food products and one for personal systems, but now the organization operates as one. Cameron affirms that, 'We have worked very hard over the last two years to get the basics right, and now they are, we can look at execution and delivering benefits.' IT strategy is now closely aligned to the business strategy in both global and regional terms, and business processes and information have to run as a single entity. Cameron further states that, 'The success of the systems convergence programme means we are now using the things we invested in. This has meant company-wide changes including the IT organization has changed significantly too. We are now driving efficiencies and implementing programmes to unify the businesses geographically.'

Unilever operates in nearly 100 countries, has 365 manufacturing sites and employs around 223,000 people. So any efficiency it can gain from its convergence programme will have significant benefits by way of reducing resource costs. The company is looking at information and back-to-business programmes centred upon its global customers, for example Wal-Mart, and also at improving customer-centred systems at regional and local levels for customers such as Sainsbury, which have a local presence but do not operate in a global marketplace. Cameron is justifiably proud of his function's achievements when he states that 'Business and technology innovations which provide things like improvements in our supply chain, reductions in cost and speeding up customer response times are fundamentally changing our business. In the UK there have been a huge number of changes to systems, including manufacturing, basic HR and supporting accounts over the past year. This has brought lots of opportunities for Unilever UK. But we must make sure we support that.'

However, Cameron does recognize that there is still a lot of work to be done. For example, Unilever is selling the majority of its European frozen food business,

Unilever's recently refurbished UK headquarters in London.

PHOTO SOURCE: REPRODUCED WITH KIND PERMISSION OF UNILEVER

including its Bird's Eye branded business. This could throw up complex requirements for IT, according to Cameron. 'If it is a trade sale, then we just have to support the buyer until they are ready to move to their own systems. But if it is bought by a private equity business we have to provide the services for it, and work out charges as well as segregating it from the rest of the business.'

The sale is part of Unilever's focus on growth, says Cameron. 'We have to focus on the business and where the growth is going to come from. The sale will be better for the business in the long term.' Systems are being standardized and consolidated with suppliers. In the UK for example, desktop supply, implementation and support are part of a standardized global deal with Dell and Unisys. Cameron says, 'These are good people to work with. Unisys handles Dell's services, and we will be transferring support to there. Global deals like this put us in great shape for execution, as well as improving efficiency and reducing costs.' Unilever also struck a deal recently for a seven-year contract with IBM to outsource financial transactional services. The contract covers more than 20 European countries and is part of the streamlining programme. The deal is that IBM will provide financial services including general accounting from its centres in Portugal, Poland and India.

Not only does IT support the sales end of Unilever, it also continues to support scientific research and product innovation. Cameron says 'We are supporting product Research and Development from an IT perspective.' He is very enthusiastic when he further adds that, 'It is very interesting and challenging working with the scientists, and trying to add something. The process goes the whole way from research and innovation concepts all the way through to product launch. Trying to get the balance right is important and the support comes from IT.'

'We are working very hard at innovation and science at the molecular level – for example V-shots have to taste of something – and there are huge scientific issues. We are doing some grid computing work on this, but frankly some of the scientists we have are much better at doing this than we are.'

Unilever has recognized not only the need to align its IT strategy with its business strategy but has also rationlized its IT systems by streamlining two systems into one more efficient and effective system. Consequently this has resulted in more efficient and successful business processes.

Thinking about the case

1 Why would Unilever seek to rationalize their IT systems?
2 What benefits would an organization expect due to such a rationalization?
3 Why is it important nowadays for organizations to align their IT strategy with their business strategy?
4 How important is it for Unilever's IT systems to be centred on its customers?
5 How might outsourcing functions such as 'financial transactions' aid in the streamlining of Unilever's IT systems?

SOURCE: CIO Magazine online at: http://www.cio.co.uk/mis100/companyprofile/index.cfm?companyid=8

Case study **1.2**

The personal touch

'The information about a package is as important as the delivery of the package itself.' FREDERICK W. SMITH, FOUNDER AND CHAIRMAN OF FEDEX

With bases from Brussels to Hong Kong, FedEx is an organization that never sleeps and for which every minute counts. On the peak days between Christmas and New Years' Eve, it typically ships more than 8 million packages. On a normal day the company transports more than 6 million packages, using over 600 aircraft and 71,000 trucks across 220 countries and territories. Inevitably, some packages miss their delivery time, some miss their destination and some are damaged. When that happens, FedEx's 4,000 customer service reps are the people customers call.

Prompt, efficient customer service is extremely important for staying in this highly competitive global shipping industry, let alone doing so with a satisfactory profit. Incoming telephone calls at FedEx's 46 call centres across the globe never stop and FedEx reps never have an idle moment on shift. Sitting in front of computer monitors in a cluster of cubicles with headsets on, these agents barely have time to stretch their limbs.

A caller in London complains that her package hasn't arrived, which is a common complaint. Another in Pretoria asks if he can change his pickup time. A third caller in Oslo is confused about signature: is he supposed to sign for the delivery or will the package just be dropped at his doorstep? The reps are confident and friendly. They welcome any question or complaint even if they have heard it a thousand times before. The words 'I am sorry' are uttered often. They are careful not to give the customers a feeling of being rushed, but try to resolve complaints quickly. Time is money.

Several years ago FedEx installed software that reps at the call centres can use to provide faster service. Many of the callers are already registered in the company's database. One of the most frequent requests is to send a FedEx worker to pick up a package. Using the software, a rep can handle such a request in 20 seconds. All she needs to do is enter a name, which leads to a post code, which in turn leads to a tracking number. That number uniquely identifies the package. Some complaints are more complex. For example, a FedEx driver misunderstood a note a caller had left for him and therefore misdelivered a package. A complaint like that takes no more than 10 minutes to resolve.

An experienced and efficient rep can handle about 10 callers in 45 minutes. Ideally, though, nobody would call. If FedEx had its way, at least six of the ten callers would use their computers to go to FedEx's global website and solve their problem by themselves. Six of ten, because about 60 per cent of FedEx's clients have a computer connected to the Internet. Like other companies, FedEx tries to save labour by directing callers to its website. Yet, many people prefer to use the phone and talk to a human helper.

Every time a customer decides to use the company's website instead of telephoning, the company saves up to €1.42. Efforts to divert callers to the site have been fruitful. In 2005, FedEx call centres received 470,000 calls per day, 83,000 fewer than in 2000. This difference in calls translates into a saving of €43.73 million per year. The company's website handles an average of 60 million requests per month to track packages. Operating the website does costs money. Each of these requests costs FedEx €0.02, amounting to €16.4 million per year. However, if all these requests were made by phone, the cost would exceed €1.03 billion per year. As it is impossible to divert all callers to the website, the company must maintain call centres. The annual costs of these call centres is €248 million. This cost might decrease over the years, as more and more customers use the website, but there will probably always be call centres, because FedEx does not want to lose frustrated customers.

Many people are still uncomfortable doing business at a website. The cost of a customer who is frustrated by the company website is incalculable. Experience shows that people are willing to encounter one or two obstacles with the website, but then they stop trying.

Since its establishment in the United States in 1971 as Federal Express Corp., the company was keen on information technologies, but over the years it used an increasing number of disparate systems for different business purposes, such as air freight, ground freight, special logistic operations and custom shipping of critical items. These discrepancies were compounded by expansion into major new territories, such as Europe and Asia in 1984 and the Middle East in 1989. By 1999, customer information was scattered across computer systems implemented over 14 years. To periodically test service, executives pretend to be customers. They discovered that customers who used more than one FedEx business were not treated consistently. For example, when claiming damages, a customer had to fill out 37 fields on a claims form, such as tracking number, ship date, pickup location and destination, even though FedEx systems already held data for 33 of those fields. The official change of 'Federal Express' to 'FedEx' started an important move: all the company units were to share the same information systems.

Meanwhile, FedEx's customer service centres were redesigned around a PC-based software desktop. If reps could pull up historical data on customers whenever they called – not just their shipping histories, but their preferences and even images of their paper bills – FedEx could provide better, faster service, both to individual customers and to businesses that sold goods through catalogues.

In 2000, management purchased customer relationship management software called Clarify. A new policy

FedEx Express employees in the company hub at Charles de Gaulle International Airport in Paris, France, help customers reach major European markets.

PHOTO SOURCE: COURTESY OF FEDEX

was established: systems and customer service experts are equally responsible for the call centres. Using PCs, reps can pull up historical data on customers whenever customers call. Customer records that are immediately available to reps include shipping histories, preferences and images of the paper bills. Customers are happier now than they were just a few years ago. So are the reps. Turnover of service reps has decreased 20 per cent.

Productivity is important, but so is the reps' service quality. They must be polite, provide customers with correct appropriate information and try not to give customers a reason to call again. Typically, callers are either determined to speak to a human or they know the help they need is too complex to be available at the company's website. Therefore, callers require more time than in the past. The company periodically evaluates the reps' performance based on clearly stated goals that take all these factors into consideration. Typically, 32 per cent of the reps' performance rating is based on the quality of their response and 17 per cent on their efficiency. The other 51 per cent is based on attendance, adherence to scheduled breaks and compliance with regulations.

Interestingly, customers are not interested in friendliness, but in quick and accurate information. FedEx constantly follows customer reactions to different help styles. Managers discovered then when reps' time is not limited, they tend to speak with customers beyond the time required to solve the problem. Customers perceive them as too talkative and they get a bad impression about FedEx. Thus, reps are encouraged to get off the phone as soon as the problem is resolved rather than try to be 'nice'.

The professionals who work for the vendor of Clarify, the CRM software, spend time with reps to see how well the software serves them. They discovered that reps often move quickly from one window of information to another and that sometimes they took extra time to find a window that 'disappeared'. The software engineers decided to modify Clarify so it interacts with Java code. This enables the reps to switch between windows and different applications of Clarify quickly during a call without reentering customer data. For instance, if a customer needs directions to pick up a package, the rep can click the tab of the mapping application. Relying on the customer's account data, the application picks up the customer's post code. Combining it with the code of the pickup centre, the software immediately produces directions, which the rep can read to the customer.

While great improvements have already been accomplished both in service speed and quality, FedEx executives continue to look for ways to improve. They refuse to discuss what their next step is because it might be copied immediately by competitors, but they do reveal that their goal is to bring call centres to the point where a rep never has to put a customer on hold.

Experts expect a single 'nervous system' for all types of customer calls by 2010. Software will accept all customer calls from the customer's PC phone or handheld device. Special software involving artificial intelligence techniques will screen all incoming calls, evaluate the problem complexity and decide whether to direct the calls to other software for resolution or to invite a human rep to intervene.

FedEx has already developed systems that integrate sales and marketing data. The FedEx Europe, Middle East, India and Africa division has developed a data warehouse that is fed data from more than 20 sources, not just CRM but also human resource (HR) systems and external sources. Immediate access is available to senior management to enable them to detect early warning signs of customer dissatisfaction. They can analyse customer activity to see if they are using competitors for their deliveries, what their preferred delivery destinations and types of service are, complaints received and so on. So customers who have the potential to become ex-customers can be targeted.

Thinking about the case

1 What is CRM in general? Give examples of *different* CRM applications.

2 Enumerate and explain the various ways in which the CRM application discussed here (Clarify) saves costs or helps in other ways.

4 Which metrics would you use to measure *before* and *after* performance regarding the information technologies implemented in this case? Consider cost, service quality, cycle time and any other performance factor and provide a specific metric (i.e., ratio, product, or absolute value).

4 As a customer, would you prefer more, or less, mechanized service in lieu of human help?

5 As an executive for FedEx or a similar company, what else would you implement using software and the Internet?

SOURCE: D. Gage, 'FedEx: Personal Touch', Baseline (www.baselinemag.com), 13 January, 2005; www.fedex.com/us, 2005; www.fedex.com/us/about/overview/worldwide/emea.html?link=4 2007

silicon.com

Case study **1.3**

Analysis: CRM – get involved

BY RON CONDON

Work with all parts of the business if you want a successful rollout . . .

Whatever the size of your business, if you're looking to roll out CRM, you must involve all parts of the organization, says Ron Condon. Recent developments, though, do favour smaller players.

When the dot-com bubble burst at the beginning of the decade, a lot of customer relationship management projects came to a grinding halt or just faded away. No wonder then that by 2002, research companies such as Gartner were saying that barely half of CRM implementations had been completed or had delivered any real benefit.

In the heady days of the boom, many companies had been seduced by the prospect of being able to track their customers' every move – and thereby gain some deep, new understanding of their own business.

Retailers especially began to construct huge data warehouses and even small corner shops started launching their own loyalty card schemes. According to those technology companies pushing the concept, CRM would give companies exciting new insights into the way shoppers think.

One example that did the rounds for a while was the close connection between the sales of beer and nappies. Analysis of customer data, it was claimed, had revealed the phenomenon of working dads popping into the supermarket on a Friday night to get the beers – and to do their paternal duty by picking up the weekly nappy supply.

Unfortunately, no other great insights emerged and the beer–nappy theory turned out to be an urban myth anyway. CRM had hit the buffers, and the whole area seemed to go quiet, with some big supermarkets such as Asda and Safeway canning their loyalty card programmes. The rewards just didn't seem to be worth the trouble and the huge expense.

But the failure of so many CRM projects cannot be blamed purely on bad timing. Giles Hutchins, head of the CRM practice with consultants Atos Origin, says: 'A lot of CRM projects were run out of the sales or marketing department, where they just wanted to capture their customer information. But CRM needs to be an overarching application across the organization, not just the front office.'

The failure to integrate it with other areas of the organization meant that CRM could only deliver limited benefits. Without links into other aspects of the business – finance, order processing, supply chain, distribution, complaints handling – the CRM system was just a glorified contact management application.

Part of the problem was that companies concentrated just on technology without seeing that a customer-centric approach to business was going to require changes in processes, procedures and also in the way people in back-office functions operated. According to Paul Brewer, head of business development for BT's CRM practice, technology should account for just 30 per cent of a CRM implementation – with people and processes taking the lion's share of the budget.

As with any system that is going to touch the whole organization, a CRM project needs board-level backing and sponsorship, plus cooperation

Beer and nappies – a CRM-inspired myth?

PHOTO SOURCE © GARY ROEBUCK/ALAMY

and input from all departments. It also has to be underpinned by real business goals, such as a greater choice of sales channels, better product availability, ability to offer better, faster service and the ability to identify the most valuable customers.

In other words, no matter what the size of the organization, CRM has to be part of an overall business strategy with a clear model of where the business wants to get to. According to Juliet Armstrong, a partner at consultancy The Berkeley Partnership, development of that strategic model will help to involve senior management from the whole business – channel management, supply chain, product development, marketing and HR – and force them to decide overall priorities at an early stage. It also stops CRM being just an IT or sales project, but one that the whole organization will use.

That in turn sets the stage for greater integration between systems. Armstrong makes the point that new integration technologies based on web services, XML and common object models now make it far easier to create the seamless flow of information that is needed. 'The challenge of integrating new technologies with legacy systems was unachievable with the tools that were available in the late 1990s', she says.

In addition, most of the big CRM applications have created open APIs to allow an interchange of information with other systems. For instance, Salesforce.com, which began life very much as a sales automation service, now reports that more than 40 per cent of all its transactions come via its API – in other words, through other applications.

For complex integration projects, where the CRM system needs to interact with three or more other applications, point-to-point links via the API can start to get messy. In those cases, Atos Origin's Hutchins recommends going for some kind of enterprise application integration (EAI) tool from the likes of BEA, IBM or Tibco.

But Berkeley's Armstrong counsels against trying to make everything integrate regardless of cost. 'Consider any integration on a cost–benefit basis but also look at the impact on business process of implementing the resultant workaround [of not doing an integration]. Usually it's best to create a strategic target architecture and justified road map to achieve that architecture. This clearly explains the reasons for integration or business process workarounds at each phase of delivery.'

Despite the far-reaching nature of a fully integrated CRM system, most practitioners advise a phased introduction, so that some success can be won early on. Hutchins says: 'Start small and adopt a phased approach. Keep phase one succinct, so you can ensure success and buy-in for the completion of the project.'

Armstrong agrees: 'Each phase should have a clear business case and consider the wider impact on customers and the business – such as customer marketing and employee training. Importantly, each phase must minimize risk to the business and consider operational data requirements.'

She also notes that any integration should take into account the need to comply with the raft of corporate governance and financial regulations. With so many applications transmitting or sharing information, the company must be able to maintain an audit trail and ensure back-up and recovery if things go wrong. This may well influence the choice of integration mechanism.

She advises: 'Synchronous message-based integration is appropriate for order management solutions but unsuitable for transferring financial data in an auditable fashion. An ETL tool is likely to be more effective.'

The availability of so much technology to help tie different applications together means that smaller companies could have an advantage in the CRM stakes. While big companies, especially the High Street banks, are struggling to integrate huge legacy systems, smaller companies are less weighed down by past investments and can make the most of a newer, more streamlined approach.

Thinking about the case

1 There is a recommendation that the introduction of a CRM system should be phased. It would seem reasonable to introduce those aspects that are simplest and/or give the greatest benefits. Draw up a shortlist of CRM subsystems that best fit these criteria.

2 Are there any disadvantages to a phased approach to CRM system implementation?

Chapter 2

Strategic uses of information systems

LEARNING OBJECTIVES

Executives know that information technology is not merely a resource to support day-to-day operations. Clever use of IT can significantly change an organization's long-term strategic position in national and global markets. Often, applying information systems to long-term planning completely changes the way a firm conducts its business. Some systems even change the product or service that a firm provides. Today, information systems are an accepted and integral part of strategic planning for nearly all organizations.

When you finish this chapter, you will be able to:

Explain what business strategy and strategic moves are.

Illustrate how information systems can give businesses a competitive advantage.

Identify basic initiatives for gaining a competitive advantage.

Explain what makes an information system a *strategic* information system.

Identify fundamental requirements for developing strategic information systems.

Explain circumstances and initiatives that make one IT strategy succeed and another fail.

BETTER BITES

USING INFORMATION STRATEGICALLY

The information systems that Better Bites had in place had succeeded so far: the business had been operating for a year and it was profitable. Paul Clermont, Sarah Odell and Christina Healy had begun to enjoy running their pushcart lunch business. Handling the food concessions for the city's major holiday celebrations had helped carry them through the summer, when there weren't as many students on campus. Now the three entrepreneurs were looking for ways to expand and increase their profits even more. An opportunity presented itself at a City Council meeting.

Looking at expansion

Christina regularly attended Council meetings to keep in touch with the local business community. She was always looking for new opportunities. After one meeting, the manager of a local shopping centre approached her with a proposal: the shopping centre manager wanted to draw more foot traffic and he thought that some small food vendors would provide a fun atmosphere and encourage shoppers to linger. He was thinking of a couple of pushcarts – would Better Bites be interested? Christina checked with her partners and they decided to expand their operations to the shopping centre.

However, the increased sales from operating three carts meant that Paul, Sarah and Christina needed to ramp up their production – and quickly. They were having trouble handling their increased cooking and food preparation load – they were in Paul's uncle's kitchen earlier and earlier to finish in time. They seriously needed to consider renting kitchen space for themselves. And they also needed to hire additional staff to help prepare the sandwiches and staff the carts – it was simply too much for Paul, Sarah and Christina to cover three carts by themselves.

A new line of business?

Customers began lining up at the shopping centre lunch carts in droves. To keep their clientele happy, Better Bites experimented with new crisp varieties – handing them out to waiting customers and getting their immediate feedback. Sarah tried parsnip crisps and baked tortilla chips in different flavours, in addition to the all-natural potato crisps they originally offered. Customers loved the new tortilla crisps and they could be made from wraps that hadn't been used the previous day, so their additional cost was minimal. With the great customer reception of the crisp line, Paul, Sarah and Christina were now considering producing and packaging the crisps for sale to other retail establishments – in other words, becoming a food manufacturer. They would definitely need to move to new kitchen facilities, but they reasoned they could use the new kitchen space around the clock eventually, if needed. The additional crisp revenue

A local shopping centre provided the first opportunity for Better Bites' expansion and introduced new strategic challenges for Paul, Sarah and Christina.

PHOTO SOURCE: © SIMON GURNEY

could help them cover the cost of the equipment and new space. They'd also need their own pots and pans, ovens and packaging equipment. None of this would be cheap, so they'd need to watch expenses and revenues closely in their spreadsheets.

Charting a strategy with information systems

Paul and Christina also investigated the option of using only organic ingredients, to appeal even more to the health-food market. They called organic suppliers and surfed the Web to gather data to plug into their spreadsheets. Doing this research helped them avoid what could have been a costly mistake – going organic would raise their prices 33 per cent and would not be a good strategic move for them right now.

New competition on the block

After Paul, Sarah and Christina had made these important decisions, they received some bad news. Word of Better Bites success had evidently spread – a local Subwich franchise had located a shop near to the University concourse to attract some of their business. The three partners were very worried about competing with a national franchise, which had much greater financial resources than they did.

To help retain loyal customers, they decided to implement a frequent buyer programme, where current customers could get a free sandwich after the purchase of ten. The three partners registered repeat customers in their database and issued cards to be punched. They hoped this additional programme would help them stay competitive with Subwich, but they knew they'd need to remain on their toes.

Strategy and strategic moves

The word 'strategy' originates from the Greek word *strategos*, meaning 'general'. In war, a strategy is a plan to gain an advantage over the enemy. Other disciplines, especially business, have borrowed the term. As you know from media coverage, corporate executives often discuss actions in ways that make business competition sound like war. Business people must devise decisive courses of action to win – just as generals do. In business, a strategy is a plan designed to help an organization outperform its competitors. Unlike battle plans, however, business strategy often takes the form of creating new opportunities rather than beating rivals.

Although many information systems are built to solve problems, many others are built to seize opportunities. And, as anyone in business can tell you, identifying a problem is easier than creating an opportunity. Why? Because a problem already exists; it is an obstacle to a desired mode of operation and, as such, calls attention to itself. An opportunity, on the other hand, is less tangible. It takes a certain amount of imagination, creativity and vision to identify an opportunity, or to create one and seize it. Information systems that help seize opportunities are often called **strategic information systems (SISs)**. They can be developed from scratch, or they can evolve from an organization's existing ISs.

strategic information system Any information system that gives its owner a competitive advantage.

In 1979 Michael Porter of Harvard Business School presented a framework for businesses to consider their strategic position in a competitive environment. He defined five forces that can affect the marketplace which can therefore be used to give a qualitative analysis of the business' position. Figure 2.1 shows diagrammatically how the forces potentially affect a business initiative. Any change in one or more of the forces may lead the business to re-asses what it is doing. In all cases, information systems can be helpful in analysing the situation, alerting us to subtle changes and trends and generally giving us market intelligence.

- Supplier bargaining power – An information system can help to analyse the relative costs of goods and materials from suppliers, investigate trends in prices and volumes and look for the best deal from our suppliers.

Figure 2.1 Porter's five forces model

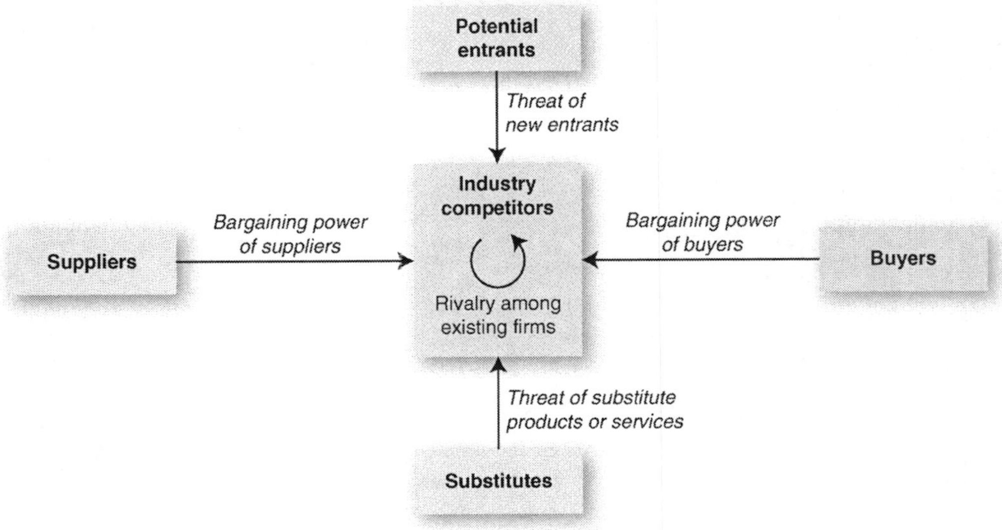

- Competitive rivalry – An information system can help analysis of our competitors, the prices they are charging, their customer base and so on.
- Buyer bargaining power – The more we know about our customers the easier it is to hold on to them. An information system that holds details of previous purchases will enable us to pitch our sale price at the right level.
- Threat of substitutes – More complicated than keeping an eye on companies in direct competition, we need sophisticated analysis that enables us to identify potential substitute products early and react accordingly.
- Threat of new entrants – Any profitable market will lead to new firms joining. We need an information system to give us early warning about these new competitors and strategic information to enable us to maintain our share of the market.

In a free-market economy, it is difficult for a business to do well without some strategic planning. Although strategies vary, they tend to fall into some basic categories, such as developing a new product, identifying an unmet consumer need, changing a service to entice more customers or retain existing clients, or taking any other action that increases the organization's value through improved performance.

Many strategies do not, and cannot, involve information systems. But increasingly, corporations are able to implement certain strategies – such as maximizing sales and lowering costs – thanks to the innovative use of information systems. In other words, better information gives corporations a competitive advantage in the marketplace. A company uses strategy to maximize its strengths, resulting in a **competitive advantage**. When a business uses a strategy with the intent to *create* a market for new products or services, it does not aim to compete with other organizations, because that market does not yet exist. Therefore, a strategic move is not always a competitive move. However, in a free-enterprise society, a market rarely remains the domain of one organization for long; thus, competition ensues almost immediately. So, we often use the terms 'competitive advantage' and 'strategic advantage' interchangeably.

competitive advantage A position in which one dominates a market; also called strategic advantage.

You might have heard statements about using the Web strategically. Business competition is no longer limited to a particular country or even a region of the world. To increase the sale of

Industry SNAPSHOT

IT and business strategy at board level

SOURCE: NCC Benchmark of IT Strategy 2006, National Computer Centre

A 2006 study by the National Computer Centre of 288 IT decision-makers in medium- to large-sized UK organizations found that the IT function is becoming more widely represented at company board level. Nearly 85 per cent of those surveyed now have IT representation at the top level compared to only 61 per cent in 2001. On the other hand 54 per cent of the respondents where IT is not represented on the board cited lack of involvement and commitment of senior managers as the cause of a poor IT strategy. The study's authors concluded that 'IT strategy is becoming a much bigger component of business strategy. This means the business drivers and consequent abilities to apply these through technology is becoming a critical issue for the business and the IT professional.'

The IT function's presence at board level is growing but, as the chapter 9 silicon.com case study illustrates, this growth remains unsatisfactorily slow for many businesses.

PHOTO SOURCE: © MAARTJE VAN CASPEL

goods and services, companies must regard the entire world as their market. Because thousands of corporations and hundreds of millions of consumers have access to the Web, augmenting business via the Web has become strategic: many companies that utilized the Web early on have enjoyed greater market shares, more experience with the Web as a business enabler, and larger revenues than latecomers. Some companies developed information systems, or features of information systems, that are unique, such as Amazon's 'one-click' online purchasing and Priceline's 'name your own price' auctioning. Practically any web-based system that gives a company competitive advantage is a strategic information system.

Achieving a competitive advantage

Consider competitive advantage in terms of a for-profit company, whose major goal is to maximize profits by lowering costs and increasing revenue. A for-profit company achieves competitive advantage when its profits increase significantly, most commonly through increased market share. Table 2.1 lists eight basic initiatives that can be used to gain competitive advantage, including offering a product or service that competitors cannot provide or providing the same product or service more attractively to customers. It is important to understand that the eight listed are the most common, but not the only, types of business strategies an organization can pursue. It is also important to understand that strategic moves often consist of a combination of two or more of these initiatives and other steps. The essence of strategy is innovation, so competitive advantage is often gained when an organization tries a strategy that no one has tried before.

CD TASK

For example, Dell was the first PC manufacturer to use the Web to take customer orders. Competitors have long imitated the practice, but Dell, first to gain a web audience, gained

Table 2.1 Eight basic ways to gain competitive advantage

Initiative	Benefit
Reduce costs	A company can gain advantage if it can sell more units at a lower price while providing quality and maintaining or increasing its profit margin.
Raise barriers to market entrants	A company can gain advantage if it deters potential entrants into the market, enjoying less competition and more market potential.
Establish high switching costs	A company can gain advantage if it creates high switching costs, making it economically infeasible for customers to buy from competitors.
Create new products or services	A company can gain advantage if it offers a unique product or service.
Differentiate products or services	A company can gain advantage if it can attract customers by convincing them its product differs from the competition's.
Enhance products or services	A company can gain advantage if its product or service is better than anyone else's.
Establish alliances	Companies from different industries can help each other gain advantage by offering combined packages of goods or services at special prices.
Lock in suppliers or buyers	A company can gain advantage if it can lock in either suppliers or buyers, making it economically impractical for suppliers or buyers to deal with competitors.

more experience than other PC makers on this e-commerce vehicle and still sells more computers via the Web than its competitors. Figure 2.2 indicates that a company can use many strategies together to gain competitive advantage.

Initiative 1: Reduce costs

Customers like to pay as little as possible while still receiving the quality of service or product they need. One way to increase market share is to lower prices and the best way to lower prices is to *reduce costs*. For instance, if carried out successfully, massive automation of any business process gives an organization competitive advantage. The reason is simple: automation makes an organization more productive and any cost savings can be transferred to customers through lower prices. We saw this happen in the car industry. In the 1970s, Japanese car manufacturers brought robots to their production and assembly lines and reduced costs – and subsequently prices – quickly and dramatically. The robots weld, paint and assemble parts at a far lower cost than manual labour. Until their competitors began to employ robots, the Japanese had a clear competitive advantage because they were able to sell high-quality cars for less than their competitors.

CD TASK

In the service sector, the Web has created an opportunity to automate what until recently was considered an activity that only humans could perform: customer service. An enormous trend towards automating online customer service began with companies such as FedEx, which initially gave customers an opportunity to track their parcels' status by logging on to a dedicated, private network and database. The same approach is now implemented through the Web. Many sites today include answers to FAQs (frequently asked

Figure 2.2 Many strategic moves can work together to achieve a competitive advantage

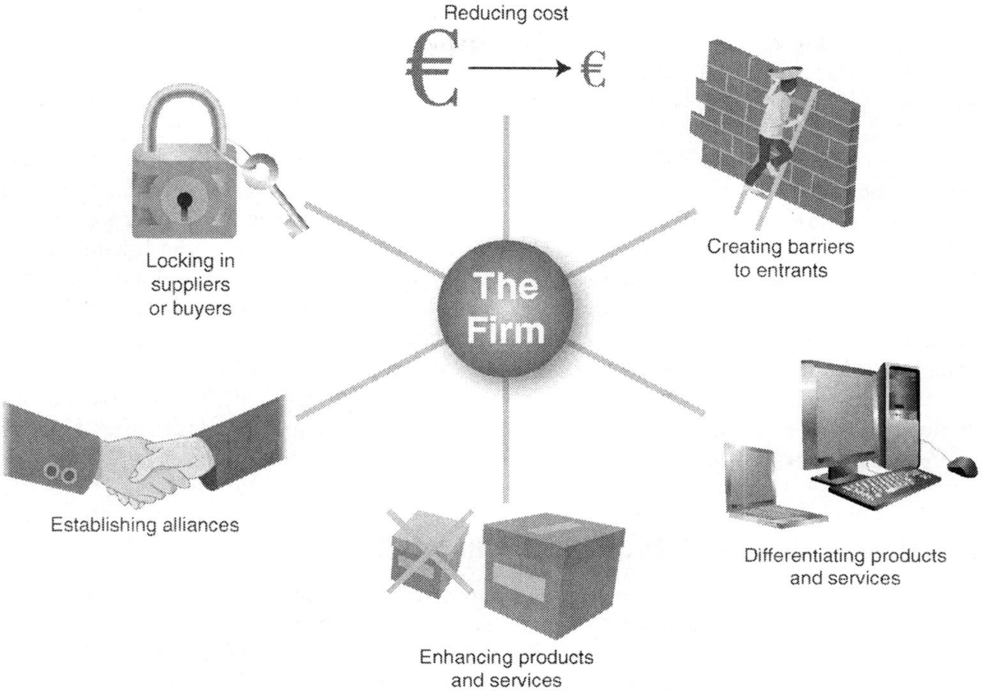

questions). Others have special programs that can respond to customer questions. Online service gives businesses two major benefits: it changes service from being labour-intensive to technology-intensive, which is much less expensive; and it provides customers easy access to a service seven days a week, 24 hours a day. It cuts the costs not only of expensive human labour but also of telephone and postal charges. Companies that are the first to adopt advanced systems that reduce labour enjoy competitive advantage for as long as their competitors lag behind.

Initiative 2: Raise barriers to market entrants

The smaller the number of companies competing within an industry, the better off each company is. Therefore, an organization might gain competitive advantage by making it difficult, or impossible, for other organizations to produce the product or service it provides. Using expertise or technology that is unavailable to competitors or prohibitively expensive is one way to bar new entrants.

CD TASK

Companies *raise barriers to entrants* in a number of ways. Obtaining legal protection of intellectual property such as an invention or artistic work will bar competitors from freely using it. Microsoft and other software powerhouses have gained tremendous strategic advantages by copyrighting and patenting software. On the Web, there are numerous examples of such protection. Priceline.com holds a patent for online reverse ('name your own price') auctioning, which has prevented competitors from entering its business space. Amazon.com secured a patent for one-click online purchasing, which enables customers to enter delivery and credit-card information once, so all subsequent orders do not have to go through a verification web page. Although the software is quite simple, Amazon obtained a patent for it in 1999 that won't expire until 2017. Amazon successfully sued Barnes & Noble (B&N) when it implemented the same technology on BN.com. Now B&N pays Amazon for its use. More recently, Amazon obtained a patent for its techniques used to decide what types of items a user might like to buy in the future. Exclusive use of the methods might give the company additional strategic advantage in online shopping. Protecting any invention, including hardware and software, with patents and copyrights provides an excellent barrier to potential entrants.

Another barrier to potential new market entrants is the high expense of entering that market. The pension fund management industry is a prime illustration. State Street Corporation is one of its most successful examples. The company maintains operations in 26 countries covering all major investment centres, including London, Frankfurt, Paris and Johannesburg. In the 1980s, State Street committed massive amounts of money to developing ISs that helped make the company a leader in managing pension funds and international bank accounts. The huge capital allocation required to build a system to compete successfully with State Street keeps potential entrants out of the market. Instead, other pension management corporations rent State Street's technology and expertise. In fact, State Street derives about 70 per cent of its revenues from selling its IS services. This company is an interesting example of an entire business refocusing around its ISs.

Initiative 3: Establish high switching costs

switching costs
Expenses that are incurred when a customer stops buying a product or service from one business and starts buying it from another.

Switching costs are expenses incurred when a customer stops buying a product or service from one business and starts buying it from another. Switching costs can be explicit (such as charges the seller levies on a customer for switching) or implicit (such as the indirect costs in time and money spent adjusting to a new product that does the same job as the old).

Often, explicit switching costs are fixed, non-recurring costs, such as a penalty a buyer must pay for terminating a deal early. In the mobile telephone service industry, you can usually get an attractive deal, but if you cancel the service before a full year or more has passed, you have to pay a hefty penalty. So although another company's service might be more attractive, you might decide to wait the full contract period because the penalty outweighs the benefits of the new company's service. When you do decide to switch, you might discover that the telephone is not suitable for service with any other telephone company. The cost of the telephone itself, then, is another disincentive to switch.

A perfect example of indirect switching expenses is the time and money required to learn new software. Once a company trains its personnel to use one word-processing or spreadsheet program, a competing software company must offer a very enticing deal to make switching worthwhile. The same principle holds for many other applications, such as database management systems and web page editors and graphical software. Consider Microsoft's popular MS Office suite; you can purchase the significantly less expensive Sun Microsystems' StarOffice, a software suite that is equivalent to MS Office. Better yet, you can download free of charge the entire suite of OpenOffice.org. Yet, few organizations or consumers who are accustomed to MS Office are willing to switch to StarOffice or OpenOffice.org.

Manufacturers of laser and ink-jet printers sell their printers at cost or below cost. However, once you purchase a printer, you must replace a depleted ink or toner cartridge with one that the printer manufacturer sells, or take a risk with non-original cartridges. As a cartridge customer, you face high costs if you consider switching to another brand. Even if comparable cartridges from another manufacturer are less expensive, you cannot use them; and if you decide to use those cartridges, you will lose your investment in the printer, because you must buy a new one. Thus, establishing high switching costs often locks in customers. Locking in customers by any means is a way to accomplish a strategic advantage and is discussed later.

Initiative 4: Create new products or services

Clearly, *creating a new and unique product or service* that many organizations and individuals need gives an organization a great competitive advantage. Unfortunately, the advantage lasts only until other organizations in the industry start offering an identical or similar product or service for a comparable or lower price.

Examples of this scenario abound in the software industry. For instance, Lotus Development Corporation became the major player early on in the electronic spreadsheet market after it introduced its Lotus 1-2-3 program. When two competitors tried to market similar products, Lotus sued for copyright infringement and won the court case, sustaining its market dominance for several years. However, with time, Microsoft established its Excel spreadsheet application as the world leader, not only by aggressive marketing but also by including better features in its application.

CD TASK

Another example of a company creating a new service is eBay, the firm that dominates online auctions. The organization was the first to offer this service, which became very popular within only a few months. While other firms now offer a similar service (e.g., Amazon and Yahoo! Auctions), the fact that eBay was the first to offer it gave eBay a huge advantage: it quickly acquired a large number of sellers and bidders, a network that is so critical to creating a 'mass' of clients, which in turn is the main draw for additional clients. It also gave eBay a great advantage in experience and allowed it to open a gap that was difficult for competitors to close, even for giants such as Amazon. eBay is an example of an entire business that would be impossible without the Web and the information technologies that support the firm's service.

eBay's success demonstrates the strategic advantage of the **first mover**, an organization that is the first to offer a new product or service. By the time other organizations start offering the same product or service, the first mover has usually created some assets that cannot be had by the competitors: a superior brand name, a better technology or method for delivery, or a critical mass. A critical mass is a body of clients that is large enough to attract many other clients. In many cases, first movers simply enjoy longer experience, which in itself is an advantage over competitors.

first mover A business that is first in its industry to adopt a technology or method.

Being a first mover is not always a guarantee of long-term success, however. One example of how a first-mover strategic advantage can be lost within just a few months is in the web browser arena. Netscape Corporation (now part of AOL) dominated the web browser market, which was new in 1994. By allowing individual users to download its browser for free, it cornered up to 95 per cent of the market. The wide use of the browser by individuals moved commercial organizations to purchase the product and other software compatible with the browser. Netscape's dominance quickly diminished when Microsoft aggressively marketed its own browser, which many perceived as at least as good as Netscape's. Microsoft provided Internet Explorer free of charge to anyone and then bundled it into the Microsoft Windows operating system software distributed with almost all PCs. Even after the court-ordered unbundling, its browser still dominated. This dominance in turn has been threatened by free browsers such as Mozilla's Firefox and Avant Force's Avant Browser, which offer similar or better features, more flexibility and fewer security vulnerabilities.

Other first movers have lost market share because they neglected to improve the service they pioneered. Few web surfers remember Infoseek, the first commercial search engine. Google, which entered the search engine arena in 1998, improved the quality and speed of web searches, offering a clutter-free home page. The strategy of its two young entrepreneurs was simple: provide the best search engine and refrain from commercialising it for a while. Over a period of about three years Google established itself as the best search engine. In time, it started to capitalize on this prominence by selling sponsored links (the right side of the results of a user's search). Most importantly, the organization never stopped improving its search algorithms and periodically has offered new services. The strategy has succeeded so much that 'google it' has become synonymous with 'search for it on the Web'.

PHOTO SOURCE: COURTESY OF GOOGLE INC

A Google employee enjoying a unique working environment.

Initiative 5: Differentiate products or services

A company can achieve a competitive advantage by persuading consumers that its product or service is better than its competitors', even if it is not. Called 'product differentiation', this advantage is usually achieved through advertising. Brand-name success is a perfect example of product differentiation. Think of Levi's Jeans, Chanel perfume and Gap clothes. The customer buys the brand-name product, perceiving it to be superior to similar products. In fact, some products *are* the same, but units sold under a prestigious brand name sell for higher prices. You often see this phenomenon in the food, clothing, pharmaceutical and cosmetics markets.

Product and service differentiation impacts not only consumers but also businesses. For example, IBM's Global Services division has created a great brand name for itself as an IT consulting firm. Interestingly, while IBM lost the corporate world's perception that only IBM computers are reliable enough to support business operations ('Nobody ever got fired for buying IBM'), it has gradually differentiated itself as a reliable and knowledgeable consulting organization.

Initiative 6: Enhance products or services

Instead of differentiating a product or service, an organization might actually add to the product or service to increase its value to the consumer; this is called *enhancing existing products or services*. For example, car manufacturers might entice customers by offering a longer warranty period for their cars and estate agents might attract more business by providing useful financing information to potential buyers.

Since the Internet opened its portals to commercial enterprises in the early 1990s, an increasing number of companies have supplemented their products and services. Their websites provide up-to-date information that helps customers utilize their purchased products better or receive additional services. Companies that pioneered such Internet use reaped great rewards. For example, Charles Schwab gained a competitive advantage over other, older brokerage companies such as Merrill Lynch by opening a site for online stock transactions. Nearly half its revenue now comes from this site. All brokerage houses followed and allow customers to trade through a website.

Other companies use the Internet to maintain their competitive edge by continually adding to and enhancing their online services. Dell is not the only company that sells computers online, for example. Other, smaller companies provide a similar service and sell comparable products, with more flexibility in 'building your own computer online', often at lower prices. However, Dell maintains the popularity of its site through continuous enhancement of the services it offers. For example, it offers a buying guide centre that clearly explains what to look for in various types of products and explains topics of interest such as software security.

Industry SNAPSHOT

Online holiday brochures

The availability of electronic brochures on holiday company websites has lead to a significant saving in printing costs as well as giving customers an improved, faster service according to www.onlinetravelbrochures.com. Operators such as Page and Moy and TrekAmerica have seen a 90 per cent decline in requests for printed brochures because they have given the customer the ability to browse a full electronic version of their printed brochures. The major tour operators (such as Thomson) have their own specially designed websites giving views of the accommodation, description of the facilities and so on but this third-party web service gives the smaller operators a chance to compete without the need for a dedicated website design. It is also reported that the availability of the online brochures leads to the average user staying with the website a further five minutes, hence opening up sales and marketing opportunities.

SOURCE: European Travel Commission, New Media Review, Online Travel Market (http://www.etcnewmedia.com) 21 December 2006

Royal Carribean International is one of a growing number of companies that use electronic brochures.

PHOTO SOURCE: COURTESY OF ROYAL CARRIBEAN CRUISES LTD

Why you should… understand the notion of strategic information systems

Although devising strategic moves is mainly the responsibility of senior management, let us remember Napoleon's words: 'Every soldier carries a marshal's baton in his knapsack.' To paraphrase: every junior manager is a potential senior manager. Thus, it is incumbent on every professional to try to think strategically for his or her organization. In fact, employees at the lowest levels have proposed some of the most brilliant strategic ideas. In today's highly competitive market, strategy might determine an organization's rise or fall.

An increasing number of strategic moves are either possible only with the aid of ISs or have ISs at the centre of their strategy – that is, technology provides the product, service or method that gains the organization strategic advantage. The potential for new business models on the Web is still great. Thus, professionals must understand how to use technology in strategic moves. Understanding how strategic information systems are conceived and implemented might help you suggest good ideas for such systems in your organization and facilitate your promotion up the organizational ladder.

Initiative 7: Establish alliances

Companies can gain competitive advantage by combining services to make them more attractive (and usually less expensive) than purchasing services separately. These alliances provide two draws for customers: combined service is cheaper and one-stop shopping is more convenient. The travel industry is very aggressive in this area. For example, airlines collaborate with hotel chains and car-rental firms to offer travel and lodging packages and with credit-card companies that offer discount ticket purchases from particular airlines or the products of particular manufacturers. Credit-card companies commonly offer frequent flier miles which can be exchanged for flights or for other goods and services through alliances. In a similar manner, the leading UK supermarket chain, Tesco, runs a customer loyalty card which can accumulate points exchangeable for not just grocery vouchers but holidays, theatre tickets and so on. In all these cases, alliances create competitive advantages. For example, by forging alliances the Tesco group can negotiate special deals with the suppliers of the 'treats'. The alliances work both ways too so that, for example, by staying at the Singapore Marriot Hotel you can earn Tesco Clubcard points!

As Figure 2.3 indicates, by creating an alliance, organizations enjoy synergy: the combined profit for the allies from the sale of a package of goods or services exceeds the profits earned when each acts individually. Sometimes, the alliances are formed by more than two organizations. Consider the benefits you receive when you agree to accept a major credit card: discounts from several hotel chains, restaurant chains, flower delivery chains and other stores, as well as free insurance when renting a car and frequent flier miles, to name a few. Similarly, travel websites such as Lastminute.com offer you the opportunity to reserve accommodation and car rental at discounts while you make your airline reservations. The company has also established alliances with hotel chains, car rental companies and health spas.

What is the common denominator among these companies? They each have an information system that tracks all these transactions and discounts. A package of attractive propositions entices clients who need these services (and most businesses do). Would this offer be feasible without an IS to track transactions and discounts? Probably not.

Figure 2.3 Strategic alliances combine services to create synergies

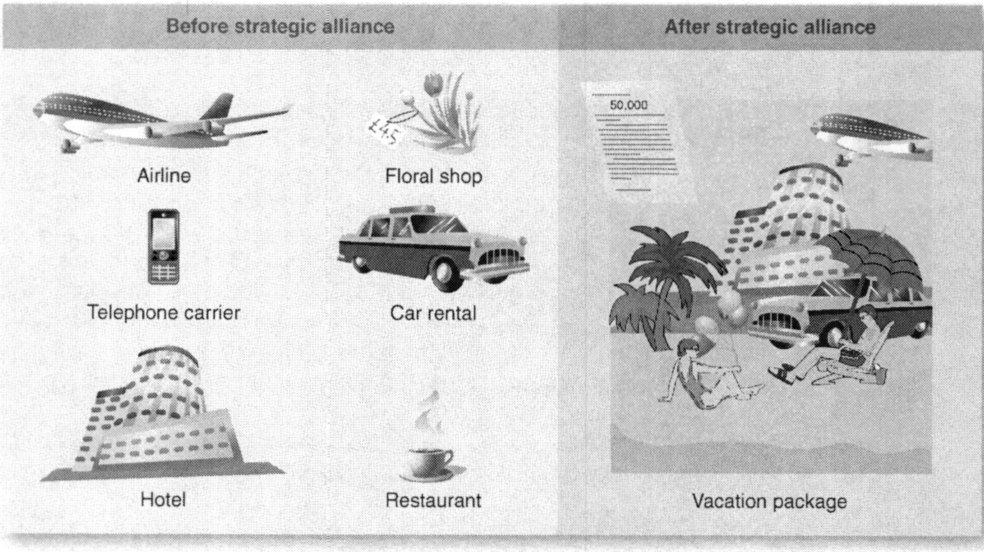

Industry SNAPSHOT

IT spending mismatch

According to statistics from the United Kingdom's National Computing Centre, gathered in August 2006, spending on IT increased from the previous year by 28 per cent to £3,891 per end user. However there is a sharp contrast between the spending from different sectors of industry. The finance sector reported a median spend of £9,864 per end user whilst the lowest-spending sectors of local government and health reported a relatively meagre spend of £2,189 and £1,713 per end user respectively.

Predictions for the future again show a contrast with the median level of spending growth at 1.9 per cent (compared to 1.6 per cent the previous year) but central government predicting a 'growth' rate of minus 2.5 per cent.

SOURCE: National Computer Centre press release 'No news is bad news for IT vendors', 1 November 2006

London's financial centre at Canrary Wharf – home to high levels of IT expenditure.

PHOTO SOURCE: © PEETER VIISIMAA

Growing web use for e-commerce has pushed organizations to create alliances that would be unimaginable a few years ago. Consider the alliance between Hewlett-Packard and FedEx. HP is a leading manufacturer of computers and computer equipment. FedEx is a shipping company. HP maintains inventory of its products at FedEx facilities. When customers order items from HP via its website, HP routes the order, via the Web, to FedEx. FedEx packages the items and ships them to customers. This arrangement lets HP dispatch ordered items within hours rather than days. The alliance gives HP an advantage that other computer equipment makers do not share. Again, it is a clever IS that enables this strategy.

CD TASK

On the Web, an obvious example of alliances is an **affiliate programme**. Anyone can place links to commercial sites on his or her personal website. When a visitor clicks through to a commercial site and makes a purchase, the first site's owner is paid a fee. Some online retailers have thousands of affiliates. The early adopters of such programmes, Amazon.co.uk, Buy.com, Priceline.co.uk and other large e-retailers, enjoyed a competitive advantage in gaining new customers. It is easy for any website holder to become an affiliate of Amazon.co.uk.

affiliate programme An arrangement by which a website promotes sales for another website through a link to the seller's site, and for which the affiliate is compensated. There are various schemes of compensation to affiliates.

Another example is the collaboration between Amazon.com and other retailers who make use of Amazon's technology. Target Corp. is one of America's largest retailers. To extend its operation to the Web, it formed a strategic alliance with the giant online retailer. If you go to Target's site, you will notice the words 'Powered by Amazon.com'. Amazon provides Target with its proprietary search engine, order-fulfilment and customer-service systems and the patented one-click shopping application, which lets customers pay for merchandise selected from the Target, Marshall Field's and Mervyns' sites from one electronic shopping cart (Marshall Field's and Mervyns are Target subsidiaries). In return, Amazon collects a percentage of all sales from Target's retail sites, as well as annual fixed fees. Have we mentioned referrals? Next to the logos of Target and its subsidiaries, you also find Amazon's logo, which serves as a link to Amazon's site (where you also see the Target logo prominently displayed). There are countless small Internet-based businesses displaying the 'powered by Amazon' logo and linking to Amazon.com, Amazon.co.uk or one of its many subsidiaries. These small businesses are often niche sites (for football programmes, local history, etc.) and they make a small amount of money for every sale that is made on Amazon via a referral from the affiliated site.

Initiative 8: Lock in suppliers or buyers

Organizations can achieve competitive advantage if they are powerful enough to lock in either suppliers to their mode of operation or buyers to their product. Possessing bargaining power – the ability to influence buyers and suppliers – is the key to this approach. As such, companies so large that suppliers and buyers must listen to their demands use this tactic nearly exclusively.

A firm gains bargaining power with a supplier either when the firm has few competitors or when the firm is a major competitor in its industry. In the former case, the fewer the companies that make up a supplier's customer base, the more important each company is to the supplier; in the latter case, the more important a specific company is to a supplier's success, the greater bargaining power that company has over that supplier.

CD TASK

The most common factor in bargaining is purchase volume. Companies that spend huge amounts of money purchasing parts and services have the power to force their suppliers to conform to their methods of operation and even to shift some costs onto suppliers as part of the business arrangement. Consider Tesco, the UK's largest retailer and fourth largest in the world. Not only does the company use its great bargaining power to pressure suppliers to lower prices, but it also requires them to use information systems that are compatible with its own automated processes. The suppliers must use ISs that tell them when to deliver products to Tesco so that the giant retailer is never left understocked or overstocked. The company is currently working towards a requirement for its suppliers to use radio frequency identification (RFID) devices in packaging, to allow more accurate tracking of ordered, shelved and sold items. This great bargaining power and tight control of inventory enables Tesco to enjoy great cost savings, which it passes on to customers, which keep growing in numbers thanks to the competitive prices. Many suppliers are locked in with Tesco because of the sheer volume of business they have with the company: some sell a third to one-half of everything they produce to this single retailer.

One way to lock in *buyers* in a free market is to create the impression that an organization's product is significantly better than the competitors', or to enjoy a situation in which customers fear high switching costs. In the software arena, enterprise applications are a good example. This type of software helps organizations manage a wide array of operations: purchasing, manufacturing, human resources, finance and so forth. The software is expensive, costing millions of dollars. After a company purchases the software from a firm, it is locked in to that firm's services: training, implementation, updates and so on. Thus, companies that sell enterprise software, such as SAP and Oracle, make great efforts to improve both their software and support services to maintain leadership in this market.

Another way to lock in clients is to *create a standard*. The software industry has pursued this strategy vigorously, especially in the Internet arena. For example, Microsoft's decision to give away its web browser by letting both individuals and organizations download it free from its site was not altruistic. Microsoft executives knew that the greater the number of Internet Explorer (IE) users, the greater the user base. The greater the user base, the more likely organizations were to purchase Microsoft's proprietary software to help manage their websites. Also, once individual users committed to IE as their main browser, they were likely to purchase Microsoft software that enhanced the browser's capabilities.

Similarly, Adobe gives away its Acrobat Reader software, an application that lets web surfers open and manipulate documents created using different computers running different operating systems, such as various versions of Windows, the Mac operating system and UNIX. When the Reader user base became large enough, organizations and individuals found it economically justifiable to purchase and use the full Acrobat application (the application used to create the documents) and related applications. Using this strategy put Adobe's PDF (portable data format) standard in an unrivalled position.

Another company, Macromedia Inc., developed software called Flash to create web page animations. It offers the Flash player for download free of charge but sells the development tool. Like Adobe, Macromedia has created a symbiotic situation to augment its market: the more individuals who download the player, the more businesses who are willing to purchase the development tool. The more companies who engage Flash modules in their web pages, the more individuals who download the player, without which they cannot enjoy those animations.

Creating and maintaining strategic information systems

There might be many opportunities to accomplish a competitive edge with IT, especially in industries that are using older software, such as the insurance industry. Insurance companies were among the early adopters of IT and have not changed much of their software. This is why some observers say the entire industry is inefficient. Once an insurance company adopts innovative software applications, it might gain competitive advantage. As you'll learn later in the chapter, when JetBlue was established, it adopted the latest technologies and this was a major reason for its great competitive advantage.

Companies can implement some of the strategic initiatives described in the previous section by using information systems. As we mentioned at the beginning of the chapter, a strategic information system (SIS) is any information system that can help an organization achieve a long-term competitive advantage. An SIS can be created from scratch, developed by modifying an existing system, or 'discovered' by realizing that a system already in place can be used to strategic advantage. While companies continue to explore new ways of devising SISs, some successful SISs are the result of less lofty endeavours: the intention to improve mundane operations using IT has occasionally yielded a system with strategic qualities.

Strategic information systems combine two types of ideas: ideas for making potentially winning business decisions and ideas for harnessing information technology to implement the decisions. For an information system to be an SIS, two conditions must exist. First, the information system must serve an organizational goal rather than simply provide information; and second, the organization's IS unit must work with managers of other functional units (including marketing, finance, purchasing, human resources and so on) to pursue the organizational goal.

Creating an SIS

To develop an SIS, top management must be involved from initial consideration through development and implementation. In other words, the SIS must be part of the overall organizational strategic plan. There is always the danger that a new SIS might be considered the IS unit's exclusive property. However, to succeed, the project must be a corporate effort, involving all managers who use the system.

Table 2.2 presents questions that management should ask to determine whether to develop a new SIS. Executives meet to try to identify areas in which information can support a

Table 2.2 Questions to answer in a strategic information system idea-generating meeting

1 What would be the most effective way to gain an advantage?

2 Would more accessible or timely information to our employees, customers, or suppliers help establish a significant advantage? If so . . .

3 Can an information system be developed that provides more accessible and timely information?

4 Will the development effort be economically justified?
- Can existing competitors afford to fund the development of a similar system?
- How long will it take the competitors to build their own, similar system?
- Can we make our system a moving target to the competition by constantly enhancing it, so that it always retains its superiority?

5 What is the risk of not developing such a system?

6 Are alternative means of achieving the same goals available, and if so, how do they compare with the advantages and disadvantages of a new SIS?

strategic goal. Only after completing the activities outlined in Table 2.2 will management be able to conceptualize an SIS that seizes an opportunity.

A word of caution regarding Question 4 in Table 2.2, the issue of economic justification of an SIS: an increasing number of researchers and practitioners conclude that estimating the financial benefits of information systems is extremely difficult. This difficulty is especially true of SISs. The purpose of these systems is not simply to reduce costs or increase output per employee; many create a whole new service or product. Some completely change the way an organization does business. Because so many fundamental business changes are involved, measuring the financial impact is difficult, if not impossible, even after implementation, let alone before. For example, if a bank is considering offering a full range of financial services via the Web, how can management know whether the move justifies the great cost of the special software? It is extremely difficult to estimate the success of such a bold approach in terms of how many new customers the bank would gain.

Reengineering and organizational change

Sometimes, to implement an SIS and achieve competitive advantage, organizations must rethink the entire way they operate. While brainstorming about strategic plans, management should ask: 'If we established this business unit again, from scratch, what processes would we implement and how?' The answer often leads to the decision to eliminate one set of operations and build others from the ground up. Changes such as these are called **reengineering**. Reengineering often involves adoption of new machinery and elimination of management layers. Frequently, information technology plays an important role in this process.

reengineering The process by which an organization takes a fresh look at a business process and reorganizes it to attain efficiency. Almost always, reengineering includes the integration of a new or improved information system.

Reengineering's goal is not to gain small incremental cost savings, but to achieve great efficiency leaps – of 100 per cent and even 1000 per cent. With that degree of improvement, a company often gains competitive advantage. Interestingly, a company that undertakes reengineering along with implementing a new SIS cannot always tell whether the SIS was successful. The reengineering process makes it impossible to determine how much each change contributed to the organization's improved position.

Implementation of an SIS requires a business to revamp processes – to undergo organizational change – to gain an advantage. For example, when General Motors Corp. (GM) decided to manufacture a new car that would compete with Japanese cars, it chose a different production process from that of its other cars. Management first identified goals that could make the new car successful in terms of how to build it and also how to deliver and service it. Realizing that none of its existing divisions could meet these goals because of their organizational structures, their cultures and their inadequate ISs, management established Saturn as an independent company with a completely separate operation.

CD TASK

Part of GM's initiative was to recognize the importance of Saturn dealerships in gaining competitive advantage. Through satellite communications, the new company gave dealers access to factory information. Clients could find out if, and exactly when, different cars with different features would be available.

Another feature of Saturn's SIS was improved customer service. Saturn embeds an electronic computer chip in the chassis of each car. The chip maintains a record of the car's technical details and the owner's name. When the car is serviced after the sale, new information is added to the chip. At their first service visit, many Saturn owners were surprised to be greeted by name as they rolled down their windows. While the quality of the car itself has been important to Saturn's success, the new SIS also played an important role. This technology was later copied by other car manufacturers.

Competitive advantage as a moving target

As you might have guessed, competitive advantage is not often long-lasting. In time, competitors imitate the leader and the advantage diminishes. So, the quest for innovative strategies must be dynamic. Corporations must continuously contemplate new ways to use information technology to their advantage. In a way, companies' jockeying for the latest competitive advantage is a lot like an arms race. Side A develops an advanced weapon, then side B develops a similar weapon that terminates the advantage of side A and so on.

In an environment where most information technology is available to all, SISs originally developed to create a strategic advantage quickly become an expected standard business practice. A prime example is the banking industry, where surveys indicate that increased IS expenditures did not yield long-range strategic advantages. The few banks that provided services such as ATMs and online banking once had a powerful strategic advantage, but now almost every bank provides these services.

A system can help a company sustain competitive advantage only if the company continuously modifies and enhances it, creating a moving target for competitors.

An Airline Reservation Systems (ARS) for travel agents is a classic example. American Airlines developed Sabre, an innovative IS, in the late 1970s to expedite airline reservations and sell travel agencies a new service. In 1976 United Airlines began installing its own ARS called Apollo into travel agencies themselves and American Airlines quickly followed. The cost savings in reducing call centre staff by getting the agents to make the booking themselves was too significant to ignore. Sabre surpassed Apollo in market share to take a dominant position, giving a return on investment (ROI) of more than 100 per cent in the late 1980s. The reservation system now encompasses hotel reservations, car rentals, train schedules, theatre tickets and limousine rentals. It later added a feature that let travellers use Sabre from their own computers. The system has been so successful that in its early years American earned more from it than from its airline operations. However, in the 1990s European airlines began developing their own reservation systems with Amadeus, owned jointly by Air France, Lufthansa, Iberia and SAS, being the market leader with a 27 per cent market share. Over the years the major players in the travel industry (airlines, traditional travel agents, tour operators, web-based travel companies) have been trying to get ahead of one another by the use of ISs and the fight goes on!

Industry SNAPSHOT

Keeping on track – A success story

TheTrainline was created by Virgin Trains in 1997 to sell rail tickets to UK destinations over the phone. In 1999 Virgin saw the potential of the Internet as a sales channel and launched TheTrainline website. The enhanced service to customers in the provision of timetable information as well as significant extra information on ticket prices and special deals was seen as an excellent way to gain competitive advantage.

The service was an immediate success and the company needed to add to its IT infrastructure to cope with demand. When the company formed alliances with other national rail companies such as Chiltern Railways and Southwest Trains as well as National Rail Enquiries, there was further growth in the company's IT support. The continued expansion of services and alliances lead to incremental growth in the IT systems but these were made in response to short-term business needs rather than a long-term, well planned strategy.

Robert Parkinson, Development Director, TheTrainline, says: 'We have grown very rapidly since the website's beginning and have become hugely successful. However, this has caused us to effect changes in an organic rather than structured fashion, which caused costs to rise. These issues are as a result of our success so are nice problems to have, but from a technical perspective they are genuine headaches.'

Therefore in 2002 the company commissioned Cap Gemini, the consultancy firm that originally created the website, to develop a plan for the migration from TheTrainline-evolved technology to a newer, more appropriate technology. The aim was to support growth, reduce maintenance costs and make site improvements easier. After considerable work on comparing alternative strategies, the company decided on a solution based around Microsoft .NET technology. System operation costs could be reduced by consolidating the number of servers from 180 machines to about 100 so there are fewer points of failure and hence increased reliability. However, the transition needed to be smooth and virtually imperceptible to the users. According to Parkinson, 'We chose this solution as it was worked out as the least risky and most cost-effective. It will enable us to transfer to the new platform gradually as we can neither afford nor countenance stopping our current system cold.'

However, it is not just in the web-based technology that TheTrainline is making strategic developments. The company have two contact centres based in Edinburgh and Dingwall, Scotland. These centres receive over 120,000 calls per week and sell train tickets worth more than £10 million per month. Although the centres were providing an essential personal service to customers, there was a need to investigate ways to make them operate more efficiently to reduce the cost per sale. One obvious way of reducing the costs is to reduce the one-to-one telephone conversations. The improvements made to the Internet-based service was one way but many customers still preferred to use the telephone. Traditional touch-tone technology is limited in the customer information that could be captured and certainly more appropriate for balance enquiries at a bank than for capturing complex travel requirements. However, something needed to be done, as 40 per cent of calls received an engaged tone, the average length of call was six minutes and 65 per cent of calls did not convert into a sale. In addition there was low morale and high turnover at the two sites.

Cable & Wireless, working with Cap Gemini, developed a system that enables a customer to use their telephone while minimizing the human operator's interaction. This is how it works:

- Calls are answered by an automated system that requests details of a planned journey (from/to, date, time, etc.). The customer responds naturally, as if speaking to a friend.
- Speech recognition software records the detail provided by the customer and feeds it into data format within the IT system.
- The 'demand' data then trigger automatic and virtually instant retrieval of all 'supply side' information (e.g. train times, seat availability, ticket prices) from rail industry databases.
- The data are sent to the screen of the appropriate sales agent and within a few seconds the customer call is patched through to that same agent, using Cable & Wireless's Intelligent Call

Manager (ICM) platform. The sale is confirmed person-to-person, payment details are taken and the transaction is completed.

Of course it was still important to make the automated part of the system friendly. A professional voice-over artist was commissioned to be the 'Voice of Virgin,' and the digitized recordings were embedded into the Cable & Wireless Advance Speech Recognition (ASR) system.

The system is even cleverer than that. Computer-telephony integration (CTI) checks the calling line identity (CLI) against a database of previous callers' CLIs. Returning callers are taken through a briefer menu than first-time callers and additionally the contact centre agent will have customer information displayed such as the caller's name, recent transactions and so on.

The benefits for TheTrainline have been huge:

- Overall operating costs have been reduced by 10 per cent, a saving of about a million pounds.
- Conversion rates for calls have increased with about 4,000 extra calls per week resulting in tickets being sold.
- Customer satisfaction has improved.
- Resource usage has improved, with CTI sharing the loading of calls and providing management reports.

According to Bill Hopkins, customer services director of TheTrainline, 'The improvement in TheTrainline contact centre infrastructure has led to significant benefits by improving the customer experience and in reducing our operating costs. As a consequence TheTrainline has been able to grow its business in a very competitive market place.'

SOURCE: http://www.cw.com/docs/why_cw/trainline.pdf 'Cable & Wireless contact centre puts TheTrainline back on track' and http://www.capgemini.com/resources/success-stories/capgemini_migration_strategy_will_help_thetrainline_to_reduce_maintenance_by_25/ 'Capgemini Migration Strategy Will Help TheTrainline to Reduce Maintenance by 25 per cent'

TheTrainline is the UK's leading independent retailer of train tickets with over 8.4 million registered users purchasing tickets for trips throughout the country.

PHOTO SOURCE: COURTESY OF THETRAINLINE

We return again to Amazon as an example of how ISs help companies maintain competitive advantage. Management believes that it must add new features to its website to attract buyers over and over again. The company continuously improves its web pages' look and the online services it provides. Amazon has moved from merely selling books through the Web to providing best-seller lists, readers' reviews, authors' interviews; selling almost any consumer product imaginable including users' own unwanted items through its Marketplace. The constant improvements help the company maintain its dominant position in online retailing.

PHOTO SOURCE: © PETER STEINER/ALAMY

A line of JetBlue planes, illustrating the rapid growth the airline has enjoyed since it was established in 2000.

JetBlue: A success story

We usually expect entrepreneurs to enter a new and profitable industry, not an old, money-losing one. However, with the proper technology and management methods, it seems that some energetic people can gain strategic advantage where others have been hurting. The US airline industry has seen mainly bad times since the industry's deregulation in the 1970s. Things got worse in the beginning of the third millennium and even worse after the terrible events of September 11, 2001. In 2001, the industry lost US$7.7 billion, but JetBlue had a profit of US$38.5 million on revenue of US$320.4 million. It continued to be profitable in 2002, 2003 and 2004 along with only one other US airline, Southwest Airlines, while all other US carriers had losses. Its revenues grew from US$998.4 in 2003 to US$1.27 billion in 2004.

JetBlue was established in February 2000 by David Neeleman, who serves as its CEO. Two decades earlier, in 1984, Neeleman cofounded Morris Air, a small airline in Salt Lake City, Utah, which was the first airline to offer ticketless travel, a programme that was developed inside the company. With a college student he developed Open Skies, a computer program that integrates electronic ticketing, Internet reservations and revenue management. Revenue management tools help an airline plan the most profitable routes and ticket pricing. Morris Air was sold to Southwest Airlines, which enthusiastically adopted the e-ticket idea. Neeleman became an executive at Southwest but left in frustration, because he believed that an airline could achieve much more efficiency with information technology. Now JetBlue has gained a great strategic advantage over larger and older airlines. The company's success is the result of understanding customers' priorities and gaining great efficiencies through automating whatever IT can automate. Management also learned to break away from practices that inhibit efficiency and agility. In a highly competitive industry that traditionally has had a narrow profit margin, JetBlue managed to gain strategic advantage by *reducing cost* and therefore reducing the price to the customer; and *improving a service*, especially in terms of on-time departures and arrivals.

Massive automation

We usually think of manufacturing organizations when mentioning automation, but great benefits can also be gained by automating services. JetBlue uses Open Skies, the software that Neeleman developed. It is a combination reservation system and accounting system which also supports customer service and sales tracking. The company avoids travel agents. Booking a flight through a travel agent costs airlines US$20 per ticket. JetBlue saves office space rent and electricity by using reservation agents who work from home (telecommuting is discussed in Chapter 5) and use VoIP (Voice over Internet Protocol, also discussed in Chapter 5) for telephoning. The company pays a flat fee of US$25 per telephone line per month for these telecommuting agents. This reduces its handling cost per ticket to US$4.50.

CD TASK

Because all tickets are electronic, there is no paper handling or expense. JetBlue encourages customers to purchase their tickets online and more than 79 per cent of them do so, saving the company much labour. The cost of handling a ticket ordered via the Web is reduced to only 50 cents, as opposed to US$4.50 paid to a reservation agent and a far cry from the US$20 a booking through a travel agent.

JetBlue automates other aspects of running an airline as well. Its maintenance workers use a maintenance information system from Dash Group to log all airplane parts and their time cycles, that is, when the parts must be replaced and where they can be found. The system reduces manual tracking costs.

Flight planning to maximize yield – the number of seats occupied on a flight – is executed on a flight-planning application from Bornemann Associates. It reduces planning costs and makes operations more efficient. JetBlue also uses an application that its team of 58 IT professionals developed in-house, called Blue Performance. It tracks operational data that is updated flight by flight. The company's intranet enables its 2800 employees to access the performance data. Managers have up-to-the-minute metrics, so critical in airline operations, which enable them to respond immediately to problems.

When on the ground, employees use wireless devices to report and respond to any irregular event, from weather delays to passenger injuries. The response is quick and the events are recorded in a database for later analysis.

CD TASK

When training pilots and other employees, no paper records are kept. An aviation training management system provides a database to track each employee's training record. It is easy to update and efficient for record retrieval.

Away from tradition

The company decided not to use the hub-and-spokes method of routing its airplanes, a method used by all major airlines. Instead of having its airplanes land in one or two hubs and undergo maintenance there before taking off for the next leg of a route, it simply uses the most profitable routes between any two cities. All flights are point to point – no hubs, no spokes.

JetBlue was the first airline to establish paperless cockpits. The Federal Aviation Authority (FAA) mandates that pilots and other air crew members have access to flight manuals. The manuals are the documents showing information about each flight, including route, weight and how the weight is spread on board, fuel quantity and even details such as how many pets are on board. Other airlines update their manuals and then print them after every update. All JetBlue flight manuals are centrally maintained and the pilots and first officers access and update the manuals on laptop computers that they carry into the cockpit. As soon as the data have been entered, employees have access to the information.

The laptops enable the pilots and first officers to calculate the weight and balance of their plane with a few keystrokes instead of relying on dispatchers at headquarters to do the calculations for them. JetBlue saves paper and time by having employees enter flight data. The company subscribes to SharePoint, a web-based portal that enables electronic updates to flight manuals. This cuts 15 to 20 minutes from preflight preparations for every flight. The result is a saving of about 4800 hours per year and planes that take off and land on time.

JetBlue continues to harness IT to maintain the strategic gap between it and its competitors. Management planned a paperless frequent flier programme, cockpit-monitoring cameras transmitting through satellites so that ground crews can monitor activity and biometric applications in airport terminals. Biometrics use physical characteristics of people, such as fingerprints and retina scans, for authentication and access to physical places and online information systems. Biometrics are more secure than access codes. The IT team is also developing a new reservation system that will have features no other airline reservation system has.

Enhanced service

Much of the technology that helps JetBlue employees provide better service is invisible to the customers, but it also has some more obvious winning features. JetBlue offers leather seats and individual real-time television on all its airplanes. Other airlines do not offer such seats on economy class and offer only recorded television programmes. The real-time TV service is offered under a contract with DirecTV.

Its use of IT technologies also placed the airline at the top of the list for on-schedule departures and arrivals, a service that is very important, especially to business travellers. Perhaps even better, JetBlue ranks at the top as having the fewest mishandled bags. Thanks to constant updates to the Open Skies system, the company has managed to maintain check-in time at less than one minute. When passengers arrive at JetBlue's terminal at JFK airport, they are directed by a large LCD display with a computer-generated voice telling them which window is available to serve them. Usually, checking baggage takes 45 seconds. When passengers arrive at their destination, they do not have to wait for their suitcases. Their electronically tagged suitcases wait for them at the baggage claim area.

Because of heightened security awareness, management decided to install hidden video cameras in the cabin and monitors in the cockpit. Technicians used the DirecTV wires to add the cameras and monitors. Customers are more comfortable knowing of this extra step to enhance their safety.

Impressive performance

The most important metric in the airline industry is cost per available seat-mile (CASM), which is how much it costs to fly a passenger one mile of the journey. JetBlue has been able to maintain the lowest or next-to-lowest CASM in its first three years of operations. While its competitors' CASM is 11 cents or higher, JetBlue's CASM is less than 7 cents. While its competitors fill only 71 per cent of seats, JetBlue fills 78 per cent.

Late mover advantage

Some observers cite the fact that JetBlue is a late competitor as an important factor in its success. The company is not burdened with antiquated information systems, or as IT professionals like to call them, legacy systems. This allowed its CIO, Jeff Cohen, to implement the latest available technologies: fast databases, VoIP, a slick website, laptop computers with the latest algorithms for fast calculation of routes and loads in the cockpit and other technologies. This situation illustrates the strategic advantage of the late mover.

late mover An organization that adopts a technology or method after competitors have adopted it.

JetBlue executives quip that while other airlines run on fuel, theirs runs on information technology. Cohen said that up to 40 per cent of the software the company was using was beta or new software. Beta software is software that the developer gives to potential adopters for trial use. Talk about being on the cutting – and possibly bleeding – edge! Yet, competitors have taken notice. Delta Airlines established a subsidiary called Delta Song. The organization mimics many of JetBlue's innovations, including live TV. Similarly, United Airlines created a nimble subsidiary airline called Ted to compete with JetBlue.

Ford on the Web: A failure story

Sometimes what seems to be a great, forward-looking strategic move ends up as a colossal failure. It might be because of lack of attention to details or simply because the innovator could not predict the response of customers or business partners. Such was the great initiative

Industry **SNAPSHOT**

A healthy IT strategy? – A not so successful story

'Securing Our Future Health: Taking A Long-Term View' – an independent review by Derek Wanless in 2002 for the UK Treasury, concluded that the government would need to devote more resources to health care in order to meet people's expectations. In particular, there should be a spending equivalent to 4 per cent of the National Health Service (NHS) turnover on business-related IT.

However, it seems, according to a British Computer Society (BCS) report in December 2006, this necessary spending is not leading to the benefits that are needed. Many NHS staff see the National Programme for Information Technology (NPfIT) as of little relevance rather than, as the NHS believes, a key enabler of essential business change.

The BCS Health Informatics Forum (BCSHIF) is made up of experts in the field of IT in health. It brings together IT experts, academics, users, suppliers and patients. According to the chair of BCSHIF, Dr Glyn Hayes, 'IT enables change, is sometimes a catalyst for change, but it is not an end in itself. This misconception has been a prime cause of large-scale IT project failure since computers first became commonplace. The problem has been heightened by NPfIT's top-down nature; the patchy reflection of NHS requirements in the procurements in 2002; and the subsequent changes in those requirements to meet the Government's NHS reform programme. We believe that this is one reason why so many NHS staff have yet to see NPfIT as a key enabler of business change and it has thus discouraged the local ownership of NPfIT implementations.'

Dr Hayes added, 'Instead of the current monolithic systems intended to meet most of the needs of users in a local health community, we need a range and choice of more innovative and agile solutions contributing to a common purpose, encouraged within national standards to deliver functionality in whatever way suits the users and suppliers. This should not be interpreted as ruling out adoption of local server provider (LSP) products where they fit the business requirements.'

It seems that money alone will not make an IT strategy. There needs to be sensible spending with support at all levels of the organization, the involvement of users and 'joined-up thinking' in making IT work for you.

SOURCE: http://www.itpro.co.uk/news/100099/bcs-calls-for-major-changes-to-nhs-it-strategy.html, 'BCS calls for major changes to NHS IT strategy', Maggie Holland, ITPro

of Jacques Nasser, the former CEO of Ford Motor Company, the second largest US car manufacturer.

The ideas

When Nasser was appointed CEO of Ford in 1999, he regarded himself as an agent of change. He was eager to push the company into the Web, which was then at the height of its hype as a commercial vehicle. 'We are now measuring speed in gigahertz, not horsepower', he said at the 2000 North American International Auto Show in Detroit. The concept cars sported, among other innovations, mobile Internet access. Ford Motor Co., he said, would put the Internet on wheels.

Ford launched Wingcast telematics, devices that would be installed in the company's vehicles and enable drivers and passengers to access the Web. To this end the company formed an alliance with Qualcomm Inc., a telecommunications company and Yahoo!

CD TASK

Ford created a joint venture with General Motors Corp. and DaimlerChrysler to establish Covisint, a website that serves as an electronic market for parts suppliers who can bid online on requests for proposals posted by the car manufacturers. Although not announced this way, the manufacturers' hope was that suppliers would fiercely compete in an open bidding process and cut their prices dramatically, so the car companies could enjoy cost cuts. This was the business-to-business (B2B) part of Nassers's grand plan.

The business-to-consumer (B2C) idea was bolder: Ford wanted to push vehicle sales to the Web. Nasser wanted to bypass dealerships and retail the vehicles online directly to consumers. Consumers would go to the website, take a virtual test-drive, see images of a vehicle in all its available colours, order a vehicle, pay for it online and then have it driven to their door. Ford would not only provide a great service but also save the dealer fees. The company called the site FordDirect.com. A special organizational unit, ConsumerConnect, was established to build the website and handle the direct sales.

Hitting the wall

Apparently, buyers were not as enthusiastic about having web access in their vehicles as Nasser predicted. In June 2001, Ford eliminated the Wingcast project. The B2B effort, Covisint, works and now includes more manufacturers, such as the French company Renault and the Japanese company Nissan. The B2C initiative failed.

The failure was not the result of faulty technology. There are excellent web technologies that would support retail through the Web. There is no reason why a car cannot be selected, paid for and delivered (with the help of companies that specialize in such delivery from the manufacturer to the buyer) via the Web. The company failed because it did not carefully consider US state laws and its relationships with dealers.

Many US state laws do not permit cutting an agent out of the sale. State franchising laws did not allow Ford to bypass its dealers. Also, since Ford would still rely on dealers to sell cars to people who do not have access to the Internet or who like to sit in a physical car and test-drive it, it could not cut the relationship all at once. Ford still needed the collaboration of the dealers, if it could overcome the legal hurdles, in order for direct sales to take off.

The retreat

The circumstances convinced Ford to abandon its plan to sell directly to consumers. The ConsumerConnect unit was disbanded. FordDirect.com is now operated jointly by Ford and its 3900 Ford and Lincoln Mercury dealerships. The site helps consumers find the vehicles they want, but they then have to find a dealer close to their homes who can deliver the vehicle. Like any car dealer, the site also offers used cars for sale, which is not what Ford would like to do. The price tag of this failed experiment was reported to be a hefty portion of the US$1 billion Ford spent on its Internet initiative under Nasser's leadership.

Ford's management can find some solace in the continued operation of FordDirect.com. Although the grand plan did not materialize, the site is the origin point of 10,000 sales transactions per month. Ford reported that it sold 100,000 vehicles through the website in 2001 and that 60 per cent of those transactions would not even have started had the site not existed. The monthly sales through the website have increased since. In April 2005 the site generated sales of 22,500 new vehicles.

Some observers say that Ford's focus on the Internet was at times greater than on making cars. While other car manufacturers were making modest profits in the period from 2000 to 2001, Ford had losses. Nasser was forced to leave the company.

Ethical and Societal ISSUES

Size matters

At what point do the public and the courts start to consider a successful strategy as a predatory, unfair business practice that makes competition from other businesses impossible, even if their products are better? For instance, should a firm that takes bold entrepreneurial steps to become a business leader be curbed when it succeeds in becoming powerful? Several court cases against Microsoft, the software industry leader, have focused on these questions. However, the questions are not simply legal issues. They are also important because they impact the economy and, as a result, society.

Historical background In the 1970s, Microsoft was a small software company headed by its young president, Bill Gates, who established the company at age 19. The company was fortunate to find and buy an operating system from a small company in Seattle, Washington, for US$50,000. An operating system (OS) is the software program that 'mediates' between any computer program and the computer. Every application is developed with a particular operating system, or several operating systems, in mind. To a great extent, the operating system determines which applications a computer can run. Therefore, it is an extremely important program. We discuss operating systems and other types of software in Chapter 4, 'Business Hardware and Software'.

So, people who purchased a computer had to consider the OS to determine which applications they could run on their computer. After Microsoft bought the operating system, it entered into a contract with IBM, the most powerful computer manufacturer at that time. IBM needed an operating system for its new creation, the IBM PC and they chose Microsoft's DOS (Disk Operating System). While Microsoft did not make much money on the IBM deal, its executives realized the strategic potential of contracting with 'the big guy'.

Indeed, the strategy paid off. Soon, Compaq (now part of Hewlett-Packard) and many other manufacturers started to market IBM PC clones, cheaper computers that performed as well as IBM PCs and could run the same operating system and applications. Because Microsoft's contract with IBM allowed it to sell DOS to other parties, it made a fortune selling DOS to Compaq and others. Later, Microsoft developed Windows, an improved operating system and the success story repeated itself. To this day, the majority of buyers of personal computers also buy a copy of some version of Windows.

One major key to gaining a decent share of the new Internet market was the widespread use of web browsers. In the mid-1990s, more than 80 per cent of web surfers used Netscape's browsers. Netscape (now part of AOL) was a young, entrepreneurial company selling innovative products. Microsoft decided to increase its own browser's market share of about 15 per cent to a leading position. If a great number of people used its browser, Microsoft could expect hefty sales of related software, such as server management applications.

Controversial practices No one would deny that Microsoft's attempt to compete in the browser market was legitimate. While Netscape gave its browsers away to individuals and educational institutions but charged for-profit organizations, Microsoft gave its browser to everyone free of charge. Also, the company took advantage of Windows dominance; it started bundling its browser with Windows, practically forcing any PC maker who wanted to sell the machines with the operating system installed to also install Internet Explorer (IE). The great majority of new PC owners used IE without even trying any other browser.

The German headquarters of software giant Microsoft near Munich. Microsoft Germany is the largest European subsidiary of the U.S. corporation.

PHOTO SOURCE: © VARIO IMAGES GMBH & CO.KG/ALAMY

Within two years, a majority of web surfers were using IE. But Netscape, the US Department of Justice and many individuals considered Microsoft's tactics unfair. Microsoft used its muscle in the operating system market to compel sellers of personal computers to include a copy of Internet Explorer with Windows. Furthermore, the browser was inseparable from the newer Windows version, Windows 98. Since sellers had to include Windows on every machine and because it is practically the only operating system most buyers would accept, sellers had no choice but to succumb to the pressure. The US Department of Justice and the Attorneys General of several states filed lawsuits claiming Microsoft violated fair trade practices. Subsequently, legal authorities in other countries, such as the European Union (EU) and Taiwan, also either probed the company or sued it. In 2004, the EU's antitrust office fined Microsoft 497 million euros (US$665 million) for abusively wielding Windows' monopoly and for locking competitors out of the software market. Meanwhile, as competition in the digital audio and video media increased, Microsoft bundled its Media Player software with the Windows OS. In 2002, the US Department of Justice settled with Microsoft on this issue, requiring the company only to enable users to hide Media Player and set another application as the default player. The EU demanded that Microsoft sell Windows without Media Player.

It also demanded that the company allow all software developers access to information about Windows, so that they could develop applications that would compete well with Microsoft's own applications. The EU claimed that developers of nonproprietary software (software that is not owned by anyone and can be used free of charge) were denied access to the Windows information altogether. If the company did not stop these practices, the EU threatened it with additional fines reaching 5 per cent of the company's daily worldwide sales revenue until the company complied with the EU's demands.

Contrary to public perception, the United States, the European Union and many other countries do not outlaw monopolies. They only forbid unfair use of monopolistic power. Because anyone may compete in any market, it would be unfair to punish an entrepreneur for marketing unique products and mustering market power of any magnitude. Of concern in the eyes of US law, for example, are two issues: (1) have any unfair practices helped the company gain monopolistic power and (2) does the monopolistic situation serve customers well, or does it hurt them?

Up side, down side Microsoft argues that although it could charge higher prices for Windows, it has not, because it wants to make Windows affordable to all. Microsoft also argues that, unlike typical monopolists, it invests huge amounts of money in research and development, which eventually benefit society in the form of better and less-expensive products. Microsoft's rivals in the software industry claim that Microsoft's practices stifle true competition. Both claims are difficult to measure. Some observers argue that allowing the same company to develop operating systems and many applications is good for consumers: the applications are compatible with each other; all use the same interface of menus and icons. Others suggest that Microsoft should be broken into two organizations; one that develops operating systems and another that develops only applications and competes fairly in that market. And some organizations and individuals simply fear the great power that a single person, Bill Gates, holds in an industry that so greatly impacts our economy and society. What is your opinion? What would you do about this issue?

The bleeding edge

As you might often hear, huge rewards go to whoever first implements a new idea. Innovators might enjoy a strategic advantage until competitors discover the benefits of a new business idea or a new technology. However, taking such steps before competitors have tested a system involves great risk. In some cases, failure results from rushing implementation without adequately testing a market. But even with careful planning, pioneers sometimes get burned.

For example, several supermarket chains tried self-checkout stations in the mid-1990s. Consumers were expected to ring up their own purchases. By and large, investment in such devices failed not because the technology was bad, but because many consumers either preferred the human touch, or because they did not want to learn how to correct mistakes when the devices did not pick up the price of an item or picked it up twice. Recently, machines that are more user friendly and less error prone have been installed by several chains and consumers have been more willing to use them.

While it is tempting to take the lead, the risk of business failure is quite high. Several organizations have experienced disasters with new business ideas, which are only magnified when implementing new technology. When failure occurs because an organization tries to be on the technological leading edge, observers call it the **bleeding edge**. The pioneering organization 'bleeds' cash on a technology that increases costs instead of profits. Adopting a new technology involves great risk: there is no experience from which to learn, no guarantees that the technology will work well and no certainty that customers and employees will welcome it.

bleeding edge The situation in which a business fails because it tries to be on the technological leading edge.

Being on the bleeding edge often means that implementation costs are significantly more than anticipated, that the new technology does not work as well as expected, or that the parties who were supposed to benefit – employees, customers or suppliers – do not like using it. Thus, instead of leading, the organization ends up bleeding, that is, suffering from high cost and lost market share. For this reason, some organizations decide to let competitors test new technology before they adopt it. They risk losing the initial rewards they might reap, but if a competitor succeeds, they can quickly adopt the technology and even try to use it better than the pioneering organization.

Microsoft generally takes this approach. It seizes an existing idea, improves it and promotes the result with its great marketing power. For instance, the company did not invent word processing, but Word is the most popular word-processing application today. The company did not invent the electronic spreadsheet, but Excel is the most popular spreadsheet application. And Microsoft was not the first to introduce a PC database management application, but it sells the highly popular Access. The company joined the Internet rush late, but it developed and gave away Internet Explorer, a web browser that competed with the highly popular Netscape Navigator and now dominates the market (in part because it was given free to everyone, including for-profit businesses). You might call this approach competing by emulating and improving, rather than competing by being on the leading edge.

Sometimes, companies wait quite a long time to ensure that a technology has matured before they start using it, even at the risk of diminishing their strategic position. Although data warehousing – the organization and summarization of huge amounts of transactional records for later analysis – has been around since the mid-1990s, The Home Depot, Inc., decided only in 2002 to build a data warehouse. Home Depot is the world's largest home improvement retailer. It started the project years after its main rival in the United States, Lowe's, had implemented a well-functioning data warehouse, which it used effectively for strategic decision-making.

SUMMARY

Some ISs have become strategic tools as a result of strategic planning; others have evolved into strategic tools. To compete in the market, executives need to define strategic goals and determine whether new or improved ISs can support these goals. Rather than waiting complacently until a problem occurs, businesses actively look for opportunities to improve their position with information systems.

An IS that helps gain strategic advantage is called a strategic information system (SIS). To assure optimal utilization of IT for competitive advantage, executives must participate in generating ideas and champion new, innovative uses of information systems. In recent years, many of these ideas involved using the Internet.

A company achieves strategic advantage by using strategy to maximize its strengths, resulting in a competitive advantage.

Strategic advantage is often achieved by one or a combination of the following initiatives. Cost reduction enables a business to sell more units of its products or services while maintaining or increasing its profit margin. Raising barriers to potential entrants to the industry lets an organization maintain a sizeable market share by developing systems that are prohibitively expensive for competitors to emulate. By establishing high switching costs, a business can make buying from competitors unattractive to clients. Developing totally new products and services can create an entirely new market for an organization, which can also enjoy the advantage of being a first mover for that product and market. And if the organization cannot create new products or services, it can still enjoy competitive advantage by differentiating its products so that customers view them as better than a competitor's products. Organizations also attain advantage by enhancing existing products or services. Many new services are the fruits of alliances between companies: each contributes its own expertise to package services that entice customers with an overall value greater than that offered by the separate services individually. Locking in clients or suppliers, that is, creating conditions that make dealing with competitors infeasible is a powerful strategy to gain advantage.

In the software industry, creating standards often creates strategic advantage. A standard is an application used by a significant share of the users. To this end, many companies go as far as giving software away. When the standard has been established, the company enjoys a large sales volume of compatible and add-on software. Microsoft, the software giant, has been found guilty of using unfair trade practices in trying to establish standards and squash competitors.

Reengineering is the process of designing a business process from scratch to achieve hundreds of percentage points in improvement rates. Almost always, reengineering involves implementing new ISs.

Strategic advantages from information systems are often short-lived, because competitors quickly emulate the systems for their own benefit. Therefore, looking for new opportunities must be an ongoing process.

To maintain a strategic advantage, organizations must develop new features to keep the system on the leading edge. But they must be mindful of the bleeding edge, the undesirable results (such as huge ongoing costs and loss of customers) of being the first to use new technology with the hope of establishing a competitive advantage. Early adopters find themselves on the bleeding edge when the new technology is not yet fully reliable or when customers are uncomfortable with it.

BETTER BITES

BETTER BITES REVISITED

As you have seen in the continuing story of Better Bites, the three young entrepreneurs have gained experience, used information systems to research options and instituted changes to remain profitable and expand their business. They also face some new opportunities and challenges for the strategic direction of their business. The next section explores some of their strategic initiatives to see whether you think they can make improvements.

What would you do?

Through their alliance with the shopping centre owner, Better Bites has increased its business to three lunch carts. From the case at the beginning of the chapter, identify some strategic moves the three have already made to help them compete. Have any of their partners operated strategically? How? Be sure to consider these ways to gain a competitive advantage:

- Reduce costs.
- Raise barriers to entrants.
- Establish high switching costs.
- Create new products and services.
- Differentiate products and services.
- Enhance products or services.
- Establish alliances.
- Lock in suppliers or buyers.

Review the decision that Paul, Sarah and Christina made not to pursue organic labels for their food. Was this decision correct, in your opinion? What further information could they use to monitor the organic food market in the future?

New perspectives

Operating from a new kitchen space and becoming a crisp manufacturer offers Paul, Sarah and Christina the opportunity to rethink completely their food preparation processes – to reengineer. Think of some options the three can pursue in redesigning their food preparation for both their lunch business and crisp manufacturing. Consider how the changes can help them compete effectively.

With the Subwich franchise as a new competitor to the pushcart lunch business, Paul, Sarah and Christina need to monitor costs and profits closely and they need to keep making changes to remain competitive. They already have a loyal customer base. How can they use their existing information systems to compete effectively against Subwich? Suggest at least three ways to help them compete. Would a website help them at all? Why or why not?

Review questions

1. In what respect does business strategy resemble military strategy?
2. What should an information system achieve for an organization in order for it to be considered a strategic information system?
3. What strategic goal can an IS attain that does not involve wresting market share from competitors?
4. What conditions must exist in an organization planning an SIS?
5. Sometimes it is difficult to convince top management to commit funds to develop and implement an SIS. Why?
6. An SIS often offers a corporation short-lived advantages. How so?
7. What is reengineering? What does it have to do with IT?
8. Software developers have made great efforts to 'create a standard'. What does creating a standard mean in the software industry and why are companies doing it?
9. What should an organization do to sustain the strategic benefits of an IS?
10. Adobe encourages PC users to download its Acrobat Reader free of charge. Macromedia encourages people to download its Flash player free of charge. How does this eventually

help them strategically? If they give the application away, how does their generosity help them make money?

11 Referring to the list of strategic moves (see Figure 2.2), classify the initiatives of JetBlue.

12 What were the reasons for the failure of FordDirect.com?

13 The executives of well-established airlines are not less smart than those at JetBlue and yet, their larger companies have not done what JetBlue has done. Why?

14 What does the term 'first mover' mean?

15 Can a *late mover* have any strategic advantage with IT? What is the risk that a late mover takes?

16 What does the term 'bleeding edge' mean?

Discussion questions

1 Can an off-the-shelf computer program be used as an SIS? Why or why not?

2 The organizations that eventually use the systems, not consulting firms, develop more successful SISs. What might be the reasons for this?

3 You head a small company. You have an idea for software that can give your company an advantage over competitors. Since you do not have staff that can develop and implement the software, you decide to approach a software company. Other than the technical requirements, what should you desire of the software company?

4 Some argue that an SIS gives a company an unfair advantage and might even cause the demise of smaller, weaker companies that cannot afford to build similar systems. Is this good or bad for customers? Explain your opinion.

5 Why has the Web been the arena of so much competition in recent years?

6 ISs play a major role in almost every reengineering project. Why?

7 Accounting and payroll ISs have never become SISs. Why? What other types of ISs are unlikely to ever gain their owners' strategic advantage?

8 Ford's CEO envisaged a future in which consumers log on to a car manufacturer's website, design their cars online, wait for the cars to be manufactured (design transformed into electronic blueprints) and have the car delivered to their door. Do you think we will see this in practice within the next decade? Why, or why not?

9 Give two examples of other products or services whose delivery time could be cut from days to minutes with the aid of IT.

10 What is the role of ISs in alliances such as airlines and credit-card issuers? Why would such alliances be practically infeasible without IT?

11 Many companies use new software that has not been tested by other companies. If you were a Chief Information Officer (CIO), would you use software that is still in beta (untested with live data) in your organization?

12 You are an executive for a large organization that provides services to local government. A software development firm approached you with an offer to implement new software that might give your organization a strategic advantage by reducing the service delivery cycle by several days. What would you do to avoid putting your organization on the 'bleeding edge' while still considering the new software?

13 When a software developer creates a *de facto* standard (i.e., not the official standard, but something so widely used that it becomes a standard), it has monopolistic power. Should governments intervene to prevent this practice? Explain your opinion.

14 Suppose you are a venture capitalist considering a proposal to invest a significant amount of money in a new online business. What questions would you ask the enthusiastic young people who have approached you for funds?

15 What are the potential risks of a single organization controlling much of the market of essential software?

Tutorial activities

1 Use a literature search program to find a news story on a strategic information system. Write a short report that explains: (a) the industry in which the business competes, (b) the

function(s) of the system and (c) how the system gives the company strategic advantage. For (c), identify the type of strategic move that the organization made from the list provided in Figure 2.1. Suggest how the company might improve the system to maintain its advantage in the future, when competitors mimic the system. Alternatively, find a story on a new business model. In your write-up explain (a) the term 'business model', (b) the particular business model you found and (c) how information systems support this business model.

2 Prepare a brief essay that includes an example of each of the following strategic moves: raising barriers to entrants (*Hint*: intellectual property), establishing high switching costs, creating a new product or service (*Hint*: the Web) and establishing alliances. The examples do not necessarily have to involve IT. Do not use examples already presented in the text. You may use examples from actual events or your own suggestions, but the examples must be practical.

3 A publishing company is contemplating publishing electronic books on small CDs. To read the discs, users will need a device called an electronic book reader. At least two firms have developed e-book technologies that the publisher can adopt. The publisher hires you as a strategic consultant. Write a report explaining the strategic moves you suggest. What would you advise the company to do: try to develop its own e-book reader or purchase a licence for existing technology? Who should be the initial target audience for the product? What should be the company's major goal in the first two or three years: profit, market share, user base, technological improvement, or perhaps having the largest salesforce in this industry? Should the company give anything away? Prepare a detailed report enumerating and explaining your suggestions.

4 You are a software-marketing expert. A new software development firm has hired you to advise it on pricing and marketing strategies of its new application. After some research, you conclude that the firm can be successful either by selling at a high unit price (in which case, probably only businesses would purchase licences to use the application), or at a very low price, which would be attractive to many individuals and companies. You estimate that by the end of the sixth year of the marketing effort, competing software will be offered, which will bring the number of units sold to zero. For alternative A, the price would be €400 per licence and you expect 500 adopters in the first year and an annual growth of adopters of 70 per cent. For alternative B, the price would be €30 and you expect 600,000 adopters in the first year and an annual growth of adopters of 4 per cent. Use a spreadsheet application to calculate revenue and tell the firm which strategy is expected to bring in greater revenue. Enter the prices and number of first-year adopters for each alternative only once, each in a single cell and use absolute referencing to those cells.

5 Use PowerPoint or other presentation software to present the ideas you generated in Question 1 or 2 above. Use the program's best features to make a convincing and visually pleasing presentation.

6 Do a library or web search of business journals and magazines such as the *Wall Street Journal*, *BusinessWeek*, *Forbes* or *Fortune*. Find a story on a business's strategic use of data information, or information systems. (*Note*: The writer might not have identified the strategic use, but you might find that the use served strategic goals.) Prepare a report explaining the opportunity seized. Did the organization create a new product or service, improve one, or manage to capture a significantly greater market share of an existing product or service? How did the data, information or information system play a major role in the strategic move?

7 Consider the information provided in the 'Ethical and Societal Issues' box of this chapter. Prepare two extensive lists, pros and cons. The pros should aim to convince an audience why Microsoft, or a similar company, should be left alone to practise its business manoeuvres. The cons should aim to convince an audience why governments should intervene in how corporations such as Microsoft behave and explain what such interventions are meant to accomplish.

8 Brainstorm with your team to answer the question: 'Which information technology over the past two years has epitomized a unique product or service that was "ahead of the curve" for a significant amount of time?' This

might be a physical product using IT or an online service that was, or still is, unique. List the reasons each of the team members liked this product or service so much.

9 Some information technologies had a certain original purpose but were creatively used to serve additional purposes. For example, companies have used caller ID to retrieve customer records as soon as a customer telephones. This saves labour and increases service quality. You and your teammates are consultants who work with many businesses. Offering your clients original ideas will increase your success. Select an information technology or IT feature that can be used in ways not originally conceived. How can your clients (in manufacturing, service or any other business sector) use this feature to gain strategic advantage? Prepare a rationale.

10 Someone suggested that you and your teammates establish the first web cemetery for pets. Obviously, you cannot bury any pets there, but there might be other services you can offer. Prepare a written plan that describes what you would offer, what you would charge for different features and how you can sustain your strategic position if traditional pet cemeteries go online. (*Note*: There might be some online pet cemeteries. Assume there are none.)

Companion CD questions

1 Clear the cookies from your computer. Visit Amazon.co.uk or another e-commerce site listed in this chapter. Browse the site and click on items you might buy and add them to your cart. Don't actually make a purchase. Open the cookie file on your computer. How many cookies did the site put on your computer?

2 How can Excel's goal seek function be used in strategic planning? Give an example.

Video questions

1 Do some research to determine how big the potential market for this product is. Who are its competitors (think about products that are designed to do similar things (e.g., prevent car theft) but may not be a direct competitor)?

2 Name three companies whose products or services might be potential strategic alliances with this product.

From ideas to application
REAL CASES

Case study **2.1**

Screwfix

BY SCOTT RAEBURN

Screwfix is a retail phenomenon in Britain. At one point, the managers were told 'You can't sell screws over the Internet!' But they have – to the tune of £260 million in 2005/6. Admittedly, it is now screws, other building materials and tools, but Screwfix are the third largest online retailer in the UK after Amazon and Tesco.

The start back in 1981 was inauspicious. Jon Goddard-Watts bought a small company which sold wood screws. The Woodscrew Supply Company sold its products through *Exchange & Mart*, a UK weekly magazine dedicated to advertising supplies for DIY and small business (as well as allowing individuals to sell their own goods). Over the next ten years or so, JGW and family added another two small businesses. The big change came in 1993, when the company became Screwfix Direct and set up a telephone ordering centre in Yeovil in southwest England. Turnover doubled every year from then until 1999. By then it had 470 staff, was handling 15,000 orders per week and had set up its first website. Professional managers had been brought in two years previously and had helped make the company 'e-commerce ready'.

The potential for growth in Internet sales made the company, selling a range of very basic products, part of the 'dotcom' boom. But like all growing companies, more investment was needed. The original founder and his family decided to sell to the highest bidder, a process won by the Kingfisher Group. JGW and family netted £60 million from the sale. Kingfisher were well known in the City as national and international retailers, with Woolworths, Comet and B&Q part of the group. Indeed many analysts at the time expected Screwfix Direct to become part of B&Q, a very large chain of DIY stores. But Screwfix Direct retained its independence within the Group and flourished via its telephone and online sales. David Cox, Screwfix CEO since 1997, said: 'This is a fantastic success story. Our takings have doubled every year for the last six years. With Kingfisher's resources behind us, we'll be able to expand even faster.'

Screwfix Direct continued to develop its product range, building experience in selling via the Internet and advertising to its target customers – DIY and small builders – in a range of innovative ways. One involved an ad campaign with posters in male toilets in motorway service stations. It's not recorded how successful this was, or indeed what their female customers thought.

By 2003 Screwfix Direct had 1 million customers and sales of £187 million. More importantly, the number of orders handled per week was growing inexorably, having trebled since 1999. Those familiar with the map of the UK will realize that Yeovil (in the southwest of England) is not an ideal place to have a UK-wide distribution centre promising next working day delivery anywhere on mainland Britain. Getting the stock down there, well away from major ports and 30 miles from the nearest motorway was bad enough. Getting orders despatched to the bulk of the population in the southeast, Midlands and north of England was more difficult and costly. A distribution centre in Leicester in the East Midlands had been set up a couple of years earlier but now more was needed.

It was decided to create a new distribution centre at Stoke-on-Trent in the Midlands of England. Midway between Birmingham and Manchester and just off the M6 motorway in the west Midlands, it was much nearer its customer base. Such a move, however, meant that the warehouse staff in Yeovil would be redundant – Stoke is almost 200 miles away and relocation for most would not be an option. In mid-2004 the Yeovil warehouse closed down with the loss of 500 jobs. The Stoke distribution centre took over but had problems recruiting and training staff. This caused many problems and by September that year deliveries were being affected. Screwfix took the decision to close the main website and call centre for a week to control the flow of orders

PHOTO SOURCE: COURTESY OF SCREWFIX WWW.SCREWFIX.COM

After setting up their first website in 1999, Screwfix today holds in excess of 4 million customer records, carries out over 40 per cent of transactions online and employs 1 000 people at its head office and contact centre.

and allow the distribution centre time to catch up. By the end of September, the telephone sales and Internet sales operations were back to normal, as were deliveries of more than 50,000 parcels per week.

Meanwhile, the Yeovil warehouse was becoming Head Office. Parallel developments of a supplier web portal, financial management systems and sales intelligence systems were proceeding. The supplier portal, for example, was supplied by Yantra and made dealing with more than 300 suppliers in the Far East and Eastern Europe much easier. Screwfix Direct relies on global sourcing to maintain its cost advantage over competitors.

Since then, further software contracts have led to the development of a dispatch process which can integrate the dispatch of larger items direct from suppliers' factories around the country with smaller items which come direct from Screwfix distribution centres. Esker Software supplied a system which is now handling 80,000 dispatches per week and gathers much sales information. An interesting part of this system analyses daily sales data overnight and sends summaries by text message to executives early each morning. This system also alerts technical staff by text message if there is a major power failure and the UPS (uninterruptible power supply) is activated on the main systems.

The Logic Group managed the process of integrating and upgrading the network infrastructure of Screwfix. The company now has an integrated IP (Internet Protocol) network which handles both voice and data. This led to the contact centre for sales converting to IP telephony, further managing Screwfix's cost base downward. Vecta were contracted to develop software to provide higher-quality sales information over this network, this time to telephone sales staff. The target was a detailed sales report to an operator within two clicks while on the phone to a customer. Not only does this help sales directly, but the new software also provides information for both strategic business decisions and targeted sales campaigns, making best use of all the available data.

One of those strategic decisions was taken in late 2004, following the interruption to orders because of distribution centre problems. By March 2005, Screwfix CEO John Allan had announced the year-long trial of six 'trade counters' in various locations across the UK. As well as positioning Screwfix Direct to compete with a rival joinery firm which was moving into building supplies, this would spread the load by allowing customers to collect goods from a local store. The model chosen was the 'Argos' model, with a small front area containing catalogues and several sales terminals. Customers would select goods from the catalogue, pay at a terminal after local stock was checked by sales staff and the goods would be brought to a delivery counter by picking staff. These are now being rolled out across the UK, with 14 complete by mid-2006. Interestingly, the systems do not allow the customer to check stock as is done at Argos stores.

These changes necessitated an increase in the staff complement and Screwfix Direct now employs 1900 people. Coordinating these staff members across the Yeovil Head Office, the Stoke distribution centre and local trade counters needed more new software. Coda Financial Intelligence was contracted in 2006 to eliminate as much paper handling as possible. All invoices to Screwfix from suppliers are converted to electronic images, either by the supplier or by Image Integrators, a firm which specializes in document image processing. Invoices arrive at Head Office as images only, with paper copies safely stored off-site. The system is also used for HR and personnel records and many legal documents. The proposed next stage is Goods Received Note processing which will speed up payments to suppliers and reduce disputes.

So Screwfix, a firm which had never had retail outlets and grew spectacularly with telephone and Internet sales, is now becoming a traditional supplier to the building trade and DIY markets. As other traditional companies, such as B&Q, are moving into web sales to complement store-based retail, Screwfix has found itself moving into store-based retail. Recent figures suggest that telephone orders account for 57 per cent of sales, Internet orders for 38 per cent and the trade counters account for 5 per cent.

This is a good example of the 'last mile' problem – how do you get lots of small orders quickly to your customers spread around a large area? Perhaps the Tesco online grocery solution will be the future: web orders delivered from the nearest store rather than from a distribution centre. One interesting side-effect of this is that the price advantage of Screwfix goods is falling. Prices for at least some items sold by Screwfix have risen significantly in the past two years. If you take on a traditional business model, all the software in the world won't keep your costs down!

Case study questions

1 What was Screwfix's original USP (unique selling proposition)? What advantages did this give Screwfix?

2 In what ways did the strategic use of information systems allow Screwfix to expand its operations?

3 Why does Screwfix appear to need to modify its information systems frequently?

SOURCES: www.kingfisher.co.uk, May 2007; www.esker.co.uk, May 2007; www.the-logic-group.com, May 2007; www.bbc.co.uk, 2004; *The Times*, 5 March 2005; The *Independent*, 14 March 1999; *Financial Times*, 22 July 1999

Case study **2.2**

Royal Mail Group

BY PATRICIA BRITTEN

The Royal Mail Group is a public limited company wholly owned by the British Government. The head office is in London and the organization employs almost 193,000 people in the UK, which represents about 1 per cent of the population. It operates Britain's mail services and the Post Office network and has total revenues of around £8.8 billion per year. Royal Mail became a plc on 26 March 2001 under the Postal Services Act 2000 and since then has undergone a huge transformation, turning losses of £1 million a day to a profit of £355 million at the end of 2005.

The head of IT is David Burden, CIO (Chief Information Officer). David Burden says Royal Mail Group focused on two issues in 2005: improving the delivery of letters and rolling out chip and pin to about 15,000 post offices. Of the two, the organization's reputation really stands or falls on the delivery of 83 million items to 27 million addresses each working day. Prices charged are some of the lowest in Europe, but its reputation has taken a battering in recent years. However, there is no doubt that performance has improved over the past year.

Improved postal service

Between July and September 2005, 92 per cent of first class letters arrived the day after posting – one of its best performances for a decade. By the end of 2006 this performance had improved to 94.4 per cent on time delivery for first class post and 99.1 per cent for second class post. IT has contributed enormously to this improvement across a very complex delivery process. 'We collect from 113,000 red pillar boxes and there are probably about 70,000 collection points, including large businesses', says Burden. Mail goes through a process involving 72 mail centres, 1400 delivery offices and enormous physical transportation systems which include the use of 30,000 vehicles and 33,000 bicycles.

'We have put in new processes, computing systems and communication links. We also implemented new report processing last year so that every level of the organization can validate an issue before it goes up to another level. It uses a SAP data warehouse and lots of reporting tools from different vendors', says Burden.

Letter recognition

'The really clever stuff is the letter processing systems. We have been doing an enormous amount of work with address systems,' says Burden.

The new system – which replaced an optical character recognition device – first went live in 2004, but Burden's team continues to work on enhancements. It photographs the envelope, including handwritten letters to interpret the correct address. 'It is a very sophisticated image recognition system working against a database of 27 million addresses. It is one that is very specifically aimed at identifying defects in processing.' The beauty of the new online centrally hosted system is that it can identify the correct address even when someone makes a mistake, such as omitting the postcode.

'Previously if someone got the postcode wrong it would have gone to the wrong address. If someone misses out the postcode we can detect this and put it in. If it cannot do this, we can put it on one side and rectify it', explains Burden. What happens is that a

Royal Mail's traditional red pillar boxes mark the start of an increasingly sophisticated delivery process.

PHOTO SOURCE: © TRACY HEBDEN

sorting office's computer captures the data and sends them to the central image recognition system. If there is a problem, it is sent to one of three centres where someone will resolve it', says Burden.

Chip and pin

Installing chip and pin technology in post offices has presented a different set of challenges. It required fairly substantial changes to the software systems. The organization installed new hardware at each site. 'As a result, the major challenge was the sheer scale of project', says Burden. The installation was complete in all 14,902 post offices by mid-2005.

A heavily outsourced operation, primarily to CSC, IT has also contributed to Royal Mail's drive to cut costs. 'We have been chopping back as always', says Burden. It has slashed IT operating costs by 10 per cent over the past 12 months. 'We keep very tight control and make sure that we do not have any inefficient use of IT.'

Overall, Royal Mail said that it was making more than £1 million per day – instead of losing more than £1 million per day before its renewal plan kicked in. However, Royal Mail faces many challenges to its profitability in the future.

Future challenges

The future challenges to Royal Mail's business come from the competitive and regulatory environment. Their market place is rapidly changing, with the UK postal market having been fully liberalized since January 2006, resulting in full competition from rival companies. The Postal Services Act also established a new regulatory regime with an independent regulator, Postcomm, and a consumer body, Postwatch. Royal Mail says it cannot compete on commercial terms because of the constraints on pricing imposed by the regulator. Royal Mail currently loses around 2 pence on every item handled. The amount of mail handled by rival companies in 2007 is forecast to be around 2.5 billion letters and packets (out of a total volume of 22 billion).

The postal services market is also a mature one, which has seen a decline of 2 per cent in volumes over the past year – a pattern repeated throughout Europe. This is thought to be due to the growth in electronic communications using the Internet, and the recent growth of broadband services is a key factor.

Operating losses at the Post Office have doubled to £4 million a week following the loss of government contracts to handle pensions and social security benefit payments. This has led to the decision to close many of the smaller branches (of which 7793 are rural), causing a public outcry from rural communities who depend on these retail outlets for many other services. Currently nearly 25 million customers make over 36 million visits a week to post offices.

This has put an emphasis on further improving both the efficiency and effectiveness of the services provided by Royal Mail. The modernization programme has resulted in many improvements to date, which include record quality of service, improved productivity, reduced absenteeism and substantial increases in pay for the workforce. Information technology has contributed greatly to this, but further modernization of the business is required. Overall, the technology currently lags behind that of their competitors and innovative new systems are required if they are to be ahead of the game. It is estimated that around £2 billion needs to be spent on modernizing the company and renewing its premises and equipment. Consequently, it was announced in July 2006 that the UK Government would provide a £1.2 billion investment facility to help achieve the next five-year modernization programme.

New services are being provided to meet these challenges, which range from new Post Office financial services, such as personal loans and 'two-in-one' credit cards, to electronic 'stamps', online shopping facilities and data tools to help companies improve their marketing performance.

Alan Leighton, Chairman, said: 'The changes the Group will now need to make are more stretching and challenging than the gains we made during the three-year renewal plan to 2005. New technology is vital for our future.' This represents both challenges and real opportunities for the application of IT systems.

Case study questions

1 Does the letter recognition system in the case give Royal Mail a competitive advantage? Is it an example of a strategic information system?

2 Do you consider that the information technology and computer systems in use by Royal Mail, as described in the case, are 'bleeding edge' or 'leading edge'? Justify your answer.

3 Which of the six strategic initiatives described in this chapter has Royal Mail chosen to adopt to achieve its goals?

4 Carry out Porter's five forces analysis of the Postal Services industry and assess whether the application of information technology could help to alter these forces.

SOURCES: An article by James Thompson in *MIS U.K.*, April 2005; Allan Leighton, Chairman's Statement, December 2006; and www.royalmailgroup.com

silicon.com

Case study **2.3**

Offshoring – how to get it right

BY ANDY McCUE

The debate about whether – and how – to send work overseas has moved out of the IT department and into the domain of top-level business executives and the board. Andy McCue speaks to the experts about best practices for all the various options.

Globalization has had a positive impact on the way businesses can source products, services and skills in order to gain competitive advantage, cut costs and drive top-line growth – but many boardrooms still don't have a centralized and consistent strategy for sending work offshore, instead relying on piecemeal and uncoordinated efforts.

The model for using lower-cost overseas locations such as India for software development and call centre work has become a mainstream and widely accepted business practice over the last decade, led largely by the financial services sector.

That trend is only set to grow, both in volume and in the types of services that will increasingly be sent offshore. A study conducted last year by management consultants McKinsey and Indian IT trade body Nasscom predicts around $110 billion of IT and business process outsourcing (BPO) services globally will be offshored by businesses by 2010.

But how does this globalization – 'the world is flat' vision of Thomas Friedman's book of the same title – affect a company's sourcing strategy?

Devise a strategy

Businesses over the past twenty years have focused on the supplier selection and contract negotiation elements of sourcing, but Gartner says leading-edge organizations are now firmly focused on sourcing strategy and sourcing management first.

Phanish Puranam, assistant professor of strategic and international management at the London Business School (LBS), says best practice is to operate from a portfolio perspective.

He says: 'People are increasingly looking at the whole portfolio of choices and saying "let's look at the whole range of options". A big trend has also been to centralize the services function so there is a common method for evaluating these decisions.'

But in many boardrooms a complete shift in mindset is needed as the sourcing situation becomes more complex, according to Phil Morris, founding director and COO at outsourcing advisers Morgan Chambers.

Morris says: 'The whole of the executive management needs to understand the impact of their response to the globalization phenomenon on their organization. Every executive needs to understand how different types of outsourcing can be woven into the organization to make it more competitive.'

One of the reasons for the need for a group-wide sourcing strategy is the range of services and processes that can now be offshored – aside from the obvious things such as software development and tech support.

Neil Hammond, head of IT at British Sugar, experienced the first wave of offshore outsourcing as head of IT strategy for Thomas Cook in the late 1990s when he offshored IT development work

The Bangalore headquarters of Infosys – a major IT company at the forefront of the offshore outsourcing boom.

PHOTO SOURCE: © BELINDA LAWLEY/ALAMY

to India. He says globalization and offshore outsourcing can no longer be ignored or sidelined by a business.

He says: 'It must be a factor in any significant sourcing decision, new business development or process improvement strategy.'

BPO on the rise

The current offshoring buzz is around BPO which at the top end is the outsourcing of an entire end-to-end process in HR or finance and at the lower end is basic call centre outsourcing.

Analyst Forrester predicts that over the next few years organizations will centralize activities such as customer service, marketing, HR, and finance and accounting (F&A) and move non-core processes such as low-level HR or payroll activities to low-cost offshore destinations.

British Sugar's Hammond says: '[Offshoring] has moved beyond IT development and call centres into areas such as back office transaction processing, engineering and architectural design, bespoke equipment manufacture, through to buying and operationalizing "shell" factories.'

Frances Karamouzis, VP of research at Gartner, says BPO adoption is just taking hold but that the pace of growth is picking up all the time.

She says: 'The core focus in terms of volumes is HR followed by F&A. Beyond that it's procurement or CRM and call centre work.'

KPO on the horizon

The future over the next five to ten years, however, appears to be around what industry experts are labelling knowledge process outsourcing, which refers to tasks such as financial analysis, legal work and research. There are already some examples of that in action.

LBS's Puranam says: 'Processes that would have been unthinkable a decade or so ago are now on the table and that's definitely the case in financial services companies.'

Equity analysis and research is offshored by many Wall Street and City of London organizations, for example. The number crunching is done in Mumbai or some other low-cost location and then sent back to the bank for review and analysis.

According to Gartner's Karamouzis, while the numbers in terms of headcount involved in KPO are smaller than IT or BPO offshoring, the value is higher in payback and return on investment.

She says: 'The per capita savings [for KPO] are around the 50 to 60th percentile. But the savings in absolute dollar amount also don't factor in productivity. You can get those [offshore] people to produce more in less hours and you can staff two or three people doing a deeper dive into the research', she said.

Pick a model

The other factor businesses need to address is the model they choose for offshoring. The most common option is to outsource the service or process to a third-party supplier, whether that be one of the traditional 'big six' consultancies, such as Accenture or IBM, or to one of the home-grown service providers in the offshore location, such as India's Infosys, TCS or Wipro.

Other options include going down the captive route, which means setting up a wholly owned unit of the business in the offshore country. Several high-profile companies have done this including GE, HSBC and Tesco.

Then there are joint ventures or 'build, operate, transfer' deals where a third-party supplier sets up the offshore operation, gets it up and running and then transfers it to the company using it. All these different models have their own pros and cons and the decision will depend on factors like the size of the company and the type of service being offshored.

The rule of thumb is that large global companies looking to offshore work that is a core competency or closely regulated are best suited to setting up their own captive operation, otherwise it is difficult to justify the business case.

Brand is also an issue that many companies fail to take into account when setting up their own captive offshore operation. In countries such as India, where there is stiff competition for staff and high attrition rates, the company's brand reputation is key to being able to attract and retain talent.

Morgan Chambers' Morris says: 'You need to understand how your brand will be perceived in the local market. If your brand doesn't stack up against Microsoft, Oracle, etc. you will suffer high attrition.'

Crunch the numbers

But none of this matters if the figures don't stack up. There are many good reasons for offshoring including filling skills gaps, freeing up resources and speeding up product development – but cost savings are still the chief motivation for sending work overseas.

In a recent Forrester survey of business and IT executives in European companies that use offshore providers, 45 out of 47 rated cost as the principal choice behind their decision.

The most important thing here is to be realistic about the level of savings once all the extra communication, management and travel time and resources have been factored into the basic return on investment equation, according to LBS's Puranam.

He says: 'Instead of 30 to 40 per cent savings the business case is now being made on more like 15 to 20 per cent.'

Beyond cost, British Sugar's Hammond says some of the issues to consider when offshoring are the management of a remote operation, ensuring you can gain access to sufficient technological and managerial expertise, and dealing with different cultural expectations and attitudes.

The lesson for boardrooms then is to look at offshore outsourcing within the context of a company-wide global sourcing strategy to ascertain which services and processes could be sent offshore and to make those decisions in a consistent framework. This means that while price is important, it is also a balance against other advantages such as access to talent, and quality and process improvements.

As Morgan Chambers' Morris says: 'Offshoring is not just a panacea on short-term labour arbitrage.'

Thinking about the case

1 The offshoring of manufacturing has been used for many years. Technology has helped to increase 'higher level' offshoring, such as call centres. What technology drivers are there to assist the extension of these functions to even higher levels such as knowledge processing?

2 The report suggests that while HR would remain as a home-based function 'low level' HR could be offshored. What do you understand by the term 'low level HR'?

Chapter 3

Business functions and supply chains

LEARNING OBJECTIVES

In an economy that produces and consumes so much information, professionals must know how to use information systems in virtually every business activity. Managers must have an overall understanding of all elements of a system, so that they know what options are available to control quality, costs and resources. Modern information systems encompass whole business cycles, often called supply chains.

When you finish this chapter, you will be able to:

Identify various business functions and the role of ISs in these functions.

Explain how ISs in the basic business functions relate to each other.

Articulate what supply chains are and how information technology supports management of supply chains.

Enumerate the purposes of customer relationship management systems.

Explain the notion of enterprise resource planning systems.

BETTER BITES

CONTINUED GROWTH AND SPECIALISM

Something had to give: Better Bites' business expansion to more carts and to crisp manufacturing had worked so well that Paul Clermont was drowning in piles of sales receipts. He had employed a part-time assistant to help him input the receipts to the business's spreadsheet program, but that solution was no longer enough. The labour-intensive process simply had to go. Luckily, Paul, Sarah Odell and Christina Healy found a solution in a handheld personal digital assistant (PDA) with wireless mobile printer software. The sales staff serving from the carts keyed the customer's menu selections into the PDAs and printed a receipt. Later, the information was downloaded from the PDAs to the business's main accounting system. The time saved by automating the sales transactions allowed Paul to concentrate on bigger issues the partners faced: tracking sales, costs and profitability.

As part of his monthly sales analysis, Paul printed sales reports segregated by each of the three carts. When he did so, he noticed that sales from the University Concourse pushcart were dropping. Their Subwich competitor was drawing customers from the Concourse cart. Also, Paul noticed that business was even worse during colder months and bad weather. The partners needed to turn the situation around.

A new opportunity appears

Earlier Paul, Sarah and Christina had decided to find their own kitchen space to handle their increased food volume. When they were looking for rental space, they ran across a vacant shop unit in their local town. Instead of simply renting kitchen space, they decided they'd open a small restaurant with its own kitchen. That way, they could meet their Subwich competitor head on, offering dinners as well as lunches and not worrying about the change of seasons or weather. They could also use the restaurant's kitchen for crisp manufacturing when the restaurant was closed.

To handle the increased workload for the restaurant, the three entrepreneurs hired a full-time chef and kitchen staff. Sarah and the chef developed streamlined cooking procedures for both the meal and crisp operations and then trained the staff in the procedures. That freed Sarah to work on new restaurant recipes.

Advertising needs and promotions

To announce the opening of their new restaurant, Christina used a desktop publishing program to create flyers for their grand opening that could be handed out to pushcart customers or on campus. The flyers included a feedback form and those who returned the forms received discount coupons for a free beverage with the purchase of a sandwich. They hoped these special offers would attract new customers. Paul also suggested they produce radio commercials, reasoning that radio offered an affordable means of reaching their customers – college students, shoppers and commuters. They'd need professional help with that media project.

Moving forward

Better Bites had come a long way since its start, but the entrepreneurs still had decisions to make and changes to undergo. With the opening of the restaurant, the partners needed to revamp their computer systems to handle credit-card purchases. Better Bites also needed to automate and expand its employee systems. Paul had written cheques by hand when the business only had a small staff payroll to deal with. But the new chef and kitchen staff now made that system impractical. Finally, Sarah thought that their food inventory and preparation systems might benefit from automation. She had tracked

PHOTO SOURCE: © JON JAKOBSSON

her inventory closely, but with the expansion, it was getting more and more difficult to keep up. Paul and Christina agreed that an inventory control system would be a good move, so they bought the QuickBooks program. This software could help them not only with inventory control but also with online credit verifications, sales and expenses, payroll and accounting as well as other needed functions, such as tracking sales taxes, invoicing and cheque printing. With this more comprehensive system, the three entrepreneurs believed they had made a great leap forward. It was clear to them that a well-run information system was an integral part of their business, simplifying their business as activities became more complex. They'd need to remain informed about technology as they looked to the future.

Effectiveness and efficiency

CD TASK

As we saw in TheTrainline 'Industry Snapshot' in the previous chapter, the use of technology enables the contact centre staff to deal with calls more efficiently and also every call has potential added value because of the extra information that the operator has in front of them. It is often said that the use of information technology makes our work more effective, more efficient, or both. What do these terms mean? **Effectiveness** defines the degree to which a goal is achieved. Thus, a system is more or less effective depending on (1) how much of its goal it achieves and (2) the degree to which it achieves better outcomes than other systems do.

effectiveness The measure of how well a job is performed.

Efficiency is determined by the relationship between resources expended and the benefits gained in achieving a goal. Expressed mathematically,

efficiency The ratio of output to input; the greater the ratio, the greater the efficiency.

$$\text{Efficiency} = \text{Benefits} \div \text{Costs}$$

One system is more efficient than another if its operating costs are lower for the same or better quality product, or if its product's quality is greater for the same or lower costs. The term 'productivity' is commonly used as a synonym for efficiency. However, **productivity** refers specifically to the efficiency of *human* resources. Productivity improves when fewer workers are required to produce the same amount of output, or, alternatively, when the same number of workers produces a greater amount of output. This is why IT professionals often speak of 'productivity tools', which are software applications that help workers produce more in less time. The closer the result of an effort is to the ultimate goal, the more effective the effort. The fewer the resources spent on achieving a goal, the more efficient the effort.

productivity Efficiency, when the input is labour. The fewer labour hours needed to perform a job, the greater the productivity.

Suppose your goal is to design a new car that reaches a speed of 60 miles per hour in five seconds. If you manage to build it, then you produce the product effectively. If the car does not meet the requirement, your effort is ineffective. If your competitor makes a car with the same features and performance, but uses fewer people and fewer other resources, then your competitor is not only as effective as you but also more efficient. ISs contribute to both the effectiveness and efficiency of businesses, especially when positioned in specific business functions, such as accounting, finance and engineering and when used to help companies achieve their goals more quickly by facilitating collaborative work.

One way to look at business functions and their supporting systems is to follow typical business cycles, which often begin with marketing and sales activities (see Figure 3.1). Serving customers better and faster, as well as learning more about their experiences and preferences, is facilitated by **customer relationship management (CRM)** systems. When customers place orders, the orders are executed in the supply chain. Customer relationship management continues after delivery of the ordered goods in the forms of customer service and more marketing. When an organization enjoys the support of CRM and supply chain management (SCM)

customer relationship management (CRM) A set of applications designed to gather and analyse information about customers.

Figure 3.1 Business activities consist of customer relationship management, supply chain management and supporting functions

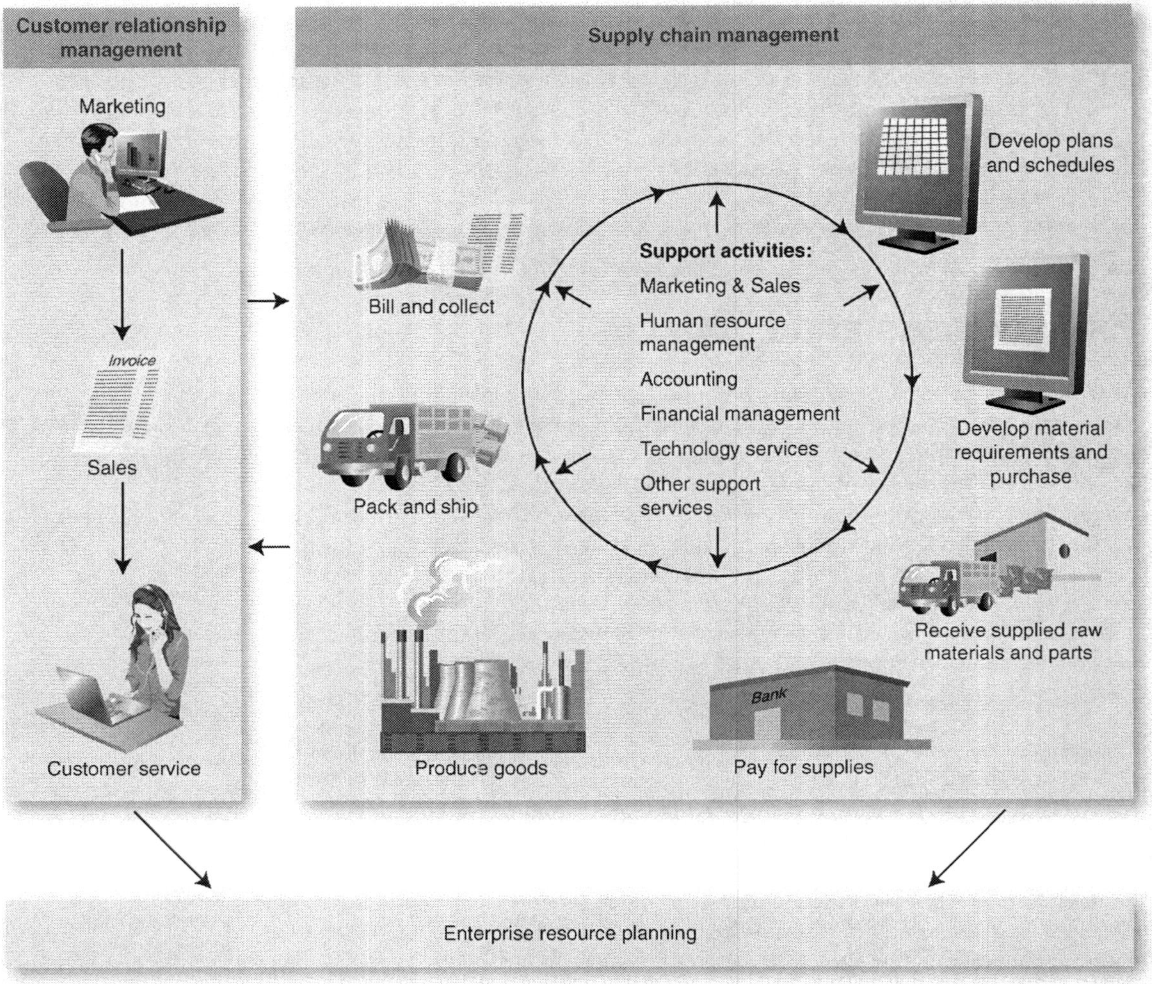

systems, it can plan its resources well. Combined, these systems are often referred to as enterprise resource planning (ERP) systems.

Figure 3.2 shows some of the most common business activities and their interdependence. For example, cost accounting systems are linked to payroll, benefits and purchasing systems to accumulate the cost of products manufactured by a company; and information from purchasing systems flows to both cost accounting and financial reporting systems. The following discussion addresses the role of information systems, one business function at a time.

Accounting

The purpose of accounting is to track every financial transaction within a company, from a few cents to multimillion euro purchases, from salaries and benefits to the sale of every item. Without tracking the costs of labour, materials and purchased services using a

Figure 3.2 Information systems in different business functions are interdependent

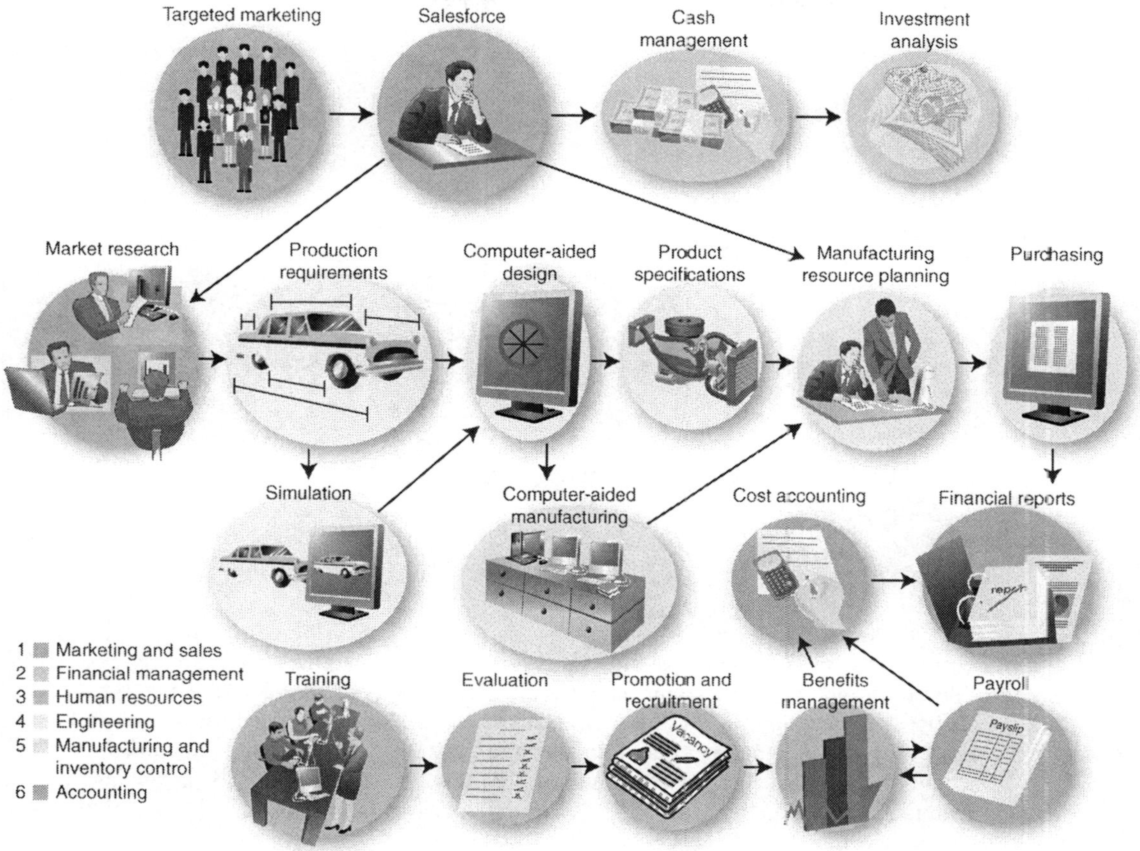

cost-accounting system, a company might discover too late that it sells products below what it costs to make them. Without a system of accounts receivable, managers might not know who owes the company how much money and when it is due. Without an accounts payable system, managers cannot know how much money the company owes each supplier and when payment is due. Without a system that records and helps plan cash flow, managers cannot keep enough cash in the bank to make payments on schedule. At the year's end, the company cannot present a picture of its financial situation – called a balance sheet – and a profit-and-loss report, unless it maintains a general ledger to record every transaction with a financial impact. General ledger, accounts receivable, accounts payable and cash-flow books conveniently lend themselves to computerization and can easily generate balance sheets and profit-and-loss statements from records (see Figure 3.3).

Typically, accounting ISs receive records of routine business transactions – such as the purchase of raw materials or services, or the sale of manufactured goods – from transaction processing systems (TPSs). Such a system automatically routes every purchase of raw materials or services to the accounts payable system, which uses it to produce cheques or transfer funds to a vendor's bank account. Whenever a sale is recorded, the transaction is routed to the accounts receivable system (which generates invoices) and other destinations. Totals of accounts receivable and accounts payable can be automatically transferred to a balance sheet. Data from the general ledger can be automatically compiled to generate a cash-flow report or a profit-and-loss report for the past quarter or year. Accounting ISs can generate any of these reports on demand, as well as at scheduled times.

Figure 3.3 Accounting information systems include features that reflect up-to-date performance of the organization in financial terms

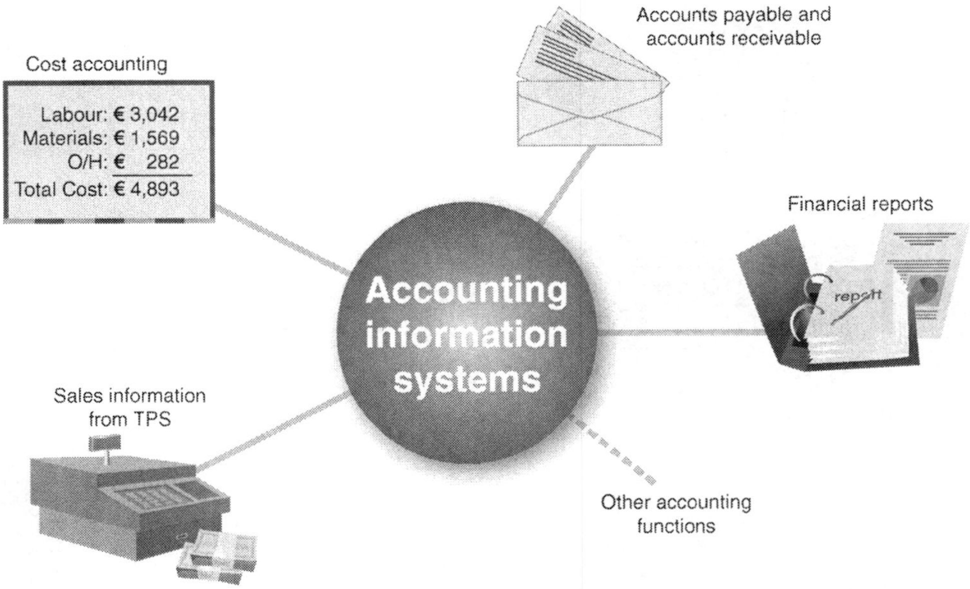

When a company develops and manufactures a new product that has never been available on the market, how can it determine a price that covers costs and generates a decent profit? It must maintain a system that tracks the costs of labour, materials, consulting fees and every other expense related to the product's development and manufacture. Cost-accounting systems, used to accumulate data about costs involved in producing specific products, make excellent use of IT to compile pricing data. ISs also help allocate costs to specific work orders. A work order is an authorization to perform work for a specific purpose. When interfaced with payroll and purchasing ISs, a cost-accounting system automatically captures records of everything spent (and originally recorded in the payroll and purchasing systems) and routes expenses to the appropriate work order. Because work orders are associated with specific products and services, the company now knows how much each product or service costs.

Why you should...

know about business functions and supply chains

Today's professionals are expected to be knowledgeable not only in their specific line of work but also in other areas, specifically information technology. In today's market, many employers look for generalists rather than specialists and focus on the techno-manager, a manager well versed in information technology.

Because many ISs serve multiple functions and interface with other systems, it is extremely important for a professional to be familiar with the way ISs facilitate work in areas outside his or her expertise. If you work for a commercial organization, you are bound to be part of a supply chain or work for a unit that supports a supply chain. Knowledge of systems in different business areas helps you cooperate with your peers and coordinate efforts that cross departmental boundaries. Because professionals often have opportunities to be promoted to positions in other disciplines, the more you know, the better your chances of being 'cross-promoted'.

Accounting ISs are also used extensively for managerial purposes, assisting in organizing quarterly and annual budgets for departments, divisions and entire corporations. The same systems help managers control their budgets by tracking income and expense in real time and comparing them with the amounts predicted in the budget. Budget applications are designed with proper controls, so that the system does not allow spending funds for a specific purpose beyond the amount that was budgeted for that purpose.

Finance

A firm's health is often measured by its finances and ISs can significantly improve financial management (see Figure 3.4). The goal of financial managers, including controllers and treasurers, is to manage an organization's money as efficiently as possible. They achieve this goal by (1) collecting payables as soon as possible, (2) making payments at the latest time allowed by contract or law, (3) ensuring that sufficient funds are available for day-to-day operations and (4) taking advantage of opportunities to accrue the highest yield on funds not used for current activities. These goals can be best met by careful cash management and investment analysis.

Cash management

Financial information systems help managers track a company's finances. These systems record every payment and cash receipt to reflect cash movement, employ budgeting software to track plans for company finances and include capital investment systems to manage investments, thus balancing the need to accrue interest on idle money against the need to have cash available. The information on expected cash receipts comes from sales contracts and the information on cash outlays comes from purchasing contracts, as well as payroll and benefits schedules. Systems that deal specifically with cash are often called cash management systems (CMSs). One common use for a CMS is to execute cash transactions in which financial

cash management system (CMS) Information system that helps reduce the interest and fees that organizations have to pay when borrowing money and increases the yield that organizations can receive on unused funds.

Figure 3.4 Financial information systems help manage cash and investment portfolios

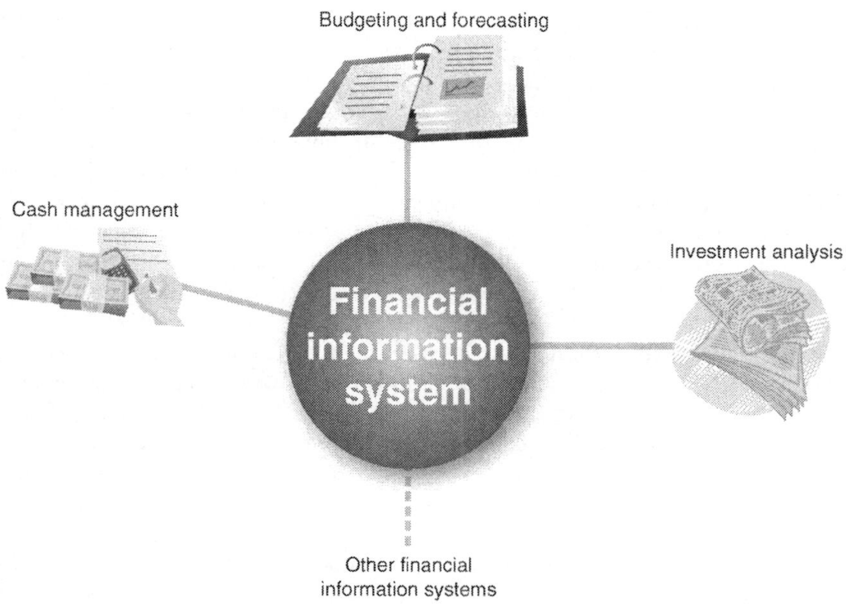

electronic funds transfer (EFT) The electronic transfer of cash from an account in one bank to an account in another bank.

institutions transfer huge amounts of money using electronic funds transfer (EFT). EFT is the electronic transfer of cash from an account in one bank to an account in another bank.

Investment analysis and service

Every investor's goal is to buy an asset and later sell it for more than it cost. When investing in securities, such as stocks and bonds, it is important to know the prices of securities in real time, that is, *right now*. The ability of financial ISs to record millions of securities prices and their changes over long time periods, coupled with the ability to manipulate numbers using software, puts powerful analysis tools in investment managers' hands. Within seconds, an investment analyst can use a financial IS and chart prices of a specific stock or bond over a given period and then build models to estimate what might happen to securities prices in the future.

Even the smallest investment firm can provide clients with an inexpensive online service for buying and selling securities, providing on-demand statements listing the stocks they own (called a portfolio), periodic yield and the portfolio's current value. Clients serve themselves through the websites of brokerage firms to place buy and sell orders. Execution of orders takes only a few seconds.

Nearly instantaneously, ISs provide subscriber brokers and their clients with financial news, stock prices, commodity prices and currency exchange rates from multiple locations across the world. Consider what happens when a foreign currency's exchange rate fluctuates a fraction of a percentage. A brokerage house can make a significant profit within two minutes of buying and selling a large block of the foreign currency. A small fraction of a very large number is still big!

Financial managers need to consider many factors before they invest in a security. Some of the most important factors these managers must consider are (1) risk, measured as the variability (degree of change) of the paper's past yield; (2) expected return; and (3) liquidity, a measure of how fast an investment can be turned into cash. Special programs help calculate these factors and present the results in either tables or graphs to allow timely decision-making.

time to market The time between generating an idea for a product and completing a prototype that can be mass-manufactured; also called engineering lead time.

brainstorming The process of a group collaboratively generating new ideas and creative solutions to problems.

computer-aided design (CAD) Special software used by engineers and designers that facilitates engineering and design work.

rapid prototyping Using software and special output devices to create prototypes to test design in three dimensions.

Engineering

The time between generating an idea for a product and completing a prototype that can be mass-manufactured is known as engineering lead time or time to market. Engineering includes brainstorming (the process of a group of colleagues meeting and working collaboratively to generate creative solutions and new ideas), developing a concept, creating mock-ups, building prototypes, testing and other activities that require investments of time, labour and money. Minimizing lead time is key to maintaining a competitive edge: it leaves competitors insufficient time to introduce their own products first. ISs can contribute significantly to this effort. Over the past decade, car manufacturers have used engineering and other ISs to reduce the time from product concept to market from seven to two years.

IT's greatest contribution to engineering is in the area of computer-aided design (CAD) and rapid prototyping (creating one-of-a-kind products to test design in three dimensions). Engineers can use computers to modify designs quickly and store drawings electronically. With collaborative software, they perform much of this process over the Internet: engineers can conduct remote conferences while viewing and developing plans and drawings together. The electronic drawings are then available to make rapid prototypes.

Rapid prototyping allows a model of a product to be produced within hours, rather than days or weeks. The model required is often a mock-up to show only the physical look and dimensions of a product, without the electronics or other

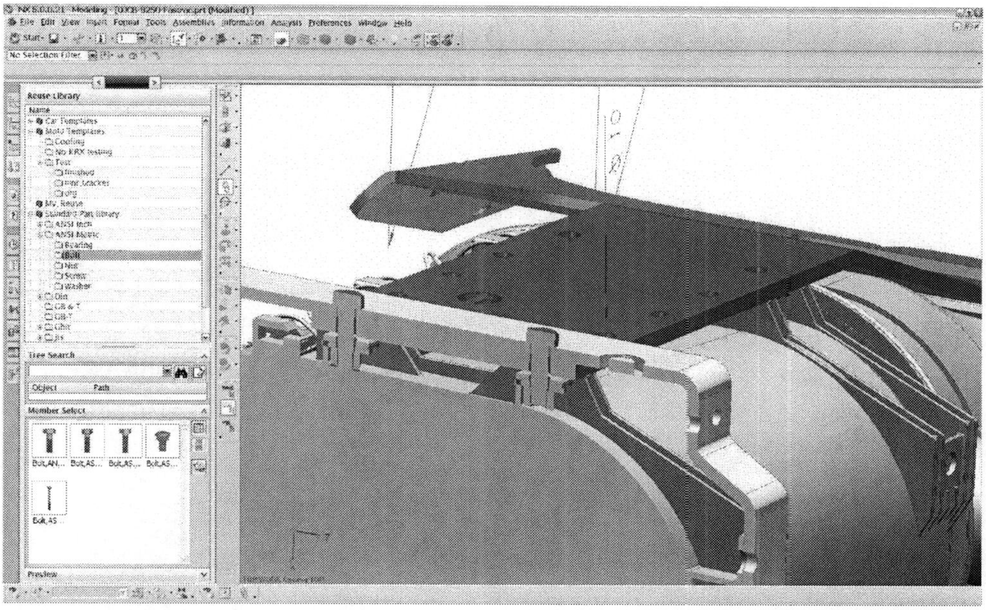

Computer-aided design systems significantly shorten the time needed to produce drawings and complete the design of new products.

components that are part of the full product. First, an image of the object is created on a computer. The computer is connected to a special machine that creates a physical, three-dimensional model by laying down hundreds or thousands of thin layers of liquid plastic or special resin. The model can be examined by engineers and marketing managers in the organization, or shown to clients.

When the prototypes are satisfactory, the electronic drawings and material specifications can be transferred from the CAD systems to computer-aided manufacturing (CAM) systems. CAM systems process the data to instruct machines, including robots, how to manufacture the parts and assemble the product (see Figure 3.5).

computer-aided manufacturing (CAM) Automation of manufacturing activities by use of computers. Often, the information for the activity comes directly from connected computers that were used for engineering the parts or products to be manufactured.

Until several years ago, car manufacturers needed four to five years to turn a concept into vehicles rolling out for sale. Now, thanks to CAD, CAM, rapid prototyping and collaborative engineering software, the lead time has been reduced to less than two years. The digital design of vehicles saves not only time but also the cost of cars crashed in tests. All the tests are performed with sophisticated software rather than with real cars.

Supply chain management

In its fundamental form, a supply chain consists of three phases: procurement of raw materials, processing the materials into intermediate and finished goods and delivery of the goods to customers. Processing raw materials into goods is manufacturing. Supply chain management (SCM) consists of monitoring, controlling and facilitating supply chains, as depicted on the right side of Figure 3.1. Supply chain management (SCM) systems are information technologies that support SCM. Such systems have been instrumental in reducing manufacturing costs, including the costs of managing resources and controlling inventory (see Figure 3.6). In retail, the manufacturing phase does not exist, so the term 'supply chain' refers only to the purchasing of finished goods and the delivery to customers of those goods. In the service industries the term is practically meaningless.

supply chain The activities performed from the purchase of raw material to the shipping of manufactured goods and collecting for their sale.

supply chain management (SCM) The coordination of purchasing, manufacturing, shipping and billing operations, often supported by an enterprise resource planning system.

As is clear from the previous discussion, much of the data required for manufacturing processes can flow directly from CAD systems to CAM systems, as well

Figure 3.5 Engineering information systems aid engineers in designing new products and simulating how they operate

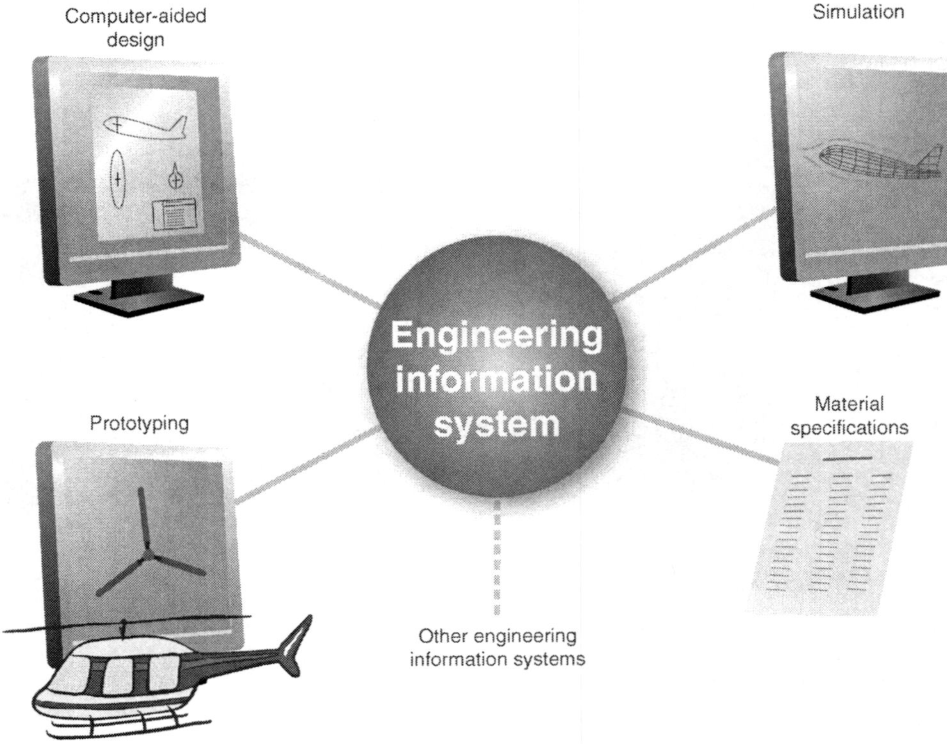

Figure 3.6 Manufacturing and inventory control information systems help reduce cycle times and the cost of maintaining inventory

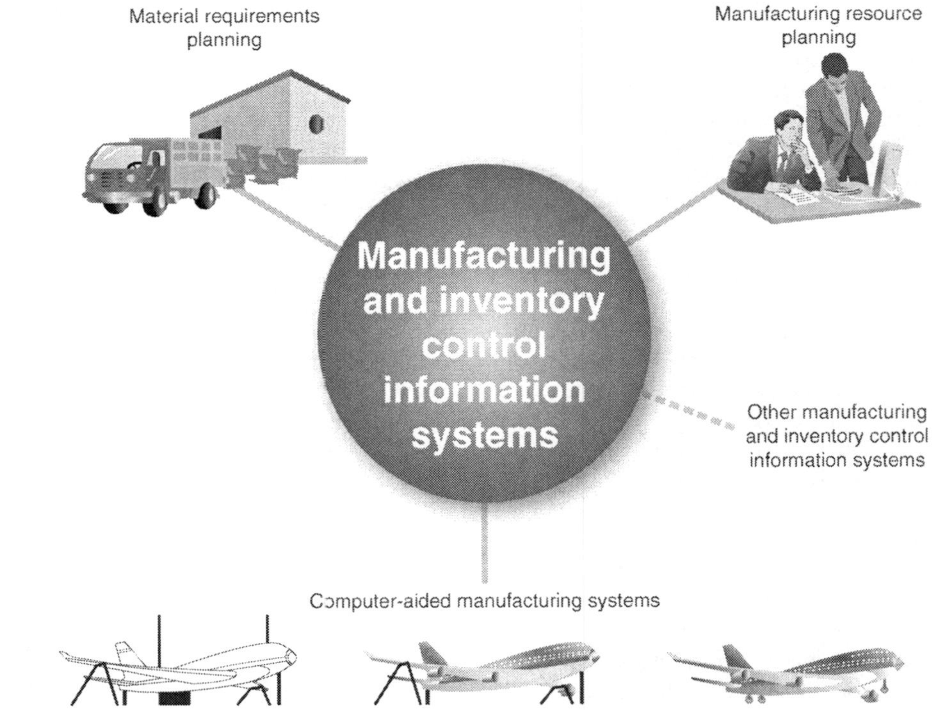

as inventory control systems and other systems that support planning and execution of manufacturing. While CAM systems participate in physical activities such as cutting and welding, other information systems help to plan and monitor manufacturing.

Information technology helps in the following manufacturing activities:

- Scheduling plant activities while optimizing the combined use of all resources – machines, personnel, tooling and raw and interim materials.
- Planning material requirements based on current and forecasted demand.
- Reallocating materials rapidly from one order to another to satisfy due dates.
- Letting users manage inventories in real time, taking into consideration demand and the responsiveness of all work centres.
- Grouping work orders by characteristics of items ordered, such as colour and width of products.
- Considering the qualifications of each resource (such as qualified labour, set-up crews and specialized tools) to accomplish its task. For instance, people and raw materials can be moved from one assembly line to another to respond to machine breakdown or customer emergency, and design changes can be implemented quickly to respond to changes in customer wishes.

Material requirements planning and purchasing

One area of manufacturing that has experienced the greatest improvement from IS is inventory control, or **material requirements planning (MRP)**. Traditional inventory control techniques operated according to the basic principle that future inventory needs are based on past use: once used up, inventory was replaced. By contrast, replenishment in MRP is based on *future* need, calculated by MRP software from demand forecasts. MRP programs take customer demand as their initial input. The main input to MRP programs is the number of product units needed and the time at which they are needed; the programs then work back to calculate the amounts of resources required to produce subparts and assemblies. The programs use long-range forecasts to put long-lead material on order.

Other important input to MRP applications includes a list of all raw materials and subcomponent demands (called the **bill of materials**, or **BOM**) and the economic order quantity of different raw materials. The **economic order quantity (EOQ)** of a specific raw material is the optimal quantity that allows a business to minimize overstocking and save cost, without risking under-stocking and missing production deadlines. A special program calculates EOQ for each item. It considers several factors: the item's cost, the discount schedule for large quantities, the cost of warehousing ordered parts, the cost of alternative uses of the money (such as the interest the money could earn had it not been spent on inventory) and other factors affecting the cost of ordering the item. Some MRP applications are tied to a purchasing IS, to produce purchase orders automatically when the quantity on hand reaches a reorder level. The purchase order includes the economic order quantity.

material requirements planning (MRP) Inventory control that includes a calculation of future need.

bill of materials (BOM) A list showing an explosion of the materials that go into the production of an item. Used in planning the purchase of raw materials.

economic order quantity (EOQ) The optimal (cost-minimizing) quantity of a specific raw material that allows a business to minimize overstocking and save cost without risking understocking and missing production deadlines.

manufacturing resource planning (MRP II) The combination of MRP with other manufacturing-related activities to plan the entire manufacturing process, not just inventory.

Manufacturing resource planning

Manufacturing resource planning (MRP II) combines material requirements planning (MRP) with other manufacturing-related activities to plan the entire manufacturing process, not just inventory. MRP II systems can quickly modify schedules to

master production schedule (MPS) The component of an MRP II system that specifies production capacity to meet customer demands and maintain inventories.

just-in-time (JIT) The manufacturing strategy in which suppliers ship parts directly to assembly lines, saving the cost of warehousing raw materials, parts and subassemblies.

accommodate orders, track production in real time and fix quality slippage. The most important input of MRP II systems is the master production schedule (MPS), which specifies how production capacity is to be used to meet customer demands and maintain inventories. Virtually every report an MRP II package generates starts with, or is based on, the MPS. Purchases of materials and internal control of manufacturing work flow, for example, start with the MPS, so the MPS directly affects operational costs and asset use.

MRP II systems help balance production economies, customer demands, manufacturing capacity and inventory levels over a planning horizon of several months. Successful MRP II systems have made a significant contribution to just-in-time (JIT) manufacturing, where suppliers ship parts directly to assembly lines, saving the cost of warehousing raw materials, parts and subassemblies.

Ideally, the ISs of manufacturing organizations and their suppliers would be linked in a way that makes them subsystems of one large system. The MRP II application of an organization that manufactures a final product would plan and dictate the items required, their quantities and the exact times they are needed at the assembly lines. Suppliers would deliver items directly to assembly lines just before they are incorporated into the final product (hence the term *just-in-time manufacturing*). Manufacturing organizations have not yet reached the point where JIT is accomplished with every product, but they have made great progress towards this ideal.

The Internet facilitates such system linking. Companies that were quick to link their systems to their suppliers' systems attained strategic advantages. One such company is Cisco Systems, a world leader in design and manufacturing of telecommunications devices. The company used to maintain many manufacturing plants. In 2001, it had sold all but two. The company's ISs are linked through the Internet to the ISs of its suppliers, some of whom purchased the very plants that Cisco sold. Through these systems managers can track orders. They can tell Cisco clients the exact status of their orders and the time of delivery. Cisco managers keep track of the products they order and know at what phase of manufacturing and delivery each item is – as if *they* were running the manufacturing plants. More than 80 per cent of what Cisco orders never passes through the company's facilities; the manufacturers deliver the products directly to Cisco's clients.

Monitoring and control

Information systems have been designed to control manufacturing processes, not just monitor them. Controlling processes is important to ensure quality. Most of the major car manufacturers use a combination of bar coding and wireless technology to ensure the quality of the assembly. Since each vehicle is assembled on a chassis, each chassis is tagged with a unique bar code. A bar-code sensor is installed at each stop of the assembly line. The sensor transmits wireless signals to computers and electronically controlled gates. The purpose of the system is to ensure that no assembly steps are skipped and that each vehicle passes a series of performance and quality tests along the way. If a step is missed, the gate does not let the vehicle leave the plant.

However, the use of ISs in monitoring and control is not limited to manufacturing. CareCaller is a computer-based alarm processing system for use in nursing environments. It monitors routine nursing calls and emergency calls, routing the request for assistance to appropriate nursing staff who carry radio phones. These events can be recorded and used to produce management reports showing, for example, average response time, how often each patient pressed his or her button and when, and so on. However, the system also has an element of control. For example, in the case of an emergency, doors which are usually kept locked for security reasons can be automatically unlocked to allow fast access by the emergency response team.

Distribution

When the process of manufacturing products is complete, the next link in the supply chain is delivery to the customer. Distribution is performed either by the manufacturer or by a hired delivery company. The variables that affect the cost and speed of delivery are numerous: length of routes, sequence of loading and unloading, type of materials (e.g., perishable, hazardous or fragile), fuel prices, road tolls, terrain and restricted roads and many more. Therefore, the use of sophisticated software to give an optimal delivery time for every customer and the cost of labour and equipment use helps companies stay competitive. Figure 3.7 shows an example of such software.

Today's lorries are equipped with computers and satellite communication hardware and software. Each can receive real-time orders from a central distribution office, especially when routing changes are necessary, and transmits information about the truck, such as current location, the previous point of loading or unloading and the next point of loading or unloading. Lorry drivers rarely reach a shipping office. These systems allow them to be on the road doing productive work all the time, thanks to constant communication with the office.

Supply chain management software in transportation helps load lorries, ships and aeroplanes in an optimal manner both in terms of space utilization and sequence of unloading. Figure 3.8 provides a visual description of an optimal loading of boxes on a lorry before its dispatch.

Figure 3.7 A software tool for optimizing utilization of human resources and equipment in transportation

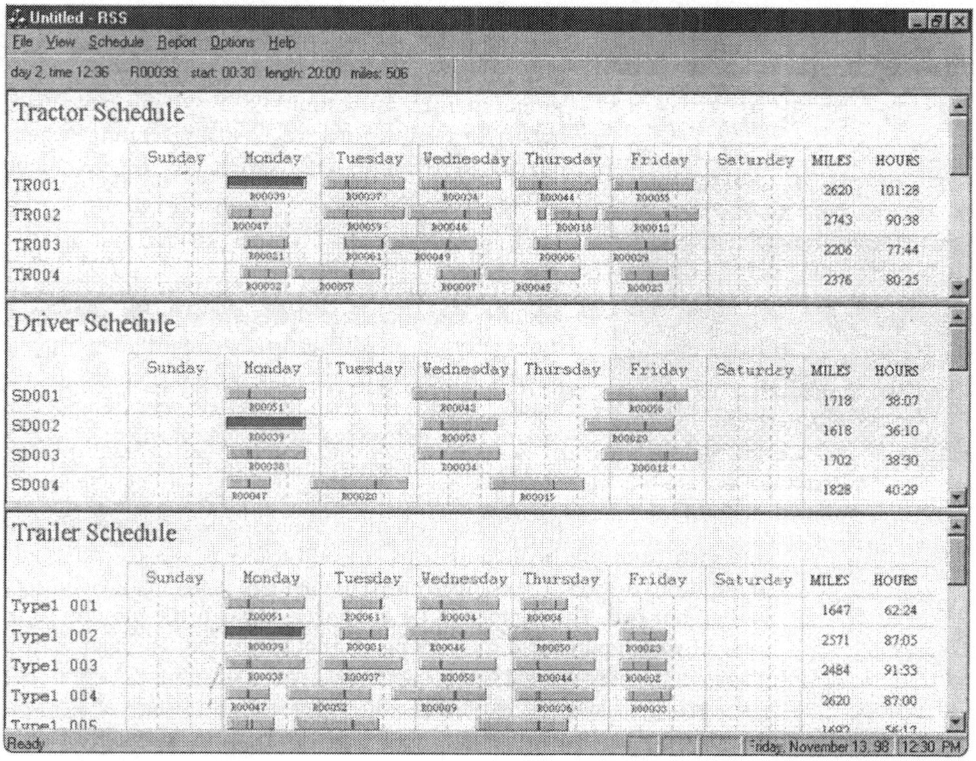

Figure 3.8 A graphical display of planned loading on a truck, as produced by shipping software

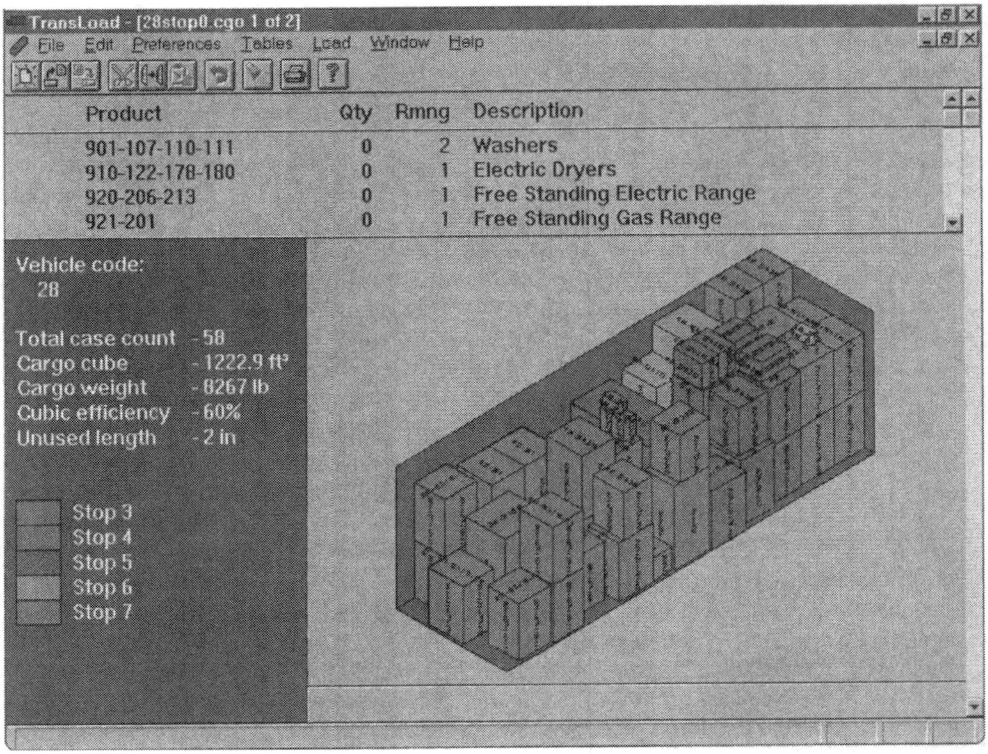

RFID in SCM

CD TASK

The most important development in hardware to support SCM has been a technology called radio frequency identification (RFID). We discuss the technology itself in Chapter 5. RFID tags contain circuitry that allows recording of information about a product. When attached to a product, it contains an electronic product code (EPC), which replaces the universal product code (UPC) with much more information. The tag can include the date of manufacturing, the plant in which the product was made, lot number, expiration date, destination and many other details that help track its movement and sale. The information can be read and also revised by special RFID transceivers (transmitter–receiver devices). Figure 3.9 shows an example of how RFID is used in a supply chain. Items with rewritable tags can contain the maintenance history of products, which helps in the maintenance of the items.

radio frequency identification (RFID) Technology that enables identification of an object (such as product, vehicle or living creature) by receiving a radio signal from a tag attached to the object.

The same technology can also be used for other purposes: detection of items that should be recalled because of hazardous components, detection of counterfeit products and accurate condemnation of expired items, such as medicines and car parts. When a pattern of defects is discovered in a product, RFID helps pinpoint the plant at which it was produced and the particular lot from which it came. Only products from that lot are recalled and replaced or fixed. It does not take too long to find out the particular manufacturing phase in which the defect was caused. When the expiration date of an item arrives, a transceiver detects that fact and alerts personnel to remove it from a shelf. Packaging of medicines and other items contain RFID tags with unique identifiers. Transceivers can detect whether the products are genuine.

electronic product code (EPC) A product code embedded in a radio frequency identification (RFID) tag. Similar to the older UPC.

Figure 3.9 RFID in the supply chain

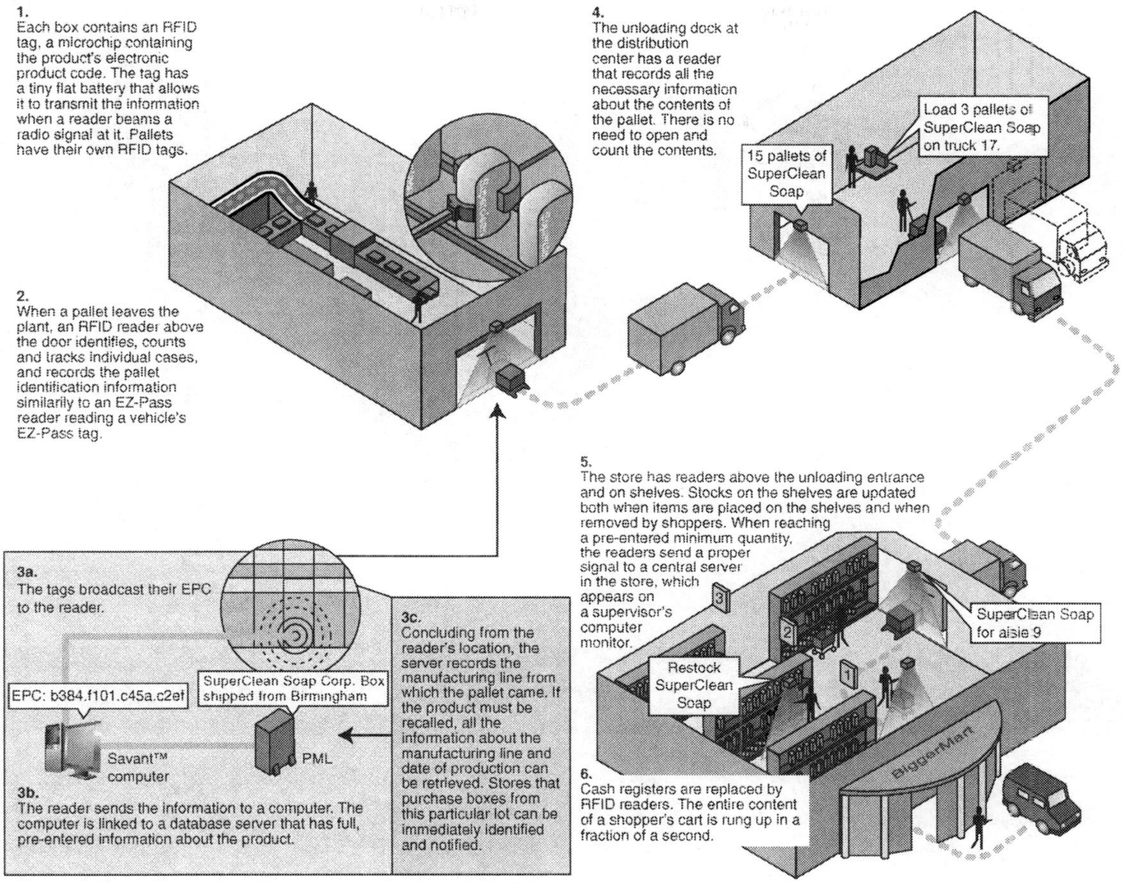

Customer relationship management

No commercial organization can survive without selling its products or services. Thus, businesses seek to provide products that consumers want and to entice them to buy what the business produces. They exert marketing efforts to pinpoint demographic groups that are most likely to buy products, to determine features that consumers desire most and to provide the most efficient and effective ways to execute a sale when a consumer shows interest in the product or service. Because these efforts depend mainly on the analysis of huge amounts of data, ISs have become key tools for conceiving and executing marketing strategies. When marketing succeeds, ISs support the sales effort; to entice customers to continue to purchase, ISs support customer service (see Figure 3.10).

Customer relationship management (CRM) systems are designed to support any and all relationships with customers. Mostly, they support three areas: marketing, sales and customer service. Modern CRM systems can help capture the entire customer experience with an organization, from response to an online advertisement to automatic replenishment of products, to proactive service. With growing competition and so many options available to consumers, keeping customers satisfied is extremely important. Many executives will tell you that their companies do not make money (and might even lose money) on a first sale to a new customer because of the great investment in marketing. Thus, they constantly strive to

Figure 3.10 Customer relationship management systems help marketing, sales and customer sevice departments target interested customers, learn from their experiences, and serve them better

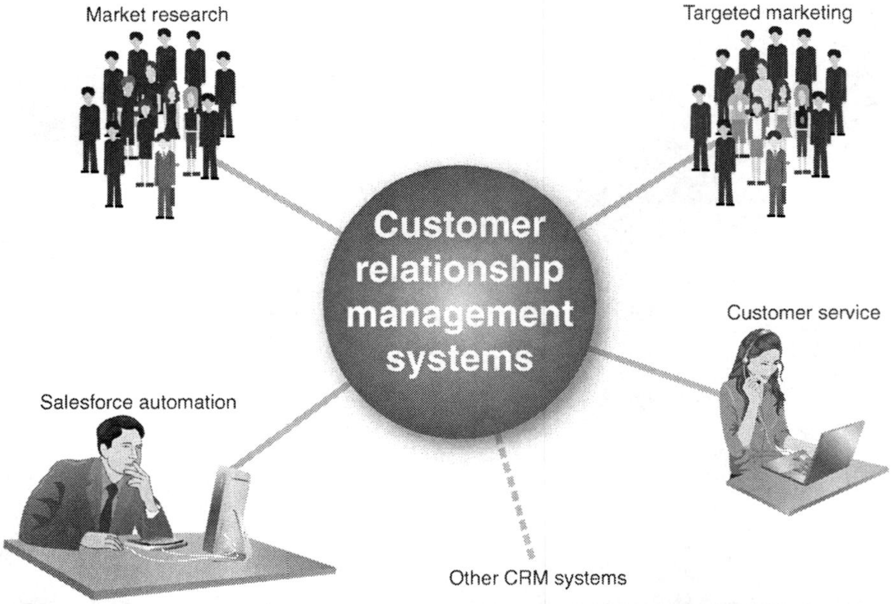

Industry SNAPSHOT

Say it with flowers – using RFID

FloraHolland is the world's largest flower auction company. It houses flowers from 7000 growers in a warehouse the size of 100 football fields. It interacts with 4000 dealers and exporters and needs to move 100,000 trolleys of flowers around the warehouse. Each of the trolleys are fitted with RFID tags and RFID loops are embedded in the warehouse floor. The movement of the flowers is captured and this information is made available to the IT systems that handle the auctions. Data about the trolley number and the products on it are displayed on an LED screen on the auction floor, alerting buyers as to which products are heading to auction. Time is an important factor, as the flowers must be moved quickly to ensure they are fresh. Customers can receive an electronic processing history of the flowers to guarantee their quality, for example ensuring that they have not spent too much time out of cold storage en route to the auction. FloaraHolland can use the data to analyse their logistics and make improvements.

SOURCE: Claire Swedberg, 'Dutch Horticultural Company Sends Flowers via RFID', *RFID Journal*, http://www.rfidjournal.com/article/articleview/2733/1/1/

PHOTO SOURCE: © DANITA DELIMONT/ALAMY

improve customer service and periodically contact anyone who has ever purchased something from them to ensure repeat sales and to encourage customer loyalty. Any information technology that supports these efforts is considered a CRM system, but in recent years the effort has been to combine applications that support all three areas – marketing, sales and customer service – to better understand what customers want, to ensure timely delivery and to be able to collect payment sooner.

CRM systems also provide an organization with an important element: all employees of the company who directly or indirectly serve a customer are 'on the same page'. Through their individual computers, all can have immediate access to the status of an order for an item or a resolution of a buyer's complaint, or to any other information that has to do with the customer. All who serve the customer are well informed and receive the information from the same source. This is especially important in a long, complex sales cycle, because it minimizes response time and improves the quality of service for customers.

Market research

Few organizations can sell their products and services without promotion; fewer still can promote successfully without market research. Market research systems help to find the populations and regions that are most likely to purchase a new product or service. They also help analyse how a new product fares in its first several months on the market.

Through interviews with consumers and retailers, market researchers collect information on what consumers like and dislike about products. When the researchers collect sufficient data, the marketing department uses statistical models to predict sales volumes of different products and of different designs of the same product. This critical information aids in planning manufacturing capacities and production lines. It is also extremely important for budgeting purposes.

Targeted marketing

To save resources, businesses use IT to promote to people most likely to purchase their products. This activity is often referred to as **targeted marketing**. Great advances in database technology enable even the smallest and poorest business to use targeted marketing. The principle of targeted marketing is to define the prospective customer as accurately as possible and then to direct promotional spending towards those people most likely to purchase your product. Perhaps the best evidence of how much companies use ISs for targeted marketing is the use of the Internet for mass communication of unsolicited promotional email, a practice called spamming. Many people loathe spamming, but it is certainly the least expensive method of advertising. Another controversial, but apparently effective, method is pop-up advertising, in which a small window pops up either in front of or behind a web browser's window.

targeted marketing
Promoting products and services to the people who are most likely to purchase them.

To define their target markets, businesses collect data everywhere they can: from sales transactions and loyalty cards, or by purchasing databases with information about organizations and individuals. Using database management systems (DBMSs), special programs to build and manipulate data pools, a company can sort and categorize consumers by age, gender, income, previous purchase of a related product, or any combination of these facts and other demographic information. The company then selects those whose characteristics match the company's customer profile and spends its promotional effort and money to try to sell to those select customers.

The great amount of personal information that corporations collect and purchase lets them prepare electronic dossiers on the interests, tastes and buying habits of individuals. The information they possess lets them target 'a market of one', namely, an individual rather than a group. Online purchase transactions and online product registrations by consumers provide a wealth of information to corporations. Vendors sort the information to send promotional material by post or email only to those customers whose profiles indicate potential interest.

Telemarketing (marketing over the telephone) makes extensive use of IT. The telemarketer uses a PC connected to a large database. The database contains records of potential or existing customers. With a retrieved record displayed on the screen, a marketer dials the number by pressing a single key or clicking the mouse. The telemarketer speaks to the potential buyer while looking at that person's purchasing record with the organization or even other organizations. Charitable organizations use the same method to solicit donations.

Computer telephony integration (CTI) is a technique enabling a computer to use the digital signal coming through a telephone line as input in a computer system. It has been used often in marketing, sales and customer service. For example, some mail-order firms use caller ID to better serve their customers. Caller ID was originally intended to identify the telephone number from which a person calls, but mail-order businesses quickly found a new use for the gadget. They connect it to their customer database. When you call to order, a simple program searches for your number, retrieves your record and displays it on a PC monitor. You might be surprised when the person who receives your call greets you by name and later asks if you want to use the same credit card number you used in your last purchase.

Techniques such as data mining take advantage of large data warehouses to find trends and shopping habits of various demographic groups. For example, the software discovers clusters of products that people tend to purchase together and then the marketing experts promote the products as a combination and might suggest displaying them together on store shelves. You will learn more about data mining in Chapter 6.

With the proliferation of set-top boxes for digital televisions, several companies have developed applications that may allow television networks to transition from the wasteful and expensive 30-second commercial to more personal advertising. Relying on information provided by households through these interactive boxes, they can select and transmit to each subscriber commercials only for products in which the subscriber is interested. For example, you will not receive commercials about pet food if you do not have pets but will receive commercials about gardening if this is your hobby.

Use of information technology for targeted marketing has taken sophisticated forms on the Web. More than just targeting a certain demographic group, web technologies enable retailers to *personalize* marketing when shopping and buying are conducted online. Special software on online retailers' servers keeps track of every visit consumers make and captures their 'click streams' (the sequence of selections they make) and the amount of time they spend viewing each page. The retailer's software combines this information with information from online purchases to personalize the pages whenever consumers revisit the site. The reconstructed page introduces information about the products that the individual visitor is most likely to purchase. For example, two people with different purchasing records at Amazon.co.uk who revisit the company's home page will find that they are looking at slightly different versions of the page. Amazon's software custom-composes the elements for each person according to his or her inferred interests in products. The ones that the software concludes might be of the highest interest are displayed or linked on the page.

Customer service

CD TASK

Web-based customer service provides automated customer support 24 hours per day, 365 days per year. At the same time, it saves companies the cost of labour required when humans provide the same service. For example, letting customers pay their bills electronically not only provides convenience but also saves (both customers and companies) the cost of postage and paper and saves the company the time required for dealing with paper documents. Online billing costs only a small fraction of paper billing. The business research firm Gartner Group estimates the average invoice-to-payment cycle at 41 days, while online invoice and payment shortens the period by at least six days. Customers appreciate the discounts that many companies offer for accepting statements and paying bills online.

Ethical and Societal ISSUES

Consumer privacy

Consider the following scenario: you agree to give some financial information about yourself to one organization in exchange for credit. At a later date, you provide some medical information to another organization. In the meantime, your credit card company has enough information from your purchasing activity to know your culinary and fashion tastes better than you do. Finally, without your knowledge or consent, yet another organization gathers all this information and puts it in one big record that is practically a detailed personal dossier. Whenever you use your credit card, you provide information about you. Whenever you interact with an organization online, you provide information about you. Do you ever stop to think where the information goes?

Organizations collect huge amounts of personal information. Every time you pay with your credit card you leave a personal record; the few details of your purchase are often used to update an already hefty dossier about your buying habits. Every time you provide personal information at a website, you either help open a new dossier with an organization or help other organizations update their dossier about you. In their zeal to market more effectively, businesses often violate consumer privacy.

What is privacy? In the context of information, privacy is your right to control information about yourself. For example, you keep your privacy if you keep to yourself your university grades, medical background or the name of the person with whom you had dinner last evening. Someone who receives such information without your permission is violating your privacy.

Business arguments Business leaders argue that they must collect and use personal data. Without personal data, they would have to waste time and money to target likely buyers. They need to know the purchasing and payment habits of individuals because these details create credit histories that help make prudent decisions on consumer risks. This ability to purchase and manipulate large amounts of consumer information makes the business world more democratic than it used to be. Small companies now have the same chances of targeting prospective buyers with good credit as big companies creating more opportunities and more competition, which eventually benefit consumers.

Consumer arguments Consumers usually accept that they must divulge some private information to receive services, but many do not accept the mass violation of privacy. They resent unsolicited junk mail and email sent by companies who know much about them although they have never provided personal details to these companies. They hate telephone calls from salespeople who obtained their records from companies that were supposed to keep their records confidential. And they are frightened by the 'dossier phenomenon': it might be the greatest concern to consumers.

Losing control In many cases, you volunteer information in return for some benefit, such as receiving a discount or participation in a competition. In others, you simply cannot receive the service or product unless you agree to give certain personal details. In such cases, you give implicit or explicit informed consent to obtain information about yourself. However, once you provide information, you have little control over it. With some newer technology, such as RFID, you might not even be aware of who is collecting information about you and when it is collected. You have just stepped out of a supermarket with a cartful of groceries. All are RFID-tagged. The supermarket systems recorded your visit and detailed what you purchased. Can you be sure that nobody else has the proper device to read and record what you purchased?

The Eight Commandments of personal data collection and maintenance In a free, market-oriented society, not allowing organizations to collect personal data is inconceivable. What can businesses do to help protect privacy? They can try to adhere to these rules to avoid misuse:

Purpose. Companies should inform people who provide information of the specific, exclusive purpose for which the company maintains its data and use the data for another purpose only with the subjects' consent. For example, this practice could protect psychiatric patients from having their insurance companies sell information about their treatments.

Relevance. Companies should only record and use data necessary to fulfil their own purposes. For example, an applicant's credit record should not contain his or her political views because that information is irrelevant in credit considerations and would only be useful if sold.

Accuracy. Companies should ensure that the personal records they maintain are accurate. For example, many loan applicants have had terrible experiences because some of the data maintained by credit companies is erroneous. Careful data entry and periodic verification can enhance accuracy.

Currency. Companies should make sure that all data about an individual are current. If currency cannot be guaranteed, then data should be discarded periodically. Outdated information can create horribly negative repercussions. For example, a person who might have been unemployable due to past illness might not be able to get a job, even though he or she might be healthy now.

Security. Companies should limit access to data to only those who need to know. In addition to passwords, audit trails (which identify every employee who accesses a personal record and for what purpose) are also very effective tools for ensuring security.

Time limitation. Companies should retain data only for the time period necessary.

Scrutiny. Companies should establish procedures to let individuals review their records and correct inaccuracies.

Sole recording. When using a recording technology, a company should ensure that no other party can take advantage of the technology to record the same information. For example, if a supermarket records an individual's purchases using RFID technology, it must ensure that the RFID tags embedded in the packaging are disabled as soon as the customer leaves the store.

All of the above 'commandments' have been embodied into legislation in different parts of the world, for example the UK Data Protection Act. Of course, many consumers will still feel that their privacy is invaded even if every business is required to comply with the legislation. How can you protect your privacy? Do not furnish your name, passport (or any other identifying) number, address, or any other private information if you do not know how it will be used. If you do provide detailed information, indicate that you do not wish the data to be shared with any other organization or individual. You can usually check a box to this effect on paper or online forms. To avoid junk mail or junk email, again check the proper box on online forms. Do not fill out any online or paper forms with detailed data unless an opt-out option is available. Of course, many services we receive depend on our willingness to provide personal data, so at least some organizations must have personal information, but you can be selective. Always carefully weigh what you gain against the privacy you might lose.

Online customer service applications have become increasingly sophisticated. They help track past purchases and payments, update online answers to frequently asked questions (FAQs) about products and services and analyse customers' contacts with the company to maintain and update an electronic customer profile. The FAQ pages of many companies have been replaced with options for open-ended questions; instead of looking up a question that is similar to what you would ask, you can simply type in your question. Employing artificial intelligence software, the site will 'understand' your question and provide a short list of links where you can find an answer.

Sales force automation

Sales force automation equips travelling salespeople with information technology to facilitate their productivity. Typically, salespeople are equipped with notebook computers that store promotional information for prospective customers, software for manipulating this information and computerized forms. Many salespeople carry laptop computers or personal digital assistants (PDAs) with all the information they need and which allow them to connect to their organizational information systems through the Internet. Sales force automation can increase sales productivity significantly, making sales presentations more efficient and letting field representatives close deals on the spot, using preformatted contracts and forms.

Information technology lets salespeople present different options for products and services on the computer, rather than asking prospective customers to wait until the main office faxes or posts the information. At the end of the day or the week, salespeople can upload sales information to a computer at the main office, where it is raw input to the order-processing department, the manufacturing unit, or the shipping and invoicing departments.

Using PDAs that can establish a wireless connection to the Internet enables salespeople to check prices, check availability of the items in which a customer is interested and place an order away from the office. The salespeople can then spend much more time on the road, increasing time spent with prospective customers.

Human resource management

Human resource management (HRM) has become more complex due to the fast growth in specialized occupations, the need to train and promote highly skilled employees and the growing variety of benefits programmes. Human resource management can be classified into five main activities: (1) employee record management, (2) promotion and recruitment, (3) training, (4) evaluation and (5) compensation and benefits management (see Figure 3.11).

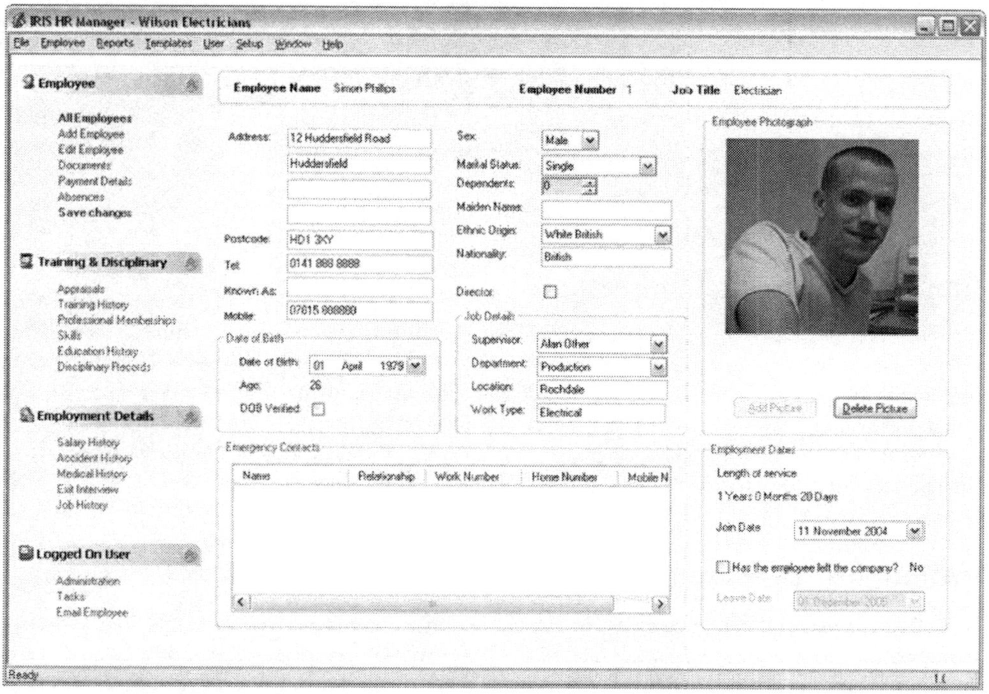

Text and pictures can be combined to store and retrieve employee records.

Figure 3.11 Human resource management information systems help managers optimize promotion and recruitment, training, evaluation and other activities

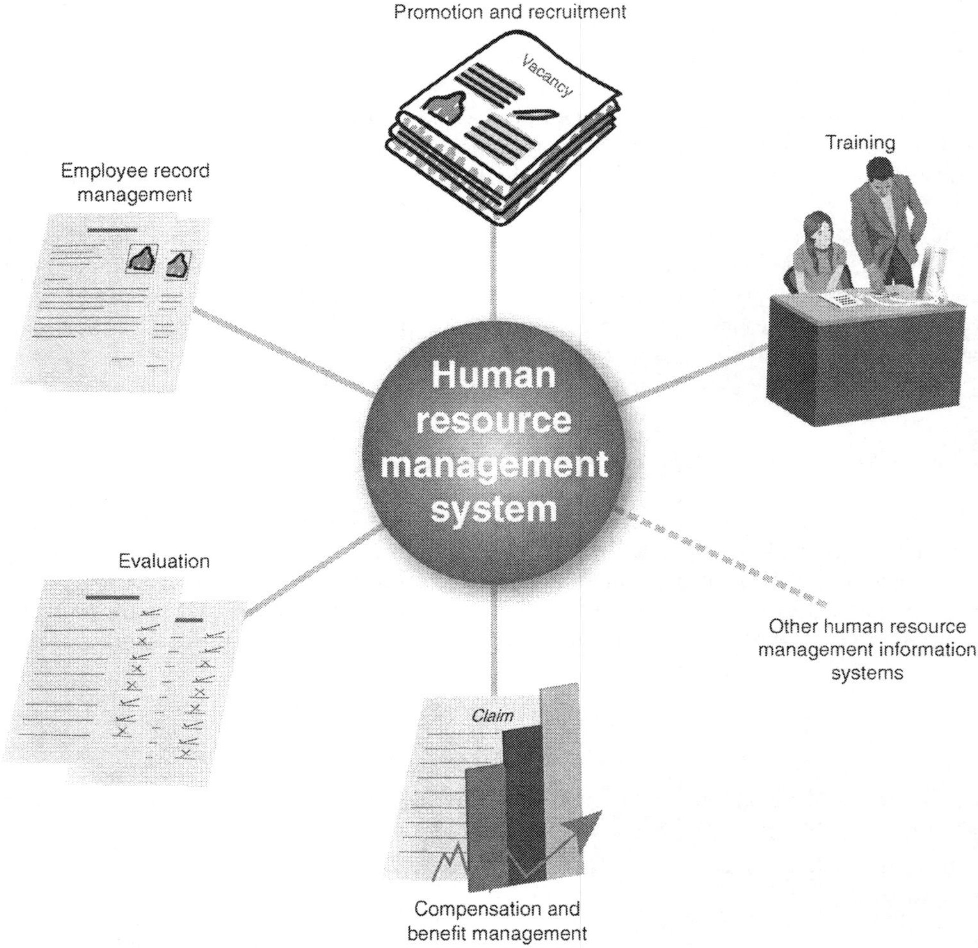

Employee record management

ISs facilitate employee record management. Human resource departments must keep personnel records to satisfy both external regulations (for example those required by law) and internal regulations, as well as for payroll and tax calculation and deposit, promotion consideration and periodic reporting. Many HR ISs are now held completely in digital form (including employees' pictures), which dramatically reduces the space needed to store records, the time needed to retrieve them and the costs of both.

Promotion and recruitment

To select the best-qualified person for a position, a human resource manager can search a database of applicants and existing employees' records for set criteria, such as a specific type and length of education, particular experience, specific talents and required licences or certifications. Automating the selection process significantly minimizes time and money spent on recruitment but does require that a current database be maintained.

Intranets (intra-organizational networks that support web applications) help HR managers post position vacancy announcements for employees to peruse and consider from their own PCs. This system is especially efficient in large organizations that employ thousands of workers and even more so at multisite organizations.

Many companies refuse to receive paper applications and curricula vitae (CVs). Some accept such documents via email, but others accept only forms that are filled out and submitted online. Using keywords, recruiting officers can then use special software to scour a database for the most-qualified candidates. HR consultants say that this process reduces the time spent on a typical search from several hours to several minutes. Some software companies sell automated recruiting and selection software to support such activities.

Industry **SNAPSHOT**

E-recruitment

A study conducted by the Institute for Employment Studies in 2003 found that organizations reported the following as being important factors in their decision to increase the use of e-recruitment:

- improve corporate image and profile
- reduce recruitment costs
- reduce administrative burden
- employ better tools for the recruitment team.

SOURCE: *e-Recruitment: Is it Delivering?*, M. Kerrin and P. Kettley IES Report 402, 2003. ISBN: 978-1-85184-329-9

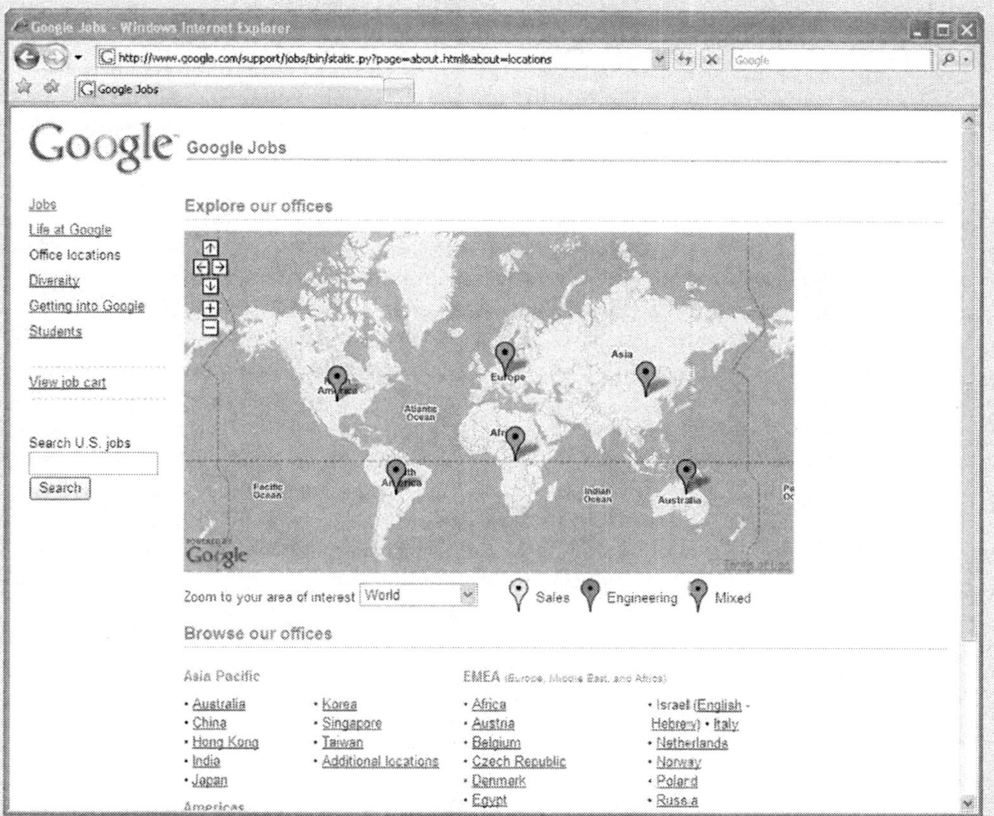

PHOTO SOURCE: ©2008 GOOGLE

Google is an example of an organization taking advantage of e-recruitment.

Some companies use the entire Web as a database for their search, which means they include in the search many people who have never applied for a job with them but have posted their CVs. Traditional recruitment methods often produce many candidates but, alas, often few (or none!) of these are suitable. The whole process can be very expensive and, worse still, a complete waste of money, and it would seem that the situation is potentially set to become worse. Demographics suggest that 35 million Europeans will disappear from the labour market in the next ten years. However, the Internet has created a significant number of 'always on' jobseekers, people who are not specifically looking for a particular job but are open to offers. Software exists that searches the Web for CVs and then matches qualified candidates with job openings. Across industries, as companies move from traditional recruiting to recruiting through the Web, the cost per hire is set to reduce significantly.

Training

One important function of human resource departments is improving employee skills. In both the manufacturing and service sectors, multimedia software training is rapidly replacing training programmes involving classrooms and teachers. Such applications include interactive, three-dimensional simulated environments. Some applications contain full-blown virtual reality components. For example, one such application trains workers to handle wrought iron that must be hammered manually. The worker wears special goggles and holds a hammer in one hand and a piece of metal in the other, over an anvil. The worker 'sees' the metal piece through the goggles, 'hears' the hitting sound through earphones and receives a programmed, realistic jolt every time he 'hits' the metal. This safely prepares the employees for the dangerous work instead of putting them at risk of injury before they have enough experience to do the actual work. Although the initial investment in multimedia training systems might be high, human resource managers find the systems very effective. Surgeons train using similar systems to operate on virtual patients rather than risk injuries to human patients.

Training software simulates situations in which an employee must act and includes tests and modules to evaluate a trainee's performance. In addition to the savings in trainers' time, there are other benefits. The trainee is more comfortable because he or she controls the speed at which the sessions run. The software lets the trainee go back to a certain point in the session if a concept is missed. Also, the software can simulate hazardous situations, thereby testing employee performance in a safe environment. And if training in a real environment involves destruction of equipment or consumption of materials, virtual reality training applications accomplish the same results in skill enhancement without destruction or waste.

Developments in IT enable organizations to reduce training costs dramatically. BUPA is the UK market leader in health and care services. Some staff spend a great deal of time travelling and need to be contactable via email. A solution was found in the issuing of Blackberry PDAs but naturally these people needed training in order to get the most out of the technology. The initial solution was to set up two-and-a-half-hour classroom-based training sessions but this proved problematical and expensive. BUPA commissioned Tata Interactive Systems, an international e-learning developer, to devise an alternative strategy for the delivery of this necessary learning. In addition BUPA introduced a learning management system (LMS) which enables the monitoring of all training programmes and the engagement of the employees with those programmes. The e-learning programme reduced the training time by an hour and also saved, on average, one and a half hours travelling time per employee with an associated reduction in training costs for the company. Staff are pleased with the flexible approach and they are also able to access refresher training at any time that they need it.

Evaluation

Supervisors must periodically evaluate the technical ability, communications skills, professional conduct and general behaviour of employees. While objective factors are involved in evaluation – such as attendance rates and punctuality – employee evaluation is often very subjective. Assessing performance and effort levels and their relative weights of importance, varies significantly, depending on who is evaluating. A supervisor might forget to include some factors altogether or might inappropriately weigh a particular aspect of performance. Subjectivity is particularly problematic when several employees are being considered for a promotion and their evaluations are compared to determine the strongest candidate. By helping to standardize the evaluation process across employees and departments, evaluation software adds a certain measure of objectivity and consistency.

In an evaluation, a supervisor provides feedback to an employee, records the evaluation for official records and future comparison and accepts input from the employee. Software helps managers standardize their employee evaluations by providing step-by-step guides to writing performance reviews, a checklist of performance areas to include in the evaluation (with the option to add or remove topics), scales to indicate how strong the employee is in each area and the ability to select the relative importance each factor should hold in the overall evaluation. Performance areas include written and oral communication, job knowledge and management skills, with each topic subdivided into basic elements to assist the supervisor in creating an accurate evaluation. A typical application guides the user through all necessary factors and includes a help guide. When the evaluator finishes entering data, the application automatically computes a subtotal for each category and a weighted grade, which can then be electronically stored as part of the employee's record.

Compensation and benefits management

ISs help HR officers manage compensation (salaries, hourly pay, commissions and bonuses) efficiently and effectively. Programs can easily calculate weekly, monthly and hourly pay according to annual salaries and can include tax tables to assist in complying with compensation regulations. This same system can also automatically generate pay cheques or direct deposits, which are the electronic transfer of funds from the firm's bank account to the employee's.

Special software helps the HR department manage benefits, such as health insurance, life insurance, retirement plans and sick leave days. To optimize benefits, some companies use special software, incorporating expert systems (ISs that emulate human expertise) that determine the optimal health and retirement plans for each employee based on factors such as marital status, age, occupation and other data.

Using intranets, many organizations allow their employees to access the benefits database directly and make changes to their preferences, such as selecting another health-care insurance programme, or adding a family member as a beneficiary in a life insurance plan. When the company engages a third party for managing pension funds or other benefits, employees can go directly to the website of that company, not involving their own company resources at all. By making the changes directly from their PCs, employees reduce the amount of work of the HR staff and decrease the company's overhead costs.

Inter-organizational supply chain management systems

According to IBM, companies that implemented SCM systems have reduced inventory levels by 10–50 per cent, improved the rate of accurate deliveries by 95–99 per cent, reduced unscheduled work stoppages to 0–5 per cent, reduced cycle time (from order to collection) by 10–20 per cent and reduced transportation costs by 10–15 per cent.

Figure 3.12 A shared supply chain management system

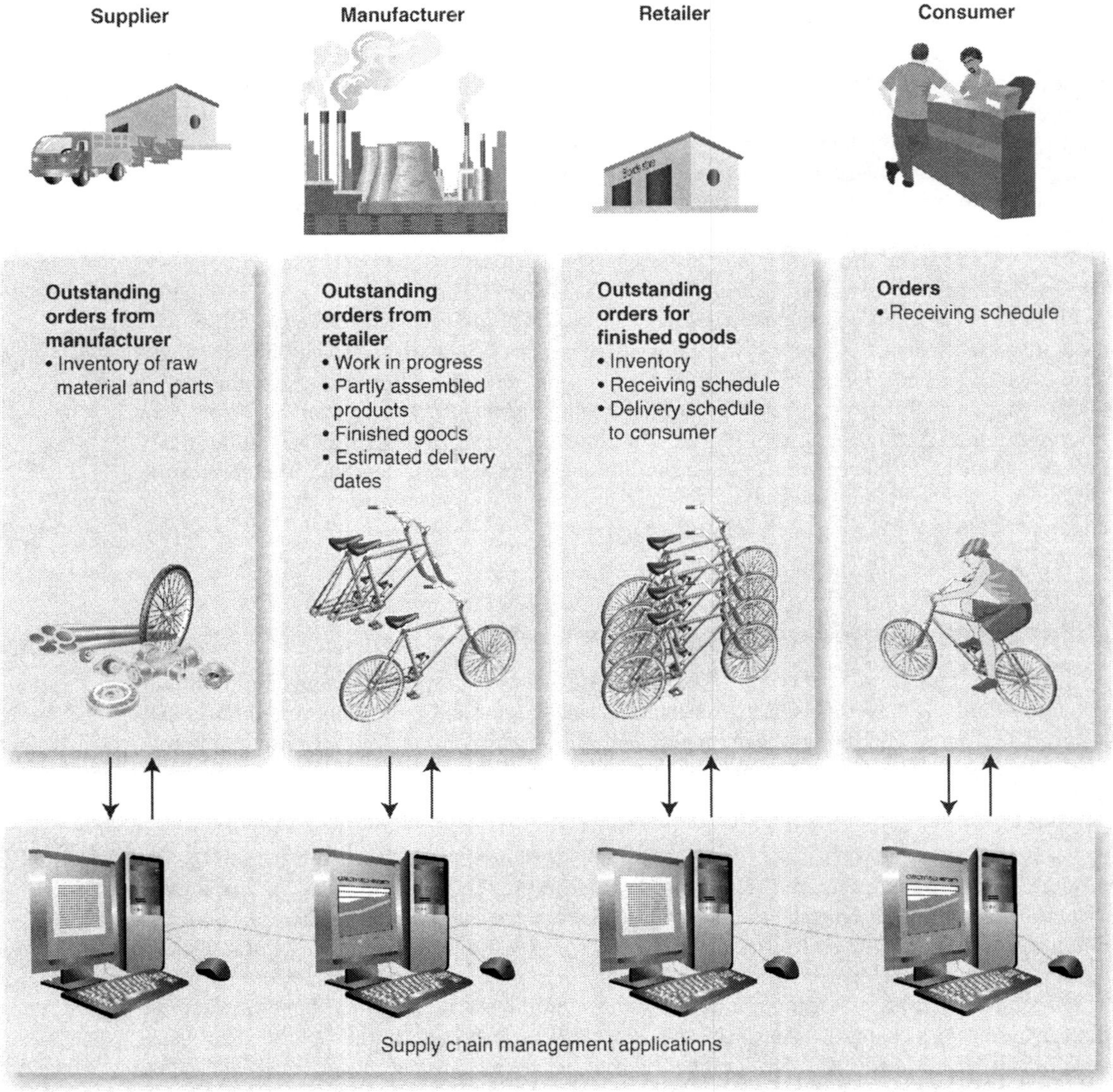

Several enterprise applications, such as ERP systems, also serve as SCM systems. As Figure 3.12 illustrates, many such systems enable managers not only to monitor what goes on at their own units or organization, but also to follow what goes on at the facilities of their suppliers and contractors. For example, at any given point in time managers can know the status of the following: an order now being handled by a contractor, by order number; the phase of manufacturing the produced units have reached; and the date of delivery, including any delays and their length. When purchasing parts, managers use the systems for issuing electronic purchase orders and they can follow the fulfilment process at the supplier's facilities, such as when the parts were packed, when they were loaded onto lorries and when they are estimated to arrive at the managers' floor or the floor of another business partner who needed the parts.

SCM applications streamline operations throughout the chain, from suppliers to customers, lowering inventories, decreasing production costs and improving responsiveness to suppliers and clients. Harnessing the global network, managers can supervise an entire supply chain regardless of the location of the activity – at their own facilities or another organization's, at the same location or thousands of miles away. Older SCM systems connected two organizations. New ones connect several. For example, a distributor can reorder products from Organization A and simultaneously alert Organization B, the supplier of Organization A. The systems let all parties – suppliers, manufacturers, distributors and customers – see the same information. A change made by any organization that affects an order can affect a corresponding change in scheduling and operations in the other organization's activities.

Companies that have adopted SCM systems have seen improvement in three major areas: reduction in inventory, reduction in cycle time (the time it takes to complete a business process) and, as a result, reduction in production cost. Companies can reduce their inventory by communicating to their suppliers through a shared SCM system the exact number of units of each item they need and the exact time they need them. In ideal situations, they do not need to stockpile any inventory, saving warehouse costs. The management consulting firm Aberdeen Group estimates that companies using SCM systems through the Internet reduce purchase order processing cycles by 70–80 per cent and pay 5–10 per cent less for the items they purchase.

The importance of trust

SCM systems accomplish the greatest efficiencies when all businesses in the chain link their systems and share all the information that is pertinent to planning production and shipment. For example, Nissan UK has a 750 acre site near Sunderland, currently the UK's biggest car plant with flexible production technology that allows different car models to be produced on the same line. The majority of the parts used come from the UK and almost all the rest come from Europe. Key components are sourced from suppliers who are located in Sunderland and are categorized as 'Synchro Suppliers' whose systems are closely linked with Nissan's production control system. It is reported that 97 per cent of parts are delivered on time and over 98 per cent of cars are completed within two hours of their allotted time slot. The inventory of parts has been reduced by 45 per cent since 2001, leading to a reduction in manufacturing costs of 16 per cent. All of this can only happen if the suppliers and Nissan are willing and able to work together, particularly with regard to their ISs.

However, not all organizations are willing to collaborate with their business partners. One reason is the fear that when Organization A purchases from Organization B and has access to Organization B's demand figures, it might disclose the information to competitors in an attempt to stir more competition and enjoy favourable prices. Another fear is that if Organization B realizes that at a certain point in time Organization A is in dire need of its raw materials, Organization B might take advantage of the situation and negotiate higher prices.

The first type of fear can be found in the initial reluctance of suppliers to share information with large buyers such as Tesco. Only the bargaining power of Tesco and its insistence on sharing such information convinced suppliers to link their systems with those of Tesco. The second type of fear is still there between General Motors and its main tyre supplier, Goodyear. Goodyear could enjoy lower inventories if it had GM's demand schedule for tyres. It could then calibrate its own order for raw materials, such as rubber, and its manufacturing capacity to suit those of GM, save money and pass at least some of the savings to its client in the form of cheaper products. It could always replenish its client's inventory of tyres before GM ran out of them. Better yet, it could deliver the tyres directly to the assembly lines just when they are needed, saving both GM and itself warehousing costs. Yet, GM is guarding its production schedule as confidential.

SCM systems can be taken a step beyond the sale. The systems can be used for after-the-sale services. For example, Beckman Coulter is an international company with operations in over 130 countries and more than 10,000 employees. It makes blood analysers and other medical devices. After it sells a machine, the company uses the Internet to link the machine from the client's facility to a computer system in its head office. Software on the computer runs seven days per week, 24 hours per day to monitor the sold machine. When a problem occurs, the computer alerts a Beckman technician, who can repair the machine before it stops working. Beckman estimates that the system saves it US$1 million annually, because malfunctions are captured at an early stage, which avoids the higher cost of fixing a more damaged machine. The added benefit is increased customer satisfaction.

The musical chairs of inventory

So sensible use of ISs can help to reduce the inventory and hence the costs involved in maintaining that inventory. However, much of the trend took place in the 1981–1991 period. Since then the situation across business and industry as a whole has remained the same. Apparently, while large corporations have the resources to install and run SCM systems to cut their own inventory, the ratio of inventory to revenue in small enterprises is growing because they do not use such systems. And sometimes, the companies that suffer the inventory ripple effect are not small. They might be powerful and they might even own their own SCM system, but their system might not be linked to their buyers' systems, so they cannot plan their own production to reduce inventory.

For an example, let us return to the relationship between General Motors and Goodyear. The world's largest car manufacturer improved 'inventory turns' 55.2 per cent between 1996 and 2001. Inventory turns are the number of times a business sells (or turns over) its inventory per year. It is calculated by dividing the sales revenue by the average value of inventory. The greater the inventory turns number, the better. During the same period, Goodyear, GM's tyre supplier, experienced a 21 per cent decrease in inventory turns. The likely conclusion is that GM avoided purchasing tyres from Goodyear until it needed them at the assembly line, but Goodyear did not have enough information on when, exactly, those tyres would be required and therefore kept overstocks. Had the SCM systems of the companies been linked, Goodyear could reduce inventory and see its inventory turns rise rather than fall. It is also reasonable to assume that thanks to the cost savings, Goodyear would be able to sell tyres to GM at a lower price. GM and other companies have created a situation where the company tries to 'sit' with a lean inventory while, inadvertently, leaving another 'standing' with an overstock. In order for all involved in a supply chain to enjoy efficiencies, the musical chairs, or 'hot potato' situation, must stop.

Collaborative logistics

The Web enables organizations from totally different industries to streamline operations through collaboration. In recent years an increasing number of businesses found a new way to cut distribution costs: they combine goods for delivery with other businesses, sharing their own lorries or the vehicles of delivery companies. The collaboration reduces partially empty lorries, or empty vehicles between stops. To this end, the companies connect their SCM systems to the site of a company that specializes in optimization of logistics, such as UK-based company Translogistica. The company manages the site and uses sophisticated software to calculate the shortest routes between departure and arrival points and the best combination of loads from two or more companies to share trucks and routes. The SCM systems of subscribing companies provide daily data into the shared system. The IS takes into consideration the type of freight to ensure safety and adherence to regulations. For example, the software is designed not to combine chemicals with food. Therefore, typical allies of food manufacturers have been paper manufacturers, for instance. The cost savings have been impressive.

A group of companies operating in Northern Ireland and the Republic of Ireland from small to medium enterprises (SMEs) to global brand names worked with the European Logistic Users, Providers and Enablers Group (ELUPEG) and InterTradeIreland on a project to demonstrate how collaboration could bring down costs and improve competitiveness. Their prediction is not only massive savings but also a positive environmental contribution through better utilization of vehicles and reduced traffic congestion.

Another area where some companies have explored collaboration is warehousing. The principle here is the same: try to maximize the use of warehouse space and if you cannot use all of it, allow other businesses to use the extra space. The way to accomplish this, again, goes through the Web: a third party specializing in warehousing optimization combines warehousing needs and availability from member companies to offer optimal solutions.

Enterprise resource planning

A growing number of organizations elect to replace old, disparate ISs with enterprise applications that support all or most of the business activities we have described. As mentioned before, these systems are often referred to as **enterprise resource planning (ERP) systems**, although they are used not only for planning but also for managing daily operations. Designers of ERP systems take a systems approach to an enterprise. For example, the manufacturing resource planning (MRP) component of the system uses the information recorded on a sale to retrieve product specifications; the data are used to generate purchasing information such as items, quantities and the timetable for suppliers to deliver for the purchasing department. As products are manufactured, the system tracks the stages of the work in progress. When items are ready to be delivered, the distribution department can retrieve information on the items for its operations. The system keeps delivery information such as content and destination, along with billing information, to help produce delivery and billing documentation. The system also records financial transactions involved in such activities, such as payment made from a bank account. The accounting component records the transactions. In addition, ERP systems also provide human resource modules for payroll, employee benefits management and employee evaluation software. CRM components are also available and are tied to other components through orders applications and sales records.

enterprise resource planning (ERP) system An information system that supports different activities for different departments, assisting executives with planning and running different interdependent functions.

ERP packages are quite complex. Because they are not tailored to the needs of specific clients, they often require adjustment and fine-tuning for specific organizations. Therefore, their installation and testing involve experts who are usually employees of the software vendor or professionals who are certified for such work by the vendor. The most visible software companies specializing in ERP systems are SAP and Oracle.

ERP applications represent a significant expense for a business. Installation and modifications represent further major spending. Installation often takes many months to complete. Implementation of ERP systems can fail because of formidable challenges: the gap between system capabilities and business needs, lack of expertise on the consultant's part and mismanagement of the implementation project. The business research firm Standish Group found that only 10 per cent of ERP implementation projects are completed as planned, on time and within budget. Fifty-five per cent are completed late or over budget (which usually means loss of business and revenue) and the other 35 per cent of such projects are cancelled because of difficulties. At Hewlett-Packard, one of the world's largest computer and IT equipment makers, a US$400 million loss in the third quarter of 2004 was blamed on poorly managed migration to a new ERP system.

SUMMARY

Effectiveness is the degree to which a task is accomplished. The better a person performs a job, the more effective he or she is. Efficiency is measured as the ratio of output to input. The more output with the same input, or the less input for the same output used in a process, the more efficient the process. ISs can help companies attain more effective and efficient business processes. Productivity is the measure of people's efficiency. When people use ISs, their productivity increases.

ISs have been integrated into almost every functional business area. In accounting and payroll, because of the routine and structured nature of accounting tasks, the systems automatically post transactions in the books and automate the generation of reports for management and for legal requirements.

Financial ISs help managers track cash available for transactions, while ensuring that available money is invested in short- or long-term programmes to yield the highest interest possible. Investment analysis ISs help build portfolios based on historical performance and other characteristics of securities.

Computer-aided design (CAD) systems help engineers design new products and save and modify drawings electronically. Computer-aided manufacturing (CAM) systems direct machines in manufacturing parts and assembling products.

Supply chain management systems optimize workload, speed and cost in the supply chains: procurement of raw materials, manufacturing and distribution of goods. ISs, especially MRP and MRP II systems, facilitate production scheduling and material requirements planning and shorten lead time between idea and product. Shipping ISs help speed up delivery and cut costs. RFID technology helps promote and operate supply chain management (SCM) systems. Radio frequency identification (RFID) tags carry product information that can be tracked and updated.

Customer relationship management (CRM) includes the entire cycle of relationships with customers, from marketing through sales to customer service. CRM ISs collect information about shoppers and customers and help target the most likely buyers of a product or service. Online customer service systems help customers help themselves via the Web 24 hours per day, seven days per week and save the company labour and telephone expenses. Salesforce automation allows travelling salespeople to spend more time with customers and less time in the office.

Human resource management systems expedite staff selection and record keeping. An increasing amount of recruiting is done via the Web. Managers often use evaluation software to help assess their subordinates' performance. Employees can use expert systems to choose health care and other benefits programmes that best suit their situation.

Companies can link their SCM systems to monitor the status of orders not only at their own facilities but also at those of their business partners, usually their suppliers. Such cooperation can create further efficiencies, but it requires a high degree of trust between organizations.

Rather than use disparate ISs for business functions, many organizations opt to install a single system that encompasses all their business processes, or at least the major ones. They employ enterprise resource planning (ERP) systems to support their supply chain management and customer relationship management.

BETTER BITES

BETTER BITES REVISITED

Better Bites has grown in the past two years from a single pushcart to a business with many sites, different products and more customers. The partners have noticed that their activities are becoming more specialized as the business grows and that they need information systems to support those activities. Help them sort through their systems.

What would you do?

Using the classifications in this chapter, identify the business functions within Better Bites. Which information systems do Paul, Sarah and Christina use now to streamline their operations? What other applications could they use?

Do you think that Better Bites should invest in an ERP system at this time? Why or why not? If not, which types of information systems mentioned in this chapter would be appropriate short of an ERP system?

New perspectives

A large snack-food manufacturer has noticed that Sarah's crisp line is very successful. The manufacturer is now proposing that Better Bites license its crisp business – the partners would get a percentage of the profits from the expanded sales and the manufacturer would have a new healthful crisp line to round out its snack-food product line. What information could the three entrepreneurs use to help them decide whether this opportunity would be a good idea? Suggest how they could obtain this information.

Review questions

1 What is a supply chain? What is the purpose of supply chain management systems?
2 What is the purpose of cost accounting ISs?
3 What is the relationship between CAD and CAM systems?
4 What are the concerns in cash management and how do cash management ISs help financial managers?
5 What is time to market? How have ISs affected time to market?
6 In brief, what is the purpose of customer relationship management systems?
7 What are the typical components of ERP systems?
8 Although technologically the full linking of the SCM systems of suppliers and buyers is feasible, many buyers are reluctant to do so. Why?
9 Why do the ERP installation and testing of systems require that experts be involved? Why does the implementation of so many ERP systems face severe challenges or totally fail?
10 What is EOQ? Which two problems do ISs that calculate EOQ help minimize?
11 What is JIT? How do MRP and MRP II systems help achieve JIT?
12 For the human resource managers of some organizations the entire Web is a database of job candidates. How so?
13 What information technologies play a crucial role in marketing?
14 Many sales reps have no offices, yet their productivity is great. Explain how that is possible.
15 What is RFID and what role does it play in SCM?
16 In the supply chain, distribution software helps mainly in two ways. What are they?

Discussion questions

1 You established a small shop that manufactures a single product that you sell by mail. You purchase raw materials from several vendors and employ five full-time employees. For which business functions would you certainly use software?

2 Which of the ISs you listed for Question 1 would you link to each other and for what purpose?

3 Why is it so important to have a quick response of online investment ISs? Give two examples of how such systems are critical.

4 Some experts say that ISs have great potential in manufacturing. Explain why. (*Hint*: business process reengineering.)

5 Over the past decade, banks and investment firms have offered many services that would be impossible without ISs. Describe three such services and explain how IT makes them possible.

6 CAD systems replace older, manual tools in engineering, but they also contribute by maintaining all information in electronic form. How does this facilitate the work of draftspeople and engineers? How do such systems help the transition from engineering a product to manufacturing it?

7 ISs in both the manufacturing and service sectors often help to *optimize*. Give two examples of what they optimize.

8 The Web has significantly cut the cost of collecting data about shoppers and buyers. Explain how.

9 Sellers of consumer products argue that targeted marketing serves not only them but also their consumers. How so?

10 If you had to evaluate your own colleagues, would you prefer to evaluate them in written, open-ended form, or would you prefer to use employee evaluation software? Why?

11 As an employee, would you prefer that your supervisor evaluate you with the aid of employee evaluation software or without it? Why?

12 Try to remember the last time you gave someone your personal data. What was the reason for asking for the data?

13 Some consumer advocates argue that organizations should pay a small fee to every individual whenever they sell data about him or her to another organization. Do you agree? Why?

14 Examine the list of precautions suggested in 'Ethical and Societal Issues' for ensuring minimum invasion of privacy when businesses use personal data. Which steps can be taken without, or with minimal added cost? Which steps would impose financial burdens on businesses? Why?

15 RFID tags are increasingly embedded in almost every type of good, from washing powder to clothing items. Consumer advocates fear that the technology might cause massive violation of privacy. Describe at least two ways in which this can happen. What controls or limitations would you impose on RFID tags and use to minimize the fears of invasion of privacy?

Tutorial activities

1 Choose three distinct but related business functions (e.g. inventory control, purchasing, payroll, accounting, etc.). Write a short paper describing how interfacing the information systems of these three functions can improve an organization's performance.

2 Select a business process (possibly at a local firm) not mentioned in this chapter. Write an essay explaining how IS technology could make the process (1) more efficient and (2) more effective.

3 Write a three-page essay titled 'Factory of the Future'. Your factory of the future will not require anybody in the manufacturing organization to enter any data into information systems. All the necessary information will come from customers at one end and suppliers at the other end. There will also be no need to type in any data for payments and collections. Explain how all this will work.

4 Many companies use email to advertise their products. Your company is trying to sell a new product and is advised to use email. The profit on each unit sold is 200 euro. Developing the attractive email message, use of 2,750,000 email addresses and sending the message would cost 25,000 euro. Experience shows that 5 per cent of the initial recipients forward such messages to friends and family. Experience also shows that 2 per cent of all recipients actually click the web address included in the message and visit the commercial site. Of these visitors, 0.5 per cent end up purchasing the advertised item. Using Microsoft Excel or another spreadsheet, answer the following

questions: (1) Would you generate a profit if you used this advertising opportunity? (2) Would you profit if you could email only 1,000,000 people?

5 Form a team and design an IS for a small business that sells manufactured parts to other businesses. The system must handle customer order processing, sales, salesperson commissions, billing and accounts receivable. Prepare a report describing the system's different components and their points of interface. What files are necessary? How will the business use data in each file? If you have command of Microsoft Access, create the tables for the above objects and populate each one with three to five records.

6 Assume that you and your teammates are about to start a web-based business for sporting goods. You wish to email information to potential customers. Determine the demographic characteristics of your target audience. Search the Web for companies that sell consumer data that can serve you. Prepare a report about three such companies: their names, services and prices (if available).

Companion CD questions

1 Create a database with at least five records that could be used by a company such as TheTrainline.

2 Research systems that distribution companies can use to track products throughout the distribution process. List at least two such systems and summarize how they work.

Video questions

1 What practices used by Krispy Kreme might Better Bites be able to adopt for their business?

2 Use PowerPoint or another presentation program to create a figure showing what you think the supply chain looks like for Krispy Kreme.

From ideas to application **REAL CASES**

Case study **3.1**

Banking on IT

The Bank of Ireland employs over 18,000 people and has assets of 87 billion euro, making it the number one banking institution in the Republic of Ireland. It has been in existence since 1783 and in that time has had to adapt to many changing circumstances in the national and global economy. Like any business, it faces the need to maximize its use of resources and minimize its costs. To this end the Bank realized the need for an integrated approach to its business functions, particularly finance, human resources and procurement. Over the years, fragmented and disparate IT systems had developed to improve specific

A view from Trinity College, Dublin, showing the statue of Edmund Burke overlooking the original Bank of Ireland building.

PHOTO SOURCE: © DAVID DEAR

business processes, often with multiple, non-integrated systems to handle similar problems in different parts of the organization. For example, various human resource systems existed, generally not linked to payroll which in itself was not standardized throughout the group. Significantly there was no group procurement system and therefore no way to properly monitor supplier contracts and spending budgets.

The Bank commissioned the company Systems Applications and Products in Data Processing (SAP) to analyse their requirements and develop an integrated set of IT solutions. SAP is the world's largest business software company with more than 38,000 customers worldwide from all aspects of business.

Hugo Flinn, then general manager for finance and business services at the Bank of Ireland, described their requirements. 'One of the key elements of our vision was to provide information more quickly and to enable faster action. The main business driver behind the project was to improve productivity in both finance and HR through the implementation of shared services. From a procurement point of view, we wanted a better way of buying.'

Integration was the key. The Bank decided that it was a better solution, and cheaper in the long run, to standardize processes across the group rather than build interfaces between the separate systems.

The group had about 30 non-integrated general ledgers, several payroll and HR systems and no overall system for procurement. Data often had to be input twice, a cardinal sin in an IT environment as this can easily lead to inconsistencies between the 'same' items of data. With the implementation of mySAP® Financials, a suite of financial applications, staff at all levels were provided with accurate, up-to-date and consistent information in a suitable time-frame without having to search other systems or even manual records. The Bank now has one general ledger, one payroll system and one accounts payable system with integrated accounts reporting.

There were similar problems in HR with multiple and often incompatible systems which sometimes duplicated the information, again leading to problems of incompatibility as well as wasting staff time. The application mySAP® HR solved these problems by integrating recruitment, organizational management, personnel administration, payroll and time management. In addition, the functionality was increased by empowering the employees. Employee Self-Service (ESS) enables employees to view, create and maintain information relevant to their job. One of the most obvious benefits of this system, for both employees and the Bank, was the ability of employees to file their own expense reports. 'One of the key benefits of the HR solution is that employees can answer an awful lot of questions themselves through ESS', says Flinn.

The third major problem area was procurement. The group did not have a coordinated system to deal with purchasing. This disparate approach meant that no-one had an overview of procurement procedure or costs. There was no easy way for orders to be consolidated across the group. If you are ordering one chair for your office in Dublin you will get a better price quote if you bundle it up with an order for 50 chairs in the new branch in Cork. Once again the Bank used a solution from SAP, mySAP® Supplier Relationship Management (mySAP® SRM) which aims to reduce costs, increase efficiencies in purchasing, monitor buying behaviour and collaborate with business partners. It gives employees access to an online catalogue which they can browse using a standard web browser enabling them to start the procurement process. The Bank can establish supplier arrangements and pricing policies as well as define the purchasing authorization rules. The feedback suggests that employees are very comfortable with this approach as it has many similarities to personal Internet shopping, which is becoming second nature to virtually everyone. 'We are seeing benefits from process efficiency and visibility', says Flinn. 'We have enabled management to challenge costs on a transaction-by-transaction basis. Plus, we are realizing benefits from better supplier management.'

Thinking about the case

1 Give three examples of HRM activities that require access to an employee record. How could an organization benefit from integrating these activities so that they can be done in a single IS?

2 The Bank of Ireland decided to use the same developer (SAP) for the three functional areas described above, namely finance, HRM and procurement. Why do you think this decision was made? Would it have been better to look for separate solutions for each of the three areas?

3 What other developments in IT can you think of for the Bank of Ireland to improve its business functions?

SOURCE: Bank of Ireland. SAP® for banking solutions increase profitability and deliver greater control, http://www.sap.com/uk/company/success/casestudies/boi.pdf

Case Study 3.2

DHL – moving in the right direction

BY PATRICIA BRITTEN

Whether it is delivering the goods by plane, rail, sea or road, customers increasingly demand end-to-end global supply chain management (SCM) services.

DHL International (UK) is a good example of a company that has continuously used new technologies to improve its business. These include track and trace equipment, wireless technologies and business intelligence software.

Integrating infrastructure

Logistics companies, such as DHL and its competitors, often have to deliver different IT systems, documents and processes for individual sectors, such as retail or automotive. These have to be provided across many different business divisions, including warehouse or vehicle fleet management, and third-party suppliers.

As a result, a key thrust is to simplify, standardize and integrate their IT infrastructures, while driving down costs and improving supply chain visibility.

Peter Redshaw, an analyst at Gartner, says: 'Individual segments of the supply chain, such as warehousing, are already highly efficient. But many segments are not coupled together properly and a fragmented supply chain means extra cost.'

Track and trace

Even companies such as DHL that focus purely on the delivery of packages have complex operations. For instance, customers increasingly demand the capability to track and trace the delivery of products via an Internet portal.

'Track and trace functionality, delivered via self-service websites, is also cheaper and more efficient than a telephone call to a customer service centre. As a result, logistics portals are increasing in popularity and importance', says Redshaw. 'While customers expect online services, most are not prepared to pay any extra for them – unless suppliers extend them out to third parties', says Jeff Woods, principal analyst at Gartner.

Wireless technologies are also transforming the ability of logistics employees, such as truck drivers, to send data to back-office systems in real time. Companies have recently moved aggressively to replace clunky handheld devices with PDAs (Personal Digital Assistants) that connect to corporate systems over GPRS (Global Position Receiving Satellite) networks.

The real challenge for logistics companies is to integrate information held on multiple systems to generate cross-selling opportunities. To this end, logistics companies have invested heavily in data analytics tools (also called business intelligence tools) in a bid to provide a single view of customers and boost conversion rates.

Radio frequency identification (RFID) is a general term used to describe a system that transmits the identity of an object wirelessly. It is a contact-less technology and is made up of three components – the tag, the reader and the host computer system. A feature of RFID is the ability to read many tags together at once and it is not required for the 'reader' to be physically present. Furthermore, data can also be written to the tag. None of these features are possible with bar codes.

A DHL RFID tag.

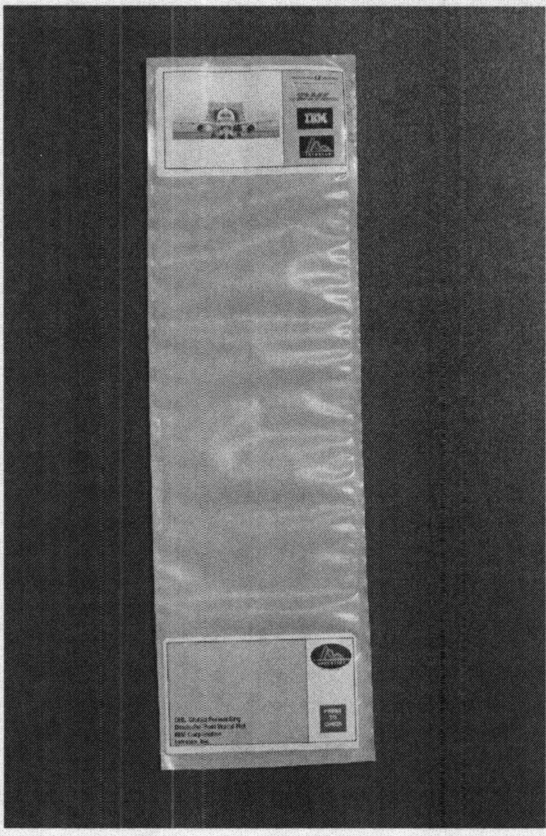

PHOTO SOURCE: DEUTSHE POST AG

In warehouses tagging technology cannot currently compete with the cheap and highly efficient bar code technology. Woods said, 'I do not think RFID will replace bar code in structured warehouse environments and manufacturing facilities. The two will co-exist for a long time and the challenge for RFID comes not with when it replaces bar code but what processes it is suitable for.' Woods considered that 'RFID might make sense in environments where you are moving high volumes of pallets rapidly off a truck.'

There are, however, developments in RFID that are making tagging technology cheaper and more reliable. RFID equipment has steadily fallen in price as volumes increase and microchip unit costs fall. The tag has the ability to store several kilobytes of data in addition to the number identifier and could be viewed as a form of 'mass distributed database' that has the potential to become ubiquitous – billions of tags in daily use throughout the world on all objects produced, stored and moved.

When used in conjunction with allied track and trace technologies, RFID can remotely contact objects to determine their identity and track their position in real time. This improves the movement and control of assets, which is particularly important if these are of high value or require urgent delivery. Applications that could be of use to logistics companies such as DHL include real-time item location/item visibility and status, anti-theft/tamper evidence and authentication.

According to the IT consultancy company Accenture, early adopters stand to gain the most benefits from this new technology through accelerated learning and experience. Accenture also considers that 'companies that apply more strategic thinking to RFID will be able to develop more high-value, game-changing applications and higher performance capabilities that will help them differentiate themselves in the market place'.

Multiple projects

DHL International launched a new service in the UK in 2005 enabling customers to book online from its full product portfolio.

The UK was the first country to pilot the online booking system, before the logistics giant rolled it out globally. Tony Eccleston, DHL's UK and Ireland IT director, says UK customers can choose any domestic or international air, sea or freight delivery service.

The new service was just one of many projects DHL has rolled out since late 2003. These include upgraded handheld devices for couriers, analytics reporting tools for executives and online track and trace capabilities for customers.

The projects were designed to deliver parcels more efficiently, while providing customers and its own executives, couriers and call centre agents with near real-time information. DHL upgraded the handheld devices to GPRS connectivity in 2004. But it is DHL's process reengineering and back-office integration with the devices that is delivering the real value.

Scanning information

Couriers use the device's bar code scanner to upload parcel information to DHL's main system – where it is matched with the pre-shipment electronic document. 'Previously there was a fair degree of paperwork when couriers arrived in the morning. We have automated this processing, which saves couriers between 45 minutes and one hour per day. It is a fantastic change for us as a business. Couriers can be out on the road for one hour longer, which has knock-on benefits for customer service.'

Once a parcel has been delivered, couriers key in the final details and upload them to the central system. Data is then transmitted into DHL's global network, providing instant information on shipment availability. A parcel is scanned seven to eight times through its life cycle. DHL's service centres poll the uploaded information every 15 minutes – enabling it to update customers about status and identify any operational problems more quickly. 'We can target an issue in our operations before it becomes a major issue.'

DHL has also introduced an online track and trace service. Once logged in, customers can use their parcel identifier number to track the progress of a parcel across DHL's network. 'Big customers are interested in exceptions where something potentially goes wrong. Customers are increasingly seeing more visibility in terms of track and trace', says Eccleston.

DHL were also investigating the use of RFID technology in innovative applications to further improve their track and trace capability.

Accessing data

The company's investment in web-based reporting tools and an integrated data warehouse aims to give its executives vital data. DHL established several new data feeds into a common data warehouse, including financial, transactional, sales and operational data.

The 'dashboard' reporting tools give executives a helicopter view of their respective performances against targets. 'Historically, we did not have an integrated view. We had a system where different people came to meetings with different numbers.'

Eccleston says he and his team have delivered 36 projects since the end of 2003. 'My own role is now changing to be much more cross-functional in terms of change management and the benefits realization of IT delivery. Our focus over the next 12 months is less on building new capability, it is more about driving the value from them', says Eccleston.

Of the company's overall goals, he says: 'If you look at DHL globally, we are either number one or number two in most markets. Our aim is to get to number one everywhere and clearly IT is essential to that.'

Case study questions

1. What were the business benefits to DHL of introducing the new technologies?
2. Why is integrating the new technologies with existing back-off systems so important?
3. One of the consultants in the case has stated that he does not think that RFID tagging will be commercially viable for logistics companies in the future. Do you agree with his opinion? Can you think of any applications that might justify its use in DHL?

SOURCES: An article in *MIS U.K.* by James Thompson, April 2005; www.accenture.com and www.rfidc.com

silicon.com

Case study **3.3**

How to avoid an ERP disaster

BY ANDY McCUE

Implementing an enterprise resource planning (ERP) system is one of the biggest IT headaches many organizations will face, and while the rewards of doing it right are high, the cost of failing is often disastrous.

Examples include MFI, which was thrown £46 million into the red as a result of technical problems with the rollout of a SAP-based supply chain system, which led to inventory shortages and incomplete orders being sent out, and more recently chocolate manufacturer Cadbury took a £12 million hit on profits as a result of a chocolate glut related to problems with the rollout of a new SAP-based ERP system.

The software itself is now rarely the cause of these kinds of problems, the root cause of which can more often be linked to the massive business and process change associated with implementing an ERP system.

Yorkshire Water – now saving £12 million per year thanks to a new SAP-based supply chain system.

PHOTO SOURCE: © DIRIMAGE/ALAMY

Jenny Sener, director of IT at property services organization OCS Group, speaking at a SAP customer event, said: 'It's the change management and the process change. That's where the real challenges are. The technology works. Many organizations fundamentally underestimate the scale of process change.'

Alan Harrison, CIO at Yorkshire Water, which is now saving almost £12 million per year after spending £30 million implementing SAP since 2000, said getting the business to change the way it works is vital to a successful project.

He said: 'The business managers are leading the implementation. They are the people who can actually deliver business change.'

Dale Vile, research director at analyst Freeform Dynamics, said problems with the business and process change often come when organizations hand over the implementation of the system to someone else, which leads to misunderstanding of roles and responsibilities.

He said: 'The most critical imperative is to regard the implementation as your own. The biggest danger comes when organizations delegate responsibility to their implementation partner. Remain in the driving seat and don't put it in the hands of someone else.'

Chris Gibbons, general manager of the internal IS consulting division at WHSmith News, is in charge of a £30 million SAP rollout that has paid for itself within four years but he admitted there were difficulties in getting the business to change processes and the way it works.

He said: 'There were teething problems in the first year. It is difficult to get the business to change.'

Scope creep is another issue. ERP implementations often take years and businesses rarely stand still, with the result that requests for changes to the scope of the project can spiral out of control.

Yorkshire Water's Harrison said scope creep is why a lot of SAP rollouts get into trouble. 'Scope creep is something you have to sit on', he said.

Vile agreed that a big pitfall is often trying to do too much in one go. 'The change requests should be challenged against the business objectives – be led by the business objectives and what the software can do', he said.

The final key piece of best practice advice for a major SAP rollout is to make the system as 'vanilla' as possible – that is to say using the standard off-the-shelf package with as little customization as is feasible.

Vile said: 'The golden rule is only deviate from the standard functionality in areas that really matter.'

He said that once an organization has got the core system implemented it can then look to 'unlock value incrementally' and build things around the edges such as remote web interfaces and wireless working.

Thinking about the case

1 The report uses the phrase 'scope creep'. What do you understand by this term? Can you think of examples of development that you have been involved in, either as a developer or as a user?

2 The suggestion is that an off-the-shelf ERP package should not be customized. Do you agree with this advice? Do you see any problems with this approach?

PART TWO

Information technology

Trent Courier Services

Andrew Langston looked out of his office window and smiled when he saw another of his bike messengers pedal in from a delivery. Had it really been a decade since he began Trent Courier Services? He'd come a long way from his early days in the business, when he got a phone call, hopped on his bike, and made the deliveries himself.

During his university days in London, Andrew competed in the cycling club's races. A friend told him that he worked part-time for the local bicycle delivery service to keep in shape, so Andrew decided to sign up, too. He could use a little extra cash. That was how he'd learned the ropes of the messenger delivery business. His employer had been operating for a long time in the City of London, and working there gave Andrew a taste of a different career option. After graduation, Andrew had moved back to Stoke-on-Trent, his hometown, and started Trent Couriers. It was the best way he could think to combine his love of cycling with the need to earn a living. Besides, at the time, Stoke-on-Trent had only a handful of small messenger services.

It was slow going at first. With such a small business and few funds, he had to watch every penny. But timing had helped him survive. With the business boom in the 1990s, the pace of business transactions skyrocketed. Firms of all sizes needed additional services to carry out their day-to-day transactions, so deliveries needed to increase, too. 'Instant service' became the watchword of business in the Information Age. Meanwhile, traffic on Stoke-on-Trent's streets had grown heavier and heavier. Delays throughout the area became a frustrating fact of life. Andrew found he could zip by the cars in heavy traffic as if they were parked. He loved pumping his way up the hills and coasting down to deliver his packages safe and sound – and always on time. He was proud that he'd built his business on his reputation for reliability. Now, here he was, owner of a company with nearly 50 employees making deliveries by both bicycle and car. He'd met each challenge with the determination he'd had when he was racing. And as with his bicycle, he tried to keep his business running smoothly, although it didn't always run the way a well-oiled machine should.

Bumps in the road

There was the time that a quickly opened door of a parked car had flattened one of his first messengers and landed him in Accident and Emergency. With no way to communicate except a pager, Andrew didn't know where his messenger was until he regained consciousness and had the nurses telephone him. Andrew spent the afternoon worrying, calling local police stations, and trying to placate his customer about her missing delivery. Also, he remembered the time high winds had brought down trees all over the

PHOTO SOURCE: © IZABELA HABUR

city. No traffic – including his car messengers – could get through for a day. Trent Couriers had no system for traffic alerts then, so some messengers were stranded in the chaos. Mobile phones and emailed delivery notices had certainly helped him maintain better contact in the field. Now if a messenger didn't arrive on time, he knew it sooner and could check the problem out directly.

Early expansion and growth

Trent Couriers had expanded rapidly over its first few years as demand grew for its services. Businesses found it cheaper to use a delivery service than to waste their own employees' time running across the city to make deliveries. The price for the service was another advantage – customers could get same-day delivery at prices much lower than the large package delivery services could offer. So, Trent Couriers definitely had a niche to fill in Stoke-on-Trent's business community.

As Trent Couriers grew, Andrew gradually added staff to his payroll – both messengers and dispatchers – to handle repeat customers and routine route deliveries. The company served a variety of businesses: solicitors needing contracts signed or papers filed, architects sending plans to their clients, medical and pharmaceutical companies and suppliers to the ceramics industry who needed rush deliveries, public relations firms sending their copy to poster and sign suppliers, and other businesses needing quick deliveries to satellite offices, suppliers or clients.

Andrew set up routes within the city to handle his regular customers' needs. He also accepted requests for special deliveries from drop-off or call-in business. Standard delivery was two-hour service, with premium rates for faster service. If a business only needed same-day service, then it could opt for the economy rate. Trent Couriers made deliveries all year round, in any kind of weather. Regular service operated Monday to Friday, from 7 a.m. to 7 p.m. During the high-technology boom, Trent Couriers also added premium service delivery on Saturdays.

Moving beyond bikes

After a few years of building Trent Couriers' clientele, Andrew noticed that revenues began to plateau. His competitors were offering the same type of service, and there was only so much business to go around. He needed to think of some way to separate his business from the pack – and soon.

In looking over the customer feedback his messengers entered into their report forms, Andrew saw patterns emerging. Messengers said several of his customers that had satellite offices outside the conurbation and in nearby towns had requested expanded routes. He also had repeated enquiries to serve several pottery businesses in the area. Handling fragile ceramics and other one-of-a-kind, irreplaceable items definitely called for a safer delivery method than bicycles. So, Andrew had investigated the feasibility of adding van deliveries to his business and decided to make the move.

Maintaining a fleet and drivers took the business to an entirely new level, but it also allowed Trent Couriers to deliver a wider and more profitable range of services – deliveries no longer had to fit in a backpack or bike basket. Ultimately, adding a van service allowed Trent Couriers to double its size. It now made about 500 deliveries per day and generated revenue of roughly £500,000 annually.

With the addition of a van service, Andrew needed to develop new pricing scales and schedules. He used his financial information system to calculate all the costs that went into a delivery – such as van purchases and maintenance, fuel costs and driver wages. Then he added a profit margin. Next, he used a mapping system to compute delivery route mileage based on the post codes of sending and receiving parties. To cover the new territories, he added even more employees, especially to the central office staff to handle customer orders and other business functions. Finally, he set special rates for 'white glove' service for pottery companies and medical centres.

Customers come first

Still, even with the expansion, the key to Trent Couriers' success remained its service quality. Andrew insisted that each of his employees provide the same on-time deliveries and courteous service that he had when he biked the routes himself. Messengers were on the front lines, and they represented the company to customers, so their attitudes and hard work were critical to Trent Couriers. Over the years, he'd had some run-ins with messengers over slack work habits, and a few had quit or just didn't work out and were let go. Andrew had documented problems in employees' computerized personnel files when necessary. But overall, he considered his employees part of an extended family and valued their loyalty. Ongoing training for messengers and dispatchers was important to maintain service levels. Above all, he wanted all his employees to enjoy the work they did.

Increasing reliance on information systems

Throughout his expansions, Andrew had turned to information systems to increase his efficiency and handle growing amounts of data. Information technology had helped him in so many areas:

- Automating payroll and accounting services.
- Streamlining customer paperwork.
- Tracking equipment maintenance and supplies.
- Routing deliveries.
- Maintaining customer and messenger contact.
- Providing customized services on the Web.
- Handling customer and employee database files.

In fact, for a business that many considered low-tech, Trent Couriers has relied on very high-tech computer hardware and software.

Handheld computers had rescued quite a few new messengers who became lost in Stoke-on-Trent's back streets. They'd found their way by bringing maps up on their handheld's screen. So, information technology was certainly critical to his employees. A couple of years ago the company even added a website offering online ordering to handle increased customer demands. Customers were pleased with the new option. For his own work, there were the useful databases – without which Andrew wouldn't know who his customers were or what their needs were. He'd also lose track of his employees and their productivity. The company had certainly followed the digital wave. Looking back, he knew he wouldn't be able to sustain his business without these technologies.

Back to business

Andrew's thoughts were interrupted by Mary Thomas, his administrative assistant, who was knocking at the door.

'Andrew? Sorry to bother you. Time for our meeting with the tyre supplier. They want to discuss our upcoming needs for the year.'

'Maybe we can get a volume price break on our fleet this year', noted Andrew. 'We added two new vans, you know'. He had used the same tyre supplier since the addition of the firm's first motor vehicle. His business relationship was strong and long-lasting. He'd heard that the supplier had offered some quantity price breaks to other businesses, so he was going to pull the entire purchasing history of the supplier and use the information to squeeze out better discounts this year. Savings made could be ploughed back into the company to make it bigger and better.

Business Challenges

Throughout his business's expansion, Andrew Langston has had to meet several challenges – not the least of which was selecting and using information systems to keep his business competitive. Information systems have played a critical role in Trent Couriers' history. You explore how Andrew met those challenges in the chapters of Part Two:

- In Chapter 4, 'Business Hardware and Software', you learn how to evaluate Trent Couriers' hardware and software needs as it grows, adds employees and customers, and streamlines its business processes.
- In Chapter 5, 'Business Networks and Telecommunications', you learn about the strategies Trent Couriers uses to remain in constant contact with its messengers and customers – with the goal of improving its services.
- In Chapter 6, 'Databases and Data Warehouses', you learn the importance of one of business's most powerful tools – databases – and see how Trent Couriers uses database technology throughout its business operations.

Chapter 4

Business networks and telecommunications

LEARNING OBJECTIVES

Modern telecommunications technology allows businesses to send and receive information in seconds. Except when a physical transfer of goods is involved, geographical distances are becoming meaningless in business transactions. When using computers and other digital devices, people can now work together as if they were sitting next to each other, even when they are thousands of miles apart. Financial transactions and information retrieval take seconds, and wireless technology enables us to perform these activities from almost anywhere and while moving. Understanding the technology underlying telecommunications – its strengths, weaknesses and available options – is essential to making informed business decisions.

When you finish this chapter, you will be able to:

Describe business and home applications of digital telecommunications.

Identify the major media and devices used in telecommunications.

Explain the concept of protocols.

Compare and contrast various networking and Internet services.

List networking technologies and trends that are likely to have an impact on businesses and information management in the near future.

Discuss the pros and cons of telecommuting.

Trent Courier Services

COMMUNICATION IS KEY

Mark Johnson, one of Trent Couriers' longtime car messengers, was hopelessly stuck in traffic. A serious accident involving two lorries had snarled traffic on the bypass; it was at a dead stop. He desperately needed to contact his customer – a medical supply firm – to alert it that his delivery would be delayed. So he used his hands-free mobile phone to call the customer. His contact at the supply firm acknowledged his delay and told him that the supplies were a routine delivery to a hospital pharmacy and not to worry – as long as the hospital received the delivery sometime that day, they'd be fine. Mark apologized for the glitch and promised to get off at the next exit as soon as he could move again. Then he used his group email program to warn other messengers to stay off the bypass for the time being. Maybe he could save somebody else a headache.

From beepers to mobile phones

When mobile phone technology hit the UK, Trent Courier Services replaced its collection of beepers. Andrew Langston had seen their competitive advantage almost immediately. The company could contact its messengers instantly; they didn't need to find a phonebox. Also, text message alerts could be sent to the entire delivery fleet. Now messengers could be rerouted around trouble spots. Of course, there was always the occasional delay of one or two messengers, such as Mark Johnson was experiencing, but the problems now could be isolated.

As soon as the media began reporting a link between mobile phone use and car accidents, Andrew decided to purchase hands-free car kits so that messengers could communicate safely with customers and the office. These devices also meant that his messengers didn't miss calls while they were fumbling for their phones.

Increasing efficiency and customer satisfaction

Mary Thomas updated delivery information from the messengers' handheld computers into the database. As the business grew, however, Mary spent more and more of her time uploading data from the handheld computers. A representative from the company's mobile phone service provider told her about a wireless card that messengers could use to upload delivery information to the company's database. The messengers plug the card into a slot on their handheld computers and access the Internet through the mobile phone providers' connection. Not only did this innovation save Mary time, it also meant that messengers could update delivery information immediately upon delivery so that the company could provide this information to their customers right away. Delivery confirmations now could be sent via email directly to the senders as soon as deliveries were made. Mary Thomas in the central office no longer had to confirm special deliveries. Messengers did that immediately and copied her on their transmittals, saving her time and the company money, all while increasing customer service.

PHOTO SOURCE: © PCC/ALAMY

Competitors up the ante

Trent Couriers' competitors hadn't stood still either. One of its major competitors had improved its service by offering a standard one-hour delivery time in nearby communities – half of Trent Couriers' standard delivery time. So, Andrew responded by opening two satellite offices to get messengers to remote destinations more quickly. That allowed Andrew to match his competitor's new time frame and still make a profit on deliveries.

An additional benefit of the three-office configuration was enhanced data security. In 2004, when pipes burst and flooded the main office, Trent Couriers did not have a recovery plan. Now, every time any data is recorded at one of the offices, it is automatically duplicated on disks at the other two offices via the Internet. Andrew felt much more secure knowing that the duplication in computing services was ready, if needed.

Choosing the right network service providers

To link its three offices, Trent Couriers used an Internet service provider (ISP) offering digital subscriber line (DSL) service, and a company that specialized in installation of virtual private networks (VPNs). Andrew found the DSL service to be fast enough for his company's needs and very affordable, but the connection was not reliable enough for Trent Couriers. So Andrew and Sarah Truesdale, the office manager, found themselves looking for an alternative. They considered cable, but the companies that offered those services would have to dig their trenches to the office sites, and they couldn't get to Trent Couriers for six to eight weeks.

Some time earlier, Andrew noticed strange aerials popping up in the neighbourhood. He remembered someone mentioning that a telecom company was establishing fixed wireless service in the area. Perhaps he could use that service. Indeed, the service was available at a fee comparable to the DSL service, and Andrew subscribed Trent Couriers. The company that provided the VPN software made all the necessary arrangements to ensure that communication among the three offices remained private. Now, Trent Couriers' three offices would have high-speed wireless Internet access as well as secure interoffice communications at a reasonable rate.

Intranets and extranets

As the staff became more comfortable with Internet technology, they began to see its usefulness for other business functions. For example, the human resources manager set up an intranet to inform staff of the benefits programme options and general company news. That information could be accessed from all three offices and through the mobile phones that messengers carried. He also set up a short orientation video to introduce new employees to the company.

Sarah and Mary began to consider an extranet to expedite transactions with the firms that maintained their van and bicycle fleets. They also explored the option to use the extranet of a national office supply superstore.

Telecommunications in business

telecommunications Communications over a long distance, as opposed to communication within a computer, or between adjacent hardware pieces.

Telecommunications, which is essential to today's smooth business operations, is the transmittal of data and information from one point to another. The Greek word *tele*, which means 'distance', is part of such words as 'telegraph', 'telephone' and other words referring to technologies that allow communications over large distances. Thus, telecommunications is communications over a distance. Telephone, fax, email, the World Wide Web – none of these essential business services would be available without fast, reliable telecommunications. Networking technologies have brought several improvements to business processes:

- *Better business communication.* When no physical objects need to be transferred from one place to another, telecommunications technology can make geographical distance irrelevant. Email, voice mail, instant messaging, faxing, file transfer, mobile telephony and teleconferencing enable detailed and instant communication, within and between organizations. Telecommunications can also be used by one person to monitor another person's performance in real time. The use of email has brought some secondary benefits to business communications by establishing a permanent written record of, and accountability for, ideas. The result is more accurate business communications and less need for manual recording. Web-based instant messaging is used to support online shoppers in real time.

- *Greater efficiency.* Telecommunications has made business processes more efficient. Any information that is recorded electronically can become immediately available to anyone involved in a business process, even when the business units are located far apart. For example, as soon as an order is placed, anyone in the organization who will ever be involved with it can view it: from the marketing people, to purchasing officers, to manufacturing managers, to shipping workers, to billing and collection clerks.
- *Better distribution of data.* Organizations that can transmit vital data quickly from one computer to another no longer need centralized databases. Business units that need certain data frequently might store it locally, while others can access it remotely. Only fast, reliable transfer of data makes this efficient arrangement possible.
- *Instant transactions.* The availability of the Internet to millions of businesses and consumers has shifted a significant volume of business transactions to the Web. Both businesses and consumers can shop, purchase and pay instantly online. Wireless technology has also made possible instant payment and data collection using small radio devices, such as electronic toll collection tags. In addition to commercial activities, people can use telecommunications for online education and entertainment.
- *Flexible and mobile workforce.* Employees do not have to come to the office to carry out their work as long as their jobs only involve the use and creation of information. They can telecommute using Internet connections. Salespeople, support personnel and field workers are more mobile with wireless communication.
- *Alternative channels.* Services that used to be conducted through specialized dedicated channels can be conducted through alternative channels. For example, voice communication used to be conducted only through proprietary telephone networks, but is now also conducted through the Internet, which has decreased its cost. Radio and television broadcasts were conducted through radio frequencies and company-owned cables. Newer technologies enable organizations to broadcast over the Internet and provide telephone services over the Internet as well. Furthermore, Internet technologies allow individuals to broadcast text and sound to subscribers' computers or to web-capable mobile devices. (We discuss these technologies in Chapter 7, 'The Web-Enabled Enterprise'.)

CD TASK

At the same time you enjoy the great opportunities created by telecommunications technology, you must recognize that it poses great risks. Once an organization connects its ISs to a public network, security becomes a challenge. Unauthorized access and data destruction are constant threats. Thus, organizations must establish proper security controls as preventive measures. We discuss the risks and solutions in Chapter 13, 'Risks, Security and Disaster Recovery'.

Telecommunications in daily use

We have grown so used to networks that we no longer think much about them in daily life; however, they are pervasive. Here is an overview of the most widespread telecommunications uses.

Mobile phones

The American term for a mobile phone is a cellular phone, which derives its name from the territories of service providers, which are divided into areas known as cells. Each cell has at its centre a computerized transceiver (transmitter-receiver), which both transmits signals to another receiver and receives signals from another transmitter. When a call is placed on a mobile phone, the signal is first transmitted to the closest transceiver, which sends a signal through landlines that dial the desired phone number. If the receiving phone is also mobile, the call is communicated to the transceiver closest to the destination phone. As the user moves from one area, or cell, to another, other transceivers pick up the transmission and receiving tasks.

Using mobile phone networks, people can transmit and receive calls almost anywhere, freeing them from a fixed office location. They can also be used for email and faxing, and many are web-enabled. Many mobile phones have been merged with digital cameras, PDAs and GPS (global positioning system) circuitry. 'My car is my office' is a reality for many professionals who spend much of their time travelling. As technology advances and more capabilities are squeezed into smaller casings, some professionals can say, 'My pocket is my office.'

CD TASK

The major advantage of mobile phones is that they are attached to people, not offices. This is why, despite the higher cost of mobile phones over landline phones, some companies have decided to discard the latter and adopt the former for some or all of their employees.

Videoconferencing

People sitting in conference rooms thousands of miles apart are brought together by their transmitted images and speech in what is called **videoconferencing**. Businesses use videoconferencing to save on travel costs and lodging, car fleets and the time of highly salaried employees, whether they work in different organizations or at different sites of the same organization. From national and global perspectives, videoconferencing also reduces traffic congestion and air pollution. The increasing speed of Internet connections makes it easy for anyone with a high-speed link to establish videoconferences either by using a peer-to-peer link or by using the services of a third party, a company that specializes in maintaining videoconferencing hardware and software. In the latter case, businesses pay either a monthly fee for unlimited conferences, or every time they use the service.

videoconferencing A telecommunication system that allows people who are in different locations to meet via transmitted images and speech.

Fax

Facsimile, or *fax*, is the transmission and reception of images over telephone lines. A fax machine digitizes an image and transmits the representative bits to a receiving fax machine. The receiving machine converts the digitized codes back into an image. Fax machines provide an easy means of communicating text and graphical images. Because it is based on digital images, faxing does not have to be executed through traditional telephone lines but can go through the Internet, using special software. Fax functions can also be combined with scanning, printing and copying functions in 'multifunction' machines.

PHOTO SOURCE: © TOM GUFLER

Videoconferencing is becoming an increasingly popular cost-saving option for a range of organizations.

Why you should... understand telecommunications

As a professional, you will be responsible for ensuring that your organization maximizes its benefits from fast and reliable telecommunications. To do so, you might be involved in selecting from networking alternatives. To be a creative and productive contributor to these decisions, it is essential that you understand the fundamental promises and limitations of networking and telecommunications.

A growing number of tasks that used to be in the sole domain of highly paid specialists are becoming a must for professionals whose main occupation is not IT. For example, creating small networks in businesses and homes used to be the sole domain of technicians. Now any professional is expected to know how to create hotspots and how to use a plethora of networks: wired, wireless, mobile and Internet-based.

Wireless payments and warehousing

Radio frequency identification (RFID) technology, mentioned in Chapter 3 and covered in more detail later in this chapter, enables us to conclude transactions and to make payments quickly. Stockholm's Congestion Charging system uses a wireless payment method. Drivers are loaned an electronic tag which they carry in their car. This communicates with 'gates' over the road at various points and this will automatically create a direct debit of the driver's account. The system is flexible in that charging can vary throughout the day and even take into account exceptions to payment. For example, the Lindingo district is accessible to the mainland only via the congestion charged area. It would be unfair to charge the residents if they are only 'passing through' when they have no choice. So any vehicle that enters the congestion charge area from Lindingo and leaves within 30 minutes pays no charge. With the electronic tag this exception is dealt with easily.

RFID technology is also used in warehouses where employees can use handheld units to check a central system for availability and location of items to be picked up and stored from and to shelves or bins. When storing, the handhelds are used to update inventory databases. Such systems have made the work of 'untethered employees' more efficient compared with older systems that require physical access to a computer terminal. Wireless communications have many other uses, some of which are discussed in detail later in the chapter.

Peer-to-peer file sharing

One of the most interesting developments in worldwide telecommunications is **peer-to-peer (P2P) file sharing** through the Internet: anyone with access to the Internet can download one of several free applications that help locate and download files from any online computer. You might have heard of some of these applications: LimeWire, BearShare, Morpheus, KaZaA and others. While the concept has well served scientists who share scientific text files and application developers who exchange code, the greater use has been in downloading artistic files, such as music and video files. Because unauthorized duplication and use of such files violates copyright laws and deprives recording and film companies of revenue, these industries have sued some violators in court. These actions and the proliferation of legal services that sell individual music tracks online for a small charge per track have reduced the use of file sharing for illegal copying, but have not eliminated it.

peer-to-peer (P2P) file sharing Software applications that enable two Internet users to send and receive to each other. The technology is highly objectionable to organizations that sell copyrighted materials because the software promotes violation of copyrights.

Since some files, especially movies, could take hours to download even with fast connections, some software divides up the designated file and downloads

Industry **SNAPSHOT**

Technology and copyright

In a precedent-setting case, a Belgian court appointed an expert to look into ways of automatically identifying copyright material in P2P operations. The expert identified seven ways Scarlet, one of Belgium's largest ISPs, could block such traffic without intrusively monitoring transactions, hence maintaining customers' privacy. Scarlet were given six months to implement the technology to block copyright material or face a daily fine of €2500.

SOURCE: 'Block P2P, Belgian court tells ISP' by Stephen Withers, *IT Wire*, 7 July 2007

each segment from a different online computer. For example, BitTorrent lets you conduct a search for a file. It finds several sources, and then downloads each segment of the file from a different source. It then combines the segments back into a complete file. A movie that would take several hours to download if copied from a single computer could take only several minutes from a large number of sources. If the owner of one computer turns it off, the software automatically tries to download the segment from another computer. The application poses a threat to the film industry. What is further threatening to both the music and movie industries is that these software packages work with each other, and that BitTorrent has been incorporated into some of the other file sharing applications.

bandwidth The capacity of the communications channel, practically its speed: the number of signal streams the channel can support, usually measured as number of bits per second. A greater bandwidth also supports a greater bit rate, i.e., transmission speed.

Web-empowered commerce

CD TASK

Increasingly fast digital communication enables millions of organizations to conduct business and individuals to research, market, educate, train, shop, purchase and pay online. Whole industries, such as online exchanges and auctions, have been created thanks to the Web. Web-based commerce is the subject of an entire chapter (Chapter 7) and is illustrated with many examples throughout the book.

Bandwidth and media

While people can enjoy technologies without understanding how they work, educated professionals often do need to understand some fundamental concepts to be able to participate in decision-making when selecting networking equipment and services. This section introduces bandwidth and networking media.

transmission rate The speed at which data are communicated over a communications channel.

Bandwidth

bits per second (bps) The measurement of the capacity (or transmission rate) of a communications channel.

A communications *medium* is the physical means that transports the signal, such as a telephone line, a television cable or a radio wave. The bandwidth of the medium is the speed at which data are communicated, which is also called the transmission rate, or simply the bit rate. It is measured as bits per second (bps). Table 5.1 shows common bit rate measurements. As is often the case, bandwidth is a limited resource. Usually, the greater the bandwidth the higher the cost of the communications service. Thus, determining the type of communications lines to install or subscribe to is an important business decision.

baseband A communications channel that allows only a very low bit rate in telecommunications, such as unconditioned telephone twisted pair cables.

When a communications medium can carry only one transmission at a time, it is known as baseband. Dial-up connections through regular phone lines and

Table 5.1 Transmission speed measurement units

bps = Bits per second
Kbps = Thousand bps
Mbps = Million bps (mega bps)
Gbps = Billion bps (giga bps)
Tbps = Trillion bps (tera bps)

broadband High-speed digital communication, sometimes defined as at least 200 kbps. T1, cable modem and DSL provide broadband.

Ethernet computer network connections are examples of baseband. When a line is capable of carrying multiple transmissions simultaneously, it is said to be **broadband**. Cable television, DSL (direct subscriber line), fibre-optic cables and most wireless connections are broadband. In general, broadband offers greater bandwidth and faster throughput than baseband connections, and in common usage the term 'broadband' is associated with a high-speed networking connection, which is required for fast transmission of large files and multimedia material.

Media

There are several types of communications media, that is, means through which bits are transmitted. Media can be tangible, such as cables, or intangible, such as radio waves. The most available tangible media are twisted pair cable, coaxial cable and optical fibre (see Table 5.2). Intangible media include all microwave radio technologies, which support wireless communication. Recently, the electric power grid has also been added as a medium for communications. All can be used to link a business or household to the Internet. Later in the chapter we discuss the various Internet connection services and also refer to typical periodic cost of the services.

Table 5.2 Networking media

Medium	Availability	Bandwidth	Vulnerability to electromagnetic interference
Twisted pair cable	High	Low to medium	High
Radio waves	High	Medium to high	Low (but vulnerable to RFI)
Microwave	Low	High	Low
Coaxial (TV) cable	High	High	Low
Optical fibre	Moderate but growing	Highest	Nonexistent
Electric power lines (BPL)	Very high	High	High

Twisted pair cable Twisted pair cable is used in computer networks and in telephone networks. It consists of pairs of insulated copper wires that are twisted together to reduce *electromagnetic interference (EMI)* and encased in a plastic cover. Twisted pair cable is a popular medium for connecting computers and networking devices because it is relatively flexible, reliable and low cost. Twisted pair cable is also used in telephone networks, but in many countries, twisted copper wires are now used only between the telephone jack and the central office of the company providing the telephone service. The typical distance of this link is 1.5–6 kilometres (about 1–4 miles), and is often referred to as 'the last mile'. The central offices themselves are connected with fibre optic cables, but it is often the 'last mile' media that determine the overall speed of the connection. In recent years many 'last mile' connections have also been converted to optical cables.

twisted pair cable Traditional telephone wires, twisted in pairs to reduce electromagnetic interference.

Coaxial cable Coaxial cable is sometimes called TV cable or simply 'cable' because of its common use for cable television transmission. It is widely used for links to the Internet. Television companies use the same network they employ to transmit television programming to link households and businesses to the Internet.

coaxial cable A transmission medium consisting of thick copper wire insulated and shielded by a special sheath of meshed wires to prevent electromagnetic interference. Supports high-speed telecommunication.

Optical fibre Fibre optic technology uses light instead of electricity to represent bits. Fibre optic lines are made of thin fibreglass filaments. A transmitter sends bursts of light using a laser or a light-emitting diode device. The receiver detects the period of light and no-light to receive the data bits. Optical fibre systems operate in the infrared and visible light frequencies. Because light is not susceptible to EMI (electromagnetic interference) and radio frequency interference (RFI), fibre optic communication is much less prone to error than twisted pair and radio transmission. Optical fibres can also carry signals over relatively longer distances than other media.

Some optical carriers support bit rates of up to several terabytes per second (Tbps), expected to reach 10 Tbps (10,000,000,000,000 bits per second) in the foreseeable future. This great bandwidth enables multiple streams of both Internet and television transmission. Some telecommunications companies have laid optical fibre lines to offer households both services, directly competing with TV cable companies.

radio frequency interference (RFI) The unwanted reception of radio signals that occurs when using metal communication lines. Optical fibres are not susceptible to RFI.

microwaves Short (high frequency) radio waves. Used in telecommunications to carry digital signals.

Radio and satellite transmission Radio frequency (RF) technologies use radio waves to carry bits. There are several wireless technologies that transmit through air or space. Some of the most popular for personal and business networking, such as Wi-Fi and Bluetooth, are discussed later in this chapter. Microwaves are high-frequency radio waves that can carry signals over long distances with high accuracy. You have probably noticed the parabolic dishes on the roofs of some buildings. They are so numerous on rooftops and high towers because microwave communication is effective only if the line of sight between the transmitter and receiver is unobstructed. Clusters of microwave aerials are often installed on high buildings and the tops of mountains to obtain a clear line of sight. Terrestrial microwave communication – so-called because signals are sent from and received by stations on the earth – is good for long-distance telecommunications but can also be

PHOTO SOURCE: © COURTESY OF NASA

Large companies lease telecommunication satellite frequencies to transmit data coast to coast and across national borders.

used in local networks in and among buildings. It is commonly used for voice and television communications. When radio communication is used outside buildings, it is vulnerable to weather conditions. Thunderstorms, fog and snow might degrade communication quality.

Signals can also be transmitted using microwaves via satellite links. There are two major types of satellites: geostationary, also called GEO, and low earth orbit, also called LEO. Both types serve as radio relay stations in orbit above the earth that receive, amplify and redirect signals. Microwave transceiver dishes are aimed at the satellite, which has antennas, amplifiers and transmitters. The satellite receives a signal, amplifies it and retransmits it to the destination.

GEO satellites are placed in orbit 35,784 kilometres (about 22,282 miles) above the earth. At this distance the satellite is geosynchronized (synchronized with the earth); that is, once it starts orbiting, the satellite stays above the same point on earth at all times, without being propelled. Thus, a GEO satellite is stationary relative to the earth. Because they orbit at such a great distance above the earth, three GEO satellites can provide service for every point on earth by relaying signals among themselves before transmitting them back down to their destinations.

Because of the great distance from the earth to satellites, the communication is fine for transmitting data because delays of a few seconds make no significant difference. However, a delay of even two or three seconds might be disturbing in interactive communication, such as when voice and pictures are communicated in real time. You might have noticed such delays when reporters use devices that communicate to a television station. When the presenter in the studio asks a question, the reporter on location receives the question with a noticeable delay.

LEO satellites minimize this shortcoming. These lower-cost satellites are placed about 800–1000 kilometres (500–600 miles) above the earth. The signals' round-trip is short enough for mobile telephoning and interactive computer applications. Unlike GEOs, LEO satellites revolve around the globe every few hours. Multiple LEOs are required to maintain continuous coverage for uninterrupted communication.

Electrical power lines One communications medium that had been available for years but has only recently been tapped for telecommunications is the electric power grid. The bits in an electric power grid are represented by electric impulses, but they must be distinct from the regular power that flows through the grid. Engineers have succeeded in overcoming this technical challenge. The service is referred to as broadband over power line (BPL) or power line communication (PLC). BPL is covered in more detail later in the chapter.

From the point of view of organizations, among the important factors in choosing a networking medium are availability, current and potential bandwidth, and vulnerability to electromagnetic interference (EMI) or radio frequency interference (RFI). Your business's current and future needs for data security, as well as compatibility with an already installed network, are also factors. Cost is another important consideration. For example, one of the great qualities of optical fibre is that it is practically immune to EMI. However, it is more expensive than other options.

> **network** A combination of a communications device and a computer or several computers, or two or more computers, so that the various devices can send and receive text or audiovisual information to each other.

> **node** A device connected to at least one other device on a network.

Networks

In the context of data communications, a **network** is a combination of devices or **nodes** (computers or communication devices) connected to each other through one of the communication channels just discussed. We will often use the word 'computer' for a device that is networked, but this is only for convenience. Any compatible device that can transmit and receive on a network is part of it.

CD TASK

Types of networks

Computer networks are classified according to their reach and complexity. There are three basic types of networks: LANs (local area networks), which connect computers, printers and other computer equipment for an office, several adjacent offices, an entire building or a campus; MANs (metropolitan area networks), which span a greater distance than LANs and usually have more complicated networking equipment for midrange communications; and WANs (wide area networks), which connect systems in an entire nation, continent or worldwide. Some people also include a fourth category: PANs (personal area networks), which encompass connections between personal digital devices such as PDAs and tablet computers.

local area network (LAN) A computer network confined to a building or a group of adjacent buildings, as opposed to a wide area network.

server A computer connected to several less powerful computers that can utilize its databases and applications.

peer-to-peer LAN A local area network (LAN) in which no central device controls communications.

wireless LAN (WLAN) A local area network that uses electromagnetic waves (radio or infrared light) as the medium of communication. In recent years almost all WLANs have been established using Wi-Fi.

scalability The ability to adapt applications as business needs grow.

LANs A computer network within a building, or a campus of adjacent buildings, is called a **local area network**, or **LAN**. LANs are usually established by a single organization with offices within a radius of roughly 5–6 kilometres (3–4 miles). LANs are set up by organizations to enhance communications among employees and to share IT resources. Households might set up LANs to share a broadband link to the Internet and to transmit digital music, pictures and video from one part of a home to another.

In office LANs, one computer is often used as a central repository of programs and files that all connected computers can use; this computer is called a **server**. Connected computers can store documents on their own disks or on the server, can share hardware such as printers, and can exchange email. When a LAN has a server, the server usually has centralized control of communications among the connected computers and between the computers and the server itself. Another computer or special communications device can also exercise this control, or control can be distributed among several servers. A **peer-to-peer LAN** is one in which no central device controls communications.

In recent years the cost of wireless devices has decreased significantly, and many offices as well as households now network their computers wirelessly, or create networks in which some of the computers are wired and some are not. **Wireless LANs (WLANs)** offer significant benefits: installation is easy because you don't have to drill through walls to install wires, and you can move equipment wherever it is needed. Wireless networks offer significant savings in some environments. Wireless LANs are less costly to maintain when the network spans two or more buildings. They are also more scalable. **Scalability** is the ease of expanding a system. It is easy to add more nodes, or clients, to a WLAN, because all that is needed is wireless circuitry in any device that comes within range of a wireless network.

However, wireless LANs have a significant drawback: they can be less secure than wired LANs. On a wired network, there are several measures that might be taken to guard against unauthorized access. On a wireless network, security measures exist (which are being upgraded all the time), but at present they are limited compared with those for wired networks, are not always easy to set up and can slow down communications. Anyone using a WLAN should keep informed about the latest security measures and take them to ensure that communications are secure. Some of these measures are covered later in the chapter.

PHOTO SOURCE: © GEOGPHOTOS/ALAMY

In April 2007 The Cloud, Europe's leading wireless broadband network, launched the City of London Network.

wide area network (WAN) A network of computers and other communications devices that extends over a large area, possibly comprising national territories. Example: the Internet.

value-added network (VAN) A telecommunications network owned and managed by a vendor that charges clients periodic fees for network management services.

Internet service provider (ISP) An individual or organization that provides Internet connection, and sometimes other related services, to subscribers.

PAN (personal area network) A network of devices typically within a small radius that enables a user to use two or more devices wirelessly, such as wireless keyboard and mouse.

MANs A *metropolitan area network (MAN)* usually links multiple LANs within a large city or metropolitan region and typically spans a distance of up to 50 kilometres (about 30 miles). For example, the LAN in a chemistry lab might be linked to a research hospital's LAN and to a pharmaceutical company's LAN several miles away in the same city to form a MAN. The individual LANs that compose a MAN might belong to the same organization or to several different organizations. The high-speed links between LANs within a MAN typically use fibre optic or wireless broadband connections.

WANs A **wide area network (WAN)** is a far-reaching system of networks. One WAN is composed of two or more LANs (or MANs) that are connected across a distance of more than approximately 48 kilometres (or 30 miles). Large WANs might have many constituent LANs and MANs on different continents. The simplest WAN is a dial-up connection to a network provider's services over basic telephone lines. A more complex WAN is a satellite linkup between LANs in two different countries. The best-known WAN is the Internet.

WANs can be public or private. The telephone network and the Internet are examples of public WANs. A private WAN might use either dedicated lines or satellite connections. Many organizations cannot afford to maintain a private WAN. They pay to use existing networks, which are provided in two basic formats: common carriers or value-added networks.

A common carrier provides public telephone lines that anyone can access or dial up, and leased lines, which are dedicated to the leasing organization's exclusive use. The user pays for public lines based on time used and distance called. Leased lines are dedicated to the leaseholder and have a lower error rate than dial-up lines, because they are not switched among many different subscribers.

Value-added networks (VANs) provide enhanced network services. VANs fulfill organizational needs for reliable data communications while relieving the organization of the burden of providing its own network management and maintenance. Many businesses use VANs for their electronic data interchange (EDI) with other businesses, suppliers and buyers. However, due to cost considerations, an increasing number of organizations prefer to conduct commerce via the Internet rather than through VANs. VAN services cost much more than those offered by **Internet service providers (ISPs)**. (Many VAN providers also provide Internet links.) This issue is discussed in Chapter 7.

CD TASK

PANs A **PAN (personal area network)** is a wireless network designed for handheld and portable devices such as PDAs, mobile phones and tablet or laptop computers, and is intended for use by only one or two people. Transmission speed is slow to moderate, and the maximum distance between devices is generally 10 metres (33 feet). For example, Maria and Simon meet at a conference and exchange electronic business cards using their Bluetooth-enabled PDAs. When Maria gets back to her office, the PDA automatically synchronizes with her office notebook computer, updating the address book on the notebook with Simon's information. (Bluetooth and other wireless technologies are covered later in the chapter.)

network interface card (NIC) Circuitry embedded or installed in a computer to support proper linking of the computer to a network.

hub In networking, a device connecting several computers or other electronic devices.

Networking hardware

Networks use a variety of devices to connect computers and peripheral devices (such as printers) to each other, and to connect networks to each other. Each computer or device connected to a network must have a **network interface card (NIC)**, which connects through a cable or a wireless antenna to a hub, switch, bridge or router, which in turn connects to a LAN or WAN. A **hub** is a common device often used as a central location to connect computers or devices to a local network. A

Industry SNAPSHOT

You can take it with you

Slingbox is a piece of hardware that you can connect to your cable box, satellite receiver or digital video recorder. It then can stream your favourite TV programmes to a PC anywhere in the world. It uses wireless connection or mobile phone connection. Thus, you can access your DVR from your PC and select preferred programmes for viewing in your hotel, far from home.

SOURCE: D. Tynan, 'TV on the Run', *PC World*, May 2005, p. 136

PHOTO SOURCE: © SLING MEDIA, INC.

Sling Player Mobile also allows you to 'Slingbox from your phone'.

switch is like a hub, except that it is more 'intelligent'. Communications that go through a hub are broadcast to all devices attached to the hub; communications through a switch go only to designated devices on the network. A bridge is a device that connects two networks, such as a LAN, to the Internet. A router routes data packets to the next node on their way to the final destination. It can connect dissimilar networks and can be programmed to act as a firewall to filter communications. Routers keep tables of network addresses, known as Internet Protocol (IP) addresses, which identify each computer on the network along with the best routes to other network addresses. You are not likely to see a WAN router, but you might have seen a router used to support a LAN in a small office or in a household. A repeater amplifies or regenerates signals so that they do not become weak or distorted.

Another type of networking hardware that might be familiar to home computer users is the modem. A modem – a word contracted from *mod*ulator-*dem*odulator – in traditional usage is a device whose purpose is to translate communications signals from analogue to digital, and vice versa. For many years the only way to link to the Internet was to dial up, meaning connecting over regular telephone lines. These lines were originally designed for analogue – continuous – signals rather than for digital signals, which consist of discrete bursts. A modem turns the digital signal from your computer into an analogue signal that can go out over the phone lines. A modem on the receiving computer transforms the analogue signal back into a digital signal the computer can understand. The former transformation is called modulation and the latter is called demodulation.

A dial-up connection with a modem is very slow (usually no faster than 56 Kbps), so most users and small businesses today are turning to faster connections that use digital signals throughout the connection, such as DSL and cable connections. Even though the medium transfers digital signals, the word 'modem' is now used for the devices that connect computers to the Internet with these technologies. Thus, for example, if you use the service of a cable company to link to the Internet, the device connecting your computer's network card to the cable is called a cable modem. If you use a DSL service, the device used is called a DSL modem, and if you use a power line, the device is called a BPL modem.

switch In networking, a device that is able to direct communications to certain devices on the network. Compare with a hub which broadcasts to all connected devices.

bridge A device connecting two communications networks that use similar hardware.

router A network hub, wired or wireless, that ensures proper routing of messages within a network such as a LAN and between each device on that network and another network, such as the Internet.

repeater A device that strengthens signals and then sends them on their next leg towards their next destination.

modem (modulator/demodulator) A communications device that transforms digital signals to analogue telephone signals and vice versa, for data communications over voice telephone lines. The term is widely used for all devices that connect a computer to a wide area network, such as the Internet, even if the device does not modulate or demodulate.

Virtual private networks

modulation The modification of a digital signal (from a computer) into an analogue signal (for a phone line to transmit).

dial-up connection A connection to the Internet through a regular telephone and modem. Dial-up connections are slow, as opposed to broadband connections.

virtual private network (VPN) Hardware and software installed to ensure that a network path that includes the Internet enables employees of the same organization or employees of business partners to communicate confidentially. The hardware and software create an impression that the entire communication path is private.

A LAN is a private network, because it provides access only to members of an organization. Though a firm does not own the lines it leases, the network of leased lines might be considered a private network, because only members authorized by the organization can use it. In the Internet age, many companies that cannot afford a private network can create a **virtual private network (VPN)**. Although the Internet is discussed in Chapter 7, VPNs are important in the context of the current discussion.

A virtual private network (VPN) can be thought of as a 'tunnel' through the Internet or other public network that allows only authorized users to access company resources. The 'virtual' in VPN refers to the illusion that the user is accessing a private network directly, rather than through a public network. VPNs enable the use of intranets and extranets. An intranet is a network that uses web technologies to serve an organization's employees who are located in several sites that might be many miles apart; an extranet serves both the employees and other enterprises that do business with the organization. It is important to understand that once a LAN is linked to a public network, such as the Internet, technically anyone with access to the public network can obtain access to the LAN. Therefore, organizations that link their LANs to the Internet implement sophisticated security measures to control or totally deny public access to their resources.

Switching techniques

Imagine that your telephone could connect to only one other telephone. Of course, this limitation would render the telephone impractical. The same is true of communications when using computers. You want to be able to link your computer to every other computer on a network. Or, imagine that you can link to any other computer, but you have to wait for a specific communications path to open to conduct a conversation; no other path is available to you. So you might wait a long time until no one is using any segment of that path to make your call. Obviously, this wait would be very inconvenient. To avoid such inconveniences, data communications must have mechanisms to allow your messages to be routed through any number of paths: if one is busy, then another can be used. These mechanisms, called switching techniques, facilitate the flow of communications and specify how the messages travel to their destination. There are two major switching techniques – circuit switching and packet switching.

circuit switching A communication process in which a dedicated channel (circuit) is established for the duration of a transmission; the sending node signals the receiving node; the receiver acknowledges the signal and then receives the entire message.

packet switching A telecommunications method whereby messages are broken into groups of fixed amounts of bytes, and each group (packet) is transmitted through the shortest route available. The packets are assembled at the destination into the original message.

packet Several bytes that make up a part of a telecommunicated message.

Circuit switching In **circuit switching**, a dedicated channel (a circuit) is established for the duration of the transmission. The sending node signals the receiving node that it is going to send a message. The receiver must acknowledge the signal. The receiving node then receives the entire message. Only then can the circuit be allocated for use by two other communicating parties. Traditional telephone communication is the most common type of circuit-switching communication. The advantages of circuit switching are that data and voice can use the same line and that no special training or protocols are needed to handle data traffic. One disadvantage is the requirement that the communications devices be compatible at both ends.

Packet switching In **packet switching**, a message is broken up into packets. A **packet** is a group of bits transmitted together. In addition to the data bits, each packet includes sender and destination information, as well as error detection bits (see Figure 5.1). Each of the message's packets is passed from the source computer to the destination computer, often through intermediate nodes. At each node, the entire packet is received, stored and then passed on to the next node, until all packets, either kept together or reassembled, reach the destination.

Figure 5.1 A packet

On their way to their final destination, the packets are transmitted independently to intermediate nodes. Different packets of the same message might be routed through different paths to minimize delay and are then reassembled at their destination. This type of switching offers some advantages. Sending and receiving devices do not have to be speed-compatible because buffers in the network might receive data at one rate and retransmit it at another. The lines are used on demand rather than being dedicated to a particular call. With packet switching, a host computer can have simultaneous exchanges with several nodes over a single line. The main disadvantage of packet switching is that it requires complex routing and control software. When the load is high, there are delays. When the network is used for voice communication, a conversation with long delays might sound unnatural. Therefore, voice communication in traditional telephone systems uses circuit switching.

frame relay A high-speed packet switching protocol used on the Internet.

Frame relay is a high-speed packet-switching protocol used in WANs. The frames are variable-sized packets. The service provider's software determines the route for each frame so it can arrive at the destination the fastest. The variable size of packets allows more flexibility than with fixed-sized units; communication lines can be used more efficiently. One reason is the higher ratio of data bits to nondata bits (such as destination and source addresses) in each packet is greater. Larger packets also enable lines to stay idle for less time.

Circuit switching is ideal for real-time communications, when the destination must receive the message without delay. Packet switching is more efficient, but it is suitable only if some delay in reception is acceptable, or if the transmission is so fast that these delays do not adversely affect the communication. The switching rules in a network are part of the communication protocol. These protocols, along with increasingly faster Internet connections, enable the growing use of the Internet for packet-switching telephoning, known as VoIP, which we discuss later.

Multi-protocol label switching (MPLS) is a relatively recent packet-switching technology that enhances services such as VoIP. Messages are broken up into packets, and packets are still transmitted independently, but all are routed through the same path on the network. This minimizes the time gaps between receptions of the packets. Therefore, content that must be communicated in real time – such as voice and video – is received at higher quality than if the packets are routed through different paths.

Protocols

protocol A standard set of rules that governs telecommunication between two communications devices or in a network.

A communications protocol is a set of rules that govern communication between computers or between computers and other computer-related devices that exchange data. When these rules govern a network of devices, the rule set is often referred to as a *network protocol*. If a device does not know what the network's agreed-upon protocol is, or cannot comply with it, that device cannot communicate on that network.

In a way, a protocol is like human language and basic understanding. Human beings make certain gestures when they start a conversation, and certain words signal its end. Each element of the language, be it English, Chinese or Hindi, means the same thing to all parties who speak that language. Computers, too, need an agreed-upon set of rules to communicate. Some protocols are designed for WANs, others are designed for LANs, and some are designed specifically for wireless communications. This discussion addresses only some of these protocols. Protocols, often called 'standards', do not necessarily compete with each other. They often work together or serve different purposes. The most important and pervasive set of protocols for telecommunications and networks today is called TCP/IP.

TCP/IP (transmission control protocol/Internet protocol) A packet-switching protocol that is actually a set of related protocols that can guarantee packets are delivered in the correct order and can handle differences in transmission and reception rates.

backbone The network of copper lines, optical fibres and radio satellites that supports the Internet.

host A computer that contains files and other resources that can be accessed by 'clients', computers linked to it via a network.

Internet Protocol (IP) number A unique number assigned to a server or another device that is connected to the Internet for identification purposes. Consists of 32 bits.

DNS (domain name system) Hardware and software making up a server whose purpose is to resolve domain names (converting them back to IP numbers) and routing messages on the Internet.

static IP number An Internet Protocol number permanently associated with a device.

dynamic IP number The IP number assigned to a computer that is connected to the Internet intermittently for the duration of the computer's connection.

TCP/IP

Communication on the Internet follows mainly **TCP/IP (Transmission Control Protocol/Internet Protocol)**, which is actually a set of related protocols. TCP ensures that the packets arrive accurately and in the proper order, while IP ensures delivery of packets from node to node in the most efficient manner.

A computer connected directly to the Internet **backbone** – the highest speed communication channel – is called a **host**. IP controls the delivery from one host to another until the message is received by the host to which it was sent or one that is connected to a device to which it was sent. The host forwards messages to devices connected to it. Often, we call hosts servers. For example, your university or college has at least one email server. That email server forwards to your computer email messages addressed to you.

Every device on the Internet backbone is uniquely identified with a numerical label known as an **Internet protocol number**, or **IP number**, a 32-bit numeric address, presented in four parts separated by full stops, such as 146.186.87.220. Each of these parts can be a number between 1 and 254. If you know the IP number (also called the IP address) of a website, you can enter those numbers in the address box of a web browser. However, it is easier to remember names and words, and therefore most organizations associate their IP numbers with names. The process of associating a character-based name such as *course.com* with an IP number is called domain name resolution, and the domain name resolution service is **DNS (domain name system)**. DNS servers are maintained by Internet service providers (ISPs) and other organizations. In large organizations, a server can be dedicated as a DNS server.

If a LAN is linked to the Internet through a router and a modem, the entire network has an IP number unique on the Internet. That number is stored in the router. To uniquely identify devices on the LAN, the router assigns local IP numbers to individual computers and devices. These IP numbers identify the computers only within the LAN. It is the router that is identified uniquely on the Internet.

Servers and many other computers and devices are assigned permanent IP numbers, called a **static IP number**. A computer connected to the Internet intermittently might be assigned a temporary IP number for the duration of its connection only. Such a number is called a **dynamic IP number**. It is assigned by the host through which that computer is connecting to the Internet. Dynamic IP numbers give an organization flexibility with its limited number of assigned IP numbers: only modems seeking a connection to the Internet are assigned IP numbers. And the number is disassociated from a device that logs off. The server can then reassign the IP number to another modem that has just logged on. Some broadband providers assign static IP numbers; others assign only dynamic IP numbers.

Ethernet

The Institute of Electrical and Electronics Engineers (IEEE) sets standards for communication protocols. IEEE 802.3, known as **Ethernet**, is a highly popular LAN protocol. Ethernet uses either coaxial cable or twisted pair cable. Different generations of Ethernet support speeds from 10 Mbps (10Base-T) to 100 Mbps (100Base-T or Fast Ethernet) to over 1 Gbps (**Gigabit Ethernet** and 10 Gigabit Ethernet). Ethernet is known as a contention-based protocol, because devices on the network 'contend' with other devices on the network for transmission time. Each device constantly monitors the network to see if other devices are transmitting. A protocol called CSMA/CD (carrier sense multiple access with collision detection) ensures that there are no collisions in transmission and that each device transmits without interfering with another.

Ethernet The design, introduced and named by Xerox, for the contention-based data communications protocol.

Gigabit Ethernet A network protocol often used in local area networks (LANs) supporting up to 1 Gbps.

Wireless protocols

CD TASK

All wireless devices use radio transceivers (transmitter-receivers). The radio waves carry the digital signal, the bits. Depending on the protocol followed, the devices use different radio frequencies for their work.

IEEE 802.11 Wi-Fi **IEEE 802.11** is a family of wireless protocols, collectively known as **Wi-Fi** (for 'wireless fidelity'). The term originally applied to the IEEE 802.11b standard that supports communication within about 100 metres (300 feet) of a wireless router at a maximum speed of 11 Mbps. The more advanced 802.11g standard supports speeds of up to 54 Mbps for the same range. The g standard is backward-compatible with the b standard, meaning that you can add b or g devices to a g network. However, in a mixed b and g network, throughput for the b devices will likely be at the lower 802.11b speed. Both standards use a radio frequency in the 2.4–2.5 GHz range. This is the same frequency used by microwave ovens and some cordless phones. However, the Wi-Fi transmitting and receiving circuitry constantly looks for the best frequency (such as 2.401 GHz or 2.402 GHz) on which to communicate within that range, so 'collisions' with other devices are minimized. If interference with other devices or nearby wireless networks is a problem, the 802.11a standard is an option. The 802.11a standard operates in the 5 GHz range, and supports speeds of up to 54 Mbps at distances of about 20 metres (60 feet). However, the a standard is incompatible with the other Wi-Fi standards, and therefore is much less popular.

A single Wi-Fi router can be connected to an **access point (AP)**, which in turn is connected to a wired network and usually to the Internet, allowing tens to hundreds of Wi-Fi-equipped devices to share the Internet link. A direct link to a wireless router or AP creates a **hotspot**. Hotspots allow Internet access to anyone within range who uses a wireless-equipped device, provided logging in is not limited by controlled access codes. Figure 5.2 illustrates a home wireless LAN (WLAN).

As mentioned earlier, security has been a concern for Wi-Fi networks. The earliest 802.11 standards had serious security flaws; 802.11g and 802.11a have improved security by offering the wired equivalent privacy (WEP) protocol and the Wi-Fi protected access (WPA) and WPA2 security protocols. These protocols offer **encryption**, the ability to scramble and code messages through encryption keys that are shared only between the sender and receiver. Of course, to receive the protection of these protocols, they must be enabled on your wireless computer or device.

Wi-Fi hotspots are appearing everywhere, from airports and restaurant chains to the local library. However, businesses also use wireless LANs for many types of

IEEE 802.11 A standard for wireless communication. Several other IEEE 802.x standards have been approved by the Institute of Electrical and Electronics Engineers.

Wi-Fi A name given to the IEEE 802.11 standards of wireless communication. Wi-Fi technologies are used in hotspots and in home and office networks. Wi-Fi is usually effective for a radius of 300 feet.

access point (AP) An arrangement consisting of a device connected to the Internet on one end and to a router on the other end. All wireless devices link to the Internet through the router.

hotspot An area, usually of 300-feet radius, in which a wireless device can connect to the Internet. The hotspot is created by installing an access point consisting of a device connected to the Internet on one end and to a router on the other end. All wireless devices link to the Internet through the router.

Industry **SNAPSHOT**

Wi-Fi health concerns

A recent BBC *Panorama* programme highlighted the potential risks to school children caused by the proliferation of Wi-Fi networks in UK schools. There are calls for urgent clarification. 'Schools can't afford to delay while the scientists make up their minds', says John Dunford of the Association of School and College Leaders. And it is not only schools which are seeing the rise in such networks. Home use of Wi-Fi is growing and even if you do not have one in your home, you could be affected by your neighbour's. The increase in city-centre Wi-Fi networks is also a concern for some people. However, the Health Protection Agency (HPA) is making reassuring noises, sort of! Current evidence suggests that Wi-Fi does not represent a risk with low power signals of typically 0.1 Watt. However, the HPA does want more research. In the meantime, schools can't wait. 'Unless there is evidence that they are damaging, schools will continue to develop them – because they're finding that they're essential', says Dr Dunford.

SOURCE: 'Schools want urgent WiFi advice', Sean Coughlan, http://news.bbc.co.uk/1/hi/education/6676205.stm

PHOTO SOURCE: © LISA F. YOUNG

encryption The conversion of plaintext to an unreadable stream of characters, especially to prevent a party that intercepts telecommunicated messages from reading them. Special encryption software is used by the sending party to encrypt messages, and by the receiving party to decipher them.

operations. You will find a WLAN in almost every warehouse. Workers holding PDAs or specialized electronic units communicate with each other and receive information about the location of items by section, shelf and bin. For example, the forklifts in many warehouses are equipped with Wi-Fi transceivers to help their operators locate parts. Conference centres and universities use WLANs to help guests, students and staff to communicate as well as link to the Internet through a hotspot.

All new aeroplanes for long flights are equipped with WLANs. Boeing started equipping its large airplanes with Wi-Fi in 2003. Lufthansa, British Airways, Japan Airlines, Scandinavian Airlines System and other airlines have equipped their long-range jetliners with the technology to allow paying passengers to use a hotspot 12 miles above ground.

Utility companies are converting manually read electric, gas and water meters to wireless meters. Older versions still require a person to read the meter and record the reading, but new meters use networks that relay the signal to the utility company's office and automatically update each customer's account in the company's computers. Wireless meters save millions of labour hours and overcome common problems, such as meters enclosed in locked places, inaccurate reading and, occasionally, an aggressive dog.

Figure 5.2 A wireless home network

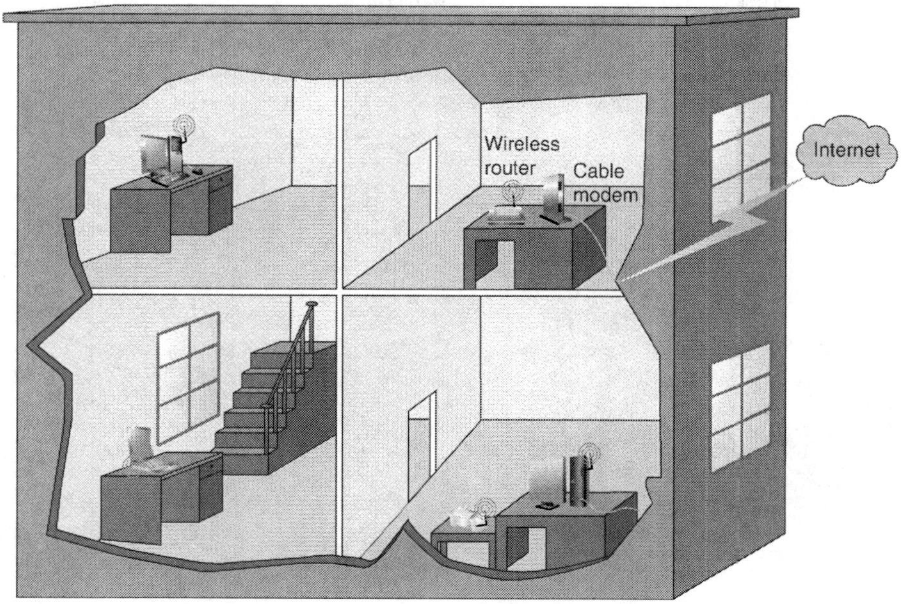

A growing number of electronic devices, such as mobile phones, PDAs, digital cameras and video game consoles, are equipped with wireless circuitry. This rids their owners of the need to physically connect a device to a computer or a router for communication. For example, with a wireless-enabled digital camera you can send digital pictures from your camera to your PC, or directly to a friend via a hotspot over the Internet.

IEEE 802.15 Bluetooth Named after a Scandinavian king who unified many tribes, the **Bluetooth** standard was developed for devices that communicate with each other within a short range of up to 10 metres (33 feet) in the office, at home and in motor vehicles. It transmits voice and data. Bluetooth was later adopted by IEEE as its 802.15 standard, which is compatible with the early versions of Bluetooth. Typical Bluetooth devices include wireless keyboards and mice, wireless microphones for mobile phones (especially for use in cars while driving), and increasingly, digital entertainment devices. For example, you can purchase a wrist-worn MP3 player that uses Bluetooth to transmit the music to earbuds or headphones, avoiding the wires that typically connect a portable player to headphones. Bluetooth is considered a personal area network (PAN) technology, because it typically supports a network used by only one person. Bluetooth use the 2.4–2.5 GHz radio frequency to transmit bits at a rate of 1 Mbps.

Bluetooth A personal wireless network protocol. It enables wireless communication between input devices and computers and among other devices within 10 metres.

IEEE 802.16 WiMAX IEEE 802.16, worldwide interoperability for microwave access (**WiMAX**), increases the range and speed of wireless communication. It might potentially reach up to 110 kilometres (about 70 miles) with a speed of 100 Mbps; however, it typically reaches 13–16 kilometres (8–10 miles). This standard can cover whole metropolitan areas and provide Internet access to hundreds of thousands of households that either cannot afford an Internet service or for some reason cannot obtain access. This has created a threat to the business of ISPs, who count on subscriber fees for revenue, because an entire metropolitan area can

WiMAX The IEEE 802.16 standard for wireless networking with a range of up to 50 km (31 miles). (WiMAX stands for the organization that promotes that standard, Worldwide Interoperability for Microwave Access.)

Figure 5.3 How WiMAX works

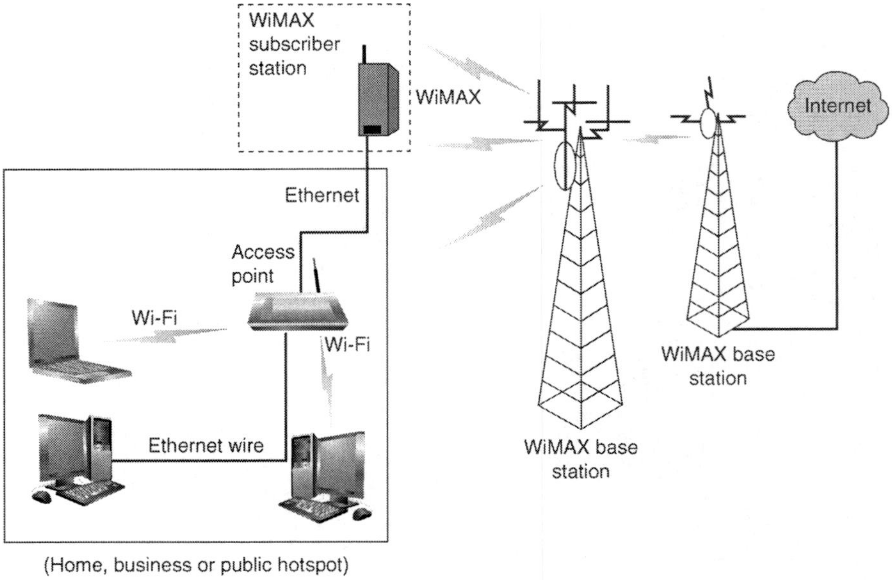

become one huge hotspot. Milton Keynes has become the UK's first trial metropolitan area for WiMAX. The trial began in 2006 and as of July 2007 there were 154 connected trialists. The feedback from them, following a survey by the company running the trial, Pipex, was generally favourable and the next step is to increase the trialist number to 500. The next area earmarked for the introduction of WiMAX is Warwick. WiMAX is a metropolitan area network (MAN) technology. Figure 5.3 shows how WiMAX works. A household, office or public hotspot can use a router to link multiple devices either by linking directly to a WiMAX base antenna that is linked to the Internet, or by using a relay antenna that receives the signal and retransmits it to the Internet-linked antenna. If a mobile user's equipment included the proper WiMAX communication device, the user could communicate with the Internet moving at speeds of up to 150 Km/H (about 94 MPH), which enables convenient use of the Internet while sitting in a moving vehicle (though the driver should not be going that fast!). An extension of this standard, 802.16e, supports mobile Internet communication. However, a newer, special standard dedicated to mobile communications is 802.20.

mobile broadband wireless access (MBWA) IEEE 801.20 standard to support continuous wireless connection while moving in vehicles.

IEEE 802.20 MBWA Mobile broadband wireless access (MBWA) functions similarly to mobile phone communications, because it controls communication from stationary towers. The purpose of MBWA is to provide mobile communication that is compatible with IP services. This should enable worldwide deployment of affordable, always-on wireless access. The principle is simple: place wireless routers on towers, so that mobile phones can use VoIP and access other Internet resources over wide areas and, eventually, globally. MBWA is expected to work at speeds over 1 Mbps, using licensed radio frequencies below 3.5 GHz. If the standard is successfully implemented globally, it will reduce subscriber fees significantly and pose severe competition to providers of mobile phone services.

The 802.20 standard is designed to be compatible with 802.11 (Wi-Fi) and 802.15 (Bluetooth). It can support Internet communication at a moving speed of up to 250 Km/H (156 MPH). MBWA promises to support practically everything that we now do with

Table 5.3 Wireless networking protocols

Protocol	Max. range	Max. speed	Main use
802.11a	19 metres (60 feet)	54 Mbps	LAN
802.11b	100 metres (300 feet)	11 Mbps	LAN
802.11g	100 metres (300 feet)	54 Mbps	LAN
802.15 Bluetooth	10 metres (33 feet)	1 Mbps	PAN
802.16 WiMax	50 km (31 miles)	100 Mbps	MAN
802.20 MBWA	Global	4 Mbps	Mobile voice, data and Internet communications

telephones and through the Internet: web browsing, file transfer, email, VoIP, video telephony and videoconferencing, audio streaming (such as listening to transmitted music), web-based gaming and file sharing. Table 5.3 summarizes relevant features of the 802.xx wireless protocols discussed here.

Generations in mobile communications

Networking professionals often refer to generations of mobile communication technologies. Each generation refers to a communication protocol or a combination of protocols. The differences among generations are mainly in capabilities (e.g., enabling a mobile phone to access additional resources) and transmission speed. The first generation, 1G, was analogue and used circuit switching. Then 2G protocols became the first to provide digital voice encoding, and they worked at faster transmission rates. They include the GSM (global system for mobile) and CDMA (code division multiple access) protocols, the details of which are outside the scope of this discussion. They lack security measures. Then 2.5G, between 2G and 3G, stepped up the speed of digital mobile communication to 144 Kbps and enabled limited Internet access by mobile phones through packet switching. The 2.5G protocol combines digital mobile telephoning with some IP capabilities. This is the set of protocols used by most mobile phones in the early 2000s.

Industry **SNAPSHOT**

Complementary technologies

In a way, 3G mobile technologies compete with Wi-Fi, but it seems that eventually the technologies will complement each other: we will use 3G outdoors and Wi-Fi indoors. Wi-Fi is significantly less expensive to use than 3G. Fixed-mobile convergence (FMC) is a system whereby a single telephone device will contact an access point using short range wireless communication when in range and general mobile communications methods when outside the range. The user does not need to know which is being used or do anything special – the device does the work.

The 3G protocols support transmission rates of 1 Mbps. The protocols support video, videoconferencing and full Internet access. The 4G protocol devices operate only digitally and with packet switching, transmit at bandwidths of up to 100 Mbps, and include tighter security measures. Some of the protocols that comprise 4G are still under development. The high speed of the technology will enable the holder of a mobile phone handset to watch a DVD-quality video, listen to CD-quality music files, browse the Web and make a telephone call at the same time.

Internet networking services

CD TASK

Both organizations and individuals can choose from a variety of options when subscribing to networking services. The proliferation of high-speed connection services, also called broadband services, is mainly the result of businesses' and individuals' rush to the Internet.

Cable

Cable Internet links are provided by television cable firms. The medium is the same as for television reception, but the firms connect the cable to an Internet server. At the subscriber's residence, the cable is split – one part is connected to the television set, and the other is connected to the computer via a bridge that is often called a cable modem. Both television transmission and data are transmitted through the same line. The cable link is always on, so the computer is constantly connected to the Internet. The subscriber does not have to dial up any telephone number.

The major downside of cable is that cable nodes are shared by all the subscribers connected to the node. Therefore, at peak times, such as television prime time (7–11 p.m.), communication speed slows down. The speed also slows down as more subscribers join the service in a given territory.

digital subscriber line (DSL) Technology that relieves individual subscribers of the need for the conversion of digital signals into analogue signals between the telephone exchange and the subscriber jack. DSL lines are linked to the Internet on a permanent basis and support bit rates significantly greater than a normal telephone line between the subscriber's jack and the telephone exchange.

Digital subscriber line (DSL)

With normal telephone service, the telephone company filters information that arrives in digital form and then transforms it to analogue form; thus, it requires a modem to transform the signal back to digital form. This conversion constrains the capacity of the link between your telephone (or computer) and the telephone company's switching centre to a low speed of 56 Kbps.

With **digital subscriber line (DSL)**, data remain digital throughout the entire transmission; they are never transformed into analogue signals. So, the telephone

Industry SNAPSHOT

Broadband on the rise

In 2005, there were 150 million subscribers to broadband links (cable and DSL) in the world, most of them in the Asia-Pacific region. The number is expected to grow to 400 million by 2009. The gap between the number of DSL subscribers and cable subscribers is growing. The reason is simple: while there are more than 1 billion telephone subscriber lines in the world, there are only 530 million homes with cable service.

SOURCE: IMS Research, 2005

Industry SNAPSHOT

The United States, a broadband laggard

Because of little competition among telecommunications companies, the United States lags behind other countries in the proportion of households that enjoy broadband links to the Internet. Only 42 per cent of American households had broadband in 2005 (mainly through cable and DSL). The proportion was greater in Japan, South Korea, Denmark and Canada, where more broadband companies compete for business, thereby driving down the cost. In South Korea, for instance, 73 per cent of households had broadband links. The speed of broadband in those countries is greater than what Americans experience and the service is less expensive. In Japan, for example, some households reach 100 Mbps. About 20 per cent of US households could not have access to broadband even if they chose to subscribe to the service, because broadband is not offered where they live.

SOURCE: S. Lacy, 'America: Still the High-Speed Laggard', *Business Week*, 6 April 2005

company can transmit to subscribers' computers at significantly higher speeds of up to 8 Mbps. To provide DSL service, the telecommunications company connects your telephone line to a DSL bridge (often called a DSL modem). At the telephone company's regional central office, DSL traffic is aggregated and forwarded to the ISP or data network provider with which the subscriber has a contract. Often, the telephone company is also the ISP.

T1 and T3 lines There are several types of DSL, whose details are beyond the scope of this book, but they can be generally placed in one of two categories: symmetric and asymmetric. Asymmetric DSL (ADSL) allows reception at a much faster rate than transmission, that is, it is faster downstream than upstream. (Often, the respective terms 'download' and 'upload' are used.) The reason for the faster download is that home users and small businesses usually receive significantly more information (from the Web, for example) than they transmit. Symmetric DSL (SDSL) is designed for short-distance connections that require high speed in both directions. Many ADSL technologies are actually RADSL (rate adaptive DSL) technologies; the speed is adjusted based on signal quality. Some ADSL technologies let subscribers use the same telephone lines for both Internet connection and analogue voice telephone service. Symmetric DSL lines cannot share lines with telephones.

The bit rates of DSL lines are closely related to the distance of the subscriber's computer from the regional central office of the telephone company. Telecommunications companies might offer the service to subscribers as far as 6100 metres (20,000 feet) from the central office, but the speed then is usually no faster than 144 Kbps, unless the company has installed a DSL repeater on the line. Some companies do not offer the service if the subscriber's address is not within 4500 metres (15,000 feet) of the central office. Most subscribers have ADSL, so the upstream speed is significantly lower than the downstream speed.

Leased lines

Leased lines are point-to-point dedicated digital circuits provided by telephone companies. They are expensive and, therefore, only businesses that must rely on high speeds are willing to accept the high cost of subscribing to the service. Most universities, as well as large companies, use leased for their backbone and Internet connections.

leased lines Point-to-point dedicated digital circuits provided by telephone companies.

Ethical and Societal ISSUES

Telecommuting: pros and cons

Often, when you are introduced to people, you mention your occupation, and then you might be asked, 'Where do you work?' Many employed people now answer, 'At home.' They do not commute; they *telecommute*, or, as some prefer to call it, they *telework*. They have the shortest commute to work: from the bedroom to another room in the home that is equipped with a PC and a broadband Internet link. For an increasing number of workers, IT provides all that's needed to create the goods their employers sell: software, analysis reports, literature, tax returns and many other types of output. If they need data from the office, they can connect to their office intranet using VPN software and retrieve the required information. If they need to talk to supervisors or co-workers, they use their computers to conduct videoconferencing. And when they complete their product, they can simply email it or place it on a remote server.

Telecommuting on the rise According to the UK Office of National Statistics, more than 2.1 million people already work from home, with 8 million more spending at least some of their working week in their home instead of the office. In certain parts of the UK the benefits are obvious. A success story reported on www.itwales.com shows how rural locations can support telecommuting. 'Reynoldston is a small village in Gower (outside of Swansea) and is widely known not only as the home of King Arthur's stone but for its spectacular coastal views. For architectural consultant, David Clarke, Reynoldston was the ultimate retirement destination from his busy Oxford practice. However, his retirement plans hinged on one factor . . . the availability of broadband, so that he could continue work as a specialist architectural consultant. Just like hundreds of other people moving to Wales for the first time, David couldn't fathom that such a remote community could have access to broadband. But it does, thanks to the Reynoldston Community Wireless Network, a village initiative that provides a local wireless network to homes in the village. Now David's consultancy is flourishing as he benefits from a better work/life balance, reduced travel costs and more time to spend with his clients.'

Telecommuting has increased productivity and reduced employee stress. Pitney Bowes, a business communications company with 32,000 employees, noticed increased productivity in employees on their telecommuting days. Managers there believe that telecommuting increases productivity because it accommodates both the 'morning person' and 'night owl' who can work at the time of day that best fits their preferences. From an economic perspective, telecommuting saves travel cost and time. It also decreases pollution. And it might reduce unemployment by allowing people who would otherwise not work because they are not within commuting distance the opportunity to join the workforce.

Employment opportunities Telecommuting enables people who could otherwise not work to join or rejoin the workforce. This includes not only people who live far away from the offices of companies that would like to hire them but also whole groups in the population that otherwise might not be able to join certain businesses. Disabled people and parents of small children can work from home. Older people who would rather retire than commute might stay in the workforce if allowed to work at home. Organizations hungry for labour can tap a larger supply of workers if they offer telecommuting.

Saving time and money Organizations like telecommuting because it saves the cost of office space. Studies have shown that for each teleworker the annual saving on office space is US$5,000–10,000. When Nortel Networks allowed 4000 of its 13,000 employees to telecommute, it saved US$20 million per year on real estate. Studies also have shown that teleworkers are more productive by 15–50 per cent than their office counterparts. Telecommuters like their arrangement because they save the time and money they would spend on commuting. Telecommuting reduces millions of tons of pollutants, saves billions of gallons of petrol, and frees billions of personal hours for leisure time. AT&T, the telecommunications giant, reported in 2000 that its telecommuting programme increased productivity by 45 per cent and saved 50 per cent on office space costs. Another report, by British Telecom and Gartner Group, said that telecommuting reduced office space and other costs equivalent to 17 per cent of annual salary costs.

The downside However, not everyone is so enthusiastic about telecommuting. Sociologists have mixed opinions about the phenomenon. On one hand, telecommuting allows people to work who would otherwise remain outside the workforce, such as older professionals and many disabled people. On the other hand, it has been found that employers tend to pressure telecommuters to work harder than office workers. In the office an employee works a set number of hours, but the home worker has no defined workday; his or her workday is, the employer often assumes, 24 hours per day. In addition, telecommuters are more estranged from their fellow workers. For telecommuters, there is no office in which to foster new social ties and camaraderie.

The AT&T report said that teleworkers typically worked an hour more per day than their office-bound colleagues, which amounted to 250 hours per year. The British Telecom and Gartner Group report said that the average telecommuter works 11 per cent more hours than his or her office-bound brethren. Perhaps this extra time is what companies observe as added productivity. Although this extra work time is good for corporations, it is not so good for workers: when you telecommute, you work more for no additional compensation.

Telecommuting might foster isolation. Teleworkers share fewer experiences with other people. In addition, leaving the workplace behind means leaving behind one more community that gives many people a sense of belonging, even if this belonging amounts only to having a sandwich together at lunchtime and complaining about the boss. At the same time, some managers might prefer to see their employees in the office and keep them in their 'line of sight'.

On a wider level, telecommuting could severely affect some segments of national economies. Imagine the huge drop in revenue of large city restaurants during lunchtime if the number of commuters rushing to grab lunch between 12 and 2 p.m. were to halve. Some cities' dining industries could crumble if the telecommuting trend continues at the current pace. Many people live in cities mainly because of proximity to their offices, thus further movement to suburbs and remote residential areas would gut many other industries in central cities.

Many workers, given the option to work at home, have decided to return to the office. Interestingly, this happens also in the very industries that are so amenable to telecommuting, such as software development. These returning workers claim they missed social interaction with their peers, hallway chats, lunches with friends and direct communication with fellow workers and supervisors. But telecommuting has grown, and will probably continue to grow, especially thanks to greater availability of broadband services and their declining monthly fees. If the trend continues, offices occupied by organizations will be significantly smaller than they are now and will serve as the symbolic rather than physical centres of the organizations' activities.

Satellite

Businesses and households in rural areas and other regions that do not have access to cable or DSL might be able to obtain satellite services, which use microwave radio transmission. In fact, satellite service providers target these households. The service provider installs a dish antenna that is tuned to a communications satellite. Satellite connections might reach a speed of 45 Mbps. Many people use a free satellite service, the global positioning system (GPS). While a proper device is required to enable reception from the satellites (which were launched into orbit by the US government), anyone can communicate free of charge. The satellite transmits back to any GPS device its location on earth by longitude and latitude.

Fixed wireless

fixed wireless A network of fixed transceivers to facilitate connection to the Internet. Requires line of sight between transceivers.

Another alternative for households and small businesses that cannot obtain cable or DSL connections to the Internet is fixed wireless. **Fixed wireless** is point-to-point transmission between two stationary devices, usually between two buildings, as opposed to mobile wireless, in which people carry a mobile device. ISPs that specialize in fixed wireless services are often referred to as WISPs, wireless ISPs. They install microwave transceivers on rooftops instead of laying physical wires and cables. Subscribers connect their computers to the rooftop transceiver. They can communicate at speeds up to 2 Mbps. Repeaters are installed close to each other to enhance the signal, which can deteriorate in the presence of buildings and trees, and foul weather. Transmission rates depend on the distance between the receiver and the base station. Up to 14 kilometres (9 miles) from the base station, the speed is 100 Mbps; speeds drop to about 2 Mbps at about 56 kilometres (35 miles) from the base.

Fixed wireless is highly modular – the telecommunications company can add as many transceivers as it needs to serve a growing number of subscribers. Unlike cable service, the company does not need franchise licences. The technology is suitable for both urban and rural areas.

Optical carrier

OC (optical carrier) A family of several very high-speed technologies using optical fibres. Usually, the standard is marked as OC-3, OC-12, OC-48, etc.

Companies willing to pay high fees can enjoy very high connection speeds. The services are denoted with **OC**, the acronym for **optical carrier**, because all of these services are provided through optical fibre lines. The number next to OC refers to data speed in multiples of 51.84 Mbps, considered the base rate bandwidth. Thus, when available, the services are denoted as C-1, C-3, C-9, C-12, C-18, C-48, and so on through C-3072. For illustration, OC-768 (40 Gbps) enables you to transmit the content of seven CDs in 1 second. Typical businesses that purchase the services are ISPs, providers of search engines and businesses that wish to support content-rich websites and high-volume traffic. However, media companies have also purchased such services because the high speeds support streaming video. Among companies that use OC-768, for instance, are Deutsche Telecom, NBC, Disney, the US Department of Defense Advanced Research Projects Agency (the agency that developed the Internet), NASA and Nippon TV.

Broadband over power lines (BPL)

broadband over power lines (BPL) A broadband service provided over electric power lines.

As mentioned in the discussion on communications media, electric power lines are capable of carrying digital signals. Subscribers simply plug their BPL modem into standard electrical wall outlets. Usually, utility companies partner with telecommunications companies to provide **broadband over power lines (BPL)**. Interestingly, even if BPL service availability is to lag far behind cable and optical fibre in terms of subscribers and revenue, utility companies are likely to invest in the technology for their own use. They can use BPL to monitor power consumption down to the household, detect power failure in real time, track power outages by region, automate some customer services and remotely control substations. Collecting and analysing such business information might make the utility companies more efficient.

The speed and monthly service for BPL are similar to those of DSL, but the highest current speeds are lower than the highest speeds offered by DSL providers. The hope was that households in rural areas, where neither cable nor DSL service is available, could enjoy BPL. However, the density of households in rural areas is lower than the density of households where the other services are already offered. Utility companies have found that investing in the equipment required to provide BPL to a small number of households does not make business sense, and therefore it is unlikely that many rural areas will be offered BPL.

The future of networking technologies

CD TASK

This section takes a look at networking technologies and trends that are likely to have a great impact on businesses and the management of information in the near future: broadband telephoning, radio frequency identification and the convergence of digital technologies.

Broadband telephoning

While regular long-distance telephone companies charge according to the number of minutes a call lasts, Internet service providers (ISPs) charge customers a flat monthly fee for connection to the Internet. With the proper software and microphones attached to their computers, Internet users can conduct long-distance and international conversations via their Internet connection for a fraction of regular calling costs. The technology is called Internet telephoning, IP telephoning, or **VoIP (Voice over Internet Protocol)**. Organizations can purchase the proper software or use the services of companies that specialize in providing IP telephoning, offering inexpensive use of their VoIP hardware and software for PC-to-PC, PC-to-telephone and telephone-to-telephone voice communication.

VoIP (Voice over Internet Protocol) Technologies that enable voice communication by utilizing the Internet instead of the telephone network.

PC-to-PC calls can be conducted free of charge by using the service of a company such as Skype. Phone-to-phone service requires an additional modem, but it does not require a new phone or phone number, and it does not require routing calls through a home computer.

In 2007, British Telecom announced that the number of UK subscribers to its Broadband Talk and Softphone VoIP services had hit the one million mark.

In addition to sound quality, there are other differences between traditional and VoIP telephone services. Most VoIP services do not include the ability to call an emergency number such as 999. Also, when your link to the Internet is down, so is your VoIP service. Since the phone uses a modem that requires electric power, if power is out, the phone cannot be

Skype was founded in 2003 and generates revenue through its premium services such as VoIP calls to landlines and mobile phones.

used. However, VoIP providers offer some advantages over traditional telephoning. A subscriber receives a special converter into which the telephone number is programmed. The subscriber can take the converter anywhere there is a broadband link to the Internet and use it. This makes the VoIP telephone portable.

Some experts see the future of telephony in a convergence of the mobile phone and VoIP phone: you will use only one mobile phone. When outside the home or office, you will use the mobile phone network; when back home or in the office, the phone will communicate through a VoIP service. This will reduce the higher cost of mobile phone minutes.

Radio frequency identification

In Chapter 3 you learned about the great efficiency and business intelligence that companies, especially in manufacturing and retail, can gain from one particular type of communications technology: radio frequency identification (RFID). This section explains in more detail how RFID works. RFID tags can be very tiny, about the size of a rice grain, or several square inches, depending on the amount of information they need to contain and the environment in which they are used. They are not always flat; they can be cylindrical. The tags need very little power. Passive tags use power from the reader that queries them; active tags have their own tiny batteries, which increase the range of the reading range. These tiny batteries last a long time.

An RFID system works as follows: objects are equipped, often embedded, with a tag. The tag contains a transponder. A transponder is a radio transceiver (transmitter-receiver) that is activated for transmission by a signal that is transmitted to it. The tag is equipped with digital memory that is given a unique electronic product code (EPC). The interrogator, a combination of an aerial, a transceiver and a decoder, emits a signal activating the RFID tag so the interrogator can read data from it and write data to it. (Although the interrogator also writes

Industry **SNAPSHOT**

Getting under your skin

A night club in Barcelona, Spain, offers its regular customers a chance to get 'chipped' instead of bringing their wallets when they visit. A tiny RFID chip called VeriChip after the company that manufactures it is injected painlessly into their arm and resides under the skin. The chip, the size of a rice grain, is housed in a glass capsule. A reader identifies customers when they enter. Another reader charges their drinks and other expenses at the club to the customers' accounts. Removing the chip is done with the same syringe-like device with which it was injected. The same capsule can be used with patients to track diseases and treatments.

SOURCE: 'Barcelona Clubbers Get Chipped', BBC online (http://news.bbc.co.uk), 29 September 2004

An inplantable VeriChip microchip next to a grain of rice.

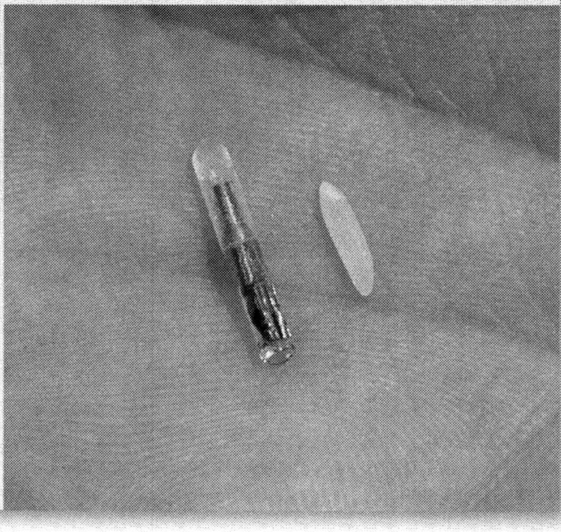

PHOTO SOURCE: © COURTESY OF VERICHIP

to the tag, it is often called a reader.) When an RFID tag enters the reader's electromagnetic zone, it detects the reader's activation signal. The reader decodes the data stored in the tag's memory, and the data are passed to a host computer for processing.

In the US, Wal-Mart, Gillette, Procter & Gamble and 84 other companies embarked on a project that might radically change supply chains. The companies use microchips that are embedded in products to replace the ubiquitous bar codes for tracking and checkout at store registers. Each microchip holds a product identification number. The microchips communicate with wireless computers, including handheld and laptop computers, as they are moved in the production line, packed, picked, shipped, unloaded, shelved and paid for by customers. As the product moves, the information about its location is communicated to a network of computers to which all businesses involved in the production and sale have access. This is often a Wi-Fi network. The big benefits are a just-in-time (JIT) system that minimizes inventory throughout the supply chain to almost zero and shelves that are always stocked. JIT, or a situation that is close to JIT, can be accomplished thanks to up-to-the-minute information about available inventory and when the next shipment from a supplier is needed. 'Smart shelves', equipped with tiny wireless transceivers, alert staff whenever the shelf is running out of units, so the staff can put more units on the shelf immediately.

RFID is used for many other purposes as well, as Figure 5.4 shows. For many businesses, the main impediment is the price of an RFID tag. As the unit cost of each tag reduces, it is likely that the uses of the technology, such as thoses as listed in Table 5.4, will increase.

Converging technologies

Recall the discussion of converging hardware technologies in the previous chapter. Convergence occurs also in networking technologies. Mobile phones used to be able to transmit and receive only through a dedicated network of analogue or digital transceivers. Now many are constructed with dual technologies, so that they can serve both as a 'traditional' mobile phone and a wireless web phone. When the circuitry detects that it is within the range of a hotspot, calling switches to VoIP to save cost. As mentioned earlier, a landline phone is no longer just a line phone but can be also a VoIP phone. And eventually, we will be able to use the same phone as a landline phone, a VoIP phone and a mobile phone, depending on availability of service and the cost and quality we are willing to accept.

At home, new television sets are designed to connect to cable, satellites and the Internet, not only alternately, but concurrently. Thus, we will be able to watch a sports game and chat online about it at the same time through the same device, using two different networking technologies. PDAs can already function as television sets and phones. Soon they will be able to do so simultaneously. For individuals, this means they can carry a single device that will connect them to any type of network, erasing the lines between radio, television, telephone and Internet surfing. To businesses this gives an opportunity to provide new information services and manage a more effective and efficient salesforce.

Wireless technologies can be combined in the same device to enhance functionality. For example, a portable digital music and video player can use Wi-Fi to communicate with your PC or another Wi-Fi device (possibly another music/video player) to download files. It can then use Bluetooth to transmit the music to your wireless earphones. When WiMAX is implemented, some local radio stations are likely to use MANs as additional broadcast channels. With proper software you can then select from the songs to which you have just listened and have them downloaded to your portable player or home computer.

Figure 5.4 RFID applications

Use	Example
Access control	Cards used to replace door keys.
People tracking	Keep children within school. Track prisoners on probation and prevent fleeing.
Animal tracking	Track pets.
Livestock management	Track life cycle of farm animals (e.g., feeding and immunization). Equip each cow with a unique ID to track diseases.
Antitheft measures	Transponders integrated into car keys. Only a legal key can start the engine.
Transportation	At airports, safety inspection of tagged luggage.
Retail	Tracking products in pallets and on shelves. Contactless payment.
Pharmaceuticals	Prevent drug counterfeiting.
Health care	Tag people who enter and leave an epidemic zone.

Table 5.4 Future uses of RFID

Use in...	Activity
Shopping	Identify dresses in your size, if you hold or wear a personal tag. Enhanced product information on your PDA/cell phone. Personalized customer service. Passive self-checkout. Dynamic pricing by demand. Return RFID tagged items without receipt.
Product information	Scan an RFID tag of an item and download additional information about it from an Internet site to your mobile phone. Use your mobile phone to check the price of an item while in a competitor's store.
Manufacturer serving customers	Send recall message to customer mobile phone or email address. Send warranty and recall messages to customer.
Appliances	Washing machine automatically sets proper wash cycle based on information on tags attached to clothes. Refrigerator alerts you about expired or recalled foods, notifies you about items consumed and prepares shopping lists. It can also log on to the Internet and search for recipes of dishes you can prepare with refrigerated items.
Agriculture	Tags attached to crops can transmit information about weather and soil conditions and trigger automatic irrigation.
Waste management	Track hazardous materials to ensure proper disposal. Sort recyclable items.

SUMMARY

Telecommunication is communication over distance, primarily communication of bits representing many forms of data and information. In the past decade, telecommunications technology has driven the major developments in the dissemination and use of information.

Telecommunications technology has changed the business environment. Businesspeople are increasingly more mobile; they can use mobile phones for greater availability to their employers and customers, using the phone for both voice and data communications. Videoconferencing brings together people who are thousands of miles apart. Peer-to-peer file sharing enables sharing of research, software code and artistic works.

Different media have different bandwidths, meaning that they are capable of carrying different numbers of bits per second (bps) without garbling messages. Wired media include twisted pair, coaxial and optical fibre cable. Wireless media include light waves (infrared) and radio waves, including terrestrial and satellite microwave.

Networks are classified according to their reach and complexity. When computers are connected locally within an office, a campus, or a home, the arrangement is called a local area network (LAN). A metropolitan area network (MAN) connects LANs within a radius of about 50 kilometres (30 miles). When computers communicate over longer distances, the network is called a wide area network (WAN). Personal area networks (PANs) connect individual devices at short range.

Although it uses the public Internet, a network can be turned into a virtual private network (VPN) by using tight security measures.

There are two ways to switch a communication line. In circuit switching, a message is communicated in its entirety from the transmitting computer to the receiving computer while the communication path is fully devoted to the exchange between the two nodes. In packet switching, data are divided into packets of bits and transmitted via several paths on the network. Internet protocols work with packet switching.

Network protocols are sets of rules to which all devices on a network must adhere. Communications on the Internet adheres to a set of protocols called TCP/IP. Ethernet has long been a popular protocol for wired LANs. Wireless protocols open great opportunities for more people to enjoy Internet links and for mobility while communicating. The most important are the IEEE 802.xx protocols, which include the popular Wi-Fi, Bluetooth and WiMAX standards.

Wireless technologies make it easy and affordable to create wireless LANs (WLANs) and hotspots. They allow workers mobility while retrieving information in warehouses and other work environments. They enable airline and retail customers to link to the Internet with portable computers. They make the reading of utility meters much less labour-intensive and more accurate.

Organizations and individuals have a variety of choices when subscribing to networking services. They can choose among digital subscriber lines (DSL), cable lines, T1 and T3 lines, satellite links, fixed wireless service, optical carriers (OC) and broadband over power lines (BPL). OC is expected to reach the speed of 10 Tbps in the foreseeable future.

As Internet links become faster, Internet telephoning, also know as Voice over Internet Protocol (VoIP), is gaining in popularity. Several companies offer the service, which is significantly less expensive than a land telephone line.

Wireless technologies support the increasingly popular RFID technologies. They support a variety of noncontact identification and payment mechanisms, from quick toll and gas payment to cattle tracking to sophisticated supply chain management, and many future uses are anticipated.

Much like hardware, telecommunications technologies are merging. The same device can now use several different networks simultaneously, such as mobile telephone networks, the Internet and television broadcasts.

Increasing numbers of employees now telecommute. Telecommuting has advantages, but it does not serve some basic human needs, such as socializing, the short hallway chat during lunch break, and the clear separation between work and family obligations.

Trent Courier Services

TRENT COURIER SERVICES REVISITED

Trent Couriers has upgraded its telecommunications systems – from beepers to mobile phones, from handheld computers to handheld computers with a wireless Internet connection, from a single local office to three networked offices, and from DSL Internet access to fixed wireless access. At each point, Andrew Langston has expanded his communications ability.

What would you do?

If Trent Couriers could have connected its offices to the Internet via coaxial cable or T1 line in time, should it have opted for either of those connections over fixed wireless access? Investigate the costs and capabilities of each and give your opinion.

Now that messengers carry mobile phones, Trent Couriers can track their movements for every delivery and know where they are at all times. Consider Trent Couriers' existing 'family' culture. Should it follow its couriers' moves to check for efficiency? Why or why not?

A local marketing company has approached Andrew to see whether he would be willing to sell his customer list to them. Providing the information would be simple for Trent Couriers. Do you think it should do so? Why or why not?

New perspectives

During a conversation with a representative from the mobile phone company, the representative suggested to Mary that Trent Couriers purchase smart phones for their messengers. What would be the advantage of smart phones over the mobile phones that they are now carrying? Would this investment be financially worthwhile?

Andrew has seen customers at Starbucks wirelessly logging on to the Web through Wi-Fi connections. What factors should he consider to determine whether Wi-Fi devices would be a good option for his business?

A traffic-monitoring company has called on Andrew to offer its service. The representative says that his company can provide real-time traffic reports in the Stoke-on-Trent area. Dispatchers would be able to receive periodic or on-demand reports through their handheld web-enabled devices and view traffic conditions as they happen. Should Trent Couriers consider this service? What does it need to know to decide? Draw up a list of questions that Andrew should ask the representative.

Review questions

1. If we could see all the paths of data communications, we might be overwhelmed. Give some examples.
2. Why can't whole bytes be transmitted over a distance?
3. What makes one channel medium capable of greater data communication speed than another?
4. On many communication lines repeaters are used. What for? What does a repeater do?
5. Networking professionals speak of 'the last mile'. What is 'the last mile', and what is its significance?
6. Would an astronomy observatory 20 miles away from a city or town be able to get DSL service?

7 What risks to organizations does the growing use of networks pose?

8 What is a virtual private network? Why is it called 'virtual'?

9 What is a network protocol?

10 What are the technical advantages of optical fibres over other communications media?

11 What is the difference between circuit switching and packet switching?

12 Why does circuit switching accommodate voice communication more effectively than packet switching?

13 What is VoIP? Since VoIP uses packet switching, why is voice quality better now than several years ago?

14 What is ADSL? What does the A stand for, and what does it mean in terms of communicating with the Internet? Why do households receive only ADSL services and not other DSL services?

15 What is BPL? Why is the technology potentially available to almost every home?

16 Explain the notions of WAN, LAN, MAN and PAN.

17 What are hotspots, and how can they help businesspeople?

18 What is the purpose of WiMAX, and why is it in competition with subscriber broadband services?

19 Mobile phones are already wireless. Why should companies be interested in equipping employees with Wi-Fi-enabled mobile phones?

Discussion questions

1 Wi-Fi is all around us. Is there any downside to its pervasiveness?

2 People express themselves differently when they speak (either face to face or via the telephone) versus when they send and receive email. What are the differences? Which do you prefer when communicating with someone you don't know personally? Which do you prefer when you know the person?

3 Every home with access to the Internet can now inexpensively become a hotspot. How so? Are there any risks in turning a home into a hotspot?

4 What are the implications of telecommunications for group work?

5 As broadband services cover larger and larger regions and become less expensive, the number of small businesses and home businesses grows. What is the relationship?

6 Some organizations stopped allocating offices to their sales representatives. Why, and is this a wise move?

7 List and explain the benefits of video-conferencing to an organization. List and explain the benefits to society.

8 Anything that does not take space can be traded solely via telecommunications networks. Do you agree? Explain your answer.

9 Do you see any undesirable effects of humans communicating more and more via computer networks rather than in person or over the telephone? What don't you like and why? What do you like about it?

10 List several industries in which telecommuting would be infeasible. Explain why.

11 Wi-Fi circuitry is now embedded in consumer electronic devices such as digital cameras and mobile phones. Give an example of what you could do with the Wi-Fi capability of a digital camera.

12 If you were given the opportunity to telecommute, would you? Why or why not?

13 Suppose that you are a middle manager. Would you allow the people who report to you to telecommute? Why or why not?

Tutorial activities

1 Ima Jeenyes completed her book, *How to Become a Millionaire upon Graduation*. She used a word processor to type the manuscript. She saved the book as a file of 5.7 MB. Ima lives in Bristol. The publisher asked that Ima transmit the book via the Internet to the publisher's office in Manchester. Ima can transmit the file at a guaranteed speed of 400 Kbps. Because each packet of data transmitted must also contain some nondata

bits, assume the total number of bits to transmit is equivalent to 6 MB.

How long (in minutes) does it take to transmit the book? Ignore the distance between the cities. Remember how many bytes make up 1 MB. Show your calculations clearly using a spreadsheet. Use measurement units throughout your calculation.

2 Justin Tyme uses a DSL modem to transmit a report from his office to headquarters. The DSL affords an average bit rate transmission (upload) of 250 Kbps. Since the transmission protocol adds additional bits to data bytes, assume that, on average, there is 1 additional bit for each transmitted byte. On average, a page contains 3000 characters, including spaces. Justin is allotted only 3 minutes for the transmission. How many pages can he transmit?

3 Find out which residential telecommunication services are available where you live and how much they cost. You might find several DSL and cable services, and perhaps also satellite and BPL services. Calculate the ratio of maximum downloaded bit rate per euro (or your local currency) to monthly fee for each service. Which service provides the 'biggest bang for the buck', that is, the greatest speed per euro of monthly fee?

4 Broadband services provided in Japan, South Korea and Canada are usually faster and less expensive than in the United States. Use the Web to research why this is so. Write a one-page report discussing the reasons.

5 Search the Web for a site that enables you to check your high-speed (broadband) link: DSL, cable, or (if you connect from university or college) leased line. Follow the instructions. Usually, you simply have to click one button. Do so and wait for the response. Print out the response. Wait a minute, and repeat the process. The speeds are likely to be different. Why?

6 You are a telecommunications guru and love to help individuals and businesses. Assume that dial-up, cable, DSL, T3 line and satellite links to the Internet are available everywhere unless the particular scenario indicates otherwise. Consider the following scenarios and suggest the best overall type of link (consider communication speed, cost and any other factor you believe is relevant). Each scenario is independent of the others. For each scenario, explain why you selected the option.

a) An author works at home writing articles for a magazine. Once per week she must transmit an article to her editor. She rarely uses the link for any other purpose.

b) A large company maintains its own website for online catalogs and purchase transactions by its customers. Hundreds of customers visit the sites daily and make purchases.

c) A small business uses the Internet for daily research. Owners have heard that some links are shared by other subscribers in the same area, which might slow down the connection or even pose security threats. Thus, they would like to avoid such a service. They do need a speed of at least 200 Kbps.

d) A farm in South Africa needs a link of at least 200 Kbps. People on the farm can receive television signals only through a satellite dish. The closest telephone central office is 12 miles away.

e) An Internet service provider specializes in hosting websites of small businesses.

f) A cruise ship wants to provide Internet service to vacationers on the third deck. The ship cruises in the Caribbean. The link's speed must be at least 250 Kbps.

7 Team up with another student from your class. Select a bank branch close to your school. Interview the branch personnel about the telecommunications equipment used between the branch and (a) other branches, (b) headquarters, and (c) other institutions, such as credit information companies, if any. Use the discussion in this chapter to identify the various communications devices that the branch uses. List the devices and state their roles at the bank.

8 Team up with two other students from your class. Each of you should send an email message to one other team member. One of you may use the university's facilities, but the other two should use a subscriber's address, such as an AOL or Hotmail address. When you receive the

messages, try to get the routing information: which servers did the messages pass through on their way to you? How long did it take the messages to get to the server from which your own computer retrieves the messages? Print out the route your computer generated.

2 Do you have a network at home? If so, which type of network is it? What made you decide on this type of network? If not, if you were to set one up, what kind would you choose and why?

Companion CD questions

1 This chapter discusses RFID as an application of wireless networking. Some people have raised privacy concerns about the use of RFID. Do some research and summarize these concerns. Do you agree with them? Why or why not?

Video questions

1 The video segment does not define Wiki. What is a Wiki?

2 Could Trent Couriers use a Wiki? In which ways?

From ideas to application
REAL CASES

Case study **5.1**

Mobile phone banking in Africa on the rise

More than 800 million mobile phones were sold in developing countries in the last three years according to FinMark Trust, a research think-tank in South Africa. Twice as many Africans have mobile phones than have land lines according to the International Telecommunications Union. Associated with this significant expansion in mobile phone usage, in Africa particularly, is a lack of physical banking infrastructure. For example, in Ingwavuma, a rural town in the KwaZulu-Ntal province of South Africa, there are just two ATMs and the nearest bank is a 90-minute drive away. These factors mean that in many African countries, including South Africa, Nigeria and the Democratic Republic of Congo, 'the use of cell phone banking is becoming relevant' according to Jeremy Leach, executive director of FinMark Trust.

A joint report 'Mobile Phone Banking and Low-Income Customers: Evidence from South Africa' from the World Bank's Consultative Group to Assist the Poor (CGAP), the United Nations Foundation and the Vodafone Group Foundation, summarizes a study they carried out of 515 low-income individuals in South Africa, 300 of whom do not yet use mobile banking, with the remaining 215 customers of Wizzit, a mobile-banking subsidiary of the South African Bank of Athens. Wizzit targets the 16 million people in South Africa, that is 46 per cent of the adult population, who are 'unbanked' or have difficulty accessing conventional banking services. Since it was launched in December 2004, Wizzit has acquired over 50,000 customers. For a new customer signing up is easy. They simply key their national identity number into their mobile phone. For existing customers Wizzit provides a call centre 15 hours per day in the 11 official languages of South Africa.

Whilst the survey recognizes its limitations in terms of sample population, the findings, particularly from the existing Wizzit customers, are encouraging. These customers generally found the system to be faster, cheaper and more convenient than traditional banking. Although customers must still visit a branch to make a deposit, most transactions such as checking their account balance, transferring money to friends and family and making payments such as utility bills can all be done without a trip to the bank. For someone living in a major European city that might not be such a big deal, but for someone on a low income in South Africa when the average journey time is 32 minutes at a cost that might represent a significant percentage of their monthly income, the benefits of mobile banking become clear. Of course the service is not free. Customers have to pay a charge to sign up and then pay a per-transaction charge, but this is a fraction of the cost of visiting a remote branch.

A mobile phone user in Soweto, South Africa.

PHOTO SOURCE: © LULIBUB

It seems that the early adopters of Wizzit's services are people with relatively higher incomes, more technologically sophisticated and well educated. The challenge now seems to be to target those poor people who either are not aware of the potential of mobile banking for them or who think that they are ineligible for a bank account at all. Traditionally to open a bank account a potential customer would need to supply documentation such as proof of income and address – many are unable to do so. These are specifically the people for whom Wizzit was designed.

If the South African model is successful then there is every possibility that it will be copied in the rest of Africa, which tends to remain a cash economy with its inherent security problems. According to Brian Richardson, Wizzit's CEO, the model is more than technology. 'We have many requests from banks to come and implement the Wizzit model. One challenge is that many IT departments feel threatened by Wizzit and believe they can develop it themselves. We are quite sure that they can but the Wizzit model is much more than technology and this point is often missed. What is of as much if not greater importance is the methodology utilized in opening accounts, educating customers etc.' Wizzit does not use mass media advertising. Instead it markets its services through 2000 'WIZZ Kids' who are typically youngsters from the target low-income population. They educate potential people on the benefits of mobile banking and earn commission for each new customer they sign up.

Thinking about the case

1 Do you think that the South African model of mobile banking will be a success? What about the rest of Africa? What about the rest of the developing world? What telecommunications infrastructure needs to be in place?

2 Are there inherent security problems with banking over a mobile phone network? How can these be resolved?

3 Is there much difference between a South African using Wizzit's mobile banking facilities and a resident of central London using conventional banking in association with Internet banking?

SOURCE: John Yarney, 'African mobile-phone banking poised for growth', IDG News Service, 17 May 2007 and Consultative Group to Assist the Poor (CGAP), the United Nations Foundation and the Vodafone Group Foundation, Mobile Phone Banking and Low-Income Customers: Evidence from South Africa , 2006

Case study 5.2

WiMAX by the sea

The traditional British sea-side resort of Brighton is also a thriving centre for new media. One in five businesses in the city is allied to the creative industries. It has a high percentage of young people involved in these industries and other related IT businesses and many became early adopters of Wi-Fi. The Loose Connections project means that nobody in Brighton is further than ten minutes from a free wireless broadband hotspot. This has proved a boon for mobile workers across the city. However, the city council realized that a more radical approach was needed to service schools and other aspects of local authority connectivity. According to Bill Parslow, Head of ICT and eGovernment, Wi-Fi has its drawbacks. 'Whilst there are clear benefits to its use, perhaps for small community mesh networks, 802.11b or g neither had the range nor the security levels that made us comfortable with sending potentially sensitive information over the airwaves. 2.4 GHz, the frequency used for WiFi, is also particularly sensitive to the odd coastal sea mist that occasionally rumbles in soaking up Wi-Fi strength.' The solution was the creation of the Brighton Metranet (Metropolitan Internet), a WiMax standard broadband infrastructure covering the whole of the city. 'Whereas Wi-Fi might have a range of 50 m in reality, the Brighton's Metranet's longest link at the moment is 7.5 km', explains Bill Parslow.

The initial pilot linked seven schools and three university sites with the main access point 140 m in the air on the rooftop of Brighton's tallest building. Line of sight helps for longer range. However, the advantage of WiMax is that it is also capable of non-line-of-sight (NLOS) connection by using multiple paths and reflections of buildings and so on. This is a principal that can be followed in many similar situations relating to local government. Local councils tend to own enough high ground such as town halls and other housing blocks. Connection to a university then gives access to academic networks, giving European and worldwide high-speed connectivity. The benefits of the Brighton Metranet are many. Obviously the original school and other council offices are connected, but it also allows the wider public low-cost, high-speed connectivity. The general public also have potential access to council IT services such as social services, the local health authority and so on. The social aspects were expressed in a bid put forward in 2006 called 'Digital City Healthy City' which aimed to integrate with the NHS Connecting for Health project by linking up several service agencies that deliver care outside the hospital context using remote patient monitoring. The following example scenario shows how the technology and agencies could be brought together for the greater good of the individual.

The lifestyle of a disabled person living independently in the community would be significantly enhanced. For example, if they have mobility problems, they could be living in a Smart House with monitoring devices, which include a smoke detector which summons emergency services, a fall detector and a bed occupancy sensor all connected to a single Wi-Fi access point. Thanks to support and tutoring from a Digital Champion at their local UK online centre, they could become a confident computer and Internet user. This would increase their ability to interact socially and combat isolation and exclusion, through participation in local blogs, chat rooms and attending online meetings.

Thinking about the case

1 The reservations regarding security of WiFi may be reasonable. Does this mean that anyone using a WiFi connection in a city or airport is subject to security problems?

2 Could the example scenario at the end of the case study work without the Brighton Metranet?

3 Can you think of any other ways that the WiMax network could help the residents of Brighton?

SOURCE: Bill Parslow, 'Brighton Unwired with WiMAX', http://www.egovmonitor.com/node/707

The Brighton Metranet's use of WiMAX's technology allows it to reach most locations within 10 km of its primary access point in central Brighton.

PHOTO SOURCE: © PAUL MCARDLE

silicon.com

Case study **5.3**

VoIP takes hold with small businesses

BY ANTHONY PLEWES

It may be a truism but, nonetheless, voice over IP has the capacity to transform how companies deal with their communications. Large enterprises have been dipping their toe in the water for several years and now it appears that small and medium-sized companies are following suit, says Anthony Plewes.

Investing in Voice over IP has become a priority for SMEs, with some 60 per cent considering investing in it during 2007, according to a survey by silicon.com and The Bathwick Group. In terms of planned investment, it lags behind only laptop and handheld computers.

This trend is significant as VoIP lies at the heart of convergence; it allows voice to be carried over data networks, eliminating the historical divergence between voice and data.

Although VoIP describes a very specific technology, there is often confusion among SMEs about exactly what it means for their business. Put simply, there are two different communications areas where VoIP plays a role. The first of these is what can be called Internet telephony, where phone calls are delivered over the Internet; and the second is IP telephony, which in essence is the replacement of the legacy PBX within a corporation. Both of these areas are relevant to SMEs and confusion between the two has served as a significant barrier to the uptake of the latter.

Internet telephony

To many SMEs, Voice over IP is synonymous with telephony over the Internet. Until recently, the lack of high-bandwidth connections made Internet telephony little more than a curiosity, but nearly all of the small businesses in the silicon.com/Bathwick Group survey now have access to broadband Internet services, and therefore the bandwidth to take Internet telephony seriously. For companies with a substantial amount of international calling or audio conferencing, it can provide massive savings on their telephone bill.

Skype has played a major role in popularizing Internet telephony and remains one of the most important players in the market. However, unlike most telephony services, Skype uses a peer-to-peer network of Skype users to deliver the calls rather than a service provider per se.

What attracts many people to Skype is the perception that it makes calling free. This is only partly true: calls are only free between Skype-enabled computers. Skype can be used to call traditional telephone numbers but this involves 'breakout' – the call must leave the Internet and be terminated on a telephone network. This service, SkypeOut, carries a usage charge which must be prepaid. The savings offered are by rating calls as local rather than national or international.

Vonage is more like a traditional operator than Skype. It offers consumers and businesses a normal telephone number but routes the calls over the Internet. Vonage says the operator has more than two million users worldwide. The number of users in the UK is confidential but Vincent Potier, director of marketing at Vonage UK, says around 20 to 25 per cent

A German businessman using VoIP.

PHOTO SOURCE: © JOCHEN TACK/ALAMY

of these are SMEs. 'Our sweet spot is companies with one to 10 employees and we have a large number of self-employed sole traders as customers', he says.

Because the telephony service uses IP, Vonage is able to offer a range of interesting features, such as allowing the user to choose their own dialling code for their business. This is useful to home-based businesses which might be located in rural areas but want to look as if they are based in London, for example. Vonage also allows subscribers to set up a whole range of virtual numbers with area codes in their main trading locations without needing to have a presence in the city. It is also possible to set up international virtual numbers in the countries in which Vonage operates.

However, Vonage and other Internet telephony services rely on customers' broadband connections, most of which do not provide high quality of service (QoS) for voice and the number of simultaneous callers are limited by the upload capacity. Vonage, for example, recommends that in order to conduct a high-quality audio call, each user will need 90 Kbps upstream and down. The problem here is that while ADSL downstream speeds are rapidly improving, the same cannot be said for upstream.

IP telephony

While Internet telephony has attracted techies, consumers and cost-conscious businesses alike, the development of IP PBX technology for SMEs is much more significant.

Guenter Junk, CEO of Sywx, one of the first companies to focus solely on IP telephony for SMEs, says: 'Communications are changing for SMEs. Where the telephone used to be the primary form of communication, it is now just one of many, and IP telephony helps companies knit it all together.'

IP telephony is a fairly major undertaking and is best broken down into three phases. The first phase is IP trunking, where multi-site SMEs can make substantial cost savings by connecting their sites together by effectively eliminating inter-site call costs. Productivity can also be improved through having a unified call plan across the business, allowing colleagues in different sites to work together better.

The next phase is to link remote or home workers into the office network using a VPN over broadband connections. Voice over IP gateways allow the remote worker to access PBX functionality remotely and collaborate with their colleagues.

Trevor Evans, business development manager in Alcatel's SME business, says: 'It is possible to connect a single person to the office network with standard broadband connections. But if the employee needs to speak to external people over the connection, they will probably need a better connection including some elements of quality of service.'

The final phase is to spread IP telephony throughout the organization with IP phones on the employees' desktop. This set-up completely eliminates the requirement to have separate sets of cabling for voice and data networks, and provides for simplified management.

IP phones on the desktop also open up a whole new world of telephony applications, as IP telephony can be very easily integrated into the company's back-end systems. For example, it only requires a simple XML application and the entire company directory can be accessed from the phone.

Steven Frost, SMB market manager at Cisco UK & Ireland, says: 'VoIP is only the starting point, the real benefits come from features such as unified messaging.' Although unified messaging can be done without VoIP, combining all communication on a single IP network makes its deployment and management straightforward. It also offers functionality such as presence and can be integrated directly into business processes. For example, companies could create a click-to-call button in their accounts package to call late payers of invoices. Features such as these are a real boon to company productivity.

Despite the clear advantages, there is still conflicting evidence about exactly how many SMEs have made it all the way to IP telephony. Alcatel, which heralds from a traditional PBX background, says it has now reached the tipping point for IP telephony sales to companies with more than 100 employees. For this market it is now selling more IP than legacy TDM systems. But in the sub-100 employee market, Alcatel is still mainly selling legacy PBXs, with IP telephony making up only a fairly insignificant 5 to 8 per cent of sales.

Alcatel's Evans says: 'Our customers are still finding barriers to deployment, particularly the cost of auditing and upgrading the LAN by putting QoS on it.' Other earlier barriers such as security and scalability have been largely overcome, although companies need to pay close attention to security if combining VoIP with Wi-Fi networks.

Even IP telephony specialists such as Cisco have found that SMEs have been slower to adopt IP telephony than larger companies. Cisco's Frost says: 'It has taken smaller companies a while to adopt VoIP partly because the technology was designed for larger enterprises, but now we have developed the right product set and the right channels to meet the SME requirements. The channel is vitally important for SMEs, because they want to buy from local companies. We've had to train them in both voice and data skills.'

The relatively slow take-up of IP telephony in the SME market is not surprising. Equipment makers have long focused on larger enterprises and it is only relatively recently that fully functional telephony systems have been within reach of the smallest companies. Businesses with more than 20 employees are well placed to benefit from the advantages of premise-based IP telephony, while smaller companies without many internal IT skills are more suited to hosted offerings.

Companies of all sizes, though, are able to benefit from Internet telephony as long as they remember its limitations and mainly use it for internal communications.

Thinking about the case

1 It seems that enterprises with few employees have been slow to take up VoIP. Why is this the case? Will improved Internet connections help to increase the take-up?

2 Are a high volume of international calls the main deciding factor in the introduction of VoIP?

SOURCE: www.silicon.com.

Chapter 5

Databases and data warehouses

LEARNING OBJECTIVES

Data are usually collected in a way that does not make them immediately useful to businesspeople. Imagine building a model palace from a pile of building blocks. You have a good idea of what you want to build, but first you have to organize the blocks so it is easy for you to find and select only the blocks you need. Then you can combine them into substructures that eventually are integrated into your model. Similarly, data collected by organizations must be organized and stored so that useful information can be extracted from the database in a flexible manner.

When you finish this chapter, you will be able to:

Explain the difference between traditional file organization and the database approach to managing digital data.

Explain how relational and object-oriented database management systems are used to construct databases, populate them with data, and manipulate the data to produce information.

Enumerate the most important features and operations of a relational database, the most popular database model.

Understand how data modelling and design create a conceptual blueprint of a database.

Discuss how databases are used on the Web.

List the operations involved in transferring data from transactional databases to data warehouses.

Trent Courier Services

THE VALUE AND USES OF DATABASES

As Trent Couriers grew, so did its reliance on databases. By the time the company had grown to a size of 90 employees, Andrew was using databases to create weekly schedules for part-time and full-time employees, track customer orders, store and access employee and customer information, organize and report financial data and provide crucial information for marketing strategies. As his database needs expanded, he transitioned from one database management system to another.

Moving up: from Microsoft Access to Oracle

In the early days, Andrew had relied on Microsoft Access and Excel for his company's database needs. When he hired his first part-time messengers, he used an Excel spreadsheet to set up weekly schedules. He stored customer and order information in an Access database. As business grew, so did the size of the database. Karen Brown, an IT consultant who worked in an office on the second floor of his building, told him that he should consider using a more powerful database management system (DBMS). When Mary Thomas suggested that Trent Couriers create an intranet so that messengers could upload delivery information through their wireless connections, the need to switch to a more powerful DBMS became urgent. Microsoft Access wouldn't be able to handle the number of concurrent users that Trent Couriers anticipated. Andrew decided to hire Karen to help the office shift to Oracle. An Oracle database would be able to accommodate both the increased size of the database and the need for concurrent access.

Tapping the power of databases

Then Andrew turned his thoughts to using his data to better his service – to maintain his existing customers and strengthen his relationships with them. He also wanted to find out who would be good potential customers. He hired Karen to run SQL queries and create reports. Surely he could find valuable information by exploring customer information and buying patterns.

First Andrew wanted to find out who his preferred customers were – those who used his service most often and provided the most revenue. The consultant used data-mining software to delve into the data and identified a profile. To his surprise, Andrew found that the legal and medical-supply firms were most profitable. He'd always thought the pottery companies were his best clients because of the special handling their objects required. But lawyers and pharmacists needed faster delivery and special services, such as delivery confirmation, which commanded premium rates and generated additional revenue at no further cost per delivery to Trent Couriers. Andrew designated those customers as VIPs and tagged their database files. VIPs would receive priority delivery on the routes from now on.

Also, Andrew was interested in the purchasing patterns of customers. He planned to target those opportunities with a promotion to gain new clients. Again, the consultant came back with interesting news: law firms with branches throughout South Cheshire used Trent Couriers' service most often on weekdays between the hours of 10 a.m. and 1 p.m. So Andrew decided to locate other similar firms and develop a direct-mail promotion to them – discounted deliveries for setting up an account and scheduling 30 orders in a month's time. Andrew also added additional messengers during that time frame to be sure to handle deliveries smoothly.

PHOTO SOURCE: © KRISTIAN SEKULIC

Managing digital data

Businesses collect and dissect data for a multitude of purposes. Digital data can be stored in a variety of ways on different types of media, as discussed in Chapter 4. They can be stored in what can be called the traditional file format, in which the different pieces of information are not labelled and categorized, but are stored as continuous strings of bytes. The chief advantage of this format is the efficient use of space, but the data are nonetheless difficult to locate and manipulate. By contrast, the database format, in which each piece of data is labelled or categorized, provides a much more powerful information management tool. Data in this format can be easily accessed and manipulated in almost any way desired to create useful information and optimize productivity.

CD TASK

The impact of database technology on business cannot be overstated. Not only has it changed the way almost every industry conducts business, but it has also created an information industry with far-reaching effects on both our business and personal lives. Databases are behind the successful use of automatic teller machines, increased efficiency in retail stores, almost every marketing effort, and the numerous online search engines and electronic storefronts on the Web. Combined with interactive web pages on the Internet, databases have made an immense contribution to commerce. Without them, there would be no online banking, no online consumer catalogues, no online searches for information, no online stock brokerages and no online chat rooms. Their impact on business has allowed fewer people to complete larger tasks, and their power has allowed organizations to learn more about us, as consumers, than we might realize. Imagine: every time you enter the address of a website, a special program performs a search in a huge database and matches your request with one of millions of addresses. Every time you fill out an online form with details such as your address, phone number, National Insurance number or credit-card number, a program feeds the data into a database, where each item is recorded for further use.

In virtually every type of business today, you must understand the power of databases. This chapter reviews approaches to organizing and manipulating data.

The traditional file approach

database approach An approach to maintaining data that contains a mechanism for tagging, retrieving and manipulating data.

There are two overall approaches to maintaining data: the *traditional file approach* – which has no mechanism for tagging, retrieving and manipulating data – and the **database approach**, which does have that mechanism. To appreciate the benefits of the database approach, you must keep in mind the inconvenience involved in accessing and manipulating data in the traditional file approach: program-data dependency, high data redundancy and low data integrity.

CD TASK

Consider Figure 6.1, which is an example of a human resource file in traditional file format. Suppose a programmer wants to retrieve and print out only the last name and department number of each employee from this file. The programmer must clearly instruct the computer to first retrieve the data between position 10 and position 20. Then he must instruct the computer to skip the positions up to position 35 and retrieve the data between positions 36 and 39. He cannot instruct the computer to retrieve a piece of data by its column name, because column names do not exist in this format. To create the reports, the programmer must know which position ranges maintain which types of data and insert the appropriate headings, 'Last Name' and 'Department', so that the reader can understand the information. If the programmer miscounts the positions, the printout might include output like '677Rapap' as a last name instead of 'Rapaport'. This illustrates the *interdependency of programs and data* of the traditional file approach. The programmer must know *how* data are stored to use them. Perhaps most importantly, the very fact that manipulation of the data requires a programmer is probably the greatest disadvantage of the file approach. Much business data is still processed this way. New data resources are rarely built this way, but the existing ones must be maintained with this challenge in mind.

Figure 6.1 The layout of a human resource file in traditional file organization

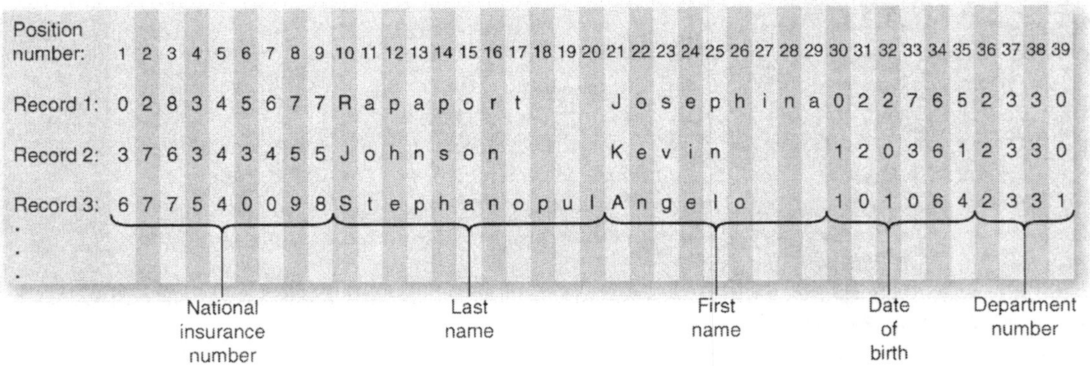

Other challenges with traditional file storage are high data redundancy and low data integrity, because in older file systems files were built, and are still maintained, for the use of specific organizational units. If your last and first name, as well as address and other details appear in the files of the department where you work as well as in the payroll file of the Human Resource department, there is duplication of data, or data redundancy, which wastes storage space (and consequently money) and is inefficient. When corrections or modifications need to be made, every change has to be made as many times as the number of locations where the data appear, which takes time and might introduce errors. If the same data were entered correctly in one place but incorrectly in another, your record is not only inaccurate, but might appear to represent a different person in each place. Inaccuracies hurt data integrity. Often, the traditional file approach to storing data leads to low data integrity.

data redundancy The existence of the same data in more than one place in a computer system. Although some data redundancy is unavoidable, efforts should be made to minimize it.

data integrity Accuracy, timeliness and relevance of data in a context.

CD TASK

The database approach

In the database approach, data pieces are organized about entities. An entity is any object about which an organization chooses to collect data. Entities can be types of people, such as employees, students or members of fan clubs; events, such as sales transactions, sports events or theatre shows; or inanimate objects, such as inventoried or for-sale products, buildings or minerals. In the context of data management, 'entity' refers to all the occurrences sharing the same types of data. Therefore, it does not matter if you maintain a record of one student or many students; the entity is 'student'. To understand how data are organized in a database, you must first understand the data hierarchy, described in Figure 6.2, which shows a compilation of information about students: their first names, last names, years of birth, enrolment numbers, departments and campus phone numbers. The smallest piece of data is a character (such as a letter in a first or last name, or a digit in a street address). Multiple characters make up a field. A field is one piece of information about an entity, such as the last name or first name of a student, or the student's street address. The fields related to the same entity make up a record. A collection of related records, such as all the records of a college's students, is called a file. Often, several related files must be kept together. A collection of such files is referred to as a database. However, the features of a database can be present even when a database consists of a single file.

entity Any object about which an organization chooses to collect data.

character The smallest piece of data in the data hierarchy.

field A data element in a record, describing one aspect of an entity or event. Referred to as attribute in relational databases.

record A set of standard field types. All the fields of a record contain data about a certain entity or event.

Figure 6.2 Data hierarchy

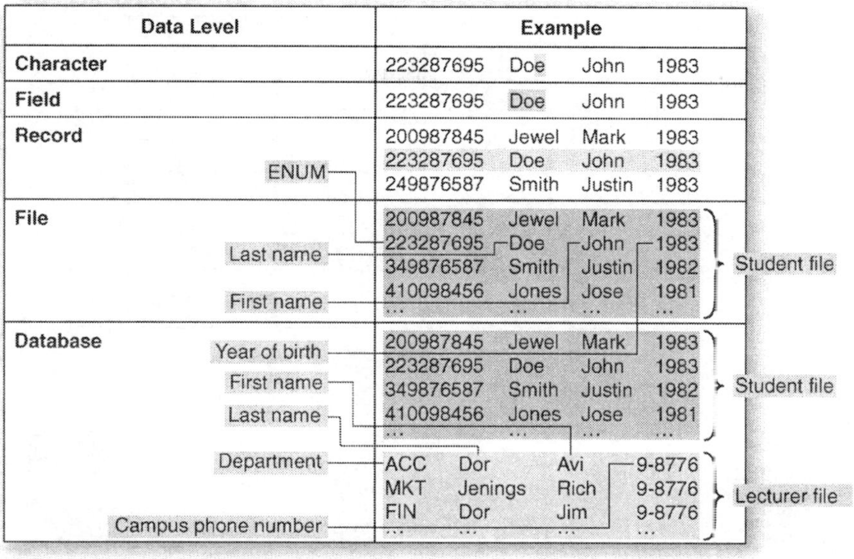

Once the fields are assigned names, including Last Name, First Name, ENUM and the like, the data in each field carries a tag – a field name – and can be easily accessed by that field name, no matter where the data are physically stored. One of the greatest strengths of databases is their promotion of application-data independence. In other words, if an application is written to process data in a database, the application designer only needs to know the names of the fields, not their physical organization or their length.

file A collection of related records, such as a customer file containing details of all customer names, billing addresses, delivery addresses, credit limits and so on.

Database fields are not limited to holding text and numbers. They can hold pictures, sounds and video clips. Fields can hold any content that can be digitized. For example, when you shop online, you can search for a product by its product name or code, and then retrieve its picture or a video clip about the product.

database management system (DBMS) A computer program that allows the user to construct a database, populate it with data and manipulate the data.

While a database itself is a collection of several related files, the program used to build databases, populate them with data and manipulate the data is called a **database management system (DBMS)**. The files themselves *are* the database, but DBMSs do all the work – structuring files, storing data and linking records. As you saw previously, if you wanted to access data from files that were stored in a traditional file approach, you would have to know exactly how many characters were designated for each type of data. A DBMS, however, does much of this work (and a lot of other work) for you.

If you are using a database, you want to be able to move rapidly from one record to another, sort by different criteria, create different types of reports and analyse the data in different ways. Because of these demands, databases are stored on and processed from direct access storage devices, such as magnetic disks or CDs. They can be backed up to sequential storage devices such as magnetic or optical tapes, but cannot be efficiently processed off such media because it would take too long to access the records.

Queries Data are accessed in a database by sending messages called 'queries', which request data from specific records and/or fields and direct the computer to display the results. Queries are also entered to manipulate data. Usually, the same software that is used to

Figure 6.3 Different database views reveal different combinations of data

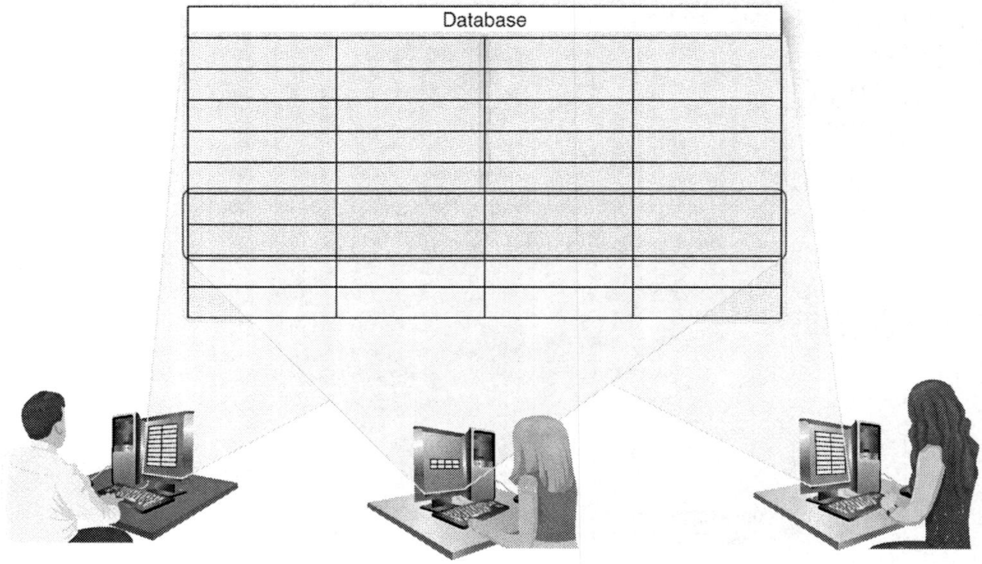

construct and populate the database, that is, the DBMS, is also used to present queries. Modern DBMSs provide fairly user-friendly means of querying a database.

Security The use of databases raises security and privacy issues. The fact that data are stored only once in a database for several different purposes does not mean that everyone with access to that database should have access to *all* the data in it. Restricting access is easily dealt with by customizing menus for different users and requiring users to enter codes that limit access to certain fields or records. As a result, users have different *views* of the database, as abstractly illustrated in Figure 6.3. The ability to limit users' views only to specific columns or records gives the database administrator (DBA) another advantage: the ability to implement security measures. The measures are implemented once for the database, rather than multiple times for different files. For instance, in the database in Figure 6.4, while a human resource manager has access to all fields of the employee file (represented by the top, middle and lower parts of the figure), the payroll personnel have access only to four fields of the employee file (middle part of the figure), and a project manager has access only to the Name and Hours Worked fields. Views can be limited to certain fields in a database, or certain records, or a combination of both.

database administrator (DBA) The individual in charge of building and maintaining organizational databases.

DBMSs are usually bundled with a 4GL (fourth-generation programming language) module. Programmers can use this module to develop applications that facilitate queries and produce predesigned reports.

Database models

A *database model* is the general logical structure in which records are stored within a database and the method used to establish relationships among the records. There are several database models. They differ in the manner in which records are linked to each other. These differences, in turn, dictate the manner in which a user can navigate the database, retrieve

Figure 6.4 Different views from the same database

View of Human Resource Manager				
NIN	Name	D.O.B.	Hire Date	Marital Status

View of Payroll Personnel			
NIN	Hourly Rate	Benefits Code	Hours Worked

View of Project Manager	
Name	Hours Worked

desired records and create reports. The oldest models, the hierarchical and network models, are still used in some databases that were built in the 1970s and 1980s, but are no longer used in newly constructed databases. Virtually all new databases are designed following the relational and object-oriented models.

The relational model

CD TASK

The **relational database model** consists of **tables**. Its roots are in relational algebra, although you do not have to know relational algebra to build and use relational databases. However, database experts still use relational algebra terminology: in a relational database, a record is called a *tuple*, a field – often referred to as a column – is called an *attribute*, and a table of records is called a *relation*. This text uses the simpler terms, as do the popular software packages: fields, records and tables.

relational database model A general structure of database in which records are organized in tables (relations) and the relationships among tables are maintained through foreign keys.

table A set of related records in a relational database.

key A field in a database table whose values identify records either for display or for processing. Typical keys are part number (in an inventory file) and National Insurance number (in a human resources file).

To design a relational database, you need a clear idea of the different entities and how they relate. For example, in a DVD store database, the entities might be Customer, DVD Rental, DVD and Distributor. A single table is built for each entity (though each table can contain from only a few to potentially millions of records). DVD Rental is an associative entity, and you can see in Figure 6.5 that the DVD Rental table associates data from the Customer and DVD tables.

Maintenance of a relational database is relatively easy because each table is independent of the others, although some tables are related to others. To add a customer record, the user accesses the Customer table. To delete a record of a DVD, the user accesses the DVD table. The advantages of this model makes relational database management systems the most popular in the software market. Virtually all DBMSs that are offered on the market accommodate the relational model. This model is used in supply chain management (SCM) systems and many other enterprise applications and local, individual ISs.

CD TASK

To retrieve records from a relational database, or to sort them, you must use a **key**. A key is a field whose values identify records either for display or for processing. You can use any

Figure 6.5 A relational database

Customer Table			
CustID	**CustName**	**CustPhone**	**CustAddr**
33091	Jill Bronson	322-4907	203 Oak Dr
35999	John Smith	322-5577	519 Devon St
36002	John Sosik	342-0071	554 Spring Dr
36024	Jane Fedorow	322-7299	101 Grant Ave

Primary key

Composite primary key

DVD Rental Table			
CustID	**CopyNum**	**Date Rented**	**Date Returned**
35999	4452-1	1-5-06	3-5-06
36002	4780-3	3-5-06	
36024	5312-2	2-5-06	5-5-06

Copy Table	
CopyNum	**TitleNum**
4452-1	4452
4452-2	4452
5312-1	5312
5312-2	5312
5312-3	5312
7662-1	7662
7662-2	7662
5583-1	5583

Primary key in *Title* and part of a composite primary key in *Copy-Title*

Title Table				
TitleNum	**Title**	**Category**	**DistribNum**	**RentPrice**
4452	Enter the Dragon	Martial Arts	277	€4.00
5312	The Ring II	Thriller	305	€4.00
7662	Star Wars III	Sci-Fi	372	€5.00
5583	White Noise	Thriller	589	€2.50

Primary key in *Distributor* and foreign key in *Title*

Distributor Table		
DistribNum	**DistribName**	**Phone**
277	HK Corp	1-877-555-0550
305	Columbia	1-888-222-3654
372	Lucas Films	1-247-233-6996
589	Booh Inc	1-866-222-9999

CD TASK

field as a key. For example, you could ask the database for the record of John Smith from the Customer table by using the CustName field as a key. That is, you enter a query, a condition that instructs the DBMS to retrieve a record with the value of CustName as 'John Smith'. A key is *unique* if the value (content) in that field appears only in one record.

Why you should... know about data management

A national car rental company knows the precise number of vehicles to hold for late-booking, high-paying travellers. A restaurant chain detects consumer buying patterns that the company then uses to boost its sales of special meals. How do businesses find this information?

Transactions are recorded at the boundaries of a company in its contacts with external entities, such as customers and suppliers. Data captured this way make up the greater part of most organizational databases. They provide the raw material for essential information that helps answer questions such as: What is the total amount of money we owe debtors? What is the backlog of a certain product that we manufacture? What was the average sales volume per employee last quarter? However, to be able to extract useful information, the data must first be organized in well-designed databases. And to know what information you can draw from a database, you must understand how databases are structured and what combinations of data can be created for you on demand.

Imagine a sales clerk who cannot immediately respond to a customer about the availability of an item or an online shopper who cannot display the details of an item that is actually available for sale at the site. Customers experiencing this are not likely to patronize the business again. Imagine a treasurer who cannot figure out in real time how much cash the company has in the bank. The company might miss an important deal. Available and reliable information is the most important resource of any business, in any industry. Thus, professionals must understand at least the fundamentals of data organization and manipulation. You will be a more productive professional if you know how databases and data warehouses are built and queried, and what types of information can be extracted from them.

Sometimes a key is composed of several fields so that their combination provides a unique key.

As you can see, database design requires careful forethought. The designer must include fields for foreign keys from other tables so that join tables can be created in the future. A table might include foreign keys from several tables, so that there is much flexibility in creating reports with related data from several tables. The inclusion of foreign keys might cause considerable data redundancy. This complexity has not diminished the popularity of relational databases, however.

If there is more than one record with 'John Smith' (because several customers happen to have that same name) in the CustName field, you might not retrieve the single record you desired. Depending on the application you use for the query, you might receive the first one that meets the condition, that is, a list of all the records with that value in the field. The only way to be sure you are retrieving the desired record is to use a unique key, such as a National Insurance number, an employee ID, or, in our example, a customer ID (CustID). A unique key can serve as a **primary key**. A primary key is the field by which records in a table are uniquely identified. If your query specified that you wanted the record whose CustID value is 36002, the system would retrieve the record of John Sosik. It will be the John Sosik you wanted, even if there are more records of people with exactly the same name. Because the purpose of a primary key is to uniquely identify a record, there must be a unique value in that field for each record.

primary key In a file, a field that holds values that are unique to each record. Only a primary key can be used to uniquely identify and retrieve a record.

Usually, a table in a relational database must have a primary key, and most relational DBMSs enforce this rule; if the designer does not designate a field as a key, the DBMS creates its own serial number field as the primary key field for the table. Once the designer of the table determines the primary key when constructing the records' format, the DBMS does not allow a user to enter two records with the same value in that column. Note that there might be situations in which more than one field can be used as a primary key. Such is the case with motor vehicles, because two different fields can uniquely identify the record of a particular vehicle: the vehicle identification number (VIN) and its registration plate number. Thus, a database designer might establish one of these fields as a primary key to retrieve records. In Figure 6.5 in the DVD Rental table both CustID and CopyNum can be used as a primary key.

composite key In a data file, a combination of two fields that can serve as a unique key to locate specific records.

foreign key In a relational database: a field in a table that is a primary key in another table. Foreign keys allow association of data between the two files.

join table In relational database manipulation, a table created by linking – that is, joining – data from multiple tables.

one-to-many relationship In a database, a relationship between two tables such that each record in the one table can be associated with several records in the other table, but each record in the other table can be associated with only one record in the first table.

many-to-many relationship In databases, a relationship between two tables whereby every record in a table can be associated with several records in the other table.

For some business needs you must use a composite key, a combination of two or more fields that together serve as a primary key, because it is impractical to use a single field as a primary key. For example, consider flight records of a commercial airline. Flights of a certain route are the same every week or every day they are offered, so the daily Virgin Atlantic flight from London Heathrow to Johannesburg – VS601 – for instance, cannot serve us well to retrieve a list of all the passengers who took this flight on 3 May 2007. However, we can use the combination of the flight number *and* date as a composite primary key. To check who sat in a particular seat, a composite key consisting of three fields is needed: flight number, date and seat number.

To link records from one table with records of another table, the tables must have at least one field in common (i.e., one column in each table must contain the same type of data), and that field must be a primary key field for one of the tables. This repeated field is a primary key in one table, and a foreign key field in the other table. In the DVD store example, if you ever want to create a report showing the name of every distributor and all the DVD titles from that distributor, the primary key of the Distributor table, DistribNum, must also be included as a foreign key in the Title table. The resultant table (Figure 6.6) is called a join table. Note that although DistribNum was used to create the join table, it does not have to be displayed in the join table, although it could be.

Since the relationships between tables are created as part of manipulating the table, the relational model supports both one-to-many and many-to-many relationships between records of different tables. For example, a one-to-many relationship is created when a group of employees belongs to only one department. All would have the same department number as a foreign key in their records, and none will have more than one department key. There is *one* department, linked to *many* employees. A many-to-many relationship can be maintained, for instance, for lecturers and students in a college database. A lecturer might have many students, and a student might have many lecturers. This can be accomplished by creating a composite key of lecturer ID and student ID. In our example of the DVD store, there is a many-to-many relationship between customers and the DVDs they have rented. The DVD Rental table enables the store manager to create a history report of customers and their rentals. It is clear that more than one customer has rented a certain DVD, and the same customer has rented many different DVDs.

The major vendors of relational DBMSs are IBM, Oracle and Microsoft, at a worldwide market share in licensing revenues of about 34 per cent, 34 per cent and 20 per cent,

Figure 6.6 A join table

Distributor	Telephone	Title
HK Corp	1-877-555-05-50	Enter the Dragon
Columbia	1-888-222-3654	The Ring II
Lucas Films	1-247-233-6996	Star Wars III
Booh Inc	1-866-222-9999	White Noise

respectively. IBM licenses DB2, Oracle licenses DBMSs by the company name, and Microsoft licenses SQL Server and Access. These DBMSs are an essential part of enterprise applications such as SCM and CRM systems.

The object-oriented model

The object-oriented database model uses the object-oriented approach, described in Chapter 4, to maintaining records. In object-oriented technology, an object consists of both data and the procedures that manipulate the data. So, in addition to the attributes of an entity, an object also contains relationships with other entities and procedures to manipulate the data. The combined storage of both data and the procedures that manipulate them is referred to as encapsulation. Through encapsulation, an object can be 'planted' in different data sets. The ability in object-oriented structures to create a new object automatically by replicating all or some of the characteristics of a previously developed object (called the parent object) is called inheritance. Figure 6.7 demonstrates how the same data maintained in a relational database at the DVD rental store would be stored and used

object-oriented database model A database, in which data are part of an object that is processed using object-oriented programs.

encapsulation In an object oriented data model, the combined storage of both data and the procedures that manipulate them.

Figure 6.7 An object-oriented database

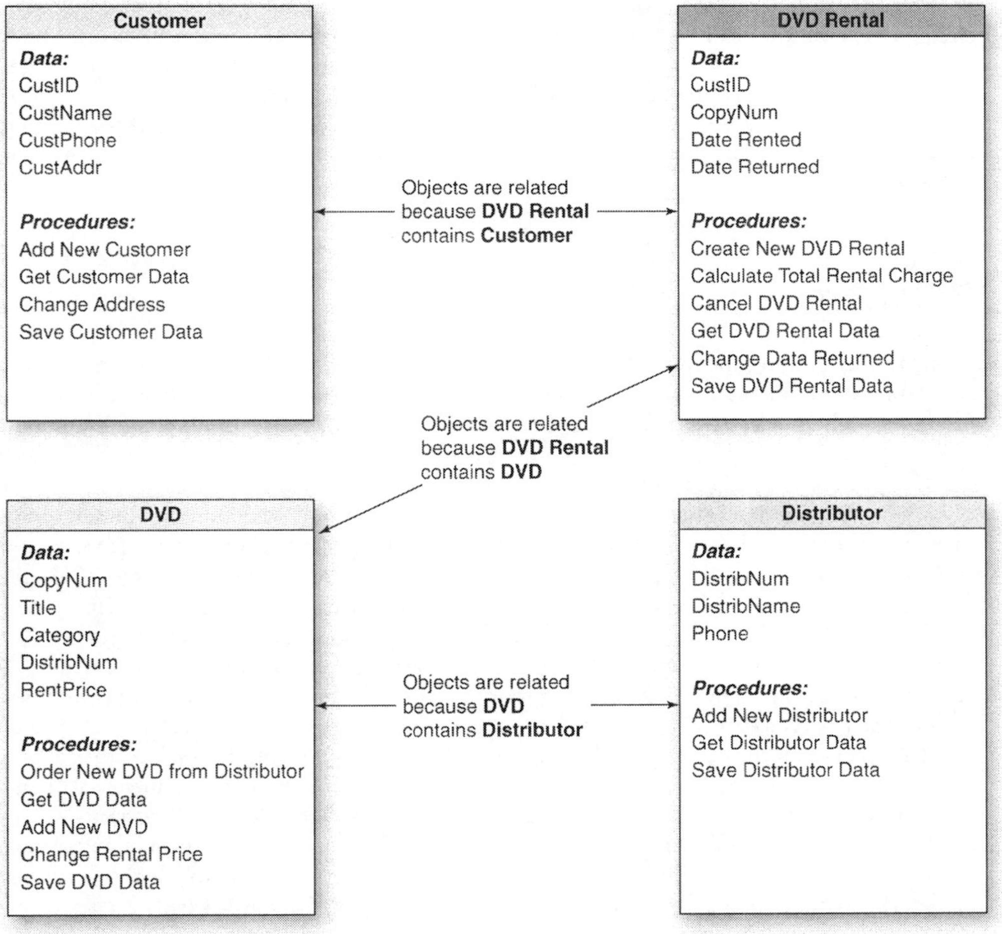

inheritance The ability in object-oriented structures to create a new object automatically by replicating all or some of the characteristics of a previously developed object.

in an object-oriented database. The relationships between data about entities are not kept by way of foreign keys, but through the relationships of one object with another. One advantage of this is the reduction of data redundancy.

Some data and information cannot be organized as fields, but they can be handled as objects, such as drawings, maps and web pages. All these capabilities make object-oriented DBMSs (OODBMSs) handy in computer-aided design (CAD), geographic information systems and applications used to update quickly thousands of web pages daily, because they can handle a wide range of data – such as graphics, voice and text – more easily than the relational model.

Similar to relational DBMSs, OODBMSs provide a graphical user interface (GUI) to manage the DBMS. The user can choose objects from 'classes', which are groups of objects that share similar characteristics. Elements of OODBMSs are often incorporated into relational databases, and such databases are sometimes known as *object-relational databases or hybrid databases*.

Object-oriented databases (OODBs) do not store records, but data objects, which is an advantage for quick updates of data sets and the relationships among them. For instance, in the example of the DVD store, in the OODB the relationship between a DVD and its distributor is not established through a foreign key; it exists because the DVD class contains the Distributor class. However, object-oriented databases also have some disadvantages, compared with relational databases. For example, there is dependence between applications and data; they are simply 'wrapped' together. Changing the structures of tables in a relational database does not require changes in applications that use the data in those tables, while it would require changes in applications in an object-oriented database. This dependence also limits the ability to enter *ad hoc* queries in an OODB, that is, to enter queries at will. While not as popular and as well understood as relational databases, OODBs are gaining adopters.

Several software companies have developed popular object-oriented DBMSs. Among them are Objectivity/DB (Objectivity Inc.), ObjectStore (Progress Software Inc.) and Versant (Versant Corporation).

Relational operations

CD TASK

As mentioned before, the most popular DBMSs are those that support the relational model. Therefore, it would be beneficial for you to familiarize yourself with a widely used relational database, such as Access, Oracle or SQL Server. To use the database, you should know how relational operations work. A **relational operation** creates a temporary table that is a subset of the original table or tables. It allows you to create a report containing records that satisfy a condition, create a list with only some fields about an entity, or produce a report from a join table, which combines relevant data from two or more tables. If so desired, the user can save the newly created table. Often, the temporary table is needed only for *ad hoc* reporting and is immediately discarded.

relational operation An operation that creates a temporary table that is a subset of the original table or tables in a relational database.

The three most important relational operations are *select*, *project* and *join*. *Select* is the selection of records that meet certain conditions. For example, a human resources manager might need a report showing the entire record of every employee whose salary exceeds €60,000. *Project* is the selection of certain columns from a table, such as the salaries of all the employees. A query might specify a combination of selection and projection. In the preceding example, the manager might require only the ID number, last name (project) and salary of employees whose salaries are greater than €60,000 (select).

One of the most useful manipulations of a relational database is the creation of a new table from two or more other tables. As you might recall from our discussion of the relational model, the joining of data from multiple tables is called a *join*. We have already used a simple example from the DVD store database (Figure 6.6). However, join queries can be much more complex. For example, a relational business database might have four tables: SalesRep, Catalogue, Order and Customer. A sales manager might wish to create a report showing, for each sales rep, a list of all of the customers who purchased anything last month, the items each customer purchased and the total amount spent by each customer. The new table is created from a relational operation that draws data from all four tables.

The join operation is a powerful manipulation that can create very useful reports for decision-making. A join table is created 'on the fly' as a result of a query and only for the duration the user wishes to view it or to create a paper report from it. Design features allow the user to change the field headings (although the field names are kept the same in the internal table), place the output in different layouts on the screen or paper and add graphics and text to the report. The new table might be saved as an additional table in the database.

Structured Query Language

Structured Query Language (SQL) has become the query language of choice for many developers of relational DBMSs. SQL is an international standard and is provided with most relational database management programs. Its strength is in its easy-to-remember intuitive commands. For instance, to create a list of all titles of thriller DVDs whose rental price is less than €5.00, the query would be:

Structured Query Language (SQL) The data definition and manipulation language of choice for many developers of relational database management systems.

```
SELECT TITLE, CATEGORY FROM DVD
  WHERE CATEGORY = 'Thriller' AND RENTPRICE < 5;
```

Statements like this can be used for *ad hoc* queries or integrated in a program that is saved for repeated use. Commands for updating the database are also easy to remember: INSERT, DELETE and UPDATE.

There are several advantages to integrating SQL in a DBMS:

- With a standard language, users do not have to learn different sets of commands to create and manipulate databases in different DBMSs.
- SQL statements can be embedded in widely used third-generation languages such as Visual Basic or C and object-oriented languages such as C++ or Java, in which case these languages are called the 'host language'. The combination of highly tailored and efficient 3GL or object-oriented statements with SQL statements increases the efficiency and effectiveness of applications accessing relational databases.
- Because SQL statements are portable from one operating system to another, the programmer is not forced to rewrite statements.

Some relational DBMSs, such as Microsoft Access, provide GUIs to create SQL queries: SQL queries can be placed by clicking icons and selecting menu items, which are internally converted into SQL queries and executed. This capability allows relatively inexperienced database designers to use SQL.

The schema and metadata

When building a new database, users must first build a schema (from the Greek word for 'plan'). The schema describes the structure of the database being designed: the names and types of fields in each record type and the general relationships among different sets of records or files. It includes a description of the database's structure, the names and sizes of fields, and details such as which field is a primary key. The number of records is never specified because it might change, and the maximum number of records is determined by the capacity of the storage medium.

schema The structure of a database, detailing the names and types of fields in each set of records, and the relationships among sets of records.

Fields can hold different types of data: numeric, alphanumeric, graphic or time-related. Numeric fields hold numbers that can be manipulated by addition,

Figure 6.8 Schema of the Employee table in an Access database

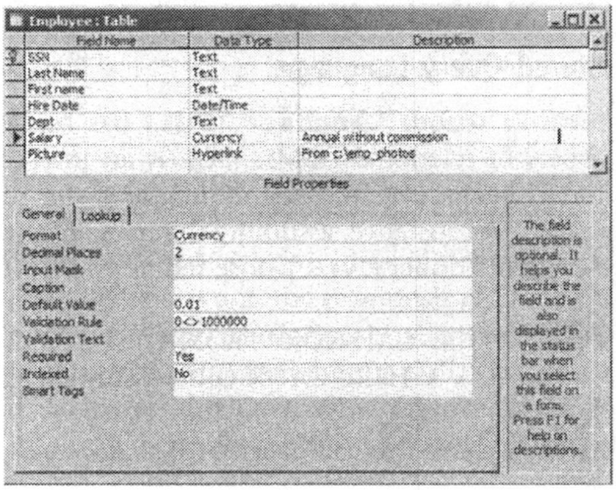

multiplication, averaging and the like. Alphanumeric fields hold textual values: words, numerals and special symbols, which make up names, addresses and identification numbers. Numerals entered in alphanumeric fields, such as National Insurance numbers or post codes, cannot be manipulated mathematically. The builder of a new database must also indicate which fields are to be used as primary keys. Many DBMSs also allow a builder to positively indicate when a field is not unique, meaning that the value in that field might be the same for more than one record.

Figure 6.8 presents the schema of a database table created with the Microsoft Access DBMS. The user is prompted to enter the names and types of fields. Access lets the user name the fields and determine the data types. The Description section allows the designer to describe the nature and function of the fields for people who maintain the database. In the lower part of the window the user is offered many options for each field, such as field size, format and so on. In Access the primary key field is indicated by a little key icon to its left.

data dictionary The part of the database that contains information about the different sets of records and fields, such as their source and who may change them.

metadata Information about the data in a database, often called data dictionary.

The description of each table structure and types of fields become part of a **data dictionary**, which is a repository of information about the data and their organization. Designers usually add more information about each field, such as where the data come from (such as another system, or entered manually); who owns the original data; who is allowed to add, delete or update data in the field; and other details that help DBAs maintain the database and understand the meaning of the fields and their relationships. (Some people prefer to call this **metadata**, meaning 'data about the data'.) Metadata include:

- The source of the data, including contact information.
- Tables that are related to the data.
- Field and index information, such as the size and type of the field (whether it is text or numeric), and the ways the data are sorted.
- Programs and processes that use the data.
- Population rules: what is inserted, or updated, and how often.

data modelling The process of charting existing or planned data stores and flows of an organization or one of its units. It includes charting of entity relationship diagrams.

Data modelling

Databases must be carefully planned and designed to meet business goals. How they are designed enables or limits flexibility in use. Analysing an organization's data and identifying the relationships among the data is called **data modelling**.

Data modelling should first be done to decide which data should be collected and how they should be organized. Thus, data modelling should be proactive. It is a good practice to create data models periodically, so that decision makers have a clear picture of what data are available for reports, and what data the organization might need to start collecting for improved decision-making. Managers can then ask experts to change the relationships and design new reports or applications that generate desired reports with a few keystrokes.

Many business databases consist of multiple tables with relationships among them. For example, a hospital might use a database that has a table holding the records of all its doctors, another one with all its nurses, another one with all the current patients, and so on. The administrative staff must be able to create reports that link data from multiple tables. For example, one report might be about a doctor and all her patients during a certain period. Another might revolve around a patient: details of the patient and a list of all the caregivers who were involved in his rehabilitation, as well as a list of medications. Thus, the database must be carefully planned to allow useful data manipulation and report generation.

Effective data modelling and design of each database involves the creation of a conceptual blueprint of the database. Such a blueprint is called an **entity relationship diagram (ERD)**. An ERD is a graphical representation of all entity relationships, an example of which is shown in Figure 6.9, and they are often consulted to determine a problem with a query or to implement changes. Boxes are used to identify entities. Lines are used to indicate a relationship between entities. When lines shaped like crow's-feet are pointing to an object, there might be many instances of that object. When a link with a crow's-foot also includes a crossbar, then all instances of the object on the side of the crow's-foot are linked with a single instance of the object on the side of the crossbar. A second crossbar would denote 'mandatory', which means that the relationship must occur, such as between a book title and author: a book title must have an author with which it is associated. A circle close to the box denotes 'optional'.

entity relationship diagram (ERD) One of several conventions for graphical rendition of the data elements involved in business processes and the logical relationships among the elements.

- In the figure, the crow's-foot on the Department end of the Department/University relationship indicates that there are several departments in one college, indicating a one-to-many relationship between University and Department. In addition, the crossbar at the University end of the University/Department link indicates that a department belongs to only one college.
- A department has many lecturers, but a lecturer might belong to more than one department; thus, the relationship between Lecturer and Department is many-to-many, represented by the crow's-feet at both ends of the link.
- A course is offered by a single department, indicated by the crossbar at the Department end of the Department/Course link.
- A lecturer might teach more than one student, and a student might have more than one lecturer, thus the crow's-feet at both the Lecturer and Student ends of the many-to-many relationship between Lecturer and Student.

Figure 6.9 An entity relationship diagram (ERD)

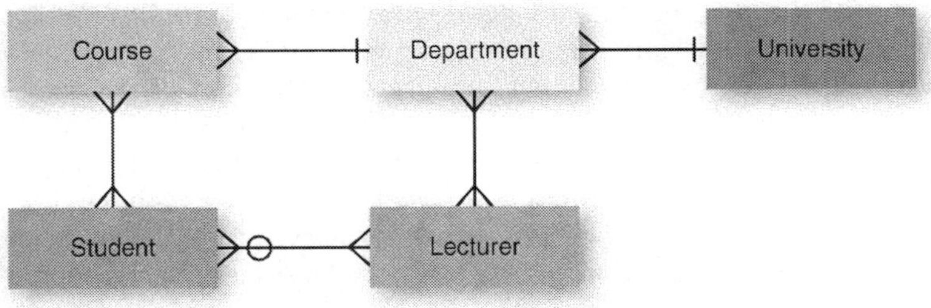

Figure 6.10 Fields of the Lecturer entity

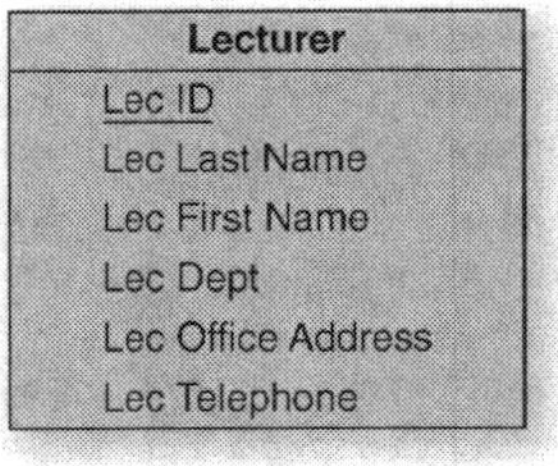

- However, the ring at the Student end indicates that a lecturer does not have to have students at all. The ring means 'optional', and is there for cases of lecturers (or professors) who concentrate on research and therefore do not teach.

Figure 6.9 provides an initial ERD. The designers must also detail the fields of each object, which determines the fields for each record of that object. The attributes are listed in each object box, and the primary key attribute is underlined. Usually, the primary key field appears at the top of the field list in the box. Figure 6.10 is an example of possible attributes of a Lecturer entity. You should be aware that database designers might use different notations. Therefore, before you review an ER diagram, be sure you understand what each symbol means.

The examples given here are quite simple. In reality, the reports that managers need to generate can be quite complex in terms of relationships among different data elements and the number of different tables from which they are assembled. Imagine the relationships among data maintained in libraries: a patron might borrow several titles; the library maintains several copies of each title; a title might be a book, a videotape or a CD; several authors might have published different books with the same title; librarians must be able to see availability and borrowed items by title, by author and by patron; they should also be able to produce a history report of all the borrowing of each patron for a certain period of time; and so on. All of these relationships and the various needs for reports must be taken into account when designing the database.

Databases on the Web

The Internet and its user-friendly Web would be practically useless if people could not access databases online. The premise of the Web is that people can not only browse appealing web pages but also search for and find information. Most often, that information is stored in databases. When a shopper accesses an online store, he or she can look for information about any of thousands, or hundreds of thousands, of items offered for sale. For example, when you access the site of Amazon.co.uk, you can receive online information (such as an image of an electronics item, price, shipping time and consumer evaluations) for thousands of items offered for sale. Wholesalers make their catalogues available online. Applications at auction sites receive enquiries by category, price range, country or origin, colour, date and other attributes and identify records of matching items, which often include pictures and detailed descriptions. Behind each of these sites is a database. The only way for organizations to conduct these web-based businesses is to give people outside the organizations access to their databases. In other words, the organizations must link their databases to the Internet.

From a technical point of view, online databases that are used with web browsers are no different from other databases. However, an interface must be designed to work with the Web. The user must see a form in which to enter queries or keywords to obtain information from the site's database. The interface designers must provide a mechanism to figure out data

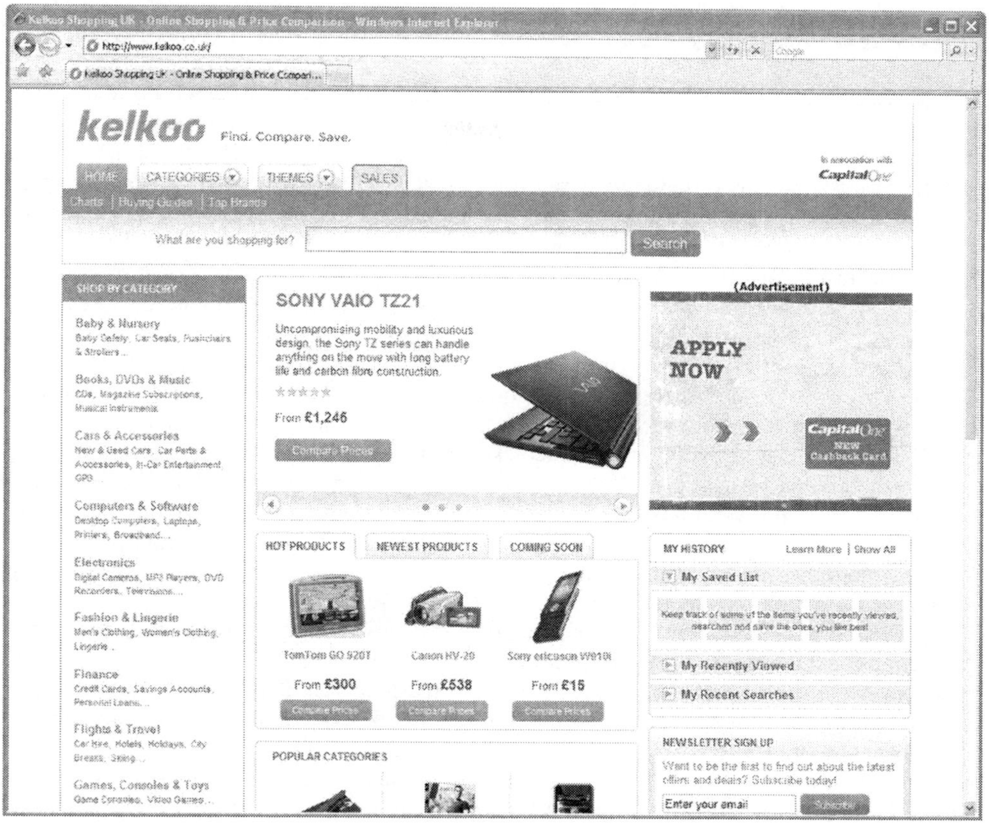

When you shop online you query databases and receive the results on your screen

that users insert in the online forms so that they can be placed in the proper fields in the database. The system also needs a mechanism to pass queries and keywords from the user to the database. There are several such interface programs, including CGI (Common Gateway Interface), Java servlets and active server pages (ASPs), as well as API (application program interface). The technical aspects of these applications are beyond the scope of this book. The process is diagrammed in Figure 6.11.

To ensure that their production databases are not vulnerable to attack via the Internet, organizations avoid linking their transaction databases to the Internet unless these are databases dedicated to online transactions, in which case the organization must apply proper security software. They must also be careful when linking a data warehouse (discussed next) to the Internet.

Figure 6.11 Active server pages and similar software enable data queries and entry via the Web

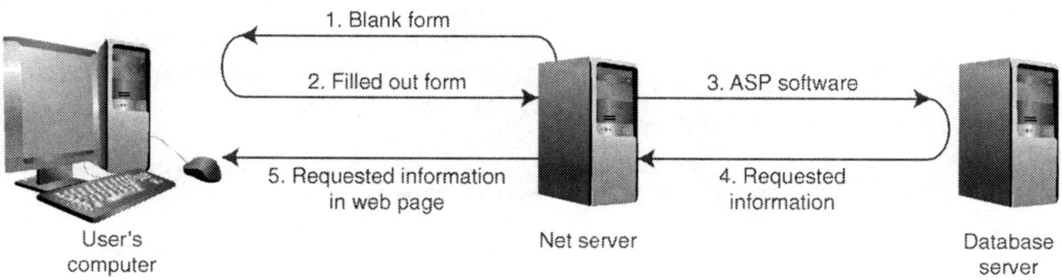

Data warehousing

The great majority of data collections in business are used for daily transactions and operations: records of customers and their purchases and information on employees, patients and other parties for monitoring, collection, payment and other business or legal purposes. The transactions do not stay in these databases long; usually only a few days or weeks. However, many organizations have found that if they accumulate transaction data, they can use it for important management decisions, such as researching market trends or tracking down fraud. Organizing and storing data for such purposes is called data warehousing.

data warehouse A huge collection of historical data that can be processed to support management decision-making.

A data warehouse is a large, typically relational, database that supports management decision-making. The database is large because it contains data, or summaries of data, from millions of transactions over many years and/or from national or global transactions rather than from a short period or a single region. It might maintain records of individual transactions or summaries of transactions for predetermined periods, such as hourly, daily or weekly. The purpose of data warehouses is to let managers produce reports or analyse large amounts of archival data and make decisions. Data-warehousing experts must be familiar with the types of business analyses that will be done with the data. They also have to design the data warehouse tables to be flexible enough for modifications in years to come, when business activities change or when different information must be extracted.

Data warehouses do not replace transactional databases, which are updated with daily transactions such as sales, billing, cash receipts and returns. Instead, transactional data are copied into the data warehouse, which is a separate database. This large archive contains valuable information for the organization that might not be evident in the smaller amounts of data typically stored in transactional databases. For example, an insurance company might keep monthly tables of policy sales; it can then see trends in the types of policies customers prefer in general or by age group. Such trends are meaningful only if they are gleaned from data collected over several years. Data from transactional databases are added to the data warehouse at the end of each business day, week or month, or might be added automatically as soon as a transaction is recorded in a transactional database. While a transactional database contains current data, which are disposed of after some time, the data in data warehouses are accumulated and might reflect many years of business activities.

data mart A collection of archival data that is part of a data warehouse, usually focusing on one aspect of the organization such as sales of a family of products or daily revenues in a geographic region.

Businesses often organize their data warehouse as a collection of data marts, smaller collections of data that focus on a particular subject or department. If data marts need to be used as one large data warehouse, special software tools can unify data marts and make them appear as one large data warehouse.

Industry SNAPSHOT

Data explosion

Albert Einstein said 'We can't solve problems by using the same kind of thinking we used when we created them.' This is also true of the technology that has lead to the vast increase in data held by companies worldwide. Typically a business today stores ten times more data than in 2000 and according to Gartner, one of the world's leading IT research and advisory companies, storage requirements are likely to increase by a factor of 30 by 2012.

SOURCE: 'Dealing with the data explosion', Richard Soundy, ComputerWeekly.com, 4 September 2007

Ethical and Societal **ISSUES**

Every move you make

The widespread use of database management systems coupled with web technologies allows organizations to collect, maintain and sell vast amounts of private personal data fast and cheaply. Millions of credit-card transactions take place in the world, each carrying private information. Millions of personal data items are routed daily to corporate databases through sales calls and credit checks. Millions of consumer records are collected and updated daily on the Web. For businesses, such data are an important resource; for individuals, such large data pools and the ways they are used threaten a fundamental human right: privacy.

Out of hand – Out of control You have just received a letter from the John Doe Investment Co. In the letter, the president tells you that at your age, with a nice income like yours, the company could provide you with innovative investment services. How did the company know about your existence? About your annual income? Could it be that some time ago you applied for a credit card? The company receiving the information sold part of it, or all of it, to the John Doe Investment Co. You now enjoy your credit card but you paid a hidden cost for it.

The Web: a source of data collection In the preceding example, you were at least aware that you gave somebody information. But many consumers provide information routinely without being aware of it. A huge amount of personal data is now collected through the Web. You might wonder why the home pages of so many websites ask you to register with them. When registering, you often provide your name, address and other details. The site asks you to create a user ID and password. If the pages you are accessing contain private data such as your investment portfolio, a user ID and password protect you, but if you are accessing news or other nonpersonal pages, a user ID and password actually serve the site operator. From the moment you log on to the site, the server can collect data about every move you make: which pages you are watching and for how long, which icons you click and in which order, and which advertising banners you click. In many cases, the organization that collects the data doesn't even own the site. The site owner hires a business such as DoubleClick to collect data. When you click an advertisement, that information is channelled into DoubleClick's huge database. What does the firm do with the database? It sells parts of it to other companies, or it slices and dices the information to help other companies target potential buyers belonging to certain demographic groups. And, no, it does not bother to tell you. While the software of such companies as DoubleClick can only identify the computer or IP number from which you logged on to a site and not you, personally, the information can be matched with you, personally, if you also use your personal ID and password.

Web bugs In addition to Web cookies, companies also use clear GIFs to track our web movements. A 'clear GIF', better known as a 'web beacon' or 'web bug', is a graphic image on a website used to monitor a surfer's activity. The image is usually undetectable because it usually consists of a single pixel. The bug links the web page to the web server of a third party, such as DoubleClick. The third party's server obtains the URL (web address) of the user as well as the URL of the site from which the user views the page. As long as the bug is 'displayed' by the user's computer, the third-party server can request session information from the user's web browser. Session information includes click stream and other activities performed by the user while visiting the site. In DoubleClick's own words: 'Companies use clear GIFs on their websites to learn more about their visitors' use of their websites and may be used to target ads to those visitors on other websites' (www.doubleclick.com/us/about_doubleclick/privacy/clear-gifs.asp).

Our health online Allowing medical staff and pharmacists to share patient medical information might help them help us. Imagine yourself being injured on a trip thousands of miles from your home. If the doctor treating you can immediately receive information about your sensitivities to certain medications, it might save your life. However, any electronic record residing on a database that is connected to a public network is potentially exposed to unauthorized access by people who do not have a legitimate need to know.

The upside In spite of the downside of collection of personal data, there is also a positive side. Database technology enables companies to provide us with better and faster services. It also makes the market more competitive. Small firms often cannot afford the great expense of data collection. For much less money, they can purchase sorted data – the same data that are available to the big, strong industry leader. So, the wide availability of data contributes to a more egalitarian and democratic business environment. The winners are not only vendors but also consumers, who can purchase new and cheaper products.

And while many of us complain that these huge databases add to the glut of junk mail and spam, better information in the hands of marketers might actually save consumers from such annoyances. After all, those annoying communications are for products and services you don't need. With more specific information, marketers can target only those individuals that might be interested in their offerings. While you shop, special tracking software can tell the online business, at least indirectly, what you do not like about the site. This enables businesses to improve their services. For example, many online retailers discovered that a hefty proportion of shoppers abandoned their virtual shopping carts just before the final purchase. Analysis of collected information discovered that some people wanted to know the handling and shipping charges before they charged their credit cards. Now, most online retailers provide clear shipping information and charges earlier.

From database to data warehouse

Unlike data warehouses, transactional databases are usually not suitable for business analysis because they contain only current, not historical, data. Often, data in transactional databases are also scattered in different systems throughout an organization. The same data can be stored differently and under other names. For example, customer names might be recorded in a column called Name in one table and in two columns – First Name and Last Name – in another table. These discrepancies commonly occur when an organization uses both its own data and data it purchases from other organizations, or if it has developed more than one database that contains the same data under a different label. When management decides to build a data warehouse, the IT staff must carefully consider the hardware, software and data involved in the effort.

The larger the data warehouse, the larger the storage capacity, the greater the memory and the greater the processing power of the computers that are needed. Because of capacity needs, organizations often choose mainframe computers with multiple CPUs to store and manage data warehouses. The computer memory must be large enough to allow processing of huge amounts of data at once. The amount of storage space and the access speed of disks are also important. Processing millions of records might take a long time, and variations in disk speed might mean the difference between hours or minutes in processing time. And since a data warehouse is considered a highly valuable asset, all data must be automatically backed up. Keep in mind that data warehouses grow continually, because their very purpose is to accumulate historical records. Retail chains such as Tesco record millions of sales transactions daily, all of which are channelled into data warehouses. Some have data warehouses that hold tens or hundreds of terabytes of data. However, not only retailers have augmented their hardware for large data warehouses. So have banks, credit-card issuers and health-care organizations, among other industries. Many organizations accumulate not only sales transactions but also purchasing records so they can produce information from which to make better purchasing decisions, such as which suppliers tend to offer lower prices for certain items at certain times of the year.

The data from which data warehouses are built usually come from within an organization, mainly from transactions, but they can also come from outside an organization. The latter

Industry SNAPSHOT

The data behemoth

Wal-Mart, the world's largest company, is well known for its appetite for retail data. With 6000 stores worldwide and 100 million people passing through its doors every week, the company is a voracious collector of data. In 2005, the company had 260 terabytes of data in its data warehouses on mainframe computers in Bentonville, Arkansas, USA, where it is headquartered. Experts estimated that this amount of data was twice as large as all the data posted on the world's websites.

ASDA, a major UK supermarket chain, is owned by Wal-Mart.

PHOTO SOURCE: © ASDA.COM

might include national or regional demographic data, data from financial markets and weather data. Similar to metadata in any database, data-warehouse designers create metadata for their large data pools. To uncover the valuable information contained in their data, organizations must use software that can effectively 'mine' data warehouses. Data mining is covered in Chapter 10, 'Business Intelligence and Knowledge Management'.

The designers must keep in mind scalability: the ability of the data warehouse to grow as the amount of the data and the processing needs grow. Future growth needs involve good planning in terms of both hardware and software.

Phases in building a data warehouse

Once an organization has ensured that it has adequate hardware and software, it can begin building the data warehouse. Three phases are involved in building a data warehouse from transactional data: extraction, transforming and loading (ETL). Figure 6.12 describes the process.

In the *extraction* phase the builders create the files from transactional databases and save them on the server that will hold the data warehouse. In the *transformation* phase the builders 'cleanse' the data and modify it into a form that allows insertion into the data warehouse. For example, they ascertain whether the data contain any spelling errors, and if there are any, they fix them. They make sure that all data are consistent. For instance, Warwickshire might be denoted as Warks, Warwicks or Warwickshire. Only one form would be used in a data warehouse. The builders ensure that all addresses follow the same form, using uppercase or lowercase letters consistently and defining fields uniformly (such as one field for the entire street address and a separate field for post codes). All the data that express the same type of quantities are 'cleansed' to use the same measurement units.

In the *loading* phase the builders transfer the transformed files to the data warehouse. They then compare the data in the data warehouses with the original data to ascertain completeness. They document the data for users, so the users know what they can find and analyse in the data warehouse.

Figure 6.12 Phases in preparing and using a data warehouse

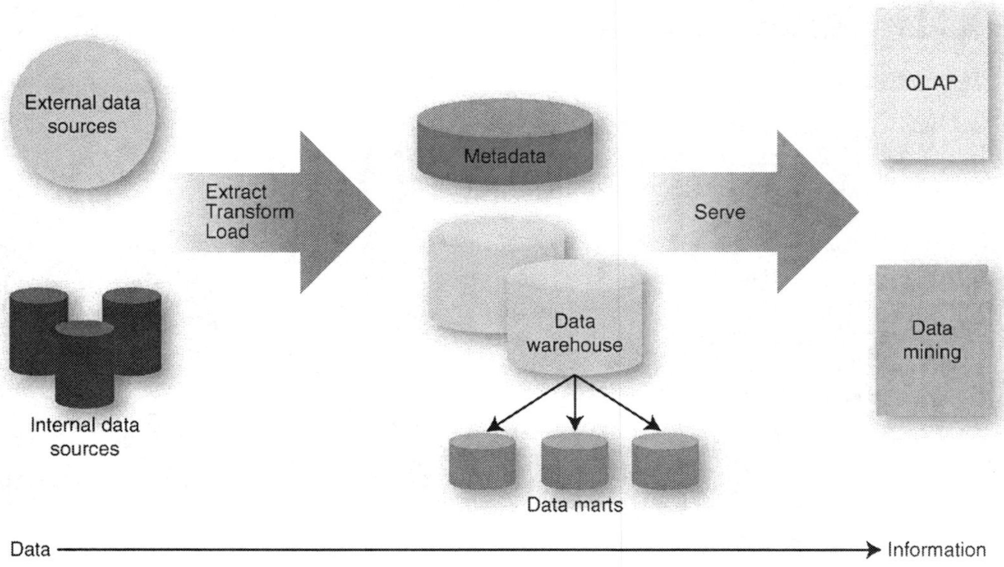

The new warehouse is then ready for use. It is a single source for all the data required for analysis, it is accessible to more users than the transactional databases (whose access is probably limited only to those who record transactions), and it provides a 'one-stop shopping' place for data. In fact, it is not unusual for a data warehouse to have large tables with fifty or more fields (attributes).

Once the data warehouse is in operation, much of the ETL activity can be automated. Depending on the needs of its users, the structure and content of the data warehouse might be changed occasionally. Once the data warehouse is ready, techniques such as data mining and online analytical processing (OLAP) can be used to exploit it. Managers can then extract business intelligence for better decision-making. Data mining, OLAP and business intelligence are discussed in Chapter 10.

SUMMARY

In their daily operations, organizations can collect vast amounts of data. These data are raw material for highly valuable information, but data are useless without tools to organize them, store them in an easily accessible manner, and manipulate them to produce that information. These functions are the great strength of databases: collections of interrelated data that, within an organization and sometimes between organizations, are shared by many units and contribute to productivity and efficiency.

The database approach has several advantages over the more traditional file approach: less data redundancy, application-data independence and greater probability of data integrity.

The smallest piece of data collected about an entity is a character. Multiple characters make up a field. Several fields make up a record. A collection of related records is a file, or in the relational model, a table. Databases usually contain several files, but the database approach can be applied to a single file.

A database management system (DBMS) is a software tool that enables us to construct databases, populate them with data and manipulate the data. Most DBMSs come with 4GLs that can be used to develop applications that facilitate queries and produce reports.

There are several database models, which are general logical structures of records in a database: hierarchical, network, relational and object-oriented. By far, the most popular model is the relational model, which is used to build most new databases, although object-oriented databases are gaining popularity. Some vendors offer DBMSs that accommodate a combination of relational and object-oriented models, called object-relational.

The links among entities in a relational database are maintained by the use of keys. Primary keys are unique identifiers. Composite keys are combinations of two or more fields that are used as a primary key. Foreign keys link one table to another within the database.

In an object-oriented database, data sets along with the procedures that process them are objects. The relationship between one set of data and another is by way of one object containing the other, rather than by foreign keys.

SQL has been adopted as an international standard language for querying relational databases. SQL statements can also be embedded in code that is produced using many programming languages.

To construct a database, a designer first constructs a schema and prepares metadata, which is information about the data to be kept in the database.

To plan databases, designers conduct data modelling. Before they design a database they create entity relationship diagrams, which show the tables required for each data entity and the attributes (fields) it should hold, as well as the relationships between tables. Then they can move on to constructing a schema, which is the structure of all record structures of the entities, and the relationships among them.

Many databases are linked to the Web for remote use. This arrangement requires web server software, such as active server pages and Java servlets, which allow users to enter queries or update databases over the Internet.

Data warehouses are huge collections of historical transactions copied from transactional databases, often along with other data from outside sources. Managers use software tools to glean useful information from data warehouses to support their decision-making. Some data warehouses are made up of several data marts, each focusing on an organizational unit or a subject.

In each addition of data from a transactional database to a data warehouse, the data are extracted, transformed and loaded, a process known by its acronym, ETL.

The low price of efficient and effective database software exacerbates a societal problem of the Information Age: invasion of privacy. Because every transaction of an individual can be easily recorded and later combined with other personal data, it is inexpensive to produce whole dossiers on individual consumers. This poses a threat to privacy. However, commercial organizations insist that they need personal information to improve their products and services and to target their marketing only to interested consumers.

TRENT COURIER SERVICES REVISITED

Trent Couriers gathers and maintains many types of data in its database. It has tried to ensure its security and safe backup while still being accessible to customers and employees. Let's explore some of the issues it faces in managing its database.

What would you do?

1. Trent Couriers' database is vital to its operations. The case at the beginning of the chapter didn't mention its supplier data. Trent Couriers has suppliers for its fleet of cars and vans and for its office supplies. What sorts of data would it likely keep about its suppliers? What controls and limits should it put on its supplier data? Make a recommendation to Andrew Langston on who should be able to review and change that data and where the data should be maintained.
2. Andrew had run into IT consultant Karen Brown many times and began talking to her about his IT concerns. When he realized that he was going to need a database management system, he decided to take her advice and purchase Oracle. What sort of research should Andrew have done to make sure that Oracle was the best solution? What advantages and disadvantages should he have considered when purchasing a new DBMS?

New perspectives

1. Trent Couriers has used SQL queries and reports to identify VIP customers and discover its most profitable clients and services. It also has a website. How could it use website tracking data to enhance its services? What departments would be interested in this information? Discuss and list as many as you can.
2. Andrew has heard that databases can also store digital images. Are there any parts of Trent Couriers' data operations that might use digital images? If so, which?

Review questions

1. It is easier to organize data and retrieve it when there is little or no dependence between programs and data. Why is there more such dependence in a file approach and less in the database approach?
2. Spreadsheets have become quite powerful for data management. What can be done with database management systems that cannot be done with spreadsheet applications? Give several examples.
3. What is the difference between a database and a database management system?
4. DBMSs are usually bundled with powerful 4GL modules. Why?
5. What are the advantages and disadvantages of object-oriented databases?
6. What is the relationship between a website's local search engines and online databases?
7. When constructing a database, the designer must know what types of relationships exist between records in different data sets, such as one-to-many or many-to-many. Give three examples for each of these relationships.
8. Can you think of a one-to-one relationship in a relational database? Give an example.

9 What is SQL? In which database model does it operate? Why is it so popular?

10 What is a data warehouse? How is it different from a transactional database?

11 Why is it not advisable to query data from transactional databases for executive decision-making the same way you do data warehouses?

12 What are the phases of adding data to a data warehouse?

13 What does it mean to cleanse data before they are stored in a data warehouse?

14 What are data marts? How different are they from data warehouses?

Discussion questions

1 Retail chains want to ensure that every time a customer returns to purchase something, the record of that purchase can be matched with previous data of that individual. What objects that consumers often use help the retailers in that regard?

2 Increasingly, corporate databases are updated by their consumers rather than corporate employees. How so?

3 Can you think of an industry that would not benefit from the promise of a data warehouse? Explain.

4 Shouldn't those who build data warehouses trim the data before they load it to data warehouses? Why do they usually not cut any data from transactions?

5 The combination of RFID and database technology will soon enable retailers to record data about consumers even when they have not purchased anything at the store. Can you think of an example and how the data could be used?

6 A retailer of household products maintains a data warehouse. In addition to data from sales transactions, the retailer also purchases and maintains in it daily weather data. What might be the reason?

7 Many organizations have posted privacy policies at their websites. Why do you think this is so?

8 Consider the following opinion shared by some people: database management systems and data-warehousing techniques are the greatest threat to individual privacy in modern times. What is your opinion?

9 The proliferation of organizational databases poses a threat to privacy. After reading the following passage, what would you say to someone in response to these statements: 'I'm a law-abiding citizen and pay my taxes promptly. I don't care if anyone reviews my university grades or my income statements, because I have nothing to hide. I have no reason to worry about violation of my privacy. All these complaints about violation of privacy are not valid. Only individuals who have something to hide need to worry.'

10 Civil rights advocates demand that organizations ask individuals for permission to sell personal information about them. Some also demand that the subjects of the information be paid for their consent. Organizations have argued that they cannot practically comply with these demands and that the demands interfere with the free flow of information. What is your opinion?

11 Organizations whose websites offer visitors some control of how their personal information is collected and used offer one of two options: 'opt out' or 'opt in'. Explain each term.

12 Some people say that as long as the concept of 'informed consent' is applied, individuals should not complain about invasion of their privacy. What is 'informed consent'? Do you agree with the argument?

13 The affordability of sophisticated DBMSs and data warehouses makes the business world more 'democratic' and puts all businesses almost on an equal footing. How so? Explain.

14 Businesses rarely allow customers to scrutinize and correct records that the organizations keep about them. Technologically, does the Web make it less expensive for organizations to allow that?

Tutorial activities

1 Acxiom.co.uk is a data services firm. Browse this company's site and research its activities at its own site and at other websites. Write a two-page summary of the company's activity: What does the company sell? How does it obtain what it sells? Who are its customers, and what

do they do with what they purchase from Acxiom?

2 Research the business of DoubleClick.com. What type of data does the company collect and sell? How does it collect the data? Who are the company's customers, and how do they use the services or data they buy from DoubleClick?

3 Research web resources to write a two- to four-page research paper titled 'Object-Oriented Databases', in which you explain the differences and similarities between relational databases and object-oriented databases, and their comparative advantages and disadvantages.

4 Mid-County Hospital holds data on doctors and patients in two tables in its database (see the tables below): DOCTOR and PATIENT. Use your DBMS to build the appropriate schema, enter the records and create the reports described.

a) A report showing the following details for each doctor in this order: Last Name, First Name and Ward. Arrange the report by ascending alphabetical order of the last names.

b) A report showing the entire record with the original order of columns of all the doctors whose salary is greater than €100,000 who work for either one of the following wards: Internal (INT), Obstetric-Gynecological (OBG), Oncology (ONC).

c) A report showing the following details for all of Dr Anderson's patients. Dr Anderson's first and last name should appear once at the top of the report. In each record, the join report should show Doctor's ID, Last Name and Ward (from the DOCTOR table), and Patient's Last Name, First Name and Date of Admission (from the PATIENT table).

5 Mr Lawrence Husick is an inventor who, with other inventors, obtained several patents. Use the search engine found at http://gb.espacenet.com/ to search the UK Intellectual Property Office to find all the patents that mention Lawrence Husick as an inventor. Type up the patent numbers along with their corresponding patent titles (what the invention is).

6 Your team is to design a relational database for an online pizza service. Customers log on to the site and provide their first and last names, address, telephone number and email address. They order pizza from a menu. Assume that each item on the menu has a unique number, a description and a price. Assume there is one person per shift who receives orders and takes care of them, from giving the order to the kitchen to dispatching a delivery person. The system automatically records the time at which the server picked up the order. The business wants to maintain the details of customers, including their orders of the past six months. The following are reports that management might require: (1) a list of all the orders handled by a server over a period of time; (2) summaries of total sales, by item, for a period; and (3) a report showing all of the past week's deliveries by server, showing each individual order – customer last name and address, items ordered, time of order pickup and last name of delivery person. (You can assume the last names of delivery people are unique, because if there is more than one with the same last name, a number is added to the name.)

a) Chart the table for each entity, including all its fields and the primary key.

b) Draw the entity relationship diagram.

DOCTOR

ID#	LIC#	Last Name	First Name	Ward	Salary
102	8234	Hogg	Yura	INT	187,000
104	4666	Tyme	Justin	INT	91,300
221	2908	Jones	Jane	OBG	189,650
243	7876	Anderson	Ralph	ONC	101,800
256	5676	Jones	Ernest	ORT	123,400
376	1909	Washington	Jaleel	INT	87,000
410	4531	Carrera	Carlos	ORT	97,000

PATIENT

NIN	Last N	First N	Admission Date	Insurance	Doc ID
055675432	Hopkins	Jonathan	01/04/06	BlueCross	221
101234566	Bernstein	Miriam	28/04/07	HAP	243
111654456	McCole	John	31/03/06	Kemper	221
200987898	Meanny	Marc	27/02/07	HAP	221
367887654	Mornay	Rebecca	03/04/06	HAP	410
378626254	Blanchard	George	30/03/07	BlueCross	243
366511122	Rubin	David	01/04/06	Brook	243

7 Your team should contact a large organization, such as a bank, an insurance company or a hospital. Interview the database administrator about the database he or she maintains on customers (or patients). What are the measures that the DBA has taken to protect the privacy of the subjects whose records are kept in the databases? Consider accuracy, timeliness and appropriate access to personal records. Write a report on your findings. If you found loopholes in the procedures, list them and explain why they are loopholes and how they can be remedied. Alternatively, log on to the site of a company that posted a detailed privacy policy and answer the same questions.

Companion CD questions

1 You and a friend would like to catalogue your CD collections. Create a simple database that will hold all of your titles in one table and your friend's titles in another table.

2 Write a query to show you which titles you and your friend both own.

From ideas to application
REAL CASES

Case study **6.1**

Coping with growth

TÜV NORD Group is one of Germany's largest technical service providers offering a wide range of consulting, testing and servicing. It is particularly well known throughout Germany for its automobile emissions testing centres and has expertise in most areas of technical safety, environmental protection and the conformity assessment of management systems and products. It has a workforce of nearly 7000 and is represented in 36 countries throughout Europe, Asia and America. It has recently merged with another company, Rheinisch-Westfälisch, leading to a potential doubling in size of its 2 terabyte SAP Business Warehouse (BW). This mission-critical database contains performance data from a vast number of company activities such as safety inspections, security testing and so on.

In addition to the doubling in size of the BW database, the merged companies expected a growth in employment in excess of 35 per cent. In order to cope with this growth the company decided to update its BW software and database management system. This allows more concurrent users without a corresponding degradation of response time.

The figures are quite mind-boggling. The group manages its IT operations with four administrators responsible for the database, operating system, server hardware and storage area network. The BW holds 2.1 terabytes (expected to increase to 4 terabytes) and is stored along with 25 multidimensional analytical data cubes, each with 16 dimensions. In addition, the company manages 24 terabytes of totally raw storage, prior to 'cleansing'. 'Our SAP system has perhaps 35,000 tables, and every table has three or four indexes', according to Sven Otromke, SAP system Manager of TÜV NORD Group. 'As we customize the system we add more indexes, but after several years it

The sign for a TÜV centre in Germany.

PHOTO SOURCE: © IMAGEBROKER/ALAMY

is difficult to remember exactly why any given index was added. With Dynamic Management Views you can see how long it has been since an index has been used, and this helps us decide when indexes can be removed. Every time we can remove an extraneous index, it means one less index needs to be maintained, and this in turn improves performance.'

It is not just the physical storage and handling of the large volumes of data that cause problems. The administrator of the Storage Area Network (SAN) needs to be aware of back-up and recovery procedures. Before the merger, the use of local tape streamers was sufficient as the data volume was less than 20 GB. However, the increase in data volume meant that TÜV NORD needed to move to a system of tape libraries located in the data centres in Hanover, Hamburg and Essen, while smaller locations are connected to the large office geographically closest to them. Depending on what they want to access, employees can access data either from a central location or via local servers in the branch offices. Backup is carried out incrementally on a daily basis and once a week TÜV NORD carries out a full backup of the complete storage volume. For legal reasons, the data held by TÜV NORD require long-term archiving. Data are transferred to media which can then be stored in a safe location away from the primary site.

The TÜV NORD Group also makes use of database mirroring. A 'hot-standby' of the live system is maintained by sending a replica of each transaction to the mirror database. Therefore with the live database in Hannover and a mirror in Hamburg the group can provide continuous working. If, for example, the Hannover centre becomes non-operational because of a fire, then the Hamburg centre can fill in immediately.

Thinking about the case

1 Does TÜV Nord need to have a different approach to operational data and archived data? Does it need a different approach to data that it archives for legal reasons and old data that it can use for strategic development?
2 The use of a mirror database seems to solve all the problems of data recovery. Is this true? What are the costs?

SOURCE: 'Germany's TUEV NORD Deploys SQL Server 2005 for 2-Terabyte SAP Business Warehouse', http://www.microsoft.com/casestudies and 'Securing Data with Software Solutions from Symantec. TÜV Nord Gruppe', http://www.symantec.com/enterprise/solutions/successes/detail.jsp?csid=tuv_nord_gruppe

Case study 6.2

Children at risk . . .

As a result of the Public Inquiry held into the child abuse case involving Victoria Climbié the Children's Bill passed into UK law in November 2004. Victoria died after years of abuse by relatives. Part of the problem was that several agencies (social services, the police, etc.) each had only part of the information about Victoria and there was no way for these pieces of information to be brought together. An important aspect of the Bill proposed the setting up of a central children's database and the UK government announced in 2005 that the database, the Information Sharing Index, would be operational by the end of 2008 with a view to improving the welfare protection of young people. The central register would be accessible to all relevant agencies and organizations with the intention of facilitating effective and speedy response to problems and concerns. This involves the establishment of 150 local authority registers coordinated by an over-arching system that creates a single identification number for all children. Any professional who comes into contact with a child, such as a doctor or social worker, can add a flag indicating a concern. Nine local authorities were chosen to pilot the scheme and as a result the Department for Education and Science (DfES) told all local authorities that they must have an Integrated Children's System (ICS) in place by January 2007. Some local authorities created systems more advanced than that required by the

The Information Sharing Index was designed to improve communication across organizations but the idea has created significant debate.

PHOTO SOURCE: © ANTHONY TUENI

DfES. According to Carey Sherman, Somerset's business and finance manager for children's social care, 'Limiting ourselves to the government's ICS requirements would confuse staff because some of the processes finished at an odd point and our social workers would have to operate two different systems.'

Whilst no one would argue with the principles behind the initiative, there are various criticisms about the implementation. According to Anna Smallwood of Socitm Consulting, there is confusion in many local authorities about the integration of the ICS with other government child care initiatives as well as with other local authority IT systems. Lack of effective training for child social workers could also be a problem. 'Social workers want better quality systems to help them analyse the information they are taking in, but some of them will need time to understand the new ways of doing things.'

However, the most stinging criticism came in a report published in November 2006 by the Foundation for Information Policy Research (FIPR) which suggested that the database will actually put children at greater risk.

'The proposed surveillance system is contrary to the basic principles of data protection and human rights law', said Professor Douwe Korff of London Metropolitan University, one of the authors of the report.

'It replaces professional discretion (in both meanings of the word) with computerised assessments of human behaviour that are inherently fallible.'

'The system violates private and family life and intrudes on children's rights without justification. The government's aims are laudable, but this is not the way to go about achieving them.'

The report suggests that the £200 million (nearly € 300 million) cost will divert money from more traditional child care. This economic argument is one made against many IT systems and is answered simply by conducting a cost/benefit analysis. Not so easily dealt with is the issue of data protection and privacy. By opening the database to so many agencies that can then draw conclusions from the data, there is a real danger of mistakes being made. The report cites an example whereby a nine-year-old child was taken into care after social workers misinterpreted medical data. In another example, police shared information about a nine-month-old child under the guise of crime prevention. With so many people, over 400,000 civil servants, having access to the database, there is potential for many more such cases. According to Professor Ross Anderson, chair of the FIPR, 'when building systems that process personal information, you can have scale, or functionality or security. You can even have any two of these, but you cannot have all three. If we are to have secure and functional child protection systems, they will have to be local rather than central.'

The most worrying aspect of the database, according to the report, is that of what it calls 'e-discrimination'. To quote part of the executive summary of the report, 'In the past, it has been well documented that children who were black, or from poor neighbourhoods or travelling families, suffered disproportionate police attention because of the expectation that they would be more likely to offend. The expectation could easily turn into a self-fulfilling prophecy. A system that attempts to predict which children will become delinquent, by totting up negative indicators from health, school and other records, runs the serious risk of recreating the same problems – especially as the information, analysis and professional opinions it contains will be made available to many of the public-sector workers who come into contact with the child. A perfectly law-abiding youngster from a difficult home background, who has perhaps struggled to overcome learning and health difficulties, may find at every turn that teachers expect less, and that police attention is more likely. As the causes of this discrimination are online, the youngster cannot mitigate them simply by dressing neatly and being polite. The data and algorithms used as a basis for discrimination might not be accessible to the victim (whether practically or at all) and thus a victim of unjustified discrimination might end up with no recourse. This raises serious data protection concerns relating to the appropriateness of collecting, processing and retaining the data.'

Child abuse is a very emotive subject and anything that can reduce the risks must be a good idea. However, as can be seen from the above arguments, there are other issues that must be taken into account when proposing the bringing together of data from a variety of sources and opening the database up to many people. Similar arguments have been raised in the UK over the introduction of identity cards and the creation of a comprehensive DNA database.

Thinking about the case

1. Professor Anderson suggests that the problem with the national database could be resolved by having 150 local, unconnected databases. Do you think this would solve the problem? Are there any drawbacks with this approach?
2. As stated above, proposals to introduce a database containing DNA data about every UK citizen has resulted in heated debate. What are the advantages? What are the drawbacks?

SOURCE: Iain Thomson, 'Children's database puts kids at risk', http://www.computing.co.uk/vnunet/news/2169272/children-database-puts-kids; Ross Anderson et al., Foundation for Information Policy Research, 'Children's Databases – Safety and Privacy', http://www.fipr.org/childrens_databases.pdf

Case study **6.3**

Tesco

BY SCOTT RAEBURN

Tesco is the UK's grocer, or so many people think. It is, of course, so much more than that. A truly colossal global company, it is the UK's market leading supermarket with over 30 per cent market share. Its leading competitor has less than 20 per cent share. But a look at the 2007 Annual Report paints a much larger picture. This group valued at more than £40 billion had revenue of £42.6 billion in the year ended February 2007. Its annual profits were £2.6 billion, or about £82 per second, 24/7. It employs 413,000 people in 1898 UK stores and 1365 other stores worldwide, including Eastern Europe, Turkey and China. When it opened its first store in the USA in late 2007 it truly had a supermarket empire 'on which the sun never sets' (with apologies to Queen Victoria).

Tesco was founded in 1919 in London's East End by a collaboration between a tea retailer (T. E. Stockwell) and Jack Cohen, who wanted to sell tea and other groceries. From a single market stall to listing on the London Stock Exchange in 1947 to being the UK's second leading supermarket grocery chain by the early 1990s, Jack and his successors proved that they could. So what changed in the mid 1990s that made them world beaters? What makes 12+ million customers use their Clubcard to shop in Tesco at least once per week? The answer is simple – data information and the way Tesco used it.

The pivotal moment was when Tesco brought in the firm of dunnhumby (yes, it is all lowercase!) to help with analysing data from a loyalty card scheme it had tried in three stores. With dunnhumby's help, the trial was extended to run through 1994, generating till data, analysing it the dunnhumby way and sending appropriate rewards to the customers.

The new insight which generated the rewards is now called 'relevance marketing' by dunnhumby. Traditional market segmentation schemes were based on what the customer was – gender, age, educational attainment, job, area lived in and so on. Customers were 'averages' of each type, according to which classification scheme was used. Dunnhumby instead worked on the concept that customers should be classified by what they bought (and didn't buy) in-store. Each individual customer should be identified and their buying patterns remembered, in an updated version of what traditional British corner shops did back in the 1950s and 1960s. Instead of sending a promotional offer to all customers, send an individual reward to each customer based on his/her buying pattern. This can encourage repeat spending for some goods and tempt the customer with offers on others. And it worked. The trial stores in and around Tesco Head Office all showed very positive customer response to the Clubcard scheme. When rolled out across the stores, it led to a step-change in Tesco's performance. About five years after introducing Clubcard, Tesco was the UK market leader. Today it is exporting its approach across the world. And it's all based on analysing data effectively.

Dunnhumby does this by adding in classifications to data as they arrive from tills and stores. Each transaction has 40–50 customer classifications added. It forms part of a time series going back to when the customer joined Clubcard. Each product also has about as many variables attached to it and the

The Tesco Clubcard's success has provided the company with unparalleled information on its customers.

PHOTO SOURCE: © EYEBYTE/ALAMY

cross-correlation of customer patterns and product attributes provides the base data for Tesco's Clubcard operations.

It is said that the dunnhumby database contains 40+ terabytes of data; that it could drill-down to find everything an individual cardholder had bought in the past ten years! Clive Humby, one of the founders of dunnhumby, saw data-mining as an art as well as a science. Normal database work is based on queries, constructed by a user in a language such as SQL (Structured Query Language), which the database then reports on. Data-mining turns that on its head and uses software to tell the user about relationships within the data; it tells the user which questions to ask! Add to that Zodiac, dunnhumby's software to find external sources of data which can supplement the till purchase data, and interesting patterns emerge. The dunnhumby database takes data from the electoral roll, the Land Registry (England and Wales) and the General Register Office (Scotland), the Office of National Statistics and others.

The UK's three large credit reference companies, Experian, Equifax and Claritas, maintain records on every adult in the UK and their credit worthiness. Dunnhumby collects data from each one, combining it with the other sources to add to the picture of its customers. Commercial companies such as Thomson Intermedia, specialists in advertising media intelligence, have struck agreements with dunnhumby which allows their knowledge of the effectiveness of advertising to be combined with dunnhumby/Tesco's customer insight. This allows dunnhumby to offer Tesco both large-scale information on buying habits for items such as 'organic products' and individual mailings reflecting what Clubcard customers bought in the last quarter.

All this has been brought together as the Crucible database, something about which Tesco and dunnhumby are very protective. All references to Crucible are now missing from the dunnhumby website (there used to be some details). It's not mentioned on the Tesco website. The *Guardian* newspaper in the UK is not impressed by this 'exhaustive – and secret' database. But neither Tesco not dunnhumby are breaking any rules. All the requirements of the Data Protection Act are met. No personal data identifying an individual is ever sold to other companies. But they know an impressive amount about their customers. It is said that during the initial trials with dunnhumby in 1994, when Humby presented three months' worth of results to the Tesco Board, Chairman Lord MacLaurin responded 'you know more about my customers after three months than I know after 30 years'. And that from 14 stores. The rise of Tesco shows the effectiveness on a national scale.

Interestingly, the final trigger for Crucible came from the UK Government. Changes to the law in 2001 allowed voters to restrict the use of their own electoral role (ER) entry. Whereas the ER used to be available to anybody who wanted it for any purpose, after the change many voters restricted their entry to the full version used for election purposes only, with no entry appearing in the version which could be sold to the public. This led to the need for replacement data sources by the credit reference agencies and their customers. Crucible was the Tesco/dunnhumby response.

The operation to mail customers four times a year is very impressive – the combined mailings represent 6 per cent of all the items handled by Royal Mail and other postal companies. It is said that the first of these mailings in 1996 was the largest single direct mailing in UK history at the time addressed to individuals (as opposed to the 'Occupier' or 'The Householder').

Of course, other companies don't want to be left out. With one-third of UK households members of Clubcard, Tesco has available real data on a sample of customers which no market research company could hope to survey. In effect, 12 million respondents are unlikely to be wrong. So dunnhumby sells a 10 per cent sample to Tesco suppliers for up to £50,000 per year, depending on volume sold. It's expensive, but Tesco buyers expect suppliers to talk the same language as themselves and Tesco is the largest buyer of these products in the UK! Companies such as Sky, Gillette and Orange also buy anonymized data based on dunnhumby data – it's the best consumer data available.

In a final, some would say almost Orwellian twist, the credit reference agency Experian has been working for several years with academics to develop Mosaic, a consumer profiling system which uses census surname data to track ethnicity, religion, colour and culture. Earlier versions of this system were used by 190 of the top 200 UK companies and the three UK political parties. The lead researcher has said that he could see no reason why Tesco shouldn't be allowed to analyse which ethnic groups buy their Asian products. This would be readily possible using Crucible data based on the surnames of Clubcard users. This is a potentially very sensitive area for database work. However, two police forces, with all the resources of the Police National Computer and government databases, have used Mosaic rather than official data to understand local policing needs. The NHS is also a customer.

So Tesco and dunnhumby may actually know more about the UK population than any other single organization (now that Tesco owns some 84 per cent of dunnhumby). Does MI5 know?

Case study questions

1 Which sources of data for Tesco come from within the company and which are external to the company?

2 This case is about growth based on effective use of data. Was the collection and analysis of accurate data enough to explain the subsequent growth of Tesco?

3 What insights can the proper use of the contents of a data warehouse give to Tesco executives?

SOURCES: The *Guardian*, 27 September 2005; *Financial Times*, 11 November 2006; *The Times*, 21 April 2007; The *Wall Street Journal*, 6 June 2006; www.tesco.com; www.loyalty.vg; www.dunnhumby.co.uk

silicon.com

Case study **6.4**

Information overload

BY STEWART BAINES

Businesses are drowning in data – but how much good is it doing them? Stewart Baines finds out how to retrieve and understand essential corporate information.

IT professionals are regularly asked to solve the 'information overload' problem but the term may be a misnomer. Almost three in five managers of the 1000 surveyed by Accenture said they miss information valuable to their jobs every day. On average, respondents to the survey of UK and US professionals spend up to two hours per day scrabbling to find data. If we're so replete with information, why can't we find what we need?

As information volumes increase, so do two other things: the number of data sources and the places to put it. Greg Todd, senior executive for Accenture Information Management Services, says: 'It's a consistent theme – there's so much information being thrown up by different technology platforms.'

RSS feeds, email, search engines and corporate intranets are competing with internal reporting systems that may not always have access to all of the data streams that employees need. An increasing

CRM Real Time Dashboards, such as this example from Netsuite, are partly an attempt to address the issue of information overload, providing users with customized data snapshots instantly.

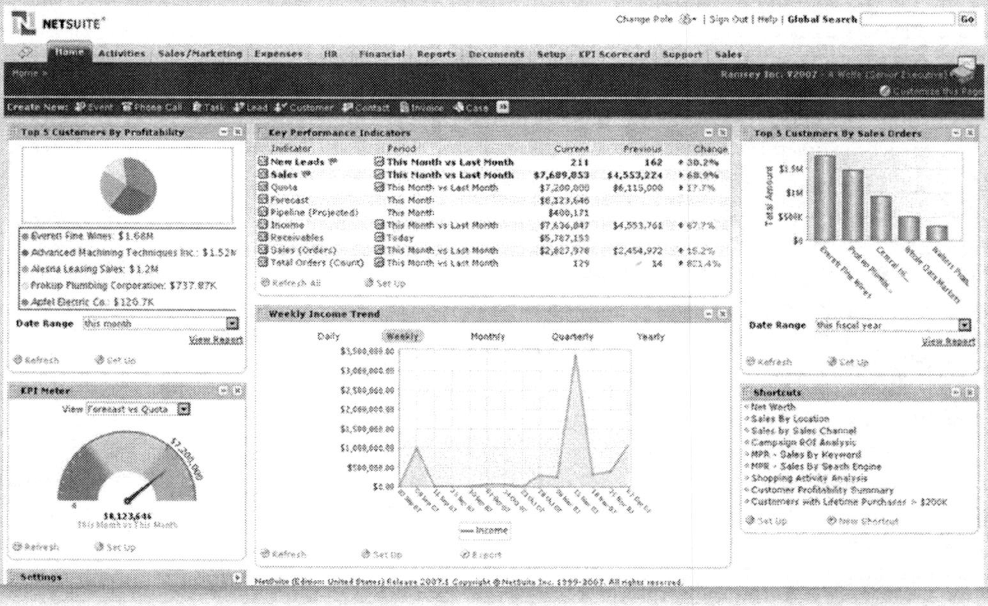

PHOTO SOURCE: © NETSUITE INC.

choice of potential storage locations (and therefore places for people to look for it) makes the mess complete.

Employees also store information on their own hard drives, which makes it difficult or impossible for others to find. IT departments compound the problem by duplicating data in different systems or storing too much of it as they frantically try to ward off future compliance problems.

Richard Kellett, head of technology strategy for SAS UK, says: 'It's a bit of a comfort blanket. If you keep everything then you can answer any question from the business, theoretically. But what you end up with is something that costs a lot and delivers little.'

Before tackling the problem, companies need to understand whether they're dealing with structured or unstructured data. Data from a company's logistics, finance or marketing activities can be pulled into a database that can then be fed to executives using a reporting system or dashboard. A collection of dials and gauges providing an at-a-glance analysis of business performance can be a crucial way to keep everyone in the business informed.

For a dashboard to work, though, a reporting system has to integrate data from separate systems, which must themselves be sophisticated enough to export it. The alternative is to move to a single platform with built-in reporting capabilities.

Netsuite, co-founded and funded by Oracle CEO, Larry Ellison, provides a hosted business management for SMEs and is carving out a niche for itself here. The company provides online CRM, shipping, inventory management and financial services, among others.

The idea is that by putting everything into the same underlying databases, managers can get a joined-up view of the business. This means no rushing around to see if you have the inventory to hand when someone calls up with a large order, for example.

Craig Sullivan, VP of International Products at Netsuite, says: 'There's a benefit to see all of your key metrics for the business in one place.'

But moving from piecemeal back-office systems to a unified platform carries its own investment overhead – and once you've moved, you have to persuade the employees to use the new system. Gavin Whatrup, group IT director at Creston, a collection of PR, advertising and direct marketing businesses, knows getting grassroots buy-in for new working practices can be a challenge.

He says: 'We suffer as an industry with unstructured data, particularly email. People use it as primary, sometimes their only, data store. It's completely wrong.

'But in marketing there isn't much top down control. People work independently and use their own processes.' He takes a hands-off approach, leaving employees to manage their own information flow on the basis that as successful businesses they must be doing it right.

Surely there are other ways to handle unstructured data, without negotiating tensions between centralized and individual ways of working? Mapping desktops to network drives and using enterprise search appliances is one way to mitigate the problem.

Another is to bring order to unstructured information in automated ways. Adrian Butcher, strategic ECM consultant at document management vendor Open Text, says 'An example would be extracting an order number or customer name from an email and using that to directly access information in a CRM or ERP system.'

That still leaves companies with the challenge of collecting the most valuable asset of all: the tacit information that exists in people's heads. How do you get 15 years of unspoken rules and experiences out of the senior support engineer's head and into a digestible format for other people? Depending on the size of the company, wikis, blogs and corporate social networking software could be a way forward.

For now, though, many companies probably have enough of a challenge managing what they already have. And while they continue to grapple with that, more of it keeps piling up.

Thinking about the case

1 Which is more important to an organization, structured or unstructured data?

2 It there a point at which the cost of extracting and processing the vast collection of data outweighs the benefits?

SOURCE: www.silicon.com.

Chapter 6

The web-enabled enterprise

LEARNING OBJECTIVES

The Web has been the most exciting development in the field of information systems and telecommunications in recent years. The combination of advanced telecommunications technology and innovative software is revolutionizing the way people communicate, shop, make contracts and payments, educate, learn and conduct business. Numerous companies throughout the world have been established thanks to the enabling power of the Web, and existing ones have used the Web to extend their operations. Firms conduct business electronically with each other and directly with consumers, using a variety of business models. This chapter focuses on web technologies and businesses on the Web.

When you finish this chapter, you will be able to:

Describe how the Web and high-speed Internet connections are changing business operations.

Explain the functionality of various web technologies.

Compare and contrast options for web servers.

Explain basic business-to-business and business-to-consumer practices on the Web.

Explain the relationship between web technologies and supply chain management.

Give examples of features and services that successful business websites offer.

Learn about online annoyances such as spam and adware, and how to protect against online identity theft.

SpareBitz.com

FIRST STEPS IN E-COMMERCE

Steve Wilson was pleased with how things were going for SpareBitz.com. His numerous meetings with Carl had caused him to think carefully about his business processes. Carl had explained that putting the business on the Web meant a review of the objectives of the current business. They needed to study the competitors, such as Ezee-fix.co.uk, and look at the service offered to customers. The good news was that, although there were competitors, Steve's initial ambitions were not particularly grand and the costs involved could be minimized, hence reducing the risks. These costs included the obvious ones such as website design. Carl persuaded Steve that the simple website needed a major overhaul and that Steve did not have the necessary skills or expertise to turn it from a 'billboard' advertising the company to a fully functional e-commerce site. At least that is how it appeared until Carl introduced Steve to a software package that allowed the building of an e-commerce application by using various templates as 'building blocks'. The user interface of the software was very intuitive and with a bit of guidance from Carl, Steve was able to create a usable e-commerce site for his small enterprise.

Maintaining the catalogue

Of course the website is only one side of the story. For the system to work properly there was a need to maintain a catalogue of products which meant taking the existing suppliers' catalogues and consolidating them into a single Microsoft Access database. The design of this was definitely beyond Steve's competence, so Carl arranged for a colleague to meet with Steve to discuss the requirements and develop a solution.

A home for the site

Another issue, which would not be just a one-off cost but require monthly payments, was the need for the hosting of the site. It did not take long to realize that having their own server was not sensible for a business such as SpareBitz so Carl recommended organizing a contract with an Internet Service Provider (ISP). 'Have you checked your domain name?' Carl asked. 'What do you mean?' Steve had a worried look on his face because he thought he knew what Carl was getting at. 'Obviously there can't be two registered users for the same name so if someone else owns SpareBitz.com then you will need to think of another.' Now Steve really was worried. 'That name has gained a reputation and changing it would cause real problems.' Luckily a quick search of the Internet showed that there was an old domain name SpareBitz.com which had now been deleted and SpareBitz.com was available. 'Let's grab it quick', Carl and Steve both said together.

The contract with the ISP also required some calculations about web traffic, that is how many customers SpareBitz.com could expect per month, the size of the downloads and so on. Steve needed to make a few wild guesses, but fortunately his contract with the ISP was flexible so that

PHOTO SOURCE ©ALEX SEGRE/ALAMY

if his online business was more successful than he had estimated he could change his ISP usage to cope.

Who will visit?

'Now what about marketing?' asked Carl. 'I thought we were relying on using our existing customer base', replied Steve. 'Well certainly that is the least costly but I think we can do a bit more for not too much extra. We can rely on conventional advertising such as leaflets in local stores but we can't expect much support from shops selling products that we are encouraging people to repair rather than buy new! There are methods of getting your site noticed by casual web surfers. We can embed keywords into your web pages so that anyone searching for Hoover, for example, will see your site in the search list. For a bit more money we can become a sponsored link that will highlight our site. We can also try some viral marketing by getting the site mentioned in blogs and other social networks.'

Web business: growing and changing

With approximately 8900 company-operated and franchised stores in more than 20 countries, Blockbuster Inc. is the world's largest video rental company. It uses a website to promote its services, but the company's online presence did not amount to more than advertising until 2003, when management decided to allow customers to rent movies through the Internet. What happened to make management change its tune? It was competition. Netflix in the United States and LOVEFiLM in the UK along with other companies throughout Europe began offering an online movie order method: pay a monthly fee, select your movies online, get them in the mail (free shipping!), mail the movies back, and they'll send you more. No need to drive to any store. This business model was popular with renters, and Wal-Mart and Netflix started nibbling into Blockbuster's revenues. Blockbuster management could not allow the company to be left behind. It decided to offer a similar service with the added convenience of the customers being able to return their tapes and DVDs to any Blockbuster store. Blockbuster, like an increasing number of brick-and-mortar businesses, had jumped on the e-commerce bandwagon.

CD TASK

Is this the most efficient way to satisfy the movie-at-home audience? Experts say that shipping a physical object such as a tape or DVD to customers will soon be a thing of the past. Movies are information, and any information can be digitized and whisked to a customer over the Web. As the number of customers with high-speed Internet links grows, enjoying a movie at home will take one of two forms: either a requested movie will be streamed to the customer while the customer is watching, or a copy of the movie will be transferred to the customer. This business model is becoming a reality in the UK with the BBC iPlayer giving viewers the ability to catch up with programmes missed over the last seven days, download and store programmes for 30 days and watch television programmes streamed over the Internet. Competitors for on-demand television include Channel 4OD and Virgin Media. As broadband increases in speed and availability, you will be able to watch films not only on your computer's monitor but also on a regular HDTV set. Just as the film rental industry has changed dramatically within a few years from in-store rental to over-the-web order to over-the-web download, other industries have changed and will continue to change thanks to faster Internet links and new web technologies. Business on the Web is growing and changing form all the time.

Web technologies: a review

Several standards and technologies enable the Web to deliver rich information. The following is a review of some nonproprietary standards and technologies.

Hypertext Transfer Protocol (HTTP) Software that allows browsers to log on to websites.

HTTPS The secure version of HTTP.

Uniform Resource Locator (URL) The address of a website. Always starts with *http://* but does not have to contain *www.*

domain name The name assigned to an Internet server or to a part of a server that hosts a website.

HTTP

In Chapter 5, you learned about protocols. The protocol used to transfer and download web information is **Hypertext Transfer Protocol**, or **HTTP**. A secure version of the protocol for confidential transactions is **HTTPS (HTTP Secure)**. Under this protocol, each web server is designated a **Uniform Resource Locator (URL)**, which is a unique address for a website. The address is the IP number (also called IP address) assigned to the site, but in most cases the site also has a **domain name** made up from letters. The term 'URL' also refers to the domain name. Each web page has its own URL, which contains the IP number or domain name of the site. Because the domain name must be unique, when an owner of a website reserves a domain name to be associated with an IP number, no other site can be associated with that domain name. Note that domain names often start with – but do not have to include – *www.*

The last part of a URL, such as the '.com' in www.thomson.com, is the top-level domain (TLD). In addition to .com, .org, and .edu, many other TLDs can be requested for a domain name, some of which are reserved for certain types of organizations and professions, and some that are not. The only organization that is authorized to approve new TLDs is the Internet Corporation for Assigned Names and Numbers (ICANN), a not-for-profit organization established specifically for this purpose.

Industry SNAPSHOT

An island domain

All countries are allocated a specific Internet domain name with the exception of the USA. The theory behind this is that in the same way as the UK invented postage stamps and does not show its name on stamps issued, the US 'invented' the Internet and so has the same privilege.

The tiny Pacific nation of Tuvalu is allocated the Internet name .tv. The government of the island had repeated requests from companies wishing to make use of the obvious appeal of these two letters and in 1998 it auctioned off the .tv domain name to a Canadian entrepreneur. The deal included a guaranteed US$50 million over ten years and a 15 per cent stake in the company selling rights to domain names ending in .tv, which effectively doubled the gross domestic product of the Pacific nation of 10,000 inhabitants. Roads have been laid, outlying islands now have electricity and schools have been built. The money has also been used to fund Tuvalu's membership of the United Nations, which requires annual fees of US$20,000. On 5 September 2000 Tuvalu became the 189th member of the UN.

SOURCE: Mark Ward, 'Net Gains for Tuvalu', http://news.bbc.co.uk/1/hi/sci/tech/1067065.stm

Citizens of Funafuti, Tuvalu's capital.

PHOTO SOURCE: © DAVID LEVINSON

While domain names consisting of catchy and meaningful words are considered prized assets, companies such as Amazon.co.uk and Google have demonstrated that the name itself is worthless unless the service provided is excellent. Few people know what these names mean (abundant like the Amazon rainforest; and googol, an impossibly large number), but everybody knows of these sites and the purpose of their business. Therefore, new Internet companies do not spend as much energy seeking an attractive domain name as they did in the past.

HTML and XML

Hypertext Markup Language (HTML) is the most common programming language for creating web pages and other information viewable in a web browser. It determines the look and location of text, pictures, animations and other elements on a web page. Extensible Markup Language (XML) enables the creation of various types of data. It is most often used not for determining the *appearance* of visual elements on a web page but to convey the *meaning* or content of the data. The World Wide Web Consortium (W3C), the organization responsible for web standards, has combined the two markup languages HTML and XML into a standard called Extensible Hypertext Markup Language (XHTML).

Hypertext Markup Language (HTML) A programming language for web pages and web browsers.

XML (Extensible Markup Language) A programming language that tags data elements in order to indicate what the data mean, especially in web pages.

XHTML A standard that combines HTML standards and XML standards.

Every file displayed on the Web is coded with a markup language such as HTML or XML. Simply put, markup languages provide a system of standardized 'tags' that format elements of a document, including text, graphics and sound. Formatting includes opening and closing tags preceding and following a part of the document, such as <b> at the start of bold text, and </b> at the end of bold text. Other tags are marked to link to another page either at the same site or another site, and others create links to email addresses. Browsers interpret HTML and XML tags and display the text in the fashion defined by the tags, or allow other software to pick up data from the page and process it or copy it into the proper place in a database.

As in HTML, tags are used in XML to mark data elements. However, XML tags define 'what it is', as opposed to 'how it looks'. The following illustrates the difference between HTML tags and XML tags:

HTML
<font size ='2'>Oz & Jones Enterprises, Ltd.</font>
<b>ST4 2DE</b>

XML
<company name>Oz & Jones Enterprises, Ltd.</company name>
<postcode>ST4 2DE</postcode>

XML tags can be used in the same page with HTML tags to indicate both what the data means (which is not visible to the user) and how each element should be displayed.

File transfer

File Transfer Protocol (FTP) is a common way of transmitting whole files from one computer to another. Every time you download a file from a website or attach files to email, you are using an FTP application. The file transmitted can be of any type: text, graphics, animation or sound. FTP is embedded in browsers and therefore is 'transparent' to the users. You can also use a separate FTP utility, many available as shareware, to manage transmitting files.

File Transfer Protocol (FTP) Software that allows the transfer of files over communications lines.

Businesses use FTP to place files on a server for sharing among professionals. FTP is also useful for placing files on a server that hosts a website. And it's convenient for retrieving large files that might exceed an email box's size limits. For example, authors can place large chapter and figure files in a folder on a server maintained by their publisher. Manufacturers often place whole assembly and maintenance manuals or videos at their website so customers can download them any time.

FTP has already changed the way in which many software firms sell their products. Instead of spending a significant amount of money copying new software on storage media, packaging it and shipping it, developers simply post their software products on their websites and let buyers download them for a fee. Music lovers can use FTP to download music files.

RSS Really Simple Syndication, a type of application using XML for aggregating updates to blogs and news posted at websites.

RSS

Really Simple Syndication (or in a newer version, Rich Site Summary) (**RSS**) is a family of XML file formats. An RSS file is installed at websites to help users check updates to the site. When users subscribe to the RSS service of a site, the software communicates to their computers short descriptions of web content along with the link to the site. Users can instruct the software to automatically transmit new or updated information to their own computers. This software is useful for news websites and sites that host blogs and podcasts (see the next sections). Subscribers to mass media sites such as newspapers and news services such as Reuters can receive the latest news without actively going to the site or receiving email messages. At some websites you might see a button with the letters RSS or XML. If you click them, the site will automatically send your computer updates of designated information, by topic.

blog A contraction of 'web log'. A website where participants post their opinions on a topic or set of related topics; these postings are listed in chronological order.

Blogs

A **blog** (a contraction of 'web log') is a web page that invites surfers to post opinions and artistic work, as well as links to sites of interest. Blog sites focus on a topic or a set of related topics, and provide an easy way to post web pages or update existing ones. Most blogs contain commentaries and humorous content. Users can simply click a button to open a window in which they type text, and click another button to post it. The text is added to the web page either automatically or after a review by the blog's operators. Some blog sites simply let 'bloggers' add comments on a topic, with the most recent comment appearing at the top, similar to the way online newsgroups work. Many companies have established blogs, and invite employees to use them for self-expression. The policy might encourage new ideas from which the company can benefit. Some, however, shun the idea, because management believes blogs are too informal and uncontrolled.

One interesting feature of some blogs is *trackback*. Trackback software notifies bloggers when their posts have been mentioned elsewhere on the Web, so they and their readers can extend the discussion beyond the original blog. Below each post there is a BackTrack button or similar option. When it is clicked, a new window pops up listing the sites mentioning the post.

The commercial potential of blogs has not escaped businesspeople. As traffic grows at some popular blogs, entrepreneurs have started selling advertising space at the sites. The old rule on the Web is still much in force: the greater the number of eyeballs, the greater the commercial potential of the site.

The importance of blogs to commercial organizations is primarily to find out what blog participants think and say about the organizations. Many organizations use special software that combs blogs for postings that mention the organizations' names. PR people then read the content and relay feedback to others in the organization as needed. For example, an anonymous blogger boasted that he could break Kryptonite bicycle locks with a pen. Within a week

Why you should... know more about web-enabled business

Web technologies continue to progress and enable a growing number of business activities. A growing proportion of revenues of traditional bricks-and-mortar businesses come from online sales. 'Pure-play' online businesses add new features to their sites almost daily. By linking corporate systems to the Web, information resources, searching software and transaction applications are increasingly tied in a way that allows employees and customers to receive the information they need in a timely manner and rich fashion. New technologies that seem to be just 'fun' all of a sudden are utilized for serious business activities. Streaming audio and video, and chat applications are just two examples. Understanding web technologies and the potential of the technologies for increased efficiency and richer experience for business customers might help you be a better-educated and more innovative professional.

the posted item was mentioned in various press articles and Kryptonite recalled the locks. Software tools exist that comb blogs, identify company names, and automatically track discussions. Such tools can turn blog data into useful market research information.

Podcasting

podcasting The practice of posting sound files at a website for automating downloading and playing by subscribers.

While blogging is publishing text and other visual material, **podcasting** is publishing sound. To podcast is to make a digital audio recording, usually of voice, and post the file on the Web so that people can download it and listen to it. RSS software called an *aggregator* or *feed reader* automatically checks for new content and downloads files from a designated site in the same way as is done for text files from online newspapers. Similarly to subscribing to such newspapers, users can subscribe to a podcast site to receive the latest audio files. The files are usually in MP3 format, which can be played on any portable player, including Apple Computer's iPod, from which the word 'podcast' was born. However, one does not need this specific MP3 player to enjoy podcasts.

Podcasting has several potential uses. It already serves as 'time-shifted' broadcast of radio stations that post their programmes for later listening. It is used by some museums for audio tours. Some schools and universities have experimented with the concept to deliver lessons to remote students. Whatever the use, people can listen to their favourite content wherever they can obtain a link to the Internet, without paying radio licence fees.

Podcasting opens business opportunities. For example, garageband.com is a website that invites aspiring musicians to post their music tracks free of charge so they can be podcast. This exposes to the world talented people who could not otherwise afford to broadcast their work. Podcasting does more than post MP3 files for downloading. By allowing computers to automatically check for new music tracks, the method helps create a following for an artist, which might result in a future fan base willing to pay for a CD or downloaded music files.

Instant messaging

instant messaging (IM) The capability for several online computer users to share messages in real time; also called chatting online.

Instant messaging (IM) offers users real-time online interactivity. It might be thought of as 'real-time email', because, unlike email, it is synchronous. IM allows a user to detect whether another person who uses the service is currently online, and the user can then exchange information with an entire group (referred to as a 'chat room'), or with only one other 'chatter' in privacy. Some IM applications include two-way video, which turns the chat into a video-conference, and most also include FTP to allow sending and receiving files.

Free IM applications are operated through a server, or a group of connected servers, which provides a directory and functions as the hub for all callers. Some IM setups, such as AOL Instant Messenger (AIM), Yahoo! Messenger, MSN Messenger and ICQ, have become the electronic meeting places for millions of people, making them an attractive target for online advertisers. To overcome the need to use multiple IM applications, some software developers produce universal IM applications that allow, for example, an AIM user to chat with an MSN Messenger user. Trillian and Pidgin (formerly know as Gaim) are two of these applications.

While IM sounds as if it is just for fun, it also can serve an important business purpose. Many online retailers post a special button on their web pages that lets shoppers establish real-time communication with a sales representative. This instant access fosters more personal service and saves telephone costs. For example, IKEA, the Swedish furniture giant, has 37 country-specific websites linked from ikea.com and most of these have a chat application that enables customers to talk to a virtual representative by clicking on 'Ask Anna'. This can help to reduce the volume of calls to the traditional call centre operatives. Generally customers will abandon the site when they cannot get answers while shopping. Using the telephone is often a bad option for those who use their telephone line for a dial-up Internet connection, and email is inefficient and time-consuming. IM enables sales agents to handle several enquiring customers at a time. Such applications also enable the company to 'push' answers from a library of answers such as sizes of furniture, instead of typing them.

CD TASK

Cookies

If you have ever surfed the Web, your computer probably contains cookies. A **cookie** is a small file that a website places on a visitor's hard disk so that the website can remember something about the surfer later. Typically, a cookie records the surfer's ID or some other unique identifier. Combined with data collected from previous visits, the site can figure out the visitor's preferences. The user can opt to allow cookies, and the option is exercised by checking a box in the browser's configuration window. On the user's hard disk, the cookie subdirectory (folder) contains a cookie file for each cookie-using website that the surfer has visited. Cookies might hold server URLs. When you instruct the browser to reach a URL from which you have a cookie, the browser transmits the information from the cookie to the server.

cookie A small file that a website places on a visitor's hard disk so that the website can remember something about the visitor later, such as an ID number or username.

Cookies have an important function in web-based commerce, especially between businesses and consumers. They provide convenience to consumers. If the cookie contains your username and password for accessing a certain resource at the site, you do not have to reenter the information. For example, when a user logs into their eBay account they can choose to keep signed in for the day even if they switch off their computer. This would obviously not be a good idea if they shared their computer with several other users! Cookies often help ensure that a user does not receive the same unsolicited information multiple times. For example, cookies are commonly used to rotate banner ads that a site sends so that a surfer receives different advertisements in a series of requested pages. They also help sites to customize other elements for customers. For example, when a retailer's site identifies a returning customer, it can build a page showing a list of items and information in which the customer might be interested based on previous purchases.

Some cookies are temporary; they are installed only for one session, and are removed when the user leaves the site. Others are persistent and stay on the hard disk unless the user deletes them. Many cookies are installed to serve only first parties, which are the businesses with which the user interacts directly. Others serve third parties, which are organizations that collect information about the user whenever the user visits a site that subscribes to the service of these organizations. These organizations include DoubleClick and FastClick.

While cookies can make online shopping, investing and reading more convenient, they also open the door for intrusion into a person's privacy. Remember that every piece of information you provide while your browser is configured to permit cookies can be recorded and kept for further use – use over which you have no control. Choices you make when selecting menu items, clicking buttons and moving from one page to another are also recorded. Such activities are often called **clickstream tracking**. Although some organizations post privacy policies at their websites and tell you what they will or will not do with the information they gather, you cannot see what information they have compiled by using cookies and how they use it. Especially worrisome are third-party cookies, which collect your browsing and shopping habits across many websites. This is akin to a spy who follows you from one store to another. Software designed to trace and report your online behaviour without your knowledge is called **spyware**. It includes cookies and other, more sophisticated applications that are installed on your computer unbeknownst to you and transmit information about you while you are online.

clickstream tracking The use of software to record the activities of a person at websites. Whenever the person clicks a link, the activity is added to the record.

spyware A small application stored surreptitiously by a website on the hard disk of a visitor's computer. The application tracks activities of the user, including visits to websites, and transmits the information to the operator's server.

Proprietary technologies

In addition to these and other widely used and usually free web technologies, many companies offer proprietary technologies. A proprietary technology is the intellectual property of its developer and is not free for all to use. These software packages include local search engines for finding information about specific items; shopping cart applications for purchase, including selection of items to place in a virtual cart and credit-card charging; wish lists, which allow shoppers to create lists of items they would like others to purchase for them; and a host of software packages that are invisible to visitors but help the site owner to analyse and predict visitor behaviour, especially shopper behaviour. The latter technologies might not be considered web technologies per se, but they analyse data that is collected from visitors accessing websites. For example, Amazon.co.uk uses software that follows the estimated age for those whom a shopper purchases items, and offers new items that fit the progressing age of the shopper's family and friends.

Options in establishing a website

A website is, practically speaking, the web pages that make up the information and links to web technologies that the site provides. To establish a web business, an organization must have access to an Internet server and the ability to control its content. Recall that an Internet server is a computer that is connected to the Internet backbone. Businesses have two options when establishing a website: installing and maintaining their own servers, or contracting with a web hosting service.

Owning and maintaining a server

Installing and maintaining a server at the business's own facility is a costly option, but it gives the business the greatest degree of control. Setting up a server requires expertise, which may

load balancing The transfer of visitor enquiries from a busy server to a less busy server.

mirror An Internet server that holds the same software and data as another server, which may be located thousands of miles away.

pure-play A business operating with clients only via the Web, as opposed to operating via stores or other physical facilities.

bricks-and-mortar A popular term for companies that use physical structure for doing business directly with other businesses and consumers, such as stores. Often used to contrast with businesses that sell only online.

web hosting The business of organizations that host, maintain and often help design websites for clients.

shared hosting An arrangement by which the websites of several clients are maintained by the hosting vendor on the same server.

or may not be available within the business. The business must obtain a high-speed physical link to the Internet backbone. It must also employ specialists to maintain the server or many servers on which the website resides. In large organizations these specialists might be employees of the company; in smaller ones, they might be contract personnel whose services the company hires. The specialists purchase a server (or several servers) for the company, connect it to the Internet through a high-speed dedicated line, register a domain name for the site, and install the proper software for managing the server and creating web pages. The specialists 'scale up' the server system when the business grows and handle issues such as load balancing to ensure quick response and to minimize the probability of site crashing. A site crashes when too many people try to log on and the software stops responding to anyone. **Load balancing** transfers visitor enquiries from a busy server to a less busy server for identical information and services. Thus, the specialist often must connect **mirrors**, servers on which the same content and applications are duplicated.

A large company whose entire business is done online, often called a **pure-play** web company, or a **bricks-and-mortar** company that owns stores but also offers the same or many of the same items for sale online, usually has its own servers and manages them fully. These companies employ crews that manage Internet networking, the hardware and software of the site, and the people responsible for updating the web pages.

Using a hosting service

A majority of organizations that have a commercial presence online either do not own servers or else they own servers but let someone else manage at least some aspect of the site. These organizations use **web hosting** services. Web hosting companies specialize in one or several types of web hosting: shared hosting, virtual private server hosting, dedicated hosting, or co-location. Some also offer free service, but this service rarely involves features beyond posting web pages. Therefore, this option is not viable for most businesses.

In **shared hosting** the client's website is stored on the host's same physical server along with the sites of other clients. The hosting company owns the server and the server management software. It offers space on the servers for hosting websites. This is a relatively inexpensive option. The client can use templates provided by the hosts for building pages, or, for an extra fee, have the host's designer design the website. However, many clients prefer to design and upload their own web pages. The service includes transaction and payment software for use by the subscribing businesses' clients. If the server is shared, the host might not be able to allow a client to maintain its own domain name, such as www.myownco.com, but only a subdomain that contains the host's domain name, such as myownco.myhost.com. However, special software employed by many hosts allows clients to use their own domain names, and although the server has only one IP address, the software directs traffic to the proper site on the server. If an independent domain name is important, this is a factor that a business must consider before selecting a hosting service.

Small businesses with a limited number of products to sell can select a host such as Freezone.co.uk for shared hosting. The company offers 'Home' hosting services but also offers two services aimed at commercial operations, BusinessPlus and Business Advanced. Large search engine and portal companies, such as Yahoo!, offer similar services. Clients have access to easy-to-use web design software tools to create the pages of their new site. This type of option is often a 'turnkey' solution for a small business that wishes to go online almost overnight. In addition to disk space and help with website design, the hosting company typically also provides a number of email addresses and a control 'dashboard', a mechanism for the client business to control remotely content and other aspects of the site. Some hosts also offer to list the new site on frequently used search sites, such as Yahoo! and Google. Many of the hosts also help with domain name registration.

In shared hosting, hundreds of businesses might share the same server and storage space. Therefore, the host often limits the storage space allotted to each client, the number of transactions performed per month, or simply the amount of data, in megabytes, that the site transmits per month. Also, a technical problem in one site could affect the functionality of the other sites residing on the server.

The purpose of a **virtual private server** is to create the impression that the client maintains its own server. Virtual private server technology enables one server to be virtually split into many addressable servers, each for a different client and with its own domain name. This option is usually less expensive than renting a dedicated server, while enjoying the same benefits, including full control of the content of the virtual server.

virtual private server Part of a server that serves as an Internet server for a client of a web hosting company, while other clients share the same physical server.

dedicated hosting An arrangement in which a web hosting organization devotes an entire server to only the website of a single client organization, as opposed to having multiple clients' sites share one server.

Some companies might want to use entire physical servers all for themselves and therefore can opt for dedicated hosting. In **dedicated hosting** the host dedicates a server to the client,

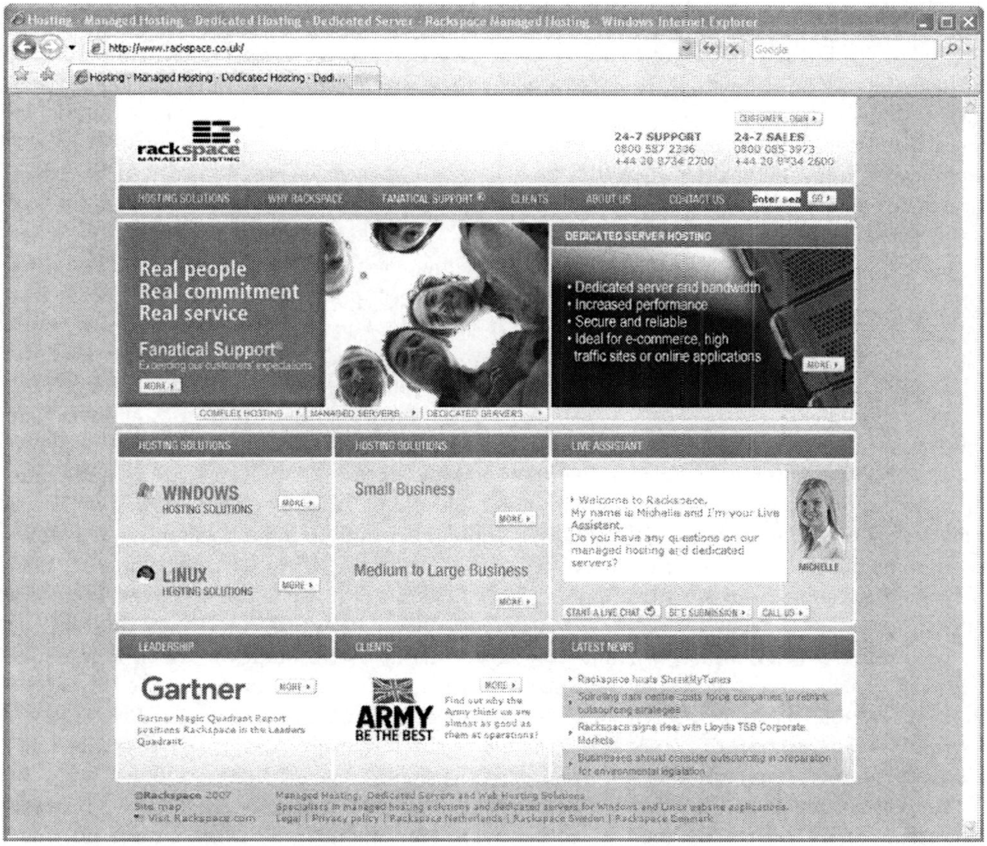

Web host companies accommodate both small and large web-based commercial sites. Large clients often prefer dedicated servers or co-location of their servers at the host's secure site

and the client can fully control the content on the server's disks. The host is responsible for networking management. For example Rackspace.co.uk offers such a service and allows the client to select from several servers. The greater the server's power, the higher the monthly fee. This service is more expensive than shared hosting, but it comes with several advantages. There are fewer restrictions on storage space and transactions, and since only one site resides on the disks, no other site can affect its functionality. Renters of dedicated servers usually have *root access*, which means they act as unrestricted administrators of that computer. The greater control of the dedicated server option comes with a price: this option is more expensive than shared hosting or a virtual private server.

co-location The placement and maintenance of a web server with servers of other subscribers of the service provider. The servers are co-located in the same facility.

In some cases a company might want to fully manage its own web servers but prefers the expertise of a hosting company in managing networking and security. Some hosting services accommodate such demand by offering a **co-location** service. The client owns the servers and manages their content, but the servers are co-located with the servers of other clients as well as those of the host in a secure (physical) site. This approach has been taken by some online retailers because it affords some advantages: the client does not have to employ hardware and network specialists, spend money on building a special secure location for the server, or ensure power supply. All these concerns are transferred to the hosting company. Co-location is usually the most expensive of hosting options. The client must purchase and run the servers, as well as pay for the co-location.

Considerations in selecting a web host

A majority of businesses do not maintain their own web servers or co-locate them; they use host services. When a decision is made to use such a service, managers must consider several factors. Table 7.1 lists the major factors. Hosts can be compared using points, for example, on a scale of 1 for the best and 5 for the worst. A simple evaluation method is for managers to compare each factor for the prospective host, compare the total scores and then make a decision. The evaluators might wish to assign different weights to the various items based on how important each item is to the business.

dynamic web page A web page whose contents change while the visitor watches it.

The business should be able to use a database management system (DBMS) for cataloguing its products and enable online shoppers to perform searches. Thus, the DBMS offered is important. It also might need to use **dynamic web pages**, pages that enable communication between the shopper's browser and the database. Such pages can be built with several programming tools: CGI, Java servlets, PHP and ASP (Active Server Pages). Since the functionality of databases and dynamic pages, as well as some features on the pages, depends on the operating system that the hosts use, all this software must be considered. For example, if the client elects to build and maintain the web pages and prefers to use ASP, notice should be taken that such software will run only on a server running Microsoft Windows. Similar restrictions apply to some page features that can be developed with the web developing tool FrontPage. Most hosting companies offer the use of a combination of software popularly called LAMP, which is an acronym: Linux for operating system, Apache for server management software, MySQL for DBMS, and PHP or Python or Perl for developing dynamic web pages. All of these resources are open source software, and therefore do not require licence fees for the host, who can thus make the service more affordable. However, many hosts also offer other software, including Windows, for higher fees. In addition to these issues, the client should ensure satisfactory shopping cart, credit-card processing and other applications at the site.

Storage space limitations might become a serious inhibitor, especially if the business expects to offer a growing number of products and augment the information provided through the site. The client should enquire about options to increase storage space on demand and its cost.

Table 7.1 Factors to consider for each web hosting company

Factor	Points
Type and quality of applications provided (shopping cart, credit-card processing, statistical analysis, etc.)	______
Storage space	______
Quality of technical support	______
Traffic limits	______
Availability of email accounts and services	______
Scalability	______
Support of page design	______
Security	______
Uptime ratio	______
Setup fee	______
Monthly fee	______

Most hosts provide technical support 24 hours per day, 7 days per week throughout the year, known as 24/7/365. The client should ensure such service and know exactly what support services are included in the contract.

Technical support involves the quality of the equipment that the hosting company provides, the security measures it maintains, the sophistication of server and load management, and the technical skills of its personnel. Companies should enquire about past downtimes and recovery time frames for the hosting company because they are an important part of technical support. If the client needs help in developing and updating web pages, the evaluators should explore the appearance and functionality of current clients of the hosting company.

Some hosting companies charge extra fees for shared hosting if the site experiences activity above a predetermined amount of data that is transferred (downloaded from the site or uploaded to it) or number of visits from web surfers, known as *hits*. In such arrangements additional fees are charged for over-the-limit data transfer or hits. Web hosting companies price their services this way because the greater the number of hits, the more bandwidth they must allocate. The size of every file that is downloaded or uploaded is recorded, and if the limit – say 200 GB – has been exceeded, there is additional charge. If the client's business grows, the cost might end up much greater than planned.

All hosting firms provide subscribers with several email addresses. Some also provide forwarding to other email addresses. Clients should examine these factors as well as the size of email boxes, autoresponding (automating email reply), and access to mailing lists.

Scalability is the ability of an organization to modify the capabilities of IT to accommodate growing needs. In this context, it is the ability for a website to grow – an important factor for most businesses. It is best to select a hosting company that has the hardware, software and expertise to accommodate varying traffic levels and that can demonstrate its ability to develop a site from a simple, static one (one that does not require interactivity) to a heavily trafficked, interactive one. This applies to disk space, growing sophistication of software used, faster backup mechanisms and other resources.

Smaller businesses often need help with the design of their web pages. They need to discover whether the hosting company maintains experienced and available web design personnel.

The host's physical site must be well secured against physical entry as well as intrusion through the Internet. Clients should ask for information about security measures. Some hosts are so careful as to not even advertise where they keep servers. Yahoo! is one such host.

Businesses want their websites available all the time. Downtime denies them business and damages their reputation. Hosting companies usually advertise their uptime as a percentage. For example, they might say they guarantee 99 per cent uptime. This means that the client should expect the site to be down 1 per cent (87.6 hours) of every year. Companies that need a higher uptime, such as 99.9 or 99.99 per cent, should take notice of this and ensure that the host has the resources to claim such a high number of 'nines'. Such resources often include the availability of power backup and redundancy, the placing of the site on two or more servers.

Setup and monthly fees are self-explanatory. Some hosting companies offer large discounts to clients that sign multiyear contracts.

More than meets the eye

However a business chooses to run its website, there are several elements that must be present to conduct business, which are illustrated in Figure 7.1. While the shopper (a consumer or corporate purchasing officer) sees only web pages, several applications and databases actually support online shopping and purchasing: an application that provides an enquiry interface for the shopper, which is connected to a catalogue that is actually a database consisting of visual and text product descriptions; an application that takes the order, which is connected to an inventory application that is also connected to the product catalogue database; a credit-card application that verifies authenticity of credit-card details and balance; and, in many cases, an order-fulfilment system that displays on monitors located in warehouses which items are to be picked off shelves and where they should be shipped. The latter system might include an automated conveyor system that picks the items with little human labour.

B2B Business-to-business, a term that refers to transactions between businesses, often through an Internet link.

B2C Business-to-consumer, a term that refers to transactions between a business and its customers, often through an Internet link.

Web-enabled business

Web-enabled business is often classified by the parties involved in the interaction: business-to-business (B2B) and business-to-consumer (B2C). Some people also add government-to-consumer and government-to-business. Auction sites, such as eBay.co.uk are sometimes referred to as consumer-to-consumer (C2C) sites, but we consider them B2C, because the business does intervene in several parts of the transaction, as well as charging the parties commissions. Following are descriptions of the business models of the most pervasive types of web-based business.

B2B trading

Business-to-business (B2B) trading takes place only between businesses. Consumers of the final goods and services are not involved. In general, the volume of e-commerce between

Figure 7.1 The components of a web-based retailing operation

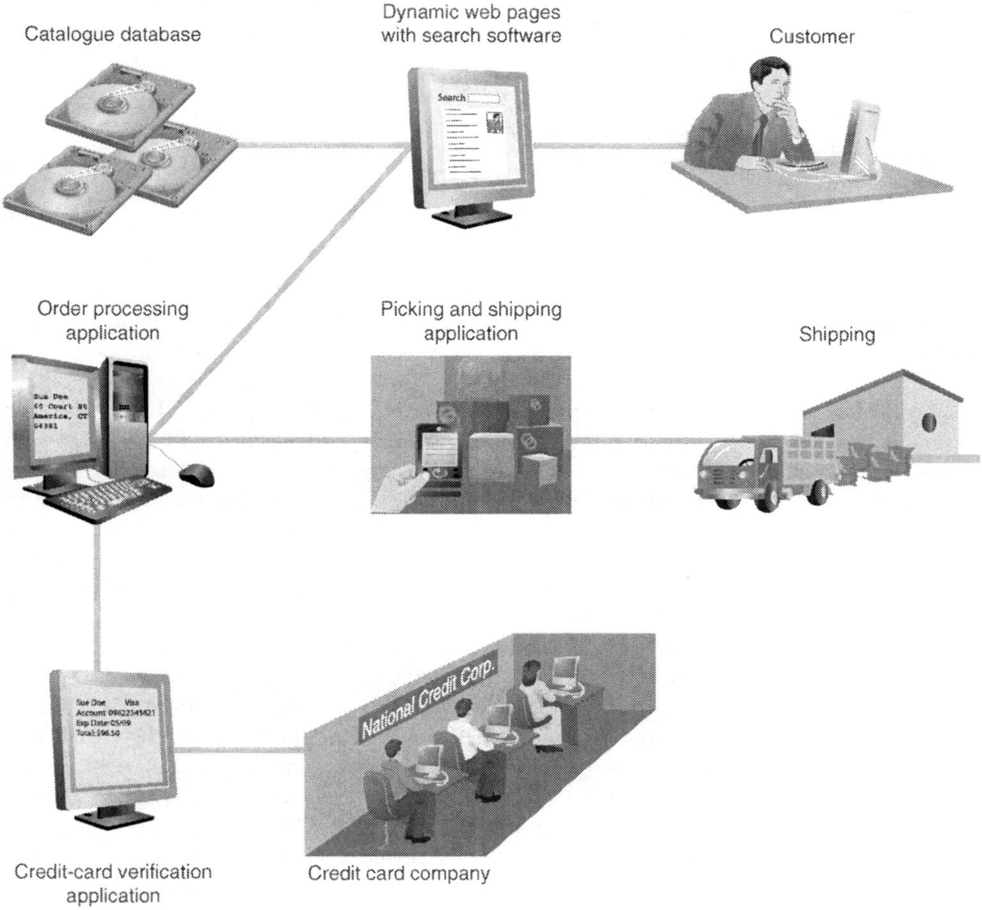

Industry SNAPSHOT

B2B commerce, the old way . . .

In June 2005, CitiBank, one of the world's largest financial institutions, discovered that some tapes it shipped with UPS were lost. The tapes included the names, Social Security numbers, account numbers and payment history of 3.9 million customers. They were en route to a credit bureau, one of several that use such information to maintain and sell people's credit history and rating. CitiBank management decided that it would start transmitting such information, encrypted, over communication networks. The question arises: why did the company wait so long to use technologies that had been available for years?

A Citibank branch in London.

PHOTO SOURCE: © FERRUCCIO/ALAMY

businesses is about ten times as great as that of business-to-consumer e-commerce. And although not all electronic B2B transactions take place on the Internet, most do. This section discusses the major forms in which businesses communicate with each other and undertake intra-business transactions.

Advertising

Online advertising is done mainly in two ways: through search engines and through banners. Although advertising on the Web is aimed not just at consumers, most of it is directed to them. Regardless of media, advertisers are interested in reaching as many people who might buy their goods or services as possible. On the Web, advertisers are interested in what they call 'traffic volume', that is, the number of people who come across their messages. As the number of people who log on to the Web increases, so does advertiser interest in this medium. According to www.internetworldstats.com, the estimated number of people online is approaching 1.2 billion in 2007, nearly one-fifth of the world population. With this traffic volume, advertisers are willing to spend a lot of money on web advertising. The research firm eMarketer estimated that the world's corporations spent nearly €4 billion on search advertising in 2005; that is, they paid the owners of search sites, such as Google and Yahoo!, to ensure that their company names either came up at the top of search results or were listed as 'sponsored' sites in the search list that appears. Because in 2005 search engine advertising was estimated at about 45 per cent of all web advertising, we might conclude that total spending on web advertising was about €8.6 billion – and the trend is upwards.

search advertising Placing ads at search engine websites.

banners Advertisements that appear on a web page.

Search advertising, which is any form of advertising through an online search site, is regarded by businesses as being highly effective. Shoppers have discovered that the fastest way to find a business that can sell them the product or service they need is by looking up the product or service on the Web, and the most effective searches are through the best-known services and those that identify the largest number of web pages: Google, Yahoo!, MSN and AOL (see Figure 7.2).

Banners are images placed on a website that link to the site of the company selling the product or service. Usually the image is wide horizontally, or elongated

Figure 7.2 Spending on search advertising

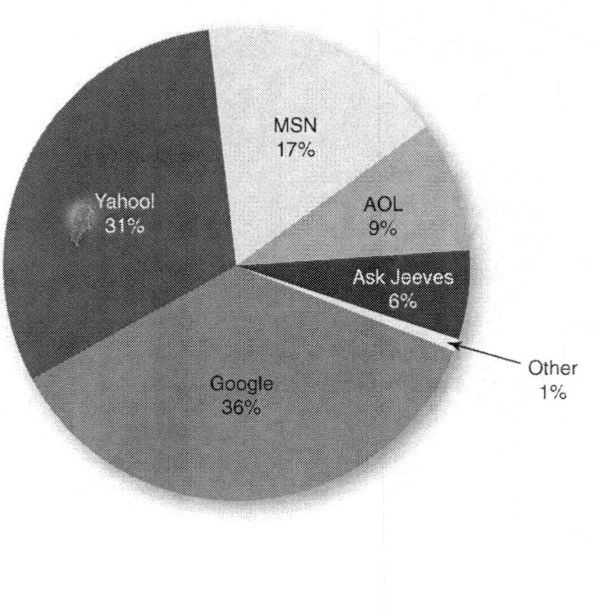

vertically, hence the term 'banner'. However, any image placed for advertising is referred to as a banner. In recent years, a growing number of online newspapers and journals have placed banners in interesting articles. Popular blog sites also attract advertisers.

How does a potential advertiser know how much traffic a site attracts? The most basic metric that can be measured at a site is the number of impressions. An **impression** occurs whenever a browser downloads the page containing the banner. More useful metrics are provided by several companies that rate website visits similar to rating television viewing. For instance, comScore, an online rating firm, maintains a panel of 1.5 million English-speaking online consumers from around the world whom the firm polls periodically. The companies produce several metrics for subscribing companies. Usually, subscribers of online rating firms are high-traffic sites that generate large revenues from advertising.

impression In web advertising, the event of an ad displayed on a surfer's monitor.

In addition to impressions, rating companies measure other metrics. One is *unique visitors per month*. If the same person visited a site several times during a given month, the person is counted only once. The reason? Advertisers are interested in reaching many people, not the same people with many visits. Another metric is *unique visitor pages*, which are the number of different pages at the site that a single visitor accessed. The reason for this metric is that the same visitor is exposed to different ads at the site. **Reach percentage** is the percentage of web users who have visited the site in the past month, namely, the ratio of visitors to total web population.

reach percentage The percentage of web users who have visited a site in the past month, or the ratio of visitors to the total web population.

As in print advertising, the site owner charges the advertiser by the ad's size (so many pixels by so many pixels) and by the number of impressions. Using the IP numbers of computers accessing the pages with the banners, the advertiser can easily count impressions.

It is said that word of mouth might be the most effective advertising at no cost. Free advertising on the Web often takes the form of multiple mentions on blogs and other social networking sites. In August 2006 a four-piece band from Sheffield, the Artic Monkey's, achieved the distinction of having Britain's fastest-selling debut album; and yet their fame and success was all built without the usual media-industry hype associated with new, probably manufactured, bands. Neither was it as a result of a reality television show and associated marketing. Their early tunes and gigs were made available to fans for free and were subsequently shared on MySpace and other social networking sites. Their fame snowballed so that by the time their debut album was released its success was assured, all without any conventional marketing.

Exchanges and auctions

In the old days, a meeting place of buyers and sellers had to be tangible such as a marketplace or a shop. Until recently, finding a buyer for scrap metal, used scientific equipment, or any other commodity might have taken a long time. Also, the buyer and seller had to pay high finder's fees to individuals and firms that specialized in such intermediary trade. On the Web, the marketplace can include as many sellers and as many buyers as wish to participate, as long as they have access to the Internet.

An **intranet** is a network used only by the employees of an organization. An **extranet** limits site access to the employees of particular organizations, usually business partners. An extranet might be viewed as connecting intranets of business partners.

intranet A network using web browsing software that serves employees within an organization.

extranet A network, part of which is the Internet, whose purpose is to facilitate communication and trade between an organization and its business partners.

An exchange is an extranet for organizations that offer for sale, and bid on, products and services of a particular type. Unlike a public auction site such as eBay or uBid, access is usually limited to subscribers, and the subscribers often pay a periodic fee to the site's operator. Auction sites whose purpose is to serve as a meeting place of buyers and sellers in a particular industry are sometimes operated by an industrial association. Others are established by entrepreneurs for the sole purpose of making profit. When the purpose is only to provide a place where sellers compete for the business of a single buyer, the buyer operates the site.

When the site is established by a private business as a meeting place for multiple buyers and sellers, the operator is impartial and profits from transaction fees paid either by one party or both, the seller and buyer, whenever a sales transaction is signed. One of the largest of these exchange sites is ChemConnect, where sellers can auction off chemicals, plastics and natural gas. ChemConnect has 9000 client members in 150 countries. The president of a petroleum company who makes 15 per cent of his natural gas purchases and sales at the site summarized the advantage of such exchanges to businesspeople. In the past he had to spend a day and use the phone to find buyers or sellers for a single purchase or sale. Now, he posts the information online and 150 interested people see it.

Auction sites sell a great variety of items, including live ones. PEFA.com, in Zeebrugge, Belgium, is a private auction site for fresh fish. More than 500 buyers, usually large companies from all over Europe, purchase 60 different species of fish – fresh, farmed, processed and frozen – worth several hundred million euro through the site from sellers in 18 ports. The site accommodates buyers and sellers in seven languages. It also allows subscribers to use PEFA's database, so they can receive rich information on market conditions and statistics. The database is available in 11 languages.

Some electronic markets are established by a single buyer or by an organization that represents many buyers. For example, ChoiceBuy.com is a site operated by Choice Hotels International, a company that franchises the hotels Comfort Inn, Quality, Clarion, Sleep Inn, Econo Lodge, Rodeway Inn and MainStay Suites. The total number of hotels it franchises is over 5000 worldwide. In 1999, the company established the website so it could concentrate all the purchases for the hotels through a single channel. The site invites sellers to offer their products. For the sellers this is an opportunity to obtain big contracts. For the hotels, this is a way to enjoy great discounts, which ChoiceBuy.com obtains through its buying power. For Choice Hotels it is a way to generate revenue from the transaction fees that the bidders pay, and

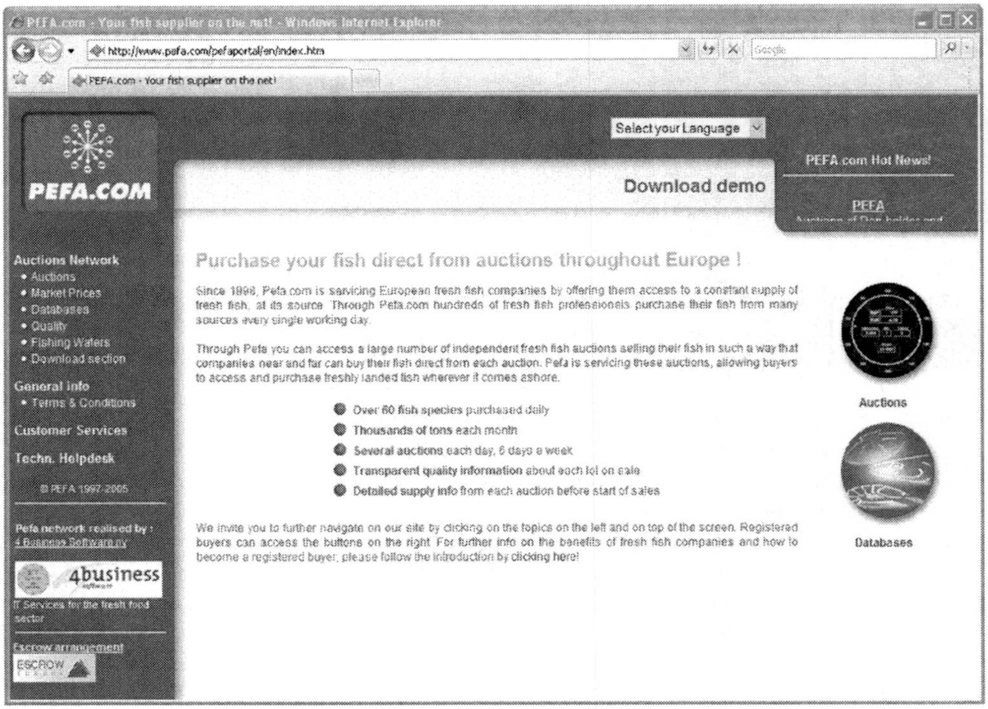

The home page of PEFA.com.

PHOTO SOURCE: © PEFA

indirectly a way to attract more franchisees that, of course, pay the company franchise fees. Independent hotels are allowed to make their own purchases, and they do buy for €1 billion annually, but an increasing number of the purchases are made through the site. In 2004, ChoiceBuy.com processed 5236 orders for toilet paper, towels and other supplies for more than 1000 hotels in its franchise. Processing orders through the site not only saves money for the hotel operators but also enriches Choice Hotels. Since all transactions are electronic, they are automatically recorded and provide valuable data from which useful information can be gleaned.

Many exchanges require businesses to register as members and to pay an annual fee. Many guarantee sellers that they will receive payment even if the buyer defaults, an important and attractive consideration for sellers. Electronic marketplaces bring markets closer to what economists call perfect markets. In a perfect market no single buyer or seller can affect the price of a product. On the Internet, all buyers and sellers have access to the same information at the same time. Thus, no single buyer or seller has an information advantage over competitors.

Online business alliances

Companies in the same industry – competitors – often collaborate in establishing a website for one or several purposes. One major purpose might be to create buying power by consolidating purchases. Another might be to create a single place for customers, assuming that a greater choice will benefit the group. The concept is not new. In America estate agents or 'realtors' have collaborated in the multiple listing system (MLS), whereby multiple agencies have access to real estate that is registered for sale with one of them. This system, which was in place way back in the early twentieth century, is now managed on the Web.

In some cases, the purpose of an alliance site is the same as an auction site operated by a single company, but the operator is a business that works for the allied companies. The purpose of such a site is to set the prices of purchased products and services. Big players in an industry, such as airlines or car manufacturers, establish a shared company that operates the site. Suppliers are invited to sell through the site and compete among themselves. The competition drives prices down. The allies enjoy lower costs and greater profit margins.

Star Alliance is one of several airline alliances, such as OneWorld, SkyTeam and Orbitz. Star Alliance established an extranet for two purposes: to concentrate purchases from parts and service providers, and to represent the group to its clients, airline passengers. The alliance includes Air Canada, Air New Zealand, Austrian Airlines, Lufthansa, Scandinavian Airlines, United, Varig and other companies. On the consumer side, the airlines collaborate in frequent flier programmes: you can fly with any of them and accrue miles with the entire alliance rather than with a single airline. The Star Alliance site provides several useful services for travellers of all member airlines. On the B2B side, the alliance solicits bids from suppliers of aircraft parts and maintenance services, food, ground equipment, office supplies and other products and services. The allies use the extranet to share information about inventory levels, facilitate joint planning and forecasting for material requirements and facilitate communication and business transactions between the airlines and suppliers. The hub for joint purchasing has saved the allies millions of euros annually.

Similar alliance sites have been established by firms in the general retail industry, the food industry and the hospitality industry (hotels).

B2C trading

Although business-to-business trading on the Internet is much larger in volume, online business-to-consumer (B2C) trading has caught the headlines in recent years, and that has prompted the establishment of a multitude of Internet companies.

E-tailing

CD TASK

You can shop the Web for virtually any item you want, from collectibles to cars, order these items online and receive them at your door. At various retail sites, shoppers can use sophisticated search applications to find information on desired items, read other shoppers' reviews of items such as books and music CDs, post their own opinions, drop an item in a virtual shopping cart, change their minds and remove the item, or decide to buy the item and pay by providing a credit-card account number or through a debit service such as PayPal. Online retailing – *e-tailing* – continues to grow throughout the world for several reasons: greater availability of faster communication lines to households, growing confidence in online purchases and the increasing ability to find the item one searches and rich information about it.

Buy.co.uk, Amazon.co.uk and the e-tailing arms of bricks-and-mortar retail chains such as Tesco and WH Smith are among thousands of e-tailers. Their sites combine friendly and enticing web pages, database management systems and transaction software to provide shopping and buying convenience. Companies that sell online have smaller expenses than those selling from stores because they do not have to buy or rent shops and use labour to operate cash registers. They do, however, maintain large warehouses and pay for picking, packing and shipping, three activities known as **fulfilment**. In some cases, however, they do not even need to maintain their entire inventory because they can simply route orders directly to manufacturers, who ship the items directly to the customer.

fulfilment Picking, packing and shipping after a customer places an order online.

An important element of online retailing is selection. Compare the variety of products that can be offered at a web storefront with the selection offered by a bricks-and-mortar store: a typical CD store offers about 25,000 different titles, while Amazon offers 500,000 titles, just about every CD title, available for sale. There are also fewer returns because shoppers have more information at hand before they make their purchases. So, shoppers are more satisfied with their buying decisions, and web businesses save the costs of dealing with returns. Another explanation for fewer returns is the creation of what marketers call one-to-one relationships. Using cookies, the website software can track the clickstream of shoppers who browse the site and track their interests. When the same shopper logs on again, the software offers new items that fall within his or her interest area. And with every visit, the software learns more about visitors and their preferences.

As Table 7.2 summarizes, consumers find several advantages to shopping online: convenience, time-saver, search mechanism, comparative shopping and product reviews. E-tailers

Table 7.2 Web-shopping benefits

Benefit	Because shoppers can . . .
Convenience	Shop from anywhere at any time of the day.
Time-saver	Visit numerous online stores in a few minutes; it would take them hours to do so at shopping malls.
Search mechanism	Find who sells a specific item within seconds by using search engines.
Comparative shopping	Quickly compare quality and price across multiple sellers.
Product reviews	Read product reviews by independent experts and other shoppers, often on the same web page that describes the item.

face mounting challenges, however. The competition is just a click away, so it is critical to offer a wide selection and excellent service, in addition to low price. E-tailers provide easy-to-use online tools to track shipments, and many make returns easy. Some bricks-and-mortar retail chains allow returns to physical stores.

The greatest challenge for e-tailers is turning shoppers into buyers and then turning the buyers into repeat buyers. To this end, many e-tailers have linked their customer relationship management (CRM) applications, discussed in Chapter 3, to their websites. Using cookies and other software, they not only collect large amounts of information about individual shoppers, but also constantly update their profiles. The purpose of **consumer profiling** is to know the consumers better so the business can serve them better while streamlining its marketing and sales operations.

consumer profiling The collection of information about individual shoppers in order to know and serve consumers better.

While consumer profiling might sound benign, many privacy advocates claim that it violates privacy rights. Imagine that every time you log on to a site, this fact is recorded. Then, when you click on an icon, it is recorded, too. The software at the server side also records the time you spent at each specific page, assuming the longer you spent, the more interested you are. Chances are the site will send you promotional emails about the items displayed on that carefully viewed page. Also, the next time you log on to the site, you might find that this particular page appears on your computer monitor faster than before. These subtle changes result from intelligent analysis of the information you provided knowingly or unknowingly to the site – and perhaps other sites that forwarded the information to this retailer. Many retailers also sell the information they collect to data brokers such as Acxiom, who combine personal data and sell the records to other companies. Privacy advocates object to such observation and sales of data without the user's consent.

Affiliate programmes Many e-tailers, as well as other online businesses, offer affiliate programmes to website owners. The affiliate, the website owner, places a link, usually a banner, to the e-tailer at the site. Affiliates are compensated in one of several ways: *pay per sale,* in which only if a visitor ended up purchasing something is the affiliate paid a fee; *pay per click*, in which the affiliate is paid a small fee whenever a visitor clicks the banner; or *pay per lead*, whereby a lead means that the visitor clicked through to the advertiser's site and filled out a registration form to receive periodic information. Retailers usually use the pay per sale model.

Some e-tailers have hundreds or even thousands of affiliates. Amazon.com and other large e-tailers probably have tens of thousands of affiliates. These programmes provide huge, effective advertising for online businesses.

Some companies make money by being affiliate aggregators. LinkShare (www.linkshare.com) and Commission Junction (www.cj.com) let you choose from hundreds of affiliate advertisers, some offering commissions of up to 40 per cent. You can pick the ones you want to mention at your website.

Competition Amazon.co.uk has taken a step beyond affiliate programmes to cooperate with competitors. It includes its competitors on its own site. When you use the search engine at the company's site for a certain item, it brings up the product description and price from Amazon.co.uk's database and also the same type of information from other companies' databases. Although these companies are direct competitors, Amazon benefits from this cooperation in two ways: it attracts more shoppers to visit its site first, because they know there is a high probability that they will find the item they want at the site, even if they end up buying from another company; and it receives a fee from these affiliated companies whenever they sell through Amazon's site.

conversion rate In marketing, the proportion of shoppers who end up buying from the organization. The term also applies to online shopping.

Conversion One measure of online retail success is **conversion rate**, the proportion of site visitors who make a purchase to the total number of visitors in a period of time, usually one year. This proportion has steadily increased over the years from a mere fraction of a per cent in the late 1990s to several percentage points now. Interestingly there is a geographical skew in conversion rates. The Internet media and market research organization Nielsen//NetRatings found in a survey that Internet shoppers in the UK and Australia show a high conversion rate, probably because the English-speaking population have an easy access to US eCommerce suppliers. Hong Kong, on the other hand, has one of the lowest conversion rates despite having an Internet environment that is based on high-speed connections. The low conversion rate is probably because the urban environment of Hong Kong is suitable for traditional physical shopping and therefore most potential e-shoppers use the Internet to make price comparisons and learn about products but then purchase in person. In general, pure-play e-tailers, companies that sell solely over the Web, enjoy higher conversion rates than bricks-and-mortar retailers who also sell online.

Auctions and reverse auctions

Similar to auctions among companies, some websites serve as auction hubs for individuals. The most prominent of the sites is eBay, but there are others, such as eBid and CQOut. The business model is simple: sellers list information about the items or services they offer for sale, and if a sale is executed, the site owner collects a fee. Because the sites provide only a platform for a transaction that eventually takes place between two consumers, some people like to call online auctions consumer-to-consumer e-business. To participate in auctions one needs to register as a member. To help bidders know better to what extent they can count on the integrity of the seller, eBay publishes the number of feedback comments it receives on a member, and the number and percentage of positive feedbacks.

reverse auction (name-your-own-price auction) An online auction in which participants post the price they want to pay for a good or service, and retailers compete to make the sale; also called a name-your-price auction.

The ability of websites to serve as prompt exchanges of information has supported another popular business model, the **reverse auction** or **name-your-own-price auction**. Priceline.com invites consumers to post requests for services and prices they are willing to pay. Although they also deal in home mortgages, the services are mostly for travel, such as flights, cruises, lodging and car rentals. Customers can post the destination, day and time of a flight, as well as the maximum price they are willing to pay. Then, airlines are invited to consider the requests. The first airline to accept the terms wins the offer. Shoppers are required to transmit a credit-card account number. The account is charged as soon as an airline accepts the deal. Priceline.co.uk's revenue comes from the fees that airlines and other businesses pay to use the service.

Content providers

On the Web, content means information, such as news, research results, statistics and other useful information, as well as artistic works such as music, pictures and video clips. The definition of content could also be extended to include job postings and online dating services. Over the years, individuals and organizations have spent increasing amounts of money on content. Although most news can be obtained free of charge, many articles cannot. Some audiences welcome for-fee content, especially if it is highly specialized. Given a choice, many people prefer to read the same information online rather than on paper because they can use search operations to quickly find specific articles. This might be one reason why many prefer to subscribe to the electronic version of a newspaper. Content revenues also have grown since companies such as Apple started selling individual song files online.

Industry SNAPSHOT

Auction tools

The success of on-line auctions has spawned another industry – that of software specifically designed to make the most of these sites. For example, Auctionlotwatch.co.uk offers tools for alerting buyers about lots that are soon due to finish without any bids, hence representing a potential bargain bid. Another piece of software looks for common misspellings. An item that has been listed for, say, a CD by the Beetles will not be found by most sellers looking for a Beatles CD – potentially another bargain for someone using the wrong spelling as a search word. There are also tools for sellers. Auction Harvest looks at the final selling price of similar items to give the seller an idea of the selling price for their item.

PHOTO SOURCE: © AUCTION LOTWATCH

Bill presentment and payment

Because it is so easy to transfer funds online from one bank account to another, and it is so easy to send information, including bills, by email, many utility companies try to convince customers to accept electronic bills and pay them online. Some customers accept the option of electronic bill presentment but refuse to sign an agreement that would enable the company to automatically charge their bank account. Obviously, banks are always a participant in electronic payment if the charge is to a bank account (which is how most utility and mortgage companies want to be paid), but some banks, for their own reasons, refuse to join such trilateral initiatives.

Electronic bill presentment and payment (EBPP) saves utility companies and financial institutions that bill customers regularly a significant amount of money. The bills are presented automatically, directly from the companies' information systems to payers' email addresses, and therefore save labour, paper and postage. Direct charge to a bank account saves the labour involved in receiving and depositing cheques. Yet, EBPP is spreading slowly. Most people still prefer to pay their bills by cheque and through the mail, partly because fraud on the Internet has increased in recent years, especially through a practice called **phishing**, discussed in the Ethical and Societal Issues feature. Figure 7.3 illustrates the practice. Note that the fictitious site is not secure. The legitimate one is secure; note the 's' in https://. Also note the bank warnings to customers. This particular email was sent to a person who does not even have an account with the bank.

phishing The criminal practice of luring Internet users to provide their personal information via email or the Web. Phishing almost always results in fraud or identity theft.

Figure 7.3 Phishing plagues web commerce. An email arrives that prompts the recipient to update personal information at a fictitious but legitimate-looking website (bottom left). Note how similar the features in the fictitious (left) and legitimate website (right) are.

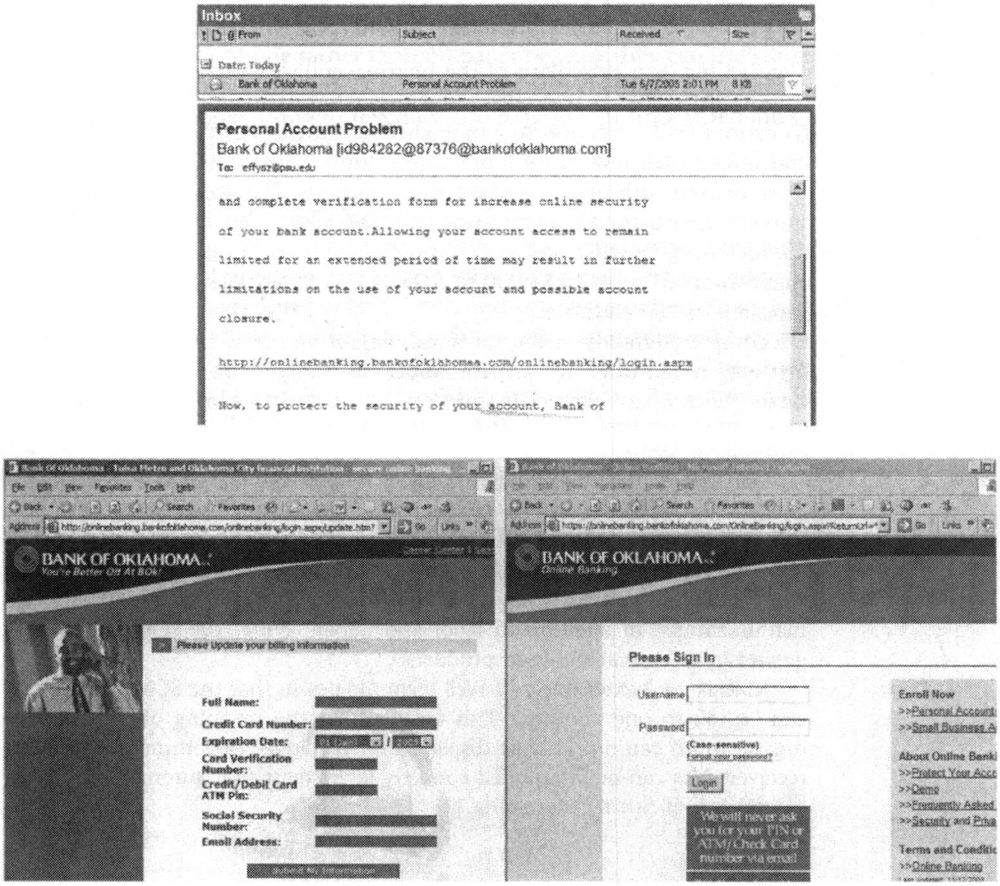

Industry **SNAPSHOT**

Anti-phish tool

When you receive an email message that sends you to your bank's website to reenter your personal details, you should ensure that the site is indeed your bank's. SpoofStick is a free add-on to your browser, which you can download from www.spoofstick.com and install on your computer. Whenever you direct your browser to a site, a line underneath the URL box will tell you the correct site, such as: 'You're on Barclays.co.uk.com' or 'You're on 218.97.169.53.' The former is the legitimate site. The latter is the site for the link the phishers sent you.

Dispersed workforce

The Web enables companies to purchase labour from many more people than their own employees. For example, companies can augment their intellectual pool by using the Web to employ talent beyond their own employees'. They can enjoy more labour for less money by offering cash for research and development (R&D) solutions provided by researchers outside their organizations.

InnoCentive Inc. is a subsidiary of the pharmaceuticals company Eli Lilly and Company. It operates InnoCentive.com, a website connecting scientists with companies. Companies whose R&D staffs cannot find a solution to a biological or chemical problem can post the challenge at the site and offer a cash reward for a practical solution. Scientists and researchers from around the world can register with the site and work on solutions. The site is operated in seven languages to accommodate scientists and organizations from all over the world. So far, Eli Lilly and 30 other companies, including Dow Chemical Co. and the giant consumer product company Procter & Gamble, have awarded sums of US$4,000 to US$100,000. The site has more than 150,000 registered scientists located in 150 countries.

When a company employs a staff of researchers it must pay them regardless of how fruitful their efforts are. When offering cash for solutions, many more scientists might work for the company, but the company pays only the scientist who solves the problem. The cost savings can be huge.

M-commerce

In Chapter 5 you learned about the many wireless technologies that enable people to access the Web while away from the office or home. Wireless technologies enable what some people call mobile commerce, or m-commerce. Mobile devices already let users log on to the Internet, but they can also provide an additional benefit to businesses: a device can be located with an accuracy of several feet, much like locating a mobile phone. As soon as you come within a few blocks of a store, your handheld computer or phone could beep and display a promotional message on its monitor.

m-commerce Mobile commerce, enabled by advances in technology for mobile communications devices.

M-commerce allows people to use their mobile devices to experience an event and react immediately. For example, they might view a horse race and place bets from their seat. Or, they can see a demonstration of a product at a public place and order it online. Impulse shopping will no longer be limited to shopping malls. Recall our discussion in Chapter 5 of future uses of RFID. Mobile devices might be equipped with RFID readers so their owners can use a product's electronic product code (EPC) to download information about it from the Web.

Smart mobile devices might be helpful in sales force automation. Travelling salespeople are able to access data through the mobile device almost anywhere. They are able to access corporate databases through their company's intranet. Both travelling salespeople and consumers already practice m-commerce whenever they transact while using a hotspot or a web-capable mobile phone.

Experts believe that the most attractive mobile application might not be online buying, but the delivery of highly relevant information, custom-tailored to the user's current location and activity. Location services include downloading coupons at the store in which the consumer has just entered, finding out about nearby restaurants, or reading product reviews while shopping at an appliance store.

In the United States, mobile phones manufactured as of 2006 must, by law, include global positioning system (GPS) capability, so that people can be located in case of emergency. As telephoning and other technologies are merged into a single device that can also link to the Web, the potential for marketing and pushing information might be too tempting for businesses.

So far, however, predictions about the growth of m-commerce in North America and Europe have not materialized. The only countries where m-commerce has become popular are Japan and South Korea. In Japan, subscribers to the DoCoMo's i-mode service use their smart mobile phones to purchase drinks from vending machines, buy food at fast-food

Industry **SNAPSHOT**

Surfing the Web 30,000 feet up

For several years airlines have looked at the possible use of mobile telephones on aeroplanes and with the increased functionality of mobile devices to allow web browsing there is a potential for passengers to work (or play!) rather than rely on the in-flight entertainment. However, there is an interesting contrast between the attitudes in the United States and Europe. Recent movements in the US have been away from airborne Internet access, with the Federal Communications Committee voicing concerns that mobile telephone signals have a potential to disrupt other radio communications. This negative attitude has lead Boeing to drop its plans for an in-flight web browsing service at a reported cost of US$1 billion. The opposite is the case in Europe, with regulatory bodies working towards approval. 'It's going through the approval process right now' according to Charlie Pryor, spokesman for OnAir, a potential mobile phone service provider sponsored by Airbus. 'We expect some decisions within a month'.

SOURCE: W David Gardner, 'FCC Say "No" to Cell Phones on Airplanes, But Europe Says "Yes"', *Information Week*, 23 March 2007

PHOTO SOURCE © ONAIR 2008

restaurants, and shop at Web sites of online retailers. Purchases are charged to the mobile phone service provider, NTT. It is expected that the United States and Europe will catch up to Japan and South Korea. In September 2007 the UK's five largest mobile telephone firms introduced a payment system designed to make handsets into digital wallets. Called PayForIt, the new scheme is designed for paying for goods and services that have low individual value, up to £10. Such sales could be ringtones, train tickets and parking fees.

Privacy proponents have already voiced concerns about m-commerce. Apparently, not many people are happy to find out that commercial organizations can track them down anytime when their mobile device is on. These devices not only allow consumer profiling, as already practised by many online retailers, but can also tell retailers and other organizations your exact location at any given time. The result might be 'We know who you are, what you have done on the Web, and where you are now.'

Supply chains on the Web

Supply chains extend from commercial organizations to both suppliers and buyers. Organizations connect their supply chain management (SCM) systems to their suppliers at one end, and to their buyers at the other end. Thus, an organization might be a participant among other buyers in an extranet managed by one of its suppliers, and a participant among several sellers in an extranet of a buyer. Large retailers manage extranets through which their suppliers' SCM systems can provide useful information to their own, so they can track orders and shipments, as well as collect useful information for decision-making on which supplier to select for which order. In this regard, a large retailer's extranet becomes a marketplace for many sellers and a single buyer.

In the years before the opening of the Internet to commercial activities, many companies invested in Electronic Data Interchange (EDI) systems to exchange documents electronically with business partners. EDI consists of certain standards for formatting documents such as orders and invoices, software that translates the data properly, and the networks through which the information flows between subscribing organizations. The networks are owned and managed by value-added network (VAN) companies, telecommunications companies that manage the traffic of EDI between the business partners. Subscribers pay for this service. Although EDI provides some advantages, such as a high degree of data security and nonrepudiation (inability to deny sent messages), companies that want to connect to establish similar data exchange with business partners can use the web technologies on the Internet. XML, in particular, enables business partners to set standards for data formats in web pages. Dynamic page technologies, the software that links web pages with databases, automate much of the business activity with business partners. Orders can automatically trigger notices to warehouse personnel on their stationary or handheld computers to pick and pack items for shipping. The information automatically flows into the accounting ISs as well as SCM systems of both the buyer and seller. Figure 7.4 illustrates how information flows between organizations.

Companies encourage their suppliers to join their extranets. For example, Tesco, the UK's leading supermarket, allows its suppliers to access the same databases that are used by Tesco's staff. These suppliers can gain information about stock levels at different stores, delivery requirements and so on. Similarly Cisco, the worldwide leader in networking for the Internet, allows their suppliers to connect to their internal systems using a password. This security feature means that suppliers are not able to view company confidential information or details about competitive suppliers. However, they are able to identify market trends and provide a better service to Cisco.

XML is used extensively in web technologies so that the SCM systems of two organizations can 'speak to one another'. This ensures that the meaning of data exchanged between the

Figure 7.4 Online supply chain management

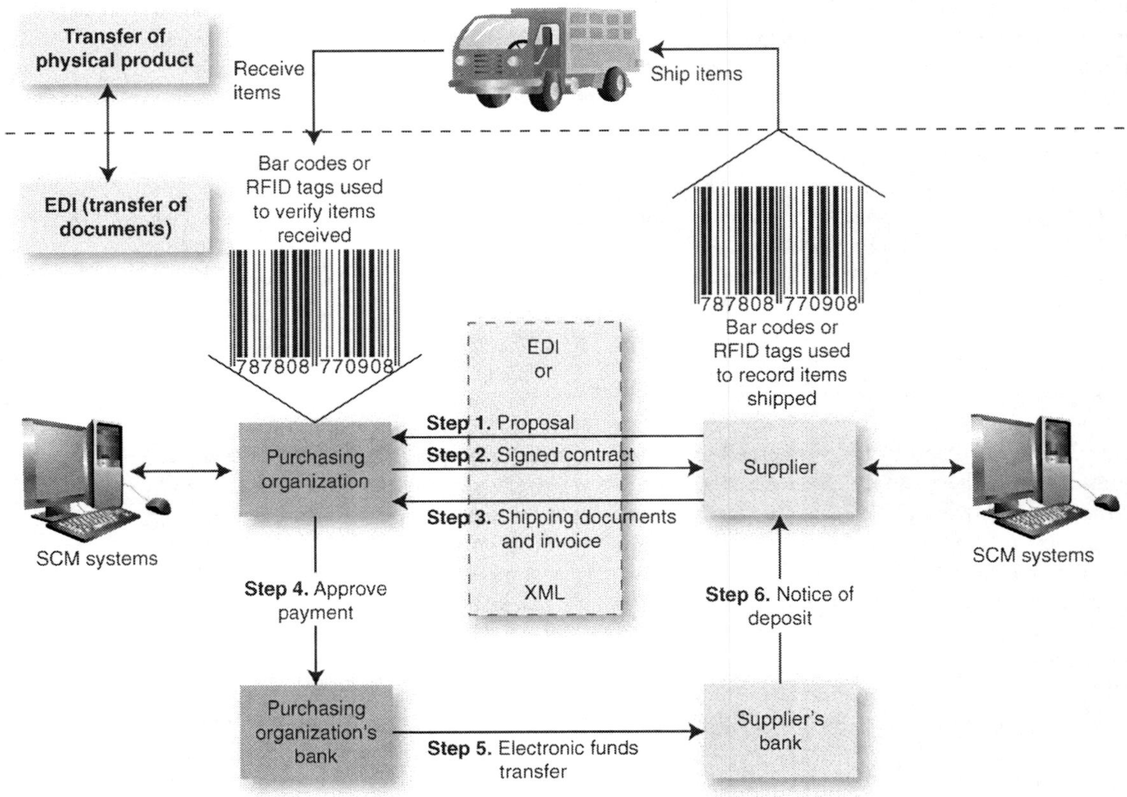

organizations can not only be displayed for employee eyes through web browsers but that the received data can be interpreted correctly by systems that automatically capture and store it in a database for further processing.

Rules for successful web-based business

Most organizations that operate a website do so to sell either products or services. Web software and the ability to connect web servers to organizational information systems open great opportunities. Often, whether online business succeeds depends not only on availability of the proper software but on how it is used. There are several elements to consider, especially if the site is to support B2C commerce.

Target the right customers

Targeting the people or organizations that are most likely to need the products and services you offer has always been the most important effort in marketing, with or without the Web. On the Web, targeting includes identifying the sites your audience frequently visits. For

Ethical and Societal ISSUES

Online annoyances and worse

The Web provides excellent opportunities, but its wide availability combined with ingenuity have created some practices that range from mildly annoying to criminally dangerous.

Spam Spam is the term for unsolicited commercial email. Spam does not have to be camouflaged to be so. The mere fact that it is not invited makes it spam. The reason for spam is simple: it is the most cost-effective marketing method. Even if a fraction of a per cent of the recipients end up purchasing the product or service touted, the spammer profits. Both individuals and organizations dislike spam. Individuals have to wade through a long list of unsolicited emails to get to useful emails. Organizations face an increasingly costly burden. Consider: if spam makes up half of the email the organization receives, the organization must employ twice the bandwidth it really needs for communications and twice the space on email servers. Obviously, it pays twice as much as it could for operating an email system. Screening software, known as antispam software, has helped to some extent, but spam is still on the rise and still causes waste of resources. By some estimates, spam constitutes about three-quarters of all email flowing on the Internet.

The Direct Marketing Association (DMA) defends the right of businesses to send unsolicited commercial email as a legitimate and cost-effective way of doing business. Indeed, the method gives small, entrepreneurial businesses a chance to compete. The DMA sees no difference between junk 'snail' mail, which most of us reluctantly tolerate, and spam.

On the other hand, the European Coalition Against Unsolicited Commercial Email (EuroCAUCE) calculated the amount of spam we might soon receive unless new laws stop the phenomenon. Their calculations are as follows. 'EUROSTAT's Yearbook for 2000 included figures for the number of businesses in various territories in 1996. There were 18.444 million businesses in the 15 countries comprising the European Union, ranging from "No Salaried Staff" (i.e. smaller even than "very small") to "Large". So take 1 per cent of that, and we get 184 440 possible senders, each of whom, for the purposes of this thought experiment, sends one message' per year 'complete with instructions for "opting out"'.

'Let's take a working year: 52 weeks less 4 weeks annual leave less an additional 5 days for legal holidays gives us 47 weeks. At 35 hours per week (this is Europe, after all) we get 47*35 = 1645 hours over a working year to deal with these 184 440 messages. That works out to 184 440/1645 = just a little over 112 messages per hour, or a bit less than two messages per minute. Not every sender makes it easy or convenient to "opt-out": some require using a different reply address, others require a visit to a website, and so on, which means that some time must be allowed to parse the message for the relevant information. This calculation does not take excessive downloading time into account, but assumes that the messages appear in time to be dealt with.'

Opting out, then, is not a realistic option but EuroCAUCE does not believe that opting in – avoiding receiving email unless you specifically ask for it – would solve the problem either. Antispam legislation in many countries has not reduced spam. According to most laws, spam is a crime only if the sending party hides its true identity.

Is unsolicited commercial email a legitimate marketing tool, or is it a nuisance that should be eradicated by strictly enforced laws? Would it be fair to outlaw an efficient way for businesses, especially entrepreneurial businesses, to approach potential customers?

Pop-up windows You browse the Web, stop to read an interesting article, and a few seconds later a window pops up, partially covering the text you were reading. The pop-up contains an advertisement. You look for the little X to close the window. It is not in the normal top-right corner. You finally manage to close the window, but as soon as you do, another one pops up. And so on, and so forth, more and more windows. When you finally close the main site's window, you discover that several other windows popped up *behind* the window. The site owner is paid by advertisers to run these pesky windows, which is legitimate. However, many people are quite annoyed by the practice. Some employ special applications or turn on a browser option that prevents pop-up windows. Is this a good solution? Not always. Many sites have links that open a little window, such as a help screen or an explanation of a term. If you block all pop-up windows, such windows do not open. If you use a selective pop-up 'killer', you have to program it to allow pop-up windows for individual sites. Thus, even with a solution, pop-up windows waste surfers' time. Web surfers might not like pop-up windows, but advertisers love them, because they are an effective marketing tool.

Adware A growing number of organizations use adware, software that delivers ad banners or pop-up advertising windows on the Web. Often, the banners hide large parts of the information on the page. Adware is often tailored to users, based on their profiles, such as previous interests. Some companies use adware that pops up deliberately to cover banners of competing companies that paid to advertise at the site a user visits. The visitor might not even know that the ad is not originating from the website, but from another one.

Spyware A more disturbing 'ware' is spyware. As discussed in this chapter, spyware is software that uses the Internet connection of a computer to transmit information about the user without the user's knowledge or permission. Usually, the software transmits information about users' activities with their computers, including their every move on the Internet. It sits on the computer's hard disk, secretly collects information, and transmits it to the computer of a company, usually for marketing purposes, but also for industrial espionage. Some surreptitious software is also designed to pop up windows. Some countries have criminalized adware and spyware, but in much of the world the software does not violate any law.

Phishing A growing number of web users receive a special kind of spam that intends not to sway them to buy something but to defraud them. The practice is called phishing, a play on 'fishing'. Criminals send thousands of messages that look as if they were sent from a bank, a credit-card company, or any other financial institution or an organization where the recipient has authority to withdraw funds. The email provides a web link where the recipient is urged to go and supply personal information, including codes that are used to withdraw or transfer funds. One of many 'reasons' is 'explained' in the message: your account must be renewed, the bank lost your details, you need to verify your personal information or the account will be revoked, and many others. Thousands of people have fallen prey to the con artists, who use the information to withdraw funds. The most obvious sign that an email message tries to phish is a message from an institution with which you have never transacted, such as a bank where you do not have an account. A more subtle sign is the URL that appears in the browser once you click the link: the domain name is not the one of the legitimate organization. Suspect every email message that asks you to update your personal information online. Call the organization using the legitimate number you have on file and ask if the message is genuine. Banks and other institutions rarely use email to ask for an 'account information update'. Phishing continues to grow. Industry statistics suggest that 5 per cent of recipients of a phishing email subsequently visit an associated website and hand over personal data.

instance, a business that sells sporting goods should create clickable links at sites that cover sporting events and provide sports statistics. Banks that offer mortgage loans should create links at estate agents' sites. And any business that targets its products to young people should do so at popular music sites. This principle should also apply to blogs and popular podcasts. Podcasting can include visual advertisements displayed by the player software.

CD TASK

Capture the customer's total experience

By using cookies and recording shoppers' movements, CRM software can create electronic consumer profiles for each shopper and buyer. The shopper's experience with the site then becomes an asset of the business. Such marketing research fine-tunes the portfolio of products that the business offers and tailors web pages for individual customers. It also can be used to 'market to one' by emailing the shopper about special deals on items in which he or she has shown an interest.

Personalize the service

CRM software and web page customization software can be combined to enable customers to personalize the pages and the service they receive when they log on to the site. Letting shoppers and readers select the type of email content they want is welcome, but sites should respect privacy by letting customers opt in rather than opt out. Opting in means that the customer can actively check options to receive email and other promotions, while opting out requires the customer to select *not* to receive such information – an annoyance to many customers.

The Web also enables companies to let consumers tailor products. IKEA, the Swedish furniture retailer, offers a kitchen design service online allowing customers to plan their room, selecting from IKEA products. The finished design is then linked to an order making a seamless link between requirements and fulfilment.

Shorten the business cycle

One reason people like to do business on the Web is that it saves them time. Businesses should keep looking for opportunities to shorten the business cycle for their customers, from shopping to paying to receiving the items they ordered. Fulfilment, the activities taking place after customers place orders online, is one of the greatest challenges for online businesses.

Those who can ship the ordered products fastest are likely to sustain or increase their market shares. Some have decided to outsource the entire fulfilment task to organizations that specialize in fulfilment, such as UPS's e-Logistics and FedEx's Supply Chain Services. E-Logistics, for example, offers to receive and store the business's merchandise in its warehouses, receive orders online, and then pick, pack and ship them to the online business's customers. It also offers a product return service. A shorter business cycle is not only important for customer satisfaction but also enables the company to collect faster because credit cards are usually charged upon shipping.

Let customers help themselves

Customers often need information from a web-enabled organization. Such information includes the status of an order, the status of a shipped item and after-sale information such as installation of add-on components and troubleshooting. Placing useful information and downloadable software at the site not only encourages customer loyalty but also saves labour.

Practically every online business now sends email messages with the status of the order, a tracking number and a link to the shipping company for checking the shipping status. Hardware companies can post online assembly instructions for their 'assembly required' products. In addition to including Frequently Asked Questions (FAQs) information, some companies have used knowledge management software (discussed in Chapter 10) that can answer open-ended questions.

Be proactive and de-commoditize

Expecting customers to visit your website every time they need your service might not be enough in today's competitive marketplace. Customers now demand not only prompt email replies to their queries but also proactive alerts. For example, the travel websites Orbitz and Travelocity email airline customers gate and time information if a customer's flight is delayed or if gates change. Some manufacturers email customers about product recalls or to schedule periodic service appointments.

These initiatives, as well as many others, are efforts to *de-commoditize* what companies sell. A commodity is any product that is sold for about the same price by a multitude of vendors in a highly competitive market, usually with a thin margin of profit. By adding a special service or additional information, the company keeps the products it sells from becoming a commodity. Adding an original service or information to the product differentiates the 'package' that online shoppers purchase from the 'package' sold by competitors.

E-commerce is every commerce

You might have noticed that the title of this chapter does not contain the term 'e-commerce'. You might have also noticed that this is not the only chapter in which web-enabled business activities are discussed. In fact, every chapter in this book gives examples of what is popularly referred to as e-commerce. Web technologies have been integrated into the business world to a degree that makes it difficult at times to realize which activities take place inside the organization and which involve information flowing from other places through the Internet. We have become so used to the integration of the Web into our daily activities, especially the commercial ones, that the lines between commerce and e-commerce have been blurred. We will eventually stop using the term 'e-commerce' and simply consider the Web another means of supporting business, much the way we consider technologies like the telephone and fax.

SUMMARY

Some industries have changed dramatically and continue to change thanks to web technologies. Any product whose sole purpose is to deliver information or any other product that can be digitized will eventually be delivered over the Web.

HTTP is an Internet standard that enables addressing of web servers with domain names. HTTPS is a secure version of the protocol for confidential transactions. HTML is a markup language for presentation of web pages. XML is a markup language for delivery of information about data communicated through web pages. XHTML combines features of HTML and XML. FTP is a protocol for uploading and downloading files. RSS is software that uses XML to automatically update text and audio from the website that posts it to subscriber online devices. It is the main enabler of podcasting. Blogs enable people to conveniently create discussion web pages by posting comments and responding to them. Instant messaging online chat services enable people to correspond in real time and help businesses serve online customers. Cookies help websites to personalize the experience of visitors. Along with other software that spies on unwitting web surfers, they might provide detailed information about web users.

In addition to a large number of nonproprietary web technologies, many more are developed and licensed to organizations by software vendors.

An organization has two options when deciding to do commerce online: own and maintain its own web servers at its own facilities, or contract with a web hosting company. When contracting with a web host, there are several degrees of service: shared hosting, virtual private servers, dedicated hosting and co-location.

When selecting a web hosting company, organizations should consider several factors: type and quality of application provided, storage space, quality of technical support, traffic limits, availability of email accounts and services, scalability, support of page design, security, uptime ratio, setup fee and monthly fee.

Web-enabled commerce can generally be classified as business-to-business (B2B) or business-to-consumer (B2C). In the former, businesses use networks to trade with other businesses, possibly through an extranet. In the latter, businesses advertise and sell goods and services to consumers via the Web. The greater volume of e-commerce is conducted between businesses.

Business-to-business trading often relies on electronic data interchange (EDI), which is conducted over value-added networks. XML facilitates interorganizational online trading similar to EDI. When linked to internal ISs, web technologies enhance supply chain management. Online interorganizational commerce often takes place through an extranet.

With the proliferation of wireless handheld computers and smart mobile phones, the next wave in B2C might be mobile commerce, popularly called m-commerce. It is already popular in Japan, but to a much smaller degree in Europe and the United States.

To be successful, an online business must target the right customers, capture the customer's total experience, personalize the service, shorten the business cycle, let customers help themselves and be proactive.

Spam, and to a lesser degree spyware, adware and pop-up windows, have become online annoyances. Society is trying to strike a balance between allowing these phenomena to continue as a form of commercial promotion and free speech, and curbing them to reduce the public's waste of resources. Phishing has become a pervasive crime, defrauding people and stealing their identities.

SpareBitz.com

SPAREBITZ REVISITED

The SpareBitz website included a customer feedback form and Steve noticed that there were several negative comments about the late delivery of items. Some of these were down to Steve and staff not being able to fulfil orders quickly enough, but most were because of delays in deliveries from suppliers and delays by the Royal Mail.

What would you do?

1 What changes to his own order fulfilling system can Steve take to minimize the customer complaints?

2 What can be done about the external problems in the process (Steve's supplier's and Royal Mail)?

New perspectives

1 Steve wants to find out more about who is visiting his site, what they are looking at and whether the visit turns into an order. What methods can Steve use to help him in this analysis?

Review questions

1 What is streaming video and on what does the success of companies that stream video rather than rent DVDs depend?

2 What is HTML, and why is it needed to use the Web?

3 What is XML? How is it different from HTML, and what purpose does it fulfil in web commerce?

4 What is the relationship between a domain name and an IP number?

5 When you visit a website and click a Download button, you activate software that adheres to a certain protocol. What protocol is that?

6 What is instant messaging (IM), and how can it support business operations? How does IM reduce telephone costs?

7 What is RSS, and for which industry is it especially useful?

8 What is blogging, and what potential does it have for businesses?

9 What is podcasting, and how is it different from radio broadcasting?

10 In the context of the Web, what is a cookie? What is the benefit of cookies for online shoppers? What is the risk?

11 What is the difference between first-party cookies and third-party cookies? Which is usually disliked more by consumers, and why?

12 What is an intranet, and what purposes does it serve?

13 What is an extranet, and what purposes does it serve?

14 When contracting with a web hosting company, what is the difference between a shared server and a dedicated server?

15 What is co-location? What are its benefits?

16 When selecting a web hosting company, one of the important factors to consider is uptime ratio. What is it, and why is it important?

17 What does 'unique monthly visitors' mean in online lingo? Who uses this metric and for what purpose?

18 What is a reverse auction? Would it be practical without the Web? Why or why not?

19 What is phishing? How do people get 'phished'?

Discussion questions

1 Streaming movies to subscribers' homes over the Web has already replaced video stores in some parts of the world. What other services do you think will change business models when large parts of the population have high-speed broadband connections?

2 Sun Microsystems Corp. coined the slogan 'The network *is* the computer.' What does that mean?

3 Some top-level domains (TLDs) are reserved for certain organizations. Why is this important? Would you prefer that anyone could register a TLD of his or her choice?

4 Podcasting is said to allow subscribers to 'time-shift'. What does that mean, and does this give listeners a benefit they do not have with radio programmes?

5 E-tailers can use their software to charge different shoppers different prices. This is called price discrimination, and it is legal. Some observers say that shoppers discriminate based on price when they decide from whom to buy, and therefore it is ethical for e-tailers to price-discriminate. Do you agree?

6 Do you see blogging and podcasting as a threat to the written and broadcast media? Explain.

7 One of the most frustrating types of events to an e-tailer is shopping cart abandonment. From your own online shopping experience, what are the things that would cause you to abandon an online shopping cart?

8 M-commerce will give organizations the opportunity to send location-related advertising, that is, they will send to our handheld devices advertising based on where we are. What is your feeling about this?

9 Some parts of the world have legislated voting through the Internet. There are thoughts of a wider 'teledemocracy'. At present online voting is restricted to 'big issues', such as the selection of State Representatives in some states in America. But the technology could easily be used for voting on wider issues such as new taxes, budget cuts and so on. Do you favour this teledemocracy? Why or why not?

10 Gambling on the Web is growing fast. Do you see a danger in this phenomenon more than in gambling in traditional ways? Does web gambling have more or less social impact than casino gambling?

11 You have a new home business. You sell a consumer product for which you have a patent. You believe there will be much demand for it. To promote it, you decide to purchase a list of 2,000,000 email addresses of people who fit into the demographic groups that are likely to purchase the product. The seller told you that these were addresses only of people who did not opt out from receiving messages from businesses. After you emailed the promotional message, you received hundreds of angry email messages, including one from the European Coalition Against Unsolicited Commercial Email (EuroCAUCE). Was there anything wrong in what you did? Why or why not?

12 The owners of a small business tell you that they would not be able to reach enough customers to survive if they couldn't use mass, unsolicited email. You strongly object to spamming. How do you respond to them?

13 Scott McNealy, CEO of Sun Microsystems, said: 'You already have zero privacy. Get over it!' Some observers say that expecting privacy when using the Internet is ridiculous; the Internet is a public network, and no one should expect privacy in a public network. Do you agree? Why or why not?

14 A student established a website that serves as an exchange of coursework. Students are invited to contribute their marked work and to search for assignments that other students contributed. When criticized, the student claims that this, too, is a way to do research. He argues that the moral responsibility rests with those who access his site, not with him. Do you agree? Why or why not?

15 There have been international efforts to harmonize laws addressing free speech on the Web. Do you think such efforts can succeed? Why or why not?

Tutorial activities

1 Find three commercial sites that operate in three different markets and offer affiliate programmes. Write up a summary: What do they sell? What do their affiliate programmes promise, and in return for what? Classify each programme as pay per sale, pay per click, pay per lead or another type, and explain why you classified the way you did.

2 Choose a topic in which you are interested. Select three different search engines (e.g., Google, Yahoo!, and MSN) and use them to look for information about the subject. Rank the performance of each site. A long list of sites that provide too broad a range of information is bad; a shorter list of sites that provide more narrowly defined information is good. Explain your ranking.

3 You have been hired by a pizza delivery service to design a website. The site should be attractive to families and young professionals and should allow them to order home delivery. Use a web page development application to build the home page of the business. Submit your page to your instructor.

4 The following table contains some of the elements offered by a web hosting firm. Assume that all other elements are satisfactory. Explain in writing to a person who has never learned about the subject what each of the shown elements means, including restrictions. Your 'student' is a small-business owner who sells 500 unique dolls and is interested in also selling online. Will this be a good option for her in the short run? Explain. If you need to make some reasonable assumptions that are not mentioned here, do so.

Feature	Description
Storage	5 GB
Your own domain name	Yes
Monthly data transfer	110 GB
MySQL database	Available
Shopping cart	Available
Email accounts	30
Website templates	Available
Setup fee	None
Monthly fee	€29.95

5 Prepare your curriculum vitae as an HTML document. If you wish, include your scanned photograph. Submit your work by email, or post it to your website and email the website link to your professor.

6 Consider the following options for a business that wishes to use a website: maintaining their own server at their facility, using a host for a shared server, using a host for a virtual private server, using a host for a dedicated server. You are a consultant. Consider each of the following scenarios independently of the others, and recommend the best hosting option to the business. Consider all the relevant factors, such as purpose and cost.

a) A family store at a shopping centre. The owners want to make the public aware of what the store offers. They want to pay as little as possible for this web presence.

b) A large retail company. Management wants to be able to execute purchases from suppliers through the new website, and to allow their own customers to shop and buy through the site. It is willing to employ its own team and facility for the servers.

c) A small business. The owners insist on having their own domain name. They wish visitors to have every sense that the site is run and controlled by the owners.

d) A small business. Management does not want to register and pay for its own domain name.

e) A large pure-play (Internet-only) e-tailer. It needs to change the list of products daily. Its web design team might want to change the DBMS, shopping cart application and other applications when the need arises. It already owns the servers but no longer wants to manage networking, backup, redundancy and security.

f) A bricks-and-mortar retailer that wants to extend its sales operations to the Web. It has a web design crew that is capable of changing content and is expert at using and modifying web applications such as dynamic pages and shopping cart applications. However, management does not want to purchase servers or manage their networking and security.

7 Team up with another student to analyse the privacy policies of three companies that specialize in collecting consumer information on the Web. All must be companies that install third-party cookies. There are at least ten such companies. List the common factors of the three companies. Then list the factors in which they differ. For each of the differing elements, which company treats consumers better, in terms of less invasion of privacy and more disclosure of its activities? Among other factors, see if the companies offer opt-in or opt-out options.

8 With two other team members, prepare a rationale for an original business idea that could generate revenue on the Web. Prepare the rationale in a way that would convince a venture capitalist to invest money in this new business.

Companion CD questions

1 Have you paid for a product or service using e-cash? If so, describe your experience. Would you do it again? If not, would you consider using e-cash? Why or why not?

2 Visit three sites that use e-commerce. Compare the look and feel of each site. Is it easy to make a transaction on the site? Does the site have any features that make doing business extremely easy or difficult? What are they?

Video questions

1 Have you downloaded music from an online site? If so, describe your experience. Would you do it again? If not, would you consider doing it? Why or why not?

2 Do you think pay-as-you-go music services are a good alternative to illegal music file sharing? Why or why not?

From ideas to application
REAL CASES

Case study 7.1

Ocado: an Internet supermarket

BY MARTIN RICH

An Ocado delivery van delivering Waitrose shopping in Cheam, Surrey, England.

PHOTO SOURCE: © HELENE ROGERS/ALAMY

Ocado is an Internet supermarket based in Hatfield, twenty miles north of central London. When it started in 2001 it delivered to customers only in a distinct area close to its base, but from 2003 onwards it also delivered in a number of urban areas of the United Kingdom outside London. Though Ocado carries goods which are also sold by the established Waitrose chain of supermarkets, it has been set up as an autonomous company in which the John Lewis Partnership (which owns Waitrose) has a 25 per cent stake. The company was started by three former bond traders who had worked at Goldman Sachs, and was originally named 'Last Mile Solutions' because of its emphasis on reengineering the final stage of the delivery process to customers' homes.

Although long-established – it has been in existence for around 100 years and has been owned by John Lewis since the 1930s – Waitrose covers a relatively small geographical area, up to around 150 miles from London. Also, while Waitrose has expanded the number of stores that it operates in recent years, these stores are typically medium-sized supermarkets; they have few very large outlets and they have not, on the whole, developed small outlets in the same way that some of the large national chains have. Where they have opened new large outlets recently, they have branded these as 'food and home' and have sold household goods, similar to those stocked in John Lewis department stores, alongside groceries.

Ocado started operations in 2002, in conjunction with the logistics firm GIST, whose depot they initially used, and using computers from Sun Microsystems and an established suite of e-commerce software from Intershop. The John Lewis Partnership already had some experience of using Intershop software as a platform for its online department store.

Ocado is carefully branded as being 'in association with Waitrose' so that it benefits from the established brand and from Waitrose's existing supply chain, and carries Waitrose's own-brand products, but is nevertheless perceived by customers as being a distinct service.

Superficially, Waitrose, as a regional player in the traditional supermarket business, would appear a good candidate to introduce an Internet supermarket with greater geographic coverage. In practice, however, Ocado started with a very limited geographic range and took two years to begin significant expansion outside London. Ocado does now service some major cities where there are few, if any, Waitrose outlets. Conversely Ocado does not, on the whole, operate in rural areas where drops are likely to be further apart and the logistics more difficult. In these areas Waitrose offers a simple store-based home delivery service. Within urban areas it makes sense for an Internet supermarket to be very focused on specific areas, partly because this makes it possible to deliver to many customers in a short time, partly because the supermarket's vans themselves are an effective form of advertising, and partly because the supermarket can build up very detailed information about buying patterns among customers in a particular area.

Ocado's advertising has been carefully targeted at relatively cash-rich time-poor customers, notably at affluent families with young children and two working parents.

By late 2006 Ocado considered the possibility of opening further distribution centres, but their business model continues to be based on serving a large area from a single centre. Ocado's delivery vans use 'demountable pods' to carry the food, so six of these can be loaded onto one lorry for the first part of their journey to customers, and each pod can then be transferred to a different van for the last mile. This is in contrast with Tesco, which is both the largest supermarket chain in Britain and the largest online food retailer, which fulfils most of its Internet orders from local supermarkets. Ocado's approach needs economies of scale to work (compared to Tesco's which could be introduced on a small scale with relatively limited investment), but if implemented well, can offer accurate time-slots and few substitutions, where customers are asked to accept different goods from those that they originally ordered.

For many years the trend in grocery retailing (and many other forms of retailing) has been towards customers picking items off shelves for themselves. This has been driven partly by a will to give customers choice (for example, by choosing loose fruit and vegetables) but mostly to save cost. Internet retailing reverses this trend, and its emergence raises the issue of how the cost of paying staff to pick items off shelves can be justified.

Ocado's core target market is firmly middle-class and pressed for time. Waitrose is already differentiated, in London at least, by presenting itself as a slightly more exclusive supermarket than its rivals. A lot of early advertising was directed to consumers who were thought to be open to Internet shopping, and who already had Waitrose or John Lewis store cards – to the extent of sending aprons and other free gifts to their target customers before the service started.

Ocado does aim to have an edge over their competitors in terms of logistics. Purchasers are offered a 'green van' option, where they can choose a slot when a van is already scheduled to be in their area. This is promoted as something that would appeal to environmentally conscious customers, but it also means that customers help Ocado to cluster deliveries in one area close together, which simplifies their logistics. Because the business model is based on customers choosing their delivery slots early, and on monitoring stocks in the central warehouse closely, the aim is to keep substitutions down to 2 per cent of all goods delivered. Complex routing software and satellite navigation in the vans are used to ensure that they can offer one-hour delivery slots: an ambitious service given the amount and unpredictability of traffic in London. Ocado waives their delivery fee on most orders over £75 (they have recently introduced a complex structure for delivery charges), so they rely on the efficiency and scale of their central warehouse to keep costs down.

Despite the business model, it is impossible to avoid substitutions completely, because there will always be occasions when a supplier is unable to fulfil, or predictions about demand are inaccurate.

In 2003 it was reported that Ocado had already lost £76.8 million, and although Ocado's directors expressed a wish to move into profit 'soon', the real objective was to expand the business by 5 per cent a week. In practice, the business has expanded by 50 per cent in each year of operation so far, and showed an operating profit (though it still had a lot of debts) for the first time in early 2007.

Case study questions

1 How easy would the Ocado idea be to replicate? Is there the possibility that another player could take Ocado's ideas and implement them more effectively?

2 Despite the attractiveness of the distribution centre approach, in practice cheap and simple approaches such as Tesco's have a better record of being profitable. What is necessary to achieve the economies of scale needed for Ocado's approach to be more profitable?

3 What concerns can you see if Ocado continues to expand into broader geographical areas? What would be a realistic aim in terms of expanding their coverage?

4 What sort of synergy exists with the John Lewis Partnership as part-owners? What do they get out of putting investment into Ocado?

5 What alternative strategies can you see for Ocado in the future?

6 What possible further applications can you see for the business model adopted by Ocado?

SOURCES: K. Boyer and M. Frohlich, 'Ocado – An Alternative Way to Bridge the Last Mile in Home Delivery?', Michigan State University, 2002; G. Clapperton, 'Supermarket Switch', *Guardian*, 17 November 2003; M. Feisst, 'Ocado on road to profits and site expansion', *Daily Telegraph*, 7 September 2006

silicon.com

Case study **7.2**

Amazon reaches out beyond its border

BY ELIZABETH BIDDLECOMBE

Businesses are learning to use technology to collaborate not only within their organizations but outside them too. Amazon.com is one example. Elizabeth Biddlecombe explains how they've done it.

From the outset Amazon.com has epitomized the e-commerce era. This is not just because of its use of the Web as its window to the customer, but also because of the systems it has used to connect with retail partners.

The company has exposed its technology platform and product data to third-party developers who have found all manner of ways to link words in text documents and weblogs – and even data from MP3 files – to goods for sale on Amazon.com.

Craig Berman, director of platform and technology communications at the Seattle-based company, says this diverse group includes developers creating applications that enhance associate sites. Others have commercial applications 'that help marketplace sellers manage business on Amazon.com', he says.

They are lured by the commission they make on each sale, while at a very basic level, Amazon reaps the reward of increased traffic through its virtual checkout.

'The great thing about enabling third parties to sell on the site is that it does provide low prices and great selection to customers', Berman explains. 'The flip side is that it allows developers to build their own profitable businesses.'

This open approach has spawned its own industry, with people writing books on how to make money through the Amazon e-machine. Two years after its launch in July 2002, some 65,000 developers had signed up to the web services platform.

One such developer is UK-based consultancy Inside C, which has developed an alternative method for customers to shop at Amazon. Its Inside Messenger application is based on the MSN Messenger instant messaging client and allows shoppers to query Amazon's database for particular products. Users keep a dedicated address in their contact list, which they click to search for an item on Amazon, though they never leave the IM client to do so.

Such applications are based on the company's E-Commerce Services (ECS) platform – itself using XML and Linux – which allows access to detailed product and pricing information.

When Amazon released version 4.0 of the platform, it incorporated new features such as the ability to link to images of products, the retrieval of all the customer reviews for a particular product or, if they prefer, particular reviews written by a specific reviewer. More sophisticated searches can be incorporated and developers can add the shopping cart functionality to their website.

At the end of January 2005 Amazon announced that ECS 4.0 was also available on its French and

Amazon is increasingly 'personalizing' its website for each of its customers.

Canadian sites, rounding out the capabilities to all six of its localized websites.

This is one part of Amazon Web Services (AWS) with another component being the web-crawling Alexa Web Information Service.

Suppliers themselves benefit from being able to plug into these systems. They can download the latest product information, manage their inventory, submit refunds and work out pricing for their goods.

Oregon-based consultancy Monsoon LLC is set up to help retailers, particularly smaller outfits with limited technological resources, plug into Amazon Web Services.

One sector that has benefited from this interfacing of systems is second-hand thrift shops that can now sell their books via Amazon. For instance, one US thrift store chain called Savers has been able to log into the system, price books competitively and then sell them. The company found itself making $8000 in book sales per week while before using AWS it would have been recycling them.

But obviously another key reason for Amazon's e-commerce prowess is its customer-facing technologies.

Berman says the company focuses on providing three things to seed the customer experience: low prices, a vast selection of products and a convenient, enjoyable experience online.

Part of that experience is driven by Amazon's use of personalization – the way it recognizes repeat customers, logs their past purchases and tries to prompt further spending.

Berman notes a collection of ways that Amazon tries to achieve the latter – in customer reviews, product ratings, the uploading of images and wish lists. Its recent investment in a weblog called 43 Things might signify that it is planning to tap into blogs as the latest way to create a community and motivate sales.

However, Berman will not provide comment on the rationale behind the investment. Nor, he says, does Amazon comment on speculation as to how the company might incorporate blogging, social networking or any other technology into its strategy.

Yet if history is any indication, Amazon will no doubt continue to find ways to use technology to reach out to partners, suppliers and customers.

Thinking about the case

1 Amazon seem to be 'giving away' access to its e-commerce applications to third-party developers. Does this seem like good business sense?

2 Can you think of ways that Amazon might use technology in the future to 'reach out to partners, suppliers and customers'?

Chapter 7

Challenges of global information systems

LEARNING OBJECTIVES

A growing number of organizations operate globally or, at least, in more than one geographic market. These organizations face some challenges that have a considerable impact on their information systems. The organizations have to meet the challenge of operating globally by providing international information systems to accommodate the free flow of information both within a single company's divisions and between multinational corporations. These issues have always been important to multinational companies but are of increasing relevance because so many companies operate a website, and websites are accessible globally.

When you finish this chapter, you will be able to:

Explain why multinational corporations must use global information systems.

Provide elementary advice for designing websites for an international audience.

Cite the cultural, legal and other challenges to implementing international information systems

SpareBitz.com

EXPANDING GLOBALLY

It came as a bit of a surprise to Steve Wilson when SpareBitz received its first order from Canada. It seemed that the customer had drawn a blank on finding the right spare part for a lawnmower he had shipped out there when he emigrated. He didn't want to throw it away and buy what he considered to be an inferior local mower. When he happened onto the SpareBitz website he was delighted to see the promise that the part would be found and delivered within a week. Steve put all his efforts into meeting this special order and had to overcome several new hurdles, not least sorting out customs clearance. When he sat down and analysed this sale he realized that he hadn't made any profit on it if you costed in all his time and the extra postage. So should he change his website so that it was only possible to order parts for delivery within the UK? His business brain kicked in. Could this be a profitable income stream? How much potential was there for overseas sales? With a few tweaks to his e-commerce operation, Steve was able to be prepared for requests for spares from virtually any part of the globe. He really was 'World Wide' now! Some of the considerations were to do with currency. A link to a currency converter was made available to website visitors, although the site automatically allowed potential customers to view their order in UK pounds, US dollars or euro at the touch of a button. At this stage Steve decided that language was not an issue. The volume of sales did not make it worthwhile to offer multilingual versions of the website.

Backwards and forwards

'There's something very odd here.' Charlie Evans, the Warehouse Manager, had just walked into Steve's office. 'It seems that this washing machine part that we have shipped in from Poland is just about to be sent out to a customer – in Poland!' Further investigation showed that many of the overseas orders were going a very roundabout route from supplier to customer. 'What we need is a set of agreements with our overseas suppliers, similar to those we have with UK suppliers that will ship the items directly to the customers.' When the company's accountant, Debbie Long, heard about this plan she realized that she needed to be involved. 'At the moment we pay import duty on the spares and the customer then pays import duty to receive the part from us. Do UK trading rules apply even if the object of the sale has never reached our shores? After all, the website is UK-based.'

Personal data

SpareBitz maintains a database of customer details. Many of its sales came from repeat customers.

PHOTO SOURCE: © DAVID FREUND

While deliveries are being instigated either from the company itself or from UK-based suppliers, Steve is happy that they are fulfilling the requirements of the UK Data Protection Act. However, if they were to give overseas suppliers customer information such as an address for delivery then there is a concern that, unwittingly, SpareBitz could be falling foul of the law. Steve called to his secretary. 'Sally. Can you get me the company lawyers on the telephone please. We may have a problem.'

Multinational organizations

An increasing number of the world's corporations have branched into countries all over the globe, becoming true multinationals. While they might have headquarters in a single country, they operate divisions and subsidiaries in different countries to take advantage of local benefits. For instance, a company might establish engineering facilities in countries that offer large pools of qualified engineers, build production lines in countries that can supply inexpensive labour, and open sales offices in countries that are strategically situated for effective marketing.

Because of this spread of operations, a company's nationality is not always obvious. For example, consider IBM and Philips. While IBM is known as an 'American' corporation because its headquarters and most of its research activities are in the United States, the company has numerous subsidiaries in other countries. These subsidiaries are registered and operate under the laws of the respective countries, and they employ local workers. Likewise, Philips' headquarters is in the Netherlands and yet it owns one of the largest US sellers of electric razors, Norelco. Similarly, Intel, an American company, has major research and development facilities in Israel, where some of its latest microprocessors have been developed.

One hundred of the 500 largest Canadian companies have majority US ownership, and 90 per cent of US multinational companies have Canadian offices. Japanese companies own whole US subsidiaries in every imaginable industry. British companies have the largest foreign investment in the United States. Thanks to the North American Free Trade Agreement (NAFTA) and agreements between the United States and the European Union, we might witness the internationalization of many more American, Canadian, Mexican and European corporations.

Multinational corporations must use **global information systems**, which are systems that serve organizations and individuals in multiple countries. These companies might have unified policies throughout their organizations, but they still have to abide by the laws of the countries in which each unit operates, and be sensitive to other local aspects of their interaction with other businesses as well as consumers. Therefore, unlike organizations that operate in a single country, multinational companies have the burden of ensuring that their information systems and the information flowing through the systems conform to laws, cultures, standards and other elements that are specific to countries or regions.

global information system Any information system that crosses national borders.

The Web and international commerce

CD TASK

The emergence of the Web as a global medium for information exchange has made it an important vehicle for both business-to-business (B2B) and business-to-consumer (B2C) commerce. In 2004, more than 888 million people regularly logged on to the Internet across the globe. About two-thirds of them come from non-English-speaking countries, as Figure 8.1 shows, and more than half of all e-commerce revenues come from these countries. The ratio of non-English speakers to English speakers has steadily grown over the years.

Figure 8.1 Two-thirds of Internet users come from non-English-speaking countries

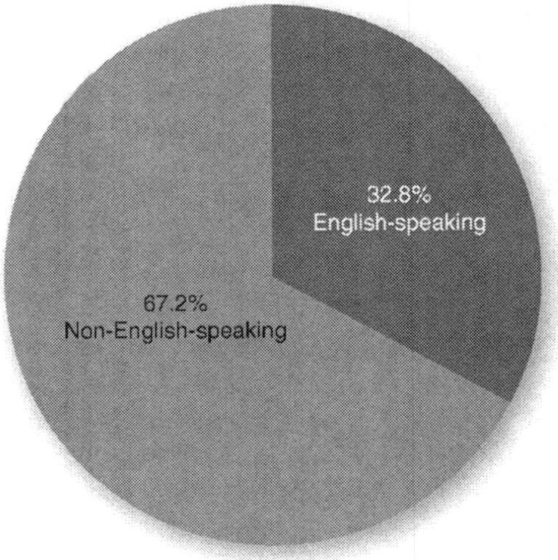

SOURCE: INTERNET WORLD STATS (WWW.INTERNETWORLDSTATS.COM)

The spread of Internet use opens enormous opportunities for businesses the world over. Some of the countries with current low participation rates have the greatest potential, such as China. About 87 million Chinese logged on in 2005, but the growth in Internet usage in Asia from 2000 to 2007 is over 250 per cent compared to the rest of the world's growth in the same period of just under 200 per cent. The Chinese market is expected one day to be the world's largest in terms of consumer spending.

The Web offers opportunities not only to increase revenue but also to save on costs. Consider, for example, how much money is saved when, instead of printing product and service manuals on paper and shipping them to customers, companies publish them on the Web, ready to be downloaded at a user's convenience. Furthermore, imagine the convenience if the manuals were prepared using not only text and graphics but also animation for easier and more informative use. Some companies place video clips to instruct buyers how to assemble the products they purchased. Many companies have stopped enclosing manuals with their retail products. They invite you to log on to their website and peruse the product's manual in your own language. This saves not only paper and printing, but also much of the labour involved in customer service. By placing maintenance manuals in multiple languages on their websites, some companies cut as much as 50 per cent of their customer service costs.

Industry **SNAPSHOT**

Low penetration but room for growth

In 2007, the world population was estimated at 6.6 billion people. About 18 per cent of the population used the Internet on a regular basis. Africa is second only to Asia in population size, with 933 million people. Yet, only 33.5 million of Africa's inhabitants (3.6 per cent) used the Internet regularly. In contrast, 69.5 per cent of the inhabitants of North America used the Internet regularly. However in the period 2000–2007, the growth in Internet usage in Africa was a staggering 643 per cent. The growth in the Middle East over the same period approached 500 per cent.

SOURCE: www.internetworldstats.com

Table 8.1 Imperatives to heed when designing websites for an international audience

Plan	Plan the site before you develop it. A site for an international audience requires more planning than a national one.
Learn the preferences	Learn the cultural preferences, convention differences and legal issues, or use experts who know these preferences. Tailor each local site (or the local section of your site) to the way in which the local people prefer to shop, buy and pay.
Translate properly	Use local interpreters to translate content for local audiences. Do not use software or other automated methods, unless humans review the translated material. Experienced translators are attentive to contemporary nuances and connotations.
Be egalitarian	Do not let any audience feel as if it is less important than other audiences. Keep all local sections of your site updated and with the same level of information and services.
Avoid cultural imperialism	If the local language or culture has a word or picture for communicating an idea, use it; do not use those of your own country. Give the local audience a homey experience.

Organizations that wish to do business globally through their websites must be sensitive to local audiences. Thus websites should be tailored to the audiences they are meant to reach. A majority of web users prefer to access the Web using a language other than English, so organizations must provide their online information and services in other languages, as well as English. As Table 8.1 shows, organizations must plan and carefully design their global sites so that they also cater to local needs and preferences, a process sometimes called **glocalization**.

glocalization The planning and designing of global websites so that they also cater to local needs and preferences.

Glocalization is a combination of universal business models and management philosophy with some adaptations for local audiences. One example of an organization that glocalizes is McDonald's. While the restaurant chain's logo and many other features are the same throughout the world, it makes some menu changes to appeal to local palates. Sometimes, other elements are changed. For example, in France, the restaurant chain replaced its familiar Ronald McDonald mascot with Asterix the Gaul, a popular French comic book character. Much like the presence of a global restaurant chain, websites are present everywhere someone can link to the Web. Therefore, website designers must keep glocalization in mind.

Think globally, act locally

Marketing experts often advise companies that operate internationally to 'think globally, act locally'. Acting locally means being sensitive to regional customs and language nuances. When interest in the company's business increases, especially from consumers, it is advisable to open a local office and let a local team handle both the website and fulfilment operations. Recall that fulfilment in online business includes picking, packing and shipping. When most of the business comes from one country or region, the business, its website and its information systems are managed centrally, but when a growing proportion of transactions take place in other regions, businesses find that they must decentralize control.

Thinking globally and acting locally might sound like contradictory ideas, but they are not. Recall our discussion of strategies in Chapter 2. Thinking globally has to do with the company's strategic planning. It involves decisions such as product lines and business alliances. However, the same strategy can be followed with a local flavour. For example, the same product, in whose

Why you should...

learn about challenges of global ISs

By default, every business that establishes a website in some way uses a global information system. Multinational corporations have used global information systems many years before the advent of the Web. They used private international banking systems and other EDI systems. All businesses can benefit from the use of global ISs, but they also face challenges. Neglecting to pay attention to such issues as different cultures, language nuances, conflicting national laws and different standards can hurt the

Businesses that cater to international audiences must 'glocalize' their websites as shown below. Emirates has succeeded in meeting this challenge, providing a sophisticated online presence that caters for a diverse range of cultural requirements on a global level.

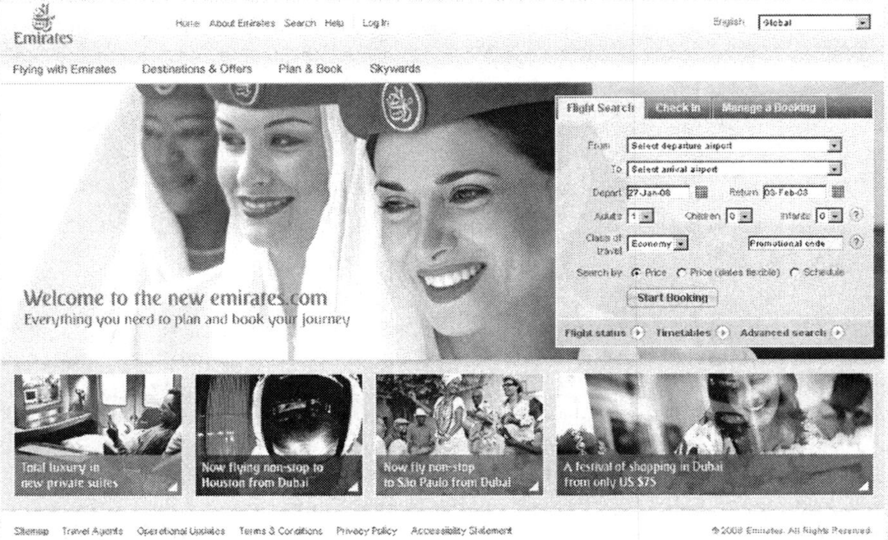

PHOTO SOURCE: © COURTESY OF EMIRATES AIRLINE

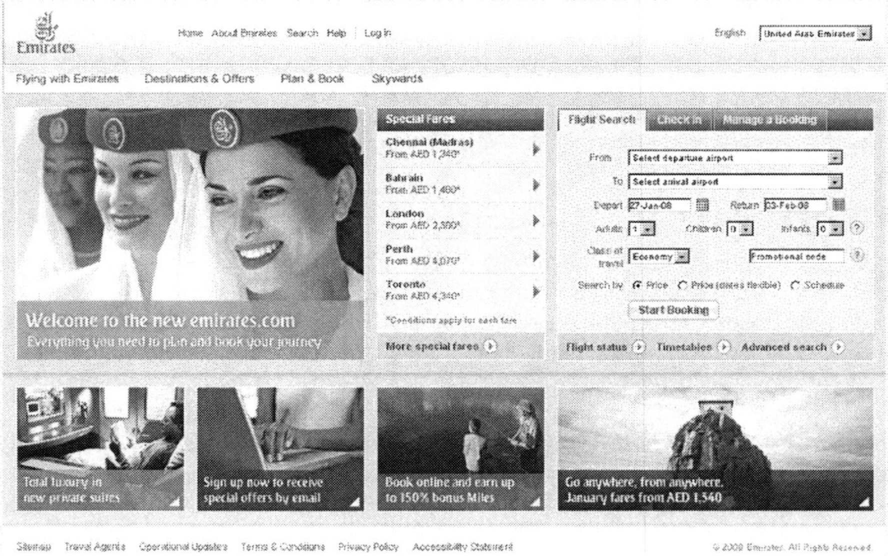

PHOTO SOURCE: © COURTESY OF EMIRATES AIRLINE

business's reputation and cause loss of revenue. Professionals who work for companies that conduct international business or for organizations that might do so in the future must be aware of the challenges involved in designing websites and using ISs for international trade.

PHOTO SOURCE: © COURTESY OF EMIRATES AIRLINE

design and production the company holds a competitive advantage, can be packaged and advertised with local motifs. The local branch of the company might still recruit the engineers with the same excellent qualifications as those of their peers in other countries, but apply different interview tactics and social benefits, which fit the customs and holidays of that country.

Challenges of global information systems

While the Web offers great opportunities for establishing international ISs, global ISs are not without their challenges, both for B2B and B2C commerce. Some of the challenges that businesses must address are technological barriers, regulations and tariffs, electronic payment mechanisms, different languages and cultures of the audiences, economic and political considerations, different measurement and notation standards, legal barriers and different time zones. These challenges are discussed in the following sections.

Technological challenges

Not all countries have adequate information technology infrastructures to allow resident companies to build international ISs. International ISs, especially those using the Web, often incorporate graphics to convey technical or business information, and those applications, as well as interactive software, require increasingly fast (broadband) communication lines. The bandwidth available in some parts of the world, for example many African countries, is too narrow for high-volume transmission of graphically and animation-rich web pages. Thus, companies might have to offer two versions of their sites, one for wide bandwidth and another for narrow bandwidth. Often, companies use one site, but provide the same content in both graphically rich and text-only pages, or the same video for download at different speeds.

Another technological challenge has to do with language. You might recall the earlier discussion of how characters are represented by bytes in computers. This setup is fine for languages with up to 256 (2^8) characters, such as English and other languages whose alphabetic root is Latin. But eight-bit bytes are not sufficient for languages with larger numbers of characters, such as Chinese. The solution for this obstacle is to ensure that computers can use **Unicode**, with double-byte characters – allowing for up to 65,536 (2^{16}) characters. However, if only the servers are programmed to accommodate Unicode, while the other systems (such as databases and applications on computers interacting with the servers) work with single-byte characters, then these back-end systems will record and display gibberish. Thus, entire systems must be reprogrammed or use special conversion software. As computers convert to operating systems that support Unicode, displaying different character sets should be less of a problem.

Unicode An international standard to enable the storage and display of characters of a large variety of languages – such as Asian, Arabic and Hebrew – on computers.

Other points that might sound trivial can also wreak havoc in international ISs or prevent individuals and companies in some world regions from transacting with companies that did not make their websites and applications flexible. For example, fields such as telephone numbers should be set for variable length, because the number of digits in telephone numbers varies by country. Similarly virtually every country uses some form of postal code but the structural rules of, for example, a UK post code are very different from a US zip code. Web forms must be able to accept various formats, hence sacrificing error-checking that might be carried out if the form was only to be used in one country.

Regulations and tariffs

Countries have different regulations on what may or may not be imported and which tariff applies to which imported product. While many executives know they might be missing out on great deals with overseas businesses, they are afraid that exploring international opportunities would entail too many hassles. They are also afraid that even with the proper research, employees might not know how to comply with the laws of destination countries, let alone calculate how much the organization would have to pay in taxes, tariffs, custom duties and other levies on exported or imported goods.

Companies such as NextLinx help exporters and importers who use the Web for commerce. The NextLinx software is integrated with a company's ERP systems and website. When a business from another country places an order, the information – such as type of item and destination country – is captured by the software, and an export manager can see how much the company will have to pay in tariffs, receive an estimate of how long the goods will stay in the seaport or airport before they are released from customs and, if the manager wishes, also receive information on regulations, licence required, shipping companies in the destination country and other useful information. Since the software is linked to the Web, it is continuously updated and provides useful information immediately. The software also calculates, on the fly, the total cost of delivering the goods to the buyer's door. It also provides more than 100 forms that exporters can fill out and save electronically. The logistics component of the application offers shipping options with land, sea and air carriers; books shipping space; and tracks shipping status. Several studies have shown that US companies have turned away about 80 per cent of online orders that come from other countries because they are not familiar with export regulations. This service can expedite the process.

Differences in payment mechanisms

One of the greatest expectations of e-commerce is easy payment for what we buy online. Credit cards are very common in North America and are the way businesses prefer to be paid online. However, this practice is not widespread in other regions of the world. The high rate of stolen credit cards, especially in Eastern Europe, attaches risk to such payments and deters potential online customers. The *Economic Times* reported in May 2007 that in India a mere 1 per cent of total spending (not just online purchases) is made using credit cards with only 28 per cent of the 'affluent' population owning a credit card, compared to 90 per cent in Hong Kong. And it is not just the developing world where lack of credit card ownership can have an effect on potential e-commerce sales. In Austria only 32 per cent of the population own a credit card according to the Lafferty Group. Americans are more willing to give credit-card details via the Web than people from other nations. Until citizens of other countries become willing to do so, payment through the Web, and therefore B2C trade, will not reach its full potential.

Americans pay with credit cards in 20 per cent of all transactions and in almost all online transactions. In Japan, on the other hand, only 8 per cent of transactions involve credit cards, and most Japanese are reluctant to use credit cards for online purchases. This calls for a different mechanism of payment. In Japan, many people who order merchandise online prefer to pick it up at convenience stores called '*konbini*', and pay there for what they purchased. Since shipping companies are reluctant to leave parcels unattended when the recipient is not home, the alliance of e-tailers and *konbini* affords not only payment confidence but also convenience. E-tailers from other countries who want to operate in Japan must be aware of these preferences.

Language differences

To communicate internationally, parties must agree on a common language, and that can create problems. For instance, data might not be transmittable internationally in real time because the information must first be translated (usually by human beings). Although some computer applications can translate 'on the fly', they are far from perfect. Another hurdle is that national laws usually forbid businesses to run accounting and other systems in a foreign language, leading to an awkward and expensive solution: running these systems in two languages, the local one and English, which is the *de facto* international language.

Companies that are in the forefront of web-based e-commerce have translated their original websites into local languages. They localize their sites by creating a dedicated site for each national audience. But translation can be tricky. For instance, the Taiwanese use the traditional set of Chinese characters, but people in the People's Republic of China prefer the simplified character set. Spanish terms in Spain might be different from those in Latin America. In addition, mere linguistic translation might not capture cultural sensitivities. Therefore, some companies prefer to leave web design and translation to their local overseas offices.

Several companies, such as TRADOS Inc., offer translation software and services to companies involved in global commerce. TRADOS' software package by the same name translates web pages into many languages, including those requiring special characters such as Hindi, Chinese, Greek and Hebrew, but also ensures consistency of terms and sentence structure in different languages. When web pages are translated, the software ensures that the XML tags and statements are retained from the original languages, so that the company maintaining the website can continue to use the same XML code for online transactions with companies and shoppers in its new markets. Other tools translate MS Word documents into multiple languages. One such tool is Wordfast.

Cultural differences

Cultural differences refer in general to the many ways in which people from different countries vary in their tastes, gestures, preferred colours, treatment of people of certain gender or age, attitudes about work, opinions about different ethical issues and the like. ISs might challenge cultural traditions by imposing the culture of one nation upon another (cultural imperialism). Conservative groups in some countries have complained about the 'Americanization' of their young generations. Governments might be inclined to forbid the reception of some information for reasons of undesirable cultural influence. An example of such fear is the French directive against use of foreign words in government-supported mass media and official communications. A similar example is the ban by the Canadian province of Quebec on the use of non-French words in business signs. These fears have intensified with the growth of the Internet and use of the Web. Because the Internet was invented and first developed in the United States and is still used by a greater percentage of Americans compared with any other single nation, its predominant culture is American.

As mentioned previously, companies that use the Web for business must learn cultural differences and design their sites accordingly. Web designers need to be sensitive to cultural differences. People might be offended by the use of certain images, colours and words. For example, black has sinister connotations in Europe, Asia and Latin America; the index-finger-to-thumb sign of approval is a rude gesture meaning 'jackass' in Brazil; the thumbs-up sign is a rude gesture in Latin America, as is the waving hand in Arab countries; and pictures of women with exposed arms or legs are offensive in many Muslim countries.

Conflicting economic, scientific and security interests

The goal of corporate management is to seize a large market share and maximize its organization's profits. The goal of a national government is to protect the economic, scientific and security interests of its people. Scientific information is both an important national resource and a great source of income for foreign corporations, so occasionally those interests conflict.

For instance, companies that design and manufacture weapons have technical drawings and specifications that are financially valuable to the company, but also valuable to the security of their country. Hence, many governments do not allow the exchange of weapon designs. Often, products whose purpose has nothing to do with the military are included in the list of prohibited trade items, because of the fear that they could be converted for use against the country of origin. In recent years, the list has included some software packages. The result is that, although home divisions of a company can use such software, their sister divisions in other countries cannot.

Consider some of the encryption applications offered by software developers. When Phil Zimmermann, developer of PGP (Pretty Good Privacy), offered this encryption application for free downloading, he was faced with federal criminal charges and severe penalties. His purpose was to allow individuals and companies to scramble their communications via computer networks. Companies use such software to protect corporate information. However, strong encryption methods are on the US federal government's list of restricted exports because, like weapons, they could compromise America's national security. Under public pressure, the government dropped the charges. In 2001, when it was found that the 9/11 terrorists used the software to encrypt their communication, Zimmermann expressed regret.

Some nations are afraid that cross-border information flow promotes cultural imperialism.

Another problem that arises with international information interchange is that countries treat trade secrets, patents and copyrights differently. Sometimes business partners are reluctant to transfer documents when one partner is in a country that restricts intellectual property rights, while another is in a country that has laws to protect intellectual property. On the other hand, the employees of a division of a multinational corporation might be able to divulge information locally with impunity. Intellectual property is tightly protected in the United States and Western Europe, and American trade negotiators and diplomats have put pressure on some countries to pass and enforce similar laws. Reportedly, the legislatures of several Asian nations have passed such laws or have revised existing laws in response to this pressure from the West.

Political challenges

Information is power. Some countries fear that a policy of free access to information could threaten their sovereignty. For instance, a nation's government might believe that access to certain data, such as the location and quantity of natural resources, might give other nations an opportunity to control an indigenous resource, thereby gaining a business advantage that would adversely affect the resource-rich country's political interests.

Governments are also increasingly recognizing software as an important economic resource, leading some countries to dictate that companies operating within their borders must purchase software from within their borders. For example, until 1997, Brazil's authorities

Industry **SNAPSHOT**

Collaborating with the censors

Companies that wish to do business in a large market where political interests limit freedom of speech often yield to government pressure. Microsoft Corp. cooperates with China's government in censoring the company's Chinese-language web portal. The company's policy of cooperation affects blogs. It works with the authorities to omit certain forbidden language. Bloggers are not allowed to post words such as 'democracy', 'human rights', and 'Taiwan independence'. Attempts to enter such words generate a message notifying the blogger that such language is forbidden. Several groups have tried to pressure executives at Microsoft, Yahoo!, Google, Cisco Systems and other companies to urge the Chinese government for reforms on free expression, but free speech is no match for the economic interest of these companies. China's estimated online population is 87 million, second only to the United States.

SOURCE: C. Woodward, 'Microsoft Censors Blogs at Chinese Portal', Associated Press, 13 June 2005

Google's corporate headquarters in Beijing, China.

PHOTO SOURCE: © DIRECTPHOTO.ORG/ALAMY

allowed local businesses to purchase software from other countries only after demonstrating that the software was not available domestically. The rule was enforced even if the business was owned by a foreign company. These policies can hinder standardization and compatibility of international ISs by preventing use of the same software throughout a multinational corporation.

As mentioned in Chapter 4, however, the recent trend in less rich countries is to adopt free open source software to avoid high costs. National governments in South America as well as local governments in Asia and Europe have adopted policies of using only open source software whenever it is available. Global corporations must ensure compatibility with the software adopted by governments and corporations in such locales.

Companies must also be aware of limits that some governments impose on Internet use. China, Singapore and many Arab countries impose restrictions on what their citizens can download, view and read. Free speech is not a universal principle. In practical terms, this means that executives might want to rephrase or cut out some content from their websites or risk their sites being blocked by some governments. This is an especially sensitive issue if a company enables employees or customers to use blogs at its website, in which they express their personal opinions.

Ethical and Societal **ISSUES**

Legal jurisdictions in cyberspace

Imagine: you surf the Web and come across a virulent site that preaches hatred and violence. You file a complaint in court, but the court cannot do anything because the site is maintained in another country that does not uphold your country's law. Or, you shop on the Web and purchase an item from a site that is physically maintained on a server in another country. When you receive the item, you discover that it is of a lower quality than promised. When you contact the site, the owners are rude and unresponsive. You decide to sue, but under which country's laws? These problems are two examples of the legal challenges in today's electronic global markets.

Global free speech In the spring of 2000, the International League against Racism and Anti-Semitism (LICRA), the Movement against Racism (MRAP), and the Union of French Jewish Students (UEFJ) filed a lawsuit against the American Internet company Yahoo! in a French court. The organizations complained that Yahoo!'s auctioning of more than 1200 Nazi-related items amounted to 'banalization of Nazism', which violates French law. The Nazi items offered for sale on the site included everything from Nazi flags and uniforms to belt buckles and medals. In November 2000, Judge Gomez ruled that a French court had jurisdiction over Yahoo! for violations that occur within France. He ordered Yahoo! to block French citizens' access to auctions of Nazi items within three months or face a fine of 15,000 euro per day.

Like many global e-commerce sites, Yahoo! did not require its webmasters to maintain a dedicated site for each language. French users merely saw a customized overlay using the main Yahoo! pages that are viewed by all visitors. This technique has enabled Yahoo! to offer country-specific and language-specific versions of its site at relatively low cost. Yahoo! screened out the items from its French site, but this did not satisfy the court because French citizens could still view the items via the general site.

To countries that have been subjected to a ruthless occupation, free speech is less important than preventing offences such as 'banalization of Nazism'. In the United States, however, free speech is legally protected even when someone's opinion or trade of objects is offensive. Yahoo! decided to remove such items from all its servers, but also took up the case in the US courts, arguing that foreign courts should not be able to negate the First Amendment of the US Constitution which concerns freedom of speech. After the original ruling and several appeals, the only thing that is clear is that the situation is unclear!

Consider this example: a ruling against a company registered in India by a court in Germany, and an appeal in a court in India of a court decision made under the laws of Germany. This legal tangle is the result of doing business globally. More than one law might govern a business practice or communication of ideas. The legal environment used to be confined to national boundaries, and jurisdiction used to refer to a territory. No longer so. Now the 'territory' is cyberspace. It is difficult to define jurisdictions in cyberspace. The lingering question is, 'Whose law applies?'

Consumer protection by whom? Where can consumers sue for e-commerce transactions gone wrong? Suppose you purchased an item from a site located in another country, and the item has a defect or arrived after the time promised. Because your request for compensation or another remedy has not been answered satisfactorily, you decide to sue the e-tailer. Where do you file the lawsuit? Your own country? The e-tailer's country? The venue of e-commerce lawsuits is still undecided in many parts of the world.

In November 2000, the European Union (EU) passed a law that lets consumers file lawsuits against an online business in any of the member countries composing the EU. Before the amendment to the 1968 Brussels Convention (which regulates commercial-legal issues in the Union), consumers could sue an online business only in courts in the country of the online business. Now, if a website has directed its business at consumers in a certain country, the consumers can sue the website's owner in their own national courts. Businesses vehemently opposed the move, but consumer advocates said people would be more confident about online shopping if they knew they could get redress in their local courts.

Two approaches to jurisdiction As you have seen, the issue of e-commerce jurisdiction is broad. The US Federal Trade Commission and European government organizations have examined the issue in an attempt to reach an international agreement such as the one reached within the EU.

There are two approaches to such agreement. One approach is the *country-of-origin* principle, whereby all legal matters are confined to the country from which the site operates. Under this principle, the laws of that country apply to the operations and conduct of the site and whoever interacts with the site, regardless of their own location. Therefore, a lawsuit could be brought only in the country of the website and would be adjudicated according to that country's laws. Under this principle it is likely that many firms would opt to establish websites in countries with lax consumer protection laws.

The other approach is the *country-of-destination* principle, whereby the laws of the country to which the site caters apply regarding dealings with the site, regardless of the site's country. The EU adopted this approach within its territory. It might take several years until there is international agreement on e-commerce jurisdiction.

Different standards

Differences in standards must be considered when integrating ISs internationally, even within the same company. Because nations use different standards and rules in their daily business operations, sometimes records within one company are incompatible. For instance, the bookkeeping records of one division of a multinational company might be incompatible with the records of other divisions and headquarters. As another example, the United States still uses the English system of weights and measures (inches, feet, miles, quarts, pounds and so on), while most of the rest of the world (including England) officially uses the metric system (centimetres, metres, litres, kilograms and the like). There are also different standards for communicating dates, times, temperatures and addresses. The United States uses the format of month, day, year, while the rest of the world records dates in the format of day, month, year. A date recorded as 10/12/08 might be misinterpreted. The United States uses a 12-hour time notation with the addition of a.m. or p.m., while other parts of the world use a 24-hour notation (called 'military time' in the United States because the US military uses this notation). The United States uses Fahrenheit temperatures, while other countries use Celsius temperatures. Americans communicate addresses in the format of street number, street name and city name. Citizens of some other countries communicate addresses in the format of street name, street number and city name.

Using different standards can be extremely costly. In 1999, NASA lost track of a spacecraft that it sent to Mars. Reportedly, an investigation found that an error in a transfer of information between the Mars Climate Orbiter team in Colorado and the mission navigation team in California led to the spacecraft's loss. Apparently, one team used English units, and the other used metric units for a key spacecraft operation. The information was critical to the manoeuvres required to place the spacecraft in the proper Mars orbit. The cost to US taxpayers was US$125 million.

Companies that want to operate globally must adapt their ISs to changing formal or *de facto* standards. In recent years the growing number of countries joining the European Union (EU) imparted significant power to this bloc. Corporations in non-EU countries have grown accustomed to adapting their systems to those of the EU. For example, in 1976, Europeans adopted the 13-digit **European Article Number (EAN)**, while American companies used the 12-digit **Universal Product Code (UPC)**. The additional bar in the EAN barcode identifies the product's country of origin. For seven years the American Uniform Code Council (UCC) promoted the use of the European standard. In 2004, the organization officially adopted it. Retailers embarked on a hectic effort to modify information systems to recognize, record and process UPCs of 13 bars instead of 12 bars so they could meet the January 2005 deadline. Most barcode readers could already read the extra bar, but the software in back-office systems – such as sales, shipping, receiving and accounting systems – had to be modified. Best Buy, the large electronics and appliance retailer, spent 25,000 hours of staff and hired consultant time to ensure that cash registers, several software applications and databases could process and store the extra digit.

European Article Number (EAN) A European standard of product code, similar to UPC but containing more information.

Universal Product Code (UPC) A code usually expressed as a number and series of variable width bars that uniquely identifies the product by scanning.

Global Trade Item Number (GTIN) A number that uniquely identifies products and services. The GTIN is a global standard succeeding the EAN and UPC.

The UCC is trying to expand product codes to 14-digit **Global Trade Item Numbers (GTINs)**. This code is large enough to identify more than 100 times the number of products and manufacturers that the 12-digit UPCs could. GTINs are designed to support global supply chains. Eventually, manufacturers and retailers might have to use either GTINs or another standard of larger codes embedded in RFID tags. The major push for using RFID tags is taking place in the United States, and American standards could expand to Europe and the rest of the world.

CD TASK

Legal barriers

The fact that countries have different laws has a great impact on global business in general, and on e-commerce in particular. The differing laws can pose serious challenges to international transfer of data, free speech and the location of legal proceedings when disputes arise between buyer and seller.

Privacy laws Although many of the challenges involved in cross-border data transfer have been resolved through international agreements, one remains unresolved: respect for individual privacy in the conduct of international business. Interestingly, despite the importance attached to privacy, that value is not even mentioned in the constitutions of the United States and many other countries. Nonetheless, a majority of the democratic nations try to protect individual privacy. An EU working party concerned with privacy recently wrote to Google regarding the latter's policy of retaining log data for two years on queries that identified the search term, the Internet server and other information derived from cookies. The response

Industry SNAPSHOT

International Hall of Shame

Privacy International (PI) is an international organization that monitors governments and commercial organizations around the world for violations of privacy. Each year, the members and affiliated organizations of PI present the 'Big Brother' awards to the government and private sector organizations in their countries that have done the most to threaten personal privacy in their countries. Since 1998 more than 40 ceremonies have been held in 16 countries and hundreds of awards have been given out to some of the most powerful government agencies, individuals and corporations in those countries. A 'lifetime menace' award is also presented. To counterbalance the shameful awards, PI also gives awards to individuals and organizations that have made an outstanding contribution to the protection of privacy. You can read more about it at www.privacyinternational.org/bba.

from Google was to reduce this period to 18 months. Whether this is satisfactory to the EU and where other search engines such as Yahoo! fit in this dispute remain to be resolved.

Countries differ in their approaches to the issue of privacy, as reflected in their laws. Some are willing to forgo some privacy for the sake of a freer flow of information and better marketing. Others restrict any collection of personal data without the consent of the individual.

Data protection laws from various countries can be generally described by three different criteria:

- Whether the laws apply to the collection and treatment of data by the private sector (companies), the public sector (governments) or by both.
- Whether the laws apply to manual data, to automated data or to both.
- Whether data protected under the law are only those concerning human beings or those concerning both human and 'legal' entities (that is, organizations).

Except for the US and Canadian privacy acts, privacy laws apply to both the public and private sectors; that is, government and private organizations are subject to the same regulation of collection, maintenance and disclosure of personal data. More than half the laws (including US federal statutes) encompass manual and computerized record-keeping systems. Denmark, Austria and Luxembourg are among the countries that protect the privacy of some types of corporations.

Countries that support protection of corporate data argue that it is difficult to separate data about individuals from data on business activities involving or performed by individuals, especially with small businesses. For example, the financial information of a small business also reveals financial information about the people involved with and/or running the business. Furthermore, a large corporation might unfairly compete against a smaller firm if it has access to the smaller firm's data.

The European Union (EU) enforces a privacy law called the Directive on Data Privacy. The EU defines personal data as 'any information relating to an identified or identifiable natural person; an identifiable person is one who can be identified, directly or indirectly, in particular by reference to an identification number or to one or more factors specific to his physical, physiological, mental, economic, cultural, or social identity.' Some of the principles of the directive are in stark contrast to the practices of US businesses and therefore limit the free flow of personal data between the United States and the EU. For example, consider the following provisions and how they conflict with US practices:

- Personal data can be collected only for specified, explicit and legitimate purposes and not further processed in a way incompatible with those purposes. However, in the United States, businesses often collect data from people without having to tell them how the data will be used. Many US corporations use personal data for purposes other than the original one, and many organizations purchase personal data from other organizations, so subjects do not even know that the data is used, let alone for what purpose. Obviously, these activities would not be allowed under the EU directive.
- Personal data can be processed only if the subject has given unambiguous consent or under other specific circumstances that the directive provides. Such circumstances are not required by American laws. In the United States, private organizations are allowed to process personal data without the subject's consent, and for practically any purpose.
- Individuals or organizations that receive personal data (the directive calls them 'controllers') not directly from the subject must identify themselves to the subject. In the United States, many organizations purchase personal data from third parties and never notify the subject.
- People have the right to obtain from controllers 'without constraint at reasonable intervals and without excessive delay or expense' confirmation that data about them are processed, to whom the data are disclosed, and the source that provided the data. They are also entitled to receive information on the 'logic involved in any automatic processing of data concerning' them at least in the case of automated decision-making. Decision-making, practically speaking, means using decision-support systems and expert systems to make decisions on hiring, credit extension, admittance to educational institutions, and so forth. None of these rights is mandated by any US law.
- People have the right to object, 'on request and free of charge', to the processing of personal data for the purpose of direct marketing, or to be informed before personal data are disclosed for the first time to third parties or used for direct marketing. Furthermore, controllers must expressly offer the right to object free of charge to disclosure of personal data to others. American companies use personal data *especially* for direct marketing, never tell subjects that they obtain data about them from third parties, and rarely offer subjects the right to object to disclosure of such data to other parties.

American companies are very busy collecting, buying and selling personal data for decision-making and marketing purposes. The American view is that such practices are essential to efficient business operations, especially in marketing and extension of credit. Thus, this huge discrepancy between the European and American approaches does not allow unrestricted flow of information.

The EU directive is only a framework within which member states may maintain their own, more restrictive, laws. Consider, for example, the French law, which states, 'An individual shall not be subject to an administrative or private decision involving an assessment of conduct which has, as its sole basis, the automatic processing of personal data defining his profile or personality.' This provision limits the use of a computer as a decision aid in certain circumstances. For instance, this law forbids automatic decisions for credit applications or admittance to a college. While the latter decision is often accompanied by human intervention, the former is often automated in the United States and other countries.

The EU directive recognizes that countries outside the EU use personal data that are transferred from the EU. It therefore provides that when a 'third country does not ensure an adequate level of protection within the meaning of [the directive], member states shall take the measures necessary to prevent any transfer of data of the same type to the third country'. This provision has created an interesting situation: agents of the European Data Protection Authorities (DPAs) arrive at least monthly in the United States to monitor American companies that process personal data of European citizens to ensure that the EU Directive on Data Protection is obeyed regarding these citizens. These representatives monitor the ISs of companies such as Visa, MasterCard, American Express and other credit-card issuers. Companies that want to do business in EU member states must accept the restrictions of the directive on their practices. Business leaders on both continents hope that a way can be found to bridge the gap between the two approaches to data privacy, but it seems that a legal solution will not come before a change in culture.

In the meantime, a practical solution has been sponsored by the US federal government. The EU agreed that the US Department of Commerce could establish a **Safe Harbor**, an arrangement for US companies that have agreed to comply with the EU directive regarding EU citizens so that European companies can trade with these US companies without fear of violating the directive. By June 2005, 739 US companies had joined the list. You can view information about the Safe Harbor arrangement and the list of companies that have joined at www.export.gov/safeharbor.

Safe Harbor A list of US corporations that have agreed to conform to European Union data protection laws with regard to EU citizens. The arrangement enables the corporations to continue to do business with European companies.

Since privacy laws regarding employees – not just consumers – are also different in the United States and the European Union, American companies employing European citizens must comply with EU laws regarding transfer of employment information. They must comply with the DPAs. Under the Safe Harbor arrangement, claims of European citizens against US companies regarding privacy are heard (with some exceptions) in the United States. To be sure they are not breaking the law, European companies that wish to transfer personal data to US companies can simply check at the above-mentioned website to see if those US companies are listed.

Applicable law As discussed in the Ethical and Societal Issues box in this chapter, countries have differing laws regarding free speech, which can have a grave impact on what a company may or may not display from its servers. Some of the other laws that can affect online business address gambling, auctioning and sales of alcoholic beverages and drugs. After establishing online business in some countries, some companies discovered that their practice was not in compliance with a local law. For example, eBay discovered that Dutch and Italian laws required that a certified auctioneer be present at any auction. This made its online auctions illegal in these countries. Some countries have changed their laws to accommodate online business, but others have not. Such legal discrepancy among jurisdictions should not come as a surprise to executives; they must research the legal environment in every jurisdiction where they intend to do business. The lessons of Yahoo!, eBay, and other online pioneers prompted many companies to employ legal research experts before they started business in a new jurisdiction. Often, this effort is part of a larger effort to research the local culture and practices. Some companies have hired local experts to help them in assessing local considerations and in some cases executives decided to avoid doing online business in certain countries altogether.

Different time zones

Different time zones must be considered by all organizations that do business in multiple countries.

PHOTO SOURCE: © LISA GAGNE

Companies that operate in many global regions, especially multinational corporations, must craft policies for the work of both their employees and information systems. Teleconferencing systems must be available much of the day, and in many cases, 24 hours per day, so that employees in many time zones apart can communicate to discuss problems that need immediate resolution. Teams in support centres might have to work in shifts to accommodate clients worldwide. For example, when arranging for a teleconference between offices in New York,

London and Sydney it is very difficult to find the time that is least inconvenient. There is an interesting website, http://www.timeanddate.com/worldclock/meeting.html which tries to help by showing when participants are liable to be in the office, at home or asleep!

In their global supply chain management systems, managers must be aware of what might seem to be incorrect time stamping in shipments and payment records. For example, consider interaction between a corporation's German manufacturing plant and its South Korean assembly plant. Because South Korea is seven hours ahead of Germany, shipping records could show that subassemblies were shipped from Germany a day before they were ordered in South Korea. To eliminate confusion, the systems at both locations can be designed to record the local times of both locations, or only that of a single location, such as the company headquarters' time.

SUMMARY

As more and more companies use the Web for business, both B2C and B2B, they realize that they must accommodate non-English-speaking audiences and tailor their sites to local preferences. They also must be carefully attuned to the cultural differences and payment preferences of different world regions, as well as be aware of legal and tariff issues.

Organizations that engage in international trade, especially through the Web, must also be aware of the linguistic, cultural, economic and political challenges involved in such trade.

One important unresolved issue is the discrepancy between the laws governing the collection and manipulation of personal data in two economic powers, the United States and the European Union, which have incompatible data privacy laws. This difference restricts the flow of personal data between the United States and the EU. The Safe Harbor arrangement enables EU companies to do business with US businesses that comply with EU policies on handling personal data of its citizens.

Several cases have demonstrated that the old legal approach of territorial jurisdiction is inadequate when so much information is communicated and so much business is conducted on the Internet. Issues such as free speech and consumer litigation of e-tailers have brought to light the need for an international legal reform for cyberspace.

SpareBitz.com

SPAREBITZ REVISITED

SpareBitz.com came from very humble origins. However, it has continued to expand not just nationally but internationally. It does not just deal with spare parts for household appliances but also the appliances themselves, mostly manufactured in Eastern Europe.

What would you do?

1. Contracting with manufacturers in another country involves communicating with the company, understanding the laws of the country and uncovering political, economic and technological issues that might affect trade. Describe the obstacles you think SpareBitz might face if it chose to expand to manufacturing in other countries such as China.
2. Sales to overseas customers are rising rapidly, with customers from the European Union, North America and even some from Africa. How should SpareBitz deal with payment and currency issues with regard to these sales?

New perspectives

It is becoming apparent that the original website, designed for UK customers, needs to have a multinational flavour. How should the company go about this? Should there be just one site that suits all nationalities and cultures? Is language the only problem?

Review questions

1. What is meant by the term 'global information systems'?
2. Executives of multinational corporations are advised to think globally and act locally. What does this mean?
3. Manufacturers and retailers have used product bar codes for many years. What information does the 13-digit European Article Number (EAN) contain that the 12-digit Universal Product Code (UPC) did not, and why is this information important?
4. Is every website a form of global IS? Why or why not?
5. Using software for automatic translation of web pages into other languages for local audiences saves much labour cost and time. If you were an executive for a company that maintains a multilingual website, would you settle for software-based translation only? Why or why not?
6. Many organizations, especially multinational corporations, must consolidate reports to ensure smooth operations. These reports include currency, measurements and dates. How would you help them receive reports 'on the fly' that are in the desired currency and format?
7. Many European countries have stricter privacy laws than the United States. What is the impact of this discrepancy on multinational corporations with offices on both continents? In terms of business functions, which activities, in particular, are affected?
8. Give three examples of cultural imperialism. Why do you think your examples reflect cultural imperialism?
9. Some countries have laws restricting collection and maintenance of data on small companies. Do such laws make sense to you? How can they protect the privacy of individuals? Give an example.
10. What are the implications of different time zones for global supply chain management systems?
11. Countries can adopt either a country-of-origin law or a country-of-destination law. What is the difference between the two approaches? Which is more helpful to consumers and which is more helpful to e-tailers? Explain.

Discussion questions

1. Test yourself: What are the 'nationalities' of the following corporations? Consider nationality to be the country where the corporation is registered: Total (petroleum), Bull (computers), Olivetti (office appliances), BP (petroleum), CheckPoint (security software), LG (electronics), Corona (beer), Heineken (beer), Thomson (electronics), Goodyear (tyres), JVC (electronics), Braun (small appliances), Siemens (electronics), Nokia (mobile telephones).
2. Some observers said that modifying applications and databases to move from 12- to 13-digit product bar codes was similar to the efforts to address the Y2K problem in the years leading to 2000. Search the Web to learn about the Y2K issue. In what way are the two issues similar?
3. The US Department of Commerce has relaxed restrictions on the export of encryption (scrambling) software for communications, but it still bans the export of many such applications. Do you agree with this policy? Why or why not?
4. Thirteen of the European Union countries use the euro as their common currency. Does this help or hinder international ISs? Explain.
5. Do you agree with the rule of the French court in the Yahoo! Nazi item auctions case? Why or why not?
6. Consider sensitivity to privacy in Europe. Are Europeans more sensitive to *government* handling of private information or to *business* handling of private information? Now answer the question regarding the USA.
7. Apparently, the EU has stricter privacy laws than the United States, and not many US companies are willing to comply with the EU Directive on Data Protection. The Safe Harbor arrangement is one way to resolve the issue, but only several hundred companies have subscribed. How would *you* resolve the conflict?
8. If a non-English-speaking country had established the Internet, do you think that country would impose its own 'cultural imperialism' on the Web? Why or why not?
9. Which legal approach do you prefer for e-commerce: country of origin or country of destination? Answer the question as a business person, then answer it as a consumer.
10. If some countries clearly adopt the country-of-origin approach for legal issues of e-commerce, online retailers might move to operate from those countries. Why?
11. An American company employs engineers in California and in several Asian and European countries. The engineers exchange emails and communicate via VoIP, teleconferencing and collaborative project management tools. The Americans often use phrases such as 'Let's touch base in a week', 'Right off the bat' and 'all the way to the end zone'. An executive instructs them to avoid such phrases in communication with colleagues from other countries and perhaps even with any colleague. Why?

Tutorial activities

1. You are an executive for Bidway.com, an auction site that has successfully competed with eBay and Yahoo! in the UK. Management decided to open use of the site to residents of all countries. You were given an important assignment: collect intelligence that will ensure that the company's move from a national business to an international business is smooth. If you envisage that there might be too many difficulties in certain countries, management will accept your recommendation to block bidding by residents of those countries, but you must be careful not to miss potentially profitable markets. Prepare an outline of all the aspects about which you will collect intelligence for each country and explain why this item is important.
2. The United States is the only country that still uses English measurement units rather than metric ones. Even the English officially moved to the metric system many years ago. The US Congress has unsuccessfully attempted to make the official move. Research on the Web and summarize your findings in two pages: Why does the United States still use the English system? When was the last attempt to officially move to the metric system? Does the use of English measurement units put US companies

at a disadvantage when competing on international contracts? How has software solved the challenge? Give examples of engineering software that resolves this challenge.

3 You are the international sales manager for Aladdin Rugs Ltd, a multinational company headquartered in the UK. At the end of every month, you receive reports from the national sales managers of your company's operations in South Africa, Germany and Japan. The products are sold by area. The managers report the units sold and income from sales in their national currencies: Rand (R), euro (€), yen (¥) and pounds sterling (£). Use your spreadsheet program to consolidate the sales reports you received, as follows.

   a) Under 'Totals', enter formulas to convert square yards to square metres and enter another formula to total the area in square metres for all four countries.

   b) In a financial newspaper such as the *Financial Times* or on the Web, find the rates of exchange for the three currencies against the pound on the last business day of last month. Enter a formula that will convert all non-sterling currency to pounds. (Extra challenge: program a macro to do the calculations.)

   c) Test all formulas with actual numbers.

4 Google and other sites offer web-based translation services. Test the quality of such tools. Write a message of 50 words in English. Use the tool to translate it into German or another language with which you might be familiar. Copy the translated text, paste it to be translated, and translate it into English. Compare the original and translated English messages. How good is the translation tool? About how much of the text in the translated version came out identical to the original? Did you find anything funny in the back-translated text?

5 Team up with three other students. Decide on three keywords with which the team will conduct a web search. All of you should use the same search engine. One team member should record the number of sites found in the United States, another in Germany, another in France and another in the Netherlands. Also, record the sites the team found whose domain name is non-US but that used English rather than, or in addition to, the local language.

   Prepare a brief report detailing what you recorded. Write your own conclusion: how dominant is English on the Web? Do you think the Web is 'Americanized'? Do you consider what you found to be cultural imperialism?

6 'Electronic immigrants' are residents of one country who are employed by a company in another country. They are the result of what some people call 'off shoring' of jobs. They deliver the results of their work through the Internet or private communications networks. Your team should conduct research with four companies in four different industries, one of which is in software development. The title of your research is 'The Electronic Immigrant: Economic and Political Implications'. Contact the human resource managers of the four companies, present the issue and ask for the managers' opinion: can the company use 'electronic immigrants'? Can it be hurt if competitors use them? Do the HR managers think the national economy can gain or lose from the phenomenon? Do they foresee any political ramifications? Your team should use a word processor to prepare a neat report starting with half a page of background on each company.

Companion CD questions

1 The version of MS Office you own probably has been manufactured for use only in the country in which you live. Why would software manufacturers limit sales of software versions to various countries?

2 Assume you have built a website for SpareBitz. The company now wants to sell its products overseas. Other than modifying the site to accept other currencies, what other changes have to be made to the site?

From ideas to application
REAL CASES

Case study **8.1**

Export with confidence

The products of Fairchild Semiconductor are installed in a large array of items, from satellites and motor vehicles to mobile phones, medical devices and home appliances. The company is a world leader in design and manufacturing of microprocessors that control power. It calls itself The Power Franchise. The company has manufacturing facilities in the United States, South Korea, China, Malaysia, Singapore and the Philippines, and 36 offices in 17 countries. It sees the entire world as its market. Fairchild ships more than 17 billion units of products annually. Some products are shipped to as few as 6 countries, while others are shipped to as many as 45 countries.

The microchips are designed in the United States and South Korea. Manufacturing starts in the United States. Then, the chips are sent to plants in Asia for assembly and testing. The products are then shipped to customers around the globe. Customers can order products online at the company's website. Over the

The Petronas Towers in Kuala Lumpur, Malaysia, where Fairchild has one of several assembly and test plants that play a central role in the global development of their products.

PHOTO SOURCE: © ROBERT CHURCHILL

past decade Fairchild established additional design and manufacturing facilities in Korea and China. With facilities as well as customers in a growing number of countries, complying with both US and other countries' export and import laws became complex. Work-in-progress is often shipped from one country to another, and then to another or back to the original country for further processing. Logistics managers decided to use the services of a company that specializes in software that helps manage such complex operations. Fairchild approached NextLinx, a company with expertise in software that supports online logistics.

Together, the companies configured and implemented NextLinx software called Trade Export Solution, which automates Fairchild's global logistics. The software provides information on laws and regulations of each country where Fairchild transacts, as well as customs duties. For each shipment it figures out the fastest and least costly carriers as well as the minimum duties to be paid. The application provides digital forms that enable employees to enter details on content, value and destination of a shipment. The various costs are calculated automatically for the country and particular seaport or airport. The system ensures full compliance with each country's regulations. In recent years, many new regulations have had to do not with economics but with homeland security. They may forbid the export of certain types of microchips to some countries, or the export of certain items from some countries. All this information is closely monitored by NextLinx and added to the documentation and automated forms.

The software has been implemented in every facility of the company in the world. It is integrated into Fairchild's enterprise resource planning (ERP) systems as well as into the shipment application of its major shipping carrier. Shipping clerks can check easily retrievable trade documentation and be sure that all shipping complies with the destination country's regulations. This saves the typical labour-intensive search for trade compliance documentation. This helps the company to clear 90 per cent of its shipments with the proper authorities before the shipment reaches the destination country. The system also shortened shipping durations and reduced shipping delays. As a result, Fairchild could reduce the amount of raw materials inventory it carries.

The use of the new system reduced the number of employees involved in shipping processes, but it also had another positive effect. It standardized shipping procedures and records worldwide. The same shipping procedures and records are maintained at every facility of the company, anywhere in the world. This enables the company to easily implement the procedures and documentation in new facilities it might establish in the future.

Thinking about the case

1 The software Fairchild integrated into its ERP system reduces risk. What risk?
2 The software saves costs. What costs?
3 Why is it important to integrate an application such as NextLinx's to the ERP system of the adopting global company?
4 Why is standardization of processes so important to a company such as Fairchild?

SOURCES: www.nextlinx.com/news/casestudies/case_fairchildsemi.shtml, 2005; www.fairchildsemi.com, 2005

Case study **8.2**

Frontier TV

For several years the European Commission have been considering revising and extending the 'TV without Frontiers' directive of 1989, last amended in 1997. This was prompted by changes in market trends and the introduction of new technology. The old directive was effectively becoming obsolete as it was drafted when video services were available only through traditional TV channels. The switch from analogue to digital technology suggests that the number of digital pay-TV subscribers will increase significantly, with a corresponding rise in the number of channels available. Similarly so-called non-linear video services make the application of the old EU law inappropriate. Non-linear technology provides on-demand services which are very difficult to regulate prior to transmission, as the viewer can choose to view the content at any time. For content from established providers such as the BBC, regulation of on-demand services is difficult, and for providers that rely on content provided by the general public, such as YouTube, regulation is virtually impossible without stringent censorship. In

May 2006 organizations and companies from seven European countries objected to the initial proposals of the EU. These companies included Yahoo!, Vodaphone, NTL and Cisco. The organizations included the UK Confederation of British Industries (CBI), the Federation of German Industries and the Confederation of Netherlands Industry and Employers. Their main complaint was that regulators would be unable to find and track the multitude of online publishers of video content, including bloggers offering video and other online interactive services.

In October 2006 a UK Parliamentary Committee heard evidence from, amongst others, Jeremy Beale, the head of the CBI's e-business group, who told them that putting restrictions on the European online market place would push consumers to services outside the EU, stunting development of Internet TV in the UK and Europe. The same committee also heard concerns about attempts to weaken the 'country of origin' principle which allows broadcasters to offer pan-European services, while complying with laws of the country of their home-base.

Probably as a consequence of these and similar objections throughout the EU, the final directive has taken a pragmatic view. A press release from Brussels in March 2007 states that 'At the heart of the new Directive is the country of origin principle, which was already the cornerstone of the original 'Television without Frontiers' Directive of 1989. This principle has played a pivotal role in boosting cross-border satellite TV and the progressive establishment of pan-European TV channels since the end of the 1980s. It will in future also ensure that audiovisual media service providers other than broadcasters (such as providers of video-on-demand, news-on-demand, sport-on-demand or providers of downloadable audiovisual content for mobiles) will have to comply only with the legislation of the country where they are established, and not with 27 different national legal systems.'

However, in addition to this flexibility there is also a requirement that member states take measures to protect minors and prohibit content that would incite religious or racial hatred. There are also indications that the EU supports the concept of national regulatory authorities that are independent from national governments to encourage democracy and media pluralism.

On a more commercial note, the 'TV Without Frontiers' allows more advertising and 'product placement' – putting a sponsor's product in a TV show.

Member countries may add to theses regulations by setting stricter national rules that will apply to all companies based in their country.

The introduction of digital television is presenting European regulators with new challenges.

PHOTO SOURCE: © CHRIS BEDDOE

Thinking about the case

1 Is it right that the EU should produce overarching regulations that apply to all member countries?

2 How does this affect non-EU countries? For example, Yahoo! has sites based in many countries of the world. Is it acceptable to post a video that promotes racial hatred if the site is based in the USA but not if it is based in the UK?

3 What would be the economic consequence for European TV companies if the regulations are over restrictive?

SOURCES: 'Can Internet TV have frontiers', Rand Corporation, www.rand.org; 'Boosting the Diversity of European TV and On-Demand Services', Press Release, 9 March 2007, Europa.eu/rapid/pressReleasesAction.do; 'EU sets new digital media rules', news.bbc.co.uk, 25 May 2007

silicon.com

Case study **8.3**

China's Internet revolution

BY DAN ILETT

China is a booming Internet society, but how are its many constituent parts embracing the medium? Dan Ilett found a mix of priorities and a few surprises.

They say a wise man learns from others' mistakes. In China's case that appears to be true.

As development rumbles on at incredible speed (8 per cent GDP growth last year), China's people are harnessing the power of the Internet to trade, talk and learn.

Beijing hotel manager Jason Shan says: 'I use the computer for talking to friends and meeting new people. I sometimes download songs and pictures and upload them to my mobile phone. I also play some games and my wife keeps some documents for her study. People at our level use computers for this sort of thing but we're not technicians.'

There is nothing special about people using computers to do any of these things, except when you consider that huge communities on the Internet are forming and changing the way people live and learn in China.

According to research by Ipsos Insight, the mean number of hours spent online in China (17.9 in one month) surpasses all other countries.

Porter Erisman, VP for Chinese trading website Alibaba says: 'The Internet is at the core of community. If you look at online communities in the West . . . in China it's like that but on steroids. The culture is incredibly social and people always want to be connected to friends and family.

'People absorb new technologies so quickly. In China a few years ago not only did you not have *Auto Trader* magazine, you didn't have autos [but now China has both]. So everything in China leaps to the next level very quickly.'

There are currently 110 million Internet users in China – a figure estimated to rise to 184 million by 2010 according to data from eMarketer.

Chat rooms, bulletin board systems (BBS) and blogs have become extremely popular in Chinese culture. So much so that people base their buying decisions largely on recommendations – just as in other countries. But in China some would argue that traditional media are not as trustworthy as advice from a neighbour.

T.R. Harrington, MD of Shanghai-based Darwin Marketing, says: 'The BBS forums have a tremendous influence. If you look at media in China, the government controls it, so it's not always what the people believe. They feel like they get the best opinions from their fellow men from the bulletin boards.'

Community posts are becoming so popular that advertisers such as Harrington have teams of people posting information on them.

He adds: 'It's labour-intensive but labour is cheap here. If someone can provide value then I'm willing to listen. It makes sense not to push a product but to try and contribute something.'

Sage Brennan, MD of analyst house Pacific Epoch, believes it is waves of young people who are creating these online communities.

He says: 'BBS really reflects what young people are interested in. Chinese people are looking around at what things to buy, what to consume. I'm

An upmarket internet cafe in Guilin, China.

PHOTO SOURCE: © DBIMAGES/ALAMY

sure that a lot of the recent growth in China's consumer economy is being driven by this new communication. The buying focus is still ultimately made by recommendations from friends and family.'

Computer games are fuelling a society that almost lives in a virtual world. According to Chinese government figures, around four million PCs are bought every year in China as the popularity of computer games fuels the demand for Internet cafés.

Alibaba's Erisman says: 'I went on a two-month bike ride in rural China and in every town I couldn't get a seat in the Internet café. The villages are just beginning to get them.

'But if you're a young woman with some disposable income, you could be up at 1:00 a.m. chatting online comparing products. Just as guys are crazy about online games, women are crazy about buying things online.'

China is riding a wave of consumerism, part of which is undoubtedly fuelled by the Internet. One website helping people to trade online is called Taobao – a China-specific consumer marketplace owned by Alibaba, which competes with eBay.

Erisman says: 'It's all about friends getting together and shopping. China went from no consumer e-commerce to being crazy about it in about two years. We launched [Taobao] three years ago. The market wasn't there then so we had to build it.

'eBay came here first. They had a four-year head start. The problem was that they never created a local product. Our team built something totally unique for China and surpassed eBay very quickly.'

One word that seems synonymous with the Internet in China in the Western media is censorship. Yahoo! China, which is also operated by Alibaba, is one US media company that has come under heavy criticism for agreeing to cooperate with government rules on what it can publish.

Erisman says: 'I don't spend any time worrying about censorship. I would only work in a job where I was making a positive impact. There's no question that Internet companies foreign and local have had an overwhelmingly positive impact on the lives of most Chinese.

'Our model on censorship is no different to foreign media in China. Then you have to ask whether we can do more good than harm by following the laws. Of course the answer is yes.

'People have blogs in China where they can chat and say just about anything they want. The international critics are focused on the one per cent of things you can't do. But when you look at the 99 per cent of things you can do it's not even an ethical dilemma. You can pursue profit and do the right thing at the same time. They're not mutually exclusive.'

Thinking about the case

1 The debate about censorship on the Internet in the West focuses on issues such as pornography and libel. Is there any difference between these arguments and those concerning government-approved content on Yahoo! China?

2 It seems that chat rooms, BBS and blogs are increasing their influence on buying patterns in China. Could the same be said of potential customers in other parts of the world?

Chapter 8

Managers and their information needs

LEARNING OBJECTIVES

Information is needed for decision-making and operations at all levels of management, but managers at different levels of an organization's hierarchy need different types of information. By making information available to virtually every level of an organization, ISs are changing the way organizations operate.

When you finish this chapter, you will be able to:

Explain the link between an organization's structure and information flow.

List the main functions and information needs at different managerial levels.

Identify the characteristics of information needed by different managerial levels.

Recognize the influence of politics on the design of, and accessibility to, information systems.

Describe the ways in which information technology personnel are deployed in organizations.

List and explain the advantages and disadvantages of various personnel deployments.

Explain the importance of collaboration between IS managers and business managers and describe the relationships between the two groups.

URBAN SCENE

SLICING AND DICING THE INFORMATION

Martin Tate, Urban Scene's chief information officer, was meeting with Mike Roberts, the Croydon operational shop manager, and Anita Belleville, one of his four regional IS managers. The company's new enterprise resource-planning system was installed in the southeast regional shops and had been running for two months now. Martin was following up to ensure that the system was generating needed information for individual managers. He was stunned to find that Mike had avoided using the system's new capabilities. Mike was accustomed to printing out his weekly sales reports and he'd continued with his old ways, despite the system's new capabilities.

Overcoming resistance to the new system

'Mike, you know that with our new system you can view data in several ways, right? I know you've always looked at total weekly sales for the women's and men's clothing lines. Did you know you can view them on screen whenever you want? Not only that, but you can drill down to see which size of jeans, in which colour and style, are selling best. You can also change the view to see which shop floor staff are selling more items – and what they're selling.'

Mike raised his eyebrows. 'Really? I always check informally with the staff on the floor to get their read on daily sales. But I didn't know the system could track actual sales down to the specific inventory item.'

'Sure, we track the items through their bar codes entered in the transaction-processing system so we know when a particular item was sold and by whom. That data is stored in the database, so you can look at real-time data or historical sales for trends – I call it 'slicing and dicing' the information. That flexibility is why Shirley wanted to implement the new system. She can pull up sales data in her headquarters office and view sales across the business as a whole, regionally, or down to individual shop sales to get a big picture of how we're doing to make long-range plans. James, your regional manager, looks at the same data for the southeast region. He's most interested in ensuring that overall sales are doing well and that your inventory system is supplying you with new stock when you need it. But you can look at more detailed information for your own shop to keep

PHOTO SOURCE: © SEAN LOCKE

your finger on the pulse of day-to-day operations. Anita will walk you through the steps to use the system.'

A convert is born

A half-hour later, Mike was pulling up data into tables, bar graphs and line graphs. 'I see that our signature lines sold well after our new advertising promotion. The sales jumped a few days after the newspaper ads came out. I'll tell Tony Martin that his marketing department's advert worked.'

Martin nodded. 'I'm sure he'll appreciate hearing from you. But he accesses the system himself to check whether his print, radio and TV spots are boosting sales. And if sales are lagging in certain regions, then he plans different campaigns or changes their frequency. But if you or your staff have any ideas for your particular shop, just send him an email. You work directly with your customers and can convey any of their concerns or needs.'

'Okay, will do. Thanks for checking in with me.'

'Sure. Work with the system awhile and let Anita and me know if you have any problems. Once you're proficient, I'd like to have you speak to the managers from the north-east region. Could you make time in your schedule? They're next in the ERP implementation and I think you can help troubleshoot some issues for them. They'll appreciate hearing your perspective and can learn from you.'

Reorganizing systems and staff

Urban Scene's growing pains were showing. The company had expanded to 40 stores and was considering expansion to Europe. In addition, it was planning to develop an e-commerce website. With these changes, it was obvious that the company was outgrowing its old ways of operating – and its information systems. Martin Tate, the chain's CIO, was increasingly involved in more aspects of the store's operations and strategic planning.

Creating order from chaos

As Urban Scene grew, it inherited each store's information system (IS). With each addition, the IS staff had to learn the details of more systems, and it became difficult to maintain them all. A few years back, Martin's staff had reached the breaking point – systems were failing and managers had no uniform method of communicating important information to each other and headquarters staff. So, under Martin's direction, Urban Scene implemented its new enterprise resource planning (ERP) system. The new system allowed a centralized IS organization. In contrast, the stores system only collected data from transactions and immediately transmitted the data to a database at headquarters. The company had chosen to overhaul its systems to simplify its hardware and software systems, streamline collection and reporting of data and make planning for the future easier. Since many problems could be addressed by IS staff through the Internet, the new centralized system was easing the daily troubleshooting and assistance his staff had to provide for other staff to do their work.

Revamping the IS organization

Since ISs were so central to Urban Scene's business processes – and to its overall success – Martin believed he needed to change his IS staff organization, too. He reviewed the existing practice of local store control over the IS function and decided that it was inefficient. IS staff had little support or direction from top management. So, he devised a system that centralized the organization's network and ERP planning and services, but still provided technical support for each store. He hired or promoted four regional IS managers. Those managers oversaw ten stores each and served as an information centre. Each manager supervised two systems administrators, who were responsible for five stores each and made routine visits. All IS staff reported to the central IS unit and attended periodic training sessions that Martin organized. Martin also set up an agreement with his ERP consultant to provide additional technical backup when needed. The consultants worked closely with his staff to ensure that Urban Scene's system functioned reliably. The on-site IS presence in stores was essential to ensure that sales staff needs were met.

Establishing an e-commerce website

Following a recent strategic planning meeting, Suzanne Granger and James Block, Urban Scene's north and south district store managers, had been working on a plan to develop an e-commerce site. Their mandates from CEO Shirley Steiner had been to be sure that e-commerce sales did not hurt local stores and that the website carry the same brand image as the recently completed store redesign. James had worked out a plan so that any sales on the company's website would be fulfilled by the store closest to the customer. That way, the site would improve store sales and tap into existing transaction-processing and warehousing systems.

Fulfilling the second mandate was proving more challenging. A group of local sales associates were so excited about setting up a site for their friends to buy Urban Scene clothes that they had begun designing a site on their own, without oversight or approval. Suzanne met with them to explain that the site needed to be controlled from headquarters and be a seamless part of Urban Scene's sales effort. She stressed that they needed to work with Martin's staff to coordinate their efforts and tie the site into the existing sales system. The sales associates were disappointed that the website design they'd done so far might not be used, but Suzanne assured them that they would have a chance to meet with Martin and his staff and present what they had developed so far. She told them that whatever path the site development took, they would certainly be able to provide feedback.

Managers and information

Generally speaking, managers at different levels of an organizational hierarchy make different types of decisions, control different types of processes and therefore have different information needs. While companies have many different organizational structures, this chapter will discuss the most common: a generic pyramid-shaped hierarchy with a few leaders at the top and an increasing number of workers at each subsequent managerial and operational level (see Figure 9.1). There has long been a fairly close correlation between the level of work a person does in an organization and the type of IS he or she uses. But today, with computers on every desk, that relationship is no longer as clear. The availability of increasingly flexible and powerful information systems throughout all organizational levels has had a profound effect on organizational structure. For instance, in the past, companies had specialized staff whose main task was to process data and generate information to meet managers' requests. Now, the ability to generate information has been placed directly in managers' hands, all the way up to the chief executive officer, which has contributed to the downsizing of middle management.

Figure 9.1 The management pyramid

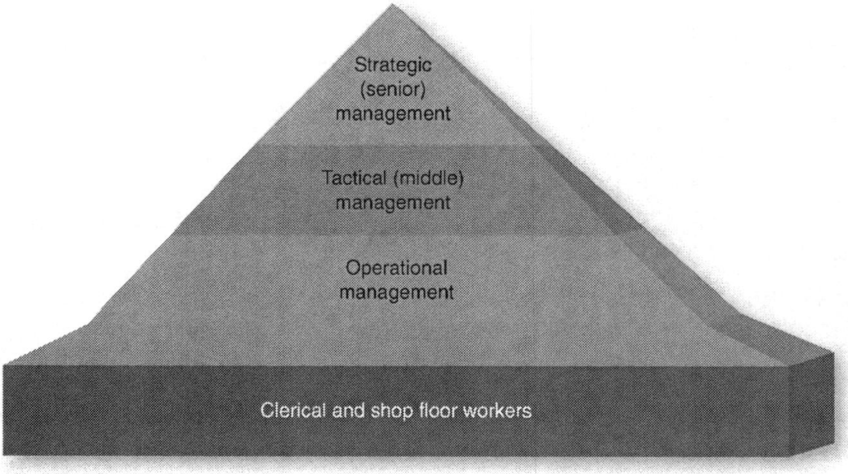

Most organizations will recognize the importance of information systems and technology and that there are often competing or conflicting requirements from different parts of the business. There is therefore a need for management of the IT function to ensure that resources are used sensibly and fairly throughout the business processes, typically headed by the chief information officer as discussed in Chapter 1. This post is concerned with the strategic use of IT in the business but also the management and control of IT projects and operational IT systems. Technology aside, the politics of information within an organization can undermine optimal business decision-making. Trying to retain power in their hands, and realizing that information is power, managers sometimes oppose the trend of making both data and processing tools available throughout a company. Problems often arise when the potential politics are not considered when developing systems and deciding how people will support those systems.

The traditional organizational pyramid

Every organization needs leadership. The top-level leaders of an organization are a small group of people responsible for running the organization and reporting to one person in the group, who usually bears the title *chief executive officer (CEO)*. Some small, knowledge-intensive companies use a *matrix* organizational structure. A matrix structure distributes leadership among several people, varying by project, product or discipline. However, the management of most organizations still follows a *pyramid model*: the CEO at the top, a small group of senior managers one level down who report to the CEO, a larger number of middle managers who report to the senior managers, many more lower-level managers who report to the middle managers, and so on down the line (see Figure 9.1).

In general, at the bottom of the organizational pyramid are clerical and shop floor workers; in the next layer up are operational managers, who are responsible for overseeing the day-to-day operation of a company; next up is a much narrower layer of middle managers; and at the top are a few senior managers. Due to the nature of their decisions, managers in the top two layers are often referred to as tactical (middle) and strategic (senior) management. Strategic managers are expected to establish corporate strategies with a long-term view, and tactical managers are expected to figure out how to achieve the strategies. Variation in this structure exists among organizations; not every organization has exactly three layers, and there are often sub-layers in the management levels. Also, the distinction between operational and middle managers is not always clear, nor is it necessarily important. Remember that this rough categorization is just for the purpose of discussing information needs. It is best to think of managerial levels as a continuum between two ends, the lowest level being operational managers, and the highest level being top management. It is very likely that your first managerial position will be as an operational manager.

Clerical and shop floor workers

In many organizations, *clerical and shop floor workers* make up the largest group of employees. Included in this group are all types of service workers, such as cashiers in banks, receptionists in hospitals and sales staff in retail stores, as well as traditional production employees in manufacturing organizations. The main characteristic common to workers at this level is that they are not managers. Although they may have high levels of expertise in a particular technology, equipment or process, the scope of their decisions is typically narrower and focused on the work at hand. However, they are not required – and are not expected – to make management-level judgements. Many of these workers operate at their organizations' boundaries, where they interact with other organizations or individuals, including customers. Many take orders for products and services, provide customer service, record sales, issue invoices, record shipments of raw material received and services performed, provide

The central warehouse of Amazon Germany.

maintenance services for equipment leased or sold by their company, and perform any other non-managerial work.

Operational management

Operational managers are in charge of small groups of frontline workers. Examples include the foreperson on a shop floor, a department manager in a department store, and a manager in a bank or insurance company who is in charge of a small unit and authorized to obligate the company for small amounts of money. The people in these positions typically follow general policies handed down by their superiors. Within these policies, they make decisions that affect their units in the short term, that is, within days. For instance, if a subordinate calls in sick, an operational manager in a manufacturing setting is empowered to decide whether to call another employee in from home, in which case the person will probably report late, or to ask another worker to stay for another shift, in which case the company must pay time and a half. In a service industry such as an airline, an operational manager might help ticket agents solve a problem that has cropped up with a passenger's luggage.

Tactical management

Tactical managers, also called middle managers, receive general directions and goals from their superiors and, within those guidelines, make decisions for their subordinates, affecting the near and somewhat more distant future. Usually, they are in charge of several operational managers. Tactical managers are so called because they are responsible for finding the best means (tactics) to accomplish their superiors' strategic decisions. As you remember from Chapter 2, 'Strategic Uses of Information Systems', a strategic decision focuses on *what* to do, while a tactical decision concentrates on *how* to do it.

For example, corporate management may make the strategic decision to provide more of a bank's services electronically: over the telephone and online via personal computers. This broad goal leaves the tactical managers to determine *how* to provide those services. Should the bank develop the necessary computer software in-house? Should it hire a consulting firm? Which services should be offered first? How should the bank educate staff and customers about the new offerings? Tactical managers are expected to provide the best solutions to these problems and refer issues to the strategic level only if their decisions may affect the general strategy outlined.

Strategic management

It is easier to determine which managers make up the strategic level than it is to discern who belongs to the other two levels. The reason is simple: these people are the highest-ranking officers of the organization. In many companies, the president and vice presidents make up the strategic management. When members of the board of directors play an active role in the company's business, they, too, contribute their share to strategic decision-making. However, do not be misled by titles. Some corporations, such as banks, grant vice presidential titles to thousands of their managers. Title alone does not place those people in the strategic level of their organizations.

Strategic managers make decisions that affect the entire organization, or large parts of it, and leave an impact in the long run. For example, such decisions may include merging with and acquiring other companies, opening branches overseas, developing a completely new product or service, moving operations to the Internet, or recommending a major restructuring of an organization.

Amazon's president, Jeff Bezos, inside his company's huge Seattle warehouse.

Characteristics of information at different managerial levels

People in different management levels have different information needs. As shown in Figure 9.2, the information needed by different managerial and operational levels varies in the time span covered, level of detail, source and other characteristics over a broad spectrum. For instance, clerical workers need data that allow them to fulfil daily operations but not necessarily make decisions. To serve customers and other workers, they must have access to information such as how many units of a certain item are available for sale, how much a certain customer service costs, and how much overtime a certain employee worked last week. Usually, these people make *ad hoc* enquiries to satisfy immediate information needs.

On the other hand, most of the information that managers require is used to make decisions. Operational managers need information based on data that are generally narrow in scope, gathered over a short period of time and useful for decisions that have an impact in the short run, that is, hours, days and weeks. The decisions middle managers make affect a greater number of organizational units for longer periods of time, and they require information extracted from data that are broader in scope and time, and that information may come from outside their departments.

The decision-making process of middle managers and above is less structured than that of operational managers; despite the broader scope of the data – and sometimes *because* of it – there are no proven methods for selecting a course of action that guarantees a predicted outcome.

The decisions that senior managers make affect whole divisions or the entire organization and have long-standing impact. Their decision-making is very unstructured. Senior managers need information gleaned from vast amounts of raw data that have been collected over long periods of time from many or all of an organization's units. The original data for the information come from internal organizational sources as well as external sources, such as the mass media, the Web, national and international trade bulletins and consulting firms.

Data scope

Data scope refers to the amount of data from which information is extracted, in terms of the number of organizational units supplying data or the length of time the data cover. For example, data gathered from just one department have a narrower scope than data from every department of the organization. In addition, one department's data from several months have a broader scope than the same department's data from one week.

Figure 9.2 Characteristics of data and information for different levels of management

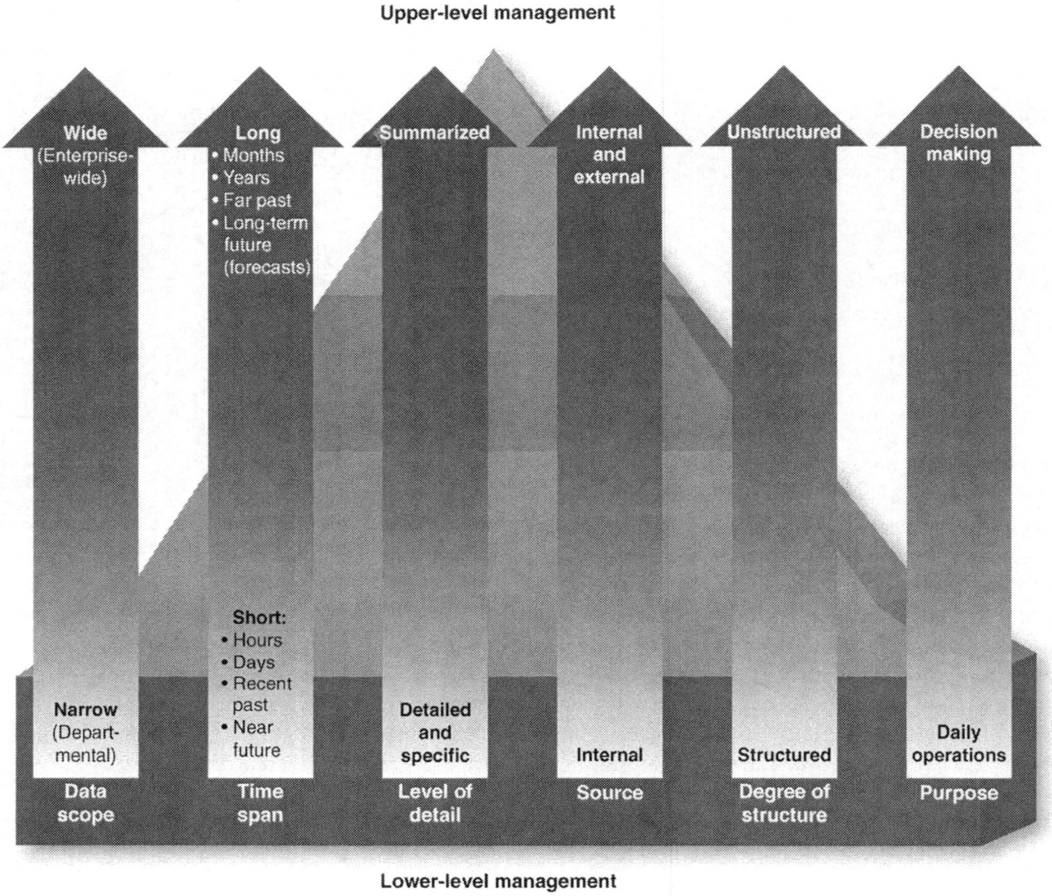

Data scope is different from level of detail. When a lot of data is summarized into a few figures, such as totals and averages, the level of detail is low; however, the data scope may be high if the data are about numerous people, departments or events. Data scope refers to the number of individuals, departments or events about which data were collected.

To make a strategic decision, top management may need a single figure that is calculated from a wide range of data, such as the average monthly expenditure on television advertising of sports shoes. The data are collected on as many sport shoe manufacturers as possible to produce information that reflects the entire industry, not a single company or a small number of companies. Although the information provided is a single figure, it is derived from vast amounts of data spanning a long time and many corporations. Therefore, the data scope is wide. At the other extreme, the manager of a shop in a manufacturing plant may need only information that is extracted from data collected within that organizational unit. The data scope is then narrow.

Time span

The *time span* of data refers to how long a period of time the data cover. Data that cover hours or days (the time span usually needed by lower-level managers) are said to have a short time span relative to data that cover months, years or decades, which are said to have a long time span. Senior managers typically use data that reach far into the past. They also make extrapolations based on the patterns of performance in the past to forecast what might happen in the future. Data warehouses, which accumulate historical data, are an excellent source for data collected over a long time span. Data mining may produce a pattern that can help make strategic decisions such as a radical way in which a certain item is marketed, or a fundamental change in the disbursement policy of an insurance company because it discovered patterns of fraud in insurance claims. Such decisions might not come about without collecting data over a long time span.

Level of detail

The *level of detail* is the degree to which the information generated is specific. When a department manager looks at the number of shoes sold every day of the week broken down by style, the information is, obviously, very detailed. Operational managers usually consider highly detailed information. Senior managers, in contrast, typically consider information that is highly summarized. This type of information includes totals and averages for categories of products (rather than individual products) over long periods of time. These different levels of detail serve the different operational purposes. Operational managers typically examine actual facts relating to present events so they can control immediate situations, while senior managers are often interested in trends to formulate strategies. The difference can be compared to looking at only several pieces of a puzzle or looking at the entire picture the puzzle forms.

Usually, the more detailed the information, the closer it is to the data from which it is derived, and thus proportionately less processing is involved in generating it. Daily totals of sales in the shoe department are more detailed than an annual total for the entire chain of stores. The latter requires significantly more processing because it combines data from many sources.

Source: internal vs. external

internal data Data collected within an organization, typically by transaction-processing systems, for example the number of sales per month, the value of outstanding credit owed to the organization.

external data Data that are collected from a wide array of sources outside the organization, including mass communications media, specialized newsletters, government agencies and the Web.

Internal data are collected within the organization, usually by transaction-processing systems, but also through employee and customer surveys. **External data** are collected from a wide array of sources outside the organization, including mass communications media such as television, radio and newspapers; specialized newsletters published by private organizations; government agencies; and the vast sources of news and statistics on the Web. For instance, to plan the expansion or contraction of a national supermarket chain, top managers cannot rely only on their organization's internal data. They must track national trends. Thus, they need information on national annual demographic changes. Without it, they may spend resources on increasing the number of shops, only to find, a few years later, that their customer base has shrunk. Multinational corporations rely on even more external data; the data they use come from many different parts of the world, from many different sources and often in many different formats. For example, they must rely on demographic and economic statistics of several nations rather than one.

In some industries, almost all the information comes from external sources. For example, managers of mutual funds and pension funds must track changes in the prices of stocks and other securities daily (sometimes even hourly) to be able to optimize the capital gains of the funds. The data they analyse come mainly from stock exchanges. Firms that operate websites that generate advertising revenues rely on data from companies that rate web traffic.

Structured and unstructured data

Structured data are numbers and facts that can be conveniently stored and retrieved in an orderly manner for operations and decision-making. The sources of such data are primarily

Why you should...
be information conscious

Imagine you are in charge of eight sales offices, each covering a different part of the world. You want to find out which offices sell well and which do not, which products sell better than others overall, and which products sell better in each region. But you cannot – you have neither the data nor the applications to help you. You know you are missing an opportunity to make better decisions for your company.

Managers are rarely physically involved in the production of their organizations' products and services. Rather, managerial work involves facilitating the generation of products and services. The 'material' managers use in their daily activities is information. They either extract information by themselves or have someone else extract it for them; they exchange information with other managers and with subordinates, and they communicate instructions to their subordinates to attain objectives.

To do all that, managers must know the best sources and applications for producing useful information and the best ways to communicate information. The flow of information is closely linked to the organizational structure. In fact, we often enquire about an organization's structure by asking, 'To whom do you report?' – a question referring to the direction of information flow.

As a manager, you must know which type of information, derived from which type of data, serves your needs best. But more information is not necessarily better; too much information may be confusing and time-consuming to analyse. Understanding what data to rely on, and how to best extract information from it, helps managers optimize their efforts.

internal files and databases that capture transactions. Drawing from transactional databases, data warehouses, too, hold highly structured data. Unstructured data are drawn from meeting discussions, private conversations, email messages, instant messaging records, textual documents, graphical representations and other 'non-uniform' sources.

Structured data are used for daily operations and decisions that are relatively easy to make with the help of proven models. The higher a managerial position, the less structured decisions a manager faces; therefore, unstructured data are extremely valuable in managerial decision-making, especially at the higher levels of an organization.

The nature of managerial work

Managers are paid to plan and control (see Figure 9.3). They plan to minimize uncertainty and reduce risks; they exercise control to ensure adherence to plans. Both responsibilities involve decision-making and leadership. Information systems are a great support throughout the management process.

Planning

In an ideal world, managers would have some way of knowing what the future portends. Then, they could make their decisions accordingly. Unfortunately, managers do not have a crystal ball. But through both short- and long-term planning, they can have something better: a hand in *shaping* the future, not just living through it. As illustrated in Figure 9.4, planning starts with a long-term mission and includes establishing goals and objectives, as well as resource-planning and budgeting for both the short and long term. Most of all, good planning requires good information. The better the information, the clearer the picture managers have of the present and the past and the more prepared they are to plan for the future. By

Figure 9.3 Managers plan and control

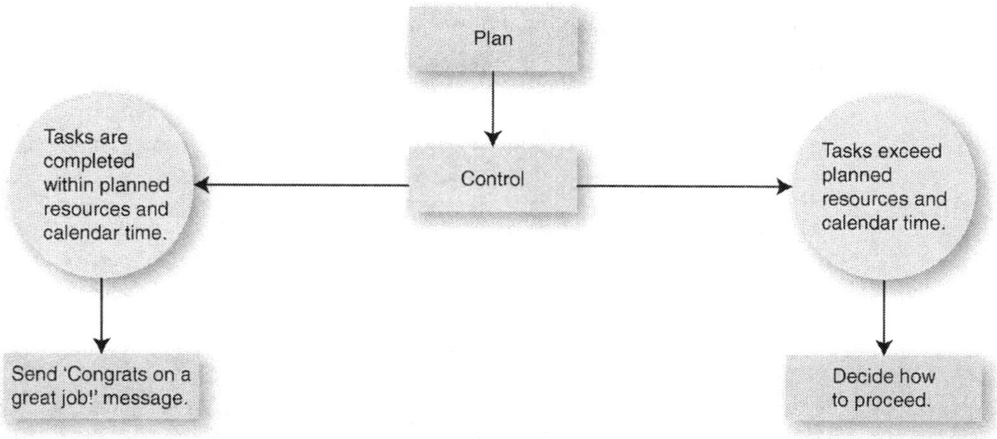

Figure 9.4 An example of a mission statement, strategic goals and tactical objectives for an in-line skate manufacturer

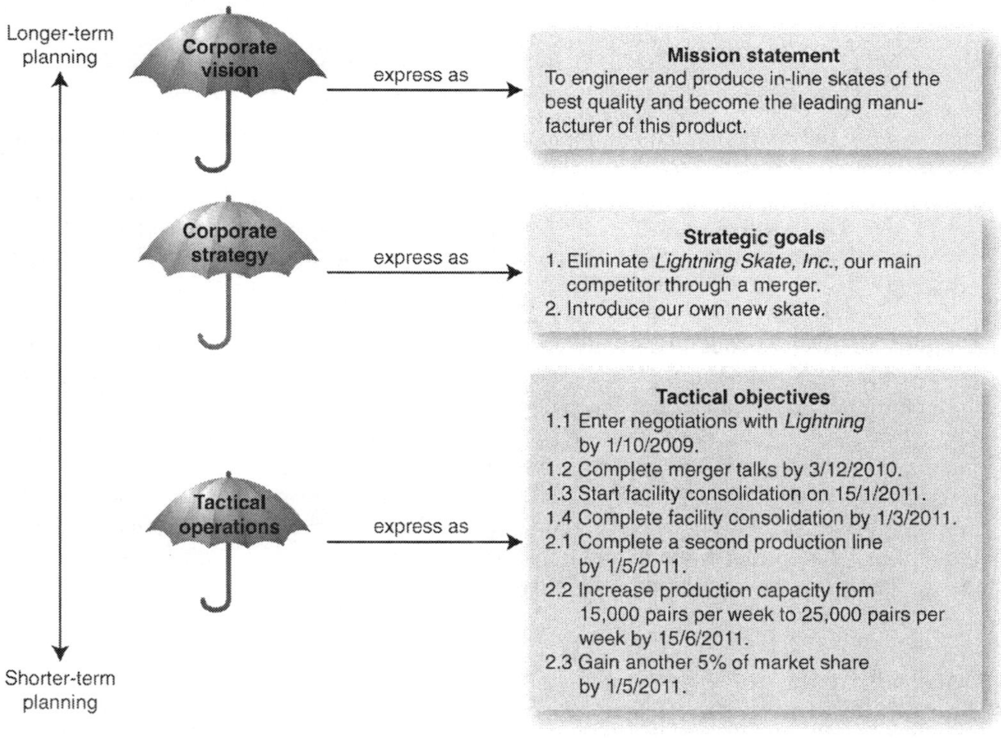

extracting only the most useful facts from raw data, ISs can provide the most salient information. Examples of the most important planning activities are shown in Figure 9.5: scheduling, budgeting and resource allocation.

As any entrepreneur will tell you, the first step in planning is to create a mission statement. How do you envisage the organization in one year, five years and ten years? Within the

Figure 9.5 The main ingredients of planning

framework of the mission statement, top management sets goals. Goals are a wish list without specific quantities or dates. Goals roughly correspond to strategy. Within the framework of each goal, top managers and middle managers set objectives. Unlike goals, objectives are specific in monetary terms, such as revenues and profits; percentages, such as market share and inventory turnover; dates, such as completion dates for tasks and other results that can be measured. Whereas the mission statement is the basis for long-term planning, objectives are the basis for medium- and short-term planning.

After objectives are outlined, planning includes steps such as the calculation of person-hours required to complete a project and, thus, the size of staff needed; the detailing of a master production schedule; and the specification of quantities of raw materials and their supply lead times. Probably the most important part of any business plan is the budget. The organization's budget is the aggregate of the budgets of all its units.

A growing number of organizations have implemented enterprise-wide ISs, some of which are popularly called enterprise resource-planning (ERP) systems. The reason that ERP systems are so called is that while they support daily operations, they also collect vast amounts of data that can be processed into useful planning information.

Controlling

Any plan, in itself, is useless unless used as a basis for control. *Controlling* consists of monitoring and taking action. *Monitoring* is knowing what is happening. Once plans are in place, managers use them to control ongoing activities by comparing the planned outcome with the actual results, as shown in Table 9.1. Thus, plans are the control tools of an organization. When discrepancies between planned and actual performance are found, managers determine the reason for the variance. If the performance is better than planned, then the plan may be modified. If the performance is worse than planned, then the cause of the discrepancy is investigated and corrected, if possible, or the remaining plan is revised to be more realistic.

Table 9.1 Examples of processes used to control projects

Reviewing project resources and updating milestones
Tracking receiving times of raw materials
Tracking shipping dates
Periodically comparing actual expenditures wih budgetary figures
Periodically examining exception reports
Discussing project progress
Periodically examining project progress reports
Periodically examining performance ratios (for example, revenue per employee, inventory turnover)

Different levels of management use different parts of plans to control operations for which they are responsible. For instance, strategic and tactical managers are concerned with allocating resources to projects, while operational managers are usually concerned with allocating resources among the tasks of a project. So, once a budget for hiring temporary workers to complete a project is approved, department managers decide how to use these workers' time. In controlling, too, ERP systems play a major role by providing daily or even up-to-the-minute facts and figures. So do online analytical processing (OLAP) applications, which are discussed later in this chapter.

Decision-making

Both planning and control activities involve decision-making. Decision-making is covered in Chapter 10, 'Business Intelligence and Knowledge Management', but you may remember from previous chapters that a decision is a commitment to act. A decision is made when a person has to select a course of action from several possible courses. For the time being, let it be said that the higher the level of management, the less routine the manager's activities are, the more open the options are, and the more decision-making is involved. For instance, operational managers usually make relatively simple decisions, such as resolving problems with individual customers, scheduling work shifts and evaluating employee performance. Many of their other activities require fulfilment of tactical managers' directives. At the very top of the organizational pyramid, on the other hand, virtually all of an executive's workday is devoted to meetings to reach decisions. All along the managerial hierarchy, information systems are used to provide information to support decision-making activities.

Managing by exception

Some people think that more information is always better than less. However, there is a limit to the amount of information that managers can handle. A better goal would be to provide managers with information that communicates the most important facts. Too much information creates *information overload*, a situation in which a person is confused and cannot make optimal decisions.

Figure 9.6 An example of a budgetary exception report

10 Percent Exception Report

Plant: 3706 Cockpit Wiring

Period: 1/1/2008–31/3/2008

Item	*Budget Amount*	*Actual Amount*	*Deviation*
Wages	€12,236,000	€10,236,876.34	(−16.4%)
Telephone	€4,700	€5,202.87	10.7%
Office Supplies	€2,500	€3,002.00	12.8%

management by exception A method of management whereby managers review only exceptions from expected results that are of a certain size or type, assuming that smaller deviations are immaterial.

One method of reducing the amount of information managers must consume is management by exception. With this approach, managers review only exceptions from expected results that are of a certain size or type, assuming that smaller deviations are immaterial (see Figure 9.6). For example, a department manager may ask for a periodic report that compares actual and budgeted expenditures and highlights only those line items that are greater than 110 per cent or less than 90 per cent of the budgeted figures. (In this example, the 10 per cent deviation is referred to as the *tolerance*, because it is the limit of deviation that is tolerated.) Or a periodic report on a project schedule may include only activities that have not been completed within seven days of scheduled dates. These exception reports require a manager to determine the cause and make a decision about how to deal with the situation. If 95 per cent of the deviations of time, money and other resources fall within the tolerances, the manager saves much time that would otherwise be devoted to detailed investigation of what caused the deviations.

ISs now can be flexible enough to let managers set their own preferences in reports. Usually, they will want to get reports that show actual expenditures against forecast expenditures, but focus on the exceptions. They can simply set the report software application to boldface, italicize or colour the exceptions to highlight them. Increasingly, reports are not paper reports, but on-demand, on-screen reports.

Leading

Reviewing exception reports focuses on adhering to an organization's agreed-upon plan, which is only a small part of a manager's job. Managers must also lead, which requires having a vision and creating confidence in others to follow that vision. Leadership requires a manager to make work more efficient and effective, create new techniques to achieve corporate goals, inspire subordinates, present a role model for desired behaviour, take responsibility for undesired consequences of decisions made under his or her direction and delegate authority.

Grace Hopper, the late rear admiral in the US Navy who was a pioneer in the field of programming in the middle of the last century, once said that the problem with many companies is that they have enough people with MBA degrees but too few leaders. A person may technically be a good manager and still not be regarded as a leader. Many experts hold that true leadership is an innate trait that may be honed but cannot be learned. Therefore, leadership 'skills' are really techniques that hone existing traits. Although some aspects of leadership may depend on personal qualities – inspiring confidence and communicating well – information systems can help managers become better leaders. ISs can provide an overall picture of an organization's operation that supports brainstorming and generation of new ideas – another important element in leadership. They may inspire innovation and the pursuit of new goals as well.

For instance, two important aspects of good leadership are motivating employees and delegating authority. Employees are motivated when they know that their superiors rely on them. One way to motivate subordinates is by granting them access to more resources such as data, information, knowledge and applications. By so doing, leaders communicate that they trust their subordinates. The subordinates, in turn, appreciate the trust and feel involved and responsible for the organization's well-being.

Trends in organizational structure

Information technology (IT) is the most powerful tool available for increasing efficiency, solving problems and making decisions in businesses today. Its impact contributed to vast organizational restructuring in the 1980s and 1990s, with a trend towards downsizing and 'flattening', which often eliminated levels of management. In the early 2000s, the Internet helped make many companies even leaner, because so many activities could be automated and immediately communicated with little need for human labour.

IT flattens the organization

Before the introduction of computers into business, lower-level managers spent much of their time processing data to produce useful information for their supervisors. Over the past two decades, many companies have used ISs to automate these activities, eliminating the need for several layers of middle managers, leading to increased unemployment amongst managers and other professionals, highly skilled people whose services were no longer needed. Rising productivity thanks to IT means that one professional can now do the work of several professionals, and that fewer managers are needed to monitor and control resources. This shift has led to flatter organizational structures (as shown in Figure 9.7) and has been a major force behind the enormous downsizing in both the manufacturing and service sectors. Studies have been conducted showing that as IT proliferates, organizational staffing in general becomes leaner.

Strategic and operational managers have been affected much less by this trend. Strategic managers are still needed because of their responsibilities for setting the organizational course, and operational managers run the daily operations of the organization. Today, easy-to-use graphical user interfaces and affordable data communications allow senior managers

Figure 9.7 Information systems flatten managerial layers.

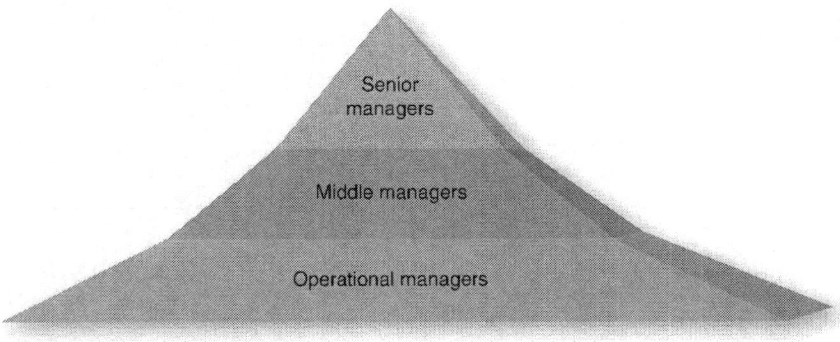

to produce their own information and communicate directly with lower-level managers, who used to be at least two or three layers away. In many small organizations there are simply *no* middle managers between strategic managers and operational managers.

In some companies that make heavy use of the Internet for business, not only is the middle management layer 'lean and mean', but the operational management and office worker layers are as well. For instance, when more and more consumers use corporate websites to purchase products and obtain customer service, there is less need for staff workers to help with these activities. Many organizations also claim that email has flattened their structure because every employee can communicate with any other employee – including top executives. That ability does not necessarily flatten an organization, however. In many organizations the policy is that top executives, including the president, respond to all email messages, which they can receive from any employee at any level. But this electronic correspondence does not affect the actual management of the company. If you take a look at the organizational structure of these companies, you will see that most of them have a clear pyramid with several layers of management. They are not flat organizations.

The matrix structure

The increasing power of information systems in organizations led to an organizational experiment: matrix management. *Matrix management* replaces a strict hierarchical structure with a flexible reporting structure, whereby people report to different supervisors, depending on the project, product or location of the work. While this structure has been successful in some small entrepreneurial organizations that consist predominantly of knowledge workers (such as young high-tech companies), it was less successful in larger, low-tech organizations.

Figure 9.8 shows how a matrix organization might work, with the personnel of each unit reporting to both a divisional and a functional manager. The manager of the personnel in cell 1 reports to both the vice president of marketing and sales and the general manager of Division A. The vice president of marketing is responsible for the marketing of all the company's products and services. The general manager of Division A is responsible for all the activities related to Division A products and services, including engineering, manufacturing *and* marketing. Technologically, IT supports a matrix structure, because both divisional and functional managers can have access to cross-sectional information. Following the example in

Figure 9.8 An example of a matrix organization

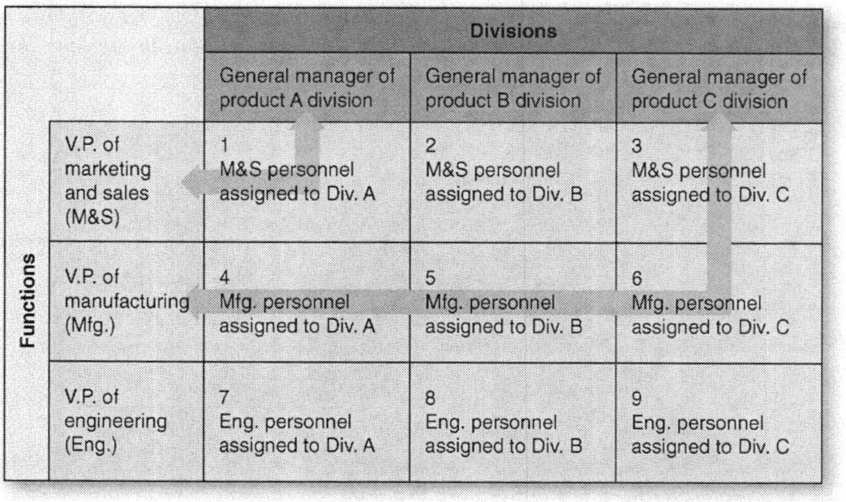

Figure 9.8, the same database can provide executive information to the vice president of engineering for all three divisions and product information to a division general manager for marketing, manufacturing and engineering activities related to the product.

The matrix structure came about because sometimes divisional supervision (by geography or product, for instance) and functional supervision are equally important. If so, then top management has to be composed of both divisional executives (such as general managers of the divisions and corporate vice presidents) and functional executives (such as vice presidents of finance, marketing, engineering and the like).

Unfortunately, human nature sometimes stands in the way of ideas that look good on paper. Many problems arise when people report to more than one authority, especially when business is not going well or when an individual's performance is in question. Also, power plays may interfere with and undermine rational decision-making. As a result, most of the organizations that tried matrix management abandoned it for the traditional pyramid, in which each manager reports to a single supervisor.

Still, a matrix structure facilitates flow of information because all employees have easier access to their managers. They do not need approval to pass information outside an organizational unit because the lines of reporting are more flexible than in a hierarchical structure. With more vertical and lateral lines of communication, there is less of a tendency to block access to information. The freer communication does have an impact on information needs, and thus on the design of ISs. To serve a matrix organization well, ISs must be integrated, and they must provide easy access to, and incorporation of, different databases and applications.

Managers and their information systems

Employees at different levels in an organization must make decisions that vary in scope and type, as mentioned earlier in this chapter. Figure 9.9 shows the traditional view of the types of information systems needed for an organization's different operational and managerial levels. While these relationships generally hold true, information needs vary widely in practice. With ISs making information available throughout organizational hierarchies, these traditional correlations can become blurred.

Figure 9.9 Types of information systems typically used at different levels of an organization's hierarchy

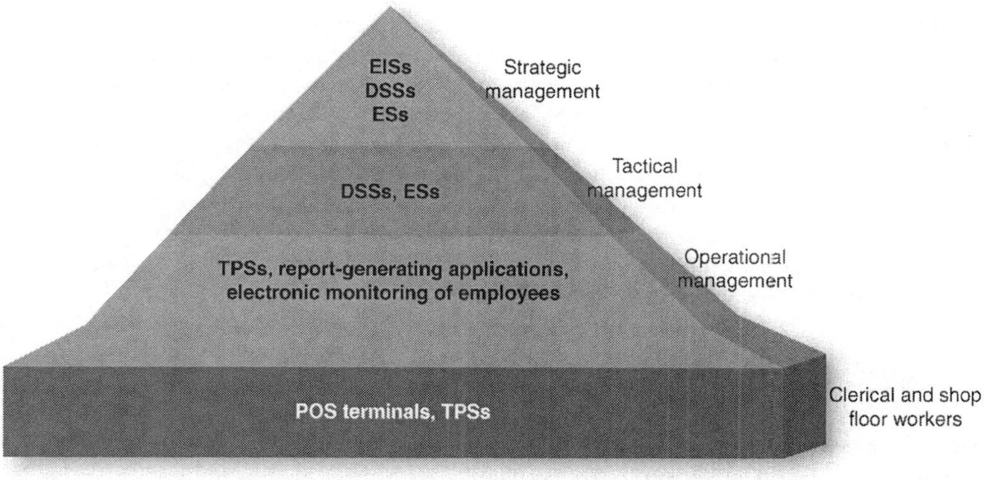

Transaction processing systems

As you may remember from Chapter 1, 'Business Information Systems: An Overview', workers at the bottom of the organizational hierarchy use point-of-sale (POS) terminals, order entry systems, and other transaction-processing systems (TPSs) to enter data at its source at the time transactions take place. These data are the raw materials for producing useful information. TPSs are linked to applications that provide clerical workers and operational managers with up-to-date information, such as the quantity on hand of a certain inventory item, the latest deposit in a customer's bank account, the shipping date and contents of a customer's order, or the latest prescription filled for a customer in a chemist. Clerical workers use the systems to perform their routine responsibilities: serving customers, placing purchase orders with suppliers, and providing information to other employees. TPSs are also used by operational managers, mainly to generate *ad hoc* reports, usually on-screen.

Decision support systems and expert systems

Middle managers must solve problems that are typically more complex and non-routine than those faced by operational managers. Their decision-making tasks require significantly more data. Therefore, they use computer-based decision aids, including decision support systems (DSSs) and expert systems (ESs), to assist them.

Senior managers, too, use DSSs and ESs, although historically they have been more reluctant to use computers in their decision-making. Until several years ago, it was rare to find a PC on the desk of a corporate president or vice president. This reluctance was partly because they perceived desktop computers to be more appropriate for lower-level managers and clerical staff. The sophistication and ease of use of such systems nowadays has probably contributed to the adoption of the systems by many high-ranking executives.

Executive information systems

In addition to the more traditional DSSs and ESs, executive information systems (EISs) provide managers with timely and concise information about the performance of their organization. EIS are often an easy-to-use interface that is linked to online analytical processing (OLAP), data mining, and business intelligence software, which retrieve the data for their analysis from data warehouses. EISs deliver summarized and concise information that helps managers quickly grasp business conditions. For instance, summary information (such as revenue per employee in a specific region) may attract the attention of a manager. Then, the manager can use an EIS to 'drill down' and isolate the data that are related to the cause of a problem.

Many executives also have their PCs connected to external commercial services that provide business and general news, including economic indices, stock and commodity prices and summaries of information sorted by industry on a regional, national and international basis.

While there is a general correlation between managerial level and type of IS, it is important to note that nothing prevents any member of an organization from using any type of IS. Of course, management may not put an EIS at the routine discretion of a clerk, but clerks may use DSSs, ESs and sometimes even EISs for their work. Also, while we discuss different types of ISs, many applications are actually combinations of several types of such ISs. For example, some decision support systems are combined with expert systems techniques and OLAP capabilities to serve as sophisticated EISs.

Information, politics and power

We assume that employees make all their work-related decisions based on what is best for the company and its goals. However, human nature being what it is, employees – including

Industry SNAPSHOT

Not necessarily counter-productive

While many employers are concerned about the increasing time employees spend on the Web, one study found an interesting correlation. The National Technology Readiness of the University of Maryland and Rockbridge Associates, Inc. found that employees spent an average of 3.7 hours per week surfing the net, on the job, for personal purposes. However, the same employees also spend an average of 5.9 hours per week online, *at home*, for work-related purposes.

SOURCE: 'Did You Know?', *PC World*, April 2003, p. 23

Evidence suggests that employees surfing casually at work also tend to work more at home online.

PHOTO SOURCE: © LAJOS REPÁSI

managers – often consider their personal interests and their close peers' interests, even when they are making work-related decisions. Politics and power influence daily interactions in organizations. They are doubly important in the context of information systems, because information is often perceived to be a source of power.

Politics

Unfortunately, the process of developing and controlling ISs often involves problematic politics. Politics arise when an individual's or group's interests are put ahead of the organization's as a whole. In contrast, rational decisions are made to achieve organizational goals. Politics can affect ISs adversely in a number of different ways – for instance, when managers are motivated to control systems rather than to make them responsive to the corporation's needs or when managers refuse to use systems that are not designed specially for their organizational unit.

When the interests of individual managers are aligned with those of the organization, both benefit. This alignment of goals is often the case, but not always. For example, a manager may resent other departments' access and use of information that his department creates and maintains because he believes it subjects him to scrutiny. Because of his fears, a manager may oppose expanded access to the information even though it would be in the best interests of the organization as a whole.

Politics also take the form of personal alliances among managers. The unspoken agreement between managers that they will help each other out is common in organizations, but can sometimes undermine their success. For instance, if a senior manager in the IS department has an alliance with a manager in one of the other units, the IS manager may work on the information needs of his friend rather than the more urgent needs of other managers.

The negative impact of politics is also at play when a manager decides not to pull the plug on a development project to save face, even though he knows the project cannot be completed successfully. Organizations invest large amounts of money in the development of new ISs, and about a third of these systems are never completed (for various reasons). However, money could be saved if managers stopped them before the financial loss (and often loss

Ethical and Societal **ISSUES**

Electronic monitoring of employees

It seems that electronic monitoring of employees is a growing trend for employers who wish to manage productivity and also to provide evidence to be used in law suits brought by employees, customers or the general public. However, the monitoring itself may land the company in the law courts. A landmark case in the European Court of Human Rights ruled in favour of an employee of Carmarthenshire College, South Wales. Lynette Copland took the UK government to court after her personal Internet usage and telephone calls were monitored by her boss. The favourable ruling of €3000 in damages and €6000 costs is obviously significant for her, but more importantly it means that private use of company telecommunications, including Internet access, may be protected by European Human Rights legislation.

There is an interesting conflict here in that in the UK the Regulation of Investigatory Powers Act (RIPA) 2000 has clear guidance regarding the monitoring of work communication, but personal communication at work may be subject to more stringent legislation. Article 8 of the Convention on Human Rights states that 'everyone has the right to privacy and family life, his home and his correspondence'. In this particular case the college had no policy in place informing employees that their communications might be monitored even though Lynette Copland, personal assistant to the College Principal, had her private communications intercepted by the deputy principal. In its ruling, the court stated that 'according to the court's case-law, telephone calls from business premises are prima facie covered by the notions of "private life" and "correspondence" for the purposes of Article 8. It follows logically that emails sent from work should be similarly protected under Article 8, as should information derived from the monitoring of personal Internet usage. The applicant in the present case had been given no warning that her calls would be liable to monitoring, therefore she had a reasonable expectation as to the privacy of calls made from her work telephone. The same expectation should apply in relation to the applicant's email and Internet usage.'

The most important part of the ruling seems to be that the employee did not know that her communication would be monitored. However, there is a wider issue as to what is reasonable monitoring. After all, is it not reasonable to try to prevent employees from accessing inappropriate (pornographic) websites whilst at work? But then who defines 'inappropriate'? What about monitoring performance? A survey in 2005 by the American Management Association involving 526 US companies found that computer monitoring exists in many forms including tracking keystrokes and time logged in as well as use of global positioning systems to monitor mobile phones. According to the survey, 80 per cent of the companies inform employees that they are monitoring content, keystrokes and time logged in. So if they tell the employees, does that make it acceptable?

of morale) grew. People do not like to admit failure because they fear it will tarnish their image. So, often managers decide to continue projects to save their own reputation, resulting in a decision that is out of sync with the good of the organization.

This happened in the United Kingdom with the Pathway project, aimed to develop electronic smart cards for executing and tracking benefits payments. The project was cancelled only after the British government spent (and lost) £698 million on it. In all, the British government is said to have lost more than £1.5 billion on failed IT projects during the period between 1996 and 2002. The US federal government is reported to have lost close to US$10 billion over the past decade and a half because of cancelled information systems development projects. While some losses are unavoidable in any development project, observers say that significant portions of these losses could be prevented if high-ranking decision makers did not try to 'save face'.

Power

Anyone who has worked for an organization recognizes that having access to information is often the road to acquiring power. And power is something that people do not give away willingly. When management decides a new IS should be implemented, department managers usually concur on several issues. But often questions arise for senior executives. For instance:

- *Who owns the system?* Unfortunately, many managers make decisions based on wanting to look powerful, regardless of the consequences. They follow the rule that the more resources they control (people, machinery, funds and so on), the more power they have. Building information system 'empires' is just another way to look – and sometimes to be – powerful. Usually, the department that owns an information system also controls it. That department may have the final say in determining its features and in modifying it. When a system serves more than one department, managers often struggle for control, leading to a system that is not used properly or at all by those who have been denied ownership. Management is often forced to announce which unit owns the system and what rights other units have to it. To resolve disputes when a system serves more than one department equally, top managers sometimes say that they are the owners of the system. Making the proper decision and educating employees about sharing systems is especially important when enterprise applications such as ERP systems are being implemented.
- *Who pays for developing the system?* Everyone wants something for nothing, and managers are no different. So, when several units are going to share a new system, their managers often try to offload the cost of development and operation on each other. Top management's challenge is to allocate the development and operating costs fairly among departments, preferably based on the benefits each group will receive.
- *Who accesses what information?* As noted previously, many managers make decisions to gain power. Since information is power, these managers often try to gain access to as much of it as they can while denying access to as many other people as possible. Many managers don't like their information accessed by people from outside their departments. They dislike scrutiny and don't want to give outsiders an opportunity to judge and question their decisions. Also, many managers feel more powerful when others who need information turn to them first.
- *Who has update privileges?* Update privilege is the authority to modify information in files and databases. Some managers make some decisions based on data collected by departments they do not control. So, if you control the data, you can influence their decisions. Management should give 'view access' on a 'need-to-know' basis. Update access should be given only to users who must update data or applications as part of their jobs. Often, these employees are the database administrator or another high-ranking MIS officer and some of his or her staff. These decisions must be made carefully in order not

to alienate other managers. The decisions must be explained satisfactorily to those who may not be given privileges they think they deserve.

Political struggles are especially harmful when several organizational units share systems. Some managers use subversive tactics to undermine the successful implementation of a system. Some managers insist on adding features for the sole purpose of giving themselves more control. Other managers may try to derail the implementation effort by not cooperating with the developers or consultants or by promoting an alternate system. As an increasing number of businesses adopt enterprise-wide applications such as supply chain management systems, these issues become extremely important, because such systems consist of modules that are often implemented one at a time. The implementers must have the cooperation of all business functions that are to be supported by the system. Managers of the various functions must collaborate to ensure success, and they must understand that one of the major purposes of such systems is the sharing of information, and therefore sharing what they may perceive as power.

The not-invented-here phenomenon

Sometimes, managers do whatever they can to *not* use an IS. The reason is known as the not-invented-here (NIH) phenomenon: managers and their subordinates often believe that if the new system is the fruit of an outsider's idea, it will not serve them well. They may know this is not true, but they may still deny others credit for something they feel *they* should have invented. Again, managers may use a variety of tactics to undermine a new system in their department. They may try to convince top management that the system is not needed, or that it does not satisfy their 'unique' business needs.

Top management must be aware of these issues and distinguish valid arguments from political ones. For instance, a manager may ask for IS systems or services that serve both his own interests and the organization's. Such requests are legitimate. But he could damage the organization if the request serves only his own goals, or the goals of his unit. Since an increasing number of ISs are not developed or implemented for individual departments, but for the entire organization, managers must be vigilant to the motives of staff members.

Management of information technology resources

Organizations have their own distinct managerial styles, most of which fall somewhere between two extremes on a spectrum. One extreme is centralized management, which designates staff positions and departments in a strict vertical hierarchy and places control of the organization in a few hands. The other is decentralized management, which delegates authority to lower-level managers. In most organizations, the management and structure of information systems follow the same pattern as the organization's overall management: centralized management tends to want centralized control over ISs; decentralized management is more likely to be comfortable with decentralized management of ISs.

As a growing amount of commerce is carried out online, organizations have faced new challenges of managing their websites, including linking internal applications and databases to those sites. Large organizations, especially, have more than one server linked to the Internet. So, they must question whether individual organizational units should manage their own websites or whether the company should manage all web activities through a single home page – essentially a central website. Different business functions can use the Web for different purposes. For instance, marketing and sales can promote products and services. Human resources can recruit employees, and finance can make electronic payments. Should the design and implementation of these various functions be the responsibilities of individual departments, or should they be cleared through a central department or manager?

The question becomes even more important in multinational organizations, with regional headquarters in different countries. Because many workers today can easily design and create web pages for their departments, managers are often tempted to establish their own unit's website, independent of the central IS organization's priorities. Also, senior executives of some organizations have actually left the IS unit out of the loop when deciding on web design and operational issues, not realizing that problems can arise later – when the website evolves from a mere presence to an important e-commerce vehicle involving many internal resources such as transactional databases and data warehouses. Thus, in many companies the issue of management of IS resources has become more complicated as technology advances.

Centralized vs. decentralized management

How management of any type of resource is conducted depends on the general philosophy of corporate executives. Some organizations emphasize central management of resources, especially resources of expensive types of equipment or investments in assets that may have an impact on the entire organization or large parts of it. Other organizations leave much of the decision-making about acquisition and control of resources to local organizational units and lower-level managers. 'Local' may be actually local in geographic terms, when the organization has multiple locations, or a business unit within a single-site organization. Preferences for managing human and other IT resources are similar. Some organizations concentrate all, or almost all, decisions on hiring IT workers and acquiring IT assets – hardware, software and networks – at corporate headquarters, and some delegate such decisions to the managers of business units. Each approach often impacts the deployment of IT professionals: a centralized approach often results in a relatively large IT unit that is responsible for almost all IT-related issues (Figure 9.10), while a decentralized approach results in a smaller corporate IT group and IT professionals deployed at the business units (Figure 9.11), with significant authority to make decisions on the local unit's information resources.

Figure 9.10 Centralized management of ISs

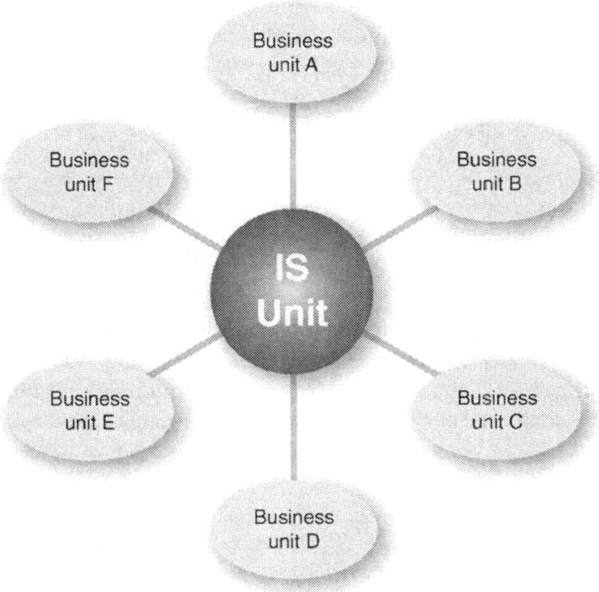

Figure 9.11 Decentralized management of ISs (in fully decentralized management, the central IS unit would not exist)

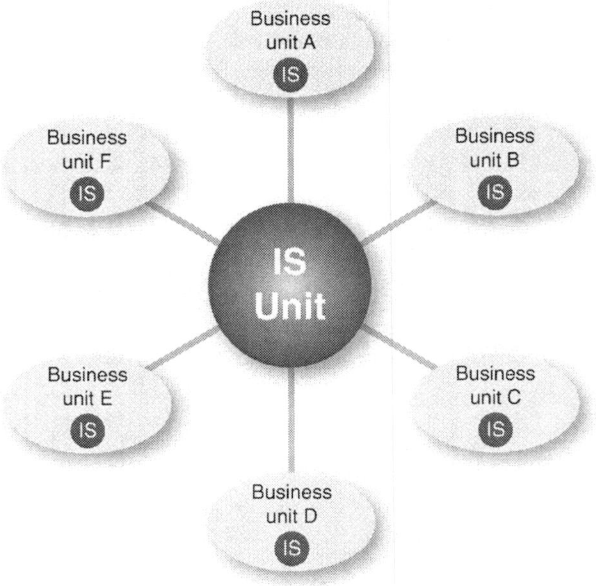

Advantages of centralized IS management

Centralized IS management, as illustrated in Figure 9.12, has several major advantages:

- *Standardized hardware and software*: Centralized ISs can establish corporate software and hardware standards, which saves time and money in purchasing and installation and simplifies interdepartmental sharing of data and information. Standardizing software is particularly important for facilitating data exchange and the sharing of applications. This benefit is especially enhanced by the ability of multi-site organizations to share applications and data by using them off central servers.
- *Efficient administration of resources*: A centralized administration of contracts, licences, and inventories of hardware and software assets is more efficient, and often effective, than dispersed administration. It also supports standardization of hardware and software.
- *Effective staffing*: Because professionals at a corporate central IS unit are usually more knowledgeable about IT and IT skills than other managers, they can do a better job in identifying the most competent individuals to fill IT positions. They speak the same professional lingo as the interviewed candidates, and therefore the communication in the recruiting process is fast and effective.
- *Easier training*: Training employees to use information technology, often a major expense in a company's budget, is much more efficient and less expensive when an organization uses standardized hardware and software. The training staff can do a better job when they can specialize in a small variety of hardware, software and telecommunications standards.
- *Common reporting systems*: Central IS management can easily standardize reporting systems and formats across departments, which many companies and some laws and regulations require for accounting or tax reporting. With standardized reporting, managers do not have to 're-map' the information they receive from one unit to a report with a different format used by another unit. This uniformity saves time and increases clarity. When reports need to be merged, it is easier to merge them (using spreadsheets, for instance) when they share the same format.

Figure 9.12 Centralized vs. decentralized IS trade-offs

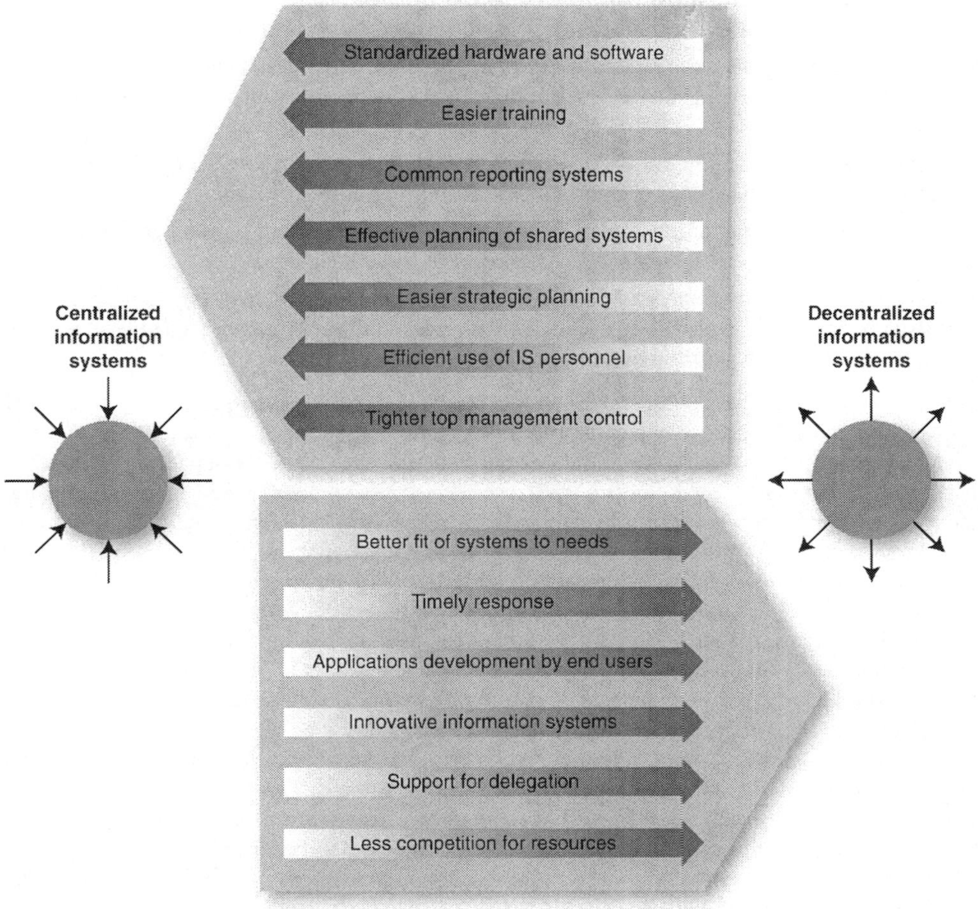

- *Effective planning of shared systems*: Large and complex systems that are shared by several organizational units can best be developed by a central IS department that knows the 'big picture'.
- *Easier strategic planning*: Strategic IS planning considers an organization's entire IS resources. It is easier to link an IS strategic plan to an organization's overall strategic plan when IS management is centralized.
- *Efficient use of IS personnel*: With a centralized IS department, an organization is more likely to employ highly specialized IS professionals who are better qualified to develop information systems, especially the larger and more complex ones, than are IS professionals who are dispersed in non-IS organizational units.
- *Tighter control by top management*: A centralized IS management allows top management to maintain control over the often vast resources spent on ISs.

Advantages of decentralized IS management

Historically, most organizations have moved from a centralized IS management to a decentralized management. Decentralized IS management has several advantages, illustrated in Figure 9.12:

- *Better fit of ISs to business needs*: The individual IS units can use their familiarity with their departments' information needs to develop systems that fit those needs more closely.

- *Timely response of IS units to business demands*: Individual IS units can arrange IS development and maintenance to fit their business units' priorities. They can be more responsive because their responsibility is more focused.
- *Encouragement of end-user development of applications*: In a decentralized setting, end users are usually encouraged to develop their own small applications to increase their productivity.
- *Innovative use of ISs*: Since a business unit's IS team knows its clients better than a centralized one, it has a better chance of implementing innovative ISs.
- *Support for delegation of authority*: Decentralized IS management works best if top management wishes to delegate more authority to lower-level managers.
- *Less competition for resources*: When a business unit manages its own ISs and IS budget, it usually does not have to compete for IT resources with other units. This saves the organization efforts wasted in struggles among managers.

Although you will find many companies with centralized IS management, fully decentralized IS management is rare. Because telecommunications technology is so pervasive and there are so many advantages of sharing information, systems that may have started as separate ISs years ago are usually networked now. Relatively speaking, decentralized management is more advantageous if an organization has divisions that produce completely different products and services. That way, each unit's information needs can be more closely served. Then, the decentralized units can share resources through networking. Some types of systems are usually managed centrally even if they span many different business units, however. With enterprise applications, such as ERP systems, the large integrated system must be managed by a single team.

The main disadvantage of decentralized IS management is that in most cases, important decisions about IT are made by managers who are not knowledgeable enough to make such decisions. Consider the following case. The manager of a unit that provides service to clients asked his two-person group, skilled programmers, to develop an application that field engineers could log into to manage projects. He requested an application that would enable the engineers to create bills-of-materials (BOMs) of assemblies, and access inventory databases, resource availability files, timelines and due date charts. The manager and his programmers struggled to understand the issues involved, and eventually developed a system that failed miserably. The results were: (1) much time wasted while the manager's team worked on understanding the project issues and deciding what approach to use, (2) wasted effort of the IT professionals, and (3) a bad decision on implementation, which resulted in redoing the project almost from scratch. The project was taken over by the corporate IT director and completed successfully.

On the other hand, the main disadvantage of centralizing IS management is that the individual business units that need to use the resource may feel that they do not have enough control. This can cause much friction within the business, particularly if the IS unit is being funded by top-slicing departmental budgets. An alternative funding strategy of the departments buying in IS services from the central unit may help, but still has potential for problems as the departmental manager will see only the service that they are receiving rather than a whole-company picture.

Organizing the IS staff

Now that you have seen the advantages and disadvantages of centralized and decentralized IS management, let's turn to the organization of the IS unit itself. There are various ways to deploy IS staff, even if an organization operates from a single site. This section discusses the two extremes of organizing IS professionals: central IS organization and dispersed IS organization. Not surprisingly, decentralized IS management often calls for dispersed organization of the IS staff.

In *central IS organization* there is a corporate IS team to whom all units turn with their IS needs. In *dispersed IS organization* there is a separate IS team for each business unit. Some arrangements combine elements of both. The approach selected has a direct effect on how IS professionals are positioned in the organizational structure of the business. But regardless of the structure, the goal of any IS organization is to optimize IS services to fit the organization's goals and culture.

Central IS organization

As seen in Figure 9.13, the most common central IS unit organization has the IS director overseeing several departments. One department implements and maintains current systems. Another department runs the information centre, whose function is to provide *ad hoc* advice about hardware, software and telecommunications to business units. The communications department develops and manages local area networks and access to wide area networks. And the data administration department develops and maintains corporate databases, data warehouses and data management and analysis applications. In large organizations there may also be a research and development department, which keeps the IS unit abreast of technological advances and develops ideas for the strategic uses of ISs.

A central IS unit is usually involved in virtually every aspect of IT in an organization. It determines which computers and peripheral equipment are approved for purchase; in some cases it is the only unit that is authorized to purchase hardware. It approves or rejects software purchases, is in charge of training new users and (except for small and simple programs) is the only body that is authorized to develop ISs for business units.

The advantages and disadvantages of a centrally organized IS unit are essentially the same as those for centralized IS management. When centrally managed, the IS unit ensures compatibility of hardware and software and provides the interface between different systems that must work together, such as purchasing and cost accounting; payroll, accounts payable and cost accounting; and sales and accounts receivable. This approach helps all top managers share an organizational vision of how information technology can serve the corporation in the future. It also supports planning of enterprise applications such as supply chain management systems, which are shared by several business functions, and often by many or all of the organization's sites.

Figure 9.13 An example of central IS organization

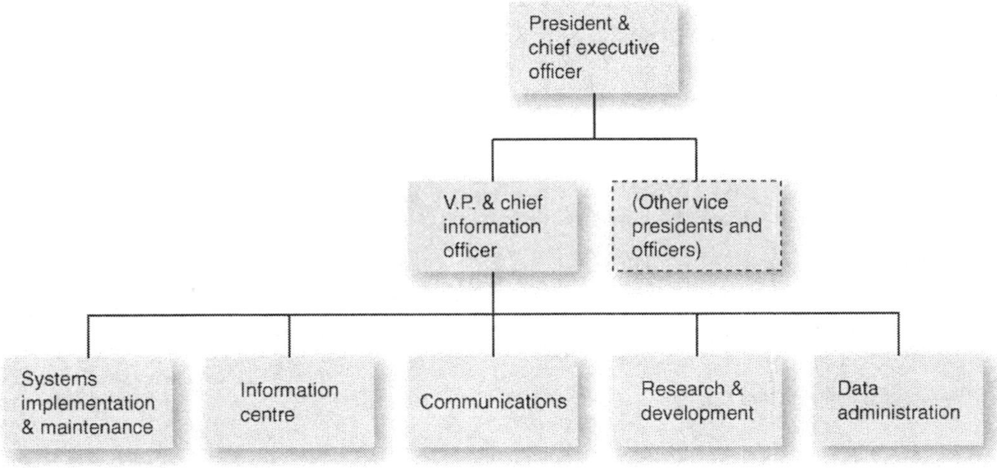

Central IS management often includes a *steering committee* with representatives from a variety of key business units. It establishes priorities for systems development and implementation of communications networks, it considers and prioritizes requests for new systems and it commits funds to projects. It is the organizational institution in charge of the budgets for all or most of the IS services.

In recent years the great majority of organizations have adopted ready-made software such as ERP systems. Others have outsourced some or all of their IS functions. Some now use the services of application service providers (ASPs). But the central IS unit still oversees the implementation of ready-made software, outsourcing and relationships with ASPs.

It is often easier to integrate an IS plan into an organization's overall strategic plan with centralized IS management than with decentralized IS services. On the other hand, when only a central department is available, business units often find themselves overly dependent on – and at times resentful of – the department. The resentment often springs from the lack of control over the services the IS department renders, as other units depend on it for their success. Under a centralized IS organization, business units must receive approval for almost anything they do with computers, software and networks – a situation that can discourage the development of applications by end users, even if they are technologically knowledgeable enough to do so.

Dispersed IS organization

At the other end of the IS staffing spectrum is the approach whereby each unit fulfils its IS needs independently, deciding for itself which systems it needs and how to develop them (see Figure 9.14). There is usually still an IS unit at corporate headquarters, but it is relatively small and serves to coordinate IS needs for departments that cannot handle their own needs. Only large and complex systems, especially those that affect several departments or sites, are implemented under the auspices of this unit.

Each business unit has one or several IS professionals who report to the unit's manager. These workers know their non-IS colleagues' daily operations well and understand their information needs better than central IS personnel do.

In a dispersed IS organization, funds for the development and maintenance of the unit's ISs always come from the unit's own budget, which is intended to optimize the use of resources.

Figure 9.14 An example of dispersed IS organization

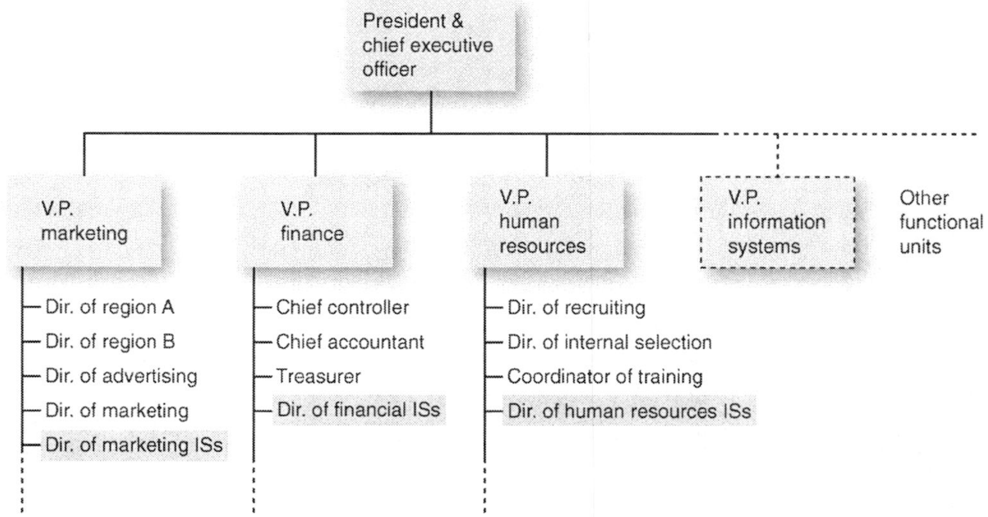

While the unit's IS professionals may seek input from their central IS colleagues, decisions are made by the units fairly independently. In this environment, IS professionals are often involved in many aspects of operations that do not necessarily involve IT, and they may be promoted from an IT position into another type of position within the business. Such a system enhances their chances of advancing up the organizational ladder to general managerial positions.

As Figure 9.14 indicates, an organization that chooses the dispersed IS staffing approach may still have a corporate IS director, possibly a vice president, who oversees a small central IS unit, consults with dispersed IS units and concentrates on larger, more complex enterprise wide IS projects. However, the IS personnel of the various units do not report to the central IS unit.

A hybrid approach

Small companies typically use the central approach to IS personnel because their IT staff levels are small. Among midsize and large companies, a purely central or dispersed IS organization is rare. Most of them use elements of both central and dispersed organization of IS personnel. For instance, a large corporate IS unit may have liaisons in the units who report to the corporate IS unit. Gillette, the world's largest supplier of shaving blades and other toiletry products, has established such an arrangement and found it very beneficial. A relatively large corporate IS unit coordinates intraorganizational systems, while the different sites (including international divisions) develop and maintain their own local systems. This approach helped the company remain on the leading edge of IT while maintaining a strong sense of ownership at the local sites.

In many organizations you will also find employees of other companies serving alongside the IS personnel. These professionals handle services that have been outsourced by the company to an IS service firm. These people may work in a central IS unit or anywhere else in the organization, depending on the contact signed with the service firm. Outsourcing is discussed in detail in Chapter 12, 'Choices in Systems Acquisition'. Many organizations also hire consultants for several weeks or months to help find and implement IT solutions to *ad hoc* problems or to seize opportunities. Again, these consultants work alongside the organization's employees as if they, too, were its employees. Senior consultants often take part in top management meetings.

Regardless of the approach to managing IS personnel and other resources, surveys show that IS implementation is handled differently according to the position of the highest IS officer in the organizational structure. If this person reports to the vice president of finance or another vice president, it is a sign that top management has decided that IT can help automate processes, but cannot change the company's strategic position significantly; the IS personnel then tend to provide primarily technical solutions to business problems. However, if the highest-ranking IS executive reports to the CEO, it is a sign that management considers IT as holding the potential to change significantly the organization's future; the IS professionals are then significantly more involved in strategic planning, and they also search for opportunities rather than just solve problems. The trend has been to upgrade the position from reporting to a vice president to reporting to the chief executive officer because of the importance of ISs to companies' survival.

Challenges for IS managers and business managers

For ISs to be developed and maintained successfully, IS managers and business managers must understand what each party expects from the other and must find the best ways to respond to those expectations. By 'business managers', we mean all managers in charge of areas other than ISs. A growing number of IS managers refer to their non-IT colleagues as customers, and treat them as such. Business managers, for their part, expect to be treated as customers, especially when the cost of the IS services rendered are covered from their unit's budget. What are the expectations?

Why you should... be interested in the deployment of information systems

You are a marketing manager for Gadgets4Fun. Several months ago you sent a request to your IS department for the development of a website. The site would provide information about the different products Gadgets4Fun sells and allow shoppers to purchase them via the site. You and your staff are still waiting for the site to be established. Calls to the company's central IS department keep yielding the same answer: 'We have a priority list. We will get to it shortly.' Several of your subordinates have told you that they could easily develop the catalogue themselves, including scanned pictures, so that shoppers could at least see what the company offers. Later, IS professionals could add the transactional components. You are not sure your organization would allow your unit to begin. What is the policy? Can your department establish and maintain its own website? Will heads roll if you take the initiative? And if you are allowed to take the initiative, who will later help your personnel upgrade the site?

Knowing how information technology and personnel are deployed in an organization helps managers know how to enquire about, and obtain, useful information. Thus, all managers – both IS and business managers – must be involved in the organization of IS resources in a business. To ensure convenient access to data, managers must not rely on IS professionals to dictate deployment, responsibilities and charges; they should be proactive and participate in the decisions leading to organizing and managing IS resources and adopting policies.

In today's businesses, managers are expected to be knowledgeable consumers of information services. Thus, they should have a clear picture of the organization of ISs and the responsibilities of different IS professionals, whose job it is to satisfy the information needs of business managers.

Business managers' expectations of an IS unit

The first thing that business managers must remember is that they should have a continual dialogue with the company's IS managers, to explore new ways to help their operations. Although business managers are not expected to be well-versed in IT's cutting edge, they should collaborate with the IS manager to explore new technologies to support the work of their subordinates. Business managers need the following from the IS unit:

- *A broad understanding of the business activities*: IS professionals are expected to understand the nature of the activities of the business unit they support: whom does the business unit serve? Where do its raw data come from? What information does it use? What systems do the business unit's systems interface with? Understanding the business helps IS professionals put themselves in the users' shoes and develop systems from the users' point of view.
- *Flexibility and adaptability*: IS professionals are expected to serve their clients under uncertain and changing circumstances. They need to accept changing requirements for systems and services, and accept imprecise requirements for acquisition of new systems. They need to help their clients define requirements.
- *Prompt response to the information needs of the business unit*: Business managers are often disappointed with the long time it takes IS units to react to business needs. A business unit that cannot elicit a prompt response from the IS staff may resort to finding haphazard – and ultimately problematic – solutions to its information needs.
- *A clear, jargon-free explanation of what the technology can and cannot do for the business unit*: To show off their expertise, IS professionals sometimes use technical jargon to communicate ideas. While use of technical terms facilitates communication among same-field

professionals, it may cause problems for lay users and professionals of other fields. Business managers and their employees may be reluctant to admit that they do not understand certain terms, so communication can break down, resulting in costly misunderstandings. If technical terms must be used, IS professionals should explain them.

- *Candid explanations of what information systems can and cannot do*: Business managers and their employees count on IS professionals to tell them not only what marvels a planned information system will accomplish, but also what the system's limitations are. Outlining the limitations of a system can eliminate disappointment and ensure proper usage of the system. In particular, business managers expect IS managers not to use their budgets for the sake of experimenting with new technology to satisfy professional curiosity.
- *Honest budgeting*: If any of the services rendered to a business unit are carried out at the expense of that unit, business managers depend on IS managers for an honest, detailed assessment of the resources needed to develop a new IS and maintain an existing one. Time and budget overruns often occur in systems development projects. IS managers must detail the work that will be done, how much it will cost in terms of person hours and other resources and how much time each project phase will take.
- *Single point of contact*: To serve the business units after an IS is installed or modified, IS managers should assign one contact person to respond to the business units' questions and problems.

In general, IS managers should treat business managers as clients, although they all work for the same organization. This approach has been adopted in an increasing number of companies. Some have taken the client/vendor model to such an extreme that business managers are allowed to use outside IS vendors if the internal IS unit cannot offer comparable services at comparable prices.

IS managers' expectations of business managers

IS managers are expected to keep themselves abreast of developments in the IT field, suggest adoption of new technologies and make recommendations to improve business operations. To do this job well, IS managers also need clear communication from business managers in three basic areas: basic business planning, general systems planning and specific systems development.

- *Business planning*: To plan ahead, IS managers need to know their own business, but they also need to know their clients' (the business units') plans and needs. For instance, if a business department is planning to hire ten new people to introduce a new product, the IS manager must be informed to budget for purchasing and installing new equipment, installing new software and training the new employees to use it. Business plans for, say, three years into the future will become a part of the organization's overall IS plan, which in turn is a part of the organization's overall strategic plan.
- *Systems planning*: Once an IS unit is called on to develop a new system, it needs a clear explanation of business processes that need support. An IS manager can develop an effective IS only if business managers and their employees clearly communicate the exact processes they want automated.
- *Systems selection or development*: Once the general automation plan is agreed on, the IS manager needs to know what features the business manager wants in the new system. Although IS professionals are more familiar with IT than many users, they still need to know how a new system will be used in daily operations to design or install it correctly. The business manager is responsible for communicating what features are needed in a new system.

- *Participation and partnership*: Much as business units want the IT staff to be partners in meeting their needs, IT managers want the business units to help the IT staff. Business managers are expected to be involved in development and modification of ISs, participate in testing of new systems and provide frequent feedback. They are expected to provide feedback before, during and after development of the systems. This has both technical and psychological benefits: the effort may result in technically better systems, and the morale of the IT staff will be kept high.

This information helps IS professionals include all input, processing and output mechanisms, as well as user interfaces that are intuitive, easy to learn and easy to use.

SUMMARY

Organizations are run by managers. The majority of organizations are structured in a pyramid model with several layers of management. Managers can be roughly classified into these levels: strategic (at the top of the organizational hierarchy), tactical (below top managers) and operational managers (below tactical). Managers at the three levels have different information needs, and typically use different types of information systems to satisfy these needs.

Senior managers make decisions that affect the entire organization, or large parts of it, in the long run. They use highly summarized information that is based on a wide data scope, both in terms of the number of organizational units that the data cover, and the time span: long historic periods, and periods well into the future. The lower the managerial level, the greater the information's level of detail. Most data for decision-making come from internal sources, but some come from external sources. Senior managers operate in highly unstructured environments. The typical information systems they use are executive information systems (EISs), decision support systems (DSSs) and, to a smaller extent, expert systems (ESs).

Middle managers receive strategic decisions as general directives within which they develop tactics to achieve specific objectives. The information they use is processed from data that cover narrower organizational units and shorter time spans. Their typical information systems consist of DSSs and ESs. Like top managers, they must make unstructured decisions.

Operational managers are responsible for daily operations. They make relatively simple decisions that affect only their departments in the short run. The information they need reflects transactions of their own small units and very narrow time spans. However, the information is very detailed and usually comes from more structured data, such as numbers and other data that can be tabulated. Too much information can result in information overload, or the inability to comprehend the meaning of facts and figures. One way to avoid overload is to examine cases that fall outside certain parameters, called management by exception.

Operational managers use transaction processing systems to generate reports. Much of their work involves monitoring, sometimes including electronic monitoring of employees, which may infringe on the employees' right to privacy.

Clerical and other workers typically carry out their supervisors' orders. They use transaction-processing systems to record transactions and satisfy queries from other employees, customers and suppliers.

A major task of middle managers in the past was to screen information and pass it on to higher-level managers. Since information technology allows top managers to extract their information directly and conveniently, many organizations have reduced whole layers of middle management, resulting in a flatter organizational structure.

Information systems help managers to monitor, control and make decisions. They can also help managers be better leaders.

Effective information conveys a message with minimum necessity for interpretation. Many applications allow users to present information in the form that best suits their individual preferences: tabular or graphical, or as dynamic representation of real-time events.

Online analytical processing (OLAP) applications link managers to data warehouses and enable them to produce useful information such as purchasing trends and fraud patterns.

Because information is power, occasionally managers try to obtain power by controlling ISs beyond their real business need. Sometimes, they reject new ISs because the systems were 'not invented here'. Politics harm the effort to deliver and share information for the benefit of the organization as a whole.

Information technology provides very effective and inexpensive means for monitoring employees on the job. As the use of email and the Web becomes pervasive in the workplace, most workers' use of the resources is monitored. Employers say it is their legitimate right to do so, but privacy advocates argue that some practices infringe on workers' right to privacy.

There are many ways to organize the IS staff. At one extreme is a centralized IS organization whereby all of the IS professionals report to the CIO or another person who is the highest IS authority. At the other extreme is dispersed IS organization, which places IS staff within an organization's business units.

Central IS management usually includes a steering committee, whose members are drawn from key business units. Regardless of organization approaches, IS staff are responsible for systems implementation and maintenance, communications networks, research and development, data administration and the information centre.

The advantages of centralized IS management are: standardized hardware, common software, easier training, common reporting systems, effective planning of shared systems, efficient use of personnel and the ability of management to maintain tight control of the company's ISs.

The advantages of decentralization of IS management are: a better fit of systems to particular needs of business units, timely response to requests by business units, encouragement of end-user computing, encouragement of innovation and accommodation of decentralized management style.

Successful use of IS technology depends on understanding and collaboration between managers of business units and IS managers. IS managers must have a broad understanding of business activities. They are expected to respond promptly to the information needs of business units, use jargon-free language when dealing with their non-IS clients, explain what is and what is not possible with ISs, detail the resources that would be needed to implement and maintain a new IS and designate personnel who will be responsible for resolving problems reported by the users.

IS managers expect business managers to project their future information needs, clearly explain the business processes that ISs should support and thoroughly detail the features they desire in a new IS.

URBAN SCENE REVISITED

Urban Scene has implemented a new enterprise-wide information system to standardize its hardware and software and enable increased communication. The new system also has enhanced capabilities, providing quicker, more accurate information to staff. Several levels of managers use the system for their specific needs, but there has been resistance also. The new enterprise resource planning system spurred a reorganization of the IS staff. The company is also setting up an e-commerce site. Examine some of these changes at Urban Scene more closely.

What would you do?

1 Shirley Steiner, Urban Scene's chief executive officer, is concerned that her retail chain stay lean and mean – with the fewest levels in its organization chart to avoid unnecessary costs. She has asked you to categorize the levels in her organization's management pyramid. From the information provided in the Part 3 case and this chapter's opening case, draw a chart and categorize the employees according to strategic, tactical and operational management and clerical and shop floor workers. Do you think that Urban Scene is a relatively flat organization? Why or why not?

2 Now that you have identified different levels within Urban Scene, take another look at this chapter's opening case. What types of data are they interested in at each level? Would you allow managers at all levels access to all the information, or would you 'tie' the level of aggregation to the managerial level? Why?

3 The chapter discussed three ways of organizing an IS staff: central IS organization, dispersed IS organization and a hybrid approach. Which type of organization do you think Urban Scene has? Support your answer with details from the opening case.

New perspectives

1 When he visits the Croydon shop, Martin is shocked to find that Mike Roberts, the shop manager, isn't using the new system to its full capabilities. Why do you think Mike continued to use the new system in his old ways despite the fact that the new capabilities have been announced? Is there anything Martin can do to help ensure other managers begin tapping the power of the new system? Give Martin some suggestions.

2 Urban Scene is using internal sales information in a variety of ways. What types of external information might the company's managers want to know for better decision-making? Where could they get that information?

3 In planning for the company's new website, Suzanne Granger had to explain to some sales staff why they couldn't head up the website development – that the IS staff needed to lead that effort. Take Suzanne's role and write a list of arguments she would have used to explain the reasons to the staff. Be prepared to present your list to the class.

Review questions

1 What are the major tasks of managers in the three levels of management?

2 There is a class of workers whose jobs are information-intensive, although they may not be in managerial positions. Give several examples of these workers.

3 What does the term 'flat organization' mean? Why is information technology said to have flattened some organizations?

4 Operational managers usually do not use DSSs. Why?

5 The amount of information used by senior managers (in terms of number of figures or lines of text considered) is often smaller than the amount of information used by operational managers. Why? Explain and give an example.

6 Give five examples of external information sources and how they are important in decision-making.

7 Why do senior managers rely on external information? Give three examples of external data and the organizations from which they can be obtained. How would an executive use the information for decision-making?

8 'Detailed information must come from a wide range of data in terms of time and number of organizational units.' Do you agree with the statement? Explain.

9 Senior executives often use information that they have recorded on small notes. How would you describe this type of information in terms of how structured it is? Why don't these executives use spreadsheets to record the information?

10 What is the connection between access to information and politics?

11 What methods do managers use to dodge corporate management's attempts to implement a new IS for their departments?

12 What are the main reasons why companies monitor their employees' email and web surfing?

13 We refer to 'management of IS resources'. What do these resources include?

14 A corporation that is a conglomerate of businesses in different industries is likely to have decentralized management of ISs. Why?

15 Some types of IS resources can be well developed and controlled only under centralized management. Give two examples.

16 What are the advantages of centralized and decentralized IS management?

17 Why should IS managers understand business processes, even though their expertise is IT?

18 What is professional jargon? In what circumstance is it appropriate to use professional jargon, and in what circumstances should it not be used?

19 What types of businesses are most likely to adopt a centrally managed IS organization?

20 What types of businesses are most likely to adopt a dispersed IS organization?

Discussion questions

1 Why are the majority of organizations structured like pyramids?

2 Often, it is difficult to distinguish between middle managers and operational managers. Why?

3 Explain the generally accepted adage, 'The higher you are in the organizational hierarchy, the more decisions you have to make.'

4 Executives are sometimes impatient and say, 'Give me the bottom line.' Explain why, in terms of data and information.

5 'A picture is worth a thousand words.' Is this always true? Why or why not? Give an example of a situation in which you would prefer information in tabular rather than graphical form.

6 Managers often strive to put resources under their control. Would you expect fiercer control for information resources than for other resources? Why or why not?

7 When an IS is shared by several departments, a power struggle over ownership may occur. One solution to this may be to pronounce that the system is owned by corporate management. What is the downside of this approach?

8 One benefit of centralized IS management is economies of scale. What does this mean, and how can it be implemented in the context of hardware and software?

9 Why is standardization of hardware and software so important in organizations?

10 One advantage of decentralized management of IS resources is a better fit of ISs to business needs. Why?

Tutorial activities

1 You are the marketing manager of the irrigation products of Voda, Inc. The following are your budgeted and actual figures.

Voda, Ltd.

Irrigation Products Department Budget, Quarter 1

Item	*Forecast*	*Actual*	*5 per cent exception*
Income			
Model P12 Sales	1,250,000	1,452,375	
Model P15 Sales	13,500,000	12,788,992	
Drip Valve V2 Sales	450,000	452,344	
Expenditures			
Sales Reps' Commission	750,000	763,000	
Advertising	500,000	425,000	
Packaging Materials	270,000	298,000	
Telephone	5,200	5,790	

Using a spreadsheet, create an exception report to aid in making decisions as to which items to investigate. Add the '5 per cent exception'. Have an asterisk (*) appear in every column for which the actual expense of an item deviated by at least 5 per cent from the budget. (*Hint*: Try the absolute value function.)

Use the appropriate fonts and styles, as used here. Turn in (1) a printout showing the reports and (2) a printout showing the formulas, where applicable.

2 The Web offers much external information that is not available in the more traditional external sources, such as newspapers, printed bulletins, trade journals and newsletters. Assume that you are a human resource manager looking to hire qualified chemical engineers for your petrochemical company. Explore the Web for three sites offering candidates. Prepare a short report answering the following questions: What are the advantages or disadvantages of using the Web, compared with advertising in newspaper help-wanted ads? What are the advantages or disadvantages compared with using a 'headhunting' firm? Include your impression of the sites and the quality of information and service they provide.

3 Team up with another student from your class. Interview managers from administrative units of your college or university. On the basis of the information you collected, write a brief report in which you conclude and explain which type of IS management the institution has: centralized or decentralized.

From ideas to application
REAL CASES

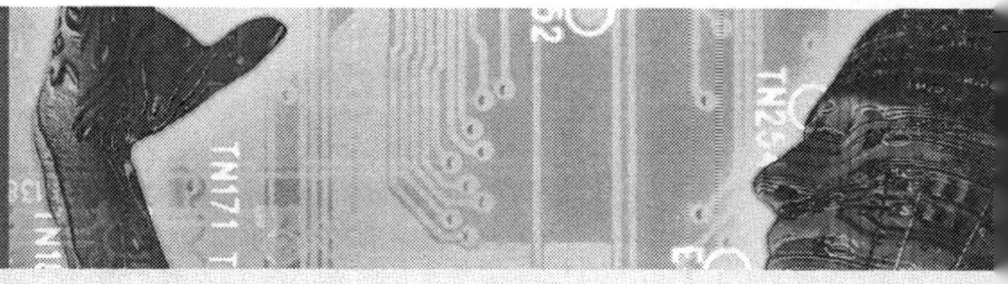

Case study **9.1**

Companies' increasing use of online technology for business meetings

BY ALAN HOGARTH

Business meetings generally get a bad press, as normally very little gets accomplished during them. The majority of meetings are unstructured, uninspiring and unproductive. But they don't have to be that way. Although meetings are part and parcel of any business, the traditional approach to meetings could soon be a thing of the past and it appears that few employees will regret this demise. There is a prevalent view that they have spent too much of their working lives in boring and unnecessary meetings in their organizations generally being lectured at by managers pushing their own agenda. Now, information and communication technology (ICT) is dramatically altering the way in which business meetings take place. We live in a global economy, and people in far-flung locations still need to meet. Increasingly they are doing so via web conferencing services, which let both small and large groups of people share presentations and documents in real time over the Web. The services also deliver handy tools for collaboration such as chat rooms, whiteboards, document annotation, application sharing, web polls and web tours. With most of the services, the audio portion of the conference is handled via the standard phone conferencing.

European organizations are now aware that meetings such as these are a substantial drain on their resources. This tends to be borne out by a number of research projects. For example, a recent survey by Bibby Financial Services indicated that up to 2 million hours a year were wasted by small to medium enterprises (SMEs) in meetings that were seen at best as pointless and at worse as fractious. Many people who attended the meetings were either unprepared, did not stick to the agenda or they were continually interrupted by mobile phone calls. Further, this cost the sector around £25 million annually. David Scott, Communications Manager of PC World Business, states that, 'Businesses often fall into a routine, having a sales meeting every Friday, say, when there may be nothing new to discuss.'

In order to eliminate some of the problems highlighted, companies can now use technology to facilitate their business meetings. For example, replacing face-to-face meetings with phone or video conferencing using a broadband connection, webcam and conference software such as Skype can replicate a business meeting online. Jerry Roest of PC World Business maintains that, 'In a world where travel is seen as increasingly high-cost, a waste of time and with ecological implications, and where IT costs such as video conferencing are coming down, It's a no-brainer!' Peter Scargill of the Federation of Small Businesses agrees when he argues that 'for routine business meetings, an electronic solution is the answer. Teams can use technology to avoid the necessity of having (face-to-face) meetings.'

Some companies are even questioning the need for meetings at all. It is suggested that one way of avoiding meetings is to put all relevant company reports and documents on the organizations' intranet so that they are accessible to all who want to review them. Alternatively a simpler and more secure approach could be just to email the documents to the relevant parties.

Dedicated videoconference rooms are an increasingly common sight in the offices of major European companies.

PHOTO SOURCE © SEAN NEL

At Difference Corporation, a communications company, meetings are rarely held. Essentially business planning meetings are held only twice a year in quiet periods such as January. Difference handles all aspects of communication such as email, phone, text and fax for clients that include Yu!Sushi and the National Trust for Scotland. Their services are technology-focused and include giving customers online access to their reports so they are always kept up to date. The company cuts travel costs and time by using video conferencing and phone conferencing and on one-to-one chats rather than holding group meetings. The company does not like meetings, as they take up too much time. No time is spent discussing past sales figures as 'People will already have seen online information about sales and product approaches and billing', says Serge Cren the managing director. 'There is no need to go over what happened in the past in planning meetings.' Clients are met only at the start of a contractual agreement and then, if contact has to be made, it is done via email, online and phone where other parties can be patched in. With 12 locations in the UK, internal conference calls are essential. Cren says, 'And it's better for the business. There's better interaction within the company and with the clients, people are not forced to sit through meetings that don't concern them.'

However, there can be problems with ICT for meetings. For example, many organizations are concerned about the increasing email burden in the workplace. Research conducted by Loughborough University has identified that 'email communication within the workplace costs UK businesses millions of pounds in lost productivity'. The cost per year was placed at £9.8 million. Another report by NTL: Telewest Business showed that on average office staff spent 42 minutes a day chasing response to 'urgent' emails and 27 minutes responding to voicemails. Stephen Benyon, managing director, states that 'Communication tools that once contributed significantly to productivity have started to become a drain on it. This means that employees can be faced with working longer hours unnecessarily.'

However, despite these cases, there is no doubt that technology can be effective in dealing with internal and external communication, but it must be properly implemented. Roest says, 'There is no point in sending out lots of emails if your company makes a few high-value products for a very select market. It is more appropriate if you want to sell 100,000 items with a £1.00 profit margin and have a potential market of 20 million people.'

Another new development adapted for business is blogging or online diaries. These are useful for keeping staff informed of organizational developments. Scott says, 'The beauty of blogs is that everybody can add comments and ideas. It can be more productive because you are not forcing people to go to meetings and you can see the train of thought in the dialogue. But it is only really for companies that are quite comfortable with IT.'

Case study questions

1 What are the typical problems associated with a traditional business meeting?

2 In what ways can information and communications technology (ICT) alleviate the problems associated with traditional business meetings?

3 What might be the pitfalls of using ICT alone for conducting meetings?

4 Suggest how the problem of excessive emails and voicemails identified in the NTL: Telewest survey might be alleviated?

5 As a client of a business that uses ICT for meetings and reporting, what benefits would you expect to accrue from such an approach?

SOURCE: Sarah Bridge, 'Time Mangers Set the Agenda', article, *Sunday Times*, 4 February 2007

Case study **9.2**

Varied approach to Vista adoption

The introduction of any new software or hardware is a significant consideration for an IT manager, but deploying Microsoft's Windows Vista operating system in every PC in the organization is potentially a major headache. Early indications are that IT managers are moving slowly, worried that there will be compatibility problems with existing software, hardware and networks. Bucking this conservative approach, Papa Gino's Inc. and D'Angelo Sandwich Shops wanted to move quickly, as it saw it as an improvement in the protection of customer credit card data. It consequently applied for membership of Microsoft's Vista Technology Adoption Program (TAP). Chris Cahalin, network manager at Papa Gino's says, 'We already have a district manager with Vista on his laptop and through TAP we have a direct line to Microsoft in case of trouble. The best way to find the kinks is to use it and these resources have really made things happen for us.'

PHOTO SOURCE: © MICROSOFT CORPORATION

The desktop of Windows Vista.

However, as an early adopter Papa Gino's has found some major 'kinks', such as an incompatibility problem between Vista and the company's Cisco network. Cahalin blames Cisco Systems for a lack of preparedness in making sure that Vista could communicate properly with its Secure Socket Layer (SSL) Virtual Private Network (VPN). However, there is a 'Catch 22' situation in that it is likely that Cisco are slow to undertake the necessary work on compatibility because so few of its customers are deploying Vista! For example, Quintiles Transnational is a health care provider with 20,000 employees in over 50 countries including China, India, Africa and Australia. Steven Dietz, Network Manger for Quintiles, is very concerned with security. 'Because we are a pharmaceutical testing company, we do business with all the large pharmaceutical companies and we have to keep data separate and independent from client A and client B. There can't be any confusion and we need to make sure data from client A isn't accidentally sent to client B.' Microsoft boasts that Vista is the most secure operating system yet, which would suggest that adoption should happen as soon as possible. However, Dietz is worried that security features in Vista could conflict with existing built-in security measures, leading to unintended data leakage. Consequently Dietz, like many other computing professionals, is taking a much slower route that Papa Gino's, putting Vista through extensive testing to ensure there are no surprises. Significant deployment will be delayed for at least a year.

However, it might prove difficult to delay for some organizations. StillSecure creates and sells a variety of third-party network software and is struggling to make its products Vista compatible. But as Alan Shimel, chief strategy officer, says 'Every time someone buys a new PC or laptop it comes out of the box with Vista. The world is being forced into the Vista universe kicking and screaming', he said, 'so vendors can't afford to move as slowly as IT shops can. Vista will find its way into corporate IT a lot sooner than most people would like. The more new machines are purchased with Vista pre-installed, the faster we all have to move.'

Thinking about the case

1 Would the problems indicated above have been as significant if the issue had been concerned with new hardware (such as new PC technology) rather than new software (an operating system in this case)?

2 Is it better to be an early adopter (like Papa Gino's) and get the help from Microsoft rather than delay (like Quintiles)? Will Quintiles be forced to deploy before they are ready?

3 Do you think that Microsoft have any moral obligation to the third-party vendors such as Cisco and StillSecure?

SOURCE: Bill Brenner, 'When Microsoft Vista and VPNs don't mix', 25 May 2007 and 'Big Microsoft Vista concerns Big Pharma', 19 June 2007, Computer Weekly.com

silicon.com

Case study **9.3**

CEO and CIO still don't see eye to eye

BY GEORGE COLONY

A lot has changed in big business's relationship to technology in the last couple of decades. But, Forrester Research's George Colony argues, there still isn't enough trust between the CEO and the CIO.

Throughout my career, I have watched the 'odd couple' of the chief information officer and the chief executive officer try to live together.

In the 1980s and for most of the 1990s, their paths rarely crossed – the CEO didn't think much about technology, and the CIO rarely interacted with executives beyond his boss, the chief financial officer. With the exception of some techie leaders like Ned Johnson at Fidelity, Fred Smith at FedEx or David Glass at Wal-Mart, chief executives perceived IT/BT (I now refer to information technology as business technology, or BT) as an important underpinning of company operations, but not as a critical strategic tool.

Added to this general ambivalence were the high-profile cases of chief executives having their reputations and budgets scorched by IT/BT projects gone awry: perpetual IRS systems overhauls, Citibank's futile effort to create a 'single customer view' in the mid-1980s, and SAP R/3 'kitchen sink' leaps of faith in the early-1990s come to mind.

Then the dot-com collective insanity hit and CEO panic set in (Amazoning, etc., etc.). In those days, I ran a tech session at the Harvard Business School for CEOs. To prepare for the session, I surveyed chief executives at 25 large companies. When I asked them how much time they spent on technology issues, the response was '25 per cent'. They were lying: CEOs – even the techies – could not afford to devote a quarter of their time to systems.

But they were certainly spending more time on tech than they had five years earlier – even Jack 'I've never used email' Welch, on his way out the door at General Electric, got religion and started to preach about the digitization of business. Michael Porter, every CEO's favourite academic, got into the act with a naive *Harvard Business Review* piece on the Internet in early 2001, just as the curtain came crashing down on The Web, Act 1.

Fast-forward to 2007. How's the odd couple today? Forrester just surveyed 75 global CEOs, and here's the punch line: 60 per cent of CEOs are satisfied with the overall performance of IT/BT, but only 28 per cent see IT/BT as a proactive leader in innovation. And only 30 per cent see IT/BT as a proactive leader in process improvement.

Now, you can analyse this data simply and conclude that CIOs are in pretty good standing with CEOs, but they have not stepped up to the plate as innovation and process mavens. I interpret the results quite differently.

The fact that 60 per cent of chief executives believe that CIOs are doing a satisfactory job is bad news, not good. Think comparatively: If only 60 per cent of your top executives were satisfied with the performance of the CFO, that would signal meaningful distrust in the financial operations of your company. Chief executives' satisfaction in IT/BT has

Influential Harvard academic, Michael Porter, whose much-discussed 2001 paper, 'Strategy and the Internet', urged business planners to recognize the internet as an 'enabling technology'.

PHOTO SOURCE: © HUW JONES/ALAMY

certainly risen through this decade, but 60 per cent is still too low.

And the fact that CEOs are not looking to the CIO to be a proactive leader in innovation and process is not bad news. Rather, it is a frank assessment by the chief executive that the CIO should not be, indeed cannot be, the driving force in these two areas.

Why? In most companies, the CIO is too busy keeping the ship's engines running smoothly to come up onto the command deck and make suggestions to the captain on course changes. Leading business innovation and process change is not in the skill set of most CIOs – nor should it be.

Does the CIO have a role in process change? Absolutely. IT/BT typically supports and manages the process backbone – think enterprise resource planning – of most companies. When technology is injected into a company, the effort will fail unless it incorporates process change (the way you do work) and organizational change (the way you are organized to do work). I call this the critical triad – technology/process/organization – and the three must always be viewed collectively and as acting in concert. While the CIO brings technology to the table, business executives (especially the CEO) must spend political capital to change process and organization. This is a collaborative effort, with the CIO working with the business people to get the right mix.

How about innovation? Obviously the CIO is always working on systems innovation – that's part of keeping the engines running smoothly. But when it comes to business innovation, he is again not the proactive driver, but rather the steady partner with business executives who are chartered to lead business innovation.

Here's the key: For business executives to effectively drive process change and innovation, they must have a solid understanding of technology. They must be, to coin a term, technology-knowledgeable businesspeople (TKBPs) able to adeptly bring the potential of technology to bear on business change. The goal is to field vice presidents of marketing, executive VPs of strategy, and presidents of divisions who know how to apply technology to get the company to achieve its goals. The CIO must be in the business of educating and teaching the businesspeople so that they can make the leap. IQ (intelligence quotient) and EQ (emotional quotient), must be joined by TQ (technology quotient). And teaching TQ is the province of the chief information officer.

If that happens chief executives' satisfaction with CIOs will head into the 70 per cent and 80 per cent range – where it belongs. And boards of directors will come to praise the chief information officer if that person can work to develop a TKCEO – a technology-knowledgeable CEO. And that's when the odd couple will see eye to eye – to the benefit of the organization and shareholders.

George Colony is chairman and chief executive officer of Forrester Research.

Thinking about the case

1. The suggestion is that CIOs should be less concerned with 'blue skies thinking' but more concerned with the education of CEOs in how technology can be used. Do you agree with this demarcation?
2. Is there room in today's business world for a true hybrid, a CEO who not only understands what can be done with IT but also how?

SOURCE: www.silicon.com.

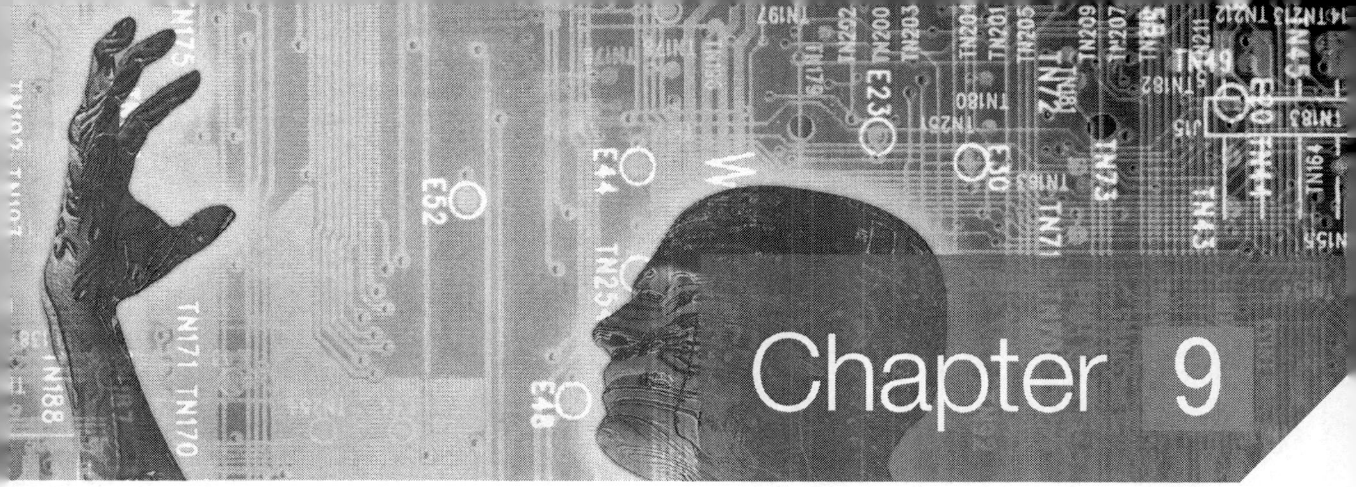

Chapter 9

Business intelligence and knowledge management

LEARNING OBJECTIVES

As more and more business operations are managed using information from information systems and sometimes automatically *by* information systems, large amounts of data are collected and stored electronically. With proper software tools, data stored in databases and data warehouses enable executives to glean business intelligence, information that helps them know more about customers and suppliers, and therefore helps them make better decisions. Information technology also enables organizations to organize stored knowledge and garner knowledge from vast amounts of unstructured data.

When you finish this chapter, you will be able to:

Explain the concepts of data mining and online analytical processing.

Explain the notion of business intelligence and its benefits to organizations.

Identify needs for knowledge storage and management in organizations.

Explain the challenges in knowledge management and its benefits to organizations.

URBAN SCENE

LOOKING FOR CLUES

Things were going well for Lucy Slade and her chain of shops selling clothes to teens. She had confidence in her management team and they had embraced the new technology aimed at streamlining her business. But there was a nagging worry at the back of her mind. As the empire grew from 40 to nearly 100 shops the impression was that some were performing better than others, but she didn't have the facts to back up her reservations.

She had visited many of the stores as they had implemented the new enterprise resource-planning system and found the staff to be generally in favour of the changes, and yet there seemed to be a lack of consistency in the day-to-day operations of the stores. With her business experience this did not surprise Lucy. She realized that some styles and designs were better sellers in certain areas than others. However, there was a need for someone to see the whole picture to see if there was a chance to bring 'best practice' to all the stores.

When she next had a meeting with Martin Tate, the CIO, she asked him about the possibility of using the knowledge of the best store managers and analysing sales data across all of the stores. 'Sounds to me like you're talking about data mining', replied Martin. 'Leave it to me.'

Analysing the sales

It wasn't long before Martin got back to Lucy with some very interesting proposals. What he wanted was a system that would analyse data about sales, the layout of the stores, special offers in place, what was sold with what, time of day of sale, and so on. Most of these details were readily available and all that was needed was a database to store all of this historical data and then the appropriate software to allow analysis in a variety of dimensions. Lucy, being the dynamic CEO that she was, gave him the go-ahead (with an appropriate budget!).

It wasn't long before the system was bearing very useful fruit. Analysis of the data showed that certain accessories, such as belts and hats, sold better when displayed next to fashion items that they naturally complemented. That in itself wasn't rocket science, but it was interesting to note which branches were doing better in this respect. The good practice was passed on to those branches which were missing this point.

Returns

An interesting by-product of the system was an analysis of returns. Whenever an item of clothing was returned as being unsuitable, it was customary to take details of the customer. The system could take an overview of this and produce a report showing the branches where there seemed to be an unusually high level of returns. Better than that, it could identify specific customers who regularly returned items a few days after purchase. Whilst there could be perfectly legitimate reasons for this, it was more likely that the customer was 'borrowing' the dress for a night out and then getting their money back. The new system could indicate to the

PHOTO SOURCE: © TONY TREMBLAY

branch manager that the customer had demonstrated such a profile so that some searching questions could be asked, the item of clothing inspected to ensure that there were no marks on it and so on.

Loyalty

'I think we should also investigate the idea of a loyalty card', Martin told Lucy at their next meeting. 'That way we can store details of every sale, who made it and when, what they bought with what and so on. This gives us massive potential for more analysis of our sales.' Lucy held up her hand. 'Hold on. I think an in-depth study of that is needed before we invest a great deal of money in such a scheme. Of course everyone knows Tesco's have benefited greatly from their Clubcard scheme but Sainsbury's abandoned theirs because it was costing more than alternative methods of business intelligence. I will not say "No" but let's do our homework first.'

Data mining and online analysis

Recall from our discussion in Chapter 6 that data warehouses are large databases containing historical transactions and other data. However, data warehouses in themselves are useless. To make data warehouses useful, organizations must use software tools to process data from these huge databases into meaningful information. Because executives can obtain significantly more information about their customers, suppliers and their own organizations, they like to call information gleaned with such tools **business intelligence (BI)**. There are two main uses of these databases: data mining and online analytical processing.

business intelligence (BI) Information gleaned from large amounts of data, usually a data warehouse or online databases; a BI system discovers not-yet-known patterns, trends and other useful information that can help improve the organization's performance.

data mining Using a special application that scours large databases for relationships among business events, such as items typically purchased together on a certain day of the week, or machinery failures that occur along with a specific use mode of the machine. Instead of the user querying the databases, the application dynamically looks for such relationships.

Data mining

Data warehouses could be regarded as a type of mine, where the data are the ore, and new useful information is the precious find. **Data mining** is the process of selecting, exploring and modelling large amounts of data to discover previously unknown relationships that can support decision-making. Data-mining software searches through large amounts of data for meaningful patterns of information.

While some tools help find predefined relationships and ratios, they do not answer the question that more powerful data-mining tools can answer: 'What are the relationships we do not yet know?' This is because the investigator must determine which relationship the software should look for in the first place.

Industry SNAPSHOT

Growing demand for intelligence

Market surveys show that corporations intend to increase their spending on BI software and the rise is even more significant in Europe. According to IDC, a global intelligence and advisory firm spending on BI software and tools in Central and Eastern Europe (CEE) is set to rise to over 100 million euro by the end of 2007. Worldwide, spending on business analytic software alone will grow annually by more than 10 per cent over the next five years, whereas in CEE the growth will be 20 per cent, nearly double the worldwide trend.

SOURCE: IDC Press Release, June 2007, http://www.idc-cema.com/?showproduct=31083

To answer this question, other techniques are used in data mining, including artificial intelligence techniques.

To illustrate the difference between traditional queries and data-mining queries, consider the following examples. A typical traditional query would be: 'What is the relationship between the amount of product X and the amount of product Y that we sold over the past quarter?' A typical data-mining query would be: 'Discover two products most likely to sell well together on a weekend.' The latter query lets the software find patterns that would otherwise not be detected through observation. While data have traditionally been used to see whether this or that pattern exists, data mining allows you to ask *what* patterns exist. Thus, some experts say that in data mining you let the computer answer questions that you do not know to ask. The combination of data-warehousing techniques and data-mining software makes it easier to predict future outcomes based on patterns discovered within historical data.

Data mining has four main objectives:

- *Sequence* or *path analysis*: Finding patterns where one event leads to another, later event.
- *Classification*: Finding whether certain facts fall into predefined groups.
- *Clustering*: Finding groups of related facts not previously known.
- *Forecasting*: Discovering patterns in data that can lead to reasonable predictions.

These techniques can be used in marketing, fraud detection and other areas (see Table 10.1). Data mining is most often used by marketing managers, who are constantly analysing purchasing patterns so that potential buyers can be targeted more efficiently through special sales, product displays, or direct mail and email campaigns. Data mining is an especially powerful tool in an environment in which businesses are shifting from mass-marketing a product to targeting the individual consumer with a variety of products that are likely to satisfy that person. Some observers call this approach 'marketing to one'.

Table 10.1 Potential applications of data mining

Data-mining application	Description
Consumer clustering	Identify the common characteristics of customers who tend to buy the same products and services from your company.
Customer churn	Identify the reason customers switch to competitors; predict which customers are likely to do so.
Fraud detection	Identify characteristics of transactions that are most likely to be fraudulent.
Direct marketing	Identify which prospective clients should be included in a mailing or email list to obtain the highest response rate.
Interactive marketing	Predict what each individual accessing a website is most likely to be interested in seeing.
Market basket analysis	Understand what products or services are commonly purchased together, and on what days of the week.
Trend analysis	Reveal the difference between a typical customer this month and a typical customer last month.

Industry SNAPSHOT

Dealing with the devil

Large retailers are investing in a system to get rid of customers! These are the so-called 'devil customers' with behaviours ranging from the legal (but loss-making and inconvenient to the retailer) to fraudulent. Many retailers will accept a returned item even if you cannot show a receipt. Some people take advantage of this and 'return' stolen goods for cash. On a less fraudulent level, many customers are guilty of 'wardrobing', the practice of buying an expensive item of clothing, wearing it for one night with the labels tucked in and then returning it the next day. To minimize theses phenomena, most retailers collect customer details when they return goods, which can then be used to investigate that customer's previous return history. John Lewis uses software from London-based IntelliQ to sift through transactions carried out at all of its shops. 'We have business protection teams who identify the sorts of bad things that criminals do, and the software allows us to look at millions of transactions and identify suspicious ones that match the modus operandi of these criminals', says Peter Kaye, John Lewis's head of business protection. 'An experienced investigator can see what's happening and say "Yes, that transaction is a fraud", or "this one is suspicious".'

The Californian-based company, The Return Exchange, has several retailers using their software, giving them the ability to share information from a larger customer transaction data warehouse. The company uses statistical models to determine if certain 'customers' engage in fraud. If the software determines that a person has defrauded retailers, the stores will stop accepting the person's returns. However, neither the retail chains nor the company disclose the criteria used to make the decision. Return Exchange does not allow retailers to share customer information.

SOURCE: 'How to get rid of "devil customers",' FT.com, 13 June 2007

A John Lewis department store on Oxford Street, London.

PHOTO SOURCE © KEVIN FOY/ALAMY

Predicting customer behaviour Data mining is also used in banking, where it is employed to find profitable customers and patterns of fraud. It is also used to predict bankruptcies and loan payment defaults. Various behaviour patterns can be finely tuned into customer profiles. The data are then clustered into smaller groups of individuals who are using banking services that do not best support their activities. Bank employees can then contact these customers and offer advice on services that would serve them better. The result can be greater customer loyalty (measured in fewer accounts closed and fewer moves to other banks). The people who are contacted will hopefully think that the bank is trying to take good care of their money.

Companies selling mobile phone services face a growing challenge of *customer churn* (switching to a competitor). Some surveys show that more than 50 per cent of mobile phone users consider switching to a competitor at any given time, and 15 per cent plan to switch to a competitor as soon as their contract expires. Mobilcom GmbH, a German company with 4.56 million customers and 1100 employees, uses data mining to identify such customers and approach them with inducements to continue or renew their contract before they switch. The company uses an application called DB Intelligent Miner from IBM. The software periodically looks for patterns of customer churns, and assigns each customer a score representing the likelihood of cancelling the contract. The software considers many variables, among which are the number of days to expiration and complaint history. Customer loyalty is extremely important because the cost of obtaining a new customer far exceeds the cost of retaining an existing one, especially in a highly competitive market such as mobile telephones.

To ensure a steady flow of customer data into their data warehouses, companies in almost every industry – from airlines to hotels, dining and gambling – operate customer loyalty programmes similar to the original frequent flier programmes. Membership is often free, and customers leave a record every time they make a purchase even if they do not use a credit card to pay. In many cases mining such data provides business intelligence to target individual customers.

Utilizing loyalty programmes Loyalty programmes such as frequent flier and consumer clubs help organizations amass huge amounts of data about their customers. Some supermarket chains, for example, issue special offers only to the most loyal customers. Harrah's Entertainment Inc., the gambling and hotel chain, uses its data warehouse to target individual customers, rather than groups. The techniques – whose specifics the company refuses to disclose for obvious reasons – enables Harrah's to tailor hotel, dining and gambling packages that are attractive to its customers. It helps discern the small spender from the big spender and decide how to price those services by individual spending patterns at the company's facilities. Harrah's relies heavily on its software applications to price-discriminate. It gives sales agents instructions to charge people who have a history of little spending on gambling higher per-night rates than they charge big gamblers.

Inferring demographics Some companies use data-mining techniques to try to predict what customers are likely to purchase in the future. As mentioned in previous chapters, Amazon.com is a leader in exploiting customer data. The company registered US Patent Number 6,865,546, titled 'Methods and systems of assisting users in purchasing items'. The software developed by Amazon determines the age of the recipient of an item purchased by a customer. The age range is estimated based at least in part on a customer order history of gifts purchased for the recipient. The first gift is associated with the first 'age appropriateness designation'. The second gift is associated with a second age appropriateness designation. An age range associated with the recipient is estimated. The recipient's age progression is calculated, and the company uses it to offer the customer gifts for that person when the customer logs on to the site. So, if you purchase gifts from Amazon.com for your baby niece, do not be surprised if Amazon entices you to purchase items for a young girl, a young woman, and an older woman over the next few decades. Here is another example of what this data-mining tool can do: if you purchased perfume a week before Valentine's Day, it will infer that you bought the item as a Valentine's gift for a woman and offer certain colours for the wrapping paper.

Online analytical processing

Another type of application to exploit data warehouses might not be as sophisticated in terms of the analysis conducted, but is extremely fast in response and enables executives to make timely decisions: online analytical processing (OLAP). Tables, even if joining data from several sources, limit the review of information. Often, executives need to view information in multiple combinations of two dimensions. For example, an executive might want to see a summary of the quantity of each product sold in each region. Then, she might want to view the total quantities of each product sold within each city of a region. And she might also want to view quantities sold of a specific product in all cities of all regions. OLAP is specially designed to answer queries such as these. OLAP applications let a user rotate virtual 'cubes' of information, whereby each side of the cube provides another two dimensions of relevant information.

online analytical processing (OLAP) A type of application that operates on data stored in databases and data warehouses to produce summary tables with multiple combinations of dimensions. An OLAP server is connected to the database or data warehouse server at one end and to the user's computer at the other.

The power of OLAP OLAP applications either operate on data that are organized especially for such use or process data from relational databases. A dynamic OLAP application responds to commands by composing tables 'on the fly'. To speed up response, databases can be organized in the first place as dimensional. In dimensional databases – also called multidimensional databases – the raw data are organized in tables that show information in summaries and ratios so that the enquirer does not have to wait for processing raw data. However, it is then possible for the user to drill down to more specific data about the source of those summaries. Many firms organize data in relational databases and data warehouses but also employ applications that automatically summarize that data and organize the information in dimensional databases for OLAP. Oracle, Cognos, Hyperion and many other companies sell multidimensional database packages and OLAP tools to use them.

CD TASK

dimensional database A database of tables, each of which contains aggregations and other manipulated information gleaned from the data to speed up the presentation by online processing applications. Also called multidimensional database.

OLAP applications can easily answer questions such as, 'What products are selling well?' or 'Where are my weakest-performing sales offices?' Note that although the word 'cube' is used to illustrate the multidimensionality of OLAP tables, the number of tables is not limited to six, which is the number of sides of a real cube. It is possible to produce tables showing relationships of any two related variables contained in the database, as long as the data exist in the database. OLAP enables managers to see summaries and ratios of the intersection of any two dimensions. As mentioned in Chapter 6, the data used by OLAP applications usually come from a data warehouse.

multidimensional database *See* dimensional database.

OLAP applications are powerful tools for executives. For example, consider Figure 10.1. Executives of a manufacturing company want to know how the three models of their product have sold over the past quarter in three world regions. They can see sales in dollar terms (top table) and then in unit terms (second table). They can then drill down into summaries of a particular region, in this case North America, and see the number of units sold not only by model but by model and colour, because each model is sold in three colours. This information might lead them to recommend to the dealer to stop selling Model 3 in blue in North America, because sales of blue units of this model are quite low in this region. While still investigating last quarter's sales in North America, the executives might want to examine the sales performance of each dealer in this region. It seems that Dealer 3 enjoyed brisk sales of Model 1, but not of Models 2 and 3. If the sales picture is the same for another quarter or two, they might decide to stop sales of these models through Dealer 3 and increase the number of units of Model 1 they provide to that dealer.

drill down The process of finding the most relevant information for executive decision-making within a database or data warehouse by moving from more general information to more specific details, such as from performance of a division to performance of a department within the division.

In a similar manner, Ruby Tuesday is a US based restaurant chain that has an expanding franchise operation in Europe. A problem was identified at one of its restaurants. Managers who examined performance by location discovered that some restaurants were performing well below the chain's average in terms of sales and profit. Analysing the information revealed that customers were waiting longer than normally for tables, and for their food after they were seated. There could be many reasons for this: an inexperienced cook, understaffing or slow waiters, to name a few.

Figure 10.1 Using OLAP tables

Sales (US$ 000)			
	Model 1	*Model 2*	*Model 3*
North America	115800	136941	53550
South America	72550	63021	25236
Asia	65875	53781	17136
Total	**254225**	**253743**	**95922**

Sales (Units)			
	Model 1	*Model 2*	*Model 3*
North America	4632	6521	2975
South America	2902	3001	1402
Asia	2635	2561	952
Total	**10169**	**12083**	**5329**

North America (Units)			
	Model 1	*Model 2*	*Model 3*
Red	2401	1785	2512
Blue	1766	527	52
White	465	4209	411
Total	**4632**	**6521**	**2975**

North America Dealerships (Units)			
	Model 1	*Model 2*	*Model 3*
Dealer 1	102	556	2011
Dealer 2	1578	2450	108
Dealer 3	2358	0	10
Dealer 4	20	520	57
Dealer 5	574	2995	789
Total	**4632**	**6521**	**2975**

Managers at headquarters decided to take a look at the average time between when a customer's bill was opened at the cash register and the time the customer paid. In the restaurant industry this is an indication of an important factor: how long it takes to move from one party to another at a given table. The shorter the time, the better. The average time 'to close a bill' at Ruby Tuesday's restaurants is 45 minutes. At some locations it was 55–60 minutes. Examining additional information, management concluded that the reason for the longer wait was increased demand thanks to an economic boom in the region. The company sent people to change the layout of the kitchen, positions of the cooks and the placement of food. Cooking took less time, serving was faster and the wait time decreased by 10 per cent. More customers could be served, and revenue went up.

OLAP applications are usually installed on a special server located between the user's computer and the server or servers that contain a data warehouse or dimensional databases (although OLAP might also process data from a transactional database). Since OLAP applications are designed to process large amounts of records and produce summaries, they are usually significantly faster than relational applications such as those using SQL (Structured Query Language) queries. OLAP applications can process 20,000 records per second. As mentioned before, when using pre-organized dimensional tables, the only processing involved is finding the table that corresponds to the dimensions and mode of presentation (such as values or percentages) that the user specified.

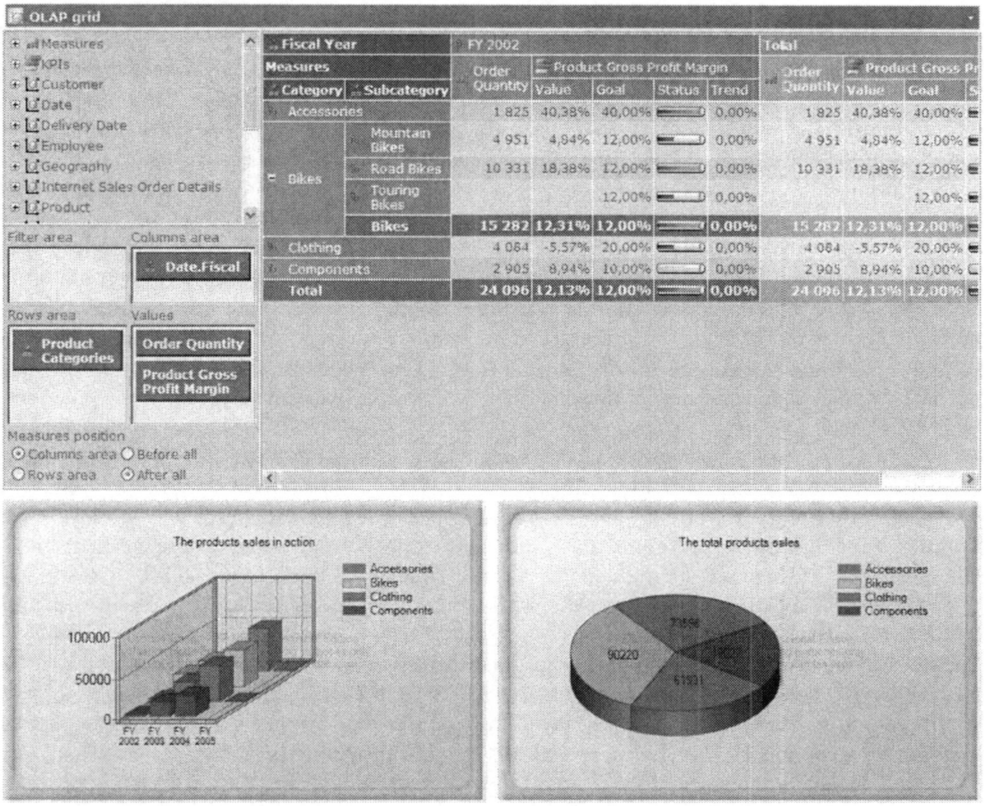

OLAP software, such as this example from Radar-Soft, performs multidimensional analysis of business data, allowing sophisticated trend analysis and data modelling.

OLAP in action OLAP and similar techniques help managers and other users to analyse quickly what is happening in the business. Managers in some companies now track information about their products from the purchasing of raw materials to the receipt of payment not only for operations but so that they can learn more about their clients and their own business. For example, Ben & Jerry's, one of the world's best-known ice cream makers, collects data about every container of ice cream it sells, starting with the ingredients. Each container is stamped with a tracking number, which is stored in a relational database. Using OLAP software, salespeople can track how fast new types of ice cream gain popularity, and which remain stagnant, on an hourly basis. Matching such information with about 200 telephone calls and email messages the company receives weekly, managers can figure out which supplier's ingredients might have caused dissatisfaction with a certain product.

Employees who know very little about programming and report design are discovering that BI software is becoming easier and easier to use. Intelligent interfaces allow them to enter questions in free form or close to free form. A part of the application that is called the semantic layer parses the question, which has been written as if you were speaking to a person, translates it into instructions to the computer to access the appropriate data mart or the proper columns of a data warehouse, and produces the answer, which is a number of charts showing trends. In a few seconds a manager at Tesco's Lands' End store can find out which type of yoghurt was the company's bestseller across the country over the past six months. BI software has become so popular in large companies that Microsoft decided to integrate such software into its popular database management system, SQL Server.

More customer intelligence

CD TASK

Customer relationship management (CRM) has been discussed in several chapters. The major effort of most businesses, especially retail businesses, is to collect business intelligence about customers. Both data-mining and OLAP software are often integrated into CRM systems for this purpose. Since an increasing number of transactions are executed through the Web, managers can use data that are already in electronic form to analyse and strategize.

The challenge is to address the right customer, at the right time, with the right offer, instead of spending large amounts of money in mass marketing or covering numerous websites with ads. Many companies find that using only the data that they collect directly from consumers does not provide a full picture. They approach third parties, companies that specialize in collection and analysis of consumer data from multiple sources. The companies, such as DoubleClick and Engage, use cookies and spyware (explained in Chapter 7) to track web users' clickstreams.

By compiling billions of consumer clickstreams and creating behavioural models, these companies can determine individual consumers' interests from the sites they visited (what do they like?), the frequency of visits (are they loyal?), the times they surf (are they at work or at home?), and the number of times they click on advertisements or complete a transaction. Then, sites can display ads that match the typical interests at sites where the likely customers tend to visit. They can use software that will change the advertisement for each visitor by using cookies that identify the user.

Site Intelligence is a company based in Oxfordshire, UK. They have several high-profile customers for their Visitor Behaviour Information System (VBIS), with Tesco being a notable recent addition. Stuart Gregory, Tesco.com comments: 'We wanted a robust web analytics system that we could manage in-house and was flexible enough to meet the growing demands of all our business managers. VBIS from Site Intelligence will provide us with online marketing intelligence ensuring all our marketing campaigns are measured, evaluated and consistently improved.' VBIS will run on Tesco's own system, analysing customer data from Tesco.net, Tesco Personal Finance and Tesco.com and producing integrated reports which will hopefully lead to improved website design and hence increased customer conversion and retention.

Executive dashboards

dashboard A graphic presentation of organizational performance. Dashboards display in an easy-to-grasp visual manner metrics, trends and other helpful information that is the result of processing of business intelligence applications.

To make the use of BI tools convenient for executives, companies that develop BI tools create interfaces that help the executives to quickly grasp business situations. The popular name of such an interface is **dashboard**, because it looks something like a car dashboard. Car dashboards provide information in the form of clock-like indicators and scales. BI dashboards use similar visual images. They include speedometer-like indicators for periodic revenues, profits and other financial information; plus bar charts, line graphs and other graphical presentations whenever the information can be presented graphically. Dashboards are available from Business Objects and XeoMatrix, providers of BI software. Similar dashboards are parts of BI tools offered by other vendors, including Siebel, Cognos and SAS. ERP vendors, such as SAP and Oracle, also include dashboards in their applications. Dashboards are often designed to quickly present predefined business metrics such as occupancy ratios in hotels and hospitals, or inventory turns in retail.

At TruServ, a member-owned hardware cooperative of 7000 retailers in 54 countries, executives use dashboards to monitor revenue and sales of individual items. Using the dashboard to conduct analyses, managers can pinpoint trends and changes over time and

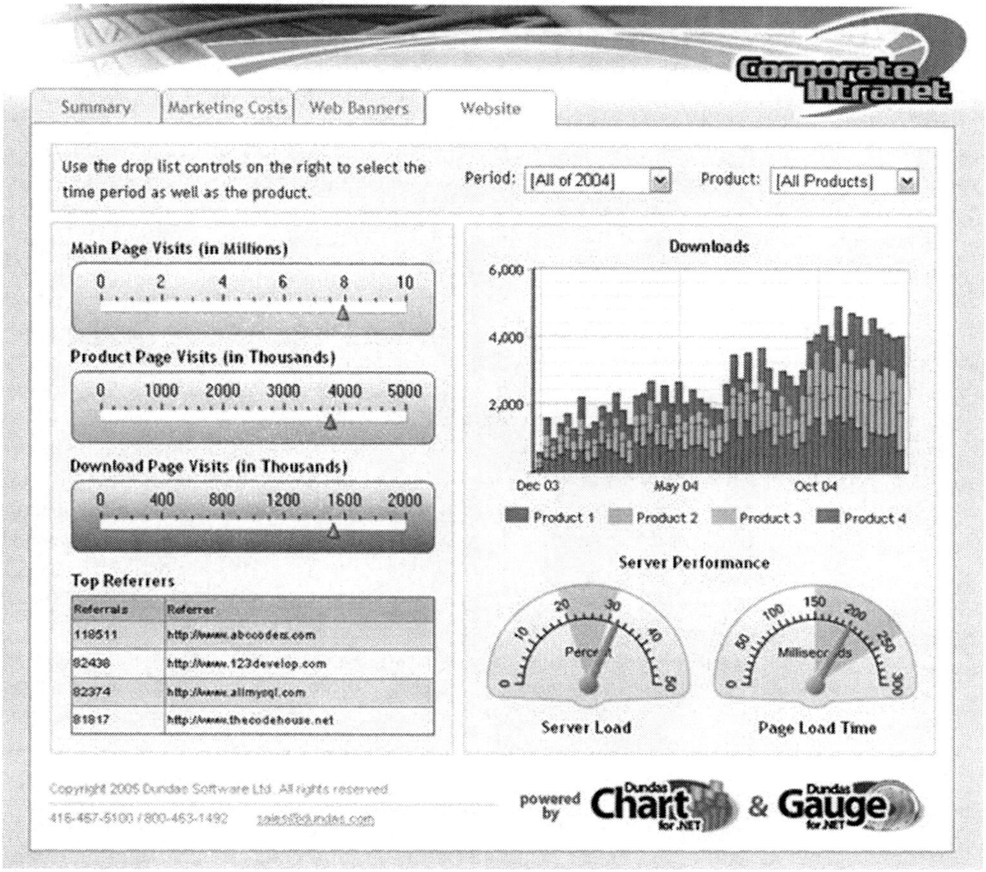

PHOTO SOURCE: © DUNDAS DATA VISUALIZATION INC. WWW.DUNDAS.COM

An example of an executive dashboard from Dundas.

receive alerts to help monitor, interpret and make decisions. They can better track inventory. In the past, 20 per cent of the cooperative's inventory was in the 'red zone'. Red zone inventory is either liquidated or sold for a loss after a promotion is ended. The executive dashboard was instrumental in helping TruServ reduce this loss inventory to 5 per cent.

Why you should... learn about BL and KM tools

Information technology has advanced from fast calculation machines to systems that produce useful information from structured data to software that turns unstructured information into knowledge. Knowing how to use BI tools will help you to independently produce highly useful information from data warehouses and other large data sources. In your work you will also need to use other peoples' knowledge. Much of this knowledge exists in the recorded work and in the minds of colleagues and experts outside your organization. Knowing how to use these tools will help you as well as others perform better. As a knowledge worker you will be able not only to use your own, limited knowledge but also augment it with the experiences of other people.

Knowledge management

Imagine you work for a consulting firm. Your supervisor assigns you to a new client. As a smart professional, the first thing you want to check is whether your firm has had previous experience with this client and what knowledge has been accumulated about the experience. You heard that two ex-employees had contact with this client several years ago. It would be great to discuss it with them, but they are gone. Their knowledge was available to the firm, but it no longer is, because it is not recorded anywhere. The data recorded about the financial transactions with this client cannot provide the knowledge you are seeking: How easy or difficult was the interaction with the client's executives? What are the strengths and weaknesses of that organization? In engineering companies, engineers might want to see if colleagues have already encountered a problem they are trying to solve, and what the solution to that problem was then. IT professionals might want to know if their colleagues have encountered a similar repeating failure with a network management system.

An organization can learn much about its customers, sellers and itself by mining data warehouses and using OLAP software, but such techniques still do not satisfy another important challenge: how to manage knowledge, expertise that is created within and outside the organization. As discussed in Chapter 9, expertise in narrow domains can be programmed in expert systems. However, there is much more knowledge that organizations would like to garner and manage. Effective management of knowledge can help both employees and customers.

knowledge management The combination of activities involved in gathering, sharing, analysing and disseminating knowledge to improve an organization's performance.

Samuel Johnson, the author of an early English dictionary, said that one type of knowledge is what we know about a subject, and the other type is knowing where to find information about the subject. The purpose of knowledge management is mainly to gain the second type of knowledge. **Knowledge management** is the combination of activities involved in gathering, organizing, sharing, analysing and disseminating knowledge to improve an organization's performance.

Information that can be gleaned from stored data is knowledge, but there is much more knowledge that organizations would like to store that they currently do not. The knowledge that is not maintained in information systems is typically of the type that cannot be extracted from readily captured data at websites or other electronic means of transactions. It is accumulated through experience. Much of it is kept in people's minds, on paper notes, on discussion transcripts and in other places that are not readily accessible to a company's employees. Therefore, knowledge management is a great challenge. Knowledge management is the attempt by organizations to put procedures and technologies in place to do the following:

CD TASK

- Transfer individual knowledge into databases.
- Filter and separate the most relevant knowledge.

Industry SNAPSHOT

Chemical mining

By some estimates, 85 per cent of recorded corporate knowledge is in text files. Using a software tool called ClearResearch from Clear Forest Corp., the research staff at Dow Chemical Co. has extracted useful information from various unstructured sources: abstracts of chemical patents registered over the past century, published research articles and the company's own files. The software has reduced the time it takes Dow's researchers to decide what they need to read.

SOURCE: D. Robb, 'Text Mining Tools Take on Unstructured Data', Computerworld (www.computerworld.com), 21 June 2004

- Organize that knowledge in databases that allow employees easy access to it or that 'push' specific knowledge to employees based on prespecified needs.

Knowledge management (KM) software facilitates these activities. As the cost of storage media continues to decrease and database management packages are increasingly more sophisticated and affordable, storage and organization of unstructured information have become less of a challenge. The more difficult issue is development of tools that address the third challenge: quickly finding the most relevant information for solving problems.

Capturing and sorting organizational knowledge

The research company IDC argues that almost half of the work that *knowledge workers* do in organizations has already been done, at least partially. This work includes researching a certain subject, preparing a report and providing information as part of a consulting contract. It estimated that labour worth 2000–3600 euro per knowledge worker is wasted annually because workers try to solve the same problem that other workers have already solved. Organizations could save this duplication, or replication, by collecting and organizing knowledge that is gained by members of the organization.

To transfer knowledge into manageable online resources, some companies require workers to create reports of their findings. Others, especially consulting firms, require their employees to create reports about sessions with clients. However organizations collect information, the results might be several terabytes of potential knowledge, but the challenge for employees is to know how to find answers to specific questions. Some software tools have been developed to help.

Electronic Data Systems Corp. (EDS), an IT consulting firm, requires all of its 130,000 employees to fill out an online questionnaire about their activities once per year. With 20,000 of these employees EDS conducts surveys three times per year. Some of the questions provide multiple-choice answers, which make the input structured and easy to sort and analyse, but some of the most valuable input is in the form of free text. In the past, this part was forwarded to managers who learned and drew conclusions from it. Now, the company uses an automated system, PolyAnalyst from Megaputer Intelligence, Inc., to sort the text information and create links between topics.

Motorola, the giant manufacturer of communications equipment, has 4 terabytes of data managed by a knowledge management application. The application enabled engineers to query this huge resource. Still, unless a worker knew exactly where the proper data was or the names of people who were on a team that had solved the problem at hand, the worker could not find a proper answer. Motorola decided to implement Watson, an application developed by Intellext. Watson is installed on employees' PCs. It is embedded in Microsoft Word, PowerPoint and Outlook. It analyses an employee's document as it is being written, creates an automatic query about the subject, reaches out into the KM program, and pulls information that might be applicable to the task at hand.

Employee knowledge networks

While some tools build knowledge bases and help employees access them, others put the emphasis on directing employees to other employees who have a certain expertise. The advantage of this approach is that an expert can provide expertise that has not been captured in information systems (see Figure 10.2). Large companies, especially multisite ones, often waste money because employees in one organizational unit are not aware of the experience of employees in another unit. For example, one energy company spent €1 million on a product designed to work on oil rigs to prevent sediment from falling into wells. When the equipment was installed, it failed. The executives of another unit decided to purchase the same

Figure 10.2 Employee knowledge network

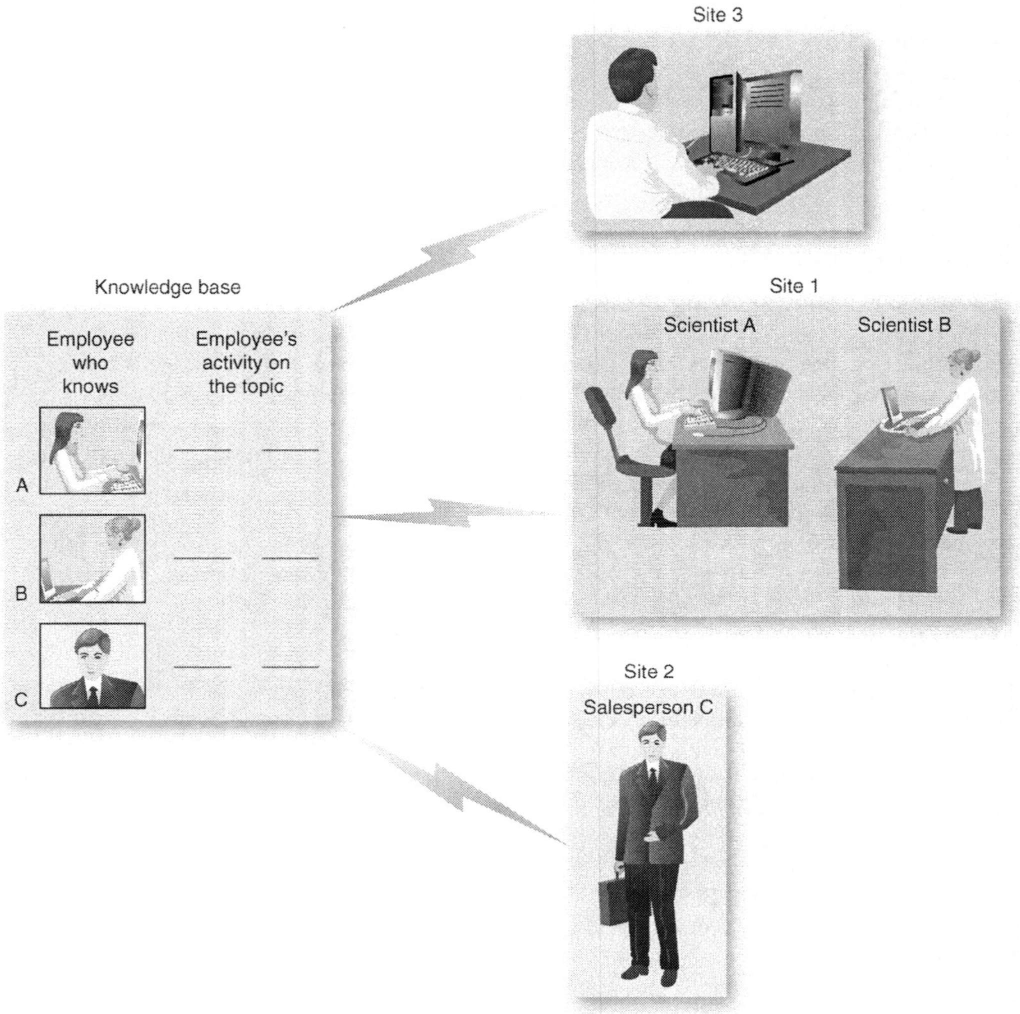

equipment, which, not surprisingly, failed in the other location. Then a third unit, elsewhere, purchased the equipment, which also failed. While one can justify the loss of the first €1 million as legitimate business expense in the course of trying a product, the other €2 million was lost because decision-makers did not know that the equipment had already been tried and failed. To alleviate similar problems, some software companies, such as Tacit Systems Inc., AskMe Corporation, Participate Systems Inc. and Entopia Inc., have developed **employee knowledge networks**, tools that facilitate knowledge-sharing through intranets. Recall that an intranet uses web technologies to link employees of the same organization.

employee knowledge network Software that facilitates search of relevant knowledge within an organization. The software points an employee with a need for certain information or expertise to co-workers who might have such information or expertise.

Tacit Systems' ActiveNet tool continuously processes email, documents and other business communications and automatically 'discovers' each employee's work focus, expertise and business relationships. The tool 'mines' this unstructured data to build a profile of each employee in terms of topics and interests. The goal is to ensure that two people who might benefit from creating a connection in a workplace

Ethical and Societal ISSUES

Knowledge and globalization

In the Middle Ages, Venice considered its expertise in making glassware not only a business trade secret but also a state secret. Divulging glassmaking knowledge to anyone outside the republic of Venice was punishable by death, because much of the state's economy depended on excluding other states and countries from such knowledge. Venice, like other states in that era, would never 'offshore' any of the work to another country. Nowadays, matters are completely different. What was expertise a year ago has become routine work this year and will become automated next year. At that point, the expertise value in the product will have diminished, and to make a profit the organization that used to have a comparative advantage in producing the product will have to use the least expensive labour available. It will offshore manufacturing to a factory in a country were labour is cheaper. The industry in the original country will lose jobs.

Information technology helps create knowledge but also expedites the turning of knowledge into routine, automated processes that can be carried out elsewhere. IT also expedites the transfer of knowledge from countries that created it to countries that can quickly use it. Software used to be developed almost exclusively in the United States and Europe. A growing amount of the software is now developed in India and China. The programmers' expertise is similar, but the wages earned by programmers in those two countries are a fraction of what US or European programmers would be paid for the same work. This is a pivotal element in what is called *globalization* – moving from national economies to a global economy. Is this bad for the US and Europe and good only for countries such as India and China?

BI and KM software is developed mainly in the West, that is the United States, Germany and the United Kingdom. However, these systems are sold anywhere and can help companies in other countries compete with companies in those 'developed' countries. This puts developing countries in a position to gain knowledge much faster than before and compete better. Now, the competition is not only in the manufacturing and service areas but also in research and development.

In the West, some observers view the issue in the following light: 'We used to be a world leader in manufacturing, but other countries now have a comparative advantage in manufacturing, and their workers have taken the jobs that our labourers used to perform. For some time we have had an advantage in providing services, but many of these services are now provided over the Internet and telephone lines by workers in other countries, so the service sector's advantage has diminished. We are still great in innovation and creation of know-how, but we are starting to see this advantage slipping away, too. And when other countries beat us in creation of knowledge, what's left with which to compete?'

Should governments take measures – legal or otherwise – that protect their economic advantages? Should they penalize companies that offshore manufacturing jobs? Should they forbid the sale of know-how to other countries? Should they adopt the Venetian model? Or, should we look at the world as one large economy where each worker and each organization should compete for a piece of the pie regardless of national borders, so that consumers everywhere can enjoy products of the highest quality for the lowest price possible?

do so, so that one can learn from the experience of another about a specific issue. By analysing email and documents, the tool extracts the employee's interests and solutions to problems, and that information is added to the employee's profile. Other employees who seek advice can access the profile, but they cannot see the original email or document created by the employee. This ensures uninhibited brainstorming and communication.

AskMe's software also detects and captures keywords from email and documents created by employees. It creates a knowledge base that holds the names of employees and their interests. An employee can access a web page at which the employee enters a free-form question. The software responds by listing the names of other employees who have created email, text documents or presentations on the subject, and the topics of their work. The employee can view the activity profiles of these people, and then contact them, via the website, by email, instant messages or paging. The responder can use the same website to respond and attach documents that might help the enquirer. AskMe's tool captures the communication, including attached documents, and adds them to the knowledge base. (Note that in this context the knowledge base is not organized as the knowledge bases in expert systems are.)

Of course this automatic capture of details on employees' expertise and knowledge raises ethical issues. Staff may not wish to share their information with other employees. It may be that they are not as involved in the area as they once were and have moved on to other things. Should it be up to the individuals to declare themselves as 'an expert'? More fundamentally, any system that trawls through the emails of employees is in danger of falling foul of privacy laws. If workers are to be allowed to send personal emails, during or outside working hours, will these emails be part of the analysis?

CD TASK

Knowledge from the Web

Consumers keep posting their opinions on products and services on the Web. Some do so at the site of the seller, others at general product evaluation sites such as epinions.com, and some on blogs. By some estimates consumer opinions are expressed in more than 550 billion web pages. This information is difficult to locate and highly unstructured. If organizations could distil knowledge from it they could learn much more than they do from conducting market research studies, such as focus groups, both about their own products and those sold by competitors.

Some companies have developed software tools that search for such information and derive valuable business knowledge from it. For example, Accenture Technology Labs, the

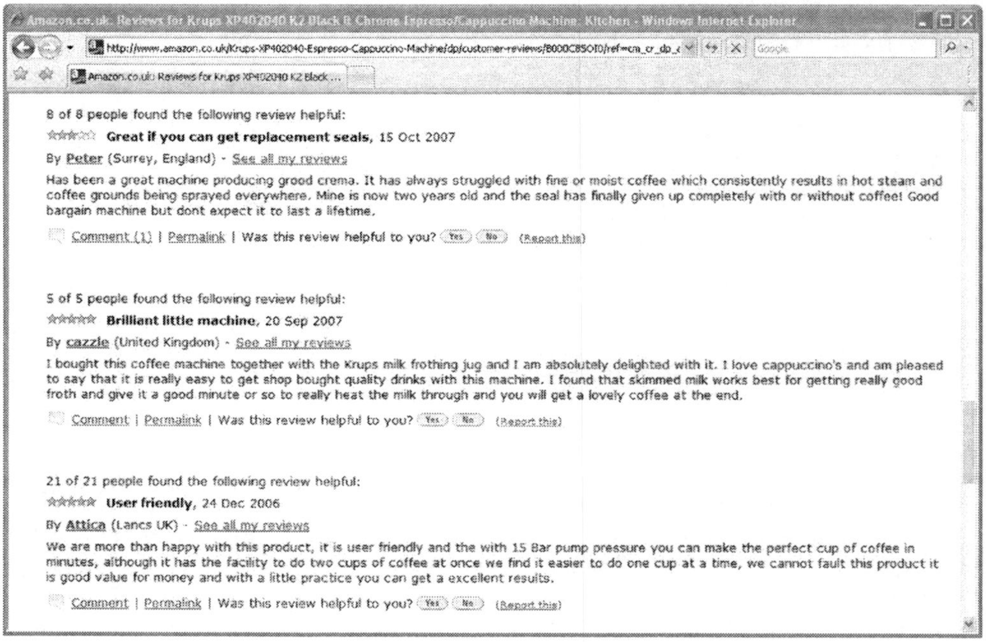

Consumer reviews of a coffee machine on Amazon UK.

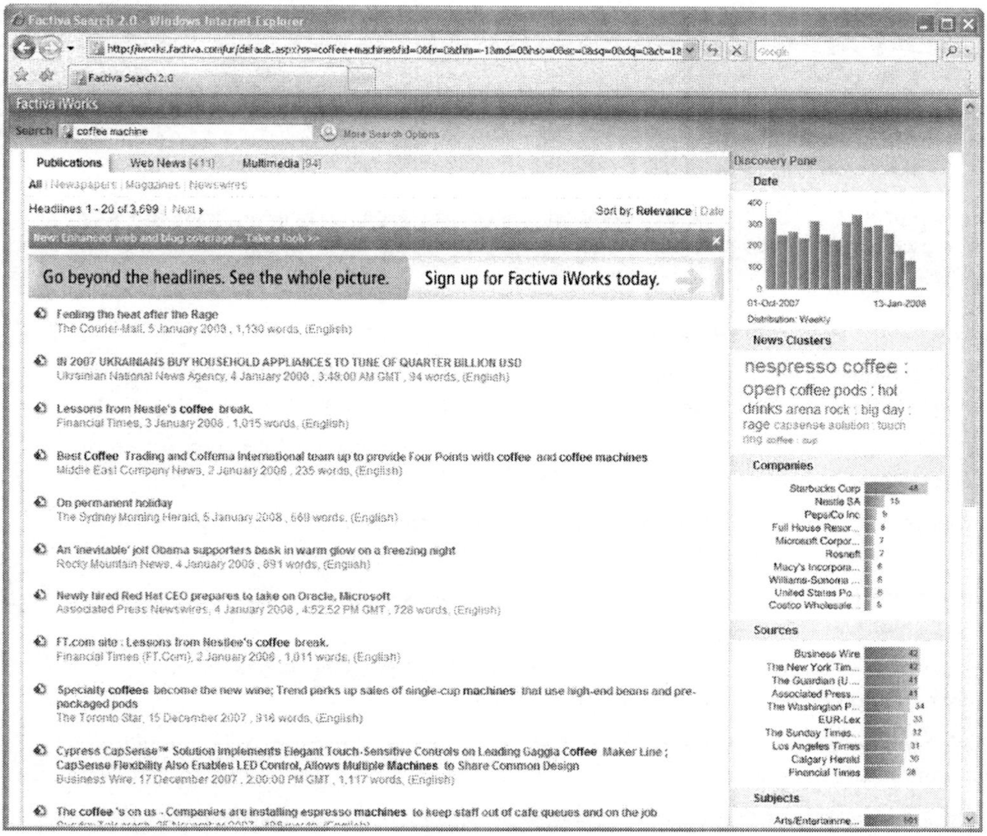

Factiva's aggregation of material on the same coffee machine reviewed by consumers on Amazon UK.

technology research and development unit of the consulting firm Accenture, developed Online Audience Analysis. The tool searches thousands of websites daily and retrieves predetermined information about specific products and services. It then uses data-mining techniques to help organizations understand what consumers are saying about corporate brands and products.

Factiva, a subsidiary of Dow Jones & Reuters, promotes a software tool by the same name. Factiva, accessible through a website, gathers information online from over 9000 sources – newspapers, journals, market data and newswires – information that amounts to millions of documents. About 60 per cent of the information is not accessible to the general public. It screens every piece of new information that is posted at any of these websites for information specified by a subscribing organization. The search can be more tailored and specific than searches performed through free search engines such as Google or Yahoo! The software helps organizations add to their knowledge base, especially in terms of what others say about their products and services. The tool takes into account factors such as the industry and context in which an enquirer works to select and deliver the proper information. For example, a key word such as 'apple' means one thing to an employee of a hardware or software organization and something completely different to an employee in agriculture or a supermarket chain.

SUMMARY

Business intelligence (BI) is any information about the organization, its customers and its suppliers that can help firms make decisions. In recent years organizations have implemented a growing number of increasingly sophisticated BI software tools.

Data mining is the process of selecting, exploring and modelling large amounts of data to discover previously unknown relationships that can support decision-making. Data mining helps sequence analysis, classification, clustering and forecasting.

Data mining is useful in such activities as predicting customer behaviour and detecting fraud.

Online analytical processing (OLAP) helps users peruse two-dimensional tables created from data that are usually stored in data warehouses. OLAP applications are said to provide a virtual cube that the user can rotate from one table to another.

OLAP either uses dimensional databases or calculates desired tables on the fly.

OLAP facilitates drilling down, moving from a broad view of information to increasingly detailed information about a narrow aspect of the business.

Executive dashboards interface with BI software tools to help users quickly receive information such as business metrics.

Knowledge management involves gathering, organizing, sharing, analysing and disseminating knowledge that can improve an organization's performance.

The main challenge in knowledge management is identifying and classifying useful information to be gleaned from unstructured sources.

Most unstructured knowledge is textual, both inside an organization and in files available to the public on the Web.

Employee knowledge networks are software tools that help employees find other employees who have expertise in certain areas of enquiry.

One important element of knowledge management is auto-categorization, the automatic classification of information. Auto-categorization has been used in online customer support web pages to reduce the labour involved in helping customers solve problems.

URBAN SCENE REVISITED

Lucy Slade sees great potential in the use of information systems in the gathering of business intelligence

What would you do?

Lucy has asked for a report on how the existing information systems can be used to supply meaningful business intelligence and what needs to be in place to improve on this situation. What might be included in such a report?

New perspectives

Knowledge management systems are being implemented in the retail industry for a variety of tasks. Search the Web for current and potential uses of knowledge management in retail. How prevalent do you think they will become? Prepare to discuss your findings in class.

Review questions

1 What is business intelligence?

2 What is OLAP, and why is it often associated with visual cubes?

3 What is the advantage of using a dimensional database rather than on-the-fly processing in OLAP?

4 Why is online analytical processing usually conducted on warehoused data or dimensional databases rather than on data in transactional databases?

5 What is 'drilling down'?

6 What are data-mining techniques expected to find in the huge data warehouses that they scour?

7 What is knowledge, and how does it differ from other information?

8 In general, what is the purpose of knowledge management in organizations?

9 What is the purpose of employee knowledge networks?

10 What is the benefit of tools that direct employees to experts rather than to stored knowledge?

11 Context is a major factor when using tools to glean knowledge from web sources. How so?

12 Data mining helps mainly in four ways: sequence analysis, classification, clustering and forecasting. Data mining helps determine whether a person has committed fraud. Which of the four types of analysis help do that? Explain why.

13 The Web is a huge resource from which almost any organization could derive knowledge, yet very few do. What is the major challenge?

Discussion questions

1 What does intelligence mean? Do you accept the use of the word in 'business intelligence software tools', or do you think the use of this word is exaggerated compared with what these tools provide?

2 You are an executive for a large retail chain. Your IT professionals use data-mining software. They tell you of the following relationship the software found: middle-aged single men tend to purchase personal grooming products and light bulbs together. Should you assign employees to research the reason for this? What should you do?

3 Employee knowledge network software keeps tabs of much of what employees create on their computers and all the email they send. As an employee, would you be comfortable with such software? Why or why not?

4 The term 'business intelligence' has been used by IT professionals to mean many different things. What might be the reason for this?

5 Can businesses use free search engines such as Google and Yahoo! to efficiently gather useful knowledge for better decision-making?

6 Recall the discussion of expert systems in Chapter 9. In what sense are employee knowledge networks similar to expert systems and in what sense are they different?

7 Consider Amazon.com's data-mining software, which infers demographic information about the recipients of gifts. Is letting software infer demographics less of an invasion of privacy than questionnaires or other forms of direct questioning? Is such inference more effective in obtaining customer information? Why or why not?

8 Some consumer advocates argue that using services such as Return Exchange (see the Industry Snapshot 'Dealing with the Devil') violate privacy, because legitimate customers who make multiple returns might be denied a legitimate right to return merchandise. The sore point is over disclosing the criteria used to determine who is probably engaged in fraud. Do you agree with this resentment, or do you think it is legitimate to use such a practice? What could be the motivation not to disclose the criteria?

9 Companies would like to have systems that would allow them to store all the knowledge that their employees have accumulated. Do you expect that such systems will exist in your lifetime? Why or why not?

10 Suppose a company found a way to debrief you at the end of each working day and store all that you have learned and experienced during the day in an information system. Would you be comfortable with this? Why or why not?

Tutorial activities

1 Search the Web for a story on an organization that successfully used data-mining techniques. Type a four- to five-page paper in which you describe what the software was able to do for the organization and how the results benefited the organization. Emphasize what information the organization now has that could not be obtained without data-mining techniques.

2 Write a one-page report explaining what one can do with an OLAP application that cannot be done with the same data in a spreadsheet or a relational database. Give at least two examples.

3 Go to www.fedscope.opm.gov. Produce the following tables for the latest year for which data is available:

a) Number of US federal employees by category size (large, medium, small) by country of service.

b) Number of US federal employees by category size, only for employees working in Australia.

c) Number of US federal employees by department within the *large* agency category, only for employees working in Australia.

Is the sequence in which you produced the three tables considered drilling down? Explain why or why not.

4 Team up with another student. Select a specific company and write a report about its knowledge management needs. Start with a description of the activities that take place. List the types of employees who could benefit from access to documented expertise. Say which expertise you would take from internal sources and which from external sources. Give examples of knowledge that the company could use.

5 Team up with two other students. The team is to prepare a plan for The Researcher Connection, an employee knowledge network, to help the staff at your institution to develop research ideas and conduct their research. List the elements of your proposed system and

convince potential users how it will help them (1) find relevant literature on a research subject, (2) learn who in the institution has done a similar study, (3) learn who in the institution would be interested in collaborating in the research, and (4) perform any other activity that is involved in conducting research and publishing the resultant article. Explain which of the resources to be used in the system already exist and will only need to be tapped (and how).

Companion CD questions

1. Think of a situation in your company or industry in which data mining could be useful. Create a database and include fields that can be used for knowledge management.
2. Assume you are setting up a website to sell products. What would you consider when setting up the website so that you can effectively mine the data you get through it?

Video questions

1. What data do you think are collected during e-voting?
2. Do some research on the current state of electronic voting. Can the data collected during electronic voting be mined?

From ideas to application
REAL CASES

Case study **10.1**

Targeting the Center Parcs market

Center Parcs is a well known brand of European holiday villages that attract visitors to its basic but comfortable bungalows set in woodland, surrounded by various sport and leisure activities and centred around a domed swimming pool that negates any problems with the uncertain weather.

Center Parcs is jointly owned by Center Parcs UK and Center Parcs Europe. The UK villages are owned and operated by Center Parcs UK whilst all other villages in the Netherlands, Belgium, Germany and France are owned and operated by Center Parcs Europe. The European operation attracts more than 3 million visitors per year and generates about 450 million euro. Part of this success comes from the excellent average occupancy of 90 per cent for its bungalows. However, traditionally this came at a significant cost. Twice a year the company would cover the continent with 5 million brochures. As technology and e-business director for the company, Richard Verhoff commented, 'We were hurt badly by mailing and printing costs.'

The technology-based solution was to reduce the number of mailings while at the same time make them better targeted. Potential customers needed to receive the right brochure at the right time. For example,

PHOTO SOURCE: © CENTER PARCS

customers are more likely to book into a village nearer to home to avoid excessive driving time. Families prefer villages with plenty of activities for their children whereas older clients prefer quieter surroundings. Timing is vitally important. The company need the brochure to drop through the letter box just as the customer is thinking about sorting out the next holiday. All of these points are fairly fundamental. The problem is identifying the customer with the criteria so that the right brochure could be sent to the right person at the right time. A software solution was needed and Center Parcs found it in PredictiveMarketing, which uses the company's customer database to rank prospects by the likelihood that they will respond to a particular campaign. Basically the package is predicting the future. It is using its algorithms to produce a score and the same principle can be used in other spheres of business – will a customer make a repeat purchase, how effective is a particular product in meeting customer needs?

As far as Center Parcs is concerned, the results speak for themselves. For example, in Germany occupancy has increased by 10 per cent even though the number of mailings has dropped from 2 million to 450,000.

Historical data are a massive resource for Center Parcs and yet at the same time a potential headache. Over the 20 European villages and 38 years of historical data there are vast numbers of business decisions that can be made based on this mass of data, but this is only possible with significant investment in hardware to store and process the data as well as software to extract and transform the data and then supply managers with timely, focused reports. The latest village being built in Reims, France, uses RFID technology to recognize the location of visitors across the whole of the park, adding to the storage headache but also increasing the potential for analysis.

Thinking about the case

1 The predictive analysis software referred to above deals only with mailings about mainland European resorts. Could the operation be extended to include Center Parcs UK? Could it be extended to cover other predictions of customer behaviour?

2 Is there a point at which a company can have too much data?

SOURCE: Linda More, 'Holiday resort speeds data processing', *Computing*, 29 March 2007 and Larry Stevens, 'Predictive Analytics Lets Companies See into the Future', *PC Magazine*, 23 August 2006, http://www.cioinsight.com/print_article2/0,1217,a=186926,00.asp

Case study **10.2**

UpMyStreet.com

BY MARTIN RICH

How do you find out about an area that you are thinking about moving to? You can discover all manner of practical information, but on its own that doesn't convey the true character of an area. For that, you really need what is termed *tacit* knowledge – a concept that was identified many years ago by Michael Polanyi, who coined the aphorism 'We know more than we can say.' This has acquired a new relevance in recent years because of the availability of technology that can store and disseminate vast amounts of information.

UpMyStreet.com is one source of information about particular areas in the UK. It was set up in 1998, by Aztec Internet (a specialist Internet advertising consultancy) to provide information about local areas in the UK. Users can type in a postcode, or the name of a town, and see a range of background information about the location. Postcodes are particularly useful here, because in residential areas they typically refer to a group of about 50 addresses, and it is possible to build a detailed picture of the area covered by an specific postcode. For each area, the site provides a range of information: average house prices, local schools, elected representatives for local and national government. Also available is a 'neighbourhood profile', which is a brief summary of the typical demographics (age, number of people in a household and so on) and buying preferences (such as what sort of food people buy and where they buy it, how likely they are to spend money on cars and holidays, what newspapers they read and what television channels they watch), associated with the area. Such a range of information recognizes the complexity necessary to build a clear picture of an area.

These neighbourhood profiles are known as *ACORN* (a classification of residential neighbourhoods) profiles. The underlying data for these is gathered by CACI – a market research company – and updated annually: they have been available to marketing professionals for many years, but until the launch of UpMyStreet.com were not available to the general

PHOTO SOURCE: © UPMYSTREET WWW.UPMYSTREET.COM

The home page of UpMyStreet.com

public. This effect, that resources that were once expensive, and only available to specialists, are now accessible to anybody with a web browser, can be referred to as *universal access*. However, a corollary of universal access is that specialists typically have access to much more detailed and comprehensive information than is available to the public.

In practice, the ACORN classifications can be inaccurate: there are only about 50 profiles to choose from, and areas can change more rapidly than the classifications can be updated. In an area where a lot of new building, or refurbishment, is taking place, very expensive new properties might be built very close to older and cheaper housing. Small as they are, individual postcode areas often include a mix of demographics. For instance, a suburban residential area might include both families with young children and older, retired people. An area with low housing costs might include a mixture of people in low-paid occupations, students and those in potentially high-earning jobs but at the start of their career. The site includes a warning not to read too much into the neighbourhood profiles. In practice, professional market researchers with access to huge amounts of data can still build a much more accurate picture of a particular consumer's preferences than could be inferred from the data available through UpMyStreet.com.

From a strategic viewpoint, UpMyStreet.com's purpose has changed over the years. Initially it was created by Aztec Internet, as much as a showpiece for their abilities to create a database as for anything else. By 2003, its financial viability appeared to be in doubt: it was clearly a good idea and had caught the public's imagination but, as with many Internet business ideas, it was unclear how the site could generate any income. It was then acquired by uSwitch.com – a price comparison site specializing in the energy sector, where customers were offered a choice of suppliers as a result of deregulation during the 1990s. Price comparison websites can be regarded as another example of universal access, since in the past it would have been a painstaking task to check and compare prices from many different suppliers. Such sites have become particularly important in the areas of consumer goods, and personal finance where it is often difficult to evaluate different products effectively. uSwitch.com makes money by taking commission payments from some energy suppliers. While originally privately owned, uSwitch.com was acquired by E. W. Scripps, a large American media company, in 2006.

Since acquisition by uSwitch.com, the scope of the UpMyStreet.com website has expanded. One noteworthy feature has been the growth of the discussion groups, known on this site as 'conversations'. These conversations provide more tacit knowledge about an area – because knowing what local people are talking about is one source of knowledge – and they also add *user-generated content* to the site. Another is that actual sold house prices are available, as well as the average prices for an area that have always been shown on the site. To view sold house prices, or to contribute to conversations, users have to register. In this way UpMyStreet.com offers one range of information to anybody browsing the site, and another, broader range of information and services to anybody who wishes to register. Further services which have been added recently also depend on users who register. In particular, the site includes a 'FindMyNearest' service which tells users details of businesses and services, such as plumbers and restaurants, close to a particular address. This has recently been extended to allow registered users to rate these businesses – another example of user-generated content.

How does UpMyStreet.com make money? Two aspects to the business have distinct revenue streams. One is advertising; because the site attracts users who are interested in a particular geographical location, it can carry advertising that is accurately targeted at people in that location. Moreover, the business has developed a sophisticated range of models for advertising, notably through sponsorship of parts of the site. Not all of these are popular with users: for instance some advertisers use pop-up windows which can be irritating, and are often suppressed by pop-up blockers in web browsers. Another revenue stream arises from the fact that UpMyStreet.com provides paid services for businesses, in parallel with offering free services to individuals. For example, they can provide content which can be included in another website, or they can provide specialist reports on an area tailored to a business's particular interests.

Case study questions

1. There are now many discussion areas on the Internet where people can carry out the sort of 'conversations' offered by UpMyStreet.com. How might UpMyStreet.com conversations be differentiated from other discussion areas?
2. Registration for UpMyStreet.com is free. Why might the site wish to persuade people to register, even if they don't directly generate an income for the site?
3. What sort of knowledge might UpMyStreet.com be able to gather about the people who register to use the site, and how might this be useful to the business?
4. What other tacit knowledge might be useful to people thinking of moving to an area, or setting up business in an area, and how could a site such as this help them to acquire this knowledge?
5. What other examples of universal access to knowledge through the Web can you think of, and how do they help with the acquisition and distribution of knowledge?

SOURCES: E-business briefing (2003), http://www.e-consultancy.com/news-blog/newsletter/view.asp?id=640; *New media age:* 'UpMyStreet relaunches with major brands in new ad deals'; W. Pavia, 'Property website reveals what you're really worth,' *The Times*, 4 February 2006

silicon.com

Case study **10.3**

Compliance made easy

BY DANNY BRADBURY

Business intelligence isn't just about enhancing performance, says Danny Bradbury – it can help your company keep the regulators happy, too.

Business intelligence (BI) – sophisticated analysis of corporate data – is often seen as a way to improve performance and increase revenue. But with industry regulators clamping down on companies, some are starting to use the technology to prove their compliance – and in some cases, to hone it.

Alison Whitby, business intelligence practice head at Diagonal Consulting, says: 'Regulations like Sarbanes-Oxley have companies realizing that they're managing their businesses on very suggestive data. So the general push for those companies has been to demonstrate that they have more rigour in terms of their budgeting process and forecasting system.' Many compliance experts are seeing BI as a way to hone that.

Take Richard Price, for example. The head of risk at the Chelsea Building Society used BI software to help tackle his Basel II banking requirements. The regulations place strict requirements on the mitigation of financial risk through judicious planning. He found himself having to marry concise business data with less tangible information for forward-planning purposes. The evidence of such planning can run into reports of up to a hundred pages for a moderately sized financial institution like his, he says.

Much of the focus with Basel II reporting has been on managing credit risk, explains Price. His company has had to think about issues such as feeding credit risk data into solvency calculations, which measure how much capital you have against how much capital you should have to cover your lending.

He explains: 'From an institution's point of view, that high-level understanding – how much capital you're supposed to have – is where business intelligence comes in.' That kind of planning requires extensive what-if analysis, he says: 'An important consideration is how you'll manage under conditions of stress. If we had another severe recession, how would we manage our capital?'

The Chelsea Building Society already had a business intelligence system in place from vendor Infor, which it had used to build a financial model of the business over roughly 15 years. The system includes its own programming language which makes it easier to handle complex analyses, Price says.

Financial data are extracted from a mainframe-based data warehouse, and married with other inputs. He says: 'The most important things that go in are the assumptions from heads of management about things like volumes or severity of house price falls. It's easy to produce actual information but it's harder to produce a coherent forecast.'

One of the most significant implementation problems from a compliance perspective is retaining all the documentation surrounding the report, Price explains. The report, published in a format called the Internal Capital Adequacy Assessment Process, has to be retained for six years.

Price says: 'It's hundreds of megabytes of data and you have to do it annually or as business

A UK branch of the Chelsea Building Society

PHOTO SOURCE: © PHOTOFUSION PICTURE LIBRARY/ALAMY

conditions dictate. Most businesses are updating their business plans as they go through the year.' Consequently many finance institutions will present two or three of these reports per year at least.

Conducting analytics for forward-looking statements is one way to meet compliance requirements, but regulators also need companies to look backwards.

BI can help with auditing too. Diagonal's Whitby explains: 'Normally compliance is ensuring that you have the right security around your data. BI systems now can not only set up different security levels but can even personalize them.' Pieces of information can be associated with specific individuals, for example, which enables you to more easily build an audit trail of events and transactions leading to a particular business event.

However, Todd Paoletti, director of client self-service solutions at BI vendor Actuate, argues that for companies to build effective audit trails using business intelligence, a clear path must be defined between the report, the business application and the source data.

Paoletti says: 'You must avoid data being "cleansed" into a different or inconsistent format with the original source, or being out of date.' One way to avoid this is to create a middleware layer between the reporting application and the disparate underlying data sources.

Ideally you will use existing performance management tools to help satisfy your compliance reporting requirements, argues Cate Zavod, who works in solutions marketing at Actuate. Reusing parts of existing BI systems enables you to guarantee that the same performance management information will be used for compliance purposes but it will also prepare you for future regulatory impact.

Zavod explains: 'There are thousands of regulatory issues pummelling the financial services industry across the world today. So the more object-oriented your approach in developing these reports and applications, obviously the more reusable they will be, "future proofing" you for the next one that comes down the pipe.'

While some companies use business intelligence tools for reporting to the regulators, others use them operationally to help meet compliance requirements on a day-to-day basis.

Diagonal's Whitby suggests that companies could use alerting systems that can be triggered when certain thresholds are met, as a way of policing internal controls. In a financial services setting, alerts could be set to prevent traders over-extending their position, for example.

Whitby says: 'Rather than having to read through the data every week, the systems push information a lot more. So you can set it up to say that you have typical traffic-light-type coding that says this is a trend we don't like, take action.' The next stage is to trigger workflow that will escalate the problem and stop it becoming a regulatory issue, she adds.

Business intelligence software is already used in many organizations to monitor effectiveness, so it seems like a no-brainer to extend that to keeping a regulatory eye on your operation – and reporting on it after the event.

Thinking about the case

1 The idea of 'future proofing' applications is put forward to deal with legal compliance issues. Can the same principle be applied to business intelligence needs for strategic decisions?

2 It is easy to see the advantage of using sophisticated BI software for compliance issues in a large enterprise. Is the same true for a small to medium enterprise?

Chapter 10

Risks, security and disaster recovery

LEARNING OBJECTIVES

As the use of computer-based information systems has spread, so has the threat to the integrity of data and the reliability of information. Organizations must deal seriously with the risks of both natural and manmade menaces. A computer expert once noted: 'The only truly secure system is powered off, cast in a block of concrete, and sealed in a lead room with armed guards. And even then I have my doubts.' Indeed, there is no way to fully secure an information system against every potential mishap, but there are ways to significantly reduce risks and recover losses.

When you finish this chapter, you will be able to:

Describe the primary goals of information security.

Enumerate the main types of risks to information systems.

List the various types of attacks on networked systems.

Describe the types of controls required to ensure the integrity of data entry and processing and uninterrupted e-commerce.

Describe the various kinds of security measures that can be taken to protect data and ISs.

Outline the principles of developing a recovery plan.

Explain the economic aspects of information security.

WORLDWIDE HOST

BATTLING BACK FROM ATTACKS

Worldwide Host's TripExpert.com site was fulfilling its promise. The site had been up for ten months now. CIO Michael Lloyd thought back to the end of the website's development project, when he had congratulated the General Data Systems staff for their hard work in getting the site up and running. At the time he did not pay much attention to the fact that the system was linked to a public network. Soon, he realized that such a link requires special consideration. The first event to draw his attention was a prank.

Website defaced

Michael's Webmaster, Susan O'Donnell, rushed into his office one day to report that someone had defaced the TripExpert home page. Since the site was so important to Worldwide, she checked it daily to ensure that it was running smoothly. She was shocked at what she saw on the site when she logged on in the morning. Someone had placed offensive images and language on the page, so she immediately took the site offline.

'It'll probably take us until early afternoon to get the site up again', she said. 'Fixing the home page takes only a few minutes, but ensuring that this doesn't happen again will take longer. We're working on it right now as our top priority.'

Michael responded, 'I'm coming down now to see for myself. We get transactions of about $90,000 an hour from that site. We've got to get it back online as soon as possible.'

Michael and Susan hurried down to the information centre, waved their badges in front of the radio ID scanner, entered their codes and opened the door. Inside, two IS staff members were working to clear the web page of the intruder's messages. All four worked furiously to find the hole that allowed the intruder to deface the home page. They quickly replaced the page with a backup copy. After several hours of hard work, they patched the server software with code that they believed would eliminate the security hole and brought the site back online.

Attacks continue

Five weeks after the defacement incident, Worldwide Host received a second blow: its site was among several that were hit with a denial-of-service attack. Requests were swamping Worldwide's servers. Michael and his IS security chief decided to disconnect the servers from the Net. Michael knew this meant a massive loss of profit, but there was nothing else he could do.

They turned the site on after an hour. Apparently, the attack had subsided, but Michael was worried that the attacker had also tried to damage databases or steal information.

'What is the extent of the problem, Jason? Did they breach any of our internal systems?'

'Doesn't look like it, but they were trying to get into our database. The secure servers that we use for transactions withstood the attempt to penetrate the customer database.'

Michael sighed with relief. 'Our security firm said that secure servers were critical to keeping our transactions private. Our system depends on the safety of our customers' information.'

'Well, the security people were right. I'll keep running my diagnostics on the damaged software', said Jason.

Irish online betting site PaddyPower.com suffered an extortive denial-of-service attack in early 2004.

PHOTO SOURCE: © STEPHEN SAKS PHOTOGRAPHY/ALAMY

'Susan is preparing a statement to post on the website to reassure our customers. We need to get that up fast. What else can we do to prevent denial-of-service attacks?'

'Since traffic load is the critical issue, we could add more servers to handle both the attacks and legitimate transactions. But the cost of those extra servers might be high.'

'Let's look into it. We need to keep our site online.'

Goals of information security

In June 2005, hackers invaded the databases of CardSystems Solutions, a company that processes credit-card transactions. Data from about 200,000 subscribers of MasterCard, Visa and other credit-card issuers were stolen. Had the hackers wanted, they could have used the same security breach to steal data from another 40 million accounts. Apparently, CardSystems Solutions did not comply with the data security policies that its clients required. The company paid a heavy toll: in July 2005 Visa and American Express stopped using the organization for their transaction processing. Visa and American Express gave merchants who used CardSystems' services ample time to switch to one of another several hundred companies that provide similar service.

As you have already seen, the development, implementation and maintenance of ISs constitute a large and growing part of the cost of doing business; protecting these resources is a primary concern. The increasing reliance on ISs, combined with their connection to the outside world through a public network, the Internet, makes securing corporate ISs increasingly challenging. The role of computer controls and security is to protect systems against accidental mishaps and intentional theft and corruption of data and application, as well as to help organizations ensure that their IT operations comply with the law and with expectations of employees and customers for privacy. The major goals of information security are to:

- Reduce the risk of systems and organizations ceasing operations.
- Maintain information confidentiality.
- Ensure the integrity and reliability of data resources.
- Ensure the uninterrupted availability of data resources and online operations.
- Ensure compliance with policies and laws regarding security and privacy.

To plan measures to support these goals, organizations must first be aware of the possible risks to their information resources, which include hardware, applications, data and networks; then, they must execute security measures to defend against those risks.

In recent years the European Union has introduced various directives and countries have passed several laws that set standards for the protection of patient and customer privacy and compliance with corporate internal controls. These laws have an important effect on securing information and, therefore, on securing information systems. However, corporate concern should not be focused only on complying with the law. It should ensure that information resources are secure to minimize situations that might practically take them out of business.

Risks to information systems

In recent years, especially because of the growth of online business, corporations have considered protection of their IS resources an increasingly important issue, for good reasons. **Downtime**, the time during which ISs or data are not available

downtime The unplanned period of time during which a system does not function.

in the course of conducting business, has become a dreaded situation for almost every business worldwide. The estimates by type of application for all industries are mind-boggling. According to a pan-European survey by Global Switch, a data centre provider, IT downtime costs businesses over €400,000 per hour.

Risks to hardware

While stories about damage to ISs by malicious Internet attacks grab headlines, the truth about risks to ISs is simply this: the number-one cause of systems downtime is hardware failure. Risks to hardware involve physical damage to computers, peripheral equipment and communications media. The major causes of such damage are natural disasters, blackouts and brownouts, and vandalism.

Natural disasters Natural disasters that pose a risk to ISs include fires, floods, earthquakes, hurricanes, tornadoes and lightning, which can destroy hardware, software or both, causing total or partial paralysis of systems or communications lines. Floodwater can ruin storage media and cause short circuits that burn delicate components such as microchips. Lightning and voltage surges cause tiny wires to melt and destroy circuitry. In addition, wildlife and human error occasionally destroy communication lines; animals gnaw cables, and farmers occasionally cut wires inadvertently while tending their crops.

blackouts and brownouts Periods of power loss or a significant fall in power. Such events may cause computers to stop working, or even damage them. Computers can be protected against these events by using proper equipment, such as UPS (uninterruptible power supply) systems.

Blackouts and brownouts Computers run on electricity. If power is disrupted, the computer and its peripheral devices cannot function, and the change in power supply can be very damaging to computer processes and storage. **Blackouts** are

PHOTO SOURCE: © COURTESY OF AMERICAN POWER CONVERSION CORP.

UPS units are a solution to extreme changes in voltage and can provide several minutes to several hours of back-up battery power.

total losses of electrical power. In brownouts, the voltage of the power decreases, or there are very short interruptions in the flow of power. Power failure might not only disrupt operations, but it can also cause irreparable damage to hardware. Occasional surges in voltage are equally harmful, because their impact on equipment is similar to that of lightning.

The popular way of handling brownouts is to connect a voltage regulator between computers and the electric network. A voltage regulator boosts or decreases voltage to smooth out drops or surges and maintains voltage within an acceptable tolerance.

To ensure against interruptions in power supply, organizations use uninterruptible power supply (UPS) systems, which provide an alternative power supply for a short time, as soon as a power network fails. The only practical measure against prolonged blackouts in a public electrical network is to maintain an alternative source of power, such as a generator that uses diesel or another fuel. Once the general power stops, the generator can kick in and produce the power needed for the computer system.

uninterruptible power supply (UPS) A device that provides an alternative power supply as soon as a power network fails.

Vandalism Vandalism occurs when human beings deliberately destroy computer systems. Bitter customers might damage ATMs, or disgruntled employees might destroy computer equipment out of fear that it will eliminate their jobs or simply to get even with their superiors. It is difficult to defend computers against vandalism. ATMs and other equipment that are accessible to the public are often encased in metal boxes, but someone with persistence can still cause severe damage. In the workplace, the best measure against vandalism is to allow access only to those who have a real need for the system. Sensitive equipment, such as servers, should be locked in a special room. Such rooms usually are well equipped with fire suppression systems and are air-conditioned, and thus protected also against environmental risks.

Risks to data and applications

The primary concern of any organization should be its data, because these are often a unique resource. Data collected over time can almost never be recollected the same way, and even when they can, the process would be too expensive and too time-consuming to recover the business from its loss. The concern for applications, especially if the applications are not tailor-made, should come second. All data and applications are susceptible to disruption, damage and theft. While the culprit in the destruction of hardware is often a natural disaster or power spike, the culprit in damage to software is almost always human.

Theft of information and identity theft

Sometimes the negligence of corporations and the careless use of technology, especially on public links to the Internet, create security 'holes' or vulnerabilities. In one case, a young man named Juju Jiang installed a program called Invisible KeyLogger Stealth on public-use computers such as those in use at airports or Internet cafes. Keystroke logging software records individual keystrokes. For one year, his software secretly recorded more than 450 usernames and passwords, which he used to access existing bank accounts and create new ones. Jiang was caught when he used an application called GoToMyPC. Subscribers to the GoToMyPC service can use an application by the same name to link to a PC from another PC and fully control the remote one as if they were sitting in front of it. Using the application, he remotely accessed and used one of his victims' PCs. Using the PC at home, this person noticed that the cursor was moving 'by itself'. The cursor opened files and subscribed to an online payment transfer service. Jiang pleaded guilty in court.

keystroke logging Automatically recording the keystrokes of a computer user. The logging is done by special software, usually surreptitiously with the intention of later using secret access codes.

In 2005 keystroke logging was put to work online on a massive scale by a criminal ring. As discussed in Chapter 7, spyware software is used for several purposes. This time spyware was used to install a keystroke logging application that recorded communication with the victim's bank, insurance company or other financial institutions. The collected data included credit-card details, usernames, passwords, instant messaging chat sessions and search terms. Some of the data were then saved in a file hosted on a server in the United States that had an offshore-registered domain name. Sunbelt, a company that develops and sells antispam and security software, managed to obtain access to a victim's computer and track what the spyware did. The company reported that the online thieves obtained confidential financial details of customers of 50 international banks. The keystroke logging software was small (26 KB), and took advantage of Internet Explorer browsers. For example, it accessed the browser's Protected Storage area, in which users often save their usernames and passwords for convenient automatic logins. Sunbelt recommended disabling this feature.

social engineering Deceptive methods that hackers use to entice people to release confidential information such as access codes and passwords. Often, the crooks misrepresent themselves as technicians who need one's password for fixing a problem in a network.

In some cases employees unwittingly give away important information such as access codes. Con artists use tricks known as **social engineering**. They telephone or email an employee who has a password to access an application or a database, introduce themselves as service people from a telephone company, or the organization's own IT unit, and say they must have the employee's password to fix a problem. Employees are often tempted to provide their password. The 'social engineers' then steal valuable information.

identity theft The criminal practice of obtaining enough personal information to pretend to be the victim, usually resulting in running up that person's credit cards or issuing new credit cards under that person's name.

Once criminals have a person's identifying details, such as a National Insurance Number, date of birth or credit-card number, they can pretend to be this person. This crime is called **identity theft**. The imposter can easily withdraw money from the victim's bank accounts, put charges on the victim's credit card, and apply for new credit cards. Since an increasing number of applications for such instruments as well as financial transactions are executed online, identity theft has become a serious problem. According to the UK Home Office, in 2006 identity theft cost the country over £1.7 billion in various sectors of the economy, from fraudulent

Industry SNAPSHOT

Losing your identity

A investigation by *Which?* magazine found that one in every four adults had either been a victim of identity theft or knew someone who had. As shocking as this statistic is, it has lead to a more useful side-effect. Two-thirds of all individuals are concerned about the problem, with many taking measures to counteract it. However, according *Which?* 33 per cent of adults do not take any precautions such as shredding personal documents, using a variety of passwords for online banking and checking personal credit files. This maybe time well spent. According to Equifax, a credit checking agency, a victim of identity theft could take up to 300 hours to clear their name. They also warn about sites such as Facebook and Friends Reunited. Putting personal information such as dates of birth on these benign websites can open the door to fraudsters wishing to steal your identity.

SOURCE: 'Identity theft affecting one in four UK adults', Silicon.com

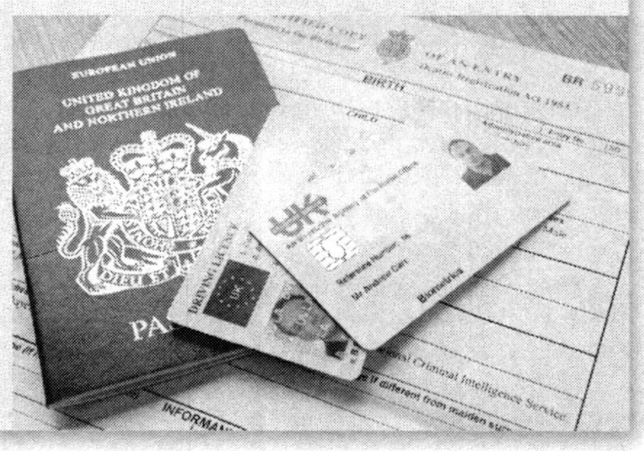

PHOTO SOURCE ©ARTHUR TURNER/ALAMY

Why you should... understand risks, security and disaster recovery planning

As explained and demonstrated throughout this book, information is the lifeblood of any modern organization. Practically every aspect of business depends on the currency of processed data and the timely provision of information. This fluent process can be achieved only if information systems are protected against threats. As a professional, you must be aware of what might happen to the ISs upon which you and your colleagues or subordinates depend. You must protect the systems against events that threaten their operation and make it impossible to carry out critical business activities. When a new system is developed, you should ask the developers to provide a system that not only supports the functions of your business unit but also incorporates controls that will minimize any compromise of the system. And to be prepared for a disaster, you should know how to implement your part of the business recovery plan to help restore operations as soon as possible.

As you can see from the snapshots and case studies in this chapter, computer disasters come in many forms but they can be summarized thus:

- They can affect hardware, software or data.
- They can be as a result of human intervention or physical problems (such as fire or flood).
- If people are involved then the problem can be because of an accident or it can be from some sort of malicious act, including terrorism.

tax and benefit claims to unpaid court fines because of a false identity being given at the time of the offence, to extra costs for ensuring the proper person turns up for a driving test and so on.

Both social engineering and breaking access codes to steal data from online databases have caused huge damage to corporations. Connecting databases to the Internet is necessary for proper operation of multisite organizations and organizations that must share data remotely with business partners. The only way to minimize hacking into such systems is to improve security measures.

In recent years identity theft has been more prevalent as part of *phishing*, a crime discussed in Chapter 9. Crooks spam millions of recipients with bogus messages, supposedly from legitimate companies, directing them to a site where they are requested to 'update' their personal data including passwords. The sites are ones constructed by the criminals who steal the personal data and use it to charge the victim's credit account, apply for new credit cards, or – in the worst situations – also apply for other documents or for loans online.

Data alteration, data destruction and web defacement

Alteration or destruction of data is often an act of mischief. Data alteration is not a new phenomenon. In 1983, a group of American teenagers accessed a computer system at Sloan-Kettering Cancer Center in New York via a modem and altered patients' records just for 'fun'. An alert nurse noticed a double – and lethal – dose of a medication in a patient's record and called a doctor. She saved the patient's life.

As mentioned before, an organization's data are often the most important asset it owns, even more important than its hardware and applications. Even if data are altered or destroyed as a prank, the damage to the organization is great. The effort to reinstate missing or altered records from a backup copy might entail expensive labour. Even if the actual damage is not great, IT staff must spend a lot of time scanning the data pools to ascertain the integrity of the entire resource, and they must also figure out how the perpetrator managed to circumvent security controls. This activity itself wastes the time of high-salaried employees.

Often, the target of online vandals is not data but the organization's website. Each day, some organizations find that their websites have been defaced. Defacement causes several types of damage: first-time visitors are not likely to stay around long enough or revisit to learn about the true nature of the site, and they might associate the offensive material with the organization; frequent visitors might never come back; and shoppers who have had a good experience with the site might leave it forever because they no longer trust its security measures.

CD TASK

To deface a website, an intruder needs to know the site's access code or codes that enable the Webmaster and other authorized people to work on the site's server and update its pages. The intruder might either obtain the codes from someone who knows them or use special 'brute force' software that tries different codes until it succeeds in accessing the pages.

Website defacing is done to embarrass an organization or as an act of protest. In June 2005 Microsoft's United Kingdom website was defaced with a banner 'FREE RAFA – HACK IS NOT A CRIME'. The banner referred to Rafael Nunez-Aponte, who had been arrested in the United States for attacks on US government websites. Zohn-h, an Estonian security firm that tracks website attacks, recorded 392,545 attacks on websites, of which 322,188 were for the mere purpose of defacement, in 2004. The firm estimated that 2500 web servers are successfully attacked daily.

The best measure against defacement, of course, is software that protects against unauthorized access, or as it is more commonly known, hacking. However, since such software might fail, the public damage can be minimized by ensuring that members of the organization monitor the home page and other essential pages frequently. When the defacement is detected shortly after it occurs, the defaced pages can be replaced with backups before too many visitors have seen the rogue pages. An increasing number of websites are restored within hours or even minutes from the defacement.

The cure to any unauthorized entry to an IS is for the organization to find the hole in its security software and fix it with the appropriate software. Such software is often called a 'patch'. Software companies that sell server management applications often produce patches and invite clients to download and install them.

honeytoken A bogus record in a database on a honeypot or productive server that is likely to draw an intruder's attention. If the intruder changes the record, the security officers know that the server has been attacked and can fix vulnerabilities.

To combat hackers, organizations use honeytokens. A **honeytoken** is a bogus record in a networked database that neither employees nor business partners would ever access for legitimate purposes. When the intruder copies the database or the part of the database that contains that record, a simple program alerts security personnel, who can start an investigation. The program that detects the incident might also reside on a router or another communications device that is programmed to send an alert as soon as it detects the honeytoken. To entice the intruder to retrieve the honeytoken when only searching for individual records, the honeytoken might be a bogus record of a famous person, such as a medical record of a celebrity in a medical database or the salary of the CEO in a payroll database.

honeypot A duplicate database on a server connected to the Internet to trace an intruder. The server is dedicated specifically for detection of intrusions and is not productive. The honeypot is there to be attacked in lieu of a productive server. The traces can be used to improve security measures and possibly catch the intruder.

To learn of security holes and methods of unauthorized access, organizations can establish honeypots. A **honeypot** is a server that contains a mirrored copy of a production database (a database that is used for business operations), or one with invalid records. It is set up to make intruders think they have accessed a production database. The traces they leave educate information security officers about vulnerable points in the configuration of servers that perform valid work. In some cases security people can follow an intruder's 'roaming' in the honeypot in real time. Note, however, that different sources have different definitions of the terms honeypot and honeytoken. For example, some define honeypot as any trap set for abusers, including a physical computer, and a honeytoken as a special case where the trap is only data.

Computer viruses, worms and logic bombs

Computer **viruses** are so named because they act on programs and data in a fashion similar to the way viruses act on living tissue: computer viruses easily spread from computer to computer. Because so many computers are now connected to one another and many people share files, people unknowingly transmit to other computers viruses that have infected their own files. Once a virus reaches a computer, it damages applications and data files. In addition to destroying legitimate applications and data files, viruses might disrupt data communications: the presence of viruses causes data communications applications to process huge numbers of messages and files for no useful purpose, which detracts from the efficiency of transmitting and receiving legitimate messages and files. The only difference between a computer virus and a worm is that a **worm** spreads in a network without human intervention. A worm attacks computers without the need to send email or open any received files. Most people refer to both types of rogue code as viruses, as does this book.

virus Destructive software that propagates and is activated by unwary users; a virus usually damages applications and data files or disrupts communications.

worm A rogue program that spreads in a computer network.

Almost as soon as email became widespread, criminal minds used it to launch viruses. The Melissa virus of 1999 was an early demonstration of why you should be suspicious of email messages even when they seem to come from people or organizations you know. In the Melissa case, an innocent-looking email message contained an attached Microsoft Word document that, when opened, activated a macro that sent an infected message to the first 50 entries in the victim's Microsoft Outlook address book. Many other viruses spread in a similar way: the recipient is tempted to open – and thereby activate – a file that is attached to a message. The program in that file then destroys files, slows down operations or does both, and uses vulnerabilities in the operating system and other applications to launch copies of itself to other computers linked to the Internet. Since Melissa, there have been thousands of virus and worm attacks, and millions of computers continue to be infected.

CD TASK

Some viruses do not affect any files, but the speed at which they spread and their repeated attacks slow down network traffic to an intolerable crawl. In January 2003 the Slammer worm struck more than 75,000 computers in just ten minutes. The number of infected computers doubled every 8.5 seconds. According to MessageLabs Inc., which scans email for viruses, in August 2003 its software detected more than 1 million copies of the 'F' variant of the Sobig virus within 24 hours of its first detection. Many organizations had to shut down their email services because of the Sobig virus.

There are many more viruses waiting for victims. CERT/CC (Computer Emergency Response Team/Coordination Centre), operated by Carnegie Mellon University, works for the US government and is one of the major distributors of information to the whole of the world on new viruses, worms and other threats to computer security. It estimated that there are at least 30,000 computer viruses somewhere on public networks at any given time; other sources estimate the number at 40,000. CERT says that about 300 new ones are created each month.

One way to protect against viruses is to use **antivirus software**, which is readily available on the market from companies that specialize in developing this kind of software, such as Symantec and McAfee. Subscribers can regularly update the software with code that identifies and deletes or quarantines new viruses, or choose automatic updates, in which virus definitions are updated automatically when the computer is connected to the Internet. However, if a new virus is designed to operate in a way not yet known, the software is unlikely to detect it. Most virus-detection applications allow the user to automatically or selectively destroy suspect programs. Another way to minimize virus threats is to program network software, especially email server software, to reject any messages that come with executable files that might be or contain viruses. Some email applications, such as Microsoft Outlook, are programmed to reject such files.

antivirus software Software designed to detect and intercept computer viruses.

Some viruses are called **Trojan horses**, analogous to the destructive gift given to the ancient Trojans. In their war against Troy, the Greeks pretended they were

Trojan horse A malicious piece of software hidden with a benign and legitimate software that one downloads or agrees to otherwise accept and install on one's computer. The Trojan horse then causes damage.

Industry SNAPSHOT

Government advice

The website for the UK Department for Business, Industry and Regulatory Reform (formerly the Department of Trade and Industry) has plenty of advice about virus protection. Its suggestions for avoiding the downloading of viruses from email include:

- Make sure people are wary of strange emails, especially if they do not recognize the sender, or if the message is unusual.
- Never rely on email to alert users to a virus infection that is carried by email. If you can, use the telephone, or have written warnings placed at entrances to workplaces or even on potentially infected machines. Users are more likely to open the virus email before the warning.
- Install antivirus software and keep it up to date. Remember that this will not only protect you and your company but may also protect your clients and other contacts. The company involved in this case study received news of its own infection from the worst possible source, a client that it had infected.
- If you outsource IT services, make sure that you provide defined procedures and requirements to your outsource agent before the contract is signed. Make security (including virus management) part of the contract, and ensure you retain the right to monitor activities.

SOURCE: www.berr.gov.uk

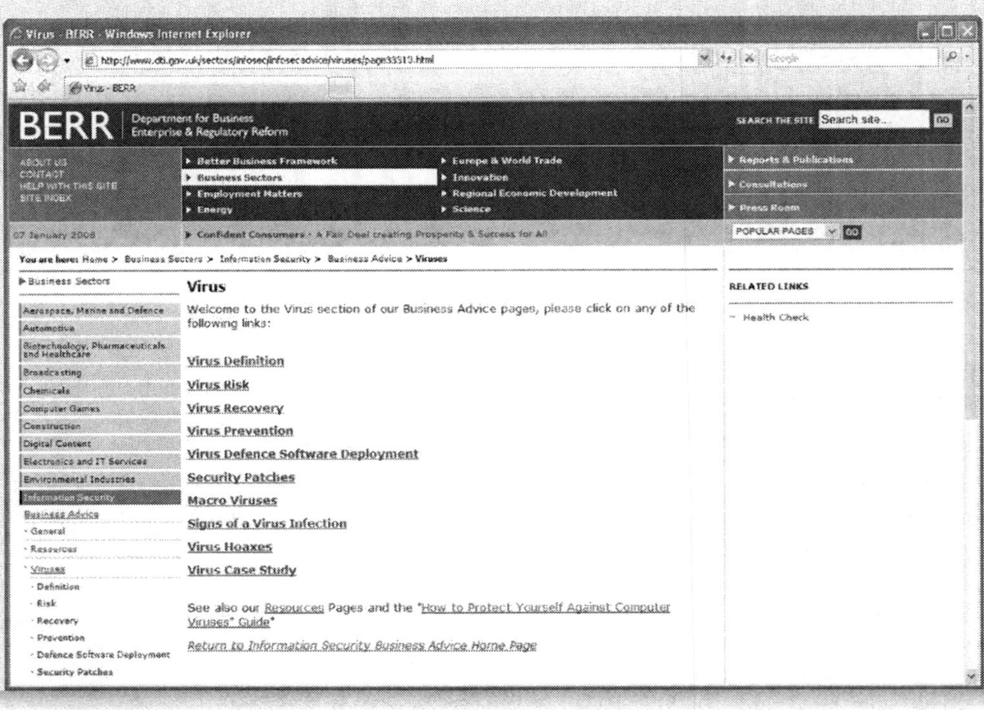

abandoning the city's outskirts and left behind a big wooden horse as a present. The Trojans pulled the horse into the city. When night fell, Greek soldiers hidden within the horse jumped out and opened the gates for thousands of their comrades, who conquered the city. In computer terms, a Trojan horse is any virus disguised as legitimate software or useful software that contains a virus. Many people also refer to spyware that comes with useful software as Trojan horse software.

A growing number of viruses and worms take advantage of vulnerable features of operating systems, most notably Microsoft Windows. Most attack this company's operating systems because the large majority of organizations worldwide use Microsoft operating systems to run their servers and computers. In the same way software vendors provide patches against direct intrusion into computer systems, they also distribute security patches against viruses and worms. However, it is up to security professionals and network administrators to implement those patches as soon as they become available. Six months before the SQL Slammer worm attack, Microsoft distributed patches to fix the vulnerability that the worm exploited. Unfortunately, many companies did not apply the patch. On 25 January 2003, the worm attacked 300,000 servers worldwide. Within 14 minutes, servers with the popular database software SQL Server started to crash on five continents. The South Korean Internet service was totally shut down for several hours, some airlines were forced to cancel flights because of problems with electronic check-in and many ATMs owned by Bank of America were disabled.

Some rogue computer programs do not spread immediately like a virus but are often significantly more damaging to the individual organization that is victimized. A **logic bomb** is software that is programmed to cause damage at a specified time to specific applications and data files. It lies dormant until a certain event takes place in the computer or until the computer's inner clock reaches the specified time; the event or time triggers the virus to start causing damage. Logic bombs are usually planted by insiders, that is, employees of the victimized organization. In one case, a man named Timothy Lloyd was convicted of planting a logic bomb on Omega Engineering's computer system after he found out he was about to be fired. Lloyd, who had worked for the company for 11 years, planted six destructive lines of code on a company network server. He had tested the bomb and then reconstructed all the files. Twenty days after he left the company, the bomb erased all of the company's contracts, designs and production programs, as well as proprietary software used by the company's manufacturing machines. The 31-year-old man's act cost the company an estimated $12 million, led to laying off 80 employees and diminished its competitive position in the electronic manufacturing market. A plant manager for the company who testified at Lloyd's trial said the company would never recover from this sabotage. Lloyd was sentenced to 41 months in prison.

logic bomb A destructive computer program that is inactive until it is triggered by an event taking place in the computer, such as the deletion of a certain record from a file. When the event is a particular time, the logic bomb is referred to as a time bomb.

Non-malicious mishaps

Unintentional damage to software occurs because of poor training, lack of adherence to simple backup procedures, or simple human error. Although unintentional damage rarely occurs in robust applications, poor training might result in inappropriate use of an application so that it ruins data, unbeknownst to the user. For instance, when faced with an instruction that might change or delete data, a robust application will pose a question such as: 'Are you sure you want to delete the record?' or issue a warning such as 'This might destroy the file.' More common damage is caused by the failure to save all work and create a backup copy. Destruction of data often happens when using a word-processing program to create text files and when updating databases.

Unauthorized downloading and installation of software that might cause damage can be controlled by limiting administration rights to employees. Many organizations instruct operating systems to deny such rights to most employees. They program ISs to accept new software installation only when the proper access codes are entered.

Risks to online operations

The massive movement of operations to the Internet has attracted hackers who try to interrupt such operations daily. In addition to unauthorized access, data theft and defacing of web pages, there has been a surge in denial-of-service attacks and hijacking of computers.

Denial of service

In February 2005, people who tried to access the websites of the Japanese prime minister and cabinet office could not do so because the sites were victims of a denial-of-service attack. Denial of service (DoS) occurs when someone launches a frequent and unusually large number of information requests to a website. The mere logging in to a site is such a request. The intention of such log-in requests is to slow down legitimate traffic on the site's server; business can slow to a halt. The server's or servers' frantic efforts to handle the massive amount of traffic denies legitimate visitors and business partners access to the site.

denial of service (DoS) The inability of legitimate visitors to log on to a website when too many malicious requests are launched by an attacker. Most DoS attacks are distributed (DDoS).

distributed denial of service (DDoS) Multiple log-in requests from many computers to the same website, so that the website is jammed with requests and cannot accept enquiries of legitimate visitors.

Such attacks are usually perpetrated from multiple computers, in which case they are called distributed denial-of-service (DDoS) attacks. In most such attacks, the perpetrator launches software that uses other people's computers for the attack – unbeknownst to them. Professionals call the computers used in these attacks 'zombies.' Zombie computers not only exacerbate the volume of calls but also make it impossible to track down the generator of the DDoS. Practically all DoS attacks now are of the DDoS type.

Because it is impossible to stop anyone from trying to log on to a website, there is no full cure for a DDoS attack, but equipment is available that can filter most of the illegitimate traffic targeting a site. The equipment detects repeated requests that come from the same IP numbers at an abnormal frequency and blocks them, and it can be programmed to block all incoming communication from suspected servers. The equipment can filter about 99 per cent, but using the equipment slows down communication, so the site's response is slowed. In addition, blocking requests might also deny access to legitimate visitors from suspected servers, especially if the server is used by an ISP who provides Internet access to thousands of people and organizations. One way to mitigate DoS attacks is for an organization to use multiple servers, which is a good idea anyway to handle times of legitimate traffic increases.

No organization is immune to DDoS. Some of the most visible websites have been attacked, including those of eBay, Amazon, CNN and the US White House. All had to shut down their sites for several hours. Amazon, eBay and other sites have lost revenue as a result. Even CERT has been forced to shut down its site. A DDoS attack sent information into its website at rates several hundred times higher than normal. One report from the University of California at San Diego estimated that there are 4000 DDoS attacks somewhere in the world each week.

Computer hijacking

You might not be aware of it, but there is a good chance your networked computer has been hijacked. No, nobody would remove it from your desk, but if it is connected to the Internet, it is used by other people. Hijacking a computer means using some or all of the resources of a computer linked to a public network without the consent of its owner. As you have seen, this has been done for DDoS, but it is also done for other purposes.

hijacking In the context of networks, when computers are remotely taken advantage of by people who are not authorized to do so by the lawful owner. The computer is 'hijacked' after a controlling application is surreptitiously installed on the computer's hard disk. Hijacked computers are exploited to participate in spamming or DDoS attacks.

Hijacking is carried out by surreptitiously installing a small program called a *bot* on a computer. Like many viruses, these programs are downloaded unwittingly by people who use chat rooms and file-sharing networks. When your computer is hijacked, your Internet connection might slow to a crawl. The damage to corporations in the form of reduced productivity can be great. The main purpose of hijacking computers is spamming: using hijacked computers to send unsolicited commercial email to large numbers of people, often millions of addresses. Spammers do so for two reasons: they hide the real source of the email so that they cannot be identified and pursued, and they take advantage of the hijacked machines'

Industry SNAPSHOT

Big rewards and a light sentence

Because so many viruses attack operating systems developed by Microsoft, in 2003 the company started offering monetary rewards of $250,000 each for informants who help arrest and convict criminals who launch such viruses. Two informants helped to arrest and convict Sven Jaschan, a German teenager who launched the Sasser worm in May 2004. Sasser exploited a flaw in Windows 2000 and Windows XP and caused hundreds of thousands of PCs to crash and reboot. The two informants shared the $250,000 reward. The 19-year old Jaschan was sentenced to 21 months of suspended arrest for a probation period of three years. While on probation, he had to provide 30 hours of community service either at a hospital or a retirement home – later he found a job as a programmer.

In an even more astounding case of 'poacher turned gamekeeper', a Chinese virus writer, Li Jun, received a four-year sentence along with several job offers, according to the *Changjiang Times*. One of the companies hit by his virus offered Li the position of technology director with a salary of a million Yuan, over € 90,000, which contrasts with the amount of money Li made from the sale of his program to online thieves at 145,000 Yuan!

SOURCES: J. Evers, 'Sasser Author Gets Suspended Sentence', CNET News.com (http://news.com.com/), 8 July 2005; http://www.securityfocus.com/brief/595?ref=rss, 25 October 2007

PHOTO SOURCE: © KRZYSZTOF ZRILI

computer resources – CPU time, memory and communications link – to expedite the distribution of spam.

Antivirus software vendor McAfee estimated that from April to June 2005, 13,000 additional computers were hijacked, an increase of 63 per cent over the same period in the previous year. In all, Symantec – another antivirus vendor – estimated that hundreds of thousands of computers were infected with bots. Other experts estimate the number in the millions. The main targets are corporate and household computers with fast Internet connections shared by two or more computers.

To hijack computers, spammers exploit security holes in operating systems and communications software, and then surreptitiously install email forwarding software, much as one would install a virus. Most users do not notice the extra work their computers do. One precaution is to check why a computer continues activity (such as hard disk work) when the owner does not use it. Computer owners can also install special software that detects email forwarding applications.

Computer hijacking is also done to turn computers into zombies to help a DDoS. Instead of exploiting the computers to send email, they are used to send repeated service requests to web servers. The MSBlast worm was programmed to launch a DDoS attach against the Microsoft Windows Update site on the 16th of each month starting in August 2003. Microsoft posted a patch against the bot and later reported that by April 2004 its update system had removed the virus from 9.5 million computers.

Table 13.1 Common controls to protect systems from risks

Program robustness and data entry controls
Backup
Access controls
Atomic transactions
Audit trail

Controls

Controls are constraints and other restrictions imposed on a user or a system, and they can be used to secure systems against the risks just discussed or to reduce damage caused to systems, applications and data. Table 13.1 lists the most common controls. Controls are implemented not only for access but also to implement policies and ensure that nonsensical data are not entered into corporate databases.

controls Constraints applied to a system to ensure proper use and security standards.

Program robustness and data entry controls

A computer program is said to be 'robust' if it is free of bugs and can handle unforeseen situations well. Robust applications can resist inappropriate usage, such as incorrect data entry or processing. The most robust programs consider every possible misuse or abuse. A highly robust program includes code that promptly produces a clear message if a user either errs or tries to circumvent a process. For example, a website invites users to select a username and password, and the operators want passwords that are not easy to guess. The application should be programmed to reject any password that has fewer than a certain number of characters or does not include numerals. A clear message then must be presented, inviting the user to follow the guidelines.

Controls also translate business policies into system features. For example, Blockbuster Video uses its IS to implement a policy limiting debt for each customer to a certain level. When a customer reaches the debt limit and tries to hire another DVD, a message appears on the cash register screen: 'Do not rent!' Thus, the policy is implemented by using a control at the point of sale. Similar systems do not allow any expenditures to be committed unless a certain budgetary item is first checked to ensure sufficient allocation. A spending policy has been implemented through the proper software.

backup Periodic duplication of data in order to guard against loss.

RAID (Redundant Array of Independent Disks) A set of magnetic disk packs maintained for backup purposes. Sometimes RAIDs are used for storing large databases.

Backup

Probably the easiest way to protect against loss of data is to automatically duplicate all data periodically, a process referred to as data backup. Storage media suitable for routine backup were discussed in Chapter 4. Many systems have built-in automatic backup programs. The data might be duplicated on inexpensive storage devices such as magnetic tapes. Manufacturers of storage devices also offer Redundant Arrays of Independent Disks (RAID) for this purpose. RAID is a set of disks that is programmed to replicate stored data to provide a higher degree of reliability.

Redundant arrays of independent disks (RAID) automatically back up transactions onto disks that can be removed and stored in a safe place.

Of course, backing up data is not enough. The disks or tapes with backed up data must be routinely transported off-site, so that if a business site is damaged by a disaster, the remote storage can be used since it is likely to be spared. In the past, many companies had a truck haul backup disks and tapes to the storage location at the end of every business day, and some might still do so. However, due to the great developments in telecommunications in recent years, most corporations prefer to back up data at a remote site through communications lines. Often, the backup disks or tapes reside thousands of miles away from the organization's business offices. For additional protection, backup disks or tapes are locked in safes that can withstand fire and floods.

Companies can also use the services of firms that specialize in providing backup facilities. The vendor maintains a site with huge amounts of disk space linked to the Internet. The online data backup service typically provides client organizations with an application that copies designated files from the client's systems to the remote disks. For obvious reasons, some professionals call this type of service 'e-vaulting'. One company that provides the service is Iron Mountain (www.ironmountain.co.uk).

Access controls

Unauthorized access to information systems, usually via public networks such as the Internet, does not always damage IT resources. However, it is regarded as one of the most serious threats to security because it is often the prelude to the destruction of websites, databases, and other resources, or theft of valuable information.

access controls Hardware and software measures, such as user IDs and passwords, used to control access to information systems.

Access controls are measures taken to ensure that only those who are authorized have access to a computer or network or to certain applications or data. One way to block access to a computer is by physically locking it in a facility to which only authorized users have a key or by locking the computer itself with a physical key. However, in the age of networked computers, this solution is practical only for a limited number of servers and other computers. Therefore, these organizations must use other access controls, most of which rely on software.

Experts like to classify access controls into three groups: what you know, what you have and who you are. 'What you know' includes access codes such as user IDs, account numbers and passwords. 'What you have' is some kind of a device, such as a security card, which you use directly or which continuously changes coordinated access codes and displays them for you. 'Who you are' includes your unique physical characteristics.

The most common way to control access is through the combination of a user ID and a password. While user IDs are usually not secret, passwords are. IS managers encourage users to change their passwords frequently, which most systems easily allow, so that others do not have time to figure them out. Some organizations have systems that force users to change their passwords at preset intervals, such as once a month or once every three months. Some systems also prevent users from selecting a password that they have used in the past, to minimize the chance that someone else might guess it, and many require a minimum length and mix of characters and numerals. Access codes and their related passwords are maintained either in a special list that becomes part of the operating system or in a database that the system searches to determine whether a user is authorized to access the requested resource.

A more secure measure than passwords is security cards, such as RSA's SecureID. The device is distributed to employees who need access to confidential databases, usually remotely.

PHOTO SOURCE: © COURTESY OF AMERICAN POWER CONVERSION CORP.

Fingerprint readers have been adopted by an increasing number of organizations as biometric controls. This mouse verifies a thumbprint in less than a second.

biometric A unique, measurable characteristic or trait of a human being used for automatically authenticating a person's identity. Biometric technologies include digitized fingerprints, retinal pictures and voice. Used with special hardware to uniquely identify a person who tries to access a facility or an IS, instead of a password.

Employees receive a small device that displays a six-digit number. Special circuitry changes the number both at the server and the device to the same new number every minute. To gain access, employees enter at least one access code and the current number. The device is small enough to be carried on a key chain or in a wallet. This two-factor access control increases the probability that only authorized people gain access. This is an example of using both what you know and what you have.

In recent years, some companies have adopted physical access controls called biometrics. A **biometric** characteristic is a unique physical, measurable characteristic of a human being that is used to identify a person. Characteristics such as fingerprints, retinal pictures, or voiceprints can be used in biometrics. They are in the class of 'who you are'. When a fingerprint is used, the user presses a finger on a scanner or puts it before a digital camera. The fingerprint is compared against a database of digitized fingerprints of people with authorized access. A growing number of laptop computers have a built-in fingerprint scanner for the same purpose. The procedure is similar when the image of a person's retina is scanned. With voice recognition, the user is instructed to utter a word or several words. The intonation and accent are digitized and compared with a list of digitized voice samples.

Several manufacturers of computer equipment offer individual keyboard-embedded and mouse-embedded fingerprint devices. For example, SecuGen Corporation offers EyeD Mouse, a mouse that includes a fingerprint reader on the thumb side of the device. It verifies a fingerprint in less than a second. Using biometric access devices is the best way not only to prevent unauthorized access to computers but also to reduce the workload of Help desk personnel. Up to 50 per cent of the calls Help desk personnel receive come from employees who have forgotten their passwords.

Atomic transactions

atomic transaction A transaction whose entry is not complete until all entries into the appropriate files have been successfully completed. It is an important data entry control. (Atom = Indivisible)

As you know, in an efficient IS, a user enters data only once, and the data are recorded in different files for different purposes, according to the system's programmed instructions. For instance, in a typical order system, a sale is recorded in several files: the shipping file (so that the warehouse knows what to pack and ship), the invoice file (to produce an invoice and keep a copy in the system), the accounts receivable file (for accounting purposes) and the commission file (so that the salesperson can be compensated with the appropriate commission fee at the end of the month). As indicated in Figure 13.1, a system supports atomic transactions when its code allows the recording of data only if they successfully reach all their many destinations. An **atomic transaction** (from the Greek *atomos*, indivisible) is a set of indivisible transactions that are either all executed or none are – never only some. Using atomic transactions ensures that only full entry occurs in all the appropriate files.

For instance, suppose the different files just mentioned reside on more than one disk, one of which is malfunctioning. When the clerk enters the sale transaction, the system tries to automatically record the appropriate data from the entry into

Figure 13.1 Atomic transactions ensure updating of all appropriate files. Either all files are updated, or none are updated and the control produces an error message

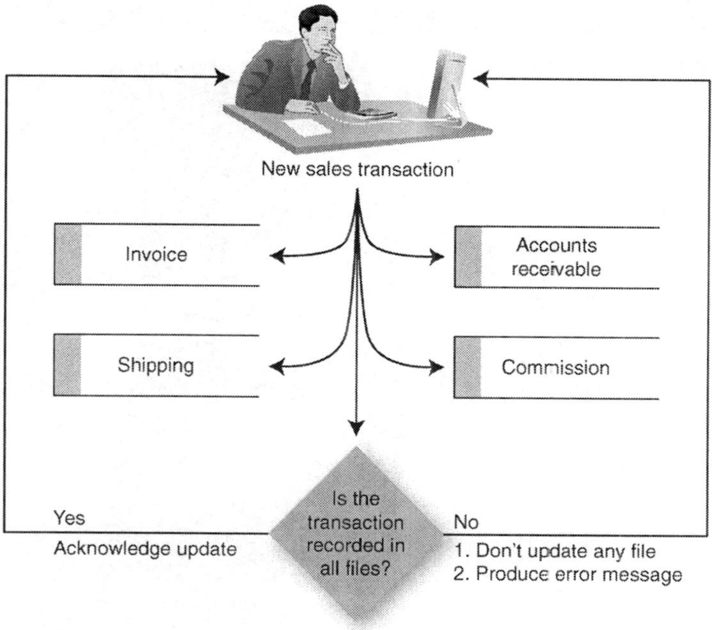

each of the files. The shipping, accounts receivable and invoice files are updated, but the malfunctioning commission file cannot accept the data. Without controls, the sale would be recorded, but unknown to anyone, the commission would not be updated and the salesperson would be deprived of the commission on this deal. However, an atomic transaction control mechanism detects that not all four files have been updated with the transaction, and it doesn't update any of the files. The system might try to update again later, but if the update does not go through, the application produces an appropriate error message for the clerk, and remedial action can be taken.

Note that this is a control not only against a malfunction but also against fraud. Suppose the salesperson collaborates with the clerk to enter the sale only in the commission file, so he or she can be rewarded for a sale that has never taken place – and then plans to split the fee with the clerk. The atomic transactions control would not let this happen.

Audit trail

In spite of the many steps taken to prevent system abuse, it nonetheless occurs. Consequently, further steps are needed to track transactions so that (1) when abuses are found, they can be traced, and (2) fear of detection indirectly discourages abuse. One popular tracking tool is the **audit trail**: a series of documented facts that help detect who recorded which transactions, at what time and under whose approval. Whenever an employee records a transaction, such a system prompts the employee to provide certain information: an invoice number, account number, salesperson ID number and the like. Sometimes an audit trail is automatically created using data, such as the date and time of a transaction or the name or password of the user updating the file. Such data are recorded directly from the computer – often unbeknownst to the user – and attached to the record of the transaction.

audit trail Names, dates and other references in computer files that can help an auditor track down the person who used an IS for a transaction, legal or illegal.

Industry SNAPSHOT

Big on biometrics

Interest in biometric technologies has steadily increased worldwide. In the United States and Europe, companies such as Alcatel, Nuance Communications and SAFLINK Corp. have developed security methods that dispense with passwords and personal identification numbers and instead use face recognition, fingerprints and vein recognition. The global biometric market was $719 million but is expected to grow to $4.6 billion by 2008. Japanese corporations are especially interested in such technologies since the Personal Information Protection Law was passed in April 2005. Japan's second largest bank, Mitsubishi Tokyo Financial Group, receives 2000 applications daily for a credit card that identifies users by the veins in their palms.

SOURCE: 'Japan's Biometric Security Firms See Demand Booming', Reuters, 16 August 2005

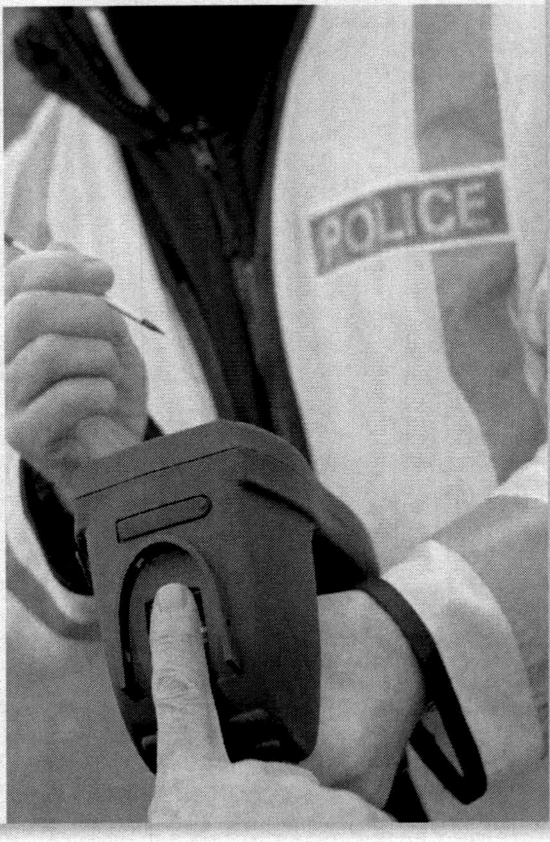

A UK police officer scans the fingerprint of a motorist using a mobile scanner.

PHOTO SOURCE: © 67PHOTO/ALAMY

The laws and regulations of many countries require certain policy and audit trail controls, and since so many operations are performed using ISs, the controls must be programmed into software. In the United States, the Sarbanes-Oxley Act of 2002 requires corporations to implement audit trails and other measures in their systems.

Audit trail information helps uncover undesirable acts, from innocent mistakes to premeditated fraud. The information helps determine who authorized and who made the entries, the date and time of the transactions and other identifying data that are essential in correcting mistakes or recovering losses. The audit trail is the most important tool of the *information systems auditor* (formerly known as the electronic data processing auditor), the professional whose job it is to find erroneous or fraudulent cases and investigate them.

Security measures

As you've seen so far in this chapter, the great increase in the number of people and organizations using the Internet has provided fertile ground for unauthorized and destructive activity. This section describes several ways that organizations can protect themselves against such attacks, including using firewalls, authentication and encryption, digital signatures and digital certificates.

Firewalls and proxy servers

The best defence against unauthorized access to systems over the Internet is a **firewall**, which is hardware and software that blocks access to computing resources. Firewalls are routinely integrated into the circuitry of routers, as discussed in Chapter 5. Firewall software screens the activities of a person who logs on to a website; it allows retrieval and viewing of certain material, but blocks attempts to change the information or to access other resources that reside on the same computer or computers connected to it.

firewall Hardware and software designed to control access by Internet surfers to an information system, and access to Internet sites by organizational users.

It is important to note that while firewalls are used to keep unauthorized users out, they are also used to keep unauthorized software or instructions away, such as computer viruses and other rogue software. When an employee uses a company computer to access external websites, the firewall screens for viruses and active attempts to invade company resources through the open communications line. It might also be programmed to block employee access to sites that are suspected of launching rogue programs, or to sites that provide no useful resources. The firewall then prohibits the user from logging on to those sites.

As Figure 13.2 illustrates, a firewall controls communication between a trusted network and the 'untrusted' Internet. The firewall can be installed on a server or on a router. Network professionals use firewall software to check which applications can access the Internet and which servers might be accessed from the organization's network.

To increase security, some companies implement the **DMZ** (demilitarized zone) approach. The DMZ is a network of computers that are connected to the company's trusted network (such as an intranet) at one end and the untrusted network – the public Internet – at the other end. The DMZ includes resources to which the organization allows direct access from the Internet. It might include a website and computers from which people can download files. A DMZ provides a barrier between the Internet and a company's organizational network, which is usually an intranet. The connection between the DMZ and the organization's trusted network is established by using a proxy server.

DMZ Demilitarized zone, a network of computers and other devices connected to the Internet where visitors are not allowed direct access to other resources connected to the DMZ. DMZs are used to serve visitors while minimizing risk of unauthorized access.

A **proxy server** 'represents' another server for all information requests from resources inside the trusted network. However, a proxy server can also be placed between the Internet and the organization's trusted network when there is no DMZ. For example, this might be the arrangement when the organization establishes its website as part of its trusted network. The proxy server then retrieves web pages for computers, requesting them remotely through the Internet. Thus, external computers requesting web pages never come in direct touch with the computer hosting the web pages. When a business hires the services of an ISP, the proxy server is often the one operated by the ISP.

proxy server A computer that serves as an intermediary between two servers on the Internet, often for the purpose of security or filtering out certain information.

Both the organizational network server and proxy server employ firewalls. In Figure 13.2, the firewalls would be installed on the server of the organizational network and the router. The router is often called a 'boundary router'. The double firewall architecture adds an extra measure of security for an intranet.

Authentication and encryption

With so much web-based commerce and other communication on the Internet, both businesses and individuals must be able to authenticate messages. That is, they must be able to tell whether certain information, plain or encrypted, was sent to them by the party that was

Figure 13.2 Firewalls

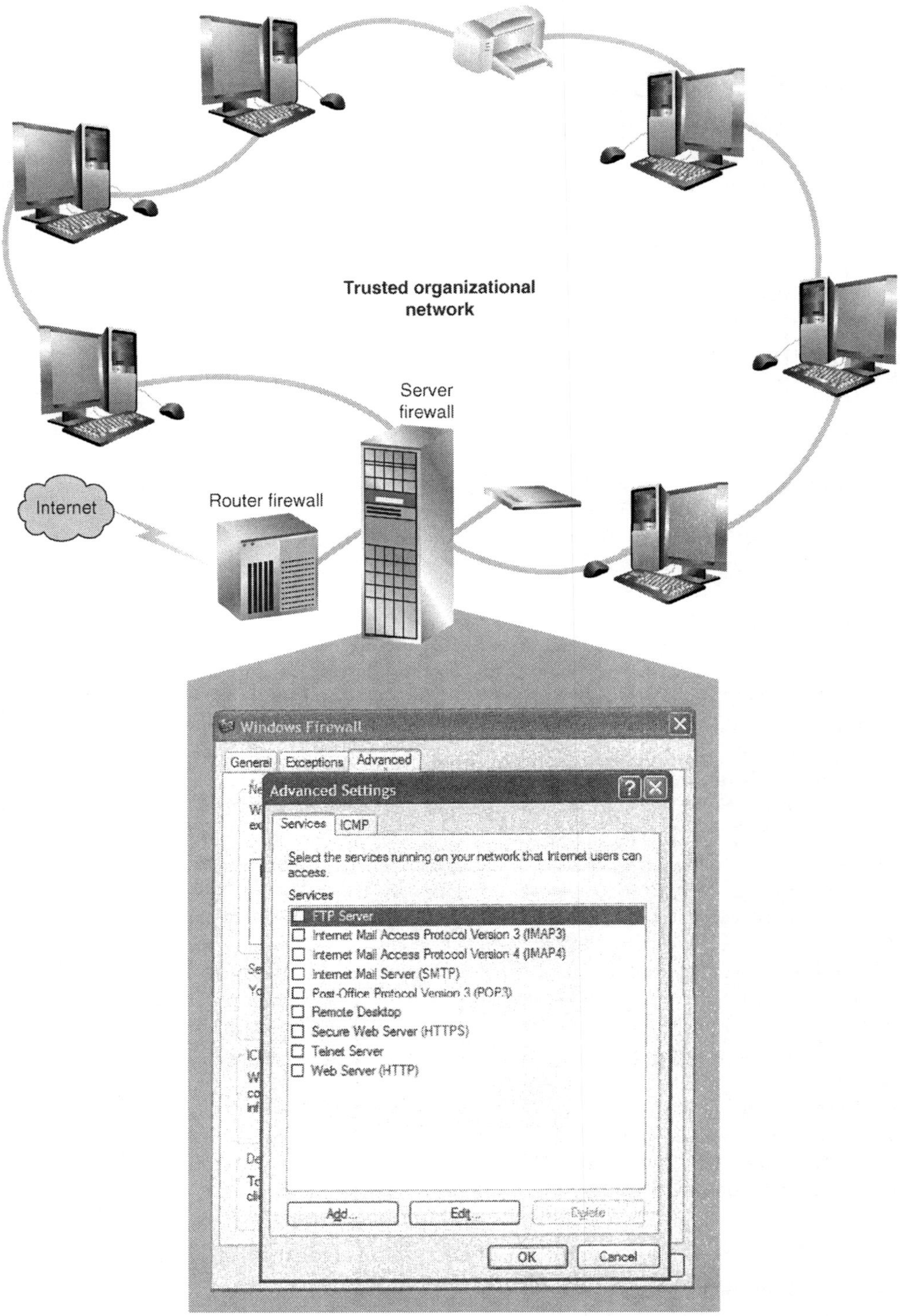

supposed to send it. Note that the word 'message' is used here for any type of information, not only text. It might be images, sounds or any other information in digital form.

authentication The process of ensuring that the person who sends a message to or receives a message from another party is indeed that person.

encryption The conversion of plaintext to an unreadable stream of characters especially to prevent a party that intercepts telecommunicated messages from reading them. Special encryption software is used by the sending party to encrypt messages, and by the receiving party to decipher them.

plaintext An original message, before encryption.

ciphertext A coded message designed to authenticate users and maintain secrecy.

symmetric (secret or private key) encryption Encryption technology in which both the sender and recipient of a message use the same key for encryption and decryption.

Authentication is the process of ensuring that the person who sends a message to or receives a message from you is indeed that person. Authentication can be accomplished by senders and receivers exchanging codes known only to them. Once authentication is established, keeping a message secret can be accomplished by transforming it into a form that cannot be read by anyone who intercepts it. Coding a message into a form unreadable to an interceptor is called **encryption**. Authentication often occurs also when an encrypted message is received, because the recipient needs to ensure that the message was indeed encrypted and sent by a certain party.

Both authentication and secrecy are important when communicating confidential information such as financial and medical records. Authentication and secrecy are also essential when transacting business through a public network. For example, millions of people now buy and sell shares of stock and other financial products on the Web, businesses and individuals make purchases through the Web and use credit-card account numbers for payment and medical clinics use the Web to transmit patient records to insurance companies. All must authenticate the recipient and keep the entire communication confidential.

To authenticate the users and maintain secrecy, the parties can use encryption programs. Encryption programs scramble information transmitted over the network so that an interceptor receives only unintelligible data. The original message is called **plaintext**; the coded message is called **ciphertext**. Encryption uses a mathematical algorithm, which is a formula, and a key. The key is a unique combination of bits that must be used in the formula to decipher the ciphertext. As indicated in Figure 13.3, the receiving computer uses the key to decipher the ciphertext back into plaintext.

Public-key encryption

As Figure 13.4 indicates, when both the sender and recipient use the same secret key (which is the case in the earlier example), the technique is called **symmetric encryption**. However, symmetric encryption requires that the recipient have the key before the encrypted text is received. Therefore, the key is referred to simply as a *secret key* or *private key*. While it is fairly simple to keep the secrecy of a message when the sender and

Figure 13.3 Encrypting communications increases security

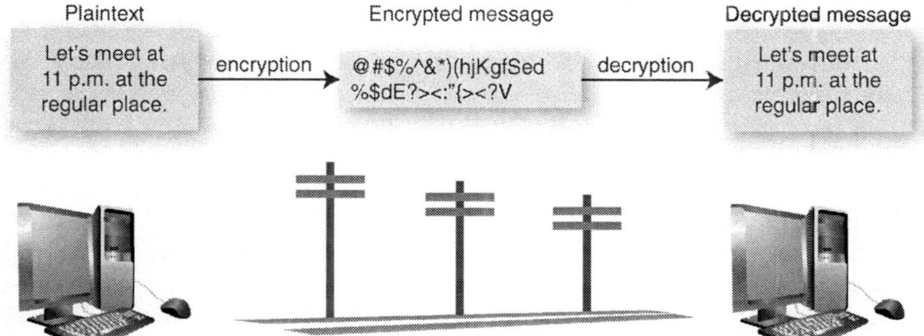

Figure 13.4 Symmetric (secret key) and asymmetric (public key) encryption

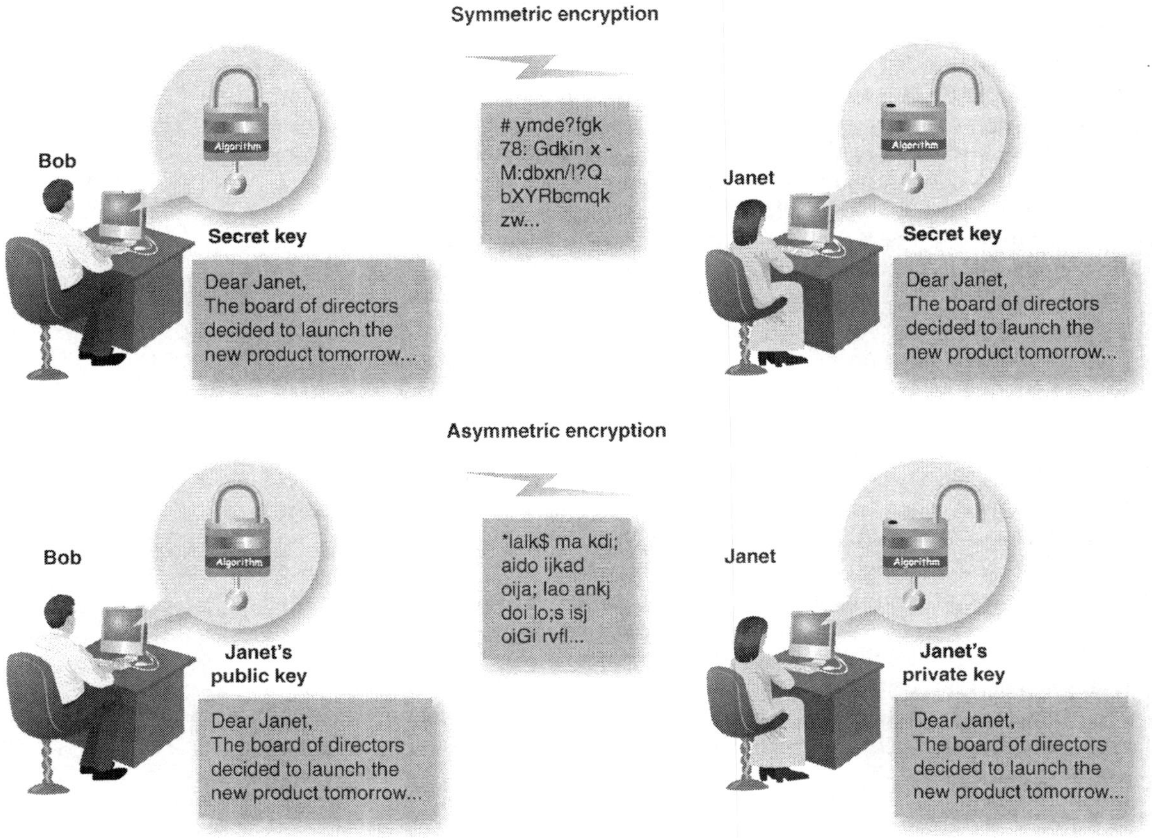

> **asymmetric (public key) encryption** Encryption technology in which a message is encrypted with one key and decrypted with another.

> **public-key encryption** Encryption technology in which the recipient's public key is used to encrypt and the recipient's private key is used to decrypt.

recipient have the same key beforehand, it is impractical in daily transactions on the Internet. For example, a retail website would not be able to function if every time a new buyer registered it required a secret key to ensure confidentiality. Therefore, in such communication, there must be a way for the sender to communicate the key to the recipient before the message is sent. To this end, the parties use an **asymmetric encryption** comprising two keys: one is public, and the other is private. It is clear why this type of encryption is also called **public-key encryption**.

A public key is distributed widely and might be known to everyone; a private key is secret and known only to the recipient of the message. When the sender wants to send a secure message to the recipient, he uses the recipient's public key to encrypt the message. The recipient then uses her own private key to decrypt it. There is a mathematical relationship between the public and private keys. The public and private keys are related in such a way that only the public key can be used to encrypt messages, and only the corresponding private key can be used to decrypt them. It is virtually impossible to deduce the private key from the public key. All applications that use public keys and private keys use the same principles. What differentiates them from one another is the different encryption algorithm each uses.

Online businesses often switch site visitors to a secure server when visitors are asked to provide secret information such as credit-card account numbers or other personal information. The secure server provides the visitor's web browser with the site's public key. The browser uses it to encrypt the credit-card number and any other personal information. The secure server uses the private key to decrypt the information. Once an encrypted exchange is established, the server can send the visitor's browser a secret key that both can use. Moreover, the server can change that key often during the session to make decryption more difficult.

Transport Layer Security

A protocol called Transport Layer Security (TLS) is used for transactions on the Web. TLS is the successor of Secure Socket Layer (SSL) and works following the same principles as SSL, with some improvements that are outside the scope of this discussion. It is part of virtually all current web browsers. Current versions of browsers use TSL with a 128-bit key. TLS uses a combination of public key and symmetric key encryption. It works as follows:

Transport Layer Security (TLS) The successor of Secure Sockets Layer (SSL), the software in the web browser responsible for secure communication.

1 When a visitor connects to an online site, the site's server sends the visitor's browser its public key.
2 The visitor's browser creates a temporary symmetric (secret) key of 128 bits. The key is transmitted to the site's server encrypted by using the site's public key. Now both the visitor's browser and the site's server know the same secret key and can use it for encryption.
3 The visitor can now safely transmit confidential information.

How safe is a 128-bit key? It would take 250 PCs working simultaneously around the clock an estimated 9 trillion times the age of the universe just to decrypt a single message. This is the reason why practically all financial institutions use 128-bit encryption, and if you want to bank online, you must use a browser that supports this key length. However, how long it takes an interceptor to decipher depends on current speed of hardware and sophistication of code-breaking software. As hardware becomes faster and software becomes more sophisticated, standard keys usually are set longer.

When you log on to secure servers you might notice that the 'HTTP://' in the URL box at the top of the browser turns into an 'HTTPS://' and a little closed padlock appears on the bottom of the browser. It is advisable not to transfer any confidential information through the Web when these two indications do not appear. HTTPS is the secure version of HTTP, discussed in Chapter 7. HTTPS encrypts communication using SSL or TSL. Luckily, all this encryption and decryption is done by the browser. When you access a secure area of a website, the communication between the site's server and your web browser is encrypted. The information you view on your screen was encrypted by the software installed on the site's server and then decrypted by your browser.

HTTPS The secure version of HTTP.

Digital signatures

A digital signature is a way to authenticate online messages, analogous to a physical signature on a piece of paper, but implemented with public-key cryptography. The digital signature authenticates the identity of the sender of a message and also guarantees that no one has altered the sent document; it is as if the message were carried in an electronically sealed envelope.

digital signature An encrypted digest of the text that is sent along with a message that authenticates the identity of the sender and guarantees that no one has altered the sent document.

When you send an encrypted message, two phases are involved in creating a digital signature. First, the encryption software uses a hashing algorithm (a mathematical formula) to create a message digest from the file you wish to transmit. A *message digest* is akin to the unique fingerprint of a file. Then, the software uses your private (secret) key to encrypt the message digest. The result is a digital signature for that specific file.

How does it work? Follow the flowchart in Figure 13.5. Suppose you want to send the draft of a detailed price proposal to your business partner. You want to be certain that the

Figure 13.5 Using digital signatures

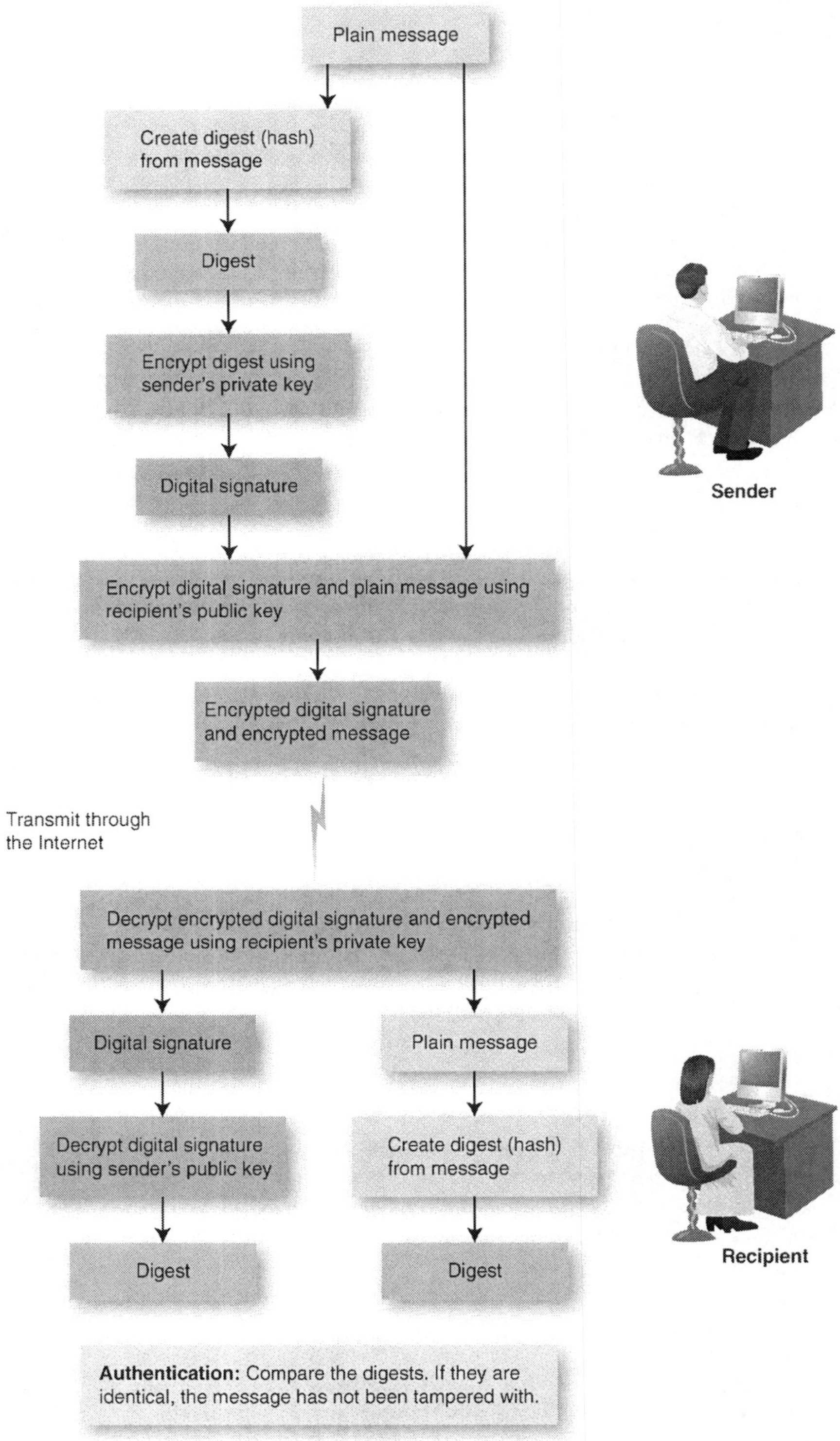

document you intend to send is indeed the one she receives. She wants the assurance that the document she receives is really from you.

1 You attach the price proposal file to an email message. The entire communication is essentially one message, indicated as 'Plain message' in Figure 13.5.

2 Using the hashing software, your computer creates a message hash, the message digest, which is a mathematically manipulated file of the message and is not readily readable by a human.

3 You then use a private key that you have previously obtained from the public-key issuer, such as a certificate authority, to encrypt the message digest. Your computer uses your private key to turn the message digest into a digital signature.

4 The computer also uses your private key to encrypt the message in its plain (unhashed) form. Your computer sends off both files.

5 Your business partner receives the encrypted files: the digital signature (which is an encrypted message digest) and the encrypted message, which usually come as one file.

6 Your business partner's computer uses her private key (which is mathematically related to her public key, which you used) to decrypt both your digital signature and your encrypted unhashed message.

7 The decrypted digital signature becomes the message digest. Hashing the decrypted unhashed message turns this message into a digest, too.

8 If the two message digests are identical, the message received is, apparently, the one you sent, unchanged.

Since the message digest is different for every message, your digital signature is different each time you send a message. As described here, senders of encrypted messages obtain the public key of the recipient from an issuer of such keys. In most cases, the issuer is a certificate authority, and the recipient's public key is included in the recipient's digital certificate, which is discussed next.

Digital certificates

To authenticate a digital signature, both buyers and sellers must use digital certificates (also known as digital IDs). **Digital certificates** are computer files that serve as the equivalent of ID cards by associating one's identity with one's public key. An issuer of digital certificates is called a **certificate authority (CA)**, an organization that serves as a trusted third party. A CA certifies the identity of anyone who enquires about a party communicating on the Internet. Some CAs are subsidiaries of banks and credit-card companies and others are independent. American Express CA, Digital Signature Trust Co., VeriSign Inc. and GlobalSign NV are just a few of the numerous companies that sell digital certificates. To view a long list of CAs you can go to www.pki-page.org. A CA issues the public (and private) keys associated with a certificate.

digital certificates Computer files that serve as the equivalent of ID cards.

certificate authority (CA) An organization that issues digital certificates, which authenticate the holder in electronic business transactions.

A digital certificate contains its holder's name, a serial number, expiration dates and a copy of the certificate holder's public key (used to encrypt messages and digital signatures). It also contains the digital signature of the certificate authority so that a recipient can verify that the certificate is real. To view the digital certificate of a secure online business, click the padlock icon in your browser (located at the end of the URL address in Windows Internet Explorer 7). The images at the bottom of page 500 show the certificate window that you would open. Clicking the Details tab brings up the version, serial number, signature encryption method, issuer name and other details of the certificate.

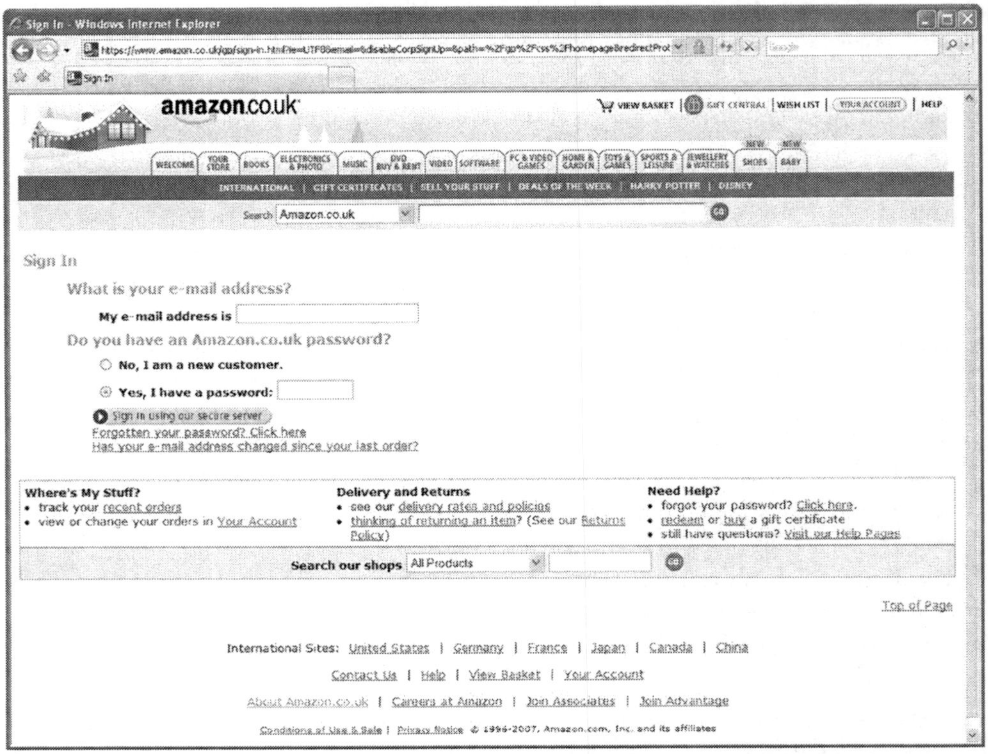

The https:// in the Address Field and the padlock icon at the end of the Address Bar indicate that you are communicating with a secure server.

Digital certificates are the equivalent of tamperproof photo identification cards. They are based on public-key encryption techniques that verify the identities of the buyer and seller in electronic transactions and prevent documents from being altered after the transaction is completed. Consumers have their own digital certificates stored on their home computers'

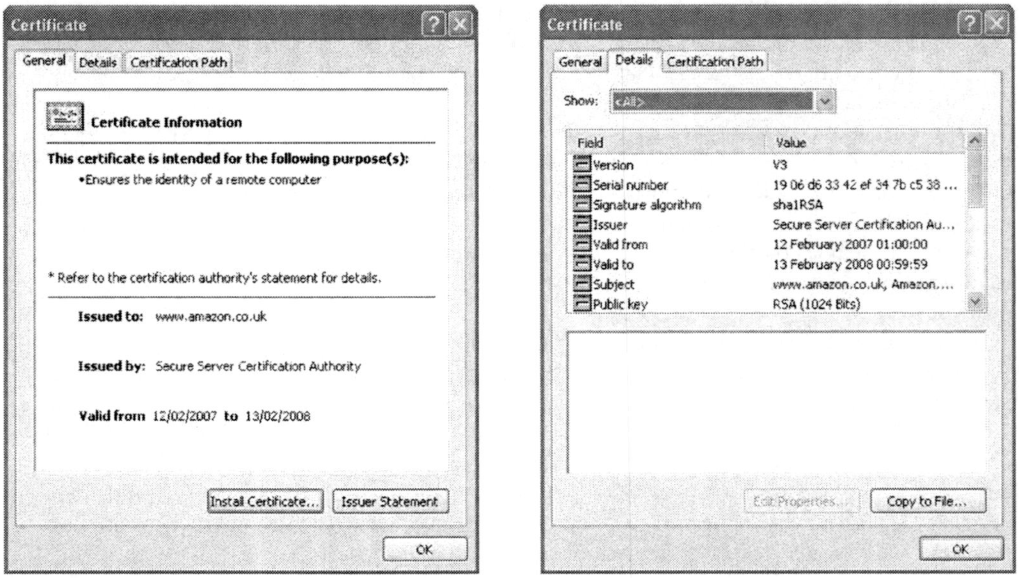

A digital certificate.

hard disks. In a transaction, a consumer uses one digital key attached to the certificate that he or she sends to the seller. The seller sends the certificate and his own digital key to a certificate authority, which then can determine the authenticity of the digital signature. Completed transaction documents are stored on a secure hard disk maintained by a trusted third party.

The recipient of an encrypted message uses the certificate authority's public key to decode the digital certificate attached to the message, verifies it as issued by the certificate authority, and then obtains the sender's public key and identification information held within the certificate. With this information, the recipient can send an encrypted reply.

When using the Web, encryption and authentication take place automatically and are transparent to the users. However, there is an indication in the browser's window if the communication is secure. In Microsoft Internet Explorer and Firefox, a small padlock appears in the lower-right corner. In Netscape, an open padlock appears in the lower-right corner if the site you reached is not secure, and a closed padlock appears if it is secure. You might see these signs as soon as the page requiring your password appears in your browser. If you double-click the padlock, a window opens with details on the digital certificate that the site uses, such as the certificate issuer's name, the date it was issued and the date it expires.

The downside of security measures

Security measures – especially passwords, encryption applications and firewalls – have a price that relates to more than money: they slow down data communications, and they require user discipline, which is not always easy to maintain. Employees tend to forget their passwords, especially if they must replace them every 30 or 90 days.

Employees are especially annoyed when they have to remember a different password for every system they use; in some companies, there might be four or five different systems, each with its own access control. A simpler solution is an approach called **SSO (single sign-on)**. With SSO, users are required to identify themselves only once before accessing several different systems. However, SSO requires special software that interacts with all the systems in an organization, and the systems must be linked through a network. Not many organizations have installed such software.

SSO (single sign-on) Enabling employees to access several information systems by using a single password.

CIOs often cite SSO as an effective way to bring down the amount of work their subordinates must do. Such was certainly the case at Welwyn Hatfield Council. The English council authority uses over 20 different IT systems to provide local government management. Much of the data on these systems are of a sensitive nature and each has its own protocols for access. A significant amount of time was being spent by the help-desk function in resetting forgotten passwords. The introduction of IBM's Tivoli Access Manager meant that users had to remember only one log-in action. Even better is that if new IT systems are introduced the SSO will 'learn' the new access protocols. The SSO has lead to a much easier log-in for users and much more efficient use of the help-desk personnel. Encryption slows down communication because the software must encrypt and decrypt every message. Remember that when you use a secure website, much of the information you view on your screen is encrypted by the software installed on the site's server and then decrypted by your browser. All this activity takes time, and the delay only exacerbates the Internet's low download speed during periods of heavy traffic. Firewalls have the same slowing effect; screening every download takes time, which affects anyone trying to access information, including employees, business partners and consumers.

IT specialists must clearly explain to managers the implications of applying security measures, especially on systems connected to the Internet. The IT specialists and other managers must first determine which resource should be accessed only with passwords and which also require other screening methods, such as firewalls. They must tell employees what impact a new security measure will have on their daily work, and if the measure will adversely affect their work, the specialists must convince the employees that the inconvenience is the price for protecting data. The IT specialists should also continue to work on methods that minimize inconvenience and delays.

Recall the discussion of virtual private networks (VPNs), which enable employees to access ISs using special security software involving passwords and encryption. This approach allows employees to access an intranet only from computers equipped with the proper VPN software and only if they remember passwords. However, it is possible to use a token (such as a keyfob) that receives a password, such as RSA's SecurID®. The password changes frequently and the user does not have to remember it, because it appears automatically on the keyfob. There is no need to use VPN software. If someone steals a password, the thief cannot use it for more than a few seconds because it then changes. This enables Wawa employees to access the intranet from any computer in the world.

Recovery measures

Security measures might reduce undesirable mishaps, but nobody can control all disasters. To be prepared for disasters when they do occur, organizations must have recovery measures in place. Organizations that depend heavily on ISs for their daily business often use redundancy; that is, they run all systems and transactions on two computers in parallel to protect against loss of data and business. If one computer is down, the work can continue on the other computer. Redundancy makes the system fault tolerant. However, in distributed systems, doubling every computing resource is extremely expensive, so other measures must be taken.

The business recovery plan

business recovery plan Organizational plan that prepares for disruption in information systems, detailing what should be done and by whom, if critical information systems fail or become untrustworthy; also called business recovery plan and disaster recovery plan. Also known as business continuity plan.

To prepare for mishaps, either natural or malicious, many organizations have well planned programmes in place, called **business recovery plans** (also called *disaster recovery plans*, *business resumption plans* or *business continuity plans*). The plans detail what should be done and by whom if critical systems go down. In principle, the systems do not have to be ISs. However, most of the attention and resources in recovery plans are devoted to measures that should be taken when ISs go down or if IS operations become untrustworthy.

The 2005 Hurricane Katrina on the US Gulf Coast was a wake-up call for many executives, reminding them in terrible terms of the need for recovery planning. Concern about disaster recovery has spread beyond banks, insurance companies and data centres, the traditional disaster recovery fanatics. Many customer service and retail firms realize that they can easily lose customers if they don't deliver services and products in a timely manner, which is why the terms 'business recovery', 'business resumption' and 'business continuity' have caught on in some circles. In interactive computing environments, when business systems are idle, so are the people who bring in revenue. Employees cannot do their work, customers cannot purchase and suppliers cannot accept requests for raw materials and services. In addition, companies' reputations can be harmed, and competitive advantage and market share lost.

Experts propose nine steps to develop a business recovery plan:

1 *Obtain management's commitment to the plan.* Development of a recovery plan requires substantial resources. Top management must be convinced of the potential damages that paralysis of information systems might cause. Once management is committed, it should appoint a business recovery coordinator to develop the plan and execute it if disaster occurs.

2 *Establish a planning committee.* The coordinator establishes a planning committee comprising representatives from all business units that are dependent on computer-based ISs.

The members serve as liaisons between the coordinator and their unit managers. The managers are authorized to establish emergency procedures for their own departments.

3 *Perform risk assessment and impact analysis.* The committee assesses which operations would be hurt by disasters, and how long the organization could continue to operate without the damaged resources. This analysis is carried out through interviews with managers of functional business areas. The committee compiles information regarding maximum allowable downtime, required backup information, and the financial, operational and legal consequences of extended downtime.

4 *Prioritize recovery needs.* The disaster recovery coordinator ranks each IS application according to its effect on an organization's ability to achieve its mission. **Mission-critical applications**, those without which the business cannot conduct its operations, are given the highest priority. The largest or most widely used system might not be the most critical. Applications might be categorized into several classes, such as:

mission-critical applications Applications without which a business cannot conduct its operations.

- *Critical*: Applications that cannot be replaced with manual systems under any circumstances.
- *Vital*: Applications that can be replaced with manual systems for a brief period, such as several days.
- *Sensitive*: Applications that can be replaced with acceptable manual systems for an extended period of time, though at great cost.
- *Noncritical*: Applications that can be interrupted for an extended period of time at little or no cost to the organization.

5 *Select a recovery plan.* Recovery plan alternatives are evaluated by considering advantages and disadvantages in terms of risk reduction, cost and the speed at which employees can adjust to the alternative system.

6 *Select vendors.* If it is determined that an external vendor can better respond to a disaster than in-house staff and provide a better alternative system, then the most cost-effective external vendor should be selected. Factors considered should include the vendor's ability to provide telecommunications alternatives, experience and capacity to support current applications.

7 *Develop and implement the plan.* The plan includes organizational and vendor responsibilities and the sequence of events that will take place. Each business unit is informed of its responsibilities, who the key contacts are in each department, and the training programmes available for personnel.

8 *Test the plan.* Testing includes a walk-through with each business unit, simulations as if a real disaster had occurred, and (if no damage will be caused) a deliberate interruption of the system and implementation of the plan. In mock disasters, the coordinator measures the time it takes to implement the plan and its effectiveness.

9 *Continually test and evaluate.* The staff must be aware of the plan at all times. Therefore, the plan must be tested periodically. It should be evaluated in light of new business practices and the addition of new applications. If necessary, the plan should be modified to accommodate these changes.

The plan should include the key personnel and their responsibilities, as well as a procedure to reinstitute interactions with outside business partners and suppliers. Because an organization's priorities and environment change over time, the plan must be examined periodically and updated if necessary. There will be new business processes or changes in the relative importance of existing processes or tasks, new or different application software, changes in hardware and new or different IS and end users. The plan must be modified to reflect the new environment, and the changes must be thoroughly tested. A copy of the plan should be kept

Industry **SNAPSHOT**

Why they invest in recovery measures

A survey carried out by SunGard Availability Services found that nearly half of the responding companies considered that they were failing to address the requirements of the new British standard for business continuity management (BCM) BS 25999. Regarding the results of the survey, Julian Thrussell, product manager BS 25999, BSi Management Systems, said, 'Clearly there remains a significant amount of work to be done but the fact that these businesses are thinking about the new Standard now is a positive sign. Organizations need to recognize the value of BS 25999 certification in terms of delivering competitive advantage and demonstrating resilience and responsible governance.'

SOURCE: http://www.sungard.com/news/default.aspx?announceID=899#Continuity

off-site, because if a disaster occurs, an on-site copy might not be available. Many companies keep an electronic copy posted at a server many miles away, so that they can retrieve it from wherever their officer can have Internet access.

Although the threat of terrorism has increased awareness for the need of recovery plans, CIOs often find the tasks of earmarking funds for disaster recovery programmes difficult because they cannot show the return on investment (ROI) of such an 'investment'. Most companies institute recovery programmes only after a disaster or near disaster occurs. Usually, the larger companies have such programmes. Even at companies that do have recovery plans, experts estimate that most of those plans are never tested. Worse, some experts observed that one out of five recovery plans did not work well when tested.

Recovery planning and hot site providers

Companies that choose not to fully develop their own recovery plan can outsource it to companies that specialize in either disaster recovery planning or provision of alternative sites. Strohl Systems, EverGreen Data Continuity and other companies provide both planning and software for disaster recovery. The software helps create and update records of key people and procedures. Fewer companies provide alternative sites – **hot sites** – chief among them is SunGard Availability Services. They provide backup and operation facilities to which a client's employees can move and continue operations in case of a disaster. These back-up centres are usually equipped with desks, computer systems and Internet links. Customers can use the duplicate databases and applications maintained for them. The company also provides hotel rooms and air mattresses for people who need to work long hours. Worldwide, the company maintains redundant facilities totalling 279,000 square meters (3 million square feet), equipped with software and networking facilities to enable a client organization to resume business within hours.

hot site A location where a client organization hit by a disaster can continue its vital operations. The structure – often underground – is equipped with hardware and software to support the client's employees.

The economics of information security

Security measures should be dealt with in a manner similar to purchasing insurance. The spending on measures should be proportional to the potential damage. Organizations also need to assess the minimum rate of system downtime and ensure that they can financially sustain the downtime.

Ethical and Societal ISSUES

Terrorism and PATRIOTism

Information technology can help track down criminals and terrorists, but it also helps criminals and terrorists in their efforts. The technology can help protect privacy and other civil rights, but it can also help violate such rights. The growing danger of terrorism and the continued effort of governments to reduce drug-related and other crimes led to controversial use, or abuse, of IT. In the UK the controversial Regulation of Investigatory Powers Act (RIPA) and the much less snappily titled Uniting and Strengthening America by Providing Appropriate Tools Required to Intercept and Obstruct Terrorism Act of 2001, the PATRIOT Act, for the USA give law enforcement agencies extra surveillance and wire-tapping rights. Similar legislation has been passed in countries throughout the world. They generally permit the reading of private files and personal Internet records without informing the suspected citizen and without need for a law enforcement agency to present to the court a probable cause. 'Our constitutional freedoms are in jeopardy. Now is the time to restore real checks and balances to the worst sections of the Patriot Act' called a web posting of the American Civil Liberties Union (ACLU) in 2005, when the law was reconsidered by the US Congress. On the contrary, said many members of Congress, the law should be enhanced to give the FBI even freer hand.

The Electronic Privacy Information Centre (EPIC) explains the major concerns with the Act, which made changes to 15 existing laws. The Act gives more power than before to law enforcement agencies in installing pen registers and trap and trace devices. A pen register is any device that records outgoing phone numbers. A trap and track device – a caller ID device, for instance – captures and records incoming telephone numbers. Similarly, the Act extends the government's authority to gain access to personal financial information and student information, even if the subject of the investigation is not suspected of wrongdoing. Agents only have to certify that the information likely to be obtained is relevant to an ongoing criminal investigation. In the past, the government had to show to a judge probable cause – a reasonable suspicion that the subject of an investigation is committing or is about to commit a crime. If a government attorney 'certifies' that the information collected is likely to be relevant, the judge must grant permission to install the device and collect the information.

Previous laws generally referred only to telephones, but the new Acts expand communication tapping to the Internet. This practically allows law enforcement agencies to record, without probable cause, email addresses and URLs. Some jurists opine that this actually allows the agencies to record not only email sender and recipient addresses and web addresses but also the content of email messages and web pages.

Even before adoption of theses various Acts, security agencies used 'packet sniffing' devices connected to the servers operated by Internet service providers (ISPs). The devices are supposed to monitor the email traffic of suspects. However, millions of other subscribers use the same servers and therefore are subject to the same surveillance.

When tapping communications, law enforcement agencies need the cooperation of a third party, such as a telephone company or an ISP. In the past, the law limited the definition of such third parties. Now in the USA under the PATRIOT Act, there is no limitation. Therefore, if a university, public library, municipality, or an airport provides access to the Internet – such as through a hotspot – all users of these services are subject to surveillance. Furthermore, that third party is prohibited from notifying anyone, including unsuspected users, of the surveillance.

Proponents of the Act want to leave all its provisions in place beyond 2005 and add two provisions. They would like to allow the FBI to demand records without first obtaining an approval from a prosecutor or a judge. Some would also amend the law to require the US Postal Service to let FBI agents copy information from the outside of envelopes in the mail.

Again, we are faced with an old dilemma: How far should we allow our governments to go in their efforts to protect us against crime and terrorism? At what point do we start to pay too much in terms of privacy and civil rights for such protection? And when terrorists strike or threaten to strike, should we give up our liberties for more security?

How much security is enough security?

From a pure cost point of view, how much should an organization spend on data security measures? There are two types of costs that must be considered to answer this question: the cost of the potential damage, and the cost of implementing a preventive measure. The cost of the damage is the aggregate of all the potential damages multiplied by their respective probabilities, as follows:

$$\textit{Cost of potential damage} = \sum_{i=1}^{n} \textit{Cost of disruption } i \times \textit{Probability of disruption } i$$

where i is a probable event and n is the number of events.

Experts are usually employed to estimate the cost and probabilities of damages, as well as the cost of security measures. Obviously, the more extensive the preventive measures, the smaller the damage potential. So, as the cost of security measures goes up, the cost of potential damage goes down. Ideally, the enterprise places itself at the optimum point, which is the point at which the total of the two costs is minimized, as Figure 13.6 illustrates.

When budgeting for IT security, managers need to define what they want to protect. They should focus on the asset they must protect, which in most cases is information, not applications. Copies of applications are usually kept in a safe place to replace those that get damaged. They should also estimate the loss of revenue from downtime. Then, they should budget sums that do not exceed the value of what the measures protect – information and potential revenues. Even the most ardent IT security advocates agree that there is no point spending €100,000 to protect information that is worth €10,000.

Calculating downtime

All other factors being equal, businesses should try to install ISs whose downtime is the lowest possible, but if obtaining a system with a higher uptime adds to the cost, they should consider the benefit of greater uptime against the added cost. Mission-critical systems must be connected to an alternative source of power, duplicated with a redundant system or both. Often, such systems must be up 24 hours per day, 7 days per week.

When the service that the business provides depends on uninterrupted power, the systems are often connected to an alternative off-grid power source, such as a generator.

Figure 13.6 Optimal spending on IT security

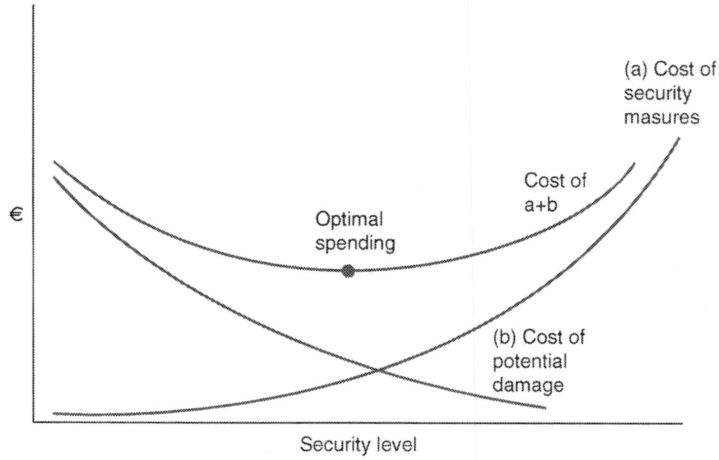

Recall the discussion of system uptime in Chapter 7. Experts can provide good estimates of the probability that systems will fail, both in terms of power failure in a certain region and for particular applications. Experience in operating certain systems, such as ERP and SCM systems, can teach the IT staff for how many minutes or seconds per year the system is likely to fail. For example, if the uptime of a system is 99 per cent ('two nines'), it should be expected to be down 1 per cent of the time, and if 'time' means 24 × 7, downtime expectancy is 87.6 hours per year (365 days × 24 hours × 0.01). This might be sufficient for a system supporting some human resources operations, but not an airline reservation system or an SCM system of a global company. For these systems, the number of nines must be greater, such as 99.999 per cent, in which case there would be only 5.256 minutes of downtime expected per year (365 × 24 × 60 × 0.00001).

More and more ISs are now interfaced with other systems, which makes them a chain or cluster of several interdependent systems. For example, if system A is connected to system B, B depends on A, and the uptime of the systems are 99 per cent and 99.5 per cent, respectively; the probability of uptime for B is the multiplication of these probabilities, or 98.505 per cent. Therefore, you could expect the systems to be down 0.01495 of the time, about 131 hours per year. This is a greater downtime than if system B operated independently. The greater the number of interdependent systems, the greater the expected downtime.

Redundancies, on the other hand, reduce expected downtime. For example, if two airline reservation systems operate in parallel, each can serve all the transactions, and the probabilities of their failures are 2 per cent and 3 per cent, the probability that the reservation service will be down is 0.06 per cent (0.03 × 0.02), just 0.0006 of the time. This downtime is significantly smaller than the downtime of a service based on either system individually. This is why so many companies rely on redundant power sources and systems, such as duplicate databases, mirrored servers and duplicate applications, especially when many of their operations are executed online, and even more so when the operations depend on constant online interaction with customers.

There might be no point in spending much money to increase the 'nines' of uptime for every system. For example, if the only purpose of an IS is to help access a data warehouse to glean business intelligence (recall the discussions in Chapters 6 and 10), spending a huge amount of money to increase its number of nines from 99 to 99.999 is probably not a wise choice. For a data warehouse, if an analysis cannot be performed immediately, it can usually be performed later without serious ramifications.

SUMMARY

The purpose of controls and security measures is to maintain the functionality of ISs, the confidentiality of information, the integrity and availability of data and computing resources, the uninterruptible availability of data resources and online operations, and compliance with security and privacy laws.

Risks to ISs include risks to hardware, risks to data and applications and risks to networks.

Risks to hardware include natural disasters, such as earthquakes, fires, floods and power failures, as well as vandalism. Protective measures run the gamut from surge protectors to the maintenance of duplicate systems, which make ISs fault-tolerant.

Risks to data and applications include theft of information, identify theft, data alteration, data destruction, defacement of websites, computer viruses, worms, and logic bombs, as well as nonmalicious mishaps such as unauthorized downloading and installation of software.

Risks to online operations include denial of service and computer hijacking.

To minimize disruption, organizations use controls. Controls include program robustness and constraints on data entry, periodic backup of software and data files, access controls, atomic transactions and audit trails.

Access controls also include information that must be entered before information resources can be used: passwords, synchronized numbers and biometrics. Biometric technologies are growing in popularity because they do not require memorization of passwords, which employees tend to forget.

Atomic transactions are an important control that ensures information integrity: either all files involved in a transaction are updated, or none is.

To protect resources that are linked to the Internet, organizations use firewalls, which are special hardware and software to control access to servers and their contents.

Encryption schemes scramble messages at the sending end and descramble them at the receiving end. Encryption is also used to authenticate the sender or recipient of a message, verifying that the user is indeed the party he or she claims to be and to keep messages secret.

To encrypt and decrypt messages the communicating parties must use a key. The larger the number of bits in the key, the longer it takes to break the encryption. In symmetric encryption, both users use a private, secret key. In asymmetric key encryption, the parties use a public and a private key.

The public–private key method does not require both parties to have a common secret key before the communication starts. To encrypt, the sender needs the recipient's public key; to decrypt, the recipient uses his or her private key. This system is a useful feature that lets consumers and organizations transact business confidentially on the Web.

TLS and HTTPS are encryption standards specially designed for the Web. They are embedded in web browsers.

Organizations can purchase public and private keys along with an associated digital certificate from a certificate authority. Digital certificates contain the certificate holder's public key and other information, such as the issue and expiration date of the certificate.

Many organizations have business recovery plans that are developed and periodically tested by a special committee. The plans identify mission-critical applications and prescribe steps that various employees should take in a disaster.

A growing number of companies also use the services of organizations that specialize in providing alternative sites, hot sites, to continue operations in case of a disaster, such as a massive terror attack, natural disaster or power outage.

When considering how much to invest in security measures, organizations should evaluate the cost of the potential damage on one hand, and the cost of security on the other hand. The more that is spent on security, the smaller the potential loss. Organizations should spend the amount that brings the combined costs to a minimum.

A system that depends on other systems for input has a greater downtime probability than if it is used independently of other systems. Redundant systems significantly reduce downtime probability.

Governments are obliged to protect citizens against crime and terrorism and therefore must be able to tap electronic communication of suspects. Such practices often collide with individuals' right to privacy.

WORLDWIDE HOST

WORLDWIDE HOST REVISITED

Worldwide Host's website has been up and running for several months now. In that time, the TripExpert site has been defaced, experienced a denial-of-service attack and has been hit with an attempt to invade the customer database. Putting its system on the World Wide Web has certainly introduced challenges to Worldwide's IS staff. Let us look at some computer security issues in more depth.

What would you do?

1. Jason Theodore, Worldwide Host's IS security chief, informs Michael Lloyd that there have been a growing number of Trojan horse attacks that target specific businesses. The perpetrators send emails to specific employees who have access to important financial information. The senders disguise themselves as a colleague and ask the employee to go to a website or open an attachment that installs a virus that is able to send sensitive financial information back to the perpetrator. Develop a list of recommendations for Michael Lloyd to distribute to employees to help safeguard Worldwide Host.
2. Severe weather is always a concern for IS personnel. If a flood or power outage hits Worldwide Host's offices, it could take down its entire operations. Michael Lloyd has asked you to help him develop a disaster recovery plan. What measures would you recommend Worldwide Host take to prepare for and recover from a disaster?
3. The chapter discussed controls on information systems to help secure them. From the description in the opening case, you know that Worldwide Host uses secure servers and physical access controls for its information systems. What other types of controls should it be using to safeguard its systems? Develop a list for Michael Lloyd and his security chief.

New perspectives

1. Worldwide Host handles thousands of transactions involving customers' credit cards. The TripExpert.com employees are complaining that the response time for the new system is much slower than their old reservations system. Michael Lloyd knows that this is the result of security measures – use of passwords, encryption and decryption, and screening of transactions. He is meeting with the travel staff to explain the security–response trade-off. Prepare an outline of his speech for him, which discusses the pros and cons of the security measures.
2. Michael Lloyd has been approached by a vendor that provides disaster recovery services at an alternative site. Should Worldwide Host consider use of such a service? If so, for what systems and business functions?

Review questions

1. What are the goals of security measures for ISs? Explain.
2. All the data of your company are concentrated in two databases. All employees use PCs or laptop computers. All use a corporate network. You are to prioritize protection of the following elements of your company: PCs and laptops, the databases, the corporate network. Which is the element about which you are most concerned, and why?
3. Data alteration and destruction are dreaded by many IS managers more than any other

mishap. Why? Is the threat of website defacement as severe as data destruction or alteration? Why or why not?

4 Some companies still make a duplicate copy of disks or tapes and transport them to a remote site as a precaution against loss of data on the original storage media. What is the preferred way of keeping secured copies of data nowadays? Give at least two benefits and one possible drawback of the new way.

5 Comment on the following statement: If your computer is connected to an external communication line, anyone with a similar link can potentially access your systems.

6 What is a honeytoken and how is it used by companies?

7 What is a honeypot and how is it used by businesses?

8 What is the difference between a virus and a worm? Which is potentially more dangerous and why?

9 Why is encryption that uses the public-key method so important in electronic commerce?

10 What is an audit trail? What audit trail information would you have for a shipping record?

11 This chapter gives an example of an atomic transaction. Give another example from any business area.

12 What is the difference between authentication and confidentiality?

13 What are biometric access controls? How are they better than passwords?

14 What is a firewall, and how does it work?

15 What is a DDoS? How is it executed, and what is the purpose of zombies in a DDoS? What can organizations do to prevent a DDoS attack?

16 What is the purpose of business recovery plans?

17 A growing number of companies have implemented business recovery plans, but there are still many without such plans. Why?

Discussion questions

1 Companies that process credit-card transactions for merchants have their computers vaulted behind concrete walls, iron bars and heavy steel doors. Employees must enter a code into a keypad to enter the vaults. Yet, every so often information on millions of credit-card accounts is stolen without any physical break-in. How so?

2 In the Blockbuster example of system controls, the cash register displays the message 'Do not rent!' when a patron reaches the maximum debt allowed. However, the customer service representative might still hire a DVD to the customer. What would you do to better enforce the chain's policy?

3 A NATO military officer in Vienna, Austria orders an item whose part number is 7954. The clerk at the supply centre in Stafford, England receives the order through his computer and ships the item: a ship's anchor, not realizing that Vienna is located hundreds of miles from any ocean. Apparently, the officer wanted to order item number 7945, a fuel tank for a fighter aircraft, but he erred when entering the item's number. What controls would you implement both at the entry system and at the systems employed at the supply centre to prevent such mistakes?

4 The average loss in a bank robbery is several thousand euro, and the culprit has an 85 per cent chance of being caught. The average damage in a 'usual' white-collar fraud is several tens of thousands of euro. The average amount stolen in computer fraud is several hundreds of thousands of euro, and it is extremely hard to find the culprit. Why is the amount involved in computer fraud so high, and why is it difficult to find the culprits?

5 To prevent unauthorized people from copying data from a database, some companies forbid their employees to come to work with USB flash memory devices and subject them to body searches. Is this an effective measure? Why or why not?

6 The majority of criminals who commit computer fraud are insiders, that is, employees. What measures would you take to minimize insider fraud through ISs?

7 Would you prefer that your identity be verified with a biometric (such as your palm or fingerprint, or your cornea picture), or with a password? Why?

8 Explain in an intuitive way why the downtime probability of a system that depends on another system is greater than if it were operating independently.

9 Employees often complain about the hurdles they have to pass whenever they need to access data and the slow response of ISs because of firewalls and encryption measures. As a CIO, how would you explain the need for such measures to employees? Would you give them any say in the decision of how to balance convenience and protection of data and applications?

10 Organizations often use firewalls to block employee access to certain websites. Do you agree with this practice, or do you think it violates employee privacy?

11 Firewalls might keep track of web pages that employees download to their PCs. Do you think this practice violates employee privacy?

12 When financial institutions discover that their ISs (especially databases) have been broken into, they often do not report the event to law enforcement officers. Even if they know who the hacker is, they do what they can to avoid publicity. Why? Should they be forced to report such events?

13 When hackers are caught, they often argue that they actually did a service to the organization whose system they accessed without permission; now, they say, the organization knows its system has a weak point, and it can take the proper steps to improve security. Do you agree with this claim? Why or why not?

14 A CIO tells you, 'We regularly review all of the potential vulnerabilities of our information systems and networks. We implement hardware, software and procedures against any potential event, no matter the cost.' What do you say to this executive?

15 Is the potential for identity theft growing? Explain.

16 Encryption helps individuals and organizations to maintain privacy and confidentiality, thereby helping protect civil liberties. However, encryption also helps terrorists and criminals hide their intentions. Some governments have laws that forbid non-government agencies to use strong encryption software. The idea is to allow people to encrypt their communication, but not enough to prevent the government from decrypting the communication in surveillance of suspected criminals and terrorists. Do you favour such laws, or do you advocate that everybody have access to the strongest encryption software possible? Explain.

Tutorial activities

1 Research the impact of the Sarbanes-Oxley Act on ISs. Write a two-page report explaining the major controls that EU corporations must incorporate in their ISs to satisfy the Act if wishing to do business in the US.

2 Log on to a secure website. Figure out which icon you have to click to receive information on the security measures used in the session. Send your professor an email message detailing the site's URL and all the information you obtained: the length of the key that is used for encryption, the type of digital certificate used, the issuer of the digital certificate, the date it was issued and its expiration date, and so forth. Explain each item.

3 Use Excel or another spreadsheet application to show your work when solving the following problems:

a A company uses three information systems that are linked sequentially: System A feeds System B, and System B feeds System C. Consider the following average uptimes: System A, 98 per cent; System B, 97 per cent; System C, 95 per cent. What is the average expected downtime (as a percentage) of System C?

b A CIO states, 'Our online transaction system has availability of five nines. However we hired the services of an ASP for using our human resources information systems. Our HR system has availability of only three nines.'

i Calculate the minutes of downtime per week for each of these systems.

ii Explain why the company must have such a high number of nines for one system but can settle for a significantly lower number of nines for the other system.

4 Team up with another student. Research the Web for recovery planning expenditures in

your country or worldwide over the past five years. Prepare a table showing the expenditure amounts. Add an analysis that explains the reasons for changes in the expenditures.

5 Your team should evaluate the business recovery plan of your college or university. If there is none, write a business recovery plan for the institution. If there is one in place, evaluate its weaknesses and make suggestions for improvement. Prepare a ten-minute, software-based presentation of your findings and suggestions.

CD questions

1 Do you run antivirus software on your home computer? Is it up to date? If not, why not?

2 What security measures have you implemented to protect your home computer? Will you do anything differently after reading this chapter?

Video questions

1 Under what circumstances would you use system restore?

2 Have you used system restore? If not, would you?

From ideas to application
REAL CASES

Case study **13.1**

The tester

The case studies in this book usually revolve around organizations. This story is about a person, a 'soldier' in the war against cybercriminals. Meet Mark Seiden, security tester extraordinaire. 'Tell me which information your bank keeps most secret', he challenged a top bank executive two years ago, 'and I'll get it anyway.' The executive complied. He told Seiden he wanted the identities of clients who were negotiating secret deals, so secret that many people inside the bank referred to them by code names. He also wanted the financial details of some mergers and acquisitions in which his bank was involved. The executive knew that those two types of information were kept under strict electronic locks by the bank.

A week later Seiden visited the executive again in his office. He gave him a printout of the secret information. He also gave the man photocopies of the floor plans of each bank office and a suitcase filled with backup tapes from which Seiden could reconstruct all the files maintained on the bank's computers. Seiden spent two weekend nights to obtain the information.

Seiden, with 35 years of experience in computer programming, is one of a small group of professional intruders, experts who are paid by corporations to find security loopholes, both in physical facilities and software. Companies hire Seiden to help improve security

Even the most sophisticated IT security systems can be compromised if the wider business environment in which they are implemented is not secure.

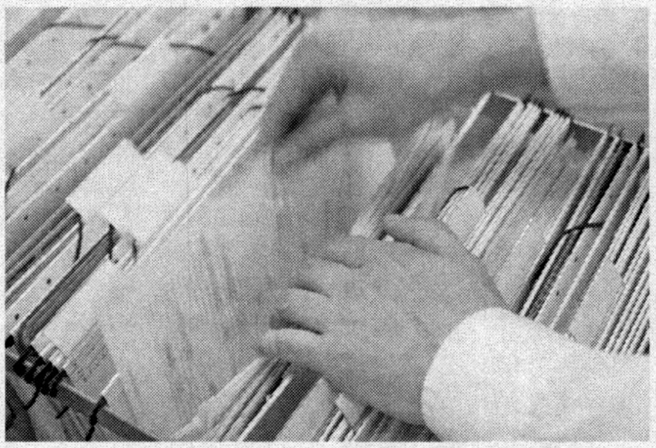

PHOTO SOURCE © FRANZISTA RICHTER

systems and procedures to protect their ISs and other sensitive corporate assets.

Business is booming for Seiden and his colleagues. As hackers increase their invasion of corporate databases and steal information from a growing number of organizations, executives are learning fast why it pays to hire the services of such people. Experts say that in the early days of the Internet, breaking into corporate ISs was mainly a matter of showing off one's prowess. Now, it has become a crime of greed. The main targets are personal information and credit-card account numbers. In a survey conducted by the FBI in 2005, 87 per cent of the polled corporations said they had routine security audits, an increase from 82 per cent in 2004. An analyst for the Gartner Group said that North American corporations spent more than $2 billion on security consultants in 2004, an increase of 14 per cent from 2003.

Much of the work such consultants do has nothing to do with hacking. Seiden has a wardrobe of uniforms and other corporate garbs. They include a uniform the FedEx drivers wear, and a windbreaker that Iron Mountain workers wear when they drive their vans to pick up backup files for credit card-processing firms. He also holds a set of tools that help him pick locks, at which he is adept. If you ask, he will tell you that the easiest way to enter a locked room is through the plenum space between the hard ceiling and the tiles underneath, space used for wiring and ventilation. Remove a tile, and you are in a safe room that is no longer so safe.

So how did Seiden get that precious information about the bank? The bank maintains some of the best security software, so Seiden did not even try to crack it. He obtained a badge that the bank often handed out to outside consultants. Wearing the badge he could enter the room where the bank's computers were housed at headquarters. He noticed that the master keys to the building as well as the building's floor plans were stored in a file cabinet that took him only two minutes to pick. Roaming freely in 'safe' rooms, he also found the backup tapes.

He then used social engineering to obtain information. Pretending he was a bank employee, he telephoned the accounting department and asked whom he should contact for assigning a code name to a project. Equipped with the name of the clerk who assigned code names, he went to her office and noticed that she placed sheets with code names in a folder and locked the folder in a file cabinet. Since the office was in a locked area, she had no reason to lock the file cabinet (which Seiden could pick anyway, if he needed to). He later explored the folder and obtained the code names of secret clients and information about confidential mergers and acquisitions that the bank was negotiating.

Seiden agrees that corporations cannot defend themselves against every intrusion, physical or otherwise. He agrees with the analogous construction of a house without windows: it can be built, but nobody would want to live in it. What corporations should do, he says, is ensure that when an intrusion occurs they know about it and take measures to ascertain that this type of intrusion does not happen again.

Thinking about the case

1 The case mentions three different ways of obtaining information illegally. What are they?

2 Why do you think corporations are spending increasing amounts of money on the services of security testers? Can you cite some recent mishaps that would prompt a corporation to do so?

3 Refer to the analogy of 'a house without windows.' You are the CEO of a large corporation. Give an example of a measure you would never take even if it enhanced security.

SOURCES: G. Rivlin, 'The Sniffer vs. the Cybercrooks', *New York Times*, Section 3, p. 1, col. 2, 31 July 2005; www.msbit.com/mis.html, 2005

silicon.com

Case study **13.2**

Plugging and preventing data leaks

BY ANTHONY PLEWES

In today's knowledge economy, getting the right information at the right time can make the difference between success and failure. However, companies need to put adequate controls in place before sharing information freely. Anthony Plewes investigates how to ensure confidential data do not fall into the wrong hands.

Before sharing information across the organization, companies need to put in place a comprehensive scheme that allows for the correct level of control over data. Simply having base-line security in place is not good enough: if security is set too high, it will impede the business, and if the bar is set too low, then confidential information may be at risk.

While most large organizations have given some thought to safeguarding their data, it's an area many SMEs have yet to confront. So while the following advice should be useful to businesses of any size, it's particularly suited to those smaller companies forming their initial data security scheme.

Information ownership

The best way to understand the security or confidentiality implications of any information is to identify its owner. Floris van den Dool, head of

The dashboard of an RBAC system from ConSentry.

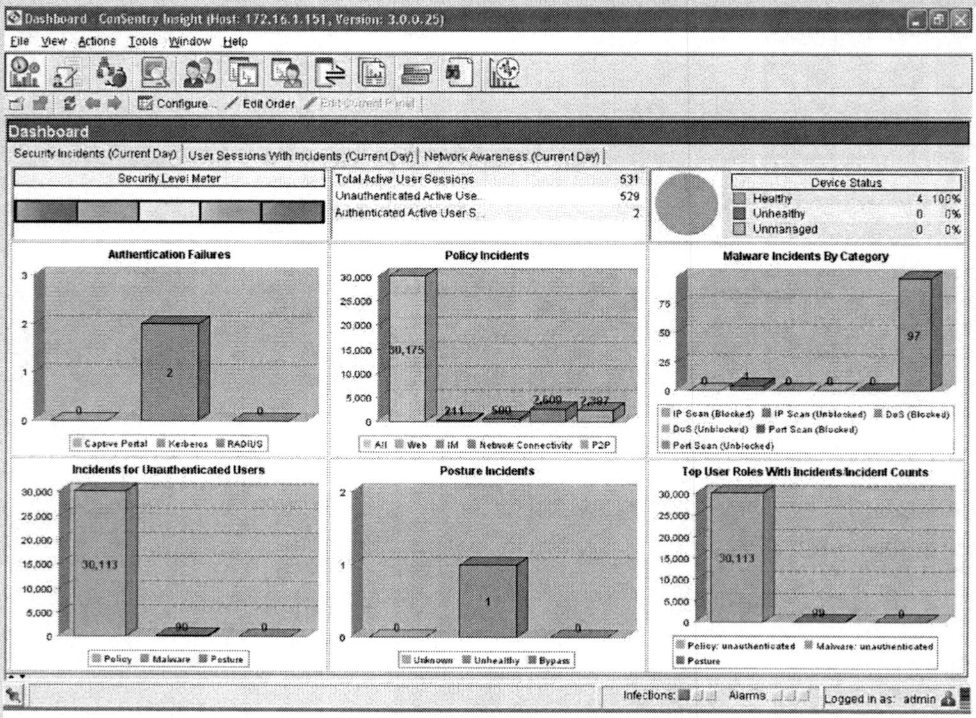

PHOTO SOURCE: © CONSENTRY NETWORKS

Accenture's European security practice, explains: 'Many smaller organizations consider that data ownership is the responsibility of the IT department but it is not – it is the business's responsibility.'

In some cases this will be obvious, such as the finance department taking ownership of the financial data, but in others the owner of the information may be more difficult to ascertain.

Building a classification scheme

Once the owner of the data has been identified, companies need to set up an information classification scheme. This practice is common in military and other security-conscious industries, but it should be used across all types of organization. A typical information classification scheme consists of four levels, such as external, company-confidential, client-confidential and classified.

The lowest level of classification is 'unclassified' information, which can be shared across the organization and with third parties. The second level should consist of all internal-use information, while the third level contains client-confidential information that can't be shared with all employees in the organization. Finally, the highest level needs to be information that very few people in the organization should have access to – such as legal matters or dealing with the security services.

This four-level classification scheme is just a starting point and it can vary widely across different companies. Applying information classification is difficult in retrospect, but fortunately companies will find it much easier to apply these rules to any new information created.

Mike Small, director of security strategy at CA, says: 'Information classification is difficult because companies built applications to solve certain business needs and the developers did not consider the requirements of data classification and compliance.' This is particularly true when classifying structured information stored in databases.

Identity management

Once the information has been classified, the next step is to enforce the scheme and the best way to do this electronically is through identity management. While it is possible to assign access rights to individuals, it is much more effective to do it based on the individual's role in the company. Role-based access control (RBAC) software packages help companies automate access control but as CA's Small points out, the tools alone are no magic bullet.

He says: 'Technology is only part of the process and projects will succeed or fail because of the soft side. Role-based access control tools only work if companies have got clear information on job roles. For example, there needs to be a single personnel system, single definition of job functions and a process to track people who change jobs. If these things are not in place, then the software will not work properly.'

It's also important to consider all possible situations whereby information could wind up in the wrong hands – and they're not all digital.

As Dave Martin, managing consultant at LogicaCMG, cautions: 'Role-based access helps companies keep electronic information secure but companies also need to address other potential sources of information leaks, such as paper left on the printer and flipcharts.'

Access control

To make sure data is secure even if it does fall into the wrong hands, companies should encrypt files. Different information will probably require different encryption policies but typically only encrypting the data when it is stored on the server will cut down on the processing overhead. It is possible to keep files encrypted even when they are being transmitted over the network, but this will require all end-user devices to have a decryption capability.

Access to specific information can even be embedded directly in documents by using DRM. This approach also allows users to take classified information out of the organization on laptops or PDAs and still manage to control who has access to certain information.

Third parties

Companies also need to think about how they can share confidential information with third parties, and this is where federated identity management comes into play. Although federated identity is still relatively unknown in smaller organizations, it will become important as supply chains become increasingly fragmented.

In a nutshell, federated identity allows companies to match job roles and trust another organization's ID management systems. They can then give access to shared information to the correct people, without having to have any knowledge about the partner company's security infrastructure.

Companies also need to consider the issue of staff working closely with outsiders. The increasing level of outsourcing often means that businesses share data with specialists such as design companies, consultants or advertising agencies who may have other customers who are competitors to your organization. Some of the information the consultants handle can be extremely sensitive and must not fall into the hands of their colleagues who are working with your competitors.

It's worth it

Securing data may seem like a lot of work but it's clearly worth it. Businesses can still benefit from sharing information across an organization, as long as they have proper information classification and identity management in place – and keep security measures commensurate with the value of the information.

In this age of strict regulations on information storage, a good information security scheme will also help companies ensure regulators that only the right people are allowed access to data.

Thinking about the case

1 Why is it so difficult to apply 'information classification' retrospectively? Are there ways of making it less difficult?

2 Will the measures outlined in the passage above deal with a situation where an employee leaves his laptop in the back of a taxi?

CHAPTER 11

The Role of Accounting in Business

AIM OF THE CHAPTER

To introduce the most common forms of business organization and to understand the reasons why people in business need accounting information, the nature of accounting information and the role of the accountant.

LEARNING OUTCOMES

After reading the chapter and completing the related exercises, students should:

- Understand the differences between the sole trader, partnership and company forms of business organization, and know, in outline, about some of the sources of business finance available to commercial organizations.
- Know in outline about some important features of the business environment including the various ways in which tax is charged on businesses.
- Understand why accounting information is produced.
- Be able to identify the principal groups in society who need and use accounting information, and to know about the principal characteristics and features of accounting information.
- Know about the functions that accountants perform in the production of accounting information.

INTRODUCTION

Accounting information is produced, quite simply, because people need it. This chapter explains the context in which accountants produce accounting information, describes the potential users of that information, and outlines the type of information that might be required. The chapter assumes no prior knowledge of accounting or finance, or indeed business in general. Students coming to these areas of knowledge for the first time are often apprehensive about them. Accounting and finance are regarded by many people as particularly difficult subjects and lecturers in accounting often face ingrained negative attitudes amongst their new students. Some of the most frequently encountered objections are considered in this introductory section of Chapter 1.

1.0.1 Special Notes for the Suspicious

If you are really looking forward to studying accounting and finance, please feel free to ignore the next few paragraphs. If, however, you are studying accounting only because of a general course requirement and if the quotations at the head of each subsection sound familiar, you might find it helpful to read the text below them.

'Accounting is boring and it's not relevant to what I'm doing anyway'

Some people are obliged to study accounting as part of a course in, say, marketing, engineering or a creative discipline. If you are a fashion student, for example, you are likely to be much more interested in creative outcomes and in developing your own skills. But people who are successful in making careers in fashion and other creative endeavours have to be very much alive to the business environment in which they work. People who have forged successful careers in the creative arts are often surprisingly well-tuned in to the business and accounting aspects of what they do.

'Accounting should be left to the accountants'

If you are looking forward to a career in, say, retail management or marketing, you may feel that you really should not have to bother with accounting – after all, there are plenty of accountants around to sort out the figures. One of the most important messages of this book is that accounting, on the contrary, is much too important to be left to the accountants. Business managers in all disciplines owe it to themselves to be able to interpret the reports that accountants present to them; such reports are vital aids to understanding what is going on in the business. Business managers should be able to question accountants from a position of understanding the accounting information. If they are not sufficiently knowledgeable to do this, they risk being quite seriously restricted in their understanding of their business and their ability to make sound decisions.

It is important to appreciate from the outset that accounting is not an exact science. Accounting has emerged in its present day form, after many centuries of development, because there is a need for it. It is, essentially, about communication between people and so it is vulnerable to all the impediments that hinder proper communication. For example, people sometimes tell lies, and accounting can be used, very effectively, to tell lies. Accounting is often imprecise, and its imprecision can be easily exploited by the unscrupulous. After studying this book, you should be much more aware of the strengths and limitations of accounting as a means of communication.

'Accounting is all about maths, and I'm no good at maths'

Accounting undeniably involves dealing with numbers. However, the study of accounting rarely involves much beyond simple arithmetic. Specifically, the principal prior skills that this book requires are the ability to add, subtract, multiply, divide and to calculate a percentage. Towards the end of the book students will be required to draw simple line graphs and to calculate compound interest. There is nothing in this book that requires knowledge beyond GCSE level (in UK terms).

What the study of accounting does involve, though, is the ability to understand what the numbers signify. This is a skill that some students find relatively difficult to acquire. The book has been written with this difficulty in mind.

'I won't be able to understand the jargon'

Accounting is no different from many other spheres of fairly advanced human endeavour in that it has its own terminology. Jargon is often baffling to the uninitiated but, inevitably, some of the jargon simply has to be learned. This book attempts to explain all the unfamiliar terms in the most straightforward way possible. There is a glossary towards the end of the book which collects together a lot of the most unfamiliar terminology so that students do not have to go back through the book hunting for the original explanation.

1.0.2 Content of this Chapter

The chapter proceeds with a brief description of different forms of business organization, and sources of finance for them. It is followed by a brief section on some important features of the business environment, including some of the ways that tax is charged on business.

The chapter then proceeds to examine the need for accounting information and the function of the accountant in providing it.

1.1 FORMS OF BUSINESS ORGANIZATION

There are three common forms of business organization: sole trader businesses, partnerships and limited companies. All three types of organization are run with a view to making profits.

1.1.1 Sole Trader Businesses

A **sole trader** operates a business himself or herself, keeping any profits which are made (after deduction of tax). This is a useful form of business for certain types of trade or profession. For example, a plumber, carpenter, financial services adviser, tax adviser, writer or nightclub singer could each operate as a sole trader business. Each of the people named offers a service to the public; each receives money in exchange for performance of the services. After deduction of the various expenses that are involved in running the business, any sum that is left over is the profit, all of which can be kept by the sole trader.

EXAMPLE 1.1

Having finished his apprenticeship, Yasin sets up in business as a plumber. He pays for a listing in Yellow Pages, subscribes to a plumbers' trade association, installs a telephone in his flat and waits to be contacted by members of the public and other businesses who require plumbing services. Yasin charges fees for his services out of which he must meet business expenses.

What are Yasin's business expenses? They will typically involve: cost of tools, expenses of running a van, telephone bills, advertising and small amounts of administrative expense, such as paying for an accountant to sort out his tax affairs.

In order to keep his business affairs in good order, he will need to keep receipts as evidence of his expenses, copies of the bills he makes out to his customers, and bank statements. It is important not to mix up the business income and expenditure with his own personal items.

Yasin or his accountant will summarize all the income he has received from customers and all the expenses of running the business on an annual basis.

Income less expenses = the profit of the business

At this point, if not before, the tax authorities (Her Majesty's Revenue and Customs in the UK – HMRC for short) take an interest in Yasin's business activities. He will have to pay tax, based upon the calculation of his profit. Later in the chapter, we will examine the tax regime in a little more detail.

Characteristics of the sole trader form of business

The sole trader is the only person responsible for the management of the business. Although he or she may employ other people as the business gets bigger, all the decision-making and risk-taking involved in the business rests on the shoulders of one individual. If the business runs into financial difficulties or faces other problems, the sole trader is on his or her own in addressing them.

Sole trader businesses tend to remain fairly small. For people who are self-employed in the types of trade or profession mentioned earlier, this type of business can work very well. However, if the business is of a type that is likely to grow very much bigger, the sole trader form of organization will need to be replaced by a partnership or limited company structure which allows more than one person to act as manager.

If a sole trader overstretches himself or herself financially, perhaps by borrowing too much, or if losses rather than profits are made, he or she is liable for all the consequences as an individual. For example, a lender would be entitled to pursue repayment of a loan even to the point where the sole trader would have to sell personal property to repay it. In extreme cases, this can result in personal bankruptcy.

The sole trader business is relatively informal and easy to set up. The business does not require registration of a separate legal entity and so it is quite likely that no legal costs will arise. In the initial stages, at least, the principal administrative issues are likely to arise with the HMRC. A competent chartered accountant can mediate between the individual and the HMRC to ensure that the correct amount is paid, and that tax does not become a problem.

1.1.2 Partnerships

A **partnership** is a business which is run by two or more people with a view to making a profit. Typically, partnerships are fairly small businesses, but there are certain types of business activity in which very large partnerships are operated. Professional partnerships, such as those between solicitors, may develop to be very large businesses indeed. There is a legal restriction which limits the number of partners in most types of partnership to 20; however, professional partnerships (solicitors, accountants, surveyors, architects, for example) are exempt from the restriction. The very largest partnerships are such big businesses that people who have barely met each other are in partnership together.

Many different trades and professions may be run through the medium of a partnership; apart from the professions noted above, doctors, pharmacists, business consultants, shopkeepers, builders, hairdressers and almost any other type of trade or business activity could be run via a partnership.

EXAMPLE 1.2

Winston and Winona start a business selling computer games; they will rent shop premises for retail sales, but will also run a mail order service from the room behind the shop. The business is established as a partnership with a business name of WW Wizard Games. The two partners decide that, as they will both be working full-time in the new business, they will share all the profits from the business equally.

As in the case of Yasin in Example 1.1, it will be necessary to keep some records of the business activities. It makes good sense to do so, as it will contribute to good relations with the tax authorities. However, unlike the case of the sole trader, Yasin, there are some legal requirements governing the records that have to be kept by the business, and the way in which the business operates. Partnerships are covered by the Partnership Act 1890. This is a relatively straightforward piece of legislation which sets out a basic structure of legal relationships between partners, minimum record-keeping requirements, and ways of resolving disputes between partners. For example, the Partnership Act states that profits will be shared equally between partners, unless they make some other agreement between themselves. Winston and Winona have agreed in any case to share profits equally; this is a common arrangement where all partners are contributing equally to the success of the business. However, they could share profits in any way that seems appropriate.

Apart from the basic legal structure set out in the Partnership Act 1890, partners may decide to draw up a formal, legal agreement between them. Typically this would set out the details of the financial and legal arrangements which are to operate; it might, for example, state that Partner A will receive 60% of the profits of the business while Partners B & C each receive 20%. It may also deal with the actions to be taken in the event of a dispute between the partners. Not all partnerships bother to have a formal agreement of this type set up, but it can prove to be very useful if relationships turn sour.

Characteristics of the partnership form of business

The success of a partnership depends to some extent on the quality of the relationships between partners. Sometimes, people who are friends, or who are related to each other, set up a business partnership together. The pressures of running a business can sometimes place an intolerable strain on what has previously been a good relationship. On the other hand, where partnerships work well, they can be highly productive, especially if the partners have a range of skills that complement each other. Winona, in the example above, is perhaps very good at selling over the counter, but lacks the attention to administrative detail that is required to run the mail order side of the business. If Winston is a good administrator, he will complement Winona's skills, and between them they will perhaps be able to run a successful business.

As well as sharing in the running of the business, the partners are likely to be able to command more resources to put into the business. At the start-up stage, each may have savings or other resources (such as equipment) which they can put into the business. If the partnership needs to borrow money, it may be in a better position to do so than the sole trader.

If the partnership loses money, or cannot repay loans, lenders are able to recover money owed by requiring the partners to sell items of property which they own personally. In this respect the partnership is no different from the sole trader, and the partners face the consequence of bankruptcy in the worst cases.

Each partner is liable under the law for the actions of his or her partners. If Winona makes a business decision which turns out badly and the partnership is left owing a large amount of money, both Winona and Winston are liable for the consequences of the decision. Winston could not claim that he knew nothing about the agreement; he would still be equally liable with Winona. (It really is important for partners to know and trust each other thoroughly.)

A partnership business is not difficult to set up. However, partners should be prepared to go to the additional trouble and expense of having a clear partnership agreement drawn up with the help of a solicitor. It will make the resolution of disputes in the future easier to resolve.

1.1.3 Limited Companies

A **limited company** is a legal arrangement for regulating the ownership of business. A company is regarded as a separate person for the purposes of the law; so, for example, a company, unlike a partnership, can enter into a legal contract. This means that, if the other contracting person sues, he or she sues the company, not the owners of the company. The company itself becomes liable for its unpaid debts, overdrafts, and so on.

This legal construction is an extremely important feature of the business world, in the UK and in many other countries. Because the company itself enters into contracts, takes out loans and so on, its owners are protected from any adverse consequences of the action. This is the concept of **limited liability**. It is an extremely useful and helpful device which protects shareholders from personal loss if the business runs into trouble.

Setting up a company (the process of **incorporation**) involves some legal formalities which must be followed strictly. It is therefore more difficult than setting up a sole trader business. However, the difficulties should not be overstated: there are specialist company registration firms which, for a modest fee, take care of all the formalities. It need cost little more than £150 to set up a company.

After the company is incorporated, there are certain regular legal formalities which must be complied with. More details are given below.

EXAMPLE 1.3

Winston and Winona decide to set up their business as a limited company, rather than as a partnership. The business is registered in the name of WW Wizard Games Limited. They divide ownership of the business between them; each owns exactly 50% of the shares in the business. Winona and Winston are both shareholders. Both are involved in the day-to-day management of the business and, as well as being **shareholders**, are also **directors**.

Characteristics of limited companies

Shareholders are liable only for the amount which they have paid into the company in exchange for shares. This is the maximum amount which they can lose if the company is, for example, sued for not repaying its loans on time.

The legal formalities involved in setting up and running a limited company are more complex than for partnerships and sole traders. The directors of a limited company are responsible for making available to the public a certain amount of financial information about the activities of the company, on a regular basis. They must do this via the Registrar of Companies, an agency which is responsible for the collection of data relating to companies. Any member of the public can obtain information about a limited company by visiting one of the offices of the Registrar of Companies or through the website (www.companieshouse.gov.uk).

Regular filings include accounting information. Information which could remain private in a sole trader or partnership organization must be made public by limited companies.

In small companies, shareholders (who are the owners of the company) and directors (who are responsible for managing it) are the same people. However, in larger companies it is frequently the case that most shareholders have nothing to do with the management of the company. Day-to-day management can be left in the hands of directors who are professional managers. Shareholders in very large companies often have virtually no contact with the company or its managers.

Chapter 7 later in the book provides more detailed information about companies and their accounting.

1.2 SOLE TRADERS, PARTNERSHIPS AND LIMITED COMPANIES CONTRASTED

When setting up a business from scratch, the founder or founders must consider carefully which form of business organization is most suitable for them. Usually, it is sensible to take professional advice on the matter as it can be advantageous for tax purposes to choose one form over another. Leaving tax to one side for the time being, the following are the principal advantages and drawbacks of the three different types of organization.

1.2.1 Sole Trader – Advantages

- It is easy to start up as a sole trader.
- There are no legal formalities on start up.
- The sole trader is self-reliant; he or she does not risk the personality clashes which can occur where more than one person is managing a business.
- The sole trader does not have to share the profits from the business with anyone else.

1.2.2 Sole Trader – Disadvantages

- A sole trader bears all of the consequences of legal action against the business for unpaid debts and unfulfilled contracts. His or her personal property may have to be sold to meet business debts.
- A sole trader organization remains small-scale.
- The sole trader bears the brunt of any losses or business difficulties.
- There is no co-manager with whom problems can be shared.
- If the sole trader is weak in some aspect of business expertise (ability to sell, to manage people, to keep track of business records) the business may suffer because there is no-one available with complementary skills.

1.2.3 Partnership – Advantages

- In a partnership, management is shared and the business can benefit from the complementary skills that the partners bring to it.
- Business decisions do not have to be taken alone.
- Business risks are shared, as are any losses which the business makes.

1.2.4 Partnership – Drawbacks

- Partners are responsible in law for the consequences of each other's actions.
- Partners face unlimited liability; they must bear all of the consequences of legal action against the partnership. Their personal property may have to be sold to meet unpaid business debts.
- The profits of the business are shared between all the partners whereas a sole trader keeps all the profits for himself or herself (but note that a partnership business, which combines the skills of two or more people, should be able to generate higher profits than a sole trader).

1.2.5 Limited Company – Advantages

- The most significant advantage conferred by company status is the limitation of personal liability. Shareholders can invest in a business knowing that they will not be pursued for further **contributions** once their shares have been paid for.
- The limited company legal structure allows for shareholders to appoint professional managers as directors.
- A limited company's shares can be used to spread the ownership of the business amongst many people.
- Shares can be sold and bought so that transfer of ownership is relatively easy and straightforward.

1.2.6 Limited Company – Drawbacks

- Setting up a company requires adherence to a set of strict formal legal requirements, and will sometimes require professional advice.
- Regular filing of financial information with the Registrar of Companies is a legal requirement; this involves additional administration and means that members of the public have access to information which would remain strictly private in a partnership or sole trader organization.

Self-test question 1.1 (answer at the end of the book)

Before moving on, make sure that you can answer the following 'true or false' questions.

a) Setting up a partnership does not involve any particular legal considerations. TRUE or FALSE?
b) A sole trader is liable personally for all losses made by the business. TRUE or FALSE?
c) A director of a company cannot hold shares in that same company. TRUE or FALSE?
d) Partners are responsible in law for the consequences of each other's actions. TRUE or FALSE?

1.3 FINANCE FOR BUSINESS

When starting a business the founder or founders must find a source of finance to pay for the setting up costs, any equipment that is needed and, probably, for the expenses of the business for the period during which it is getting established.

Most established businesses will also require finance from time to time to pay for such items as:

- Buying major items of equipment or land and buildings.
- Expanding the scope of the business (for example, opening new offices or conducting research into new product feasibility).
- Helping the business through difficult periods such as temporary recessions or decreases in sales.

In this section of the chapter we will examine the principal sources of finance that may be available to a business. Some are more appropriate than others for particular purposes. Note that Chapter 20 considers the financing of businesses in much more detail than the brief summary provided below.

1.3.1 Existing Resources

When a business starts up, the founder(s) will almost certainly make an initial contribution of their own resources. This may be in the form of cash they have saved, or won or been given. It could be in the form of motor cars or vans, premises or some other item of resource. Such initial contributions are known in accounting terms as **capital introduced**. Where partners contribute to the setting up of a business, they may contribute unequal amounts depending on the resources they have at their disposal. In such cases, it may be decided between the partners that those who contribute more will receive an extra share of the profits to compensate.

EXAMPLE 1.4

Jakes, Jones and Jessop form a partnership to conduct legal business. The total capital introduced by the partners is £190 000, constituted as follows:

Jakes – office building valued at £100 000
Jones – cash of £50 000
Jessop – cash of £30 000 plus office equipment valued at £10 000

The partners decide between them that they will allocate 10% return on each of these contributions out of the profits made by the business, before dividing the profits equally between them. The business makes £49 000 in profits in its first year, which will be allocated between the partners as follows:

	Jakes	Jones	Jessop
	£	£	£
10% on Jakes' capital: £100 000 × 10%	10 000		
10% on Jones' capital: £50 000 × 10%		5 000	
10% on Jessop's capital: £40 000 × 10%			4 000
Remaining profit split equally between the partners: £49 000 – (10 000 + 5 000 + 4 000) = £30 000.			
Split equally	10 000	10 000	10 000
TOTAL	20 000	15 000	14 000

The introduction of capital is possible at any point subsequent to the foundation of the business. Whenever the business needs more resources, the initial founders may be able to make a further contribution.

1.3.2 Retained Profits

As a business grows it makes profits. The owners of the business usually take out part of the profits as their reward for investing in it. However, they are not obliged to take out the whole of the profits; they may leave some in the business to be invested to produce growth and further profits. The amount of profit left in the business is referred to as **retained profits**. This can be a very good source of funds for further investment as it is not dependent on any outside person or organization.

1.3.3 Borrowing Money

When thinking about potential sources of finance, borrowing may be one of the first possibilities that springs to mind. However, borrowing is not always the most appropriate source of finance for a business. In some circumstances it simply may not be obtainable. Many business start-ups would not be able to borrow money, because no organization would be willing to take the risk of lending it. Lenders need to know that:

i. the money they lend will be paid back eventually; and
ii. the business will be able to pay a reasonable rate of interest on the borrowing. In order to do so the business needs to stand a good chance of being profitable.

The cost of borrowing

The cost of borrowing is the interest that must be paid on a regular basis to the lender of the money. Large institutional lenders may agree to lend money to the business but they will expect to receive interest payments on time and without fuss.

The risk/return relationship

Banks and other lenders do not always charge the same rate of interest. They make an assessment of how risky the lending is; i.e. how likely it is that the borrower will fail to repay. If the loan is perceived as more risky than average, the lender will either refuse to lend, or will charge a high interest rate on the lending. Sometimes, it may only be possible to borrow at extremely high interest rates.

Security

Sometimes banks and other lenders will not lend unless the loan is secured. For example, a bank may make a business loan to an established sole trader business, but only on condition that it is secured on his or her house. This means that if the loan is not repaid, the bank would be able to force the sale of the house in order to ensure that funds are made available for repayment. A **mortgage** is an example of a secured loan. Businesses often take out commercial mortgages to assist in the purchase of property in the form of real estate.

Overdrafts

Overdraft facilities may be obtainable through the business's bank account. An overdraft is most likely to be made available to a business if it can prove that the extra funds are needed only in the short-term and that the business is fundamentally sound.

It should be noted that an overdraft is a short-term solution. It is technically repayable on demand; this means that the bank can demand immediate repayment of the overdraft at any time. In practice, however, banks rarely demand immediate repayment.

1.3.4 Leasing and Hire Purchase

When a business makes a large purchase of an item which will be used over the medium to long-term it has to pay out a lot of cash at one time. Sometimes it makes sense to look at alternative ways of financing a major item.

Under a **leasing** arrangement, the business (the **lessee**) pays a regular amount to a **lessor** in exchange for the use of an item such as a piece of machinery. The lease often extends over a period of years. The lessor, usually a financial institution, pays for the machine which is delivered to the lessee's premises and will, typically, remain there throughout its useful productive life. The lessor organization is the legal owner of the machine but will probably never even see it. The lessee never owns the machine, but will use it, often for years, in the business.

Short-term leases are sometimes taken out on items such as photocopiers and cars. The items may be replaced regularly and each time this happens a new lease is negotiated. Again, the lessee never actually owns the item in question.

Hire purchase is a similar arrangement to the longer-term leasing described above, with the difference that, once the final agreed payment is made under the terms of the agreement ownership passes to the purchaser business.

1.3.5 Grant Finance

Businesses may be able to obtain grants from the government, local authorities or other agencies and funding bodies. Usually, grants would be awarded only in quite specific circumstances. For example, a local authority which is trying to encourage the growth of local business, might allow companies moving into the area a rent-free period in local authority business units. Although this is not a grant of cash it is a saving on the expense of rental, and it may well entice businesses into the area.

Grant finance is very advantageous in that it usually does not have to be repaid. However, there may be strings attached. In the example given above, a business taking advantage of the rent-free period might have to undertake to stay in the area for a further minimum period of time of, say, 3 years.

1.3.6 Financing Companies: Share Issues

A company (but not a partnership or sole trader business) can raise additional finance by issuing more shares for cash. If the company is doing well, it can offer existing and potential shareholders a sound investment opportunity.

1.3.7 Financing Companies: Venture Capital

Medium-sized companies may be able to seek finance from venture capitalists. A venture capital company invests for limited periods in growing companies, in order to give them a short-to-medium-term financial boost. Usually, the venture capitalist buys into the shares in the company, and will often provide management expertise as well.

1.4 SHORT, MEDIUM AND LONG-TERM FINANCE

It is important for businesses to match their needs for finance with the most appropriate form of finance. Using an overdraft to buy a new office building, for example, would be highly inappropriate. Taking out a 10-year commercial mortgage, on the other hand, would probably be the most sensible course.

The table below categorizes the different sources of finance discussed earlier into short-term, medium-term and long-term sources.

	Short term	Medium term	Long term
Existing resources	√	√	√
Retained profits	√	√	√
Borrowings	√	√	√
Mortgage			√
Overdraft	√		
Short leases	√		
Long leases and hire purchase		√	√
Grant finance	√	√	√
Share issues		√	√

Self-test question 1.2 (answer at the end of the book)

Which one of the following types of finance would NOT be suitable for a sole trader business?

a) leasing
b) overdraft
c) issue of share capital
d) grants.

1.5 FUNDAMENTALS OF TAXATION

Taxation is a fact of life for most people and businesses. This section takes a brief look at the most common taxes levied on the different types of business examined earlier in the chapter.

1.5.1 Income Taxes (Personal Taxation)

Sole traders and partners in business partnerships make profits which are chargeable to tax. The tax that is levied is not a specific business tax; it is charged according to the individual's own circumstances at income tax rates.

EXAMPLE 1.5

Cerise and Cherry are partners in a discounted clothing business. Under their partnership agreement Cerise takes 60% of the profits and Cherry takes 40%. In the tax year 2012/13 the partnership profits are £30 000. Neither partner has any other source of income.

Cerise will be entitled to 60% of the profits: £30 000 × 60% = £18 000
Cherry will be entitled to 40% of the profits: £30 000 × 40% = £12 000

Each partner will include her share of the profits in her personal tax return. Each woman will be liable for income tax on her share less any attributable personal allowances. National Insurance contributions will also be payable.

1.5.2 Corporation Tax

As the name implies, this is a tax levied on companies. Directors are paid a salary for working in the company, and they will pay tax on the amounts they earn (just like any other employee). The company itself, however, is liable to corporation tax on its profits.

The company's profit is calculated (income less expenses = profit) and then corporation tax rates are applied.

1.5.3 Capital Gains Tax

If an item such as an office building is sold at a profit, capital gains tax is likely to be charged. Capital gains tax applies to both individuals and companies, and so would be levied on sole traders, partnerships and limited companies.

1.5.4 Value Added Tax

Value added tax (VAT) is the UK's principal form of indirect tax; it is a tax on transactions in goods and services. As private individuals we frequently pay VAT on goods and services that we purchase; we have no choice in the matter, and because prices are charged inclusive of VAT we don't usually even notice that we are paying the tax.

What about VAT from the point of view of a business? Businesses act as collectors of VAT which they pay over to the government authority which collects it, the HMRC, on a regular basis. The following example demonstrates the operation of VAT:

EXAMPLE 1.6

Palfrey and Bennett Limited is a retail business which sells men's clothing from a series of high street outlets. The company adds a charge of 17.5% (the standard rate of VAT) to all the items that it sells. The company's customers pay the tax.

At the end of the 3-month period ending 31 March 2012, Palfrey and Bennett completes a VAT return. Total sales before VAT for the 3-month period are £100 000. VAT at 17.5% is £17 500. The amount of £17 500 is known as **output tax**.

Palfrey and Bennett has itself, however, paid VAT on the purchases it made. During the same 3-month period it has bought goods totalling £70 000 before VAT. VAT at 17.5% is £12 250. The amount of £12 250 is known as **input tax**.

The quarterly liability to HMRC is calculated as follows:

Output tax for the quarter	£17 500
Less: Input tax for the quarter	12 250
VAT payable	5 250

The company must complete a Value Added Tax return immediately following each quarter. In this case, by the end of April 2012 they must send the VAT return to HMRC together with payment of £5 250. HMRC is very strict indeed about deadlines.

Each of the businesses supplying Palfrey & Bennett will also be obliged to fill in VAT returns and make payments to HMRC. People in business often complain about the large administrative burden imposed by accounting for VAT. However, once a business has set up systems to cope with VAT, filling in the VAT return is usually straightforward.

This section provides only a very general introduction to the taxation of businesses. For the purposes of this book it is regarded as general background business knowledge. Detailed knowledge of tax is not required for any part of the material which will be covered in the rest of the book. In almost all cases, the exercises ignore the effects of taxation in order to avoid adding an unnecessary layer of complication. However, students should bear in mind that the effects of taxation can be a significant factor in the real world.

Self-test question 1.3 (answer at the end of the book)

A company sells a building at a profit. Which one of the following statements is correct?
The profit is taxable:

a) as a capital gain
b) under income tax rules on the company's directors
c) as a VAT input
d) at the end of the VAT quarter.

1.6 THE NEED FOR ACCOUNTING INFORMATION

Quite simply, accounting information is produced because people need it. The reasons why they need it vary from one group of people to another. This section considers, for each of the main types of business organization identified earlier in the chapter, the range of accounting information that might be required, and the purposes for which it is needed.

1.6.1 Sole Trader

A sole trader business, because it usually remains small, is not complex in its organization. There is one manager, the sole trader, who may employ a few staff. The sole trader does not have to make information about his or her business profitability generally available. The HMRC may be the only external consumer of financial information about the business.

Annual information

Tax returns to HMRC have to be made once a year, within the stipulated deadline. The sole trader needs to prepare simple accounting statements to accompany his or her tax return. There will be a statement showing the calculation of profit or loss for the year, and, possibly, a statement which shows the resources owned by the business. These statements are known as the income statement (sometimes referred to as the profit and loss account) and the **statement of financial position** (sometimes referred to as the balance sheet)

- The income statement shows the revenue for the business for the year, less the business expenses. The remainder is either a profit or loss.
- The statement of financial position shows the resources owned and controlled by the business at a single point in time. It also shows any amounts owed, for example, loans taken out from the bank and payments due to suppliers of goods.

Every business has a year-end date. The income statement is prepared for the year ending on that date, and the statement of financial position shows resources less amounts due on the same year-end date.

Quarterly information

If the sole trader is registered for VAT, a quarterly VAT return will have to be prepared. As explained earlier, this contains a summary of sales and purchases transactions which have taken place in the quarter, and a calculation of input and output tax, in order to arrive at the net amount payable to HMRC. Failing to meet the deadlines for submission of the return and the amounts due must be avoided at all costs. Therefore, the sole trader business has to be able to keep accounting records sufficiently well to be able to provide the required information quickly.

Accounting information within the business

As well as the information provided for external authorities, the sole trader needs more frequent information to help to manage the business efficiently, and to assist in decision-making. At the simplest possible level this means keeping an eye on the state of the bank balance. At a slightly more sophisticated level, it is usually helpful to prepare regular accounting statements. A sole trader should keep records of sales and receipts of cash, and of the payment of expenses. From these it should be possible to prepare a simple monthly statement of profitability. This will not be used for reporting outside the business; it is an internal document for sole trader's own use.

Recording and summarizing information

In most cases, sole trader businesses do not employ an accountant. It would be far too expensive, and, besides, because accounting information needs are relatively modest, there would be little point. If the sole trader is equipped with some basic knowledge of record keeping, has the time to do it, and is sufficiently well organized to keep the records straight, the cheapest and most straightforward option is to do the job himself or herself.

Some sole traders pay a book-keeper for a few hours a week to keep the records straight. Where staff are employed it is particularly important to keep good records and to make accurate calculations of pay, income tax and National Insurance contributions due.

In almost all cases, the sole trader is well advised to use the services of a qualified accountant for assistance with preparing annual financial statements, preparing tax returns and ensuring that the correct amount of tax is paid. Unless some very complex advice is involved, this kind of service can usually be purchased for a few hundred pounds each year.

In summary, the sole trader produces financial information to be used outside the business by HMRC. No other external party can require information from the sole trader. Financial information for internal use will be produced as frequently as necessary to provide the sole trader with the information needed to run the business.

1.6.2 Partnership

A partnership, as noted earlier, does not need to make financial information generally available to the public. However, it must, in the same way as the sole trader, prepare annual financial statements which form the basis for tax calculation by HMRC. Also, quarterly financial information will probably have to be made available to HMRC in the form of summaries of sales and expenses and input and output tax totals supplied on the VAT return every quarter.

In most respects the information requirements are, so far, very similar to those of a sole trader. However, there is one important difference: in a partnership the annual income statement provides the profit figure which will be split between the partners in accordance with their profit-sharing arrangements. The annual financial statements, therefore, take on an additional dimension of importance in a partnership. The partners themselves need to be satisfied that the accounts have been prepared properly and that they present a reasonably accurate figure for profit.

Audit

In some cases, the partners may decide to have an **audit** conducted, to ensure that the annual financial statements are properly prepared and fairly stated. There is no stipulation in the law for audit of partnership accounts, but partners may decide, in drawing up the partnership agreement, that an audit should be carried out annually.

So, what is an audit? It is an independent examination, by a properly qualified person, of the financial records and financial statements of an entity. One of the important qualities of a well-conducted audit is that the auditor should be independent of the management of the business he or she is auditing. A partnership which requires an audit would appoint a professionally qualified auditor to conduct the examination of the records and give an impartial opinion on whether or not the annual financial statements have been properly drawn up. The opinion takes the form of an **audit report** which is attached to the financial statements. In addition to providing reassurance to the partners themselves, the fact that an audit has been conducted may be reassuring to HMRC. However, it should be emphasized that there is no legal requirement for the audit of partnerships (or of sole traders).

Accounting information within the business

We saw earlier in the chapter that sole trader businesses will find it helpful in running their businesses to produce accounting information such as monthly statements of profit.

Partnership businesses tend to be larger than sole trader businesses (because more people are involved) and the need for internal accounting information may be greater because of the increased size and complexity of the business. As a business increases in size, its managers will usually find that they need more detailed information to help in decision-making.

EXAMPLE 1.7

Poste, Ponsonby and Peppard is a partnership of solicitors. As well as the three partners, the practice employs three other qualified solicitors and several administrative staff, including a full-time book-keeper. The partners have a monthly management meeting where they make decisions on important issues. In order to help them, they have instituted a system of internal financial reports. The book-keeper prepares the reports which are confidential, to be seen only by the partners.

The principal reports are:

- Income statement for the month.
- Billings summary for each solicitor for the month.
- Summary of hours worked by each solicitor for the month.
- List of client invoices unpaid.

These reports allow the partners to see whether any of the solicitors are falling behind target in their monthly billings. They also allow for an assessment of profitability so that if, for example, monthly profits are tending to fall, the partners can take stock of the situation and decide whether action is necessary.

The list of unpaid client invoices informs the partners of any clients who are taking an excessively long time to pay. They can then make the necessary telephone calls and send out letters to prompt the client to pay up.

1.6.3 Limited Company

Accounting information needs within the sole trader and partnership types of business organization are, essentially, very similar. However, the picture changes when we examine accounting for limited companies.

Provision of financial information outside the business

Limited companies are required to publish financial information via the Registrar of Companies. Because everyone has access to the information held at Companies House, the information is potentially available to a very large number of people. In fact, the financial information of most companies remains undisturbed because there are very few people who would be interested in it, apart from the shareholders. The company's shareholders are informed, in any case, of the financial condition of the company because they are entitled to receive a full set of annual financial statements.

However, it is possible that other groups of people, apart from the shareholders, could be interested in the information. People or organizations who have been asked to lend money to the company are likely to be interested in the financial status of the company. People who are affected by a company's existence (for example, those living near the premises of a chemical company which regularly breaches environmental legislation) may also take an interest. Later in the chapter we will consider the different categories of people who might be interested in a company's financial information.

Companies are required to submit tax returns and VAT returns, and financial reports must be made available to HMRC in the same way as in sole trader and partnership organizations.

Separation of ownership and management

In smaller companies the shareholders and directors are often the same people. Because they are engaged in the day-to-day management of the business, directors who are also shareholders really do not need annual financial information to tell them what is going on. They have access to as much internal financial information as they need.

However, the position is different for shareholders who are not directors. In large companies, most of the shareholders are remote from the activities of the business; they receive **dividends** and an invitation to the Annual General Meeting of the business, but have no other contact with it. If they are shareholders in a listed company, they will be able to follow movements in the share price by consulting the financial press, but they are not entitled to the regular detailed internal financial information which the directors use in managing the business.

The relationships between the company, the directors, and the shareholders are expressed in Figure 1.1:

FIGURE 1.1 Separation of ownership and management in a limited company

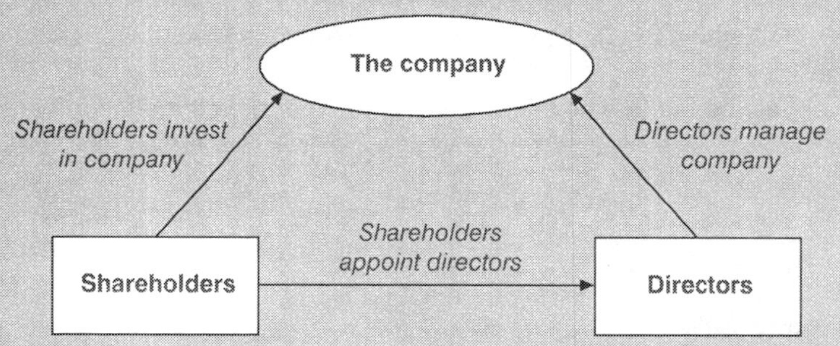

The diagram demonstrates the separation between the ownership of the company and its management. Shareholders appoint directors (who in larger companies are professional managers) to manage the company on their behalf: the directors act as agents of the shareholders, or, to use an old-fashioned term, as stewards on their behalf.

The **stewardship** function requires directors to act in the best interests of the company at all times. In order to demonstrate good stewardship, they should report on a regular basis to shareholders – hence the requirement in company law that full annual financial statements are sent to shareholders. Company law also requires in some cases that financial statements are independently audited, which provides reassurance to shareholders that the financial statements present a true and fair view. The legal requirement applies only to larger companies, although there is nothing to stop smaller companies volunteering to have an audit.

Clearly, where shareholders are remote from the management of their company, there is potential for the directors to take action which benefits themselves, rather than benefiting the shareholders. This is one of the potential problems of the agency, or stewardship, relationship. For example, a current, and recurring issue, is that of directors' remuneration in very large companies. Criticisms are often voiced in the press of the very large increases in salary, and substantial bonuses which directors award themselves. Shareholders are in a position to take action if they do not approve of directors' remuneration packages (via their votes at the Annual General Meeting) but, in practice, they rarely challenge the directors.

Accounting information within the business

With the exception of the very large professional partnerships which are permitted by law, all larger businesses in the UK are constituted as limited companies. As a company grows in size, its management needs ever larger quantities of internally generated accounting information in order to keep control of the business, and to make good quality decisions. Larger companies, especially those involved in the complexities of say, manufacturing or banking, tend to produce highly complex and sophisticated information for use by management.

Self-test question 1.4 (answer at the end of the book)

Explain which types of business are required by law to have an annual audit of their financial statements.

1.7 USERS OF ACCOUNTING INFORMATION

Different groups of users of financial information can be identified. In this chapter we have discussed many of them already. Table 1.1 lists the principal user groups and summarizes the most likely reasons for their interest.

TABLE 1.1 Principal groups of users of financial information

User group	Reason for interest in financial information
Shareholders	To assess the performance of management in their role as stewards of the company
	To use the information to make decisions on whether or not to sell the investment in the shares of the company, or perhaps whether to buy more shares in the company
Potential shareholders	To make decisions on whether or not to invest in the shares of a company
Investment analysts	To assess the performance of the company in order to be able to advise their clients on investment strategy
Lenders and potential lenders	To assess the ability of the business to make repayments and to meet regular interest payments
Employees and trade unions	To assess the viability of the business and the extent to which it is likely to be able to (a) continue to offer employment; (b) increase pay and improve employees' conditions
Suppliers	Where suppliers offer credit terms, they need to be able to assess the likelihood of being paid promptly
Special interest groups	In the case of an environmental activist group, for example: to assess the extent to which the company has set aside funds for environmental clean-up operations

TABLE 1.1 Principal groups of users of financial information *(Continued)*

Government: tax collecting agencies	To assist in the assessment and collection of taxes
Government: other agencies	To assist, for example, in the collection of national statistical information
Financial journalists	To obtain information about a company's activities and profitability which will be of interest to the journalist's readers
Academics and students	To assist in the study of business activity
Customers	To assess the likelihood of the business continuing in existence, and continuing to supply the goods or services required by the customers
The general public	Anyone, not covered by any of the categories above, who has an interest in the activities of the company

1.7.1 Access to Information

Because company financial statements are made publicly available all the above categories of users have access to them. In many cases the user groups are making important decisions on the basis of the information, answering questions such as:

- Should I sell my shares in this company?
- Should my bank be making an overdraft facility available to this company?
- Is the company doing well enough to make it safe for me to carry on working for it?
- How risky is it to supply goods on credit to this company?
- How well are the current management looking after my interests as a shareholder?

Company accounting information is called upon to be useful to a wide range of users in making decisions. In the next section of the chapter we look at the characteristics of useful financial information.

1.8 CHARACTERISTICS OF USEFUL FINANCIAL INFORMATION

Ideally, financial information produced by businesses would have the following key characteristics:

It should be:

- *Relevant:* to the decision being made. For example, the information should be prepared shortly after the events being reported so that it is not out of date by the time it is used
- *Reliable*: the information should be properly prepared and free from error or bias in its preparation
- *Comparable*: where financial statements from more than one period are being prepared, the information should be prepared on the same basis, so that it is comparable
- *Understandable*: the information in the financial statements should be capable of being understood.

In practice, it is not always possible to achieve information which fulfils all of the above characteristics. In large and complex businesses collecting accounting data and processing it into a set of financial statements is a time-consuming process. By the time it is published (usually 3 to 4 months after the year-end date in a very large company) circumstances may have changed and the information may be of limited use for decision-making. Also, the information that is reported is all historical: i.e. it relates to events that have already occurred. The extent to which past events are a reliable guide to the future is questionable in a fast-changing business environment.

Accounting information should be understandable, but, again, this is not always easily achievable. The financial statements of very complex organizations tend, inevitably, to reflect that complexity. People who are reasonably knowledgeable about business matters should be able to understand financial statements, but even their ability to understand is sometimes tested by the complex financial statements of major listed companies.

1.9 FINANCIAL ACCOUNTING AND MANAGEMENT ACCOUNTING

There are two distinct strands to accounting in organizations. **Financial accounting** refers to the processes and practices involved in providing users external to the business with the information that they need. Companies, because they provide a relatively large amount of information to outside users relative to partnership and sole trader entities, tend to devote substantial resources to financial accounting. This type of accounting is also referred to as **financial reporting**, and both terms are used in this book.

Management accounting is the accounting that a business organization carries out for its own internal uses. It assists management in controlling the business and in making decisions.

Both financial and management accounting use information generated by the accounting system of the business. Clearly, the accounting systems of businesses are likely to vary enormously, depending upon the complexity and size of the business organization. However, all accounting systems have certain characteristics in common. The flow of information in an accounting system and its relationship to financial accounting and management accounting is demonstrated diagrammatically in Figure 1.2.

Data and information about events and transactions flows in and out of the business. For example, when a business makes a sale of goods to a customer which it supplies on credit (i.e. the customer is not obliged to pay cash straight away) the following events and information flows take place:

At each stage details about the event are 'captured' by the accounting recording system. Periodically, data which share common characteristics (e.g. all sales invoices) are analyzed and the analysis is used to produce reports for both financial and management accounting purposes. See Table 1.2.

TABLE 1.2 Events and information flows relating to the sale of goods

Event	Information flow
An order is placed	Data about the nature and quantity of the goods required flows into the business and is recorded
Goods are assembled, packaged and sent out	A record of despatch is produced within the business and is sent out with the goods to the customer
An invoice is raised through the business recording system	The invoice is sent out from the business to the customer – information leaves the business
The customer sends payment	Information is received in the business and is recorded. The cheque is banked – information again flows out of the business

FIGURE 1.2 The production of financial reports and management accounting reports

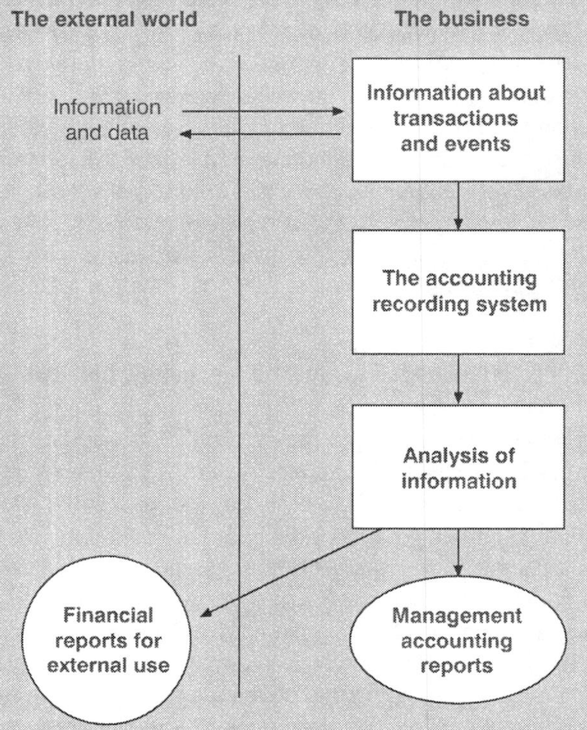

1.10 THE ROLE OF THE ACCOUNTANT IN BUSINESS ORGANIZATIONS

As we have seen, there are two separate strands in business accounting: financial reporting to user groups external to the organization, and management accounting for reporting to managers within the organization. This variation in function is reflected in the organization of the accounting profession and in the training of accountants.

1.10.1 The Accounting Profession

The accounting profession includes the following types of accountant:

Independent accounting practitioners: these accountants work outside industry and business in professional practices. These are the accountants who provide taxation and accounting services to a wide range of businesses. If they are **registered auditors**, they are authorized to carry out the audits of companies and other organizations.

Accountants in business: these are the accountants with whom business managers work in organizations. Broadly, they are either **financial accountants** or **management accountants**, depending upon whether they specialize in the external or the internal provision of accounting information.

Professional accountants may have one or more accounting qualifications. These days almost all professional accountants have a university degree, although it is not necessarily in accounting or a related subject (the author of this book for example, is a chartered accountant with a degree in Russian). After university they enter into a period of 3 or 4 years training with an employer during which they take some very tough examinations. Not everyone who embarks on accountancy training will manage to qualify because the examinations are so demanding.

The following are the principal professional accounting bodies in the UK which have their own qualification systems:

- ICAEW: the Institute of Chartered Accountants in England and Wales (members have the letters ACA or FCA after their names).
- ICAS: the Institute of Chartered Accountants of Scotland (members have the letters CA after their names).
- ACCA: the Chartered Association of Certified Accountants (members have the letters ACCA or FCCA after their names).

The members of these organizations are found in both professional independent accounting practice and in business. Students of ICAEW and ICAS usually train in professional accountancy firms. Students of ACCA are found in both professional and business environments. Usually those who go into business specialize in financial accounting and reporting rather than in management accounting.

Finally there is CIMA: the Chartered Institute of Management Accountants (members have the letters ACMA or FCMA after their names). As the name of this organization implies, its members work principally in management accounting, and its students train exclusively in the business environment.

People who have trained as accountants are often found at the most senior levels in business organizations. It is not unusual in the UK to encounter chief executives and senior directors who started their careers as accountants before moving into more general business management.

1.11 ORGANIZATION OF THE REMAINDER OF THIS BOOK

Chapters 2 to 7 inclusive are concerned with financial statement preparation, including the fundamental principles and practices involved in preparing income statements, statements of financial position and statements of cash flow. Chapters 8 and 9 are concerned with understanding the financial reports of businesses. Chapters 10 to 18 inclusive are concerned with the acquisition of skills and knowledge related to management accounting information. Chapters 19 and 20 explain the fundamentals of financing a business.

CHAPTER SUMMARY

This chapter provides a framework of information about accounting which underpins the remainder of the book. First, the three principal types of business organization were introduced, followed by a description of the characteristics of each type. Then the chapter proceeded to examine some aspects of business financing. (This topic will be examined in much more detail in Chapter 20.) The next section was concerned with taxation because it is important to have a broad outline knowledge of how the different types of business are taxed. However, it should be noted that a detailed knowledge of taxation is not required in order to achieve the aims of this book.

The chapter then turned to accounting information. The need for accounting information was examined in the context of the three types of business organization introduced earlier in the chapter: sole trader, partnership and limited company. Each organizational type needs to make some information available to people or organizations outside the business. In addition, accounting information is needed to assist management in running the business.

The provision of information to outsiders is a much more important issue for limited companies than it is for partnership or sole trader organizations. The general public has access to company financial information through the medium of the Registrar of Companies. As well as filing information at Companies House, companies are also obliged by law to make annual accounting information available to their shareholders. The chapter explained the important issue of the separation between the ownership and management of limited companies, which is especially noticeable in larger companies.

There is a long list of potential users of accounting information: shareholders, potential shareholders, investment analysts, lenders and potential lenders, employees and trade unions, suppliers, special interest groups, the government, financial journalists, academics and students, customers and the public at large.

The chapter went on to discuss some of the important characteristics of useful financial information: it should be relevant, reliable, comparable and understandable.

The distinction between financial accounting and management accounting was described and discussed, and then the role of the accountant in business organizations was described. There are several different professional accountancy qualifications and the main ones were noted.

INTERNET RESOURCES

The following websites may be of use in finding out more information about certain aspects of this chapter:

www.hmrc.gov.uk – the website of Her Majesty's Revenue and Customs

www.companieshouse.gov.uk – the Registrar of Companies' website, which provides information about all UK companies.

Book's companion website summary

www.cengage.co.uk/gowthorpe3 contains the following resources in respect of Chapter 1:

Students' section

Quiz containing 15 multiple choice questions

Four additional questions with answers

Lecturers' section

Answers to end of chapter exercises 1.13 to 1.18

Four additional questions with answers

ExamView testbank

Instructor's manual

PowerPoint presentation

EXERCISES: ANSWERS AT THE END OF THE BOOK

1.1 Which one of the following statements about the sole trader form of business is correct?

a) A sole trader has to pay corporation tax.
b) Sole traders submit annual information to the Registrar of Companies.
c) The sole trader is entirely responsible for the management of the business.
d) Because a sole trader business is simple it is not necessary to keep any records.

1.2 Which one of the following statements about the partnership form of business is correct?

a) Partnerships are always very small businesses.
b) Partners are obliged by law to put £50 000 into the business when it starts up.
c) Partnerships are very difficult to set up because of the amount of information demanded by the Government.
d) Partners are personally liable for the debts of the partnership business.

1.3 Which one of the following statements about the limited company form of business is correct?

a) A limited company is a separate person in law.
b) Limited companies cannot be sued.
c) It costs a great deal of money to establish a limited company.
d) Shareholders in a limited company are obliged to act as directors.

1.4 Select from the following list the most appropriate form of finance for purchasing a new office building:

a) 10-year mortgage loan
b) loan repayable in 6-months' time
c) overdraft
d) hire purchase.

1.5 Select from the following list the most appropriate way of financing a new office photocopier:

a) grant finance
b) issue of new share capital
c) lease
d) mortgage.

1.6 You are a small business adviser. A new client, Arnold Tapwood, has come to you for advice. Mr Tapwood explains that he is the sole proprietor of a small building business. One of his friends, Simon, who is a carpenter, has suggested that he and Arnold should join forces in a partnership. Arnold is not sure about the extra legal responsibilities which would be involved in becoming a partnership, and he asks you to explain in outline the legal formalities which would be required.

1.7 Geoffrey is a keen dangerous sports enthusiast. He would like to set up in business as a sole trader organizing dangerous sports events and activities. His business idea is that people would pay an annual subscription which would allow access to his website and a range of discounts on the fees for dangerous sports events. While he expects the idea to be a winner, because there are so many like-minded enthusiasts, he feels it likely that he will need some start-up finance to equip an office, install a couple of telephone lines and pay for some help with administration. He estimates that he will need about £10 000 to get things up and running before the subscriptions start to appear in large numbers.

Geoffrey has just left university with accumulated debts of around £8 000 so he has no money to put into the business. His parents refuse to give him any money for the venture. He has come to you for advice on the best ways of financing the start-up.

1.8 Which one of the following statements about the regulations governing a sole trader business is correct?

a) A sole trader does not need to supply any accounting information about his or her business to anyone.
b) A sole trader must employ an accountant.
c) Sole trader businesses are exempt from completing VAT returns.
d) A sole trader must submit a tax return annually.

1.9 Which one of the following statements about the regulations governing partnership businesses is correct?

a) Partnerships are obliged to have an annual audit of their financial statements.
b) Partnerships must prepare annual financial statements as the basis for the calculation of tax.
c) At least one of the partners is obliged to hold a book-keeping qualification.
d) Each partner must submit his or her own VAT return.

1.10 Which one of the following statements about the regulations governing limited company businesses is correct?

a) All limited companies are obliged by company law to have an annual audit.
b) A limited company must send annual accounts to all of its shareholders.
c) All shareholders have unlimited access to their company's management accounting information.
d) The general public can access information about a company only by applying in writing to the directors.

1.11 Podgorny & Weaver Limited is involved in the wholesale of fashion goods to retailers. The company directors have a monthly meeting to discuss strategy and to make decisions. The directors are presented with the following reports prepared by the company accountant each month:

- list of amounts owed by the retail businesses which the company supplies
- summary of the value of fashion goods items currently held in inventory
- summary of the orders received during the month
- income statement for the last month.

Explain how the directors would be able to make use of each of the reports listed in order to improve the management of the company.

1.12 A group of environmental activists is interested in the activities of Burnip Chemicals plc, a company which has been regularly fined in the past for emitting toxic waste into the river which runs past the factory premises. What kind of information would the activist group be seeking about the activities of the company? To what extent are the annual financial statements likely to be helpful to them?

EXERCISES: ANSWERS AVAILABLE ON THE LECTURERS' SECTION OF THE BOOK'S WEBSITE

1.13 One of the following statements about the limited company form of business is correct:

a) A limited company must submit information on a regular basis to the Registrar of Companies.
b) Directors of limited companies are always selected from amongst the shareholders.
c) Limited companies are not eligible to apply for grants.
d) Directors of a limited company are personally liable if the company is sued.

1.14 Select from the following list the most appropriate way of financing the build up of stocks of Easter eggs in a chocolate business:

a) grant finance
b) overdraft
c) issue of new share capital
d) lease.

1.15 Marie Deutsch is a fashion designer who, after graduation with a degree in fashion, obtained a very good job as designer in a lingerie company. She has decided that she would like to leave her job and set up in business with an old friend from college who also trained as a designer. Marie has heard that it is more sensible to set up as a limited company because it would mean that she and her friend would not be personally liable for the debts of the business. However, she says she is sure that there must be some strings attached, and would like you to tell her about any disadvantages in limited company status.

1.16 Which of the following statements is correct?

The stewardship function requires directors of limited companies to:

a) Act at all times in the best interests of the company.
b) Allow shareholders to see detailed accounting records upon request.
c) Hold regular monthly meetings to answer shareholders' questions.
d) Consult the shareholders over particularly difficult management decisions.

1.17 Ponderosa & Smythe plc is a shoe manufacturing business, specialising in children's shoes. The finance director has just received the following letter from a shareholder who has recently bought some shares in the company:

'Dear Mr Pershore

I have just read a most interesting article in the Financial Times about the decline in the market for children's shoes. The article suggests that, because of demographic changes the market will decline by 3-4% each year over the next 10 years. In the circumstances I think our company should branch out into women's shoes. I would like the directors to discuss this at the next board meeting. Could you please send me a copy of the sales budget for the coming year, so that I can see whether or not you have taken the declining market properly into account.'

What are the principal points that the finance director should make in response to this letter?

1.18 Mohsin, a bank manager, is looking at an application for a loan from Boxer Burstall Limited, a local company. The company has included a copy of its most recent annual accounts which are for the year ending 31 December 2011. The accounts show that a modest profit has been made in the year. It is now March 2013.

Required:

i. What type of information will Mohsin be looking for from the annual accounts to help him in making a decision on whether or not to lend the money?
ii. How relevant is the accounting information which the company has provided to Mohsin's decision?
iii. Is Mohsin entitled to request any further information?

CHAPTER 12

Financing the Business

AIM OF THE CHAPTER

The aim of this chapter is to know about and understand the principal sources of finance available to businesses of all sizes.

LEARNING OUTCOMES

After reading the chapter and completing the exercises, students should:

- Understand the key issues involved in financing a business start-up.
- Know about some of the most important sources of small business finance.
- Understand the problems and opportunities presented by business growth, and some of the financing issues related to growth.
- Know about sources of finance for larger business.
- Know how the UK stock market operates, and the advantages and disadvantages of operating as a listed company.

INTRODUCTION

Chapter 1 provided an introduction to types of business organization, their financing, and the role of accounting in business. This chapter provides more detailed information about the sources of business finance. The availability of finance is often dependent upon the size of the business organization. Very large, well-established companies have access to a level and type of funding that is not, except in highly unusual circumstances, available to people starting up businesses.

The chapter provides a progression through different businesses' stages. The early sections concentrate upon financing issues relating to business start-ups. The problems and opportunities of growth are then examined before, finally, the chapter examines the particular types of financing that are available to larger businesses.

20.1 FINANCING THE SMALL BUSINESS

All businesses have to start somewhere. They mostly start small and are usually based upon a bright idea which occurs to one person, or sometimes, to a small group of people. The idea may be brilliant but impractical in business terms. It may have occurred to lots of other people so there will be a high level of competition in the market. Or it may be so good and original that it is going to make its owner a millionaire.

The basic business idea may arise out of a need for a product or service which cannot, apparently, be found, or cannot be found at the right price.

20.1.1 Sources of Finance for a New Business Start-up

In chapter 1 we examined sources of business finance in outline. Below we look in more detail at some typical sources of finance which might be used to finance the start-up of a new business. Money will be required for some or all of the following:

purchase of equipment.
supporting the owner and family while the business gets going
paying for premises
paying for staff
expenses like business rates, insurance, running costs of cars, etc.

Where does the money come from?

Existing cash resources

Existing cash resources may be available in the form of savings and windfalls. In fact, the arrival of an unexpected windfall, such as a lottery win, a convenient legacy, or a big redundancy pay-off, may even provide the impetus for the starting up of a business.

Also possible, depending upon the nature of the business, is self-financing through part-time work. In practice, many small businesses are financed in this way.

EXAMPLE 20.1

Sasha completes her degree in fine art, producing several very good pieces of work at her degree show. Two of the pieces sell, and Sasha is offered an exhibition at a local art gallery. However, even though she may be comparatively successful in her working life as an artist, it is highly unlikely that she will ever earn enough from her work to be able to provide herself with a decent living. Sasha takes a job for 15 hours per week in an art materials shop. This employment subsidizes her 'business' which is selling her own art work.

Family or friends

If the prospective business person has no resources it is possible that his or her family may be prepared to support the business in its early stages. Sometimes this can be through an injection of cash, or the loan or gift of an item of equipment. Or sometimes, a supportive partner will agree to cover living costs from his or her salary during the early stages of the business.

Even if finance can be obtained in this way, there may be a downside. If the businessman borrows from his nearest and dearest, and then loses the lot in a reckless business start-up, family relationships can be scarred or even terminated. Business failure can, and often does, contribute to the breakdown of long-term relationships.

Grant finance

Grants can be an excellent source of start-up finance, as they usually do not need to be repaid. However, they are available only for quite specific purposes (such as employment of local people in areas of high unemployment), and almost never serve to finance all of the expenses of a start-up. Also, once a grant is given, the granting authority will normally keep quite a close check on the progress of the business.

Commercial borrowings

Generally speaking, anyone proposing to start up a small business is likely to be reluctant to borrow money from external sources such as banks, if it can possibly be avoided. There are several sound reasons for this reluctance:

- Banks charge commercial rates of interest on loans. This can add substantially to the costs of a business start-up and can make the difference between potential success and failure.
- Bankers will not lend to just anyone. In fact, they usually will not lend to anyone who does not have a record of success in business. This is not a problem if you are embarking on start-up number ten, with nine successful businesses to your credit, but, realistically, most people without a good track record in business are likely to face a refusal when they ask their bank for a start-up loan.
- Bankers want to know that their loans will be repaid. They will maximize the likelihood of repayment by insisting upon **security** for the loan. This means that an arrangement is made so that, if the loan is not repaid on time, the bank can take an item, or items, of at least equal value from the business or the individual in settlement of the debt. The bank will usually insist upon a legally binding agreement known as a **charge**, to ensure that the loan gets repaid.

EXAMPLE 20.2

Des starts up in business with a bank loan of £50 000. The bank stipulates a legal charge over Des's house. The business goes bust after 2.5 years, still owing the bank the original £50 000 plus £3000 in unpaid interest. Because the bank has the legal charge, the house must be sold to meet the debt, and Des and his family will, effectively, be evicted and may be made homeless. This may seem harsh but the charge is a legal document, and the bank is quite within its rights to insist upon repayment via the sale of the house.

If security is not available in any other form, bankers may ask for a guarantee from someone who is sufficiently wealthy to repay the loan if the business fails. This type of arrangement is fine, provided that the guarantor (i.e. the person giving the guarantee) thoroughly understands the possible consequences if the business fails. There have been unfortunate cases where the guarantor has not understood that he or she stands to lose a very large sum of money if the business goes bad.

A secured loan is less risky, from a bank's point of view, than an unsecured loan. The nature of the loan and the value of the security tends to affect the interest rate. The greater the risk, the higher the rate of interest. Therefore a loan made by a bank on good security will have a lower interest charge than an unsecured loan.

20.1.2 The Business Plan

When seeking finance in the form of a loan or a grant, it is usually necessary to produce a **business plan**. Even if the production of a business plan is not strictly necessary (because external finance is not being sought), it is worth producing one because the process of writing down plans and projections for a new business can help to clarify ideas. The business plan normally includes most or all of the following elements:

- Description of the business concept.
- Detailed description of the product or service which the business will offer.
- The market for the product or service. Market research. Analysis of the competition.
- Profile of entrepreneur: a personal profile detailing relevant experience (including possibly a CV) and an analysis of personal strengths and weaknesses.
- Initial investment required. Type and cost of equipment, premises and similar items.
- Details of other people involved. If the plan is to employ people straight away, details are required of how they will be recruited, and how much it will cost to employ them.
- Insurance requirements. Any relevant legal issues.
- Professional advisers. Details of the type of professional advice that may be required, and how much it is likely to cost.
- Detailed financial projections. A budget will be required for at least the first year, showing the projected profit and cash flow (see Chapter 16 as a reminder of what is involved in the budgeting process).

20.1.3 Why Do Businesses Fail (and Why Do Some of Them Succeed)?

It can be quite difficult to estimate the failure rate for businesses. A statistic that is often quoted is that, of every ten new business start-ups, only one or two will remain in business after 5 years. However, there is some evidence to suggest that the true position is more encouraging; the Small Business Administration Office of Advocacy in the USA estimates that seven out of ten new employer businesses (that is, businesses that employ people) survive for at least 2 years, and around half of the ten survive for at least 5 years. During the recent recession, the rate of business failure increased, as might be expected. For example, the number of company liquidations increased in 2009 to 19 077 from 15 535 in 2008, an increase of 22.8%.

The Association of Business Recovery Professionals in the UK (www.r3.org.uk) provides a range of useful publications. Their publication 'Understanding Insolvency' cites the most common reasons for corporate insolvency. These are as follows:

- 'Loss of market: where companies have not recognized the need to change in a shrinking or changing marketplace, because their margins have been eroded or because their service has been overtaken technically.
- Management failure to acquire adequate skills, either through training or buying them in, over-optimism in planning, imprudent accounting, lack of management information.
- Fraud.
- Loss of long-term finance, over-gearing, lack of working capital/cashflow.
- Other reasons include excessive overheads, new venture/expansion/acquisition.' (pages 3-4)

This is all very depressing, especially for anyone who is seriously thinking about setting up a business. However, many businesses do succeed and prosper. The factors which tend to lead to success include: adequate financing, a cautious approach to risk-taking, existing management experience and experience and sheer good luck.

Self-test question 20.1 (answer at the end of the book)

Briefly describe the advantages and drawbacks of obtaining the following types of finance for a business start-up: (i) grant finance; (ii) borrowing from family or friends.

20.2 STAGES IN BUSINESS GROWTH AND EXPANSION

This section of the chapter examines the problems and opportunities that may arise in the growing business. It then examines sources of finance for the growing business.

20.2.1 Employing People

Many businesses do not grow past the point where they generate an income for one person and his or her dependants. A self-employed tradesperson, such as a plumber, small builder or garden designer may have no particular need or wish to expand the business to the point where employing another person becomes necessary. However, some business people will see the need for expansion, and employing another person is often the first step towards expansion.

Advantages of employing people in a small business

There is an opportunity to increase the skills base of the business. As noted earlier in the chapter, one of the reasons why businesses fail is because of poor management. A sole trader is particularly vulnerable to this type of problem; he or she has to marshal a range of skills including selling abilities, financial management skills, organizational ability, self-discipline, and so on. If any one of these is missing the business may fail. One way around the problem of missing skills is to either go into partnership with someone whose skills are complementary, or, in some cases, to employ a person who can contribute skills lacking in the proprietor.

Employing people is likely to increase the volume of trade in goods or services. Two pairs of hands can achieve more than one. If the right person is employed, he or she may be able to contribute to the profitability of the business.

EXAMPLE 20.3

Kingsley is a self-employed furniture designer who undertakes commissions for the provision of original, well-designed furniture for businesses. He started up in business 2 years ago, and he has been very successful in generating work. He now has more than he can easily cope with. He is working 7 days a week from early morning until late at night and his relationships with friends and family are suffering. Also, he has received some unpleasant letters recently from suppliers including a threat from the electricity utility company to cut off his supplies unless he pays his bill within 7 days.

It is pretty clear that Kingsley needs help. Administering a small business can take a disproportionately large amount of time. While Kingsley may not be ready to take on a full-time administrator he should examine the possibility of employing a part-timer who can keep control of the paperwork. This would, presumably, free up part of Kingsley's time so that he could get on with more productive work.

The other area in which he probably needs help is in the design work. This is a much more difficult issue to resolve than the administration. People award Kingsley design commissions because they like his work. If he delegates some of the work to an assistant the design values may suffer. Unless Kingsley is prepared to carry on working all hours, he will have to make a decision on whether he keeps the business very small by turning down any commissions which he cannot manage himself, or, alternatively, whether he is prepared to share the design work with someone else. The first course of action involves a risk; if he turns down too much work, the supply of commissions may dry up altogether. The second course of action also involves a risk; will the quality of work suffer? And does Kingsley have the necessary management skills to control the work of one or more designer employees?

Disadvantages of employing people in a small business

There is a very significant risk attached to employment. If a poor choice of employee is made, the mistake can threaten the survival of the business. Mistakes can be made in employing someone with whom there is a personality clash, or someone who is less competent than they appeared from their CV and the interview. Many employers will make an employment decision which, sooner or later, they come to regret.

Employing people costs money. Many successful small businesses pass through an awkward stage where there is too much work for the sole trader or partners to handle by themselves but where the financial risk of taking on an employee is unacceptable. The business proprietor(s) must be sure that they have the financial resources to pay for employment.

Employing people involves a great deal of paperwork. If staff are employed, the business becomes involved in the administration of Pay As You Earn (PAYE) and National Insurance Contributions (NIC) on behalf of the employee. Detailed records must be kept, and these are liable to be inspected periodically by HMRC. Business people often complain bitterly about the amount of work they have to undertake as tax collectors on behalf of the government. The amount of administration which is involved acts, potentially, as a disincentive to employing people (although it should be noted perhaps, that the administrative burden in the UK is probably less than in some other countries. France, for example, imposes a notoriously heavy administrative burden on the employer). The example below illustrates some of the practical financial considerations involved in the decision about whether or not to employ somebody.

EXAMPLE 20.4

Recently, Kelly started a business importing and selling ornamental lamps, vases and similar items to retailers. The business has been successful, making profits of £35 000 in its first year and £38 000 in its second. Kelly has realized that, if the business is going to be able to grow, she will have to employ someone to assist her in selling goods to retailers. The ideal employee would have a good track record in selling and would be able and willing to travel 4 or 5 days a week visiting retailers' stores.

What financial factors does Kelly need to consider in making a decision about employing an assistant?

- *Salary*. Kelly needs to look carefully at how much she will have to pay in order to ensure the right employee. She needs someone with experience and who is prepared to act on his or her own initiative. Part of Kelly's annual profits will have to go to paying the employee. In addition to the annual salary, there will be the cost of providing transport (presumably an additional car will be required).
- *Employer's National Insurance and administration costs*. The employer must pay employer's National Insurance Contributions, and the cost of administering the payroll must be taken into account. Kelly may be able to do this herself (the cost of doing this is the time taken up which could be used on something else), or may have to pay her accountant a little extra to do it.
- *Balancing costs and benefits*. If Kelly succeeds in employing someone who is good at selling, the benefits could far outweigh the costs of employment. Suppose the total cost of employment is £30 000 per year; provided the employee can generate additional business which makes more than this amount in profit then it makes good business sense for Kelly to employ him or her. There may be other less obvious benefits – if Kelly gets flu and has to spend a week in bed the business, at the moment, grinds to a halt until she is better. If she could depend upon an employee, the business could be kept going more or less as normal.

20.2.2 Developing the Business Organization

As a business grows and starts to employ more people, the way in which it is organized becomes more of an issue. There is a tendency in most business organizations to establish manageable units according to the functions they carry out. For example, in a typical manufacturing organization, it may be appropriate to establish separate departments for marketing, production, despatch, design, personnel, accounting and general administration. In the early days of the business only one or two people will be employed in each function, and the business proprietors are likely to retain firm control over all of the operations of the business. However, as the business grows, it becomes increasingly difficult for its owners to control every aspect of its functions. It is important for proprietors to be able to recognize when this stage has arrived, and to be prepared to delegate control to others.

Professional management

People who have started up successful businesses are often very reluctant to concede any part of their control to others. However, in most cases, it eventually becomes necessary to employ professional managers – people who have the experience and knowledge to manage functions such as marketing and personnel. Conflict sometimes ensues between the managers and the original founders of the business as they disagree about the right way to manage change and growth.

Communication issues

As the business grows and departmental structures emerge, a range of communication problems can arise. Departments develop their own identities, and can, if not properly managed, become narrow in outlook, fighting territorial battles with other departments to protect their own status. Where this type of 'in-fighting' occurs, the overall objectives of the business tend to be forgotten.

Growth in bureaucracy

As we have already noted in this chapter, a certain amount of unavoidable record-keeping and administration is imposed on businesses by government regulation. As businesses grow and organizational functions separate, the business itself starts to require more complex records. An accounting department is usually required in order to keep the financial records straight. Some kind of authorization and control procedures are, inevitably, required, but a great deal of management skill is required to make sure that the generation of paperwork does not get out of hand. Organizations with excessive administration procedures may ultimately fail because they have become too inwardly focused. For example, staff become demotivated by the requirement to produce what they see as excessive paperwork. Perhaps the need for prompt and thorough organizational reporting starts to take priority over activities such as production quality control and establishing new sales contacts.

20.2.3 Sources of Finance for the Growing Business

Expansion and growth of a successful business usually involves moving into new areas. Sometimes, this involves expanding the range of products and/or services on offer. Or, new opportunities may arise to expand the market that the business serves. Expansion requires finance, which sometimes has to be sought from sources outside the business.

The sources of finance mentioned earlier in the chapter as suitable for the small business may also be appropriate for this stage, although some are likely to be more appropriate than others. For example, commercial borrowing is unlikely to be obtainable for a business start-up, but is more likely to be available to a growing business with a sound record of profitable trading. Conversely, finance from family and friends (unless they are wealthy) is less likely to be available for an established, growing business. A source of finance that may be appropriate, and which has not been mentioned so far in the chapter, is venture capital.

Venture capital

Venture capital is funding provided by institutional investors and/or individuals who wish to invest in growing companies with very good prospects for the future. Venture capital investors typically set up a dedicated venture capital firm or fund which seeks to invest in particular types of business, often within a restricted industry sector. These firms are sometimes referred to as 'private equity' providers.

The type of funding provided by venture capitalists is typically for the medium to long-term (often between 5 and 10 years). The funding is provided in exchange for an equity stake in the business, and the venture capitalist(s)/private equity investor(s) will typically take an active role in the management of the business. The 'hands-on' management role of the venture capitalist is often one of the most attractive aspects of the deal for the managers of the growing business as it can give them access to experience and contacts that would not otherwise be available to them.

Venture capital is usually provided for a fixed term, after which the venture capitalists withdraw from the business, perhaps by selling their equity stake back to the original founders of the business, or by realizing their investment when the successful business is floated on the stock market (the next section of this chapter contains more information about stock market flotation).

Individuals: 'angels' and 'dragons'

Individual investors may become involved in the provision of finance to growing businesses via an intermediary like a venture capital organization, as described above. Alternatively, they may provide finance to a business without an intermediary, by direct investment. Traditionally, such investors have often been referred to as 'business angels'. A relatively new piece of terminology is the business 'dragon', a term which refers to a very successful television format – 'Dragons' Den' that originated in Japan but which has been exported successfully around the world. The format in the UK involves people with business start-ups or established businesses that require new funding pitching their business idea to five 'dragons' who are successful and often well-known entrepreneurs. Most of the pitches fail miserably, thus providing much entertainment value, but a few are successful. Those who are successful are rewarded with an input of cash in exchange for an equity stake in the business from one or more of the dragons, plus their direct management input into the business.

Leasing

The acquisition of non-current assets may require a significant outflow of cash. One way of acquiring assets without a large cash outflow is to lease them. There are, broadly, two types of lease. Operating leases are for relatively short periods, and involve regular rental payments for the use of an asset. Operating lease arrangements are often used for assets such as photocopiers and motor vehicles. Finance leases cover most or all of the life of an asset, and are in essence a way of purchasing an asset in instalments. The business that leases the asset (the lessee) pays the provider of the lease (the lessor) regular amounts of cash, agreed in advance. Finance lease arrangements, as the name implies are arrangements for financing the acquisition of an asset. The regular payments include an element both of capital payments in respect of the asset acquisition, and interest payments (the finance cost related to the lease).

Leasing can be an appropriate way of financing asset acquisitions for businesses of any size. However, they may be particularly helpful for the growing business which must carefully balance working capital requirements with its need to acquire assets.

Self-test question 20.2 (answer at the end of the book)

Briefly outline the principal features of venture capital financing.

20.3 SOURCES OF FINANCE FOR LARGE BUSINESSES

There are many possible sources of finance available to large businesses, including commercial borrowing, leasing, issues of new shares, flotation on the stock market and investment by venture capitalists. Some of these are possible only where the business is structured as a company. Financial reporting by limited companies was covered earlier in the book, in Chapter 7, and some of the information below should be familiar.

20.3.1 Issue of Shares

Upon the initial formation of a company, ordinary share capital is issued to the first shareholders of the company. In the case of small businesses, the number of shareholders is usually low, often no more than one or two people. As companies grow, they may issue more shares to other people. Private companies (companies with 'limited' after their name) are not permitted to issue shares to the general public, or to have their shares quoted on a stock market. Public limited companies (companies with 'plc') after their name, on the other hand, are permitted to issue shares to a wider public. Some plcs are quoted on a stock market and so are able to issue their shares widely to the general public. It is important to note that not all plcs are quoted companies, but that only plcs (and not private companies) may have their shares quoted on the stock market.

The ordinary shares of companies are often referred to as **equity shares**. They have a nominal value such as £1.50p or 25p; this is the basic denomination of the share. Shares that are quoted on a stock market have a share price – a market value which is, usually, greater than the nominal value. For example, a listed company has 5 000 000 shares with a nominal value of 50p each and a market value of £3.75. This gives the company a total nominal value of 5 000 000/50p = £2 500 000; this is the nominal value of its issued share capital. The total market value (its market capitalization) of the company is: 5 000 000 × £3.75 = £18 750 000.

20.3.2 Rights of Shareholders

Ordinary (equity) share capital entitles its owners (shareholders) to a vote which they can exercise at the general meetings of the company. The other principal right of shareholders is to receive dividends. Dividends are paid out to shareholders, often on a regular basis; dividends constitute the income received by shareholders on their investment. Very large companies usually have two regular payment dates each year for dividends (an interim dividend and a final dividend). The company's directors decide upon the level of dividend to be paid out; it is usually expressed as an amount in pence per share, for example: 'the directors have declared an interim dividend of 5p per ordinary share in issue'.

20.3.3 Benefits of Limited Companies

The liability of shareholders in companies is limited. That means that, even if the company fails, the shareholders cannot be called upon to contribute any further cash.

Because the capital of limited companies is split up into many shares, it is possible for a shareholder to sell a very small proportion of the total share capital of the company to another person. This can be useful where, for example, the original shareholders of a company have decided that they wish to spread the share ownership more widely, perhaps to other family members.

Usually, if a business becomes really large, a limited company is the only realistic business vehicle for it. It allows for multiple shareholders, each owning, perhaps, a very small proportion of the total business. Sole traders, for obvious reasons, usually own very small businesses. Similarly, partnerships, except in a few special cases, tend to be small or medium-sized businesses. The special cases tend to be professional firms (such as firms of accountants, lawyers, architects or other professionals) where very large partnerships do exist. In most cases, however, if a business grows to be very large, it will be in the form of a company.

Sometimes, the directors of a company may choose to raise finance by obtaining a listing on the Stock Exchange. This involves selling shares to a wider public than family, friends and business associates. In the next two subsections we look at various aspects of the operation of the UK stock market.

20.3.4 The London Stock Exchange (LSE)

A stock market is a place where stocks are traded. So, what are the stocks referred to in the term 'stock market'? The LSE is the UK's stock market. It trades in, principally, the shares of quoted companies. Quoted companies comprise both UK based companies, and overseas companies which have a quotation in the UK. The market also trades in British Government bonds (these are known as 'gilts' or 'gilt-edged stock'), other types of shares and company bonds (also known as **loan stock** or **debentures**).

So, where is this 'place' where stocks are traded? In former times the principal stock market location in the UK was the trading floor of the LSE. This was a place in the City of London where the agents of people and organizations which wished to trade in stocks and shares met in person to arrange transactions. This physical location is no longer necessary following the far-reaching reforms and reorganization of trading which has taken place over the last 25 years. Transactions in shares are now arranged and dealt with electronically, so the 'place' occupied by the stock market is, nowadays, a virtual location.

The LSE is a powerful organization which regulates the trading in shares and organizes their listing. The LSE operates in two principal capacities: as a 'primary market' and as a 'secondary market'.

Primary market

The primary market function allows companies to raise capital via the LSE. In order to exploit the capital-raising potential of the LSE new entrants to the market apply for a listing and, if successful, float the company on the stock market. This means that they are entitled to offer shares, either newly issued or existing shares, to the public.

Companies which already have a stock market listing may decide that they need to raise more finance. Such companies can issue more shares and sell them for cash.

Secondary market

The secondary market function allows trading in shares to take place between willing buyers and sellers. This is an extremely useful function which allows for easy liquidity in shares. Liquidity means, in this context, that shares can be bought and sold easily. High liquidity is extremely attractive to investors; it means that they are not tied into their investment over long periods, but can liquidate (turn into cash) their investment whenever it suits them to do so. One of the problems of investing in unquoted companies can be that it can be difficult (or downright impossible) to sell the investment to anyone else.

20.3.5 Organization and Operation of the LSE

The LSE's market is split into two: the main market and the Alternative Investment Market (AIM).

The main market

The main market is the most important element of the market provided by the LSE. Companies on the main market have a full listing and are subject to the full range of regulation applicable to listed companies. In order to obtain a listing on the main market companies normally have to have been in business for at least 3 years and to have a full record of accounts for that period.

The Alternative Investment Market (AIM)

The AIM is a market which deals in shares of smaller and/or newer companies than those which are eligible to obtain a full listing. Many relatively small companies choose to obtain a quotation on this market. Investing in these companies is potentially riskier than investing in companies with a full listing because: (a) the business venture may be inherently riskier; and (b) the shares of AIM companies are often quite illiquid – that is, they may not be traded very often or in very large volumes. This could make a holding of shares in an AIM company more difficult to sell than a holding listed on the main market.

However, some AIM companies are highly successful; they may move on to a full listing once they have built up a trading record.

Share prices

There are over 2000 UK companies quoted on the LSE at any one time, plus several hundred overseas companies. Although many companies have been listed for years, the list is constantly changing as new companies come to the market (at a rate of some 200-300 per year), and existing companies leave (because they have failed and go into liquidation, or because they are taken over, or because their directors decide to de-list).

Shares in quoted companies have a market price which can fluctuate a great deal. Shares in the larger, better known companies, are traded very frequently, and their price can change from minute to minute. It is possible to obtain share prices with a delay of approximately 15 minutes from many sources nowadays. One of the best and most reliable is the LSE's own website (www.londonstockexchange.com).

Shares in smaller companies, especially those on the AIM, may be traded infrequently, i.e. their trading volume is low. Prices for such shares may remain quite static with long periods of inactivity.

Share prices will tend to rise when a company is doing well, or when some piece of good news is announced (for example, the company has obtained new business or it has sacked an incompetent director). Conversely, bad news often results in a fall in share price. However, sometimes movement in share prices has relatively little to do with individual companies' activities and is the result of a general market sentiment. For example, there was a huge general drop in share prices following September 11th, 2001. This affected all companies, but those involved in aerospace, insurance or tourism were particularly badly affected.

Stock market indices: the FTSE

Anyone who watches television news, or who listens to radio news, will have heard the (usually) brief reports about the financial markets which sound something like: 'Bad news on the financial markets. The Footsie 100 fell 54 points to close at 5729.2.' While the first sentence makes sense, the second sounds like gibberish to the financial novice. Let's pick the important pieces out of the statement:

'Footsie' is the usual verbal reference for 'FTSE' which stands for 'Financial Times Stock Exchange'. The FTSE organization, which is owned by the LSE and the Financial Times newspaper, runs a series of indices both for the UK stock market and worldwide. The FTSE 100 is an index which relates to the changes in value of the top 100 listed UK companies. The index started originally with a value of 1000. Each of the 100 constituent companies figures in the index according to the relative size of its capital. The minute by minute changes in the value of the 100 companies' share prices are fed into the index calculations. For most interested observers, daily tracking of the index value tells them all they need to know, but it is possible for people and organizations who are deeply involved in investing, to find the current value at any time during the LSE trading hours.

So, if the index falls by 54 points, it reflects an overall, average, fall for the day in the share prices of those companies which make up the index. Some of the companies' share prices may have gone up; some have fallen, and overall, the average movement for the day is slightly downwards.

The reported index total (5 729.2) is only really helpful to a person who keeps a regular eye on the movements in share prices. The index figure on its own means very little.

Which companies are in the FTSE?

At regular intervals the FTSE committee reviews the membership of the FTSE 100; the principal criterion for membership is size which, of course, fluctuates. The FTSE 100 account for over 80% of the market capitalization of companies listed on the LSE. The committee also reviews membership of the other principal stock market company classifications:

There are indices for the following:

- FTSE 250 – these are the 250 companies which are next in order of size after the FTSE 100. They account for around 15% of the total market capitalization of companies listed on the LSE.
- FTSE All-Share – the FTSE 100 and FTSE 250 plus a group of smaller, but still significant companies classified as FTSE SmallCap.
- FTSE Fledgling – these are fully listed companies which do not qualify in size terms for the FTSE SmallCap.

Information about the current values of all of these indices, and the rules which operate for their calculation, can be found at the FTSE website: www.ftse.com

20.3.6 Flotation and Other Types of Share Issue

Floating a company

As noted earlier, between 200 and 300 companies become publicly quoted each year. The process is time-consuming (it can easily take up to a year to organize and carry out), and may deflect directors' attention from running the business. A great deal of professional advice is required in order to conduct a successful flotation. Corporate finance advisers, stockbrokers (usually referred to simply as 'brokers'), lawyers and professional accountants are involved in ensuring that the process is successful.

Flotation for most companies involves a **placing** of the shares. This means identifying prospective buyers (usually institutional investors such as pension schemes, life assurance companies, venture capitalists, investment trusts and asset managers), and arranging to sell a portion of the shares. In the case of a placing, there is no invitation to the general public to buy into the new shares. An **offer for sale**, by contrast, does involve a general invitation to the general public and the institutions to buy shares in the company. It involves preparation of a detailed **prospectus** which contains a great deal of information about the history and prospects of the company.

In either case, once the shares are floated they can be bought and sold in the secondary market. However, in most cases of smaller companies coming to the market for the first time, the principal or only buyers of the new shares are likely to be half a dozen or so of the well-known institutional investors.

Other types of share issue

New issues Once a company has been floated successfully it may issue further blocks of shares in order to raise new capital. If there is sufficient demand for the shares, the new issue is likely to be successful.

Rights issues It is commonly the case that, where a listed company wishes to raise cash via a new issue of share capital, it will do so via a **rights issue**. A rights issue is an offer to existing shareholders to purchase additional shares. It is usually expressed in such terms as 'a one for three rights issue'. This would mean that for every three shares already held in the company, the shareholder could buy one additional share. Taking up the rights issue allows an individual shareholder to retain the same percentage shareholding as before, as the following example illustrates.

As in the Wendover example, it is usually the case that the rights issue price will be pitched below the current market value of the share, in order to make it attractive to shareholders. If the rights issue fails

EXAMPLE 20.5

Wendover Household Goods plc has a total issued share capital of 1 000 000 £1 shares whose current market price is £5.30 each. It requires a fresh injection of capital to finance the building of a new factory. Wendover's corporate finance advisers tell the directors that the best way of raising the money is via a rights issue. They suggest an issue of 1 for 4 at £4.40. How much cash will this rights issue raise for the company? An issue of one share for every four held will result in the issue of an additional 250 000 £1 shares. Each of these will be sold for £4.40, resulting in a cash inflow of £1 100 000.

Jeannie Lemmon is one of Wendover's principal shareholders. She holds 170 000 of the issued shares. How much will Jeannie have to pay if she takes up the rights issue? Jeannie's holding is 170 000 shares. She will have the opportunity to buy 170 000 ÷ 4 = 42 500 shares. Therefore, she will have to pay 42 500 × £4.40 = £187 000 if she decides to take up the rights issue.

(in that existing shareholders do not take up the issue) then it would be possible to try to raise additional capital by a placing or an offer for sale. However, existing shareholders could be assumed to have a particular interest in the company; if they aren't interested in investing more money in the company, it is even less likely that outsiders will wish to do so. A real-life example of a rights issue is described below.

EXAMPLE 20.6 (REAL-LIFE)

Lloyds Banking Group (LBG)

Following the financial crisis in 2007, the UK government persuaded Lloyds TSB to merge with the failing Halifax banking group. Subsequently, in 2009, LBG sought to refinance itself, partly by launching the largest rights issue ever to take place in the UK. The group's 2.8 million shareholders were asked to buy up a rights issue. The terms of the issue were 1.34 new shares for every existing share held, at a price of 37p each. This price was deeply discounted, compared to the quoted price of a LBG share at the time, by around 60p per share. In December 2009, it was announced that the issue had been successful.

Mergers and acquisitions

Where a full-scale effort is made by one company to purchase a majority of another company's shares, this is referred to as a **takeover bid**. What happens is that the bidding company offers to purchase shares from existing shareholders at a stated price. The existing shareholders do not have to accept the offer; the offer has to be pitched at a price which will make it sufficiently attractive to induce a large number of the existing shareholders to sell. Takeovers are a common feature of the stock market environment. A **hostile bid** refers to a bid by one company which is rejected by the target company's directors. Not all takeovers, however, are hostile.

The consequences of a successful takeover bid are often far-reaching. The purpose of a takeover, in principle, is to allow a better quality management to take on the control of the operations of the target company. Ideally, takeovers should lead to improved efficiency and better returns for shareholders of the company which is taking over the other. In practice, it appears that takeovers do not always have the desired effect.

Mergers and acquisitions (M&A) is a general term which refers to any bringing together of companies either by agreement or as a result of a hostile bid. (Note that both 'mergers' and 'acquisitions' have specific meanings for accountants, but it is beyond the scope of this book to examine those meanings.)

Self-test question 20.3 (answer at the end of the book)

Identify the following statements as either TRUE or FALSE:

1 All takeover bids are hostile bids.

2 A rights issue is an offer to sell shares to existing shareholders in proportion to their existing holdings.

3 An offer for sale of shares is limited to a few major financial institutions.

4 The LSE trades in corporate bonds, as well as shares.

20.3.7 To List or Not to List?

It may not be easy for the directors of a limited company to decide on whether or not to list. There are advantages and drawbacks.

Advantages of listing

- The principal advantage of listing is that the company can raise more finance for new projects and investments.
- Listing increases a company's general profile and credibility and may enhance its reputation.
- Listing may allow the founder members of a company to turn their hard work in the past into cash by selling part or all of their holding of shares.
- Listed companies shares can, in most cases, be liquidated easily. Listing is, therefore, likely to increase the pool of potential investors, and may increase the value of the company.

A survey carried out jointly in 2001 by the LSE and Eversheds (a firm of business lawyers) found that the most popular reason cited for seeking flotation was 'to raise funds' (mentioned by 64% of respondents), followed by 'to increase the company's profile and credibility' (mentioned by 23% of respondents).

Drawbacks of listing

- A listed company is in the public spotlight. Financial journalists are likely to become much more interested in a company's activities once it is listed. This may work to the company's advantage when everything is going well and the publicity is welcome. However, if the company is struggling, or if it is engaged in some controversial activity, publicity may be a major drawback.
- A listed company may become a 'takeover target'. A company can take over another company by buying up a majority of the shares in order to obtain control over it. The directors of the target company usually find themselves in a difficult position in these circumstances and they often lose their jobs.
- There is increased pressure on companies' management to produce consistent and ever-improving results. This pressure may result in short-termism, where investment in the long-term future of the company may suffer in order to produce the kind of short-term results that satisfy City commentators.

- Obtaining a listing is not cheap. A great deal of accounting and legal work must be paid for, plus underwriting costs. The total costs usually amount to at least 10%, and occasionally as much as 20%, of the amounts of cash raised by the flotation.
- The additional layers of regulation are onerous and compliance with them can be very expensive. It is usually necessary to employ additional staff.
- Movements in the company's share price can be worryingly difficult to explain or predict.

In the LSE/Eversheds survey referred to earlier, the principal drawbacks to being a public company were identified as 'additional reporting requirements and associated costs' (mentioned by 57% of respondents) and 'volatility of share price, often with little correlation to business fundamentals' (mentioned by 18% of respondents).

CHAPTER SUMMARY

There are many different potential sources of finance for businesses of all sizes, but the financing options available are more numerous and more flexible for larger and more successful businesses. The financing of very large businesses, such as the FTSE 100 companies, often involves complex arrangements such as the LBG's rights issue mentioned in the chapter. However, the more well-known a business is, the more likely it is that information about it, and its financing arrangements, will be publicly available in the form of newspaper articles, blogs and other commentaries.

It is worth following up some of the Internet resources listed below in order to develop knowledge of the types of finance available.

INTERNET RESOURCES

www.ftse.com – the website of the FTSE organization which is responsible for the indices used on the LSE. The website explains in detail the composition and operation of the indices.

www.londonstockexchange.com – the LSE's own website contains information about all companies currently listed, including news items, current share prices, hyperlinks to companies' own websites, information about what is involved in listing, and a great deal besides.

www.bvca.co.uk – the website of the British Venture Capital Association

www.bbc.co.uk/dragonsden – the BBC's Dragons' Den website includes videos of pitches by hopeful entrepreneurs and an online version of the series.

Book's companion website summary

www.cengage.co.uk/gowthorpe3 contains the following resources in respect of Chapter 20:

Students' section

Quiz containing ten multiple choice questions
Four additional questions with answers

Lecturers' section

Answers to end of chapter exercises 20.10 to 20.15
Four additional questions with answers
Case study
ExamView testbank
Instructor's manual
PowerPoint presentation

EXERCISES ANSWERS AT THE END OF THE BOOK

20.1 Erika is planning to become a self-employed graphic designer working from a small one room office in a new development in the middle of town. You are a small business adviser and she has asked you for help in producing her business plan.

Required: prepare a list of questions to ask Erica at your first meeting, based upon the major headings which you would expect to see covered in the business plan.

20.2 Ben has a degree in public relations and a huge list of useful contacts in the aerospace business which he has established over a period of several years while working for Amis & Lovett, a large PR agency. He would like to set up his own PR agency. He plans to employ a new graduate and a secretary immediately in order to avoid being regarded as a 'one man band'. He is confident that his savings (£45 000) will tide him over the first couple of months while he finds enough work to get started.

Required: list the main risks which you see in Ben's plan for the new business start-up.

20.3 Nancy is a self-employed hairdresser. She runs a salon with the assistance of one untrained employee who takes bookings, tidies and sweeps up, and makes tea and coffee for the clients. Nancy would like to expand the business; this would involve employing a fully trained stylist. There is sufficient space in Nancy's existing premises for another person to work.

Required: advise Nancy on the costs, risks and potential benefits involved in employing a stylist.

20.4 Oleander Enterprises Limited is a small holiday company run by its two principal directors and shareholders, Libby and Lisa. The company organizes exclusive (and expensive) holiday tours of French chateaux. During the 4 years since it was set up the company has gone from strength to strength. It now employs six people and it makes substantial annual profits. The company has a cash surplus and the directors have been considering ways of using the surplus to expand the business, possibly by starting up operations in new countries. Recently, the directors have been approached by Loretta, the managing director of another holiday company, Oxus Orlando Limited, which organizes holiday tours in Turkey. Loretta is the principal director and shareholder of Oxus Orlando. She would like to sell her company and retire on the proceeds.

Required: advise Libby and Lisa on:

i) The advantages and drawbacks of expanding by buying into another company
ii) The type of information they will require in order to be able to make a decision on whether or not to buy Oxus Orlando.

20.5 Ashton Longton plc, a listed company, has issued share capital of £8 000 000 comprising shares of £1 nominal value. The current quoted price per share is £3.85.

What is the company's market capitalisation?

20.6 The Alternative Investment Market is a market for:

a) companies that do not currently wish to proceed to full listing
b) companies that promote alternative lifestyles
c) British Government securities
d) overseas companies without a trading history.

20.7 Warminster Toys plc has a total issued share capital of £3 000 000 in 50p shares. The company decides to make a rights issue of 1 for 5 at a price of £5.42 per share. To take up the rights the holder of 50 000 shares will have to pay:

a) £27 100
b) £135 500
c) £54 200
d) £271 000.

20.8 Yolande Brighton is the managing director of Brighton Bestwines plc, a company which supplies the licensed trade. The company has been very successful but has now reached the point where it needs to expand its warehousing capacity if it is to continue growing. The directors have been contemplating applying for a listing on the AIM. The company will issue a further 500 000 shares (it already has 1 000 000 shares in issue). It hopes to be able to sell the shares at around £2.50 each.

The directors have invited you to their board meeting to discuss the flotation. They are keen to raise the finance, but one or two of them are wondering about potential drawbacks to being quoted on the AIM, and they would like you to give them an outline of any possible problems they face.

Required: prepare a list of potential drawbacks for discussion at the meeting.

20.9 Speke Septima Limited was started up 3 years ago to market a range of designer kitchen products. The company has been very successful, but now needs finance to expand into overseas markets. The directors have discussed a range of financing options, and have reached the tentative conclusion that they should approach a venture capital firm. In outline, they propose to sell 30% of the company in exchange for an equity investment of £3 million, and a seat on Speke Septima's board. They have asked you, a financial adviser, to identify any potential drawbacks in entering into a venture capital arrangement of the type proposed.

Required: identify and describe drawbacks to the proposed venture capital arrangement.

EXERCISES: ANSWERS AVAILABLE ON THE LECTURERS' SECTION OF THE BOOK'S WEBSITE

20.10 Norman and Naylor Partners is a business which runs corporate events. Sam Norman and Sally Naylor founded the business about 5 years ago, and it has been very successful. The partners share profits equally. It now employs five full-time staff and calls upon a pool of up to 40 additional staff who can be employed part-time for specific events. Sally is several years older than Sam, and would now like to pull out of the business. She plans to take out her share of the value of the business with a view to buying and running a vineyard in Italy.

Required: identify the business problems and risks which Sam must deal with as a result of Sally's decision. What are the financial implications (in broad terms) for the partners?

20.11 Lionel is an experienced chartered surveyor with many years of experience. He is employed by a large property company where he receives a good salary and a performance-related bonus. He has recently been approached by an old friend, Leo, who is one of three partners in a firm of surveyors. The other two partners are nearing retirement age, and they have decided that they need to bring in some 'new blood'. The partnership has been in operation for nearly 20 years and has carved out a sizeable niche in commercial property management. Leo tells Lionel that the partnership has been valued by a business valuation specialist at £1 200 000. If Lionel accepts the invitation to join the partnership he will be required to pay £300 000 in cash for a quarter share of the business. In exchange he will be entitled to one-quarter of the profits made by the partnership in the future.

Required:

i) Advise Lionel on the type of information he will need to examine in order to be able to make a decision on whether or not to buy into the partnership.
ii) Identify possible sources of finance which might be available to Lionel to fund his investment in the partnership.

20.12 Lucinda and Lister are sole (and equal) shareholders and directors of L&L Limos Limited, a company which runs a small fleet of limousines for hire for weddings and parties. Each year the company has gradually increased its revenue and has developed a reputation for reliability. There is no direct competitor for their service in their own town, and increasingly often the company is asked to undertake business in neighbouring towns and cities. Quite often these days the directors have to turn business away because all of the available cars are booked. The option of expanding the fleet and taking on new driers looks increasingly attractive.

Required:

i) Describe the sources of finance that might be suitable to finance the proposed expansion.
ii) Identify the additional costs which might be involved in the expansion.
iii) Briefly identify and describe any risks associated with the expansion and its financing.

20.13 Amery Chorlton plc, a listed company, has issued share capital of £4 000 000 comprising shares of 25p nominal value. The current quoted price per share is 98p.

What is the company's market capitalization?

20.14 Willoughby Wooster plc has a total issued share capital of £1 000 000 in 25p shares. The company decides to make a rights issue of 1 for 2 at a price of £2.70 per share. How much will the holder of 30 000 shares have to pay to take up the rights?

a) £40 500
b) £10 125
c) £20 250
d) £7 500.

20.15 Tatiana, a friend of yours, has recently been left approximately £50 000 of listed company investments in her grandmother's will. She has been trying to read the Financial Times in order to see what is happening to her investments. She has found some information about three of them:

i) Turtlehammer plc rose to 215p on speculation of a hostile bid from a competitor, but fell back to 210p by the end of the day's trading.
ii) The share price of Teddington Tilmain plc has risen by 26 pence following the announcement that it has obtained an important new export contract.
iii) Tolson Tortellini plc has announced today that it is making a rights issue of 1 for 4 at £2.30

Tatiana frankly admits that she doesn't understand any of this. She asks you to explain each of the pieces of news in terms that she can understand. She would like to know if any of it is likely to be good news for her.

CHAPTER 13

Understanding Financial Reports: Trend Analysis

AIM OF THE CHAPTER

To develop a range of skills which assist in the understanding of financial reports for various types of business.

LEARNING OUTCOMES

After reading the chapter and completing the related exercises, students should:

- Understand the potential usefulness of financial reports to various interest groups.
- Understand the principal features of the analysis of trends in financial statements.
- Be able to perform an analysis based on horizontal and/or vertical analysis of financial statements.
- Understand the problems which can arise in comparing businesses with each other.

Techniques of analysis will be developed further in Chapter 9.

INTRODUCTION

One of the most important aims of this book is to help students appreciate that financial information actually means something. The formal figures that are set out in reports may not look very interesting in themselves, but the underlying reality that the numbers symbolize is almost always fascinating, especially for those involved.

Many of the examples and exercises in Chapters 2 to 7 have emphasized the importance of accounting figures in helping people to understand what is going on in a business. However, this chapter and Chapter 9 look much more closely at the analysis of financial information as a route to understanding. The two chapters cover a range of techniques and calculations. However, those students who are less than totally confident about their numeracy skills should not be put off; none of the techniques covered in the chapters involves anything more difficult than simple arithmetical skills of the type already utilized. The important skill, in fact, lies in the interpretation of the results; this is a skill best achieved through practice.

In this chapter we will, first, briefly examine the various groups of people who are interested in accounting information, the reasons for their interest, and the aspects which might be particularly useful to them. Then the chapter proceeds to examine simple analytical techniques which compare one figure or group of figures with another.

(Note that this chapter of the book considers the analysis of the formal financial reports which we have covered in Chapters 2–7 inclusive. In the second section of the book (beginning with Chapter 10) attention will be turned to the type of management accounting information which is generated within a business for use by owners and managers in making plans and in controlling the business activities.)

8.1 USEFULNESS OF FINANCIAL REPORTS TO VARIOUS INTEREST GROUPS

8.1.1 Owners and Investors

Previous chapters have included several examples of sole trader owners using periodic financial information to inform them about the progress of their business. However, it must be recognized that most unincorporated business owners will have available to them other, more comprehensive, sources of information about their business performance. For example, an annual financial statement does not provide any information about the state of the business's order book, but the current levels of demand for products and services would be regarded by business owners as an absolutely vital means of assessing business prospects. So, although it is not unrealistic to suggest that owners of businesses use annual financial reports as aids to understanding, it should be recognized that they have other, potentially more useful, sources of information available to them.

The situation is rather different, however, for investors in limited companies. Unless they are also directors, they do not have any privileges of access to information beyond their right to receive the annual report and accounts. An investor who buys 100 shares in Marks & Spencer plc, for example, (or any other listed company) obtains some rights (the right to receive a part of any dividend declared and the right to vote at the AGM). However, he or she does not have the right to wander in off the street to the company's head office demanding to see the monthly accounts.

Investors in companies who do not have access to information other than the annual report and accounts, are likely to be interested in the answers to some or all of the following questions:

- How is my investment doing?
- Should I buy more shares/ sell the shares I've already got/ hold on to the investment I've already got?

- Is the dividend likely to increase?
- What are the chances of the company going out of business?

8.1.2 Potential Investors in a Business

People who are thinking of investing in a business will usually take steps to obtain the most recent financial reports. If the company is listed on the London Stock Exchange (or a stock exchange elsewhere), access to this type of information is usually very easy; all UK listed companies are obliged by the Companies Act 2006 to have websites. These corporate websites contain the most recent published financial reports for the company and they may also contain other useful pieces of information like the preliminary announcement of results, information about directors, and more detailed information about the company's activities. Unlisted companies, as we saw in Chapter 7, are obliged to file accounting information with the Registrar of Companies, and it is possible to obtain copies of this information quickly in exchange for a fee of a few pounds.

It may, however, be impossible to obtain any financial information about other forms of business because sole traders and partnerships are not obliged to make information public. However, if a business is interested in attracting buyers there is an incentive to provide recent, reliable financial information to potential investors.

It should be recognized, however, that financial information such as the income statement and statement of financial position is essentially backward looking; these statements report events which have already occurred, and these may not be a reliable guide to what is going to happen in the future.

Potential investors tend to be looking for answers to some or all of the following questions:

- What are the risks involved in this business? How likely would I be to lose money? Would my investment be safe?
- How much can I make from investing in this business? Will the return be better than I could make if I were to:
  - Put the money into some other business?
  - Leave it in the bank?
  - Risk it on a bet on the horses/dogs/a card game?
- What are my chances of getting seriously rich?

8.1.3 Creditors

In Chapter 7 we looked at the example of Tommy, who supplied goods on credit to a limited company but was unable to obtain payment for them before the company became insolvent. Businesses and individuals who supply goods on credit to limited companies take the risk that they will not be paid. As noted in the discussion in Chapter 7, one of the ways of reducing the risk is to examine the financial reports of a company to assess its financial condition.

Suppliers of goods and services, like anyone else, are entitled to obtain the financial information that is filed at Companies House (although remember that this information is quite limited in the case of small companies). Alternatively, they may prefer to use the services of a credit agency which, for a fee, supplies a detailed report on the credit-worthiness of a named company. (See, for example, the range of services offered by Dun & Bradstreet – www.dnb.com.)

In the case of sole traders and partnerships, there is no publicly available source of financial information, and suppliers must base their decision on whether or not to offer credit on other factors (they may, for example, ask the trader or partnership to supply references from some reputable person like a bank manager).

If a bank or other financial institution lends to a business it becomes a creditor, possibly for the long-term. In such cases, the bank is usually in a position to demand financial information, regardless of whether the business is a sole trader, partnership or company, and indeed, this may be part of the lending deal.

When undertaking an analysis of financial reports, creditors are interested in obtaining answers to the following questions:

- How likely is it that I will be paid?
- How likely is it that I will be paid on time?
- Will my interest (where applicable) be paid regularly?
- Is there a risk that this business will go bust before I get paid?

Financial statements, especially those produced by limited companies, tend to be principally oriented towards the information needs of investors and owners. However, other interested parties such as creditors will also find a great deal of information which is relevant to their needs.

8.2 ANALYTICAL TECHNIQUES: CHANGES IN FIGURES

The most straightforward analytical technique can be one of the most effective: comparing two or more figures with each other to assess the differences between them.

EXAMPLE 8.1

Ilse is a sole trader, who runs a shop selling imported fabrics and furnishings. Her revenue figures for the 3 years ending 31 March 2012 are as follows:

	2012	2011	2010
	£	£	£
Revenue	217 300	209 220	204 240

It does not take a financial wizard to see that Ilse's revenue has gone up between 2010 and 2012. Sometimes, this kind of straightforward pointing out of the obvious is all that is needed in financial analysis. However, the analysis could be refined, without much additional difficulty, by calculating the percentage increase year-on-year, as follows.

Between 2010 and 2011

Revenue has risen by £209 220 – 204 240 = £4980

£4980 can be calculated as a percentage of the 2010 figure, as follows:

$$\frac{£4\,980}{204\,240} \times 100 = 2.4\%$$

Between 2011 and 2012

Revenue has risen by £217 300 – 209 220 = £8080

£8080 can be calculated as a percentage of the 2011 figure, as follows:

$$\frac{£8\,080}{209\,220} \times 100 = 3.9\%$$

What does this mean?

By calculating the percentage increases we have added a little to our slender stock of knowledge about Ilse's sales. If we know, for example, from local Chamber of Commerce information, that traders in Ilse's part of town have experienced an average annual growth in sales of 8% between 2010 and 2012 it suggests that Ilse's business performance is in relative decline.

In order to increase the value of the information about Ilse's sales, we need some point of comparison. The point of comparison may come from outside the business (e.g. the information provided by the Chamber of Commerce) or from inside the information. For example, suppose Ilse tells you, as her new financial adviser, that she invested a lot of additional working capital in a new line of stock during 2010 and 2011, expecting to boost sales by 20% per annum, you might well conclude that her efforts to expand the business had been relatively unsuccessful.

A great deal depends upon the context of the financial information.

8.3 ANALYTICAL TECHNIQUES: HORIZONTAL AND TREND ANALYSIS

Horizontal analysis is a fancy piece of terminology, describing, essentially, the type of analysis we carried out above on Ilse's sales figures. Where there are at least 2-years' worth of information, it is possible to conduct some type of horizontal analysis.

In some cases several years' worth of information is available, and it becomes possible to carry out a **trend analysis**. This type of analysis includes figures over several years and attempts to track longer-term business trends.

Moving rapidly up the size scale from Ilse's business we will now consider the publicly available information provided by Burberry plc, a FTSE 100 listed company. Listed companies commonly provide 5-year summaries of information (sometimes the summaries even extend to a 10-year period). In the next example, we will examine some elements of the 5-year record of information for Burberry plc.

EXAMPLE 8.2 (REAL-LIFE)

The following table shows extracts from Burberry plc's financial statements for the year ending 31 March 2009.

	2009	**2008**	**2007**	**2006**	**2005**
	£m	**£m**	**£m**	**£m**	**£m**
Revenue	1,201.5	995.4	850.3	742.9	715.5
Gross profit	665.8	617.7	521.3	446.1	424.2
Loss/profit before tax	(16.1)	195.7	156.3	157.0	166.2

This is just a small part of the information disclosed by Burberry plc in its annual financial statements. What does it tell us?

Scanning the revenue line quickly we can tell that the business has improved its revenue each year over the period since 2005. If revenue increases we could expect to see a corresponding improvement in profit figures. This is true of the gross profit figure, which has increased each year, but not the case for profit before tax which is much less even. The business has recorded profits in the years 2005 to 2008, but the corresponding figure in 2009 is a loss.

We can extend the horizontal analysis by calculating year-on-year percentage increases, in the same way as for Ilse's business. The percentage increases can be neatly presented in a table like this one:

Annual percentage increases (decreases) in a selection of key figures: Burberry plc

	2009	2008	2007	2006
	%	%	%	%
Revenue	20.7%	17.1%	14.5%	3.8%
Gross profit	7.8%	18.5%	16.9%	5.2%
(Loss)/profit before tax	(108.2%)	25.2%	(0.4%)	(5.5%)

The horizontal analysis using percentages highlights some of the general trends in the business. There have been impressive rises in revenue in each year since 2005, but the trends in profitability are much less consistent. Gross profit has risen each year but the increases are not consistent with the trend in revenue growth. Except for the increase in profit before tax calculated for the 2008 financial year, there has been a drop in profit before tax in each year. It is only in the most recent financial year, however, that the drop is of great significance.

More detailed figures for the year ended 31 March 2009 show that there have been some unusual expenses, mostly relating to losses in value of non-current assets. During the worldwide recession experienced in 2008 and 2009, such losses in value were by no means unexpected. The 2008 and 2009 results must be viewed in the context of prevailing economic trends. Given the circumstances, the large increases in revenue are impressive, as the company has evidently been able to increase its appeal to consumers. (Burberry plc sells womens', mens' and childrens' clothing).

Self-test question 8.1 (answer at the end of the book)

Jamal is a sole trader selling a range of pre-packaged foods. He has a small food processing factory and employs several staff. Just over 3-years ago, in 2008, he made the decision to employ a full-time sales manager. The manager, Jared, claimed at the interview that he would be able to achieve 15% sales increases each year.

Jared is asking for a substantial increase in his annual salary effective from the start of 2012. He tells Jamal that he thinks he's worth it, because of the contribution he's made to the business. The final accounts for the year ending 31 December 2012 have just been finished in draft form by the accountant. Jamal is now reviewing his annual sales figures which are available as far back as 2004 when he started the business. The following table shows revenue for each year:

Year	£
2004	250 031
2005	347 266
2006	441 179
2007	531 150

Year	£
2008	523 622
2009	545 331
2010	590 942
2011	679 244
2012	771 485

Required: examine the horizontal trends in Jamal's revenue figures, and, briefly, advise him on whether or not Jared's claim for an increased salary appears justified.

8.3.1 Some Problems with Horizontal Analysis

There are two principal problems which are likely to arise in respect of horizontal analysis:

Changes in the business

Very rapid changes can take place in business. These may mean that figures are not really comparable over a period of years. Also, new accounting rules and standards may make a difference to the presentation of the figures. The figures of Burberry plc which we examined earlier will have been adjusted for any effects of this type so that a proper and meaningful comparison can be made. In the case of unlisted companies and smaller businesses, which do not usually include 5-years' worth of comparative figures in their financial statements, the analyst must be careful to make any necessary adjustments.

Failure to take the effects of inflation into account

Although it is possible to adjust accounting figures for the effects of inflation this is not usually done in UK accounting. In recent years the general rate of inflation in the economy has not been high, and its effects are often regarded as negligible. However, this can be misleading, as the following example shows:

EXAMPLE 8.3

A 5-year analysis of the sales of Trevor Fine Art Productions Limited shows the following figures:

	2012	2011	2010	2009	2008
	£	£	£	£	£
Revenue	683 084	657 469	634 868	617 576	590 530
Percentage increase on previous year	3.9%	3.6%	2.8%	4.6%	

Between 2008 and 2012 sales have increased in total by the following percentage:

$$\frac{£683\,084 - 590\,530}{590\,530} \times 100 = 15.7\%$$

Looking at the individual years we can see that there has been an increase each year. So far, so good, but if we take inflation into account the picture changes somewhat. Suppose that in each year between 2008 and 2012 the average rate of inflation in the economy has been 3% per annum. We can see that in most years the sales increases were only slightly above inflation and the increase between 2009 and 2010 was actually a little below the rate of inflation. The sales increases are not as impressive as they first appear to be.

8.4 ANALYTICAL TECHNIQUES: VERTICAL ANALYSIS AND COMMON SIZE ANALYSIS

Vertical analysis is a simple analytical technique which can be useful and informative. It involves expressing each figure in the income statement and statement of financial position as a percentage of one key figure (sales in the income statement and – usually – net assets in the statement of financial position). The next example explains the application of vertical analysis.

EXAMPLE 8.4

Bore & Hole Limited makes mining equipment. The company income statement and statement of financial position for 2012 are shown below, together with an extra column of percentage figures. In the income statement all percentages are calculated by reference to the value of sales, and in the statement of financial position, by reference to the equity total.

Bore & Hole Limited: Income statement for the year ending 31 December 2012

	£	%
Revenue	4 490 370	100.0
Cost of sales	(3 521 348)	(78.4)
Gross profit	969 022	21.6
Administrative expenses	(454 432)	(10.1)
Distribution and selling costs	(407 480)	(9.1)
Other operating income	16 210	0.4
Operating profit	123 320	2.8
Finance costs	(33 900)	(0.8)
Profit before tax	89 420	2.0
Tax	(26 461)	(0.6)
Profit after tax	62 959	1.4

NB: Each item is calculated as a percentage of sales (to one decimal point):
For example:

$$\frac{\text{Administrative expenses}}{\text{Revenue}} \times 100 = \frac{£454\,432}{4\,490\,370} \times 100 = 10.1\%$$

Bore & Hole Limited: Statement of financial position at 31 December 2012

	£	£	%
ASSETS			
Non-current assets		3 975 750	99.1
Current assets			
Inventories	586 404		14.6
Trade receivables	430 580		10.7
Cash at bank	10 110		0.2
		1 027 094	
		5 002 844	

	£	£	%
EQUITY AND LIABILITIES			
Equity			
Share capital		800 000	19.9
Retained earnings		3 213 632	80.1
		4 013 632	100.0
Long-term liabilities			
Borrowings		390 000	9.7
Current liabilities			
Trade and other payables		599 212	14.9
		5 002 844	

What does the vertical analysis statement tell us? It is a single period statement only, so its information content is limited. The percentage column is helpful in that it tends to draw attention to the relative size of the figures. For example, we can see from the statement that operating profit as a percentage of revenue is only 2.8%, and that profit after tax is a mere 1.4% of revenue. These percentages suggest that the business is not performing well.

Turning to the statement of financial position we can see that it is dominated by non-current assets; this is a manufacturing business, and non-current assets could be expected to be high. Cash is negligible and the business has long-term borrowings of almost 10% of the net asset value.

Common size analysis extends vertical analysis across more than one accounting period. In the next example we will extend our knowledge of Bore & Hole Limited by examining the vertical analysis percentages in the company's income statement over 4 years.

EXAMPLE 8.5

The income statement in example 8.4 shows vertical analysis of all the items, based upon sales, for the year ended 31 December 2012. Below, the comparative vertical analysis figures are repeated for the 2012 income statement, and are set alongside the comparative figures for the previous 3 years.

	2012	2011	2010	2009
	%	%	%	%
Revenue	100.0	100.0	100.0	100.0
Cost of sales	(78.4)	(78.3)	(77.2)	(77.0)
Gross profit	21.6	21.7	22.8	23.0
Administrative expenses	(10.1)	(7.3)	(7.4)	(7.2)
Selling and distribution costs	(9.1)	(10.0)	(9.3)	(9.7)
Other operating income	0.4	0.4	–	–
Operating profit	2.8	4.8	6.1	6.1
Finance costs	(0.8)	–	–	–
Profit before tax	2.0	4.8	6.1	6.1
Tax	(0.6)	(1.4)	(1.8)	(1.8)
Profit after tax	1.4	3.4	4.3	4.3

This statement is expressed entirely in percentages; it gives no indication as to the value of each component. (Revenue is the base figure and therefore is 100% in each year.) However, the statement does help understanding by presenting the trends in the figures quite clearly.

For example:

Gross profit as a percentage of revenue has fallen in each of the 4 years. If this trend continues the business could ultimately fail.

Administrative expenses have remained at a fairly constant level compared to revenue for 3 out of the 4 years reviewed. Suddenly, however, in 2012 the percentage leaps. There could be many explanations for this change; for example, perhaps there has been a change of management and the new management are not controlling costs very well. Or, there may have been a major new investment in non-current assets whose related depreciation charges are shown as part of administrative expenses.

Finance costs feature for the first time in the 2012 income statement, suggesting that in previous years borrowings were either non-existent or negligible.

Overall, although we have relatively little information about the company (compared, for example, with what is available in a full set of financial statements) the common size income statement does allow the analyst to draw some tentative conclusions about the performance of the business over time.

8.5 COMPARING BUSINESSES WITH EACH OTHER

So far in this chapter we have analyzed single businesses, generally by reference to the increases and decreases in elements of accounting information over time. However, interested parties will often need to make comparisons between businesses. They can do this by:

a) Comparing the results and statements of financial position of two or more businesses.
b) Comparing the results and statements of the financial position of a business with industry averages.

8.5.1 Problems in Comparison

The regulation surrounding accounting, especially accounting by limited companies, goes some way towards ensuring that financial statements are prepared to the same set of rules and in the same way. The International Accounting Standards Board, for example, sets out four key characteristics which accounting information should have:

- relevance
- reliability
- comparability
- understandability.

Comparability is accorded a great deal of importance precisely in order to allow meaningful comparisons between accounting statements to be made. However, despite the best intentions of the regulators, there are often problems in ensuring that a valid comparison can be made. Some of these are briefly described below.

Differences in accounting policies

Accounting policies are the principles of accounting applied in preparing the financial statements. Despite a fairly extensive level of regulation, there are many areas in which a business can make legitimate choices about the amounts at which items are stated, and the way in which those items are presented. The following example will illustrate the point:

EXAMPLE 8.6

Spanners Limited and Gasket Limited operate within the same business sector. A financial analyst is examining the results of the companies on behalf of a client. Extracts from their income statements show the following information (together with vertical analysis percentages):

	Spanners Limited		Gasket Limited	
	£	%	£	%
Revenue	984 742	100.0	1 096 880	100.0
Cost of sales	673 938	68.4	756 993	69.0
Gross profit	310 804	31.6	339 887	31.0

The companies appear to be similar in size in that they generate similar levels of turnover, and the percentage of gross profit to sales is close. It seems a fair conclusion, on the face of it, that their performance is virtually identical.

However, the analyst finds out that the companies' policies on inclusion of costs in cost of sales are not the same. Specifically, Spanners Limited includes depreciation of vehicles within cost of sales, whereas Gasket Limited includes the same type of cost within selling and distribution costs. Gasket's vehicle depreciation is £28 977 for the year under review.

In order to compare like with like the analyst must make an adjustment to Gasket's cost of sales:

$$\text{Adjusted cost of sales} = £28\,977 + 756\,993 = 785\,970$$

Building this adjusted cost into the income statement analysis results in the following changes (vertical analysis percentages are re-calculated for Gasket Limited):

	Spanners Limited		Gasket Limited	
	£	%	£	%
Revenue	984 742	100.0	1 096 880	100.0
Cost of sales	673 938	68.4	785 970	71.7
Gross profit	310 804	31.6	310 910	28.3

The re-calculation makes the comparison appear in a rather different light. Gasket's gross profit is 28.3% of revenue, as compared to Spanners' at 31.6%.

Financial statement analysts have to be alert for this type of difference. As the example shows, application of different accounting policies can make a lot of difference. The example illustrates the point in relation to cost classification but there are many other potential areas of difference, including, for example, depreciation and amortization methods.

Differences in business activities

No two businesses are entirely alike. Comparison of two apparently similar businesses can lead to incorrect conclusions, if the differences between the two are not fully appreciated.

EXAMPLE 8.7

A financial analyst is comparing the results of two companies for 2012 and 2011. Pool & Splash Limited and Dive & Float Limited are both involved in swimming pool installation and maintenance. Companies in the industry are generally performing well.

Revenue figures for the two companies for 2012 and 2011 are as follows:

	Pool & Splash Limited		Dive & Float Limited	
	2012	2011	2012	2011
	£	£	£	£
Revenue	1 662 997	1 357 549	1 842 791	1 543 360

The analyst calculates that the revenue of Pool & Splash Limited has increased by 22.5%, whereas Dive & Float Limited's revenue has increased by only 19.4%. On the face of it, Pool & Splash appear to have performed better in terms of revenue growth.

However, the picture changes when we are supplied with information about the breakdown of revenue. Pool & Splash Limited's sales and maintenance contracts are in respect of domestic sales only. Dive & Float Limited, on the other hand, undertakes contract pool maintenance for local authorities. A breakdown of the revenue figures shows the following:

	Pool & Splash Limited		Dive & Float Limited	
	2012	2011	2012	2011
	£	£	£	£
Revenue – domestic	1 662 997	1 357 549	1 430 111	1 135 910
Maintenance contracts – local authorities	–	–	412 680	407 450
Total	1 662 997	1 357 549	1 842 791	1 543 360

From the more detailed figures the analyst can calculate a more meaningful comparison. Dive & Float's domestic revenue has, in fact, increased by 25.9% as compared to Pool & Splash's increase of 22.5%.

Industry averages may be misleading

Comparison of a single company against a range of industry averages may be misleading.

EXAMPLE 8.8

Wellington Burke Limited and Ashington Smith Limited are two companies operating in the same industry, but in different parts of England. According to a recent trade survey, the average increase in revenue in the industry in the year ending 31 December 2012 was 13.8%.

The two companies show the following levels of revenue growth over that period:

Wellington Burke Limited	14.2%
Ashington Smith Limited	11.6%

It appears as though Wellington Burke Limited is the clear leader in terms of sales growth. However, the average increase in revenue published in the trade survey masks wide regional variations

Average growth in the North of England	9.7%
Average growth in the South of England	17.9%

If we know that Wellington Burke Limited operates in the Home Counties, while Ashington Smith Limited is based in Yorkshire, the comparison starts to look different. It appears that, in fact, Ashington Smith Limited may have outperformed other Northern based firms in the industry, whereas, relatively speaking, Wellington Burke Limited has under-performed in terms of revenue growth.

Comparisons between businesses, then, must be approached with caution, because apparently obvious facts may be misleading.

Self-test question 8.2 (answer at the end of the book)

Barnes & Jack Limited and Carleen Baker Limited are competitors in the aquarium supply business. Both companies supply, install and maintain aquariums. Revenue figures for the two companies for 2012 and 2011 are as follows:

	Barnes & Jack Limited		**Carleen Baker Limited**	
	2012	**2011**	**2012**	**2011**
	£	**£**	**£**	**£**
Revenue	2 044 032	1 743 906	1 850 490	1 564 774

a) Which company has produced the more impressive growth in revenue? (calculate growth to one decimal place)

b) Does the answer differ with the addition of the following information about revenue?

Barnes & Jack's sales are principally to the domestic and pet shop market. However, in addition, the company sells to zoos. Revenue growth in the latter area has been slow in recent years due to cuts in public funding. Carleen Baker Limited would like to break into the zoo market, but currently supplies only the domestic and pet shop market.

Barnes & Jack's sales to zoos were £450 800 in 2011, increasing to £488 307 in 2012.

8.6 SEGMENT ANALYSIS

Large companies usually operate in a range of different markets and conduct varying business activities. Listed companies are required by international accounting standards to produce additional information about the business segments in which they operate. This can be very useful for the analyst in providing an insight into which segments of the business yield the most revenue and which are most profitable. The next example looks at some of the segment information provided by Burberry plc.

EXAMPLE 8.9 (REAL-LIFE)

Burberry plc is a fashion business. It publishes information about revenue from different segments by business category and also by destination. This allows the analyst to see which product categories are dominant in the business, and which are the company's most important export markets.

Burberry plc: Revenue by product category

	2009	2008	2007	2006	2005
	£m	£m	£m	£m	£m
Womenswear	412.8	345.2	305.5	249.3	242.1
Menswear	298.4	247.8	227.0	206.2	194.5
Accessories	366.3	289.7	211.2	189.2	185.0
Childrenswear/other	41.4	27.9	20.5	17.1	15.5
Licensing	82.6	84.8	86.1	81.1	78.4
Total	1 201.5	995.4	850.3	742.9	715.5

This information can be analyzed in different ways. For example, we can calculate the contribution of each of the major product categories to Burberry's overall revenue for each year:

Burberry plc: Contribution of product categories to total revenue

	2009	2008	2007	2006	2005
	%	%	%	%	%
Womenswear	34.4	34.7	36.0	33.5	33.8
Menswear	24.8	24.9	26.7	27.8	27.2
Accessories	30.5	29.1	24.8	25.5	25.8
Childrenswear/other	3.4	2.8	2.4	2.3	2.2
Licensing	6.9	8.5	10.1	10.9	11.0
Total	100	100	100	100	100

What does this additional information tell us about Burberry's revenue for the 5-year period covered by the figures? We can see from the table that, relatively speaking, menswear and licensing revenue have both declined in importance, while the contribution to total revenue of womenswear has changed relatively little. Both accessories and childrenswear have become relatively more important to the company. However, it should be emphasized that revenue in all categories has actually increased (this is evident from the first table). What has changed is the relative contribution of the different categories.

We could extend the analysis by looking at the year-on-year increases or decreases in revenue in the various categories.

CHAPTER SUMMARY

In this chapter we first examined the usefulness of financial statements to certain interest groups: owners and investors, potential investors and creditors. The rest of the chapter was devoted to the study of a range of simple analysis techniques:

- Horizontal analysis – involving analysis of the financial statements of at least two consecutive accounting periods.
- Trend analysis – horizontal analysis taking place over several years.
- Vertical analysis – expressing figures in a financial statement as a percentage of one key figure (commonly sales in the income statement and net assets in the statement of financial position).
- Common size analysis – vertical analysis taking place over more than one accounting period.

We examined some of the problems of comparability which can arise when the analyst attempts to compare accounting information from two or more businesses:

- Accounting policies may be different.
- There may be differences between the activities of the businesses.
- Industry averages may be misleading.

Finally, the chapter looked at segment analysis, which uses more detailed information about a business's activities in various business segments. It can provide very useful insights into business operations.

INTERNET RESOURCES

Book's companion website summary
www.cengage.co.uk/gowthorpe3 contains the following resources in respect of Chapter 8:

Students' section
Quiz containing ten multiple choice questions
Four additional questions with answers

Lecturers' section
Answers to end of chapter exercises 8.7 to 8.10
Four additional questions with answers
Case study
ExamView testbank
Instructor's manual
PowerPoint presentation

EXERCISES: ANSWERS AT THE END OF THE BOOK

8.1 Ronald's trading business operates from a shop in a large city centre. Extracts from Ronald's most recent income statements for 2012 and 2011 show the following key figures:

	2012	2011
	£	£
Revenue	110 450	95 544
Cost of sales	(72 058)	(62 075)
Gross profit	38 392	33 469

Ronald belongs to a trade association which has recently carried out a confidential survey of its members. The survey found that between 2011 and 2012 the average increases in revenue and gross profitability of the membership were:

Increase in revenue	12.6%
Increase in gross profit	15.2%

Which of the following statements is correct? A horizontal analysis of Ronald's revenue and gross profit figures shows:

a) Higher than average increase in revenue, and lower than average increase in gross profit.
b) Lower than average increase in revenue, and lower than average increase in gross profit.
c) Lower than average increase in revenue, and higher than average increase in gross profit.
d) Higher than average increase in revenue, and lower than average increase in gross profit.

8.2 Rory's income statement statements show the following figures for the period 2009 to 2012 inclusive:

	2012	**2011**	**2010**	**2009**
	£	**£**	**£**	**£**
Revenue	562 064	539 409	520 665	505 500
Cost of sales	(410 619)	(392 802)	(378 879)	(368 509)
Gross profit	151 445	146 607	141 786	136 991

Which of the following statements is correct? Analyzed horizontally, these figures show:

a) A gradually increasing percentage of revenue growth and a gradually increasing percentage of gross profit growth.
b) A gradually decreasing percentage of revenue growth and a gradually increasing percentage of gross profit growth.
c) A gradually increasing percentage of revenue growth and a gradually decreasing percentage of gross profit growth.
d) A gradually decreasing percentage of revenue growth and a gradually decreasing percentage of gross profit growth.

8.3 Inge Larsen is the principal shareholder in Larsen Locations Limited. Her company provides services to businesses who are in the process of moving from one location to another. Inge and her staff plan the moves in detail, ensuring that all arrangements are made and that the move goes smoothly. Lately, the company has itself moved into larger premises and has taken on more staff.

Tom Wilton runs The Wilton Group plc, of which he is the major shareholder; the company's principal activity is similar to Larsen's. He is considering making an offer to Inge to buy the business from her, so that he can consolidate Wilton's position as market leader in the region. He does not want Inge Larsen to know anything about his possible interest in her company until he has completed some basic financial analysis.

Tom obtains Larsen's company accounts for the last 3 years from Companies House. Some of the extracted income statement information is summarized in the following table:

	2012	2011	2010	2009
	£	£	£	£
Sales of services	3 709 480	3 690 900	3 502 404	3 497 983
Administrative expenses	1 446 437	1 204 448	1 109 932	1 100 555
Operating profit	756 734	841 525	795 046	787 046

Over the period 2009 to 2012 The Wilton Group plc has experienced steady growth in revenue, administrative expenses and operating profits of 2-3% per year.

Required: analyze Larsen's revenue, administrative expenses and operating profits horizontally, reporting briefly on how the trends in these items compare with those of The Wilton Group plc.

8.4 Chapter Protection Limited is a security firm. Its income statement for the year ending 31 December 2012 is as follows:

	£
Revenue	188 703
Cost of sales	(115 863)
Gross profit	72 840
Administrative expenses	(14 260)
Distribution and selling costs	(20 180)
Operating profit	38 400
Finance costs	(1 200)
Profit before tax	37 200
Tax	(7 450)
Profit after tax	29 750

Required: prepare a vertical analysis statement of Chapter Protection's income statement, on the basis that the revenue figure is 100%.

8.5 Causeway Ferguson plc is a trading company specializing in the supply of tea and coffee and related products. Jason has a small shareholding in the company which was left to him by a relative. He has never taken much interest in the company's activities but has noticed that the company pays a regular twice yearly dividend which never seems to vary much.

Jason has recently started reading the financial press on a regular basis and one day he finds a brief news item about tea and coffee suppliers. Causeway Ferguson is mentioned in passing: 'Causeway Ferguson, a fine old name in British tea supply, is quietly withering away. Its lacklustre management team has failed to tackle new competitors in the market – at this rate, it starts to look like a modest takeover target for one of the food industry big boys.'

Jason never throws anything away, and after a search, manages to dig out from a dusty pile of papers a set of unopened annual reports from Causeway Ferguson going back over 4 or 5 years. He gives the reports to his cousin, Jasper, who is a trainee accountant, and asks him to comment on the company's trading over the last few years.

Jasper extracts the following income statement information from the annual reports:

	2012	2011	2010	2009	2008
	£000	£000	£000	£000	£000
Revenue	13 204	13 561	13 602	12 430	12 003
Cost of sales	(8 012)	(8 217)	(8 213)	(7 401)	(7 085)
Gross profit	5 192	5 344	5 389	5 029	4 918
Administrative expenses	(2 184)	(2 101)	(2 097)	(2 010)	(1 975)
Selling and distribution costs	(2 086)	(2 001)	(1 977)	(1 972)	(1 951)
Profit before tax	922	1 242	1 315	1 047	992
Tax	(277)	(373)	(395)	(314)	(298)
Profit after tax	645	869	920	733	694

Required: prepare a horizontal trend analysis statement and a common size statement. Comment on the key features which emerge from the analysis of these statements. Does the newspaper report appear credible in the light of the analysis?

8.6 The 5-year financial record for Marks & Spencer plc published in the company's 2009 Annual Report includes the following information:

	2009	2008	2007	2006	2005
	£m	£m	£m	£m	£m
Revenue:					
UK retail	8 164.3	8 309.1	7 977.5	7 275.0	7 034.7
International retail	897.8	712.9	610.6	522.7	455.8
Operating profit					
UK retail	755.0	1,095.9	956.7	784.5	528.0
International retail	115.7	115.4	89.2	65.6	70.1

Required: write a brief report analyzing the information in the table. (Note: it will be helpful to calculate operating profit as a percentage of sales.)

EXERCISES: ANSWERS AVAILABLE ON THE LECTURERS' SECTION OF THE BOOK'S WEBSITE

8.7 Rasheda's sales for 2011 were £206 400, and for 2012 were £214 656.

Her gross profit margins were: 36.3% for 2011 and 36.4% for 2012.

Rasheda expects sales in 2013 to increase by the same percentage as between 2011 and 2012. Gross profit margin should improve to 36.5%.

What is Rasheda's expected gross profit in 2013 (to the nearest £)?

a) £78 349
b) £78 135
c) £81 483
d) £81 363.

8.8 Reva has a jewellery business in a well-established shop. Her most recent income statements show the following key figures:

	2012	2011
	£	£
Revenue	696 400	585 702
Cost of sales	(416 447)	(352 007)
Gross profit	279 953	233 695

A recent survey by the Jewellers' Guild shows that average jewellery sales increased by 17.3% in 2012 over the previous year. Also, it was found that the average gross profit margin in 2012 amongst the survey respondents is 38.3%.

Which of the following statements is correct? An analysis of Reva's figures shows:

a) A higher than average increase in revenue, and a higher than average gross profit margin.
b) A lower than average increase in revenue and a lower than average gross profit margin.
c) A higher than average increase in revenue, and a lower than average gross profit margin.
d) A lower than average increase in revenue, and a higher than average gross profit margin.

8.9 Isaac Prentiss Limited produce parts and components for ships' engines. The business requires a continuing investment in new machinery in order to keep production as efficient as possible. Isaac Prentiss is the founder and principal shareholder of the business, although he no longer takes an active part in management. Isaac is concerned because he feels that the business is borrowing too much.

Burgess, the managing director, assures Isaac that sales and operating profits continue to improve and that the borrowing is necessary to fund the general expansion of the business, including the acquisition of new non-current assets. In order to reassure Isaac, Burgess prepares the following statement of key extracts from the financial statements for the last 5 years:

	2012	2011	2010	2009	2008
	£000	£000	£000	£000	£000
Revenue	1 635	1 421	1 254	1 181	1 133
Operating profit	303	254	223	203	199
Finance costs	(245)	(181)	(177)	(171)	(151)
Non-current assets	5 314	4 190	3 633	3 237	2 950
Borrowing	3 944	2 921	2 766	2 510	2 431

Required: analyze the company's figures horizontally over the 5-year period, and write a brief report to Isaac on the results of the analysis. You should refer particularly to Isaac's concerns about the business borrowing.

8.10 Starkey Wilmott Limited has the following statement of financial position at 31 March 2012:

	£	£
ASSETS		
Non-current assets		704 710
Current assets		
Inventories	369 440	
Trade receivables	416 700	
Cash at bank	81 450	
		867 590
		1 572 300
EQUITY AND LIABILITIES		
Equity		
Share capital		50 000
Retained earnings		931 400
		981 400
Long-term liabilities		200 000
Current liabilities		390 900
		1 572 300

Required: prepare vertical analysis statements of Starkey Wilmott's statement of financial position at 31 March 2012 based upon non-current assets = 100.0%.

CHAPTER 14

The Income Statement

AIM OF THE CHAPTER

To enable students to understand how an income statement is prepared and how it fits together with the statement of financial position.

LEARNING OUTCOMES

After reading the chapter and completing the exercises at the end, students should:

- Understand the terminology used in an income statement, and some of the principal conventions used in presenting it.
- Be able to draw up an income statement for a sole trader from a list of account balances and explanatory notes.
- Be able to understand and comment on the basic information conveyed by an income statement.
- Combine skills gained as a result of studying Chapters 2 and 3 to draw up a set of financial statements comprising an income statement and a statement of financial position.

INTRODUCTION

An organization run on a commercial basis will attempt to make profits. In straightforward terms, it does this by selling goods and/or services at prices which will allow it to cover all the expenses of the business, with a surplus remaining. Any surplus can be distributed to the owner(s) or retained in the business to fund expansion.

The income statement reports on the performance of the business to interested parties. As noted in Chapter 1, interested parties include, for example, investors and potential investors in the business, lenders, employees and HMRC.

This chapter first explores some of the accounting terminology used in the income statement. The appearance and content of the income statement is influenced to some extent by the nature of the business being conducted, and so the terminology section is followed by a brief review of the broad categories of commercial activity. The chapter then proceeds to explain the techniques involved in drawing up an income statement for a trading business, and then introduces some techniques of financial analysis which allow the user of the financial statements to understand the messages conveyed by the income statement. This section builds upon the sole trader example, but also covers the analysis of income statement information published by a large business. The chapter then explains income statement accounting for a service business. It concludes with a longer example which demonstrates the procedures involved in drawing up both an income statement and a statement of financial position for a sole trader business.

3.1 THE INCOME STATEMENT: TERMINOLOGY

Revenue (also referred to as 'sales' or 'turnover') is the amount of goods and/or services sold, expressed in monetary terms.

Expenses are the amounts incurred by the business in purchasing or manufacturing the goods sold, and other expenditure on items like rent and telephone charges.

Profit is the surplus remaining when revenue exceeds expenditure (a desirable state of affairs in a commercial organization).

Loss is the deficit which occurs when expenditure exceeds revenue (a state of affairs which cannot persist for a long period in a commercial organization).

The **income statement** summarizes the revenue and expenses of an organization over a period of time, showing the performance of the business over the period. It gives the reader information which shows how well or how badly the business is doing. Note that 'income statement' is the description that is used by the International Accounting Standards Board; however, the term **profit and loss account** is often used in the UK.

3.2 CATEGORIES OF COMMERCIAL ACTIVITY

Commercial activities can be broadly classified into three types, as follows:

trading
manufacturing
service.

Trading organizations operate as 'middlemen'. Typically, they buy in goods that have been manufactured by another individual or organization and then sell them on at a higher price to someone else.

Manufacturing organizations are often complex operations. They manufacture goods which are either sold directly to the public or to trading organizations which then sell them on. For example, a factory manufactures woollen coats which it sells to fashion shops. The factory business sells at prices which cover the various costs of manufacture plus a profit. The shop owners sell at a higher price than they are charged by the factory business, and so they, too, make a profit. By the time the customer in the shop buys the coat at least two organizations have made a profit on the transaction.

Service organizations sell services rather than goods. For example, a solicitor is not concerned at all with the sale of goods. He or she makes a surplus out of the provision of professional services.

Some organizations have a mixture of activities. Take, for example, a commercial tennis club. It sells annual subscriptions to a range of services such as use of tennis courts and tennis coaching. It also sells a range of shoes and clothing which it buys in from all the well known sports clothing manufacturers. The club, therefore, operates both trading and service activities.

3.3 INCOME STATEMENT FOR A SOLE TRADER

The early part of Chapter 2 explained the outline content of the three main accounting statements, including the income statement, using the example of the first month of trading for JJ Hair Studio, a business engaged in providing a service. In this chapter we build upon that very basic example, firstly examining the income statement of a trading business.

The income statement of a trading business splits into two parts: firstly the profitability of the buying and selling processes are shown in the trading account, to arrive at a figure of **gross profit**, and then all the other expenses of the business are deducted to arrive at a **net profit**.

The basic layout of the income statement is as follows:

	£
Revenue	–
Less: cost of sales	(–)
Gross profit	–
Various expenses	(–)
Net profit	–

First, we will look at the calculation and presentation of the upper part of the income statement to arrive at gross profit. This part of the financial statement is known as the **trading account**.

EXAMPLE 3.1

Mary has a shop that sells cookers. For the sake of simplicity we will assume that she sells only one type of cooker at a price of £195 each. She buys all the cookers from one manufacturer at a cost of £135 each. Each cooker therefore produces a profit of £60 (£195 less £135). If Mary bought and sold only one cooker the basic trading account information would be as follows:

Mary: Trading account

	£
Sale of cooker	195
Less: cost of cooker	135
Profit	60

The standard terminology used in drawing up a trading account is to describe the deduction for the cost of the goods as cost of sales, and the profit shown in the trading account as **gross profit**. We can restate Mary's trading account using this standard terminology:

Mary: Trading account

	£
Revenue	195
Less: cost of sales	135
Gross profit	60

Naturally, if Mary is trying to make a profit out of her business she will hope and expect to sell more than one cooker. If she sells 100 cookers during the course of the month of May 2012 her trading account will be as follows:

Mary: Trading account for the month ended 31 May 2012

	£
Revenue: 100 cookers @ £195	19 500
Less: cost of sales: 100 cookers @ £135	13 500
Gross profit	6 000

Note that this trading account statement has a proper heading showing Mary's name and the period covered by the statement. It is necessary to show this information so that the reader of the financial statement can be quite sure about the scope of the information covered. Note also the use of the terminology: **revenue, cost of sales** and **gross profit**.

Self-test question 3.1 (answer at the end of the book)

This question tests the understanding of the key elements of the trading account.

Jules sells leather bags from his market stall. The bags are all to the same design but are produced in a range of different colours with slightly different fastenings. During the month of December 2012 he sells 66 bags at £23 each. He has bought the bags for £14.50 each. Show Jules's trading account for the month.

3.4 MOVEMENTS IN INVENTORY

In most trading businesses an inventory of goods has to be held at all times, so that goods can be displayed and so that there are enough items available to satisfy potential demand. For example, in the cooker business outlined above, Mary has found that she needs to have at least five cookers on display at any time in order to demonstrate minor differences in styling and colours to her potential customers. Also, she needs to have a further 20 cookers available to cope with potential demand.

Inventory is replaced when necessary in order to ensure that there are always at least 25 cookers on the premises. The factory from which she orders guarantees rapid delivery so Mary does not have to keep a large amount of inventory on the premises.

EXAMPLE 3.2

Let's explore this example further by looking at some transactions during the month of June 2012. At 1 June Mary has 30 cookers in inventory. During June she sells 76 cookers. She orders 35 cookers which are delivered on 10 June and a further 40, delivered on 24 June.

How many cookers does Mary have in inventory at 30 June? In order to answer this question we can construct an inventory movement account:

	Units	£
Opening inventory: 30 cookers @ £135	30	4 050
Add purchases: (35 + 40) 75 cookers @ £135	75	10 125
Less: items of inventory sold: 76 cookers @ £135	(76)	(10 260)
Closing inventory: 29 cookers @ £135	29	3 915

Note that items sold are expressed in terms of the price Mary pays, so that like is compared with like. This account would form part of Mary's business record keeping but would not be shown as part of the financial statements.

We can use the information about inventory movements to draw up a more informative trading account for Mary for the month of June 2012.

Mary: Trading account for the month ended 30 June 2012

	Units	£	£
Revenue: 76 cookers @ £195	76		14 820
Cost of sales:			
Opening inventory: 30 cookers @ £135	30	4 050	
Add: purchases: 75 cookers @ £135	75	10 125	
	105	14 175	
Less: closing inventory: 29 cookers @ £135	(29)	(3 915)	
Cost of sales: 76 cookers @ £135	76		(10 260)
Gross profit for month			4 560

Because this is a simple example we can double check the gross profit. Mary has sold 76 cookers and we know that the gross profit on each is £60. 76 × £60 = £4560, so the answer is correct.

Note that the column containing the cost of sales calculation has been pulled to the left-hand side: this is simply to make the trading account easier to read and understand.

Self-test question 3.2 (answer at the end of the book)

At 1 January 2013 Jules has 36 handbags in inventory. Usually, January is a poor month for sales. This January is no exception and he sells only 42 bags at £23 each. However, he decides to improve the display by buying in several of each of the full range of colours. He buys in total 68 bags in January, at a cost of £14.50 each.

Prepare an inventory movement account for Jules, showing the number of units of inventory and monetary amounts. Also, prepare a full trading account for the month of January 2013, assuming that all handbags are sold for £23.

3.5 CALCULATING COST OF SALES

The example of Mary's cooker business has been kept deliberately straightforward in order to illustrate the calculation of cost of sales. However, most businesses, even small ones, would trade in more than one product. It would become very complicated to calculate precise numbers of units in the trading account. It is also unnecessary.

Most businesses have periodic inventory-taking (referred to in the UK as stocktaking), usually to coincide with the date at which the accounts are drawn up. This allows them to keep track of inventory, to identify those items that are not selling, to dispose of any damaged items found, and to generally make sure that there have not been any significant losses through poor accounting or theft. Inventory-taking identifies the quantities of inventory, which can then be valued by reference to how much it cost. Therefore, at the date of the income statement and statement of financial position, a valuation of inventory is established.

Purchases in the period are calculated from delivery records and from the invoices that suppliers send for payment.

Because the inventory value at the beginning and the end of the accounting period are established, and because the total purchases are known, it is easy to calculate cost of sales as follows:

	£
Opening inventory	—
+ Purchases	—
− Closing inventory	(—)
Cost of inventory	—

At this point it may be helpful to check this simplified layout against the trading account for Mary in example 3.2 – note that it shows the same basic components.

Now we will look at Mary's trading account for a 1-year period.

EXAMPLE 3.3

Mary's accounting year ends on 31 October. In respect of the year to 31 October 2012 she will need information about:

Opening inventory on 1 November 2011
Closing inventory on 31 October 2012
Purchases for the whole year

At 1 November 2011 her opening inventory value was £4725.
At 31 October 2012 her closing inventory value was £6480

During the year she received total purchases of cookers of £153 900. She sold 986 cookers at the normal selling price of £195 and a further 141 at £175 in a special Christmas promotion.

This is all the information that is needed to calculate Mary's gross profit for the year.

Mary: Trading account for the year ended 31 October 2012

	£	£
Revenue: 986 cookers @ £195	192 270	
141 cookers @ £175	24 675	
		216 945
Cost of sales:		
Opening inventory at 1 November 2011	4 725	
Add: purchases during year	153 900	
	158 625	
Less: closing inventory at 31 October 2012	(6 480)	
		(152 145)
Gross profit for year		64 800

3.6 CALCULATING NET PROFIT

Earlier in this chapter, we looked at the basic layout of an income statement, which was as follows:

	£
Revenue	–
Less: cost of sales	(–)
Gross profit	–
Various expenses	(–)
Net profit	–

The calculation of gross profit has now been covered comprehensively. Provided we know the expenses of the business we can deduct them from gross profit to arrive at the net profit for the period.

3.6.1 Typical Business Expenses

Expenses vary from one type of business to another, in both type and importance. For example, one of the main expenses in a road haulier's business will be the costs of fuel and other costs associated with running a fleet of haulage vehicles. By contrast, fuel and motoring costs in a business like Mary's cooker business are likely to be minor.

Expenses could include the following:

- *Cost of premises*: rental, business rates, insurance, electricity, gas, water, repairs.
- *Selling costs and costs of distributing goods*: haulage costs, delivery services, costs of sales' staff salaries and commissions.
- *Administration costs*: telephone, stationery, administrative staff salaries, accountants' and legal fees, computer costs.
- *Finance costs*: bank charges, interest on loans.

In the next example we will continue to look at Mary's business.

EXAMPLE 3.4

In the year ended 31 October 2012 Mary's business expenses are as follows:

- *Staffing costs*: Mary works in the shop by herself on quieter days, but she employs an assistant for a few hours each day on busy days. She pays the assistant £28 per day on average and he is employed for a total of 165 days during the year to 31 October 2012.
- *Premises costs*: Mary pays an annual rental for the shop of £17 500, including business rates, any major repair costs and service charges. In addition, in the year ended 31 October 2012 she pays general business insurance of £1350, electricity bills of £1207 and water rates of £795.
- *Administration*: Mary does all of the basic book-keeping herself, and pays an accountant £585 to produce the final accounts and the tax computation for HMRC. She spends £103 on stationery, stamps, and so on. Her telephone bills for the year ended 31 October 2012 come to £312, and she spends £132 on other odds and ends (usually known as 'sundry' expenses) for use in the business. The membership subscription to the trade association, the Cooker Association of Retailers and Manufacturers (CARM) costs £87 per year.
- *Finance costs*: bank charges total £85. Mary has not borrowed any money so there are no interest charges.

From this information it is possible to complete Mary's income statement to arrive at her net profit for the year, as follows:

Mary: Income statement for the year ended 31 October 2012

	£	£
Revenue (detailed calculation given earlier)		216 945
Less: cost of sales (detailed calculation given earlier)		(152 145)
Gross profit		64 800
Expenses:		
Staffing costs (165 days @ £28 per day)	4 620	
Rental of premises	17 500	
Business insurance	1 350	
Electricity	1 207	
Water rates	795	
Accountant's fees	585	
Stationery	103	
Telephone	312	
Sundry expenses	132	
CARM subscription	87	
Bank charges	85	
		(26 776)
Net profit for year		38 024

Note that the expenses are set off in a separate column towards the left-hand side of the page; this is to make the statement easier to read.

Later in the chapter we will examine an example of how the income statement and statement of financial position fit together.

3.7 WHAT DOES THE INCOME STATEMENT MEAN?

The income statement and other financial statements are prepared for a purpose; that purpose is to communicate information to people who need to know about the business. So, what information does Mary's income statement communicate?

An obvious and important piece of information is that the business is profitable in the year ended 31 October 2012. If this is a typical year, it is possible to draw the general conclusion that the business is currently successful, and may continue to be successful into the future. This general conclusion could be taken a little further by examining gross profit and net profit.

Mary is interested in assessing whether the general trend in her business profitability is upwards or downwards. She supplies the key figures from the income statement for the previous year's trading to 31 October 2011: sales were £197 535, gross profit was £57 300, expenses totalled £24 904 and net profit was £32 396.

This information can be summarized alongside the comparable figures for 2012:

	2012	2011
	£	£
Revenue	216 945	197 535
Less: cost of sales	(152 145)	(140 235)
Gross profit	64 800	57 300
Various expenses	(26 776)	(24 904)
Net profit	38 024	32 396

3.7.1 Gross Profit Analysis

Gross profit is an important element in judging how well or badly a business has performed. However, one isolated figure has little significance on its own. We need to make comparisons between at least two figures.

Comparing two consecutive years

The increase in gross profit is £64 800 − £57 300 = £7500. This is sufficient information to be able to calculate the percentage increase in gross profit from 2011 to 2012, as follows:

2011 gross profit	£57 300
Increase in gross profit	7 500

$$\text{Percentage increase} = \frac{£7\,500}{57\,300} \times 100 = 13.1\% \text{ (to nearest decimal place)}$$

If we were further informed, for example, that the Cooker Association of Retailers and Manufacturers published figures to its members showing that there had been an increase in the gross profit on cooker sales across the UK of 10% between 2011 and 2012, we could see that Mary's business has done rather well, and certainly better than average. Mary could achieve this better than average performance by either increasing her sales prices by a rate which is slightly above average, or by negotiating lower prices than average with the supplier, or by a combination of the two factors. As a sole trader, she may well charge higher prices than a large retailer, but customers may be prepared to pay a little more for better service and after-sales advice.

Gross profit margin

'Gross profit margin' is a way of expressing, by means of a percentage, the relationship between gross profit and revenue. It simply shows gross profit as a percentage of revenue.

Two figures are needed to calculate a gross profit margin: revenue and gross profit. Mary's trading account shows both, so we can apply the following formula:

$$\frac{\text{Gross profit}}{\text{Revenue}} \times 100 = \text{Gross profit margin \%}$$

In Mary's case:

$$\frac{£64\,800}{216\,945} \times 100 = 29.9\% \text{ (to nearest decimal place)}$$

Does this tell us anything useful? Again, not unless we have more information to compare it with.
Calculating the comparable ratio for 2011 uses the gross profit and revenue figures for 2011:

$$\frac{\text{Gross profit}}{\text{Revenue}} \times 100 = \text{Gross profit margin \%}$$

$$\frac{57\,300}{197\,535} \times 100 = 29.0\% \text{ (to nearest decimal place)}$$

To summarize, Mary's gross profit margin in 2011 was 29.0% and in 2012 was 29.9%. The gross profit margin in her business has improved. This means that the difference between the selling price and the cost of sales has increased. This may be as a result of selling prices increasing, cost prices reducing, or a combination of the two.

3.7.2 Net Profit Analysis

We can analyze net profit in the same way as gross profit.

Comparing two consecutive years

Net profit for the year is £38 024, and for 2011 was £32 396. The fact that it has increased is good news for Mary, but we can extend the analysis further to look at the percentage increase in the same way as we did for gross profit:

The increase is £38 024 − £32 396 = £5628.

$$\text{Percentage increase} = \frac{£5\,628}{32\,396} \times 100 = 17.4\% \text{ (to nearest decimal place)}$$

The figures for gross profit increased by 13.1% but net profit has increased by an even greater percentage. Why? The answer lies somewhere in the figure for expenses. In 2011 expenses totalled £24 904, increasing to £26 776 in 2012, an increase of £1872.

$$\text{Percentage increase} = \frac{£1\,872}{24\,904} \times 100 = 7.5\% \text{ (to nearest decimal place)}$$

We could extend the analysis further by looking at the percentage increases and decreases in the separate categories of expense. The basic analysis shows that, although expenses have increased, the level of increase is much lower than the level of increase in gross profit. As a result net profit shows a substantial increase.

Net profit margin

Net profit margin is a way of expressing, by means of a percentage, the relationship between net profit and revenue. It shows net profit as a percentage of revenue.

In Mary's business the net profit margin for 2012 is as follows:

$$\frac{£38\,024}{216\,945} \times 100 = 17.5\% \text{ (to nearest decimal place)}$$

The net profit margin for the previous year, 2011, is as follows:

$$\frac{£32\,396}{197\,535} \times 100 = 16.4\% \text{ (to nearest decimal place)}$$

These calculations show that net profit margin has increased. The conclusion is that, on the basis of the analysis of gross profit and net profit, Mary's business performance seems to have improved substantially.

3.8 ANALYZING FINANCIAL INFORMATION IN LARGE COMPANIES

As noted in Chapter 2, the financial statements of large businesses such as those listed on the Stock Exchange are muchmore complicated than the statements of the simple, single-activity, business used in the examples above. However, the analysis techniques explained in the previous section can be used productively to understand the financial statements of all types of business. Below is a real-life example.

EXAMPLE 3.5 (REAL-LIFE)

Sainsbury plc, 2008 Annual Report (available online at www.jsainsburys.co.uk).

Sainsbury's 2008 Annual Report contains a huge quantity of figures, facts and explanations. Extracting just four of the figures from the income statement information in the report:

	2008 £ million	2007 £ million
Sales* from supermarkets and convenience stores	17 837	16 860
Operating profit*	535	429

**Sainsbury's uses 'sales', rather than 'revenue'; operating profit is gross profit less operating expenses, but before deducting costs such as interest.*

These figures show an improvement in performance: sales have increased by 5.8% and operating profit by 24.7%. Operating profit margin (operating profit expressed as a percentage of sales) was 3% in 2008, compared to 2.54% in 2007. These figures suggest that Sainsbury's performance has improved, but interested parties would probably want more information than given here in order to fully understand the business's performance. Close examination of the full Annual Report would be necessary in order to find out more.

In later chapters we will examine more closely the meaning of financial information. However, it is never too soon to start thinking about the information content of financial statements.

3.9 INCOME STATEMENT ACCOUNTING IN A SERVICE BUSINESS

A service business does not trade in goods and therefore does not need to produce a trading account. In this section of the chapter we will look at the example of a business that supplies services only.

EXAMPLE 3.6

Tony is a chartered surveyor who supplies property advice services to clients investing in commercial property. He also acts as a commercial property agent, handling the selling of office and retail buildings. He makes commission on any successful sales. He employs a full-time personal assistant and, in the year to 31 December 2012 he has employed a student from the local college's estate management course on a day release basis. Other expenses incurred in his business include motor expenses for his large BMW (Tony clocks up around 50 000 miles each year in taking prospective clients to view industrial estates and business parks), entertaining, the cost of office premises, large telephone bills for office telephone and mobile, and sundries such as professional subscriptions and stationery.

Tony is a sole trader, trading as Aisgarth & Co. He provides the following list of income and expense items from which to draw up an income statement for the year ending 31 December 2012.

	£
Premises rental	12 570
Electricity bills	2 907
Personal assistant's salary	15 788
Income: commissions on commercial property sales	68 360
Motor expenses	15 370
Office and general insurance	1 003
Professional indemnity insurance (PII)*	1 880
Entertaining	9 351
Telephone charges	3 775
Income: fees for professional advice	23 333
Student's wages	1 200
Sundry office expenses	3 720

*Many qualified professionals, such as surveyors and accountants, are obliged under the regulations of their professional body, to take out special insurance against possible liabilities for professional negligence.

From this list of balances we can draw up Tony's income statement for the year to 31 December 2012 as follows:

Aisgarth & Co: Income statement for the year ended 31 December 2012

	£	£
Fees for professional services	23 333	
Commissions	68 360	
		91 693

	£	£
Expenses:		
Premises rental	12 570	
Electricity	2 907	
Personal assistant's salary	15 788	
Student's wages	1 200	
Motor expenses	15 370	
Insurance	1 003	
PII	1 880	
Entertaining	9 351	
Telephone charges	3 775	
Sundry office expenses	3 720	
		67 564
Net profit for year		24 129

Note that sole traders can trade under a business name, like Tony's. It is quite common for professional businesses like accountants, solicitors and surveyors to trade as *Something & Co*, even though there's only one sole trader involved.

We can work out a net profit margin figure for Tony's business:

$$\frac{£24\,129}{91\,693} \times 100 = 26.3\%$$

However, in a business like this, the net profit margin may fluctuate quite significantly from one year to another. Expenses are likely to be similar from year to year, but income may vary. Commercial property transactions are usually large, and the commission on a single transaction may amount to many tens of thousands of pounds. However, Tony may have to do a lot of entertaining and travel (both of which, as shown in the income statement, cost the business significant sums) in order to bring off just one deal. Without having other years' results for comparison it is not possible to say whether 2012 was a good, bad or middling year for Tony.

3.10 PREPARING BOTH THE INCOME STATEMENT AND THE STATEMENT OF FINANCIAL POSITION

This final section of the chapter draws upon aspects of Chapters 2 and 3 to demonstrate how the income statement and the statement of financial position fit together.

EXAMPLE 3.7

Nellie sells boots from her market stall and also carries out a boot repair service. This activity has never made much of a profit, but some of Nellie's long-standing customers continue to expect the service. Nellie's year-end is 31 May, a time of year when boot sales are low, and when she has very little inventory on hand. She counts and values her inventory on 31 May 2012 and arrives at a value of £2904.

You are employed in the office of Naylor & Co, Nellie's accountants. Your boss, Nasser, asks you to prepare her accounts for the year to 31 May 2012. As well as the information about inventory you are given the following list of items as at the year-end date.

	£
Inventory at 1 June 2011	2 672
Stall rental and service charge	3 844
Bank interest received	320
Sundry expenses	313
Saturday assistant's wages	1 200
Repairs income	1 801
Purchases	42 640
Trade payables	2 497
Accountant's fees and other administration	862
Insurance	574
Cash at bank	3 422
Drawings	14 257
Repairs expenses	1 742
Motor expenses	1 252
Revenue: sales of boots	63 060
Capital at 1 June 2011	6 060
Non-current assets – display stands	960

Nasser will be having a meeting with Nellie next week to talk about her business. She feels that she isn't doing as well as in previous years. Her gross profit for the year-end 31 May 2011 was £22 831 on sales of £67 760. In addition to preparing the accounts, Nasser would like you to calculate the actual and percentage changes in gross profit and revenue between 2011 and 2012, and to compare the gross profit margins between the 2 years. He would also like you to make some preliminary comments on Nellie's business performance.

■ *Step 1: prepare the accounts*

The first step is to prepare the income statement and statement of financial position for Nellie's business. The list that she has provided is a jumbled mixture of items, so a useful preliminary step is to identify a category for each item depending upon whether it goes in the trading account, the rest of the income statement or the statement of financial position. For items in the statement of financial position (referred to below as SFP) the terminology used in Chapter 2 can be used:

- non-current assets
- current assets
- current liabilities
- long-term liabilities
- capital.

	£	Category
Inventory at 1 June 2011	2 672	Trading account
Stall rental and service charge	3 844	Income statement
Bank interest received	320	Income statement
Sundry expenses	313	Income statement
Saturday assistant's wages	1 200	Income statement
Repairs income	1 801	Income statement
Purchases	42 640	Trading account

	£	Category
Trade payables	2 497	SFP: current liabilities
Accountant's fees and other administration	862	Income statement
Insurance	574	Income statement
Cash at bank	3 422	SFP: current assets
Drawings	14 257	SFP: capital
Repairs expenses	1 742	Income statement
Motor expenses	1 252	Income statement
Sales of boots	63 060	Income statement
Capital at 1 June 2011	6 060	SFP: capital
Non-current assets– display stands	960	SFP: non-current assets
Inventory at 31 May 2012	2 904	Trading account and SFP: current assets

Note that the closing inventory always appears in both the trading account and the statement of financial position as a current asset. Inventory that remains unsold at the date of the statement of financial position is deducted, as we have seen, in arriving at the cost of sales figure. However, it is also an asset of the business, because it can be sold to make money in the following accounting period. Having categorized all the items the next stage is to pick out those that appear in the trading account, so as to be able to prepare the trading account. Then, immediately below it, the rest of the income statement items are listed, ending with net profit. Remember that a heading with the name of the business (in this case Nellie simply uses her own name – which is common among sole traders) and a description of the financial statement are always required.

Nellie: Income statement for the year ended 31 May 2012

	£	£
Revenue		63 060
Less: cost of sales		
Opening inventory	2 672	
Add: purchases	42 640	
	45 312	
Less: closing inventory	(2 904)	
		(42 408)
Gross profit		20 652
Boot repairs: income	1 801	
Boot repairs: expenses	(1 742)	
		59
Other income – bank interest received		320
		21 031
Expenses		
Stall rental and service charge	3 844	
Motor expenses	1 252	
Saturday assistant's wages	1 200	
Insurance	574	
Accountant's fees and other administration	862	
Sundry expenses	313	
		(8 045)
Net profit		12 986

Once all of the balances have been put into the income statement the remainder should all relate to the statement of financial position, which can then be prepared.

Nellie: Statement of financial position at 31 May 2012

	£	£
ASSETS		
Non-current assets		960
Current assets		
Inventory	2 904	
Cash	3 422	
		6 326
		7 286
CAPITAL AND LIABILITIES		
Capital		
Opening capital balance 1 June 2011	6 060	
Add: net profit for the year	12 986	
	19 046	
Less: drawings	(14 257)	
Closing capital balance 31 May 2012		4 789
Current liabilities		
Trade payables		2 497
		7 286

The capital account shows the resources committed to the business by its owner. As explained in Chapter 2, the balance on the capital account increases or decreases in the following ways:

Capital introduced, plus Profits retained by the business, minus Drawings, minus any losses made by the business.

Nellie's capital account, as shown in the statement of financial position at 31 May 2012, has been increased by the amount of net profit for the year (calculated in the income statement) and has been decreased by the drawings she made from the business.

■ *Step 2: calculate the actual and percentage changes in gross profit and revenue*

Change in revenue: revenue has decreased from £67 760 to £63 060, a decrease of £4 700. The percentage change is calculated as follows:

$$\frac{£4\,700}{67\,760} \times 100 = 6.9\%$$

Change in gross profit: gross profit has decreased from £22 831 to £20 652, a decrease of £2 179. The percentage change is calculated as follows:

$$\frac{£2\,179}{22\,831} \times 100 = 9.5\%$$

Gross profit margins compared:

	2012	2011
	£	£
Gross profit margin	$\frac{20\,652}{63\,060} \times 100 = 32.7\%$	$\frac{22\,831}{67\,760} \times 100 = 33.7\%$

■ *Step 3: comment on Nellie's accounts*

Revenue and gross profits have both fallen between 2011 and 2012. The gross profit margin is poorer in 2012 than in the previous year. We do not have net profit information available for 2011. Nellie may be able to pinpoint reasons for the decline in trade, and Nasser needs to make some suggestions as to how she might be able to increase revenue in future. For example, a change of suppliers might improve gross profit margin. Other observations: the boot repair service is making virtually nothing. Nellie's time could perhaps be better used elsewhere and she may like to consider finally ceasing to offer the service. Nellie's drawings are in excess of the net profit generated by the business. There may be specific reasons why this level of drawings has been made during this recent financial year, but Nellie really should be considering ways of reducing drawings if possible, at least until her trade has recovered its previous levels.

CHAPTER SUMMARY

By this point, if you have followed this chapter carefully, you should understand the basic procedures involved in preparing an income statement, and should be aware of the significance of some of the revenue and cost figures that are typically included in the statement. There are many end-of-chapter exercises and website resources that you can use to consolidate your understanding.

It is very easy to access the Annual Reports of listed businesses on corporate websites. Even at this early stage it is worth making the effort to read these reports and to understand the accounting figures in them. It might be helpful to focus upon a limited number of reports to start with – perhaps a couple of competitor businesses in a sector that you find interesting. You may find it helpful to work, where possible, with other students on this exercise.

INTERNET RESOURCES

Sainsbury's website is at www.jsainsburys.co.uk The websites of listed businesses can usually be found quite easily using Google or another search engine. Alternatively, try accessing the London Stock Exchange website (www.londonstockexchange.com) which provides links to corporate websites for UK companies. Information about companies listed outside the UK is often accessible via other stock exchange websites, for example, the Deutsche Börse (www.boerse.frankfurt.de – available in English and German) or the Australian Securities Exchange (www.asx.com.au).

Book's companion website summary

www.cengage.co.uk/gowthorpe3 contains the following resources in respect of Chapter 3:

Students' section

Quiz containing ten multiple choice questions
Five additional questions with answers

Lecturers' section

Answers to end of chapter exercises 3.12 to 3.16
Five additional questions with answers
Case study
ExamView testbank
Instructor's manual
PowerPoint presentation

EXERCISES: ANSWERS AT THE END OF THE BOOK

3.1 Jackie sells garden furniture in sets comprising a dining table and four chairs. She purchases each set for £75 from the manufacturer and retails a set for £132. At the beginning of June 2012 Jackie had 30 sets in her inventory. At 30 June 2012 she had 42 sets.

She sold 35 sets during the month.

i. How many sets of dining table and chairs has Jackie purchased during the month?

a) 107
b) 47
c) 23
d) 37.

ii. What was Jackie's cost of sales figure for the month?

a) £4 425
b) £4 620
c) £2 625
d) £1 875.

iii. What was Jackie's gross profit for June?

a) £2 745
b) £1 425
c) £6 783
d) £1 995.

3.2 Jay's business is shoe retailing. He has bought in a special purchase of 1000 pairs of trainers for £8500.

He sells 750 pairs quite quickly at a retail price of £15.50 per pair. Then, in order to clear the inventory out of the shop he reduces the selling price to £12.50 and clears a further 200 pairs. The remaining 50 pairs are put into a bargain bin at a price of £5 per pair and these sell during the shop's autumn sale. What is Jay's gross profit on this line of trainers? How much gross profit would he have made if he had been able to sell the whole consignment at £15.50 per pair?

3.3 During the year Jake sells 8000 units of inventory at £42.50 each. The gross profit on each unit is £17.50. He purchased inventory at a total cost of £197 300 and still had £17 400 in inventory at the year-end.

What was Jake's opening inventory?

3.4 Jethro sells an extensive range of childrens' toys. He likes to be well-informed at all times about the performance of his business. Part of the routine work of his administrative assistant is to draw up a monthly trading account so that Jethro can check on gross profit levels. Information about revenue and purchases relating to a 3-month period October – December 2012 is as follows:

	October	November	December
	£	£	£
Revenue	39 370	48 998	56 306
Purchases	37 085	40 830	6 250

Inventory at the beginning of October was valued at £30 863.

Inventory at the end of each of the 3 months was as follows:

October	£43 258
November	£53 190
December	£23 980

Draw up a trading account for Jethro's business for each of October, November and December 2012.

3.5 Leon runs a retail grocery business, dealing in luxury and delicatessen goods. In 2012 revenue was £295 993, with cost of sales at £242 085. The equivalent figures for 2011 were revenue of £287 300 and cost of sales of £235 920.

Calculate:

i. Leon's gross profit margin in both years.
ii. The increase in revenue.
iii. The percentage increase in revenue.
iv. The increase in gross profit.
v. The percentage increase in gross profit.

3.6 The summarized results of Louis's business for the 3 years to the end of 2012 were as follows:

	2012	**2011**	**2010**
	£	**£**	**£**
Revenue	291 318	282 400	269 340
Cost of sales	(213 916)	(206 420)	(196 071)
Gross profit	77 402	75 980	73 269
Expenses	(52 394)	(51 720)	(49 270)
Net profit	25 008	24 260	23 999

Calculate the gross and net profit margins for each year and comment briefly on the general trends in the business trading results.

3.7 Madigan & Co is the trading name of Basil Madigan, a chartered accountant. He runs a small city centre office, employing a part-qualified accountant as an assistant, and a secretary, both on a full-time basis.

In the year ended 31 March 2012 fees from Madigan's clients totalled £95 311. The assistant's salary was £19 300 and the secretary was paid £11 150. Basil's one-room office is in a run-down office building at a comparatively low rental of £10 310 which includes energy costs and business rates. There is also an annual service charge (to cover repairs, caretaking, and so on) which amounted to £3790 in the year ended 31 March 2012.

Basil paid general insurance of £794, plus PII of £1250. Subscriptions and professional registration charges were £952. Business travel expenses (mileage claims for use of own car by himself and his assistant) came to £1863. Entertainment was £342.

Telephone charges were £1103 for the year and other administration charges were £1575. Stationery was £761 and sundry expenses totalled £715. Basil made donations to local charities out of the business account to the sum of £120.

Prepare the income statement for Madigan & Co for the year ending 31 March 2012.

3.8 Norbert runs a small wholesaling business, selling imported Italian coffee machines to retailers. His business is run from a small warehouse with an office at the side on an industrial estate on the edge of a large city. The industrial estate is largely deserted at night and the crime rate is high for theft and criminal damage. Norbert has recently joined a scheme run by the local authority on behalf of tenants of its industrial units; he pays an annual contribution to a fund which pays for improved lighting and security patrols.

Norbert's accounting year-end is 31 March. He provides you with a list of figures relating to the most recent year which ended on 31 March 2012. You are required to prepare an income statement and a statement of financial position from the figures.

	£
Delivery vehicle	5 020
Revenue for the year	351 777
Staff costs: storeman's wages	12 090
Electricity	2 821
Cash at bank	3 444
Capital at 1 April 2011	18 011
Administrative costs	3 810
Opening inventory at 1 April 2011	20 762
Non-current assets in warehouse and office	3 900
Drawings	25 219
Sundry expenses	1 406
Warehouse and office rental	10 509
Insurance	3 909
Trade receivables	36 623
Water rates	1 226
Security services charge	2 937
Purchases	255 255
Bank charges	398
Trade payables	31 950
Delivery expenses	8 630
Part-time admin assistant's wages	3 779

Norbert counted and valued the coffee machines on the premises at the 31 March 2012. The total value was £22 446. Prepare the income statement and statement of financial position for Norbert's business for the accounting year ended 31 March 2012.

3.9 Refer to the example of Mary's cooker business used earlier in the chapter. Briefly describe the principal groups of users of financial information who are likely to have an interest in Mary's financial statements, and the reasons for their interest. (You may find it helpful to refer back to the list of users groups provided in Chapter 1.)

3.10 Identify two listed businesses operating in the same business sector (for example, Sainsbury's and one of its competitors such as Tesco or Morrison). From the Annual Reports of the businesses, extract the revenue and profit information for the accounting year and the comparative information for the previous year. Calculate profit margins, and the year-on-year changes in the figures and compare the two businesses. Where there are differences between the businesses, use the other information in the Annual Report to see if you can identify the reasons for the differences.

3.11 Identify a company listed on a Stock Exchange outside the UK and obtain its annual report via the Internet (for example, try using the Deutsche Börse website to access information about Daimler AG or Volkswagen AG – these reports are published in English). Extract the revenue and profit information and identify whether there has been an increase or a decline in profitability.

EXERCISES: ANSWERS AVAILABLE ON THE LECTURERS' SECTION OF THE BOOK'S WEBSITE

3.12 Jin-Ming's mail order business sells trampolines. The selling price is £400 for a standard size trampoline, and £550 for a large one. The opening inventory at 1 January 2012 was 6 standard and 5 large trampolines. The cost of the trampolines to Jin-Ming is £260 (standard) and £330 (large). In the year to 31 December 2012 Jin-Ming sold 30 standard and 17 large trampolines. He could have sold more of the large size but the manufacturer stopped making them part-way through the year. Jin-Ming's purchases for the year totalled £14 880 including the purchase of 12 large trampolines.

a) Draw up Jin-Ming's trading account for the year ended 31 December 2012.
b) Calculate the gross profit on the sale of large and standard trampolines respectively.

3.13 Jodie is a wholesaler of electrical discount goods. She buys in end-of-line and seconds quality goods from manufacturers and sells them on to small electrical retailers. She has to take advantage immediately of any special offers that manufacturers make available; if she doesn't the manufacturers will sell to one of her competitors. Therefore, her inventory levels can fluctuate substantially from one week to the next. The level of revenue is not steady from month-to-month; it depends upon what's in inventory and whether there is much demand for the items Jodie currently has in her warehouse.

At the beginning of March Jodie's inventory was valued at £93 882 and comprised principally kettles, toasters and dishwashers. An unexpected surge in demand by small retail wholesalers for these items resulted in a high level of sales in March of £89 907. By the end of March inventory dropped to £34 920. At the end of April, as the result of a special purchase of electric blankets it went up to £82 860 dropping back only slightly to £75 918 at the end of May. Jodie knows that she will find it difficult to dispose of most of this inventory before the end of the summer.

Revenue for April was £31 241 and for May, £40 270.

Purchases for each of the 3 months were:

March	£3 074
April	£65 747
May	£18 911

a) Draw up trading accounts for each of the 3 months.
b) Discuss the business and financial problems Jodie would encounter in running this type of wholesaler operation.

3.14 Lulu's revenue in 2010 was £115 399. The following year, 2011, revenue increased by 4.3%. In 2012 revenue was 7.8% higher than it was in 2011. Gross profit margin in each of the 3 years was:

2010: 19.3%
2011: 21.4%
2012: 18.7%.

Calculate cost of sales for each of the 3 years, 2010, 2011 and 2012.
Work to the nearest £.

3.15 In 2012 Lola's net profit margin fell to 9.8% from 10.2% in the previous year. Her gross profit margin, on the other hand, increased from 30.2% to 33.8%. Revenue in 2011 was £148 360 and in 2012 was £153 062.

From this information prepare summary income statements for 2011 and 2012, showing revenue, cost of sales, gross profit, expenses and net profit.

Work to the nearest £.

3.16 Mahbub runs a recruitment agency. The agency's income is earned in the form of commissions from clients who pay a percentage of the first year's salary of new employees recruited by the agency. In the year to 31 December 2012 the total of commission income earned was £115 900. Mahbub is very pleased with this record level of commission; it is 25% higher than total commissions in the previous year.

Expenses, however, also increased. Premises costs totalled £16 506, staff costs were £29 900 and administration costs were £15 981. In the year to 31 December 2011 the equivalent expenses totals were:

Premises	£13 370
Staff costs	£28 807
Administration costs	£12 773

From the information given above, prepare Mahbub's income statement for both 2012 and 2011. Calculate the percentage increase or decrease in net profit.

CHAPTER 15

The Statement of Financial Position

AIM OF THE CHAPTER

To enable students to understand how a statement of financial position is prepared, and how it assists interested parties to understand the business's position at a point in time.

LEARNING OUTCOMES

After reading the chapter and completing the related exercises, students should:

- Understand how the statement of financial position relates to the other principal financial statements.
- Understand the terminology used in a statement of financial position, and some of the principal conventions used in presenting it, and in preparing financial statements in general.
- Be able to draw up a statement of financial position for a sole trader from a list of account balances and explanatory notes.
- Be able to understand and comment on the basic information conveyed by a statement of financial position.

INTRODUCTION

This chapter introduces the study of the preparation and interpretation of financial reports for external users. The first section uses a small business start-up example to explain in outline the three principal financial statements. The rest of the chapter concentrates upon one of these three statements: the statement of financial position.

The statement of financial position conveys information to people outside the business about the resources over which it has control, and which can be used in the future to generate profits. It also contains information about liabilities, that is, the amounts of obligations such as amounts owing to other businesses and individuals. It therefore produces a financial picture of the position of the business at a given point in time.

The chapter explores some of the accounting terminology that is used in a statement of financial position, and looks at the principles and conventions involved in the preparation of financial statements. All financial statements are intended to convey information to people interested in the business, and the chapter concludes with a brief examination of some of the messages transmitted by the figures in a small business statement of financial position.

2.1 BASICS OF BUSINESS ACCOUNTING: THE THREE PRINCIPAL FINANCIAL STATEMENTS

The introductory chapter to this book discussed the objective of financial statements, and the principal groups of people who might be interested in obtaining information from them. The objective of financial statements, according to the International Accounting Standards Board (IASB) in its Framework for the Preparation and Presentation of Financial Information, is as follows:

'The objective of financial statements is to provide information about the financial position, performance and changes in financial position of an entity that is useful to a wide range of users in making economic decisions' (para.12).

In this book we will be concerned with three principal financial statements: the statement of financial position, the income statement and the statement of **cash flows**. (As noted in Chapter 1, two of these statements may be referred to by different names: the statement of financial position is sometimes known as the balance sheet, and the income statement is sometimes known as the profit and loss account. This book will use the terms 'statement of financial position' and 'income statement'.)

The statement of financial position shows readers the business's position at a particular point in time, the income statement reports on the business's performance over the accounting period, and the **statement of cash flows** shows the movement in cash between the beginning and end of the accounting period. All businesses, regardless of size, produce an income statement and statement of financial position, and most also produce a statement of cash flows. The basic form of the statements is very similar from the smallest of small businesses to the largest multinational.

This chapter is principally concerned with the statement of financial position. However, as a preliminary, the relationship between the three statements is briefly explored. The example below uses a very simple business start-up to explain the outline content of the three statements, and how they interact.

EXAMPLE 2.1

Jamie has decided to put his savings into starting a hairdressing business. He has saved £8700 for this purpose, and on 2 January 2012 he opens a bank account in the name of 'JJ Hair Studio' which he has decided will be the trading name of the business. He pays £8700 into the new bank account straight away. It takes a few days to set up Internet banking for the new account, but on 8 January he is able to make a transfer of £800 to his new landlord for the first month's rent on a salon. He also spends £3500 on equipment such as chairs, dryers, mirrors, telephone and sound systems, and so on, and opens the salon for business on 20 January. In the period up to the end of January 2012 he receives a total of £1250 in cash from customers, and pays out £200 in various expenses such as shampoos and dyes.

There are five pieces of information about business transactions in the above scenario, and, perhaps surprisingly, this is quite enough to allow us to draw up the three financial statements for the business on 31 January 2012, the end of Jamie's first month in business.

Statement of cash flows

Of the three statements, the statement of cash flows is probably the easiest to understand and, at this stage, to prepare. It shows the cash inflows and outflows summarized for a particular accounting period, explaining the movement in cash resources from the beginning to the end of a period of time, in this case 1 month. Jamie's statement of cash flows for January is as follows:

JJ Hair Studio: statement of cash flows for the month ended 31 January 2012

	£	£
INFLOWS		
Cash introduced by proprietor		8 700
Receipts of cash from sales		1 250
		9 950
OUTFLOWS		
Payment for rental	800	
Payment for equipment	3 500	
Payment for expenses	200	
		(4 500)
Balance of cash on 31 January		5 450

This financial statement provides information about cash inflow and outflow. Statements of cash flows will be examined in more detail in Chapter 6.

Income statement

The income statement shows the profitability of the business for a period; it compares revenue (sometimes referred to as sales) with the expenses incurred in order to achieve that revenue. In the case of Jamie's business, revenue for the month amounts to a total of £1250. Expenses include two items: the salon rental of £800 and the other expenses of £200. Note that these items are all the same as the cash inflows or outflows. This is partly to keep the example simple, but it is also fairly realistic in the case of sales in a hairdressing business. Later in the book, we will examine the more complex situation where revenue and expenses are made on credit terms (i.e. they do not have to be paid for straight away).

Jamie's income statement for the month is as follows:

JJ Hair Studio: Income statement for the month ended 31 January 2012

	£
Revenue	1 250
Expenses (800 + 200)	(1 000)
Profit for the period	250

Comparing the two statements prepared so far, we can see that certain items of cash inflow and outflow do not appear in the income statement. This is because they represent resources that will be used in the business over more than one accounting period. Resources like cash, and equipment used on a long-term basis, are reflected instead in the business's statement of financial position.

The statement of financial position

The statement of financial position shows the position of a business at a single point in time. The items shown in the statement of financial position can be categorized into three elements: assets, liabilities and capital. Jamie's statement of financial position is shown below, followed by a section of the chapter that explains the three elements in detail.

JJ Hair Studio: Statement of financial position at 31 January 2012

	£	£
ASSETS		
Non-current assets: equipment		3 500
Current assets: cash (from the statement of cash flows)		5 450
		8 950
CAPITAL AND LIABILITIES		
Capital introduced by Jamie	8 700	
Add: profit for the month	250	
Liabilities	0	
		8 950

The total of resources available for use in Jamie's business is £8950. This total, or 'balance', is the same as the total of Jamie's capital invested in the business. This comprises the original amount of £8700 input into the business, plus the profit for the month of January. A helpful way of thinking about this is to reflect that £8950 is the amount that Jamie as an individual is 'owed' by the business. Thinking about it in this way emphasises the fact that the business and Jamie are different entities. This is known as the '**business entity**' **concept** of accounting, and it is emphasised by the fact that the business has a different name (JJ Hair Studio).

The figure for liabilities in JJ Hair Studio's statement of financial position is £0, reflecting the fact that, on 31 January 2012, the business owes no money.

2.2 THE STATEMENT OF FINANCIAL POSITION: DEFINITIONS OF ELEMENTS

This section of the chapter examines the three elements (assets, liabilities and capital) in detail.

2.2.1 Assets

Assets are resources controlled by a business, which it will use in order to generate a profit in the future. Examples of such resources include:

- Cash in the form of notes, and coins, and cash kept in bank accounts.
- Amounts of money that people or organizations owe to the business. Such amounts are described in accounting terminology as **trade receivables**.
- Items bought by the business to sell on to somebody else, or to process or transform in some way to make saleable goods. Such items are known as **inventory** (or inventories).

Cash, trade receivables and inventory are categories as **current assets**.

This description reflects the fact that they do not remain static for long. For example, trade receivables are usually turned into cash within a short period of time, inventory is sold, and then replaced, and the business bank account balance changes very frequently.

Items bought (or sometimes leased) by the business that will be used over a long period of time are known in accounting terminology as **non-current assets**. 'Non-current' means that the assets stay in the business for a long time (at least 1 year and possibly for much longer). Examples are buildings (and the land they stand on) which are bought to house the activities of the business, vans and lorries that can be used for transporting goods and people, and computer hardware and software.

2.2.2 Liabilities

Liabilities are amounts that the business is obliged to pay to other people or organizations. Examples of liabilities include:

- Amounts owing to people or organizations that have provided goods or services on credit (i.e. they provide the goods or services without requiring immediate payment for them); these amounts are known as **trade payables**.
- Amounts owing to the government in the form of taxation, for example, in the UK, corporation tax and Value Added Tax (VAT).
- Loans that will have to be repaid in due course to banks or other lenders.

The convention used in drawing up statements of financial position is to subdivide liabilities into two major categories: non-current liabilities that do not have to be repaid for 1 year or more after the date on which the statement of financial position is drawn up; and current liabilities, amounts that are payable within 1 year of the statement of financial position date.

2.2.3 Capital

Capital is the amount invested by the owner(s) of the business. There may be one or more owners: as explained in Chapter 1, in a sole trader business all of the capital is invested by a single owner or proprietor. In a partnership the ownership of capital is split between two or more individuals. In an incorporated business, shares may be owned by very large numbers of people or, indeed, by other organizations.

As explained at the end of example 2.1, it can be helpful to think of capital as being the amount 'owed' by the business to its proprietor(s).

2.2.4 Terminology

The terminology used for the different statement of financial position elements described above (inventory, trade payables, and so on) is the standard terminology used in international accounting. Companies listed on a stock exchange within the European Union (and in many other places such as Australia and New Zealand) are obliged to use standard terminology and formats for their financial statements that are established by the International Accounting Standards Board (IASB). Smaller businesses are not obliged to use such terminology, and in the UK many unlisted businesses continue to use a slightly different set of terms; for example, trade receivables are known as debtors. An appendix at the end of the book lists older UK terms against their international equivalents.

Self-test question 2.1 (answer at the end of the book)

This question tests understanding of the descriptions of the key statement of financial position elements of assets and liabilities described above.

George's retail business sells kitchen utensils, crockery and cutlery. The following are descriptions of some of the items in his statement of financial position. For each item, fill in the adjacent box with 'ASSET' or 'LIABILITY'.

Bank overdraft	
Computer and printer used to keep the administrative records of the business	
Plates and cups available for sale to customers	
Cash float kept in the till – £100 in various notes and coins	
Loan of £20 000 from George's brother	

2.3 THE ACCOUNTING EQUATION

In the JJ Hair Studio statement of financial position in example 2.1, the total of assets was balanced by the capital contributed by Jamie, plus the profit earned since the start of the business. At any point in time, a business should be able to provide a complete list of its assets and liabilities, each having a monetary amount.

It is possible to express the three basic elements of a statement of financial position in an equation. As shown by the JJ Hair Studio statement of financial position:

$$\text{ASSETS} = \text{CAPITAL} + \text{LIABILITIES}$$

It is also true to say that:

ASSETS − LIABILITIES = CAPITAL

Also,

ASSETS − CAPITAL = LIABILITIES

The next example will examine a slightly more complex statement of financial position than that of JJ Hair Studios in order to demonstrate the accounting equation.

EXAMPLE 2.2

Robert is a wholesaler selling garden tools to garden centres. His statement of financial position at 30 June contains details of his assets, liabilities and capital, as follows:

	£	£
ASSETS		
Non-current assets: warehouse, van and equipment		60 000
Current assets		
Inventory (gardening tools)	8 000	
Trade receivables (owed by garden centres)	4 000	
Cash in the bank account	6 000	
		18 000
		78 000
CAPITAL AND LIABILITIES		
Capital (Robert's resources tied up in the business)		64 000
Non-current liabilities: amounts owed to bank	8 000	
Current liabilities: trade payables (amounts owed to the firm that supplies Robert's business with gardening tools)	6 000	
		14 000
		78 000

In this example we have a value for each of the three elements of the accounting equation: assets, liabilities and capital. Robert's capital in the business is £64 000. Although assets come to more than that (£78 000) a total of £14 000 will have to be used to pay off the liabilities. £78 000 less £14 000 is £64 000, the amount of Robert's capital.

The accounting equation holds good, in all of its forms:

ASSETS = CAPITAL + LIABILITIES (£78 000 = £64 000 + £14 000)
ASSETS − LIABILITIES = CAPITAL (£78 000 − £14 000 = £64 000)
ASSETS − CAPITAL = LIABILITIES (£78 000 − £64 000 = £14 000)

2.3.1 The Statement of Financial Position Format

It was noted earlier that the IASB requires listed businesses to use standard formats for financial statements. These are illustrated in International Accounting Standard 1 (IAS 1) *Presentation of Financial Statements*. Although the content of most of the international financial reporting standards is outside the scope of this book, it is worth noting that the prescribed format is similar to that used in example 2.2. Assets are shown first, followed immediately below by capital + liabilities. However, some businesses do adopt slightly different formats that emphasise other versions of the accounting equation. Nevertheless, it should always be possible to discern the accounting equation at work in one of its forms.

Self-test question 2.2 (answer at the end of the book)

Saqib's statement of financial position at 30 September shows the following items:

	£
Non-current assets	30 000
Inventory	5 000
Trade receivables	4 000
Cash held in business bank account	3 000
Trade payables	6 000
Saqib's capital	36 000

1 What is the total of assets in the business?
2 What is the total of liabilities in the business?
3 What is the capital of the business?
4 Write down the figures for the basic accounting equation (remember: assets = capital + liabilities).

So far, figures have been provided for each of the three key elements of the accounting equation. However, if we know two out of the three figures, we can work out the third. Example 2.3 demonstrates how this is done, and self-test question 2.3 tests your understanding of this point.

EXAMPLE 2.3

We need to supply the missing figure in each of the following incomplete accounting equations:

1 **Capital**
Assets are £15 000 and liabilities are £3 000. What is capital? Using the accounting equation in the form of

ASSETS − LIABILITIES = CAPITAL

£15 000 − £3 000 = £12 000

2 **Assets**
Capital is £6 000 and liabilities are £18 000. What is the total for assets? Use the accounting equation in the form of

ASSETS = CAPITAL + LIABILITIES

? = £6 000 + £18 000

Assets therefore = £24 000

Self-test question 2.3 (answer at the end of the book)

Amy's statement of financial position at 31 August contains total assets of £58 000 and total liabilities of £30 000. Use the accounting equation to find Amy's capital.

2.4 DRAWING UP A STATEMENT OF FINANCIAL POSITION

This section of the chapter demonstrates the link between a set of business transactions and the statement of financial position at the end of an accounting period. Like the first example in this chapter, JJ Hair Studio, it uses a business start-up, but the range of transactions and the resultant statement of financial position is more extensive and complicated. The example will illustrate some important points about the conventions used in business accounting. Remember that we have already encountered the 'business entity' convention earlier in the chapter (and see if you can remember what it is).

EXAMPLE 2.4

Salma has spent several months researching business possibilities, and decides to set up a retail business selling designer kitchenware. The business will be called 'Kitchen Kit'. She has £100 000 available to put into the new business in cash, following the sale of a previous successful business. Salma signs an agreement to rent premises from 1 February 2012, planning to open her shop on 26 February. Rent is payable in arrears, and she will not have to pay anything until the end of March 2012. In order to illustrate the construction of a statement of financial position containing the results of several transactions, the statement of financial position will be drawn up at regular intervals during the first few days of business. This is somewhat artificial, and is for illustrative purposes only; in real life a statement of financial position would be drawn up at periodic intervals, and almost never more often than once a month.

Day 1

On 1 February Salma opens a business bank account in the name of 'Kitchen Kit' depositing £100 000. Assuming no other transactions on Day 1, a statement of financial position drawn up at the end of the day would show the following:

Kitchen Kit: Statement of financial position at 1 February 2012

	£
ASSET: bank account	100 000
CAPITAL	100 000

This single transaction creates items under two of the elements of the accounting equation. Every business transaction either adds to, or depletes, two of the elements of the statement of financial position; this is known as the 'dual aspect' convention of accounting.

Conventions of presentation

The simple statement of financial position above follows certain simple presentational conventions which are the norm in many countries, regardless of whether IAS 1 is complied with or not.

1 The statement of financial position has a heading showing the name of the business (not the individual) and the date at which it is drawn up.

2 It is in vertical format – that is, the figures are arranged in a columnar form.

3 It is headed by a sign indicating the currency adopted – in this case the £ sterling.

4 The key totals are underlined.

Days 2 – 8

Salma needs to display inventory in her shop, ready for the opening on 26 February. First, she has arranged for a builder to come into the shop to install a counter and some shelving. She pays him £6500 on 8 February. What are the accounting implications of this transaction?

The counter and shelving are likely to be used in the business over a long period of time and they are therefore regarded as non-current assets. The business's cash resources have been depleted by £6500 but non-current assets increase from £0 to £6500 (note the dual aspect of the transaction – one asset is depleted, but another asset increases by the same amount). If a statement of financial position is drawn up at the end of the day on 8 February, it shows the following:

Kitchen Kit: Statement of financial position at 8 February 2012

	£
ASSETS	
Non-current assets: counter and shelving	6 500
Current assets: bank account	93 500
	100 000
CAPITAL	100 000

Note that the balance on the bank account was £100 000 before Salma paid £6500 for the counter and shelving. After the transaction has taken place, the balance on the bank account drops to £93 500. Note also that the accounting equation remains valid: assets = capital.

Day 9

Salma needs to stock the shop. She has ordered various items of kitchenware that are delivered on 9 February. Because Salma has several years of experience in business and a good credit record she has been able to obtain credit terms from suppliers, and will not have to pay for the inventory until 9 March. The cost of the inventory is £72 000. What are the implications for the statement of financial position of this transaction?

The business has acquired a new type of current asset in the form of inventory. It is classified as a current asset because it is not expected to remain in the business for a long period (unlike the shop counter and shelving). However, in this case there is no effect (yet) on the bank account because immediate payment for the goods is not required. So what has occurred?

A current asset of £72 000 arises, and current assets in the statement of financial position will increase by this amount. The other aspect of the transaction is that a current liability for the same amount arises.

Taking this transaction into account, the statement of financial position of the business at 9 February 2012 is as follows:

Kitchen Kit: Statement of financial position at 9 February 2012

	£	£
ASSETS		
Non-current assets: counter and shelving		6 500
Current assets:		
Inventory	72 000	
Bank account	93 500	
		165 500
		172 000
CAPITAL AND LIABILITIES		
Capital		100 000
Current liabilities: trade payables		72 000
		172 000

What is going on here? Why are there so many more figures in this statement of financial position compared to the previous one? Don't panic. Most of the changes from the previous statements of financial position have been made in order to make the statement clearer and more useful to the reader. Starting at the top of this most recent statement of financial position:

- Non-current assets are the same as before at £6500.
- Under current assets we now have the new asset of inventory. There are now two categories of current asset so it is helpful to summarize current assets by means of the total figure of £165 500. In order to make the figures easier to read and understand, the current assets figures have been pulled into a separate column, and only the total is shown in the column at the right of the page. Once the reader gets accustomed to this convention of presentation it makes it much easier to understand what is going on.
- The bottom part of the statement of financial position now comprises both capital and current liabilities. The new category of current liabilities arises because of the amount of £72 000 owing for inventory.

Note that the accounting equation remains valid, but that it is now slightly more complicated because of the introduction of liabilities:

Assets (£172 000) = Capital (£100 000) + Liabilities (£72 000)

Day 10

Salma has invested in inventory to sell in the shop. When she pays for it in 1 month's time she will have a bank balance, assuming no other transactions in the meantime, of £21 500 (£93 500 − 72 000). She realises that there will be many further demands on her cash in the short-term, for example, advertising, more purchases of inventory, buying a cash register, installation of a burglar alarm, and so on. She realises that she is likely to need more cash, but does not want to draw any further on her personal resources. She borrows £20 000 from her mother. This is a loan without a fixed repayment date, but her mother is happy for it to be a long-term arrangement. On 10 February Salma pays the £20 000 into the business bank account. What are the accounting implications of this transaction?

The business's cash resources have increased by £20 000. On the other hand, there is now a non-current liability. A statement of financial position drawn up on 10 February will be as follows:

Kitchen Kit: Statement of financial position at 10 February 2012

	£	£
ASSETS		
Non-current assets: counter and shelving		6 500
Current assets:		
Inventory	72 000	
Bank account	113 500	
		185 500
		192 000
CAPITAL AND LIABILITIES		
Capital		100 000
Non-current liabilities: loan		20 000
Current liabilities: trade payables		72 000
		192 000

Each transaction that we have examined makes the statement of financial position a little more complicated – and by 10 February, when the example ends, the business has yet to make a sale. It should be emphasised that the frequent drawing up of statements of financial position as in the example would be very unusual – it is done here for the purposes of illustration and explanation. Statements of financial position are drawn up on a periodic basis – at least once a year and sometimes more often, but practically never on a daily basis.

2.4.1 Changing the Value of Capital

What would it take to alter the amount at which capital is stated in Kitchen Kit's statement of financial position? An increase could occur in two situations:

1 The owner of the business might put in some more of their personal resources. In Salma's case she might, for example, sell her house or her car and put the proceeds into the business. The dual aspects of this transaction would be to increase the amount of capital in the statement of financial position, and to increase cash by the same amount.

2 The business can increase the amount of capital by making a profit. In Salma's case she will do this by selling kitchenware at prices greater than the price she paid for the goods. The difference between selling and cost price must be sufficiently large to cover all categories of expense, such as rent, rates, advertising and administration.

Alternatively, the value of capital could decrease. This could happen in two ways:

1 The owner (or owners) of the business take out some of the resources they have put into it. Where the owner wants or needs to remove some part of the assets, the total of assets decreases, and so does the amount of capital in the statement of financial position. The removal of assets (usually cash, but it could be other types of asset) by the owner is traditionally known as **drawings**.

2 The business decreases its net assets by making a loss. If goods or services are sold for amounts that do not, overall, cover the costs of the business, a loss will be made and net assets, and capital, will be depleted.

2.5 MORE PRACTICE WITH STATEMENTS OF FINANCIAL POSITION

The example of Salma in the previous section of the chapter examined a new business start-up to illustrate the basics of statement of financial position preparation. This section applies the knowledge gained from the chapter so far to established businesses that are preparing statements of financial position at the end of an accounting period.

Each business – whether a company, partnership or sole trader – has a year-end date at which point it prepares its annual accounts. Conventionally, year-ends tend to be end of month dates (31 December, 31 March etc.) although there is no strict rule about this. It would be quite acceptable to have a year-end of 5 April, for example, which coincides with the end of the tax year in the UK. The next example deals with the preparation of a statement of financial position for an established business.

EXAMPLE 2.5

Dipak has been established in business for several years in a business selling computers for home and small business use. As well as selling standard systems he also builds PC systems to customers' specifications and sells a limited range of software packages, printers and fax machines. He runs the business from shop premises that he owns on a freehold basis. The business, which trades as Computers2Go has the following balances at its year-end on 31 August 2012:

	£
Freehold premises	53 000
Shop fittings and equipment	6 300
Cash	60
Loan from brother (no fixed repayment date)	8 000
Inventory of PCs	48 000
Graphics and sound cards, cables, etc.	9 650
Bank overdraft	13 750
Trade receivables (amounts owed by customers)	5 250
Owner's capital	99 130
Inventory of software	15 000
Trade payables (amounts owed to suppliers)	16 380

First, we need to establish which categories each of the balances fall into – asset, liability or capital:

	£	Category
Freehold premises	53 000	Asset
Shop fittings and equipment	6 300	Asset
Cash	60	Asset
Loan from brother (no fixed repayment date)	8 000	Liability
Inventory of PCs	48 000	Asset
Graphics and sound cards, cables, etc.	9 650	Asset
Bank overdraft	13 750	Liability
Trade receivables (amounts owed by customers)	5 250	Asset
Owner's capital	99 130	Capital
Inventory of software	15 000	Asset
Trade payables (amounts owed to suppliers)	16 380	Liability

Classifying assets

Seven of the items on the list are classified as assets. Which are current and which are non-current? Remember that inventory, trade receivables and cash are categorized as current assets. The first two items on the list are non-current assets – i.e. freehold premises and the shop fittings and equipment; these have been, and will continue to be, used for a long time in the business.

There are three categories of inventory on the list: inventory of PCs, graphics cards, etc. and software. These three are added together to give a total for inventory:

	£
PCs	48 000
Graphics cards etc.	9 650
Software	15 000
Total inventory	72 650

As well as non-current assets and inventory, Dipak's business has trade receivables of £5250 and cash of £60, which are also current assets.

Drawing up the statement of financial position

Having done the preliminary work on classification, preparing the statement of financial position should be a relatively straightforward exercise:

Computers2Go: Statement of financial position at 31 August 2012

	£	£
ASSETS		
Non-current assets:		
Freehold premises	53 000	
Shop fittings and equipment	6 300	
		59 300
Current assets:		
Inventory	72 650	
Trade receivables	5 250	
Bank account	60	
		77 960
		137 260

	£	£
CAPITAL AND LIABILITIES		
Capital		99 130
Non-current liabilities (loan from brother)		8 000
Current liabilities		
Bank overdraft	13 750	
Trade payables	16 380	
		30 130
		137 260

2.6 COMMUNICATING MEANING: WHAT DOES THE STATEMENT OF FINANCIAL POSITION SAY?

Remember that the basic function of financial statements is to be useful to a range of users. When involved in the difficulties of fitting the figures together and getting the statement of financial position to balance it is easy to forget that the point of the exercise is to communicate a message.

What does the statement of financial position of Computers2Go in example 2.5 tell us? We know that the business sells computers, and therefore needs an inventory of PCs, software, and so on. But does the business need to have quite so much inventory? Let's say that the average price that Dipak has paid for a PC is £300. This would mean that he holds approximately 160 systems (£48 000 divided by £300) in inventory. How long will it take to sell these items, and will they be out of date soon? Similar questions could be asked about the other items of inventory.

The business owes its suppliers more than £16 000. Presumably they will expect to be paid very soon. How are they to be paid? The business has a comparatively large overdraft. Will the bank allow further borrowings on overdraft? Even if the customers who owe money were to pay up straight away, there would still be a problem. Could Dipak contribute money from his own resources to help the business meet its liabilities?

Trying to understand the messages conveyed by this statement of financial position involves asking a lot of questions, that cannot, from the information given, be easily answered. We need a lot more information.

It is important to remember at all times that the purpose of statements of financial position (and accounting in general) is not to provide number puzzles for business students, but to provide information that actually means something in the context of the real world.

2.6.1 Useful Characteristics of Accounting Information

The IASB Framework for the Preparation and Presentation of Financial Statements identifies several characteristics of accounting information that help it to be useful to people (these were mentioned briefly in Chapter 1). Four characteristics are regarded as being of particular importance:

Understandability: the IASB's view is that financial statement users should have a reasonable knowledge of business and economic activities and of accounting. Financial statements should be comprehensible by people who have this level of knowledge.

Relevance: information must be reasonably up-to-date, that is, it should have the quality of 'timeliness'. Users should be aware of the age of the information they are looking at, because it becomes less relevant with the passage of time. Where financial statements are produced annually (as is the case for most businesses), there is likely to be a timelag of at least 3 months after the year-end before the information becomes available. Even during this short space of time, the information may become obsolete. There is then a further time lag, for most businesses, of up to another 12 months before the next set of accounts becomes available. It should also be appreciated that the information provided in financial statements is backward-looking in the sense that it reflects and describes events and transactions that have already taken place. Users might prefer forward-looking information (like **budgets**) but this is very rarely made available.

Reliability: information in financial statements should be free from bias, and should faithfully represent transactions and events. It is important that financial reports are drawn up with integrity, so as not to mislead users.

Comparability: except in the case of the first year's figures, financial statements always include comparative figures (i.e. the figures from the previous accounting period) to provide a comparison. It is important that these should be prepared on a consistent basis from 1 year's end to the next.

2.7 FINANCIAL REPORTING BY LARGE COMPANIES

The examples used in this chapter are all of very small businesses. This is done deliberately so that the figures remain small and straightforward in nature. Obviously, the financial statements of large, complex businesses such as the companies listed on the Stock Exchange, are much more complicated. However, one of the reasons for adopting the presentation of financial statements prescribed by the IASB in this book, is so that readers become accustomed to the terminology and layouts. This means that, even at this stage in your studies, you can begin to understand the statements of financial position of major businesses: see the comparison with the real life example 2.6.

EXAMPLE 2.6 (REAL-LIFE)

Tate & Lyle plc, 2009 Annual Report

Tate & Lyle plc is a company listed on the London Stock Exchange. European Union regulation requires that all companies listed on the stock exchanges of the member states prepare their financial statements to comply with IASB regulations. The principal statement of financial position headings used in company's statement of financial position at 31 March 2009 are as follows:

ASSETS
Non-current assets
Current assets
SHAREHOLDERS' EQUITY
Capital and reserves
LIABILITIES
Non-current liabilities
Current liabilities

The only term that is likely to be unfamiliar after studying this chapter is 'Shareholders' equity'. However the sub-description of 'Capital and reserves' suggests that this is the equivalent of what we have so far referred to simply as 'Capital' in this chapter. So, even at this stage in your studies, it is becoming possible to read the statement of financial position of a major company in an informed way.

The financial statements of companies will be covered at greater length in Chapter 7.

Self-test question 2.4

Identify a large company in which you are interested for some reason (e.g. you are a customer of it, you have worked for it, or you have a family member or a friend who works for it). Find out the URL of the company's website (almost all large companies have websites these days) and find its most recent statement of financial position. You will probably find this in the Annual Report document which can run to well over a 100 pages, and which will often be found under the section of the website devoted to 'Investor Information' or 'Corporate Information' or similar. Identify the headings and the extent to which you recognize the terminology used. It is quite likely that you will recognize most, if not all, of the main headings. Look also at the subheadings and see if you can find familiar elements such as 'trade payables', 'inventory,' and so on.

(Note: there is no specific solution to this self-test question, but you may be able to discuss your findings in class.)

CHAPTER SUMMARY

The statement of financial position is a statement of a business's position at a given point in time. At this stage, you should be able to prepare a statement of financial position for a small business from a given list of balances, and you should understand in outline how the statement of position interacts with the other principal financial statements.

It is important to understand from an early stage the conventions of presentation and preparation that are commonly used in preparing financial statements. Before moving on, be sure that you understand the 'business entity' concept, and the 'dual aspect' concept. Other concepts will be introduced over the next few chapters. Finally, remember that the purpose of all this accounting is to convey information and to be useful to people who are interested in the performance and position of the business. Even at this early stage in your studies it is always worth trying to discern the messages conveyed by the figures.

INTERNET RESOURCES

Tate & Lyle's website is at www.tateandlyle.com, under 'Investor Relations'.

Book's companion website summary
www.cengage.co.uk/gowthorpe3 contains the following resources in respect of Chapter 2:

Students' section
Quiz containing ten multiple choice questions
Six additional questions with answers

Lecturers' section
Answers to end of chapter exercises 2.16 to 2.23
Four additional questions with answers
Chapter on double-entry book-keeping
ExamView testbank
Instructor's manual
PowerPoint presentation

EXERCISES: ANSWERS AT THE END OF THE BOOK

2.1 Alexander's business manufactures and sells biscuits to supermarkets and grocery shops. Below are descriptions of some of the items in his statement of financial position. For each item fill in the adjacent box with ASSET or LIABILITY.

Cash kept in a tin in the factory office	
Oven	
Bank loan, repayable over 5 years	
Plastic packaging for biscuits	
Flour and sugar	
Amounts payable to supplier of dried fruit	

2.2 Amir has a consultancy business which he runs from rented offices. The following are descriptions of some of the items in his statement of financial position. For each item fill in the adjacent box with NON-CURRENT ASSET, CURRENT ASSET, NON-CURRENT LIABILITY or CURRENT LIABILITY.

Value Added Tax (VAT) payable to HMRC	
Office computer	
Amount due from Lomax plc for consultancy work carried out by Amir	
Bank overdraft	
Bank loan to be repaid in 3-years' time	
Amount payable to stationery supplier	

2.3 Brian's statement of financial position shows totals for assets of £83 000 and £36 500 for liabilities. Use the accounting equation to find the total for Brian's capital.

2.4 Basil's capital in his business is £43 650. Business assets total £188 365. Use the accounting equation to find the total for liabilities.

2.5 Brenda's business has non-current assets of £12 000, current assets of £8500 and total liabilities of £17 300. What is Brenda's capital?

2.6 Brigitte's business has non-current assets of £27 000, current assets of £16 000, current liabilities of £12 000 and non-current liabilities of £10 000. What is her capital in the business?

2.7 Bryony's statement of financial position shows the following totals:

	£
Non-current assets	35 840
Current assets	16 500
Current liabilities	12 000
Non-current liabilities	6 000

Bryony's capital in the business is:

a) £70 340
b) £1 340
c) £46 340
d) £34 340.

2.8 Benito's statement of financial position shows the following totals:

	£
Non-current assets	39 497
Current assets	26 004
Current liabilities	16 777
Capital	33 058

Work out the missing figure for non-current liabilities (Hint: first, work out total liabilities using the accounting equation).

2.9 Blanche's statement of financial position shows the following totals:

	£
Non-current assets	36 609
Current assets	38 444
Current liabilities	26 300
Capital	39 477

The missing figure for non-current liabilities is:

a) £61 876
b) £9 276
c) £15 012
d) £67 612.

2.10 Callum's statement of financial position at 31 July shows the following:

	£
Non-current assets	18 337
Inventory	12 018
Trade receivables	365
Cash	63
Bank overdraft	3 686
Trade payables	2 999

a) What is the total of assets in the business?
b) What is the total of current assets?
c) What is the total for liabilities?
d) What is Callum's capital?

2.11 Ciera's business has the following balances at 31 December 2012:

	£
Inventory	18 600
Trade payables	23 700
Cash in bank account	13 000
Long-term loan	20 000
Non-current assets – premises	39 000
Trade receivables	6 500
Amounts owed to HMRC	3 800
Ciera's capital	29 600

Prepare Ciera's statement of financial position at 31 December. Use the format shown in the chapter examples. Remember to line up columns of figures neatly, and to use a proper heading for the statement of financial position.

2.12 Dan's statement of financial position at 1 May 2012 was as follows:

	£	£
ASSETS		
Non-current assets		30 000
Current assets		
Inventory	15 000	
Trade receivables	5 000	
Bank account	18 000	
		38 000
		68 000
CAPITAL AND LIABILITIES		
Capital		52 000
Current liabilities		
Trade payables		16 000
		68 000

On 2 May Dan paid £1500 for an office computer to help him keep the business accounts.

On 3 May Dan paid a supplier £3000.

Explain how his statement of financial position was affected and show the new statement of financial position at 3 May 2012 after taking account of both transactions.

2.13 Ernest runs an art gallery. He organizes exhibitions at which painters and sculptors show their work. If a piece of artwork is sold, Ernest takes a commission of 50% of the selling price. He banks the cash and then pays out what is due to the artists. He held a successful exhibition in November, and is planning the next one for January. Each time he holds an exhibition he pays for advertising and sending out leaflets to people on his mailing list, also for wine and soft drinks on the opening night of the exhibition. Putting on the exhibition in January will cost him around £4000.

Ernest has the following assets and liabilities at 31 December:

	£
Gallery premises	68 000
Cash at bank	18 600
Amounts payable to artists	16 560
Office equipment	2 260
Amounts payable to printers for publicity material for recent exhibition	1 600
Capital	70 700

1 Prepare Ernest's statement of financial position at 31 December.

2 Write a brief assessment of Ernest's business position as shown by the statement of financial position.

2.14 Explain the business entity concept of accounting.

2.15 Which of the following statements is correct?

According to the IASB's Framework, the four principal characteristics of financial statements are:

a) Relevance, timeliness, reliability, comparability.
b) Understandability, relevance, reliability, comparability.
c) Understandability, relevance, consistency, comparability.
d) Relevance, comparability, reliability, consistency.

EXERCISES: ANSWERS AVAILABLE ON THE LECTURERS' SECTION OF THE BOOK'S WEBSITE

2.16 Adrian owns and runs a restaurant. The following are descriptions of some of the items in his statement of financial position. For each item fill in the adjacent box with NON-CURRENT ASSET, CURRENT ASSET, NON-CURRENT LIABILITY or CURRENT LIABILITY

Restaurant tables	
Wages owed to waiter	
Bank account containing £3850	
Tax bill due to HMRC	
Restaurant premises	

Mortgage (i.e. loan) from bank to buy restaurant premises [ ]

Food supplies in kitchen fridges [ ]

Amounts due to baker for bread supplied over the last month [ ]

2.17 Bernie's business has liabilities of £63 000. His capital is £28 000. What is the total for assets?

2.18 Bjork's capital in her business is £97 000. The total for current liabilities is £31 000. There are no non-current liabilities. What is the total for assets?

2.19 Bashir's statement of financial position shows the following totals:

	£
Capital	68 350
Non-current assets	79 403
Current assets	16 276

The liabilities in Bashir's business are:

a) £131 477
b) £27 329
c) £5 223
d) £164 029.

2.20 Benedict's statement of financial position shows the following totals:

	£
Current assets	716 237
Current liabilities	426 663
Non-current liabilities	100 000
Capital	1 373 424

What is the total for non-current assets?

2.21 Carmela's business has the following balances at 18 October 2012:

	£
Amounts due from customers	16 303
Non-current assets – machinery	12 722
Amounts payable to suppliers for materials	6 868
Bank balance	6 993
Cash on the premises	120
Amounts payable to the HMRC	396
Long-term loan from sister	1 800
Non-current assets – office computer	1 060
Inventory of goods	17 721

Prepare the statement of financial position for Carmela at 18 October 2012.

NB: no figure is given for Carmela's capital – it has to be calculated from the information given above.

2.22 Diana's statement of financial position at 28 August 2012 is as follows:

	£	£
ASSETS		
Non-current assets		13 500
Current assets		
Inventory	10 300	
Trade receivables	1 200	
Bank account	1 000	
Petty cash	600	
		13 100
		26 600
CAPITAL AND LIABILITIES		
Capital		20 200
Current liabilities		
Trade payables		6 400
		26 600

1 Diana has saved up some money for her holiday, but decides to put it into the business instead. She pays a cheque for £2000 into the business bank account on 29 August.

2 On 30 August the business receives a cheque for £600 from one of its customers.

Explain how her statement of financial position will be affected and show the new statement of financial position at 30 August 2012 after taking account of both transactions.

2.23 Erik has a retail business selling china and glass ornaments from a small shop in a town centre. He has the following balances at his year-end of 30 November:

	£
Freehold premises	16 800
Shop fittings, computer, till, etc.	8 300
Cash – float in till	600
Loan from mother (no fixed repayment date)	2 000
Inventory	10 300
Bank overdraft	3 800
Trade payables	3 200
Payables – due to HMRC for VAT	800
Capital	26 200

NB: the trade payables include £2200 owed to one company, Ornamental Glass Products Ltd. The company has been waiting for payment for this amount since August and Erik has been rung up on several occasions by the company's chief accountant requesting immediate payment. Erik has an overdraft limit of £4000.

1 Prepare Erik's statement of financial position at 30 November.

2 Erik has asked you to advise him on whether he should ask the bank manager for an increase in his overdraft limit. Assess Erik's position at 30 November as shown by the statement of financial position.

CHAPTER 16

The Statement of Cash Flows

AIM OF THE CHAPTER

To understand the distinction between profit and cash, and the principles and practices involved in preparing a statement of cash flows.

LEARNING OUTCOMES

After reading the chapter and completing the exercises at the end, students should:

- Understand the distinction between profit and cash.
- Be able to draw up a statement of cash flows for a small business.
- Understand some of the messages conveyed by the statement of cash flows.

INTRODUCTION

Early in Chapter 2, it was noted that this book will be concerned with 'three principal financial statements: the statement of financial position, the income statement and the statement of cash flows'. The first two statements have been covered extensively in Chapters 2 to 5, so it is now time to turn to the third statement. The statement of cash flows provides additional important information that allows the user of the financial statements to understand the performance and position of the business. The statement of cash flows is constructed out of the same fundamental information as the other two statements, but it presents the information in a different way, which emphasises the flows of cash in and out of the business.

This chapter first examines the distinction between profit and cash, referring back to the principles of recognition and accruals that were examined in earlier chapters. Then it turns to the mechanics of preparation of a statement of cash flows, with demonstrations based on a business start-up and then an established business. Finally the chapter examines some of the messages and meaning conveyed by the statement of cash flows.

6.1 THE DISTINCTION BETWEEN PROFIT AND CASH

In the long run, a profitable business generates positive cash flows. The increases in cash flows can be used for new investment in the business or to pay a return to the people who invested in it. A loss-making business in the long run produces negative cash flows and cash inflows in the form of new investment will be required to prevent it going under.

In the short-term, however, profits do not necessarily equate to positive cash inflows. In Chapter 4 we examined the conventions relating to accounting recognition and to accruals and concluded that 'accounting revenue is not the same figure as cash received and accounting expenditure is not the same as cash paid'. The application of accounting conventions moves the accounting statements away from pure cash inflows and outflows by accounting for depreciation, amortization, accruals, prepayments and any other adjustment that does not represent an immediate cash flow.

It is also important to appreciate that cash can be depleted or increased by transactions that do not affect the income statement; for example, the purchase of non-current assets. When a non-current asset is purchased, the asset of cash is replaced by, for example, an item of machinery. This transaction produces no immediate impact on profits, although over time, profits will be depleted as the asset is subject to depreciation.

To demonstrate these points, Table 6.1 examines the implications for cash and profits of various common transaction types. Only in the case of the fourth transaction in the list – the sale for cash of £1600 – is the impact on cash and profit identical and simultaneous. In all other cases there is a mismatch between cash and profit.

The differences between cash and profit relate to differences in timing. For example, an outflow of cash spent on a non-current asset is likely to produce profits (and cash inflows) sooner or later, but in the meantime, there is a gap. Sometimes, if the gap between outflows and inflows is too big, the business can be at risk of going under. Later in the chapter a detailed example shows how this can occur.

TABLE 6.1 The impact of transactions on cash and profits

Transaction	Impact on cash	Impact on profits
Borrowing £10 000 at an annual interest rate of 10%. Loan to be repaid after 5 years	Cash and long-term liabilities are both increased in the statement of financial position by £10 000 After 5 years, the loan will be repaid; cash and long-term liabilities will both be reduced by £10 000	No immediate impact on profits. Each year for 5 years there will be an annual interest payment of £1 000. This will decrease both cash and profit
Purchasing a new car for £8000. The car is to be depreciated on the straight-line basis over 4 years, with the assumption of no residual value at the end of 4 years	Cash is reduced, and non-current assets are increased by £8000	No immediate impact on profits. Each year for 4 years there will be a depreciation charge of £2 000 (£8000/4), but this has no effect on cash
Drawings of £3500	Cash and capital are both reduced by £3500	There is no impact on profit. Effectively, the owner is taking £3500 of his/her capital out of the business
Sale for cash of £1600	Cash is increased immediately	The sale is recognized immediately, and sales in the income statement are increased by £1600
Sale on credit for £1600	Trade receivables are increased immediately. Provided that the debtor pays up, cash will be increased at some point in the near future	The sale is recognized immediately, and sales in the income statement are increased by £1600

Self-test question 6.1 (answer at the end of the book)

What is the effect on cash and on profit of the following business transactions?

1 Purchase of inventory for cash of £1800.

2 Sale of old delivery van for £360.

3 Long-term loan from brother of £5000.

4 Payment of interest on bank overdraft of £150.

5 Amortization of charge of £8000 relating to patent rights.

6.2 PREPARING A STATEMENT OF CASH FLOWS

A very simple statement of cash flows was demonstrated early in Chapter 2. This statement comprised two parts: cash inflows and cash outflows. In practice, where statements of cash flows are prepared it is usual to produce a slightly more complex statement with the cash flows classified in a way that is intended to be helpful to the reader. International Financial Reporting Standards (IAS 7 *Statements of Cash Flow*) prescribe a statement that is divided into three principal sections:

- Operating activities: cash flows arising from the business's trading activities, such as receipts of cash in respect of sales, payments for costs such as cost of sales, staff and rental. This section of the statement is concerned with inflows and outflows relating to **working capital** items: inventory, trade receivables and trade payables.
- Investing activities: cash flows in respect of payments for resources that will generate income for the business in the future. This would include payments for non-current assets and receipts from the disposal of non-current assets.
- Financing activities: cash flows in respect of capital, for example, receipt of cash invested in the business by the owner, or the repayment of loans taken out to finance business expansion.

For the very small businesses used as most of the examples in this book so far, there is no strict requirement to produce a statement of cash flows at all. However, a statement of cash flows can often provide useful information, even in small businesses, and it is easier to learn how to do them using simple business examples first. The division of cash flows into three sections, while again not mandatory for small businesses, is helpful because the terminology becomes familiar, and then it is easier to understand when it is encountered in the context of a large business.

6.2.1 Preparing a Statement of Cash Flows: a Business Start Up

Example 6.1 describes and illustrates the procedures involved in preparing a statement of cash flows for a new business at the end of its first year of trading. This is a useful first step in learning how to prepare statements of cash flows because the starting position at the beginning of the year is zero. Subsequently, we will look at an example of a statement of cash flows in an established business, which is a little more complicated.

EXAMPLE 6.1

Isobel Buchanan started up a new business on 1 April 2011, importing and selling handmade rugs. Her business trades as Buchanan International Designs. As well as capital of her own, she borrowed money from members of her family to get the business going. In her first year of trading Isobel bought various non-current assets and items of inventory. Her sales are made partly for cash, and partly on credit.

Isobel's income statement for the year ended 31 March 2012 and her statement of financial position at that date were as follows:

Buchan International Designs: Income statement for the year ended 31 March 2012

	£	£
Revenue		115 622
Cost of sales		(80 379)
Gross profit		35 243
Operating expenses:		
Various expenses	23 606	
Depreciation	5 351	
		(28 957)

Operating profit	6 286
Interest paid	(2 400)
Interest received	651
Net profit	4 537

The income statement above is set out slightly differently from those used in earlier chapters. This statement isolates a figure for operating profit, from which are added or deducted amounts of interest paid or interest received, thus producing a net profit figure. (In practice, many income statements include a figure for operating profit.)

Buchanan International Designs: Statement of financial position at 31 March 2012

ASSETS	£	£
Non-current assets		
Cost	22 630	
Less: accumulated depreciation	(5 351)	
		17 279
Current assets		
Inventory	19 400	
Trade receivables	4 027	
Cash	13 323	
		36 750
		54 029
CAPITAL AND LIABILITIES		
Capital		
Capital introduced	10 000	
Add: profit for the year	4 537	
	14 537	
Less: drawings	(7 500)	
		7 037
Long-term liabilities		
Loan		40 000
Current liabilities		
Trade payables		6 992
		54 029

Isobel started in business on 1 April 2011 by putting cash into a new business bank account. The total cash deposited was £50,000 comprising £40 000 she borrowed from her family, and £10,000 of her own money. One year later, we can see from the statement of financial position that, although she has made a small profit of £4537, her bank balance has fallen to £13 323, a drop of (£50 000 − £13 323) £36 677. So, although the profit figure tells a positive story, the downside is that there has been a very large outflow of cash from the business.

What has happened to the cash?

Isobel's income statement and statement of financial position convey a great deal of useful information but are not obviously helpful in providing answers to this important question. A statement of cash flows helps to answer the question by isolating the principal cash movements.

Preparing Isobel's statement of cash flows

Step 1: Operating cash flows

First of all, we must examine cash flows related to the business's operating activities, i.e. those cash flows involved in buying and selling, and generally operating the business. The starting point is the figure for operating profit, which is £6286. This figure is calculated by deducting cost of sales and operating expenses from sales revenue. However, this amount does not represent a simple inflow of cash because it is affected by the accruals convention in accounting:

- Operating expenses include depreciation, which is a non-cash item.
- Only part of the sales revenue has actually been received in cash (we know this because there are trade receivables in the statement of financial position). The amount received in cash is the sales revenue total less trade receivables of £4027.
- Only part of the cost of sales and operating expenses have been paid for in cash (we know this because there are trade payables in the statement of financial position). The amount paid for in cash is total operating costs and expenses, less the trade payables balance of £6992.
- Outflows of cash have taken place to purchase inventory (we know this because there is a balance of inventory in the statement of financial position). This outflow is not included in cost of sales, because under the accruals convention, closing inventory is deducted from cost of sales. The amount of the cash outflow is £19 400.

The table below adjusts the totals for sales revenue and operating costs by adding or deducting, as appropriate, non-cash items and the outflow for the purchase of inventory. The final column shows the total cash inflow or outflow.

	Income statement	Non-cash item – depreciation	Non-cash items – trade receivables and trade payables	Cash outflow – Inventory purchase	Total cash inflow (outflow)
	£	£	£	£	£
Sales revenue	115 622		(4 027)		111 595
Operating costs*	(109 336)	5 351	6 992	(19 400)	(116,393)
Operating profit/cash flow	6 286	5 351	2 965	(19 400)	(4 798)
Interest paid	(2 400)				(2 400)
Interest received	651				651
Net profit/cash flow	4 537	5 351	2 965	(19 400)	(6 547)

*Operating costs = cost of sales (£80 379) + operating expenses (£28 957)

The first part of the statement of cash flows sets out the information from the table in the following format which demonstrates the conventional layout used in practice:

	£	£
Operating profit		6 286
Depreciation		5 351
		11 637

	£	£
Less: increase in inventory	(19 400)	
Less: increase in trade receivables	(4 027)	
Add: increase in trade payables	6 992	
		(16 435)
Cash generated from operations		(4 798)
Interest paid		(2 400)
Interest received		651
Net cash outflow from operating activities		(6 547)

Before progressing to the next step, make sure that you can see how the figures in the first part of the statement of cash flows relate to the figures in the table.

Step 2: Investing cash flows

Investing cash flows comprise payments for resources that will generate income for the business in the future. It also comprises any receipts of cash in respect of such resources, for example, cash inflows arising from the disposal of non-current assets.

In this example, there is only one amount in respect of investing cash flows: the purchase of non-current assets at cost of £22 630.

Cash outflow	(22 630)

Remember to identify the cash outflow; it is the amount *paid* for the non-current assets, *not* the year-end carrying amount.

Step 3: Financing cash flows

Financing cash flows comprise cash flows in respect of movements in capital, for example, receipt of cash invested in the business by the owner or the repayment of loans taken out to finance business expansion. The source of information about these cash flows is the capital and long-term liabilities section of the statement of financial position. In this example, the cash inflows and outflows relating to financing are as follows:

Cash inflow: capital introduced	10 000
Cash outflow: drawings (i.e. capital withdrawn)	(7 500)
Cash inflow: loan	40 000

Step 4: Completing the statement of cash flows

At this point we can pull together all the information from steps 1 to 3 and produce a complete statement of cash flows. As with all financial statements, it requires a heading.

Buchanan International Designs: Statement of cash flows for the year ended 31 March 2012

	£	£
Cash flows from operating activities		
Operating profit		6 286
Depreciation		5 351
		11 637
Less: increase in inventory	(19 400)	
Less: increase in trade receivables	(4 027)	
Add: increase in trade payables	6 992	
		(16 435)
Cash generated from operations		(4 798)
Interest paid		(2 400)
Interest received		651
Net cash outflow from operating activities		(6 547)

	£	£
Cash flows from investing activities		
Purchase of non-current assets	(22 630)	
Net cash outflow from investing activities		(22 630)
Cash flows from financing activities		
Capital introduced	10 000	
Capital returned to owner (drawings)	(7 500)	
Long-term loan	40,000	
Net cash inflow from financing activities		42 500
Net increase in cash		13 323
Cash at beginning of period		0
Cash at end of period		13 323

The final part of the statement of cash flows shows a reconciliation between the net increase or decrease in cash, and the movements in the cash balance between the opening and closing dates. In this case, the opening balance was zero, because the example deals with a new business start-up. In a continuing business, there will be cash at both the beginning and end of the period. Note that, for this purpose, 'cash' comprises all bank balances plus any cash, such as petty cash balances.

Comments on the statement of cash flows

When deeply involved in the mechanics of preparing financial statements it is easy to lose sight of the fact that their purpose is to provide useful information. The aim of a statement of cash flows is to provide explanations for the overall movement in cash in the accounting period, by isolating and describing useful categories of cash inflows and outflows.

What additional information does the statement of cash flows for Buchanan International Designs provide? We can see that operating activities produced a net cash outflow, largely because of the cash spent on building an inventory of items for sale. The other really significant items in the statement are the substantial investments in non-current assets, which will contribute to generating revenue over more than one accounting period, and inflows arising from the initial financing of the business. At the year-end a positive balance of £13 323 remains. Further detailed analysis in the form of cash flow budgets would be required to determine whether this amount of cash would be sufficient to finance the business in its second year of trading. (Cash flow budgets are covered in detail in Chapter 16 of this book.)

Before moving on to the next section of the chapter, try this self-test question.

Self-test question 6.2 (answer at the end of the book)

Amy Binyon started a new business on 1 January 2012. Extracts from her income statement for the year ended 31 December 2012 and her statement of financial position at that date show the following information:

Revenue	89 300
Cost of sales	56 200
Operating expenses, including depreciation of £4500	22 600

Interest paid	1 000
Inventory	6 900
Trade receivables	8 500
Trade payables	9 000

Prepare a table to record adjustments between profit and operating cash flows (see the table in Step 1 of Example 6.1), and then prepare the operating section of Amy Binyon's statement of cash flows for the year ended 31 December 2012.

6.3 DIRECT AND INDIRECT APPROACHES TO CASH FLOW

There are two possible approaches to the preparation of a statement of cash flows: direct and indirect. Example 6.1 demonstrates the indirect approach: it takes the reported profit figure, and then adjusts it for non-cash items and movements in inventory, receivables and payables to calculate cash generated from operations. This requires several lines of reconciling items, as shown in the example. The direct approach to preparing a statement of cash flows is, as the name implies, more straightforward requiring simply two lines, as follows:

- receipts from operating activities
- payments in respect of operating activities.

The example 6.2 shows how to calculate and present this information.

EXAMPLE 6.2

This example uses the same information as Example 6.1. The requirement is to present a statement of cash flows for Buchanan International Designs for the year ended 31 March 2012, but this time, using the direct method.

The table that was used to chart movements in operating items in the explanation of Example 6.1 is used again here. The upper part of the table is shown again:

	Income statement	**Non-cash item – depreciation**	**Non-cash items – trade receivables and trade payables**	**Cash outflow – Inventory purchase**	**Total cash inflow (outflow)**
	£	£	£	£	£
Sales revenue	115 622		(4 027)		111 595
Operating costs*	(109 336)	5 351	6 992	(19 400)	(116,393)
Operating profit/cash flow	6 286	5 351	2 965	(19 400)	(4 798)

The two new figures required for the direct operating cash flows can be taken from this table, and inserted into the statement of cash flows, as follows:

Buchanan International Designs: Statement of cash flows for the year ended 31 March 2012

	£	£
Receipts from operating activities		111 595
Payments in respect of operating activities		(116 393)
Cash generated from operations		(4 798)
Interest paid		(2 400)
Interest received		651
Net cash outflow from operating activities		(6 547)
Cash flows from investing activities		
Purchase of non-current assets	(22 630)	
Net cash outflow from investing activities		(22 630)
Cash flows from financing activities		
Capital introduced	10 000	
Capital returned to owner (drawings)	(7 500)	
Long-term loan	40 000	
Net cash inflow from financing activities		42 500
Net increase in cash		13 323
Cash at beginning of period		0
Cash at end of period		13 323*

*operating costs total = cost of sales + operating expenses

Differences between the direct and indirect approaches are confined to the operating section of the statement of cash flows. The investing and financing sections are identical in both approaches.

6.4 STATEMENTS OF CASH FLOW IN AN ESTABLISHED BUSINESS

In example 6.1 earlier in the chapter, a statement of cash flows was prepared for the first year of trading of a new business. This meant that there were no opening balances, which simplified the example. Normally, of course, a business has both opening and closing balances. Example 6.3 demonstrates the preparation of a statement of cash flows for an established business.

EXAMPLE 6.3

Horst is in business as a sole trader, trading under the name of Box Distributors. His accountant has prepared an income statement for the business for the year ended 31 December 2012, and a statement of financial position at that date. Horst approaches you in your capacity as a small business adviser to give him some advice. He shows you the financial statements and says:

'I can't quite understand what's happened here. My revenue for 2011 was £600 227, and it's increased in 2012 to £636 636. The business is really doing quite well. I've had to replace one of the delivery vehicles during the year, because it was unreliable, but I thought I'd been quite sensible about covering that spending. I got £5200 for it and extended the long-term bank loan by another £5000 which more or less covered the cost of the new van which was £10 660. I've made a big effort to control my own spending – I decided not to replace the BMW this year, and we went camping in France instead of going on that luxury cruise we'd planned. So, drawings are only slightly higher than they were in 2011. Despite all this restraint, the overdraft was almost £8000 at the year-end. Please explain to me what has happened and what I can do to reduce the overdraft.'

The income statement and statement of financial position for the 2012 financial year are shown below:

Box Distributors: Income statement for the year ended 31 December 2012

	£	£
Revenue		636 636
Cost of sales		(452 483)
Gross profit		184 153
Operating expenses		
Selling and distribution expenses (excluding depreciation)	(62 466)	
Administration expenses (excluding depreciation)	(55 892)	
Depreciation of delivery vehicles	(6 313)	
Profit on disposal of delivery vehicle	336	
Depreciation of warehouse and machinery	(11 876)	
		(136 211)
Operating profit		47 942
Interest paid		(2 104)
Net profit		45 838

Box Distributors: Statements of financial position at 31 December 2012 and 31 December 2011

	2012	2012	2011	2011
	£	£	£	£
ASSETS				
Non-current assets				
Delivery vehicles at cost	35 897		33 650	
Less: accumulated depreciation	(16 960)		(14 196)	
Carrying amount		18 937		19 454
Warehouse and machinery at cost	118 760		118 760	
Less: accumulated depreciation	(71 256)		(59 380)	
Carrying amount		47 504		59 380
		66 441		78 834
Current assets				
Inventory	52 687		45 611	
Trade receivables	78 490		65 442	
Cash at bank	–		371	
		131 177		111 424
		197 618		190 258

	2012	2012	2011	2011
	£	£	£	£
CAPITAL AND LIABILITIES				
Capital				
Capital brought forward	137 841		128 069	
Profit for the year	45 838		58 222	
Drawings	(49 000)		(48 450)	
		134 679		137 841
Long-term liabilities				
Loan		15 000		10 000
Current liabilities				
Overdraft	7 996		–	
Trade payables	39 943		42 417	
		47 939		42 417
		197 618		190 258

A detailed analysis of the delivery vehicle account shows the following:

	£
Cost of delivery vehicles	
At 1 January 2012	33 650
Disposal of vehicle	(8 413)
Addition of vehicle	10 660
At 31 December 2012	35 897
Accumulated depreciation on delivery vehicles	
At 1 January 2012	14 196
Accumulated depreciation on disposal	(3 549)
Depreciation for the year (to income statement)	6 313
At 31 December 2012	16 960

A delivery vehicle was sold for £5200 during the year.

The statement of cash flows, prepared using the indirect approach, is set out below, followed by detailed notes on its preparation.

Box Distributors: Statement of cash flows for the year ended 31 December 2012

	£	£	Note
Cash flows from operating activities			
Operating profit		47 942	1
Depreciation		17 853	1
		65 795	
Less: increase in inventory	(7 076)		2
Less: increase in trade receivables	(13 048)		2
Less: decrease in trade payables	(2 474)		2
		(22 598)	
Cash generated from operations		43 197	
Interest paid		(2 104)	3

	£	£	Note
Net cash inflow from operating activities		41 093	
Cash flows from investing activities			
Purchase of non-current assets	(10 660)		4
Proceeds of sale of non-current asset	5 200		4
Net cash outflow from investing activities		(5 460)	
Cash flows from financing activities			
Capital returned to owner (drawings)	(49 000)		5
Increase in long-term loan	5 000		6
Net cash inflow from financing activities		(44 000)	
Net decrease in cash		(8 367)	
Cash at beginning of period		371	7
Cash at end of period – overdraft		(7 996)	7

Notes

Note 1 The statement starts, as previously, with operating profit, and then non-cash items are added back. Depreciation does not involve any movement in cash, and nor does the profit on disposal of the delivery vehicle. Remember that a 'profit' or 'loss' on disposal of a non-current asset represents either under-depreciation or over-depreciation; neither is a cash flow. (Cash is received in exchange for the asset and this will be included further down the statement of cash flows, under the heading of 'Cash flows from investing activities'.)

	£
Depreciation of delivery vehicles	6 313
Profit on disposal of delivery vehicle	(336)
Depreciation of warehouse and machinery	11 876
Total	17 853

Note 2 In order to understand the effects on operating cash flows of the changes in inventory, receivables and payables, it may be helpful to use a table, as in example 6.1

	Income statement	Non-cash items – depreciation and profit on disposal	Non-cash items – trade receivables and trade payables	Cash outflow – Inventory purchase	Total cash inflow (outflow)
	£	£	£	£	£
Sales revenue	636 636		(13 048)		623 588
Operating costs total*	(588 694)	17 853	(2 474)	(7 076)	(580 391)
Operating profit/cash flow	47 942	17 853	(15 522)	(7 076)	43 197

*operating costs total = cost of sales + operating expenses (£452 483 + 136 211 = £588 694)

Inventory: there has been an increase in inventory between the two year-ends: £52 687 – 45 611 = £7076. This difference is the total additional cash outflow for the accounting period.

Trade receivables: the amount of cash received in respect of sales revenue in the period is:

	£
Opening trade receivables	65 442
Sales revenue	636 636
Less: closing trade receivables	(78 490)
Cash received	623 588

The adjustment for non-cash items is the difference between the closing and opening balances: £78 490 − 65 442 = £(13 048), i.e. an increase in trade receivables.

Trade payables: the amount of cash paid in respect of operating costs and expenses in the period is:

	£
Opening trade payables	42 417
Operating costs total	588 694
Less: closing trade payables	(39 943)
	591 168

The adjustment for non-cash items is the difference between the closing and opening balances: £39 943 − 42 417 = £(2474), i.e. a decrease in trade payables.

Note that adjustments in respect of inventory, trade receivables and trade payables are the net movements between the two year-ends. Once you have become accustomed to preparing statements of cash flows it is not necessary to prepare complex workings like the table above – simply insert the movement in inventory etc. into the operating cash flows section of the statement.

Note 3 The interest paid figure is taken from the income statement.

Note 4 The cash outflow in respect of the purchase of non-current assets is taken from the detailed analysis of the delivery vehicle accounts. The cash inflow arising from the disposal of a vehicle is noted below that analysis.

Note 5 Drawings are a return of capital to the owner of the business, and so are shown under the heading of financing activities.

Note 6 We can see by comparing the two statements of financial position that the long-term liabilities figure has increased from £10 000 to £15 000. Therefore there has been an additional cash inflow of £5000 to the business under the heading of financing activities.

Note 7 The net inflow or outflow of cash that is calculated in the statement of cash flows should equal the change in the balance of cash between the two year-end dates. In the case of Box Distributors there has been a net outflow of cash of £8367. The final section of the statement of cash flows 'proves' the figure by calculating the difference between cash at the bank on 31 December 2011 (an asset balance of £371) and the overdraft at 31 December 2012 (a liability balance of £7996).

The second step in the exercise is to provide Horst with some advice about his cash flow. We will analyze the situation and then make some recommendations for reducing the business's overdraft.

Analysis

The overall net outflow of cash is over £8000. The principal cash inflows and outflows which have contributed to the increased overdraft are as follows:

- A substantial increase in inventory, trade receivables and trade payables of over £22 000. The total for trade receivables has increased by over £13 000, suggesting that the business has become significantly less successful at collecting money owed for credit sales. Inventories have also risen by a very significant amount. Both of these factors mean that cash in the business has been reduced.

- The net cash inflow from operating activities for the year (£41 093) is less than the total of drawings for the year (£49 000). Drawings are therefore being removed from the accumulated capital of earlier years.

Capital expenditure movements are not particularly significant in the year; the expenditure on the new vehicle is more or less covered by the proceeds of the sale of the old vehicle plus the increased borrowings from the bank.

The business is significantly less profitable in 2012 than it was in 2011. Net profit for 2011 was £58 222 on sales revenue of £600 227, a margin of 9.7%. The comparable margin for 2012 is 7.2% (£45 838/636 636 × 100). This suggests the need for better control of costs.

Action to reduce the overdraft

In the next accounting period the principal action points include the following:

- Control costs to improve the net profit margin.
- Reduce trade receivables by improving collection procedures.
- If possible, reduce the amount of drawings from the business.
- Reduce the amount of inventory held so that less cash is tied up.

Self-test question 6.3 (answer at the end of the book)

Extracts from Amy Binyon's income statement for the year ended 31 December 2013 and her statement of financial position at that date (including comparative figures for 2012) show the following information:

	£
Revenue	109 300
Cost of sales	62 700
Operating expenses, including depreciation of £5000	23 800
Interest paid	1200

	2013	2012
	£	£
Inventory	7 600	6 900
Trade receivables	8 700	8 500
Trade payables	9 700	9 000

Prepare a table to record adjustments between profit and operating cash flows (see the table in note 2 of example 6.3), and then prepare the operating section of Amy Binyon's statement of cash flows for the year ended 31 December 2013.

6.5 THE HIGH PROFIT/NO CASH PARADOX

Profitability and availability of cash do not necessarily go hand in hand in the short term. The dislocation between profits and cash can create major short-term problems even for highly profitable businesses. The final example in this chapter, 6.4, illustrates this important point.

EXAMPLE 6.4

Adèle sells computer equipment, trading as Business Computer Specialist. She started in business 6-years ago and has done well, making a profit each year. About 18-months ago her business was the first in the UK to be granted the franchise to sell the XBS 0980, a specialist business computer system. She has become established as the principal supplier of the XBS 0980 and is likely to be supplied first with the XBS 0990 when it becomes available in the UK in the autumn of 2013.

Despite more than doubling her sales and nearly doubling net profits, Adèle's business is short of cash. During her accounting year ended 31 December 2012 she had to negotiate an overdraft facility of £20 000 with the bank. This was the first time since starting the business that she had needed an overdraft facility. Later in the year, the overdraft facility was increased to £40 000 and Adèle is now concerned that if things don't improve she will need to borrow more money. She has spent a total of £89 950 on new non-current assets during the year. Two new sales reps needed company cars, a lot of additional fixtures and fittings were required in the larger rented offices that the business moved to, and the warehouse, which is owned by the business, was extended to make space for all the additional inventory.

The business income statements for the years ended 31 December 2011 and 2012 are shown below, as are the statements of financial position at both dates.

Business Computer Specialist: Income statements (summarized) for the years ended 31 December 2011 and 2012.

	2012	2012	2011	2011
	£	£	£	£
Revenue		895 755		401 003
Less: cost of sales				
Opening inventory	35 901		32 412	
Purchases	597 136		252 499	
	633 037		284 911	
Closing inventory	(78 700)		(35 901)	
Cost of sales		(554 337)		(249 010)
Gross profit		341 418		151 993
Expenses	204 016		82 278	
Depreciation	13 700		7 796	
		(217 716)		(90 074)
Operating profit		123 702		61 919
Interest received		–		988
Interest paid		(2 709)		–
Net profit		120 993		62 907
Gross profit margin		38.1%		37.9%
Net profit margin		13.5%		15.7%

Business Computer Specialist: Statements of financial position at 31 December 2011 and 2012

	2012	2012	2011	2011
	£	£	£	£
ASSETS				
Non-current assets				
At cost	218 420		128 470	
Less: accumulated depreciation	(44 620)		(30 920)	
Carrying amount		173 800		97 550
Current assets				
Inventory	78 700		35 901	
Trade receivables	95 514		34 996	
Cash at bank	–		12 804	
		174 214		83 701
		348 014		181 251
CAPITAL AND LIABILITIES				
Capital				
Capital brought forward	156 852		120 945	
Profit for the year	120 993		62 907	
Drawings	(29 000)		(27 000)	
		248 845		156 852
Current liabilities				
Overdraft	33 679		–	
Trade payables	65 490		24 399	
		99 169		24 399
		348 014		181 251

From this information we can draw up a statement of cash flows for the year ended 31 December 2012. This will help us to analyze the problems that Adèle currently faces.

	£	£
Cash flows from operating activities		
Operating profit		123 702
Depreciation		13 700
		137 402
Less: increase in inventory	(42 799)	
Less: increase in trade receivables	(60 518)	
Add: increase in trade payables	41 091	
		(62 226)
Cash generated from operations		75 176
Interest paid		(2 709)
Net cash inflow from operating activities		72 467
Cash flows from investing activities		
Purchase of non-current assets	(89 950)	
Net cash outflow from investing activities		(89 950)
Cash flows from financing activities		
Capital returned to owner (drawings)	(29 000)	

	£	£
Net cash inflow from financing activities		(29 000)
Net decrease in cash		(46 483)
Cash at beginning of period		12 804
Cash at end of period – overdraft		(33 679)

Note: capital expenditure. We are told in the introduction to the case study that Adèle has spent £89 950 on new non-current assets. It is also possible to work the figure out from the accounts, as follows:

	£
Non-current assets at carrying amount 31 December 2011	97 550
Reduced by annual charge for depreciation in 2012	(13 700)
	83 850
Non-current assets at carrying amount 31 December 2012	173 800
Difference = purchases of non-current assets	89 950

The statement of cash flows shows the principal causes of the decrease in cash/increase in overdraft. The business is expanding very quickly and therefore needs new non-current assets, resulting in a cash outflow of nearly £90 000 in the year. The next largest item has been the increase in working capital (i.e. inventory, trade receivables and trade payables) which is necessary to cope with the very rapid expansion in sales revenue. A greater volume of sales means that the business has to keep more inventory in hand, and trade receivables and trade payables are likely to increase as well. If the expansion continues at its present rate, the business may need further overdraft facilities and possibly longer-term loans to fund the acquisition of more non-current assets. So far Adèle has tried to meet the funding shortfall by increasing the business's overdraft, but this is not necessarily the best approach. If funding is required for long-term assets, it is usually sensible to borrow long-term rather than short-term.

It can be very difficult in practice to manage businesses that are expanding as fast as Business Computer Specialist. The problems encountered by rapidly expanding businesses include:

- The need to take on more staff very quickly. Poor quality personnel decisions may be made when management is under pressure to employ more people in a hurry.
- Insufficient management time. Where small businesses grow very fast, the original proprietor is often swamped by the sheer weight and pace of decision-making. Usually, in such circumstances, it is necessary to employ staff at managerial levels, but it can be difficult to get staff of the right calibre into positions quickly enough.
- Loss of control over costs and inventory. A consequence of rapid expansion is often that costs get out of hand, because the business does not have systems in place to control them properly. In the case of Adèle we can see that the business's net profit margin has in fact fallen between 2011 and 2012, although gross profit margin has actually improved a little. The worsening of net profit margin suggests possible difficulties in controlling costs.
- Failure to control receivables. Receivables should convert into cash quite easily but some debtors need chasing to make them pay up. Where management time is limited, receivables may be allowed to build up to unacceptable levels.
- Chronic shortage of cash.

The case of Business Computer Specialist shows that business success can bring its own problems. Where businesses expand very rapidly they can become victims of their own success, and may even fail. In Adèle's case, she needs as a matter of urgency, to prepare budgets for the coming year, to see how much of a problem the shortage of cash is going to be. It may be time for her to consider recruiting a qualified accountant to the management team.

6.6 STATEMENTS OF CASH FLOW IN LARGE BUSINESSES

The examples in this chapter have focused upon small, simple, businesses, so as to make it easier to learn how to prepare a statement of cash flows. However, a statement of cash flows can help in understanding all types and sizes of business. Companies listed on the London Stock Exchange are required to publish a statement of cash flows in the format (prescribed by the International Accounting Standards Board) that we have used in this chapter. Therefore, if you look up the financial statements of any listed company on the Internet you should be able to find a recognizable statement of cash flows in its annual report. Look at the real-life example below, and then look at other companies' annual reports on their websites, to see if you can a) find the statement of cash flows; b) understand the information contained in it.

EXAMPLE 6.5 (REAL-LIFE)

Majestic Wine plc

The company's annual report for the 52 weeks ended 30 March 2009 included a statement of cash flows. The key figures under the principal headings were:

	2009	2008
	£	£
Net cash generated by operating activities	11 206	18 015
Net cash utilized by investing activities	(12 602)	(8 241)
Net cash used by financing activities	(44)	(14 577)
Net decrease in cash and cash equivalents	(1 440)	(4 803)

The reduction in net cash generated by operating activities is explained by the difficult trading conditions experienced by Majestic in the financial year, which was badly affected by the recession. The Review of Operations in the annual report includes the following statement:

> *'Whilst we experienced very challenging trading conditions in the second half of the financial year, we have been encouraged that sales to our private customers have held up well. We have also been pleased with our sales to restaurant customers.*
>
> *In contrast, sales to corporate customers particularly of Champagne, have been in decline. Many of our corporate customers purchase wine for entertaining, events and gifting and in the current climate they have reduced spend on these activities.'*

Despite these factors, sales revenue for the year had increased, but overall profitability was down.

Despite the effects of the recession, the business continued to invest in non-current assets, and during the 2008-2009 financial year it also spent over £5m on acquiring a new subsidiary; these factors together account for the significant cash outflow in respect of investing activities.

The figure for net cash used by financing activities in 2008-2009 is relatively small, but it is a net figure comprising various items, including over £6m in payments of dividends (cash outflow) and new borrowing of £7m (cash inflow).

The figures and the explanations above are very broad summaries of some of the issues arising in Majestic Wine. Much more detail is available in the company's full annual report.

CHAPTER SUMMARY

This chapter started by explaining the important distinction between cash and profits. Because of the accruals (matching) convention, accounting income is not the same as cash received, and accounting expenditure is not the same as cash paid.

Most of the rest of the chapter was concerned with explaining the mechanics of preparing a third important financial statement: the statement of cash flows. The preparation of a statement of cash flows in a new business was explained, and then the chapter proceeded to explain how to prepare a statement of cash flows in an established business.

The Business Computer Specialist example demonstrated and explained the apparent paradox of a successful and profitable business running out of cash. The statement of cash flows for such a business provides answers to the very basic question: 'Where has all the cash gone?' Finally the chapter concluded by examining the key elements of a real life statement of cash flows.

The statement of cash flows enhances and explains some of the key elements of the two other financial statements covered in earlier chapters: the statement of financial position and the income statement. The statement of cash flows is of equal importance to the other statements, and can be of great assistance to users in understanding the business's performance and position. Students often experience some difficulty in understanding the preparation and significance of statements of cash flow. By carefully working through the examples in the chapter and then applying their knowledge to the end-of-chapter questions, students should find they are equipped with all the necessary skills to become proficient in the preparation and understanding of the statement of cash flows.

INTERNET RESOURCES

Book's companion website summary

www.cengage.co.uk/gowthorpe3 contains the following resources in respect of Chapter 6:

Students' section

Quiz containing ten multiple choice questions
Four additional questions with answers

Lecturers' section

Answers to end of chapter exercises 6.5 to 6.8
Six additional questions with answers
Case study
ExamView testbank
Instructor's manual
PowerPoint presentation

EXERCISES: ANSWERS AT THE END OF THE BOOK

6.1 Fergus's business incurs the following transactions in the year to 31 December 2012:

- Fergus introduces additional capital of £10 000 in cash.
- Purchase on credit of goods for resale for £8000.
- Payment received from customer for £1800.

- Purchase of a new machine for use in the business on 1 January 2012. The machine costs £12 000 and will be depreciated over 10 years on the straight-line basis, assuming no residual value.
- Sales returns of £1000 in exchange for a cash refund.
- Drawings of £1300.

For each transaction show the impact on cash, other assets and liabilities, and the impact on profits.

6.2 Gilbert's business sells a non-current asset for cash proceeds of £1300. The asset originally cost £20 700, and accumulated depreciation at the point of sale was £18 210.

Three of the following six statements are correct:

1 Profits increase by £1190.

2 Profits decrease by £1190.

3 Cash increases by £1300.

4 Cash increases by £1190.

5 The net book value of non-current assets decreases by £2490.

6 The net book value of non-current assets decreases by £1300.

Which statements are correct?

a) 1, 3 and 6
b) 2, 3 and 5
c) 1, 4 and 5
d) 2, 4 and 6.

6.3 Gaston's business prepares accounts to 31 December each year. In the year ending 31 December 2012 inventory, trade receivables and trade payables are shown in the statement of financial position, with comparative figures at 31 December 2011, as follows:

	2012	**2011**
	£	**£**
Inventory	37 669	31 470
Trade receivables	21 777	19 303
Trade payables	18 250	16 264

Gaston's net profit for the year ending 31 December 2012 is £36 790, after deducting total depreciation charges of £4585.

What is the net cash inflow from operating activities for inclusion in Gaston's statement of cash flows for the year ending 31 December 2012?

a) £47 299
b) £29 340
c) £33 925
d) £34 688.

6.4 Henrietta runs a business, trading as Spicer & Co. She prepares accounts to 31 March each year. By the year-end 31 March 2012 the business has run into overdraft. Henrietta asks you to prepare a statement of cash flows for the business for the year ending 31 March 2012 and provides you with the following information:

Spicer & Co: Income statement (summarized) for the year ending 31 March 2012

	£
Revenue	598 731
Less: cost of sales	(430 131)
Gross profit	168 600
Expenses excluding depreciation	(79 633)
Depreciation	(12 471)
Operating profit	76 496
Interest paid	(230)
Net profit	76 266

Spicer & Co: Statements of financial position at 31 March 2012 and 31 March 2011

	2012 £	2012 £	2011 £	2011 £
ASSETS				
Non-current assets				
At cost	175 630		128 547	
Less: accumulated depreciation	(67 248)		(54 777)	
Carrying amount		108 382		73 770
Current assets				
Inventory	40 747		36 600	
Trade receivables	50 661		48 730	
Cash at bank	–		7 423	
		91 408		92 753
		199 790		166 523
CAPITAL AND LIABILITIES				
Capital				
Capital brought forward	131 332		111 335	
Profit for the year	76 266		61 297	
Drawings	(45 800)		(41 300)	
		161 798		131 332
Current liabilities				
Overdraft	1 348		–	
Trade payables	36 644		35 191	
		37 992		35 191
		199 790		166 523

Note: there were no disposals of non-current assets during the year.

Required: prepare a statement of cash flows for Spicer & Co for the year ending 31 March 2012.

EXERCISES: ANSWERS AVAILABLE ON THE LECTURERS' SECTION OF THE BOOK'S WEBSITE

6.5 Flynn's business incurs the following transactions in the year to 31 March 2012:

- Purchase of inventory for cash of £1300.
- Sale of a non-current asset with a written down value of £300. The sale proceeds are £900.
- Sale on credit for £3500.
- Payment made in respect of a trade payable outstanding, for electricity bill of £6350.
- Drawings of £800.
- Purchase of a motor vehicle for use in the business on 1 April 2011. The vehicle costs £10 000 and is to be depreciated at 25% per annum.

For each transaction show the impact on cash, other assets and liabilities, and the impact on profits.

6.6 Grant's business makes an operating profit of £16 632 in the year ended 30 April 2012. One of the deductions in arriving at operating profit was depreciation of £6650.

At 30 April 2012 the statement of financial position showed inventory of £26 750, trade receivables of £12 704 and trade payables of £11 667. On 30 April 2011 the corresponding figures were: inventory £27 997; trade receivables: £11 940 and trade payables: £9975. There was no interest paid or interest received.

What is the net cash inflow from operating activities to be included in Grant's statement of cash flows for the year ending 30 April 2012?

a) £21 107
b) £18 807
c) £22 073
d) £25 457.

6.7 Gunter's business sells an item of machinery for £2660 on 30 June 2012. The balances at the beginning of the accounting year (1 January 2012) for the asset were:

Cost: £17 700
Accumulated depreciation: £15 930

Gunter charges depreciation on this class of asset at the rate of 10% per annum on cost, with a month's depreciation charged for each full month of ownership in the year of disposal. He has assumed a nil residual value for this asset.

Two of the following eight statements are correct:

1 Profits decrease by £890.

2 Profits increase by £890.

3 Profits increase by £1 775.

4 Profits decrease by £1 775.

5 Cash increases by £2 660.

6 Cash increases by £1 775.

7 Cash decreases by £2 660.

8 Cash decreases by £1 775.

Which statements are correct?

a) 1 and 7
b) 4 and 6
c) 2 and 8
d) 3 and 5.

6.8 Hamid prepares his business financial statements to 31 May each year. Because he attended an accounting course at college he knows how to prepare income statements and statements of financial position. However, the course did not include the preparation statements of cash flow and Hamid asks you to prepare a statement of cash flows for his business for the year ending 31 May 2012. He supplies you with the following information:

Hamid: Income statement (summarized) for the year ended 31 May 2012

	£
Revenue	437 500
Less: cost of sales	(298 423)
Gross profit	139 077
Expenses excluding depreciation	(62 505)
Depreciation	(7 662)
Operating profit	68 910
Interest received	634
Interest paid	(506)
Net profit	69 038

Hamid: Statements of financial position at 31 May 2012 and 31 May 2011

	2012	2012	2011	2011
	£	£	£	£
ASSETS				
Non-current assets				
At cost	82 610		38 750	
Less: accumulated depreciation	(21 462)		(13 800)	
Carrying amount		61 148		24 950

	2012	2012	2011	2011
	£	£	£	£
Current assets				
Inventory	26 980		27 420	
Trade receivables	44 349		42 760	
Cash at bank	5 354		6 642	
		76 683		76 822
		137 831		101 772
CAPITAL AND LIABILITIES				
Capital				
Capital brought forward	68 313		33 766	
Profit for the year	69 038		63 291	
Drawings	(23 250)		(28 744)	
		114 101		68 313
Current liabilities				
Loan	–		5 000	
Trade payables	23 730		28 459	
		23 730		33 459
		137 831		101 772

1 There were no disposals of non-current assets during the year.
2 Following your request Hamid supplies the following information relating to cash receipts and payments during the year:

Cash receipts	£435 911
Cash payments	£365 217

Required: prepare Hamid's statement of cash flows for the year ending 31 May 2012 using a) the indirect method; and b) the direct method.

CHAPTER 17

Financial Reporting by Limited Companies

AIM OF THE CHAPTER

To understand the nature of company financial reporting, including an appreciation of the accounting regulatory framework applicable to companies.

LEARNING OUTCOMES

After reading the chapter and completing the related exercises, students should:

- Understand in outline the regulations relating to accounting by companies.
- Understand the roles of directors in respect of company financial reports.
- Be able to draw up a set of financial statements for a simple limited company.
- Understand the need for additional financial and non-financial reporting by listed companies.

INTRODUCTION

Chapter 1 briefly examined some of the characteristics of limited companies, including the separation between ownership and management of the company that is typical of larger limited companies. That chapter also identified the principal users of financial information, which included shareholders and potential shareholders in limited companies.

This chapter examines the nature of limited companies, and their financial reporting in more detail. The important concept of limited liability is examined, and its implications are explored in a numerical example in order to set the context for the discussion of information needs that follows. This is followed by a section on regulation related to limited companies, and then the components of a set of limited company accounts are explained. Listed companies (those whose share capital is listed on a stock exchange such as the London Stock Exchange) are subject to additional requirements in respect of published information, both financial and non-financial, and these are briefly examined. A final section looks at corporate reporting on the Internet which has become commonplace for listed and other large companies.

7.1 THE LIMITED COMPANY

The limited company has been an important form of business organization since the middle of the nineteenth century in the UK. The need for this type of organization developed as industrial organizations became larger, and as greater amounts of capital were required to fund the expansion of, for example, the railway system. It is unlikely that one single individual would be wealthy enough to fund a major institution like a railway or a bank, and so a legal mechanism that allows for ownership to be shared is very useful in the development of advanced economies. Most capitalist countries have developed ownership vehicles akin to the UK limited company, and in most of Europe this development took place during the nineteenth century.

A company is a convenient form of organization in that:

- It allows for investments of differing amounts to be made by a potentially very large group of individuals or organizations.
- In the form in which it is most commonly found in the UK and elsewhere, it offers investors the protection of limited liability. This useful mechanism ensures that investors are liable for no more than their original investment.
- A company is regarded as a 'person' in law. It can sue or be sued, can hold bank accounts and other forms of assets, and it can be named as a contracting party in legal contracts. The individuals investing in it are protected by the so-called 'veil of incorporation'. This means that people or organizations with a claim against the company have no legal rights against the investors' own personal assets (example 7.1 later in the chapter explains this further).
- The structure of the capital of a limited company in the form of shares lends itself to shared ownership by many parties, and, in some cases, access to markets in which share capital can be easily exchanged for cash.
- It can offer certain tax advantages over sold trader and partnership forms of organization.

7.2 LIMITED LIABILITY

Limited liability confers a great advantage upon investors in shares of companies. By contrast, a sole trader or a partner in a partnership is exposed to unlimited liability, to the extent of his or her own personal assets, in respect of business dealings.

There is, potentially, a corresponding disadvantage for the creditors of limited liability companies. Creditors of business organizations always face the risk that they will not be paid; however, if a limited company fails to pay, the creditors may have very little chance of successfully pursuing an action against the company. If it has no assets, the creditors will simply not be paid. Consider the following example:

EXAMPLE 7.1

On 1 June 2012 Elba Limited placed an order with a supplier, Tommy, to supply stock on credit to a value of £3000. Tommy supplied the goods, but then Elba went out of business on 10 August 2012, without having paid Tommy any of the money owing to him. Elba Limited had the following statement of financial position at 31 May 2012:

	£	£
ASSETS		
Non-current assets		
Property, plant and equipment		8 000
Current assets		
Inventories	1 250	
Trade receivables	1 000	
		2 250
		10 250
CAPITAL AND LIABILITIES		
Equity		
Share capital		100
Retained earnings		1 300
		1 400
Current liabilities		
Trade payables	2 550	
Overdraft	6 300	
		8 850
		10 250

Note that some new terminology has appeared. Equity is another term for capital, which is used in respect of limited companies. It comprises the share capital of the business that has been issued to shareholders in exchange for their original investment plus the accumulated profits that have been retained in the business (described as retained earnings).

By 10 August 2012 Elba's position had deteriorated. The statement of financial position at that date was as follows:

	£	£
ASSETS		
Non-current assets		
Property, plant and equipment		8 000
Current assets		
Inventories	5 250	
Trade receivables	1 600	
		6 850
		14 850
CAPITAL AND LIABILITIES		
Equity		
Share capital		100
Retained losses		(2 490)
		(2 390)
Current liabilities		
Trade payables	8 940	
Overdraft	8 300	
		17 240
		14 850

Elba's bank manager refused to extend the overdraft any further, and the company was obliged to cease to trade.

Where does Tommy stand as regards recovering the money due to him? In this case he may recover some of his money, but probably not all of it. In total, at 10 August 2012 there were current liabilities of £17 240, of which Tommy's amount due was £3000. The statement of financial position showed total assets of £14 850, a shortfall of £2390. However, the asset values may not be realistic estimates of the amounts that can be recovered by selling the assets.

Non-current assets, as we know, are presented in the statement of financial position at cost less depreciation. The carrying amount in the statement of financial position may be higher than the amounts for which the assets can be sold. The trade receivables figure of £1600 may not be fully recoverable, and perhaps the inventories could not be sold for the full amount shown in the statement of financial position.

Suppose the assets of Elba could be liquidated (i.e. turned into cash) as follows:

Non-current assets in a forced sale	6 000
Receivables – amounts actually receivable	1 400
Inventories in a forced sale	4 500
Total amount of cash which can be raised	£11 900

Against total liabilities of £17 240 there is a shortfall of £5340, or just over 30%. The creditors (i.e. trade payables and bank overdraft) cannot be repaid in full, and are likely to receive at most about 70% of the value of the sums due to them. In practice, this proportion will be reduced by accountants' fees for doing the work of winding up the company (yes: the accountants are paid before the other 'ordinary' creditors) and by any amounts due to HMRC (who take precedence over other creditors). Note that the shareholders in Elba would lose the whole of their investment in share capital. However, the share capital amounts only to £100, and the loss is small compared to the loss which will be suffered by Tommy and other creditors.

7.3 INFORMATION NEEDS OF COMPANY CREDITORS

The situation outlined above may seem very unfair to creditors. How could Tommy have avoided losing money? Well, if he had been aware of Elba's weak position he could have either refused to trade with the company, or he could have insisted on receiving the cash in advance. Either way, he would have been protected from loss.

It is partly to protect creditors like Tommy that regulation exists to ensure that companies are obliged to make certain financial details available to the public. If creditors are in possession of accounting information they are able to make better decisions. Even so, creditors like Tommy are rarely in possession of all the relevant facts. Companies are obliged to make information available within 9 months of the year-end (6 months for some larger companies); by the time the information becomes available the company's position may have altered very significantly.

7.4 INFORMATION NEEDS OF COMPANY SHAREHOLDERS

As explained in Chapter 1, companies, especially larger companies, are sometimes owned and managed by different people. Where company directors and shareholders are two different groups of people (or two groups that overlap only partially), it is important that the directors are held to account for the way in which they have managed the shareholders' investments. (This accountability is known by the rather old-fashioned term **stewardship**.) Therefore, there are regulatory requirements to ensure that shareholders receive information in a standard form about the companies they have invested in. If the shareholders are unhappy about the way in which directors have managed the company, they can vote the directors out of office and replace them. Although there may be many shareholders, especially in very large companies, directors are voted out of office comparatively rarely.

7.5 INFORMATION NEEDS OF PEOPLE OTHER THAN SHAREHOLDERS AND CREDITORS

There are other groups of people who may be interested in the information made available by companies (see Chapter 1). These include: employees, customers, financial journalists, the government, academics and the general public.

In the next section of the chapter the nature of company regulation, especially in respect of accounting, is examined in outline.

7.6 REGULATION OF COMPANY ACCOUNTING AND OTHER ISSUES

There are few regulations governing accounting by sole traders. By contrast, accounting and financial reporting by companies is subject to comparatively heavy regulation. Some of the principal sources and features of company regulation will be explained in this section.

7.6.1 Companies Acts

Since the mid-nineteenth century the conduct of companies has been subject to legal regulation in the form of Acts of Parliament. There has been a succession of Companies Acts during the period since 1844. The latest is the Companies Act 2006 (CA 2006) which supersedes all previous Companies Acts. CA 2006 is a major piece of legislation which has, amongst other things, brought company law up-to-date in respect of issues like electronic communications with shareholders.

The CA 2006 contains many complex legal regulations relating to:

- Formation of new companies and types of company.
- Company constitutional arrangements including the issue of shares.
- Role of directors.
- The audit of companies.
- Publication and presentation of accounting information.

The 1985 Companies Act, which preceded CA 2006, introduced many aspects of European company law into UK legislation; in particular, standard formats for the presentation of company financial statements were introduced. These accounting requirements were carried into the CA 2006 in general terms. The specific content of company financial statements was covered in three related pieces of legislation which were issued subsequently: the Small Companies and Groups (Accounts and Directors' Report) Regulations, 2008; the Large and Medium-sized Companies and Groups (Accounts and Reports) Regulations 2008; and The Companies Act 2006 (Amendment) (Accounts and Reports) Regulations 2008. The accounting requirements for companies will be examined in more detail later in the chapter.

7.6.2 Company Formation and Types of Company

Setting up a limited company is quite straightforward and is an inexpensive procedure. It is usually handled by a professionally qualified accountant or solicitor, or by one of the specialist company formation firms. Certain forms have to be registered with Companies House, and there are provisions to ensure that a company is not registered with a name identical to that of an existing company.

> The private company: this has a minimum of one shareholder, and one director. The word 'limited' is attached to the name of the company (in English or Welsh).
>
> The public limited company: this must be described in its **Memorandum of Association** (see below) as a public company, its name must end in 'public limited company' or 'plc' (or the Welsh equivalents) and it must have a share capital of at least £50 000.

Larger companies tend to be plcs. However, comparatively large businesses may be private companies. In order to be permitted to issue shares to the general public a company must be constituted as a plc. Only plcs may be listed on a Stock Exchange, but not all plcs are listed.

7.6.3 Company Constitutional Arrangements Including the Issue of Shares

There are formal arrangements in law for company meetings. Traditionally an Annual General Meeting (AGM) had to take place and shareholders were permitted to vote democratically on resolutions at that meeting. However, under the provisions of CA 2006, private companies are no longer obliged to hold AGMs, although the obligation remains to involve shareholders in the decision-making process of the company. For most normal purposes, a private company can deal with decision-making via written resolutions. However, public limited companies are still obliged to hold formal AGMs. The normal agenda for an AGM would include the following:

- Acceptance of the directors' report and the financial statements.
- Authorization for payment of dividend (and confirmation of dividends already paid).
- Election of directors.
- Appointment of auditors.
- Any other business.

All companies are required to have:

- **a Memorandum of Association**
- **Articles of Association.**

The Memorandum of Association is a statement made by each of the original subscribers for shares in the company, confirming their intention to form the company and to become a shareholder in it. This document is created for incorporation purposes only and then is subsequently unchanged. The Articles of Association contain the company's internal constitution, including, for example, appropriate arrangements for appointment of directors, voting by shareholders, powers of directors and directors' expenses, pensions and remuneration.

7.6.4 Shares

The most common type of share capital is **ordinary share capital**. Each share carries the right to vote on company resolutions and the right to receive a dividend (if any). Each ordinary share has a **nominal value**, which is commonly one of the following: 5p, 10p, 25p, 50p or £1. (However, public limited companies have the option of maintaining their share capital in euro.)

Decisions on the amount of ordinary dividend to be paid are made by the company's directors. Ordinary dividends for an accounting year are often paid in two or more instalments: one or more interim dividends and a final dividend.

Some companies issue preference share capital. This differs substantially from ordinary share capital, in that preference shares carry a fixed rate of dividend (and are described as, for example, 8% preference shares), and have no voting powers in decision-making about issues such as the appointment of directors. Such shares are referred to as 'preference shares' because their dividends have to be paid out in preference to any dividend on the ordinary shares. Because there is a fixed rate of return on preference shares, they are really more akin to a long-term loan and in most cases **accounting standards** require that the shares are accounted for as long-term liabilities and the 'dividends' on them are accounted for as finance costs (i.e. in the same way as interest paid). Some preference shares are cumulative; that is, if the company does not pay the dividend on the shares the obligation to pay is carried forward to the next following year.

EXAMPLE 7.2

Pauletta Limited has ordinary share capital of £20 000, split into shares of 25 pence each. In the year ending 31 December 2012 a dividend of 4p per share is paid. Li Ming owns 5000 shares in Pauletta Limited.

a) How many shares has Pauletta Limited issued?

b) What is the total value of the dividend paid for the year ending 31 December 2012?

c) What is the value of Li Ming's dividend for the year ending 31 December 2012?

Answer

a) Each £1 of ordinary share capital in Pauletta Limited is split into 4 shares ($4 \times 25p = £1$). Therefore the number of shares issued in total by Pauletta is $4 \times 20,000 = 80,000$.

b) The dividend is 4p per share; total value is $4p \times 80\,000 = £3200$.

c) Li Ming's dividend is $4p \times 5000$ (the number of shares held by her) $= £200$.

The next example looks at both dividends in respect of ordinary shares and preference share dividends.

EXAMPLE 7.3

Birch and Beech Limited has issued both ordinary shares and preference shares, as follows:

Ordinary share capital: 30 000 £1 shares
Preference share capital: £50 000 7% preference shares

The directors of the company decided to pay an interim dividend of 5% of nominal share value in the year ending 31 December 2012. The preference dividend was also paid.

What is the total amount of dividend that was paid by Birch and Beech Limited for the year ending 31 December 2012?

Answer

	£
Ordinary dividend: £30,000 × 5%	1 500
Preference dividend: £50 000 × 7%	3 500
Total	5 000

7.6.5 Role of Directors

Company directors have important responsibilities under the law, and an appointment as a director is not to be taken lightly. Directors are required to act in good faith in the interests of the company (which may not be the same as the interests of individual shareholders). If a company loses money through the actions of directors, it may be able to reclaim the money from the directors, even if they acted in what they thought were the best interests of the company.

The following guidance to directors is given in a document summarizing some of the statements made by ministers in Parliament when debating the CA 2006.

Guidance for company directors:

1 Act in the company's best interests, taking everything you think relevant into account.

2 Obey the company's constitution [the Articles of Association] and decisions taken under it.

3 Be honest, and remember that the company's property belongs to it and not to you or to its shareholders.

4 Be diligent, careful and well informed about the company's affairs. If you have any special skills or experience, use them.

5 Make sure the company keeps records of your decisions.

6 Remember that you remain responsible for the work you give to others.

7 Avoid situations where your interests conflict with those of the company. When in doubt disclose potential conflicts quickly.

8 Seek external advice where necessary, particularly if the company is in financial difficulty.

(extract from www.berr.gov.uk/files/file40139.pdf)

In essence, the duties of directors of companies remain as they were prior to the CA 2006. However, there has been a change of emphasis in the law. According to Margaret Hodge, the Minister of State for Industry and the Regions, company law in this respect is based on a new approach: 'There was a time when business success in the interests of shareholders was thought to be in conflict with society's aspirations for people who work in the company … for the long-term well-being of the community and for the protection for the environment.… Pursuing the interests of shareholders and embracing wider responsibilities are complementary purposes, not contradictory ones.' She is referring here to Section 172 of CA 2006 which requires that each director should act in a way that he or she considers would be most likely to promote the success of the company for the benefit of its members [i.e. shareholders] as a whole, having regard to such factors as:

- The likely long-term consequences.
- The interests of employees.
- Relationships with customers and suppliers.
- The impact of the company's operations on the community and environment.
- The desirability of maintaining a reputation for high standards of business conduct.
- The need to act fairly as between members [shareholders] of the company.
- Any other relevant issues.

The more traditional view of the company, and the role of the directors, is much narrower, focusing upon the interests of shareholders only, principally the need to generate cash from the business for the benefit of shareholders.

Directors' responsibilities in respect of company financial statements

Directors must ensure that adequate accounting records are kept, and they are responsible for preparing the company's annual financial statements and for ensuring that the financial statements are filed at Companies House within the time limit permitted by law. They must also ensure that the company does not trade while insolvent (the example of Elba Limited earlier demonstrates an insolvent company statement of financial position at 10 August 2012). Breach of these rules can mean that the director is guilty of a criminal offence, and may be liable for a fine or imprisonment.

The financial statements of a company must present 'a true and fair view' (this is a legal term which has existed in company law since the 1940s) of the performance and state of affairs of the company. Although the directors themselves do not necessarily take part in the preparation of the financial statements (the task is often delegated to the finance director, or a senior accountant in the business) they nevertheless take complete responsibility in law for the preparation and filing of financial statements. Fines are quite frequently levied on directors by Companies House in respect of late filing.

Allowing a company to trade while insolvent can have very serious consequences for individual directors. Directors may be ordered by the courts to make contributions out of their personal resources if they have allowed the company to continue trading in circumstances where there is no reasonable prospect of avoiding corporate failure. If it is proven that directors have deliberately defrauded creditors a criminal offence is involved; they may be disqualified as a director, fined or even imprisoned. It is very important that people who are appointed as directors should fully understand their responsibilities and the possible consequences of failing to meet those responsibilities. As explained earlier it is cheap and simple to set up a company in the UK and to become a director of a company, but it is important to understand the responsibilities that go with the role.

7.6.6 Publication and Presentation of Accounting Information

As illustrated by the Elba Limited example earlier in the chapter, company financial information may be important to many interested parties. After companies have filed their annual financial statements at Companies House, they are available for inspection by anyone who is interested ('inspection' includes obtaining a download of a company's accounts on payment of a fee). However, the meaning of 'annual financial statements' varies depending upon the size of the company. Small and medium-sized companies are entitled to take advantage of exemptions that allow them to file quite a limited amount of information at Companies House. Small companies, for example, are not required to file an income statement, and are entitled to restrict the amount of information they give in the statement of financial position and related notes.

In order to qualify as small or medium-sized, companies must meet two out of the three criteria below relating to turnover, statement of financial position total and number of employees. The current criteria are shown in table 7.1 below.

TABLE 7.1 Criteria for small and medium-sized companies

	Turnover	Total of assets (non-current and current)	Number of employees
Small company	Not more than £5.6 million	Not more than £2.8 million	Not more than 50
Medium-sized company	Not more than £22.8 million	Not more than £11.4 million	Not more than 250

These limits are changed from time to time. The main reason for allowing small and medium-sized companies to file a reduced amount of accounting information is to ensure that competitors do not have access to information that may harm the interests of the company. The reduced filing requirements do not save small and medium-sized companies much, if anything, in costs because a full set of financial statements has to be prepared for the shareholders' use. Later in the chapter, presentation requirements for company financial statements are examined in more detail.

7.6.7 The Audit of Companies

Until a few years ago, all limited companies required a formal audit by a qualified chartered or certified accountant. The auditor examines the books and records of the business, and compares them to the final financial statements. He or she issues an **audit report** addressed to the company shareholders, which states whether or not the accounts present a true and fair view.

Gradually, over the last few years, the requirement for company audit has been progressively restricted because it was felt to be a bureaucratic burden for companies. Where there are only one or two shareholders, who are probably the company directors, it is almost always a waste of resources to have a formal audit. Currently small companies (see the previous section of the chapter for the definition of a small company) are exempted from the audit requirement. Small companies can, of course, choose to have an audit if they wish. Sometimes it can be useful to do so: if a small company wishes to borrow a substantial sum of money from a bank it may assist the case if there is a set of audited accounts available to show the bank manager.

In addition, the law allows shareholders the right to require an audit, provided that holders of more than 10% of the company's share capital give notice that they require an audit to be carried out. This provision in the law is intended to give shareholders who hold only a minority of the share capital of the company some protection against majority holders. So, if a minority shareholder (i.e. a holder of at least 10% of the share capital) in a small company suspects that directors may not be acting fairly he or she has some protection in law.

7.6.8 Accounting Standards

The Companies Act contains various requirements as to the preparation and presentation of accounting information by companies (see later section in this chapter). However, these requirements are often quite general in nature, and a need has emerged over the last 50 years or so for more detailed guidance on how specific accounting issues should be dealt with in the financial statements of companies and other business organizations. The accountancy professional bodies have been responsible for providing an additional layer of accounting regulation in the form of accounting standards.

Before 1990 accounting standards were issued in the UK by the Accounting Standards Committee (ASC) which comprised senior members of the accounting profession. The ASC issued Statements of Standard Accounting Practice (SSAPs) some of which are still current. For example, SSAP 9 deals with the subject of accounting for inventories (the UK term for inventories), and it is still in issue in 2010.

Since 1990 accounting standards in the UK have been issued by the Accounting Standards Board (ASB), a more broadly based organization which represents a wider constituency of interest groups than the accountancy profession. The ASB issues Financial Reporting Standards (FRS). Many of these are on very complex topics beyond the scope of this book, but, for example, FRS 15 deals with accounting for fixed assets (the UK term for property, plant and equipment), including regulations relating to depreciation.

It is likely that at some point in the next few years, UK standards will be replaced by **International Financial Reporting Standards (IFRS)**. Many of the more recently issued UK standards are more or less identical to the equivalent IFRS in any case. IFRS are considered in more detail below.

7.6.9 International Financial Reporting Standards

International accounting standards have been issued since the 1970s when the International Accounting Standards Committee (IASC) was established. In recent years international standards have become increasingly important as the volume of global trading has increased. Where, as is more and more frequently the case, companies and individuals are investing in companies based in other countries, it becomes important that financial statements should be comprehensible and comparable internationally. One means of achieving this goal is to have an internationally accepted approach to accounting so that people can invest across borders with some confidence in the financial information they are using as a basis for decision-making. The international standard setting body has therefore gained in importance and stature in recent years. In 2001, the IASC was replaced by the International Accounting Standards Board (IASB) which is now responsible for setting international standards, known as IFRS.

How important are international standards? The European Union decided a few years ago that all listed companies in its member states should prepare their financial statements to comply with international standards from 2005 onwards. This meant that companies listed on the UK Stock Exchange no longer adhered to UK standards after 1 January 2005. As noted earlier UK standards continue to exist, for the guidance of unlisted companies and other types of entity, but their importance will diminish and they are likely to disappear completely in due course. Unlisted companies in the UK have the option of compliance with UK or international standards, an option that is permitted by the CA 2006.

Outside Europe, too, international standards are gaining in importance. Many countries have already adopted them (e.g. Australia, New Zealand) or will adopt them soon (e.g. India), and there is a project underway in collaboration with the US standard setter to bring US and international accounting practice closer together.

It is beyond the scope of this book to examine individual international standards in any detail. Some of the standards are very long and complex documents that can be fully understood only by those who are highly skilled and experienced in financial reporting. However, the financial statements prepared in accordance with IFRS can be read with understanding by those who are reasonably financially literate. The next two chapters in this book address some of the important elements in gaining an understanding of financial statements.

Terminology

Some of the terminology differs between International and UK financial statements. Some examples have already been encountered in this chapter. Other important differences include the income statement (known in UK accounting as the income statement) and the statement of financial position (known in the UK as a statement of financial position). A glossary is provided at the end of this book.

7.7 ACCOUNTING FOR LIMITED COMPANIES

The basics of accounting remain the same, regardless of the form of organization. The accounting equation, for example, which was explained in Chapter 2, holds good whether the accounting is for a sole trader, a partnership or a limited company. However, accounting for limited companies involves the introduction of some additional complexities into the income statement and statement of financial position.

7.7.1 Components of a Set of Limited Company Accounts

Under the law, a set of accounts for a limited company comprises the following:

- an income statement
- a statement of financial position
- statement of changes in equity
- notes to the accounts
- directors' report
- auditors' report (where applicable).

In addition, IAS 7 *Statements of Cash Flow* requires the inclusion of a **cash flow statement** (cash flow was examined in detail in Chapter 6).

The contents of the income statement and statement of financial position are dealt with in detail elsewhere in this chapter and in this section of the book. The statement of changes in equity has not previously been encountered; it is explained later in this chapter.

Notes to the accounts can be highly complex in practice. They contain a great deal of supporting explanatory detail about the figures in the accounts, much of which is required by law or by various accounting standards. There are quite extensive requirements, for example, relating to the disclosure of directors' remuneration.

The directors' report is a quite formal document which must contain explanation and comment on a range of items, including:

- description of the principal activities of the company
- review of the development of the business
- a note of political and charitable donations.

7.7.2 Presentation of Accounting Information

UK company law prescribes formats for the income statement and statement of financial position statements. The CA 2006 permits companies to adopt either UK or international accounting. Because this textbook is based throughout on international financial reporting standards and their terminology, the formats shown below use international terminology and conventions. These are based upon IAS 1 *Presentation of financial statements*. The main headings are shown, and underneath each of the headings are listed some of the items that might be included in a typical statement of financial position.

Statement of financial position

ASSETS

Non-current assets
Intangible assets
Tangible assets
Investments

Current assets
Inventories
Receivables (including prepayments)
Investments
Cash at bank and in hand

Total assets

EQUITY AND LIABILITIES

Equity
Share capital
Retained earnings

Non-current liabilities
Borrowings

Current liabilities
Bank loans and overdrafts
Trade payables
Other payables, including taxation and social security
Accruals

Total liabilities
Total equity and liabilities

The format for the statement of financial position should by now look quite familiar as it has been adopted throughout the book so far. The only section that looks a little different from the layout in previous chapters is the Equity section which, because we are now looking at companies, comprises share capital and retained earnings. IAS 1 prescribes an additional financial reporting statement: the statement of changes in equity. This shows changes that have occurred to the components of equity, typically share capital and retained earnings. It includes transactions with owners. In previous chapters transactions with owners have comprised the commitment of owners' own resources to the capital of the business, for example, on start-up, and then drawings from the business once it is established. The statement of changes in equity (SOCIE) for a company comprises the same basic elements as in the sole trader financial statements explained in previous chapters: increases arising from new contributions by owners, and profits, and decreases arising from payments in the form of dividends, and loss. The SOCIE is usually shown in the form of a table, for example, in the case of a company with a 31 December year-end:

Statement of changes in equity for the year ended 31 December

	Share capital	Retained earnings	Total equity
	£	£	£
At 1 January	10 000	20 000	30 000
Issue of new capital	2 000		2 000
Profit for the year		5 000	5 000
Dividend		(1 200)	(1 200)
At 31 December	12 000	23 800	35 800

Income statement

Revenue
Cost of sales
Gross profit or loss
Selling and distribution costs
Administrative expenses
Other operating income
Operating profit
Income from investments
Interest receivable and similar income
Finance costs [i.e. interest]
Profit or loss before taxation
Tax on profit or loss
Profit or loss for the year

Self-test question 7.1 (answer at the end of the book)

Explain the current position in the UK in respect of the accounting standards applicable to companies, both listed and unlisted.

Note about taxation:

In all the questions dealt with in earlier chapters in the book we have ignored the effects of taxation. Companies are subject to corporation tax; some of the examples in this chapter will include limited references to tax but no knowledge of corporation tax (or indeed any other tax) is required. In most cases, corporation tax will be a deduction from profit in the income statement, with a corresponding liability in the statement of financial position (in the UK corporation tax is payable 9 months after a company's year-end, so the liability for tax is a current liability).

EXAMPLE 7.4

On 1 January 2012 Xenophon Limited had **issued share capital** comprising 8000 50p shares and retained earnings brought forward of £17 000. On 1 March 2012, Xenophon issued a further 5000 shares of 50p each. On 31 August 2012 the company paid a dividend of 2p per share in issue on that date. The company made a profit after tax of £5000 for the year.

Prepare Xenophon Ltd's statement of changes in equity for the year ended 31 December 2012.

Xenophon Limited: Statement of changes in equity for the year ended 31 December 2012

	Share capital	Retained earnings	Total equity
	£	£	£
At 1 January 2012	4 000 (8000 × 50p)	17 000	21 000
Issue of new capital (5000 × 50p)	2 500		2 500
Profit for the year		5 000	5 000
Dividend (13 000 shares × 2p)		(260)	(260)
At 31 December 2012	6 500	21 740	28 240

Self-test question 7.2 (answer at the end of the book)

Uppingham Telephones Limited has the following balances in its books at 31 March 2012:

	£
Intangible non-current assets	30 866
Premises at carrying amount	65 700
Vehicles at carrying amount	44 430
Fixtures and fittings at carrying amount	17 260
Inventories at 31 March 2012	42 370
Receivables	82 026
Cash at bank and in hand	13 222
Trade payables	39 210
Long-term loan	15 000
Share capital – 20 000 £1 shares issued	20 000
Retained earnings at 1 April 2011	161 479
Revenue	717 216
Cost of sales	509 582
Selling costs	63 477
Distribution costs	54 460
Administrative expenses	24 512
Dividends paid	5 000

The chief accountant must allow for a corporation tax charge for the year of £19 500.
Required: prepare the income statement and the statement of changes in equity for the year ending 31 March 2012 for Uppingham Telephones Limited, and a statement of financial position at that date.

7.8 ACCOUNTING FOR LISTED COMPANIES: ADDITIONAL REQUIREMENTS

Listed companies may have thousands of shareholders, employees, and may be of interest to a very large group of people. The nature of the information published by such companies is clearly of great public significance. Listed companies vary greatly in size – some are surprisingly small – but all are subject to additional requirements over and above Companies Act requirements.

7.8.1 Listing Regulations for Quoted Companies

Companies are described as 'listed' if they are quoted on a recognized stock exchange. Obtaining a quotation for a company opens up potentially vast sources of capital available through investment in the company's shares. The London Stock Exchange is a highly significant exchange. As well as listing UK based companies (2162 of them at the end of February 2010), the London Stock Exchange has listings for many multinational companies (608 of them at the end of February 2010), including such well known company names as Deutsche Bank, Volkswagen, Sony and Ford Motor Company.

In order to allow investors to trade in shares with a reasonable degree of security, stock exchanges tend to be highly regulated. The London Stock Exchange is no exception; for listed companies there are additional accounting and disclosure requirements beyond those which apply to companies in general. For example, listed companies in the UK are required to issue interim reports which follow 6 months after the principal annual accounts. A few companies are required to report quarterly (i.e. every 3 months). In the USA listed companies are required, as a matter of course, to produce quarterly reports. UK companies must also issue a preliminary announcement of annual results, as soon as they have been approved by the board of directors.

Listed company regulation (the 'listing rules') are overseen by the Financial Services Authority (FSA), which took over this responsibility in May 2000. The FSA has a role as the UK Listing Authority (UKLA) which involves it in, amongst other things, reviewing and approving applications from companies for listing.

7.8.2 The Annual Report for a Listed Company

The annual report produced by a listed company is often a very long and complex document. It contains all the minimum annual accounting requirements under company law (the income statement, the statement of financial position, and so on) but also a great deal of additional information. Some of the additional disclosures are voluntary and some are required by other regulation. The annual report is viewed by many listed companies as an important public relations vehicle, and a great deal of care is put into design and presentation. The report is often expensive to produce because of the high quality of paper, photography and graphics used. The example below examines the content of a real-life annual report.

EXAMPLE 7.5 (REAL-LIFE)

Marks & Spencer plc is a very well known retailer, whose shares are listed in the FTSE 100 (i.e. they are amongst the 100 largest companies in the UK). The company's 2009 Annual Report can be downloaded from its website (www.corporate.marksandspencer.com/investors). This is a 120 page document, broken down as follows:

Description	Page count
Chairman's overview ('Our plan for the future')	9
Information about the executive committee	2
Governance overview by deputy chairman	2
Group finance director's report ('Managing through the recession')	3
Key performance indicators	2
Brand and marketplace report	6
Operating and financial review	25
Governance and remuneration	28
Financial statements	43
	120

The financial statements comprise just over a third of the length of the report. Some of the items in the list are required because Marks & Spencer plc is a listed company. There are, for example, extensive additional disclosures on corporate governance and directors' remuneration. The background to these disclosures is explained below in the section below on corporate governance requirements.

It should be noted that the annual report of Marks & Spencer plc contains financial statements relating to all the companies in the Marks & Spencer group of companies. Where a company owns several others it is usually necessary in law to prepare **consolidated financial statements**, which bring together the results and the assets and liabilities of all companies under common control. Therefore, the income statement in Marks & Spencer's financial statements is referred to as a 'consolidated income statement'.

Marks & Spencer's annual report, like the annual report of most large businesses, is in part a public relations document. It is well-designed, brightly coloured and contains many photographs of the company's products. A substantial part of the content of the report comprises disclosures required by law or other regulation, but such disclosures are combined with design elements and pictures to make the report as attractive looking as possible. Although this is a lengthy report which must cost a lot to produce, it is by no means the most extravagant or substantial annual report issued by a UK company.

7.8.3 Corporate Governance Requirements

Corporate governance is the system by which companies are directed and controlled. In the UK corporate governance of listed companies became the subject of much debate during the 1990s. The debate was provoked by several major company scandals which took place towards the end of the 1980s. Failures of governance were implicated in many of the scandals, and there was a general feeling that listed companies must improve the way their boards were run.

Various reports and recommendations on corporate governance were issued (the Cadbury Report in 1992, the Greenbury Report in 1995 and the Hampel Report in 1998). In 1998 the final version of the various reports combined: 'Principles of Good Governance and Code of Best Practice', was published. It is better known as the 'Combined Code'. It has been updated frequently since then. The current version of the Code can be accessed on the website of the Financial Reporting Council (www.frc.org.uk).

The detailed contents of the Combined Code are beyond the scope of this book. Broadly, the Code addresses the following areas:

- directors
- directors' remuneration
- accountability and audit
- relations with shareholders
- institutional shareholders.

Each listed company is required to produce, as part of its annual report, statements on its corporate governance and on directors' remuneration.

7.9 ACCOUNTING FOR LISTED COMPANIES: NON-FINANCIAL INFORMATION

The annual reports of listed companies tend to be lengthy documents as we observed above in the example of the Marks & Spencer 2009 annual report. A document of well over 100 pages is quite usual, especially in the case of the largest and most publicly prominent businesses. There has been a noticeable trend in recent years towards an increase in the volume of information produced in annual reports. This is the result of a combination of factors, including the following:

- More disclosures required as a result of developments in corporate governance.
- Increases in voluntary disclosures especially in respect of social, environmental and sustainability issues.
- The introduction of more complex accounting standards that require additional explanatory notes to the financial statements.

All of these factors contribute to the inclusion of much more information that is not expressed in terms of figures, i.e. non-financial information. There are both advantages and drawbacks to the inclusion of this type of information:

7.9.1 Advantages of Publishing Non-Financial Information

- Non-financial information can often help the less financially oriented user of financial statements to understand the performance and position of the company.
- It is quite often illustrated with photographs and graphs that can help to enhance understanding.
- The presentation of non-financial information often appears much more attractive and user-friendly when compared to the financial statement section of the report; therefore it is more likely to be read.

7.9.2 Drawbacks of Publishing Non-Financial Information

- The sheer volume of information included in an annual report may be off-putting to readers.
- Non-financial information may be produced principally for public relations purposes and it may, for example, report selectively about aspects of the company's performance.
- Information in the form of graphs that accompany non-financial reports may be biased (there is academic research in this area that shows that graphs can be used to give a misleading impression).

7.9.3 The Operating and Financial Review (OFR)

The **operating and financial review (OFR)** is a special type of largely non-financial disclosure intended to set out the directors' analysis of the business, so as to provide both a historical analysis of events and an analysis of prospects for the future. UK listed companies are required to provide such a review (see the inclusion of the OFR in the Marks & Spencer plc 2009 Annual Report earlier in the chapter), and non-listed companies may provide it voluntarily.

The OFR must provide a balanced and comprehensive analysis consistent with the size and complexity of the business of:

- The business's development and performance during the financial year.
- The company's position at the end of the financial year.
- The main trends and factors underlying the development, performance and position of the company, and which are likely to affect it in the future.

Having said this, the content and level of detail in the OFR is very much a matter for the directors. It is a part of the annual report that is likely to be of great interest to shareholders and other people who are interested in the business, as it provides some insight into the directors' strategy for the business. It tends to be forward-looking. In order to ensure that it bears a close relationship to the reality of the business, the auditors are required to express an opinion on whether the OFR is consistent with the rest of the financial statements.

The following list provides an overview of the approach that could be taken in structuring the OFR:

- Description of the business as a context for the rest of the review.
- Objectives of the business, and management's strategy for achieving the objectives.
- Measures used by management to assess the extent to which the objectives are achieved.
- Operating review of the business's performance in the period.
- Returns to shareholders (such as dividends).
- Dynamics of the business.
- Commentary on the strengths and resources available to the business.
- Commentary by the directors on how they have sought to maintain business performance and to improve it in the future.
- Financial review.

- Discussion of the cash inflows and outflows for the period under review.
- Discussion of liquidity.

The best way to become familiar with the contents of an OFR is to read some examples. A good starting point would be the Marks & Spencer OFR, but anyone particularly interested in another UK listed company could search the company's web pages for the latest Annual Report, which contains the OFR.

7.10 CORPORATE REPORTING ON THE INTERNET

As soon as the World Wide Web became widely accessible in the mid-1990s large corporations began using it to disseminate information. At first it was used principally by US companies, but they were rapidly followed by listed companies around the world. By 2006 almost all UK listed companies had a corporate website, and most used it to publish their annual report. The Companies Act 2006 made it compulsory for quoted companies to make their annual report freely available on a website.

Companies have to be careful about what they publish on their websites. They cannot be seen to be creating false market expectations by the publication of exaggerated or inaccurate information. In most cases, the accounting information that is published on corporate websites comprises html or pdf files containing exactly the same information as contained in the annual or half-yearly report. Increasingly, however, companies are exploiting the Internet in more creative ways to reach their actual and potential investors. Some examples of the type of information found on the investor section of corporate websites include the following:

- Webcasts of annual general meetings and/or the analysts' meetings where directors present and discuss the financial results.
- Corporate videos with information about business activities.
- Stockbrokers' forecasts.
- Press releases containing, for example, the preliminary announcement of the financial results and significant events such as takeovers and share issues.
- E-mail links to corporate officers who can deal with queries about the business.

This type of information can be very useful. For example, listed companies generally hold annual meetings with the financial analysts who are interested in the activities of the company (and who often work on behalf of institutional shareholders). Until recently, these meetings have taken place behind closed doors. Webcasts of the meetings allow private investors and anyone else who is interested to see the directors fielding questions from analysts and discussing the financial performance and prospects of the business.

The availability of information on the Internet is particularly useful for investors outside the country where the company is based. Previously, it was often difficult to obtain the financial statements of overseas businesses, but these days, it is usually a matter of simply downloading and printing out the annual report.

Further developments in technology will allow for greater flexibility in the usage of corporate information available from websites. XBRL (Extensible Business Reporting Language) is a development of XML (Extensible Markup Language) specifically, as the name implies, for business reporting purposes. It allows the preparers of reports to 'tag' certain items of information so that they can be readily transferred into the user's software applications. If data can be transferred in a standard format, it can then be subject to analysis, summary and comparison to suit the needs of the financial statement user.

7.10.1 Accessing Corporate Websites

It is usually easy to find specific corporate websites these days. Putting the company's name into any of the reliable search engines is likely to find the site quickly. The London Stock Exchange website (www.londonstockexchange.com) contains links to UK listed companies' websites.

CHAPTER SUMMARY

This chapter contains information about the nature of companies in the UK, shares, directors, financial statements and the general regulatory structures surrounding financial reporting by companies. There is a great deal of very detailed regulation pertaining to companies, and this chapter provides only an outline of it. Some of the website references listed below provide more information for those students who wish to find out more.

The need for publication of accounting information by companies was explained early in the chapter as part of an introduction to the concept of limited liability. It was followed by an explanation of some of the key features of the legal requirements relating to companies. These have changed recently with the introduction of the Companies Act 2006, and students should take care to consult up-to-date sources of information if they need more detail about legal requirements for companies.

International and UK accounting standards form part of the overall structure of regulation. Listed companies in the UK are obliged to report under international standards, and the option of using international standards rather than UK standards is open to all other companies under the Companies Act 2006. The financial reporting sections of this book are based on international accounting standards and presentations, and so the international approach has been stressed in this chapter. However, it is worth bearing in mind that many unlisted companies continue to use UK standards for financial reporting, and so students are likely to find some unfamiliar looking accounts in practice. The glossary will help in such cases.

The later sections of the chapter examined the additional regulation of accounting information in respect of listed companies. Students should appreciate the reasons why the requirements relating to this class of companies are so much more stringent than those that apply to smaller unlisted companies.

It may take some time to assimilate the information in this chapter. Students can increase their familiarity with corporate financial reporting by working through the exercises at the end of the chapter. However, reading the financial press will also help. Reading the *Financial Times* (FT) may present some challenges to understanding at first, but it will undoubtedly increase general business knowledge very quickly. A good way to start may be to read the FT once a week, or to start with the business pages of one of the better quality newspapers (e.g. *The Guardian*, *The Times* or *The Independent*).

INTERNET RESOURCES

The Internet can be used to find out a great deal of information about UK companies and company law.

www.londonstockexchange.com – a very comprehensive site containing detailed information about share prices, stock exchange statistics and data relating to individual companies.

www.companieshouse.gov.uk – the website of Companies House. Some of the detailed information about individual companies is obtainable only upon payment of a fee, but there is some free information about individual companies. Also, the site contains a very good Frequently Asked Questions section and a lot of information about the law relating to companies.

www.opsi.gov.uk – the website of the Office of Public Sector Information. This contains, amongst many other things, the full text of the Companies Act 2006, should any student be interested in reading it.

www.fsa.gov.uk – the website of the Financial Services Authority.

Book's companion website summary

www.cengage.co.uk/gowthorpe3 contains the following resources in respect of Chapter 7:

Students' section

Quiz containing ten multiple choice questions
Five additional questions with answers

Lecturers' section

Answers to end of chapter exercises 7.10 to 7.14
Four additional questions with answers
Case study
ExamView testbank
Instructor's manual
PowerPoint presentation

EXERCISES: ANSWERS AT THE END OF THE BOOK

7.1 Two of the following four statements are correct:

1 Directors must prepare the company's financial statements themselves.

2 Directors take complete responsibility for the preparation of financial statements.

3 Directors may be guilty of a criminal offence if the accounts do not present a true and fair view.

4 Directors may be guilty of a criminal offence if it is proven that they have defrauded creditors.

Which are the correct statements?

a) 3 and 4
b) 2 and 4
c) 1 and 2
d) 1 and 3.

7.2 Bayliss Chandler Limited has an issued share capital of £20 000, split into 50p shares. In the year ending 31 May 2012 a dividend of 6p per share was paid.

Ambrose owns 10% of the issued shares in Bayliss Chandler Limited. What was the value of Ambrose's dividend for the year ending 31 May 2012?

a) £180
b) £120
c) £240
d) £360.

7.3 Peachey plc has an issued share capital of £60 000 denominated in 25p shares. On 13 May 2012 Carina, a shareholder, sold half of her total shareholding of 8000 shares to her sister Cathy. Peachey's accounting year-end is 31 December. In the year ending 31 December 2012 the company paid dividends of 10% of nominal value. Half the dividend was paid on 31 March 2012 and the remainder on 30 September 2012.

What amount of dividend did Carina and Cathy receive in the year ending 31 December 2012?

a) Carina receives £600; Cathy receives £200.
b) Carina receives £400; Cathy receives £400.
c) Carina receives £100; Cathy receives £100.
d) Carina receives £150; Cathy receives £50.

7.4 Butterthwaite plc had issued share capital on 1 January 2012, as follows:

Ordinary share capital: 68 000 £1 ordinary shares
Preference share capital: £20 000 6% cumulative preference shares

On 31 January the company issued a further 12 000 £1 ordinary shares. A dividend of 5p per share was paid on 31 October 2012. In 2011 the company failed to pay its preference dividend, but in 2012 found that it could meet its obligations in full and paid the full amount owing on 31 December 2012.

What is the total amount of dividend paid by Butterthwaite plc in respect of the year ending 31 December 2012?

a) £5 800
b) £5 200
c) £6 400
d) £4 600.

7.5 The directors of Solar Bubble plc, a trading company, have asked the company's chief accountant to prepare a draft income statement for the year ending 31 January 2013 in time for them to discuss it at their board meeting on 15th February. The directors prefer to have the information presented in the same way as in the annual financial statements.

The chief accountant identifies the following relevant balances:

	£
Administrative expenses	73 959
Opening inventory	51 240
Interest payable	1 977
Revenue	975 420
Selling and distribution costs	80 714
Purchases	603 493
Closing inventory	57 210

Notes

1 £6000 has to be accrued in respect of sales commission for the year ending 31 January 2013.

2 The corporation tax charge for the year is estimated at £60 625.

3 A preference dividend on the £10 000 8% preference shares was paid. The preference dividend is to be treated as a finance cost because the preference shares are treated as a liability in the statement of financial position.

4 Of the administrative expenses, £1270 relates to prepayment of insurance.

The chief accountant will be using the following format for the draft income statement:

turnover
cost of sales
gross profit or loss
selling and distribution costs
administrative expenses
operating profit
finance costs
profit or loss before tax
tax on profit or loss
profit or loss for the year.

Required: prepare the draft income statement for Solar Bubble plc for the year ending 31 January 2013.

7.6 Brighton Magnets Limited has the following balances in its books at 31 August 2012:

	£
Closing inventories	186 420
Delivery vans at carrying amount	120 000
Secretarial costs	51 498
Electricity (administrative office)	12 491
Trade payables	219 411
Factory and plant at carrying amount	2 518 000
Retained earnings at 1 September 2011	1 597 172
Share capital – £1 ordinary shares	800 000

	£
Administration office – telephone charges	6 964
Finance costs	1 207
Salespersons' salaries	64 299
Delivery van depreciation	12 000
Other selling and distribution costs	5 911
Office rental	42 704
Other administrative expenses	36 075
Revenue	3 796 842
Interest receivable	644
Depreciation of office computer equipment	8 390
Salespersons' commission	12 270
Office manager's salary	21 704
Directors' remuneration	59 200
Delivery van expenses	24 470
Trade receivables	321 706
Office equipment at carrying amount	151 020
Cash at bank	18 290
Cost of sales	2 712 350
Other operating income	12 900
Dividends paid	40 000

Note: corporation tax on the profits for the year is estimated at £216 470. This amount is not included in the list of balances above.

Required: prepare a income statement and a statement of changes in equity for Brighton Magnets Limited for the year ended 31 August 2012 and a statement of financial position at that date. All three financial statements are to be presented in an appropriate format.

7.7 Two of the following statements are correct:

1 Listed companies are obliged to produce a social responsibility report as part of their annual report.

2 Consolidated financial statements bring together the results and assets and liabilities of all group companies.

3 Compliance with the requirements of the Combined Code is compulsory for listed companies.

4 The London Stock Exchange is responsible for all listed company regulation.

Which are the correct statements?

a) 1 and 2
b) 2 and 3
c) 3 and 4
d) 1 and 4.

7.8 The more traditional view of the company, and the role of the directors, is quite narrow, focusing upon the interests of shareholders only, principally the need to generate cash from the business for the benefit of shareholders. Explain the change in emphasis that has taken place in respect of the role of directors in the UK as a result of the Companies Act 2006. Discuss the extent to which you agree with the traditional or the more modern interpretation of the role of directors.

7.9 Explain the status of UK accounting standards and international accounting standards in financial reporting for UK companies, and briefly outline any change to this status that is likely to take place in the future.

EXERCISES: ANSWERS AVAILABLE ON THE LECTURERS' SECTION OF THE BOOK'S WEBSITE

7.10 Three of the following six statements are correct:

1 The audit report of a company states that the accounts are correct.

2 A private limited company does not have to make any information available to the public.

3 A public limited company must have an authorized share capital of £50 000.

4 The minimum number of shareholders in a private limited company is seven.

5 Each ordinary share carries the right to a vote.

6 A listed company must present its financial statements in compliance with international accounting standards.

Which are the correct statements?

a) 1, 3 and 5
b) 1, 2 and 4
c) 2, 4 and 6
d) 3, 5 and 6.

7.11 Western Gadgets Limited has an issued share capital of £5000 denominated in 25p shares. In the year ending 30 April 2012 an interim dividend of 2p per share and a final dividend of 2.5p per share were paid.

Joan owns shares in Western Gadgets Limited with a nominal value of £1500. What was the value of Joan's dividend for the year ending 30 April 2012?

a) £270
b) £150
c) £225
d) £67.50.

7.12 Parlabane Limited has an issued share capital of 42 500 50p shares. In the year ending 31 December 2012 a dividend of 2p per share was paid on 1 December.

Jonah owns 13 000 shares in Parlabane Limited.

What was the total dividend paid and how much was paid to Jonah personally?

a) total dividend paid £850; paid to Jonah £260
b) total dividend paid £1 000 paid to Jonah £260
c) total dividend paid £425; paid to Jonah £130
d) total dividend paid £500; paid to Jonah £130.

7.13 Penge and Purley plc have in issue at 31 December 2012:

138 000 ordinary shares of 50p each
40 000 8% preference shares of £1 each, issued on 1 July 2012.

Derek owns 3250 ordinary shares in the company, and 1000 of the £1 preference shares. An interim dividend of 2.7p per ordinary share was paid, and a final dividend of 3.7p per ordinary share was also paid, as was the preference dividend.

What was Derek's total dividend from the company for the year ending 31 December 2012?

a) £184
b) £288
c) £144
d) £248.

7.14 Downside Green Limited had the following balances relating to its position at 31 December 2012:

	£
Overdraft	7 746
Share capital	100 000
Loan repayable 31 December 2018	100 000
Trade receivables	916 278
Cash in hand	260
Intangible non-current assets at carrying amount	80 000
Trade payables	868 462
Retained earnings	1 850 824
Tangible non-current assets at carrying amount	1 082 184
Inventories	841 740
Non-current asset investments	24 860
Other payables (all current liabilities)	18 290

The directors wish to see how the statement of financial position will be presented when it is sent to shareholders. Downside Green's financial controller intends to use the following statement of financial position format:

ASSETS

Non-current assets
Intangible assets
Tangible assets
Investments

Current assets
Inventories
Receivables (including prepayments)
Investments
Cash at bank and in hand
Total assets

EQUITY AND LIABILITIES

Equity
Share capital
Retained earnings

Non-current liabilities
Borrowings

Current liabilities
Bank loans and overdrafts
Trade payables
Other payables, including taxation and social security
Accruals
Total liabilities
Total equity and liabilities

Required: prepare the statement of financial position for Downside Green Limited for the year ending 31 December 2012 in the format requested by the directors.

CHAPTER 18

Understanding Financial Reports: Using Accounting Ratios

AIM OF THE CHAPTER

To add to the range of skills developed in the previous chapter in order to understand financial reports for various types of business.

LEARNING OUTCOMES

After reading the chapter and completing the related exercises, students should:

- Understand the usefulness of accounting ratios in financial analysis.
- Be able to calculate a range of accounting ratios.
- Be able to use their knowledge of accounting ratios to assist in the analysis of financial statements.

INTRODUCTION

The simple analysis techniques explained in the previous chapter can be of great assistance in understanding a business. Sometimes, however, it helps to build in some ratio analysis techniques. This chapter explains how to calculate a range of useful ratios, and how to use them in analyzing a set of financial statements.

9.1 FINANCIAL RATIO ANALYSIS TECHNIQUES

There is nothing particularly remarkable about a ratio: it simply expresses the relationship between one quantity and another. Taking a very simple example: a basket of fruit contains 8 apples and 4 oranges. The ratio of apples to oranges can be expressed in an arithmetical term such as: 8:4. It is common to reduce the smaller part of the ratio to 1, so in this example the ratio of apples to oranges is expressed as: 2:1.

Not all of the techniques and calculations commonly included under the term financial ratio analysis actually involve the calculation of a ratio of the 2:1 type calculated above. The same relationship could be expressed by a percentage (e.g. '33.3% of the fruit in this basket is oranges'). However, all of the techniques result in ways of expressing the relationships between two or more figures.

A typical set of financial statements contains many figures, and it is possible to calculate almost infinite permutations expressing their relative dimensions. Some, however, are very obviously of more use than others; it is important that the figures being compared do have some genuine causal relationship between them (i.e. a change in one causes a change in the other). In the rest of this chapter we will examine some of the more commonly considered relationships between items in the financial statements.

It can be helpful, when trying to understand accounting ratios, to group the various categories of financial relationships together. We will examine ratios in five principal categories:

- performance ratios – used to assess the relative success or failure of business performance
- liquidity ratios – used to assess the extent to which a business can comfortably cover its liabilities
- efficiency ratios – used to assess the extent to which items of asset and liability are well-utilized and well-managed
- investor ratios – used to assess various items of particular interest to investors
- lending ratios – used to assess the relationship between financing via loan capital and financing via equity capital.

9.1.1 A Word of Caution About Financial Ratio Analysis

Some of the ratio calculation techniques explained below may appear quite complicated, especially for students whose arithmetical skills are rusty. However, the purpose of their calculation, and the overriding purpose of this section of the book is to assist in *understanding* financial information. Students often concentrate on trying to memorize the ratio formulae and either forget, or have never properly understood, what the relationship between the figures means. Therefore, in each example, we will search for the meaning in the expression of the relationship between figures.

9.2 PERFORMANCE RATIOS

Students may be relieved to discover that they have already studied several aspects of the financial analysis of performance. Earlier chapters introduced the idea of a significant relationship between:

Revenue and gross profit

and

Revenue and net profit

In many of the examples used up to this point in the book, gross profit margins and/or net profit margins have been calculated, and students should by now be accustomed to the idea that these margin calculations can express financial relationships between revenue and profits in ways that are actually quite helpful. The rest of this section of the chapter examines a very significant and widely used ratio: return on capital employed.

9.2.1 Return on Capital Employed (ROCE)

Return on capital employed (also known as ROCE) is widely used as a means of assessing the performance of a business. ROCE looks at the level of profits generated compared to the amount of capital invested in the business. Unfortunately, although the ratio is easy to calculate, it does present problems in that it can be difficult to decide what is included in 'return' and in 'capital employed'.

An example should help to illustrate the issue.

EXAMPLE 9.1

Bilton Burgess plc is a trading company, which occupies its own freehold premises. It has recently obtained a listing on a stock exchange. The company has the following summarized income statement for the year ending 31 December 2012 and statement of financial position at that date:

Bilton Burgess plc: Income statement for the year ending 31 December 2012

	£000	£000
Revenue		1 600
Cost of sales		
Opening inventories	100	
Add: purchases	994	
	1 094	
Less: closing inventories	(104)	
		(990)
Gross profit		610
Various expenses		(319)
Operating profit		291
Finance costs		(80)
Profit before tax		211
Tax		(64)
Profit after tax		147

Note

A dividend of £40 000 was paid during the year ended 31 December 2012.

Bilton Burgess plc: Statement of financial position at 31 December 2012

	£000	£000
ASSETS		
Non-current assets		1 813
Current assets		
Inventories	104	
Trade receivables	170	
Cash at bank	10	
		284
		2 097
EQUITY AND LIABILITIES		
Equity		
Share capital		300
Retained earnings		900
		1 200
Non-current liabilities		
Borrowings		800
Current liabilities		
Trade and other payables		97
		2 097

Return on capital employed measures the profit made by the business against the capital invested:

$$\frac{\text{Profit}}{\text{Capital}}$$

Which profit figure should be used? There are several to choose from:

- gross profit (£610 000)
- operating profit (£291 000)
- profit before tax (£211 000)
- profit after tax (£147 000).

And how much has been invested? Should we include:

Total equity (£1 200 000)

or

Total equity plus non-current liabilities (£2 000 000)?

There is no definitive right answer; it depends upon which ratio is the most useful for the analysis. For example, if the analyst is looking at a set of accounts on behalf of a shareholder, he or she will be most interested in the return made by the shareholders' investment in the business. This means comparing the amount of return that is attributable to shareholders (i.e. profit after deduction of finance costs) with shareholders' equity. This version of ROCE is often referred to as 'return on equity' (ROE).

In the case of Bilton Burgess plc pre-tax ROE (return on shareholders' equity)

$$= \frac{\text{Profit (after finance costs) before tax}}{\text{Shareholders' funds}}$$

$$\text{i.e.} \quad \frac{211}{1200} \times 100 = 17.58\%$$

£211 is the correct figure to use here because it is what is left to the shareholders after finance costs have been deducted from profit.

Post-tax ROE might also be helpful in the analysis:

$$\text{Post-tax ROE (return on shareholders' equity)} = \frac{\text{Profit after tax}}{\text{Shareholders' equity}}$$

$$\text{i.e.} = \frac{147}{1200} \times 100 = 12.25\%$$

Both pre-tax and post-tax ROE could be useful to shareholders in order to compare the return on their investment in Bilton Burgess plc with other possible investments.

Another possibility is to look at the overall return against total investment in the business. Total investment in the case of Bilton Burgess plc is the total of shareholders' equity and long-term borrowings. The matching profit figure is the operating profit before any deduction for finance costs:

$$\text{ROCE (on total capital invested)} = \frac{\text{Profit before finance costs and tax}}{\text{Shareholders' equity and long-term borrowings}}$$

$$\text{i.e.} = \frac{291}{2000} \times 100 = 14.55\%$$

This is a very useful measure of business performance because it focuses purely on performance rather than bringing in considerations related to the method of financing the business operations.

ROCE may seem rather confusing. Try to focus upon the objective of the analysis and, above all, ensure that, where comparisons are being made, the ratio is calculated on a consistent basis. Students sometimes want to know which of the calculations explained in the example is 'right'. The answer is that the ROCE calculations are tools to be used for the purpose of analysis. The 'right' ROCE in any given situation depends upon the focus of the analysis. It is important from the outset to try to focus on the meaning of the figures and remember that accounting is an art rather than a science. Although the terminology is not always used in the same way in practice, this book will use the terms Return on Equity (ROE) to express the relationship between profit after finance costs and shareholders' equity, and Return on Capital Employed (ROCE) to express the relationship between profit before deduction of finance costs and the total of shareholders' equity and long-term borrowings.

Self-test question 9.1 (answer at the end of the book)

The following figures are extracted from Augustus Algernon Limited's income statement and statement of financial position for 2012:

Operating profit	186 000
Finance costs	(24 000)
Profit before tax	162 000
Tax	(48 000)
Profit after tax	114 000

From the statement of financial position:

Share capital	120 000
Retained earnings	1 000 000
Long term borrowings	480 000

Calculate pre-tax ROE, post-tax ROE and ROCE.

9.3 LIQUIDITY RATIOS

Liquidity ratios are used to assess the extent to which a business can comfortably cover its liabilities. The emphasis in this group of ratios is especially on current liabilities. Non-current liabilities, by definition, do not have to be settled in the immediate future. Current liabilities, on the other hand, have to be settled within, at most, 1 year of the statement of financial position date, and usually much more quickly. If the business fails to settle its current liabilities it is in danger of failing altogether.

Can the business meet its liabilities as they fall due?

Two ratios are used to provide answers to this question: the **current ratio** and the **quick ratio**. We will use data from the Bilton Burgess plc financial statements provided earlier to illustrate the calculation of these important ratios.

EXAMPLE 9.2

Current ratio

The current ratio assesses the relationship between current assets and current liabilities. If current liabilities had to be settled in full, would there be sufficient current assets to cover them?

Bilton Burgess's current assets are:	£284 000
Current liabilities are:	£ 97 000

The formula for the current ratio is:

$$\frac{\text{Current assets}}{\text{Current liabilities}} = \frac{284000}{97000} = 2.93$$

It is customary to express this relationship in the form of a ratio, i.e. current assets: current liabilities, which in this case is 2.93:1, Current assets are 2.93 times as large, in total, as current liabilities. Another way of looking at this information is to say that, for every £1 of current liabilities which has to be met by the business there is £2.93 in current assets.

Does the current ratio for Bilton Burgess look reasonable? Well, the business does not appear to be in danger of going under because of inability to meet its current liabilities. If all the creditors were to arrive in a group on the company's doorstep demanding immediate payment, there is actually only £10 000 in the bank with which to pay them. However, this is an unlikely scenario. Given a month or so, many of the amounts owed to the business will be paid in cash. It is reasonable to conclude that Bilton Burgess does not have any obvious liquidity problems.

Is there any 'gold standard' figure for current ratio? Current ratios vary widely between industries, and there is no ideal figure (although some textbooks suggest that there is). It is best used as a point of comparison: for example, if we know that the current ratio for Bilton Burgess at 31 December 2011 was 2.63, we can compare the two figures at consecutive year-ends and conclude that the current ratio has improved from 2.63 to 2.93.

Quick (acid test) ratio

The analysis of liquidity can be further refined by examining the **quick ratio**, which is also referred to as the **acid test ratio**. This works on the assumption that it takes longer to turn inventories into cash, and so it leaves inventories out of the analysis. The formula for the quick ratio is:

$$\frac{\text{Current assets} - \text{inventories}}{\text{Current liabilities}}$$

For Bilton Burgess plc:

$$\frac{284 - 104}{97} = 1.86$$

Expressed in the form of a ratio this is 1.86:1. For every £1 of current liabilities there is £1.86 in cash or trade receivables available. If this ratio drops below 1:1 there may potentially be problems in meeting liabilities. However, it is difficult to generalize about this point. A business which generates cash quickly (like a food retailer, for example) can operate on a very low quick ratio. The quick ratio calculated for Bilton Burgess does not suggest that the company has any immediate problem in meeting its liabilities. As with the current ratio, the quick ratio is most informative when used in comparisons.

Self-test question 9.2 (answer at the end of the book)

Arbus Nugent Limited has the following figures for current assets and current liabilities in its statement of financial positions at 31 December 2012 and 31 December 2011:

	2012	2011
Current assets		
Inventories	34 300	31 600
Trade receivables	42 950	42 610
Cash	10 370	640
	87 620	74 850
Current liabilities		
Trade payables	31 450	32 970

Calculate the current ratio and the quick ratio for Arbus Nugent Limited for both years, working to one decimal place. Have the ratios improved or worsened?

9.4 EFFICIENCY RATIOS

Efficiency ratios are used to assess the extent to which items of asset and liability are well-managed and well-utilized. We will consider efficiency measurement related to four items: non-current assets, inventories, trade receivables and trade payables. The following example uses the Bilton Burgess plc data given earlier in the chapter.

EXAMPLE 9.3

Non-current asset turnover

Non-current assets are employed in the business in order to generate revenue and, ultimately, profits. It can be interesting and useful to gauge the success with which non-current assets are employed to produce turnover. The **non-current asset turnover ratio** examines the efficiency with which non-current assets have been utilized in the business.

The formula is:

$$\frac{\text{Revenue}}{\text{Non-current assets}}$$

Applying the formula to the relevant figures for Bilton Burgess plc:

$$\text{Non-current asset turnover} = \frac{\text{Revenue}}{\text{Non-current assets}}$$

$$= \frac{1600}{1813} = 0.88$$

A helpful way of looking at this result is to think of it in terms of the amount of revenue generated per £ of investment in non-current assets. Each £ invested in non-current assets in Bilton Burgess plc produces, on average, revenue of 88p.

Again, there is no 'gold standard' for this ratio. Businesses differ from each other in the extent to which they use non-current assets. Some businesses are largely people-based; because the value of people does not appear on business statements of financial position, such businesses are likely to produce a high level of revenue relative to very low investment in non-current assets. Bilton Burgess plc owns its own premises and therefore non-current assets are higher than in an equivalent business where the buildings are rented. When comparing the non-current asset turnover of two businesses caution must be exercised to ensure that like is compared with like.

Inventory turnover

Where inventories are a significant factor in a business, it is of prime importance to manage them properly. Holding too much in inventory costs money (because of storage costs, insurance, working capital tied up); holding insufficient inventories may also lead to problems where there is a delay in supplying customer orders. The **inventory turnover ratio** gauges the average length of time that an item of inventory spends on the premises before it is sold.

There are two related calculations:

Inventory turnover $\quad \dfrac{\text{Cost of sales}}{\text{Average inventory}}$

Inventory turnover in days $\quad \dfrac{\text{Average inventories}}{\text{Cost of sales}} \times 365 \text{ days}$

Average inventories is taken as the average of opening and closing inventory. Extracting the relevant figures from Bilton Burgess's financial statements produces the following figure for average inventories:

$$\frac{\text{Opening inventories} + \text{closing inventories}}{2} = \frac{100 + 104}{2} = 102$$

The average could be more accurately calculated if more information were available; for instance, if monthly inventories figures were available, a fairly accurate average inventories figure for the year could be calculated by adding together the monthly figures and dividing by 12.

Bilton Burgess plc:

$$\begin{aligned}\text{Inventory turnover ratio} &= \frac{\text{Cost of sales}}{\text{Average inventories}}\\ &= \frac{990}{102}\\ &= 9.7 \text{ times}\end{aligned}$$

This means that on average inventories are replaced 9.7 times in a year. The additional calculation expresses the same information in a slightly different (possibly more helpful) way:

$$\begin{aligned}\text{Inventory turnover in days} &= \frac{\text{Average inventories}}{\text{Cost of sales}} \times 365 \text{ days}\\ &= \frac{102}{990} \times 365 \text{ days} = 37.6 \text{ days}\end{aligned}$$

This means that, on average, an item of inventory spends 37.6 days in Bilton Burgess's warehouse.

As with previous ratio calculation results it is difficult to assess the significance of this figure without some point of comparison. If we know that in the previous year inventory turnover in days was 32.7 days, we can conclude that the inventory turnover ratio appears to have worsened. Also, much depends on the nature of the inventories. If Bilton Burgess plc is in the fresh fruit supply business, 37.6 days would appear to be an excessive inventory turnover; on the other hand, if it supplies electrical components, there is probably nothing out of the ordinary with a measure of 37.6 days.

Trade receivables turnover ratio

The **trade receivables turnover ratio** assesses the length of time that trade receivables take to pay. The calculation of this ratio is as follows:

$$\text{Trade receivables turnover ratio} = \frac{\text{Average trade receivables}}{\text{Revenue on credit}} \times 365 \text{ days}$$

In the case of Bilton Burgess plc we have no data available about the opening figure for trade receivables. In such cases we can use the closing figure, but it must be interpreted with some caution.

Extracting the relevant figures from the Bilton Burgess plc accounts, and assuming that all sales are made on credit (i.e. there are no sales made for cash):

$$\frac{\text{Trade receivables}}{\text{Revenue on credit}} \times 365 \text{ days}$$

$$= \frac{170}{1600} \times 365 \text{ days} = 38.8 \text{ days}$$

NB: this is sometimes referred to as the trade receivables collection period.

This figure would be useful for making a comparison over time; if we had sufficient information we would be able to say whether or not this was an improvement over the previous year's figure.

The length of time it takes to collect trade receivables is related to the business's policy on offering credit. Let's suppose that Bilton Burgess's sales invoices state: 'Payment must be received within 30 days of despatch of goods'. The trade receivables turnover ratio tells us that, on average, customers exceed the credit terms by 8.8 days. It may be that, by improving its credit control procedures, Bilton Burgess plc would be able to reduce its trade receivables turnover figure.

Trade payables turnover ratio

The **trade payables turnover ratio** measures the length of time, on average, that a business takes to settle its trade payables. Its calculation is very similar to that used for the trade receivables turnover ratio:

$$\text{Trade payables turnover ratio} = \frac{\text{Average trade payables}}{\text{Purchases}} \times 365 \text{ days}$$

In the case of Bilton Burgess plc we have no information available about the opening balance of trade payables. In such cases it is usually acceptable to use closing trade payables, but the results of the calculation need to be treated with caution.

Extracting the relevant figures from Bilton Burgess's financial statements we can calculate the ratio as follows:

$$\frac{\text{Trade payables}}{\text{Purchases}} \times 365 \text{ days}$$

$$= \frac{97}{994} \times 365 \text{ days} = 35.6 \text{ days}$$

Given that many businesses stipulate payment within 30 days, Bilton Burgess plc are probably not taking an unreasonably long time to pay their trade payables.

Where the trade payables turnover ratio is very high, or where it has risen significantly over the previous period(s), it may indicate possible liquidity problems. To some extent, it is good management practice to take advantage of this source of interest-free credit. However, it must be kept within reasonable limits. If a business takes an unreasonably long time to settle its trade payables, there may be a consequent loss of **goodwill**, and the business may find it difficult to obtain supplies on credit.

Self-test question 9.3 (answer at the end of the book)

Armitage Horobin Limited is a trading company which makes all its sales on credit. Its income statement and statement of financial position for the accounting years 2012 and 2011 are as follows:

Armitage Horobin Limited: Income statements for the years ending 31 March 2012 and 2011

	2012 £000	2012 £000	2011 £000	2011 £000
Revenue		283.4		271.1
Cost of sales				
Opening inventories	23.7		21.2	
Add: purchases	184.8		177.5	
	208.5		198.7	
Less: closing inventories	(25.9)		(23.7)	
		(182.6)		(175.0)
Gross profit		100.8		96.1
Various expenses		(75.9)		(73.0)
Operating profit		24.9		23.1
Tax		(4.9)		(3.7)
Profit after tax		20.0		19.4

Armitage Horobin Limited: Statements of financial position at 31 March 2012 and 2011

	2012 £000	2012 £000	2011 £000	2011 £000
ASSETS				
Non-current assets		289.2		275.3
Current assets				
Inventories	25.9		23.7	
Trade receivables	33.0		28.2	
Prepayments	1.0		1.5	
Cash at bank	6.0		4.2	
		65.9		57.6
		355.1		332.9
EQUITY AND LIABILITIES				
Equity				
Share capital		40.0		40.0
Retained earnings		289.3		269.3
		329.3		309.3

	2012	2012	2011	2011
	£000	£000	£000	£000
Current liabilities				
Trade payables	24.5		20.6	
Accruals	1.3		3.0	
		25.8		23.6
		355.1		332.9

Required: calculate the following efficiency ratios:

- non-current asset turnover
- inventory turnover
- trade receivables turnover
- trade payables turnover.

In each case state whether the ratio shows an improvement or not.

9.5 INVESTOR RATIOS

Investor ratios, as the name implies, are those ratios which are likely to be of particular interest to investors and potential investors.

In Chapter 8 we identified some of the questions investors are likely to ask:

- How is my investment doing?
- Should I buy more shares/ sell the shares I've already got/ hold on to the investment I've already got?
- Is the dividend likely to increase?
- What are the chances of the company going out of business?

The group of accounting ratios classified in this section under the heading 'investor ratios' may help to suggest answers to some of these questions. Although the ratios covered in this section may be of particular interest to investors, they are likely also to provide information that is useful to other people who have some reason for wanting to know more about a business.

Note that several of the ratios which follow in this section can be calculated only for limited companies. They are not applicable to sole trader and partnership businesses.

As with the other main groups of ratios, we will use the information given for Bilton Burgess plc earlier in the chapter to illustrate calculations.

EXAMPLE 9.4

Dividend per share

This ratio calculates the amount in pence of the dividend for each ordinary share:

$$\frac{\text{Dividend for the year}}{\text{Number of shares in issue}}$$

The relevant figures for Bilton Burgess plc are:

$$\frac{40}{300} = 13.3\text{p per share}$$

Note that, in this case, the number of shares is the same as the value in the statement of financial position, because the shares are of £1 each. Care must be taken where the shares are, for example, 50p shares. In this example, if the shares were of 50p nominal value there would be twice as many to take into the calculation.

Dividend cover

Dividend cover calculates the number of times the current dividend could be paid out of available profits.

$$\frac{\text{Profits after tax attributable to ordinary shareholders}}{\text{Dividend}}$$

For Bilton Burgess plc:

$$\frac{147}{40} = 3.67$$

What does this mean? Remember that the directors determine the level of dividend payout; usually they will seek to ensure that it is comfortably within available profits and that a good proportion of profits is retained in the business. The dividend cover calculated for Bilton Burgess plc tells us that the directors could pay the current level of dividend 3.67 times out of available profits.

As with all ratios the dividend cover ratio is of limited use on its own. However, it does suggest, in this case, that dividend cover is comfortable. If dividend cover = 1 it means that all available profits for the year are being paid over to shareholders in the form of dividends. This would be a matter of concern for two reasons:

- No profit is being retained in the business.
- It may not be possible to sustain this level of payout in future years.

Earnings per share

The dividend per share is the amount that is actually paid out per share to investors in the company. Earnings per share is the amount that is theoretically available per share. It is calculated as follows:

$$\frac{\text{Profit after tax attributable to ordinary shareholders}}{\text{Number of shares in issue}}$$

This gives earnings per share (often abbreviated to eps) in pence.

The relevant figures for Bilton Burgess plc are:

$$\frac{147}{300} = 49\text{p per share}$$

(Note that even where eps is greater than 99p the amount is always expressed in pence.) It is worth emphasizing again that the eps of 49p per share does not end up in the pockets of the Bilton Burgess plc shareholders; it is a theoretical figure which expresses the amount of earnings available to shareholders. The amount which does end up in the pockets of the shareholders is (usually) a lesser amount: the dividend.

Price/earnings ratio

This is a very important stock market ratio. It expresses the relationship between earnings per share (which we have just looked at) and the price of the share. Because the calculation involves a share price, it can be performed only for companies listed on a stock exchange for which a share price is available.

This ratio cannot, therefore, be calculated for most businesses, such as sole traders, partnerships and unlisted companies.

In order to calculate the ratio for Bilton Burgess plc (which, remember, is a listed company) we would need to obtain a current share price. Bilton Burgess plc is a fictional company; if it were a real UK listed company, a current share price could easily be obtained for it by looking in the companies listings in the Financial Times or by accessing the London Stock Exchange website.

Suppose that the current share price of Bilton Burgess plc is £6.40 per share. (Yes, these are £1 shares, but the value at which they are traded on the Stock Exchange depends upon the market's perception of the value and the prospects of the company.)

The price/earnings (or P/E ratio, as it is often known) for Bilton Burgess plc is:

$$\frac{\text{Price per share}}{\text{Earnings per share}}$$

$$\frac{640\text{p}}{49\text{p}} = 13.1 \text{ (to one decimal place).}$$

So what does this mean? The P/E ratio for Bilton Burgess plc tells us that investors are currently prepared to pay 13.1 × the company's earnings for a single share. On its own, as with most ratios, it has little significance. However, it is very useful for making comparisons with other listed companies, and, especially, with companies in the same industry sector.

Suppose that Bilton Burgess's two main competitors are both listed companies, and that their P/E ratios are:

Abacus Casement plc	18.4
Carew Grapeshot plc	10.3

Investors are prepared to pay up to 18.4 × earnings for a share in Abacus Casement plc, which suggests that they regard the company more highly than Bilton Burgess plc. Carew Grapeshot plc, on the other hand, has a lower P/E than Bilton Burgess plc; investors are prepared to pay only 10.3 × earnings for a single share.

The P/E ratio is a measurement of the market's perception of a company's shares. A high P/E ratio suggests that the shares are regarded as highly desirable; this is often because they are perceived as relatively low risk. Low P/Es, on the other hand, suggest an unfashionable and, relatively, more risky share which is downgraded by the market.

Figure 9.1 shows a sample of real companies' P/E ratios in March 2010. All are 'household name' retailing companies in the UK.

FIGURE 9.1 Examples of P/E ratios of companies listed on the London Stock Exchange

Company	P/E
Clinton Cards	4.25
Marks & Spencer	11.45
Next	11.66
J Sainsbury	15.82
Tesco	15.75

It should be noted that appearances can be deceptive. A sudden fluctuation in share price can result in a significant change to the P/E so that at any point in time, the P/E may not be representative of the general trend.

9.5.1 Market Capitalization

Market capitalization is not a ratio calculation, but it is a piece of information which is likely to be of interest to investors and potential investors in a listed company. Market capitalization is the current share price multiplied by the number of shares in issue. It provides a guide as to the market's view of the current value of the company.

For Bilton Burgess plc:

Price £6.40 × number of shares in issue 300 000 = £1 920 000

Self-test question 9.4 (answer at the end of the book)

Armley Regina plc is a listed company whose current share price at 31 December 2012 is £5.08 per share. The company has 1 000 000 50p shares in issue. In the financial year ended 31 December 2012 the company reported profit after tax of £680 000, all of which was attributable to ordinary shareholders. Dividends of £220 000 were paid in the year.

Required: calculate the following:

dividend per share
dividend cover
earnings per share
price/earnings ratio
market capitalization.

9.6 LENDING RATIOS

9.6.1 Gearing

A **gearing ratio** expresses the relationship between two different types of financing of a company: (a) financing through equity i.e. ordinary shares, and (b) financing through long-term loans, i.e. debt.

Equity is contributed to a company by its ordinary shareholders who have a right to a share of any ordinary dividend that is declared by the company directors. Any undistributed profits are regarded as part of equity financing.

Debt is finance in the form of loans. Lenders are usually entitled to interest at a fixed rate on the loans, but, unlike shareholders, they do not have a vote, and are not entitled to any share of the dividend.

NB: in Chapter 7 we briefly looked at another type of capital: preference share capital. This is share capital which confers the right to a fixed rate of dividend (for example, 10% preference share capital). Preference shareholders do not have any right to a share of the ordinary dividend; even if the company does really well, and distributes a lot of money to its ordinary shareholders, the preference shareholders still receive only the fixed percentage to which they are entitled. Preference share capital has characteristics more akin to debt, and so for the purposes of the **gearing** calculation, it is usually regarded as debt.

Gearing has great significance for shareholders and potential shareholders. However, it is a ratio of general importance which is likely to be significant for many interest groups.

There is more than one way of calculating gearing:

$$\frac{\text{Debt}}{\text{Equity}}$$

Or

$$\frac{\text{Debt}}{\text{Debt} + \text{equity}}$$

The really important point in adopting one or other of these methods is to be consistent.

The effect of interest in the income statement is measured by the final ratio to be considered in this chapter: interest cover.

9.6.2 Interest Cover

Interest cover is a measurement of the number of times interest (or finance costs) could be paid out of available profits. Students who have understood the idea of dividend cover will recognize that interest cover performs a similar function. It is calculated as follows:

$$\frac{\text{Profit before interest (finance costs) and taxation}}{\text{interest (finance costs)}}$$

As for previous groups of ratios we will use the Example 9.1 from Bilton Burgess plc to illustrate the calculations.

EXAMPLE 9.5

Gearing

The relevant figures for debt and equity for Bilton Burgess plc are:

- debt (assuming that amounts due after more than 1 year all relate to long-term debt) = £800 000
- equity (share capital + retained earnings) = £1 200 000.

Gearing for Bilton Burgess plc is calculated as follows:

EITHER

$$\frac{\text{Debt}}{\text{Equity}} = \frac{800\,000}{1\,200\,000} = 66.7\% \text{ (to one decimal place)}$$

OR

$$\frac{\text{Debt}}{\text{Debt} + \text{equity}} = \frac{800\,000}{800\,000 + 1\,200\,000} = 40\%$$

Interest cover

The relevant figures for Bilton Burgess plc are:

$$\frac{291}{80} = 3.64 \text{ times}$$

9.7 THE EFFECTS OF GEARING

9.7.1 Why are Ordinary Shareholders Interested in Gearing?

A high level of debt capital relative to equity capital (i.e. a high level of gearing) means that the company faces a relatively high interest charge. Interest must be paid out of the store of available profits. If the interest profit soaks up most of the available profit there will be very little left over for the ordinary shareholders. Therefore, an investment in a highly geared company is usually seen as relatively risky for equity shareholders. However, a great deal depends upon the level of profits generated.

The following example illustrates the potential impact of gearing.

EXAMPLE 9.6

Two companies, Basket Rabbitts plc and Telford Barron plc, have very similar operations and are of very similar sizes. However, their financing varies: Basket Rabbitts plc is highly geared, and Telford Barron plc is low geared, as follows:

High gearing		**Low gearing**	
Basket Rabbitts plc	£	*Telford Barron plc*	£
Long-term debt finance		Long-term debt finance	
(10% interest)	40 000	(10% interest)	5 000
Equity finance	30 000	Equity finance	65 000
	70 000		70 000

Let's look at the effects of the gearing at three different potential levels of profit before tax:

	£
High level	12 000
Medium level	8 000
Low level	4 000

In all cases we will assume a tax rate of 30%

1 High level of profit

High gearing *Basket Rabbitts plc*	£	**Low gearing** *Telford Barron plc*	£
Profit before finance costs and tax	12 000	Profit before finance costs and tax	12 000
Less: finance costs £40 000 × 10%	(4 000)	Less: finance costs £5 000 × 10%	(500)
Profit before tax	8 000	Profit before tax	11 500
Tax: £8 000 × 30%	(2 400)	Tax: £11 500 × 30%	(3 450)
Profit after tax – attributable to ordinary shareholders	5 600	Profit after tax – attributable to ordinary shareholders	8 050
Post tax return on equity (ROE):		Post tax return on equity (ROE):	

$$\frac{5\,600}{30\,000} \times 100 = 18.7\% \qquad \frac{8\,050}{65\,000} = 12.3\%$$

2 Medium level of profit

High gearing *Basket Rabbitts plc*	£	**Low gearing** *Telford Barron plc*	£
Profit before finance costs and tax	8 000	Profit before finance costs and tax	8 000
Less: finance costs £40 000 × 10%	(4 000)	Less: finance costs £5 000 × 10%	(500)
Profit before tax	4 000	Profit before tax	7 500
Tax: £4 000 × 30%	(1 200)	Tax: £7 500 × 30%	(2 250)
Profit after tax – attributable to ordinary shareholders	2 800	Profit after tax – attributable to ordinary shareholders	5 250
Post tax return on equity (ROE):		Post tax return on equity (ROE):	

$$\frac{2\,800}{30\,000} \times 100 = 9.3\% \qquad \frac{5\,250}{65\,000} = 8.1\%$$

3 Low level of profit

High gearing *Basket Rabbitts plc*	£	**Low gearing** *Telford Barron plc*	£
Profit before finance costs and tax	4 000	Profit before finance costs and tax	4 000

High gearing		**Low gearing**	
Basket Rabbitts plc	£	*Telford Barron plc*	£
Less: finance costs £40 000 × 10%	(4 000)	Less: finance costs £5 000 × 10%	(500)
Profit before tax	–	Profit before tax	3 500
Tax	–	Tax: £3 500 × 30%	(1 050)
Profit after tax – attributable to ordinary shareholders	–	Profit after tax – attributable to ordinary shareholders	2 450
Post tax return on equity (ROE):	0%	Post tax return on equity (ROE): $\frac{2450}{65000} =$	3.8%

The example illustrates that returns to shareholders in a highly geared company are more volatile than returns to shareholders in a low geared company. Highly geared companies are, therefore seen by ordinary shareholders as more risky.

CHAPTER SUMMARY

A great deal of useful material on financial ratio analysis has been covered in this chapter. The following ratios were examined within five major groups:

- **performance ratios**
  gross profit margins
  net profit margins
  return on equity
  return on capital employed.
- **liquidity ratios**
  current ratio
  quick (acid test) ratio.
- **efficiency ratios**
  non-current asset turnover
  inventory turnover
  trade receivables turnover
  trade payables turnover.
- **Investor ratios**
  dividend per share
  dividend cover

earnings per share
price earnings ratio
market capitalization.

- **Lending ratios**
  gearing ratio
  interest cover.

There are a large number of small questions included in the end of chapter questions, so that students can become accustomed to the calculation of ratios. But remember that the purpose in analyzing accounting information is to understand it better. Ratio calculations can be a useful means to an end, but the key objective is to understand the meaning of the financial statements.

INTERNET RESOURCES

Book's companion website summary
www.cengage.co.uk/gowthorpe3 contains the following resources in respect of Chapter 9:

Students' section
Quiz containing ten multiple choice questions
Three additional questions with answers

Lecturers' section
Answers to end of chapter exercises 9.21 to 9.39
Four additional questions with answers
Three case studies
ExamView testbank
Instructor's manual
PowerPoint presentation

EXERCISES: ANSWERS AT THE END OF THE BOOK

The following information is relevant to questions 9.1 to 9.3 inclusive:

Extracts from Sigmund & Son Limited's financial statements for 2012 show the following:

	£000
Gross profit	616.4
Various expenses	(313.6)
Operating profit	302.8
Finance costs	(35.0)
Profit before tax	267.8
Taxation	(80.0)
Profit after tax	187.8
Share capital	500.0
Retained earnings	1 790.0
Long-term borrowings	350.0

During the 2012 financial year, Sigmund & Son Limited paid a dividend of £100 000 to its shareholders.

9.1 What is the pre-tax return on equity (to one decimal place)?

a) 13.2%
b) 10.1%
c) 26.9%
d) 11.7%.

9.2 What is the post-tax return on equity (to one decimal place)?

a) 3.8%
b) 8.2%
c) 3.3%
d) 7.1%.

9.3 What is the return on capital employed (to one decimal place)?

a) 8.2%
b) 11.5%
c) 13.2%
d) 10.1%.

9.4 Shania would like to invest in a company which will give her a good rate of return on her investment. She has collected information on four companies. Extracts from their most recent financial statements are given below:

	Ambit Ltd £000	Bolsover Ltd £000	Carcan Ltd £000	Delphic Ltd £000
Operating profit	983.6	647.8	726.8	1 061.4
Finance costs	(180.0)	(107.0)	(151.0)	(206.0)
Profit before tax	803.6	540.8	575.8	855.4
Tax	(240.0)	(160.0)	(170.0)	(250.0)
Profit after tax	563.6	380.8	405.8	605.4
Share capital	80.0	95.0	86.0	60.0
Retained earnings	4 550.0	3 881.0	3 928.0	7 000.0
Long-term borrowings	2 400.0	1 250.0	1 820.0	2 500.0

Which company currently has the highest pre-tax return on shareholders' funds?

a) Ambit Limited
b) Bolsover Limited
c) Carcan Limited
d) Delphic Limited.

9.5 Trixie Stores Limited has the following current asset and current liability items in its statement of financial position at 31 December 2012:

	£
Inventory	18 370
Trade receivables	24 100

	£
Cash in hand	70
Trade payables	15 450
Bank overdraft	6 400

What is the current ratio (working to 2 decimal places) for Trixie Stores Limited?

a) 1.95:1
b) 1.11:1
c) 0.51:1
d) 0.90:1.

9.6 Trimester Tinker Limited has the following working capital items in its statement of financial position at 31 December 2012:

	£
Inventory	108 770
Trade receivables	94 300
Cash in hand	1 600
Trade payables	110 650

The company belongs to a trade association which has recently published industry averages for key financial ratios based upon a survey of its members. The industry averages for current and quick ratios applicable to the business of Trimester Tinker Limited are:

Current ratio	1.62:1
Quick ratio	0.93:1

Which of the following statements is correct?

a) Trimester Tinker Limited's current ratio is higher than the industry average and its quick ratio is also higher.
b) Trimester Tinker Limited's current ratio is higher than the industry average but its quick ratio is lower.
c) Trimester Tinker Limited's current ratio is lower than the industry average and its quick ratio is also lower.
d) Trimester Tinker Limited's current ratio is lower than the industry average but its quick ratio is higher.

9.7 Upwood Sickert Limited has total revenue in the year to 31 May 2012 of £686 430. Extracts from the company's statement of financial position at that date show non-current assets as follows:

	Cost	**Depreciation**	**Carrying amount**
	£	£	£
Plant and machinery	200 000	30 000	170 000
Vehicles	106 640	46 655	59 985

What is the non-current asset turnover ratio for the year to two decimal places?

a) 2.24
b) 0.34
c) 0.45
d) 2.98.

9.8 A sole trader's inventory at 31 December 2011 was £405 000. By 31 December 2012 inventory had increased in value by 10%. Cost of sales for the year ended 31 December 2012 was £1 506 700.

What was the business's inventory turnover in days for the year ended 31 December 2012?

9.9 A company has trade receivables in its year-end statement of financial position of £218 603. Revenue for the year was £1 703 698. 70% of the revenue was in respect of sales made on credit. Trade receivables turnover in days is:

a) 46.8 days
b) 32.7 days
c) 66.9 days
d) 18.3 days.

9.10 The managing director of Winger Whalley Limited has just received a report from one of the accounting assistants employed by the business. The report shows key ratios and supplies explanations for any significant fluctuations. The MD is concerned to find that the trade receivables turnover period has worsened significantly in the period from 2011 to 2012 (it was 36.4 days at the end of 2011 and is 41.2 days at the end of 2012). The accounting assistant has supplied the following reasons for the fluctuations:

1 The company's credit controller did a parachute jump for charity about 3 months ago. The parachute failed to open properly, and because of her injuries she was away from work in the last 3 months of 2012. The temporary staff agency was unable to provide a suitable replacement for her, and during most of the 3-month period her work was simply not done.

2 Revenue has increased by 4% in the course of the year.

3 During 2012 the board of directors decided to introduce a system of early settlement discounts. Trade receivables amounts paid within 30 days would receive a discount of 0.5% of the value of the invoices.

4 A new order of revenue invoice stationery was received part-way through the year. Usually the revenue invoice stationery is printed with 'SETTLEMENT REQUIRED WITHIN 30 DAYS', but the printers had omitted this by mistake. The office general manager decided to use the stationery anyway.

Two of these reasons could be valid explanations for the increase in the trade receivables turnover period. The valid explanations are:

a) 1 and 2
b) 3 and 4
c) 1 and 4
d) 2 and 3.

9.11 A business has trade payables at its year-end of £206 460. Purchases for the year are £1 952 278, of which 90% were made on credit.

What is the trade payables turnover period?

a) 42.9 days
b) 38.6 days
c) 34.7 days
d) 11.7 days.

The following information about Waldo Wolff plc, a quoted company, is relevant to questions 9.12 – 9.15 inclusive.

Extracts from Waldo Wolff's accounts for the year ending 31 December 2012 include the following useful information:

	£000
Operating profit	1 836.4
Finance costs	(220.0)
Profit before tax	1 616 4
Tax	(485.0)
Profit after tax	1 131.4

The company has 6 000 000 shares in issue. The shares have a nominal value of 50p each. During the financial year ended 31 December 2012 the company paid dividends of £300 000.

The market price at 31 December 2012 of a share in the company was £3.11.

9.12 What is the dividend per share?

a) 10p
b) 5p
c) 50p
d) 100p.

9.13 What is the dividend cover ratio?

a) 3.77
b) 5.39
c) 2.77
d) 6.12.

9.14 What is the earnings per share (in pence)?

a) 18.86p
b) 26.94p
c) 13.86p
d) 37.71p.

9.15 What is Waldo Wolff's market capitalization at 31 December 2012?

9.16 At 30 April 2013 Wilson Streep plc had a market capitalization of £6 303 000 with 3 300 000 ordinary 50p shares in issue. The profit attributable to ordinary shareholders in its income statement for the year ending 30 April 2013 was £750 090.

What was the company's P/E ratio at 30 April 2013?

a) 16.1
b) 4.2
c) 8.4
d) 3.8.

9.17 Brazier Barkiss plc had the following capital structure at 30 April 2013:

	£
Ordinary share capital (£1 shares)	1 000 000
Retained earnings	2 739 400
Long-term borrowings (10% interest rate)	2 000 000

Profit before interest and tax for the year ending 30 April 2013 was £646 750 and finance costs were £200 000.

Required: calculate the following ratios:

i) gearing (on the basis of debt/equity)

ii) interest cover.

9.18 The directors of the Cuttlefish Biscuit Corporation Limited have calculated a set of key accounting ratios for their biscuit manufacturing business. These are set out in the following table, together with industry averages provided by the National Biscuit Manufacturers' Federation.

	Cuttlefish	**Industry average**
Gross profit margin	32.3%	31.6%
Operating profit margin	16.2%	17.1%
Trade receivables turnover (days)	36.0	38.4
Inventory turnover (days)	48.7	47.4
Trade payables	31.4	39.6
Gearing (debt/equity)	18.7%	29.4%

Required: write a brief report to the directors of Cuttlefish comparing the ratios for their company with the industry averages. Identify any areas in which you think they could make improvements.

9.19 Cryer Roussillon Limited is a trading company. At the beginning of the 2012 accounting year (which ends on 31 December) a new managing director was appointed. He made the strategic decision to alter the company's range of products. Previously, the company had concentrated on lower margin products within its industry, but the new MD decided to move into higher quality products which produce better margins. He has made several other changes to the company. He persuaded the board of directors that the company should invest in some badly needed new non-current assets, and the company took out a long-term loan to help finance the acquisitions. He has also obtained the agreement of the other directors (all of whom are shareholders) not to propose any dividend this year, so that profits can be retained in the company to help finance future growth.

The summarized financial statements for 2012 (with comparative figures for 2011) are shown below.

Cryer Roussillon Limited: Income statement for the year ended 31 December 2012

	2012	2011
	£	£
Revenue	206 470	210 619
Cost of sales	(121 198)	(141 789)
Gross profit	85 272	68 830
Various expenses	(41 459)	(47 610)
Operating profit	43 813	21 220
Finance costs	(3 000)	–
Profit before tax	40 813	21 220
Tax	(8 100)	(3 180)
Profit after tax	32 713	18 040

In the year ended 31 December 2011 Cryer Roussillon paid a dividend of £13 000 to its shareholders. In the year ended 31 December 2012 it paid no dividend.

Cryer Roussillon: Statement of financial position at 31 December 2012

	2012	2012	2011	2011
	£	£	£	£
ASSETS				
Non-current assets		129 490		68 750
Current assets				
Inventory	14 278		14 550	
Trade receivables	20 693		29 420	
Cash at bank	10 792		640	
		45 763		44 610
		175 253		113 360
EQUITY AND LIABILITIES				
Equity				
Share capital	20 000		20 000	
Retained earnings	109 783		77 070	
		129 783		97 070
Non-current liabilities				
Long-term borrowings		30 000		–
Current liabilities				
Trade payables		15 470		16 290
		175 253		113 360

The managing director has asked you, as the company's financial adviser, to write a confidential report to the board commenting upon items of significance in the accounts shown above. He would like you to calculate any key ratios which you consider to be important, and to provide an assessment of how the company is doing.

9.20 The table below presents some of the key figures from the income statement of Tesco plc, extracted from its 2009 Annual Report.

	2009	**2008**
	£m	**£m**
Revenue	54 327	47 298
Cost of sales	(50 109)	(43 668)
Gross profit	4 218	3 630
Operating profit	3 206	2 791
Profit before tax	2 954	2 803
Profit after tax	2 166	2 130
Earnings per share	27.50p	26.95p

Required: write a brief report on the performance of Tesco plc in 2009, including calculations of any accounting ratios that you think are relevant.

EXERCISES: ANSWERS AVAILABLE ON THE LECTURERS' SECTION OF THE BOOK'S WEBSITE

The following information is relevant to questions 9.21 to 9.23 inclusive:

Extracts from Sinclair Salter's financial statements for 2012 show the following:

	£000
Gross profit	896.4
Various expenses	(606.8)
Operating profit	289.6
Finance costs	(93.0)
Profit before tax	196.6
Tax	(60.0)
Profit after tax	136.6
Share capital	100.0
Retained earnings	1170.0
Long-term borrowings	900.0

During the 2012 financial year, Sinclair Salter Limited paid a dividend of £40 000 to its shareholders.

9.21 What is return on total capital employed (to one decimal place)?

a) 15.5%
b) 13.3%
c) 9.1%
d) 22.8%.

9.22 What is pre-tax return on shareholders' equity (to one decimal place)?

a) 15.5%
b) 10.8%
c) 9.1%
d) 22.8%.

9.23 What is post-tax return on shareholders' equity (to one decimal place)?

a) 15.5%
b) 9.1%
c) 10.8%
d) 6.3%.

9.24 Shirley has been thinking for a while about investing some surplus cash in an unlisted company which organizes lettings of holiday properties in France. The company is run by an old friend of hers who is looking for additional investors in order to fund a planned expansion of the business.

Shirley has received financial statements for the business for 2012 (showing comparative figures for 2011). The income statements and extracts from the statements of financial position are as follows:

	2012	**2011**
	£000	**£000**
Revenue	976.9	899.6
Gross profit	377.6	360.9
Various expenses	(102.5)	(98.6)
Operating profit	275.1	262.3
Finance costs	(18.7)	(16.5)
Profit before tax	256.4	245.8
Tax	(77.0)	(74.0)
Profit after tax	179.4	171.8
Share capital	80.0	80.0
Retained earnings	1 465.0	1 285.6
Long-term borrowings	319.0	276.0

Required:
Calculate the following financial ratios for Shirley:

i) gross profit margin
ii) operating profit margin
iii) return on shareholders' equity
iv) return on total capital employed.

Work to one decimal place.
Comment on any apparent changes in business performance between 2011 and 2012.

9.25 Tadcaster Terrier Limited has the following current assets and current liabilities in its statement of financial position at 31 May 2012:

	£
Inventory	88 700
Trade payables	90 450
Trade receivables	85 210
Bank overdraft	16 790

What is the current ratio (working to 2 decimal places) for Tadcaster Terrier Limited?

a) 1.62:1
b) 0.62:1
c) 1.90:1
d) 0.79:1.

9.26 Turnbull Taffy Limited's figures at 31 March 2013 show the following working capital items:

	£
Inventory	67 400
Trade receivables	42 660
Cash at bank	6 050
Trade payables	58 760

The company's finance director is preparing a projected statement of financial position for 31 March 2014 as part of a package of information to be presented to a bank from which the company hopes to obtain a long-term loan.

The finance director estimates that there will be the following changes to working capital between 31 March 2013 and 31 March 2014:

Inventory will decrease by 10%
Trade receivables will decrease by 15%
Cash at bank will increase by 50%
Trade payables will decrease by 5%

Required:

i) Calculate (to two decimal places) the current ratio and the quick ratio at 31 March 2013.

ii) Calculate (to two decimal places) the expected current ratio and quick ratio at 31 March 2014 based on the finance director's estimates.

9.27 Uriah Westwood plc is an advertising agency which operates from rented offices in the West End of London. Ulverstone Thunderbird plc is a company engaged in heavy engineering. It owns all of its plant and equipment and a small factory site in the North of England. Both companies have recently reported revenue in the region of £10 million. The non-current asset turnover ratio for one of the companies is 1.14 and for the other is 10.62.

From the brief descriptions given, which of the two companies is more likely to have the higher non-current asset turnover ratio?

9.28 A sole trader's inventory at 31 December 2011 was £405 000. By 31 December 2012 inventory had increased in value by 10%. Cost of sales for the year ending 31 December 2012 was £1 506 700.

What was the business's inventory turnover in days?

9.29 The following are extracts from the income statements of a sole trader business for the years ending 31 December 2012 and 2011:

	2012	2011
	£000	£000
Opening inventory	1 605.3	1 396.4
Purchases	19 360.4	19 568.9
Closing inventory	(1 565.7)	(1 605.3)
Cost of sales	19 400.0	19 360.0

Calculate the inventory turnover in days for both years. Has it improved or worsened in 2012?

9.30 A company has trade receivables in its year-end statement of financial position of £218 603. Revenue for the year was £1 703 698; 70% of this figure was sales on credit.

What is trade receivables turnover (in days)?

a) 46.8 days
b) 32.7 days
c) 66.9 days
d) 18.3 days.

9.31 Whybird, a sole trader, has been advised by his accountant to keep an eye on the number of days it takes for his trade receivables to be settled. The accountant has explained how to calculate the trade receivables turnover period but Whybird doesn't really understand. He asks you to do the calculation for him. Extracts from the last 2 years' financial statements for Whybird's business show the following figures:

	2012	2011
	£	£
Revenue	180 630	178 440
Less: returns	(1 300)	(1 060)
	179 330	177 380

	2012	2011
	£000	£000
Trade receivables	20 982	21 117
Less: allowance for bad trade receivables	(306)	(297)
	20 676	20 820

Calculate the trade receivables turnover period for Whybird for both years to one decimal place. Has the trade receivables turnover period improved or worsened in 2012?

9.32 Wiswell Limited is a trading company. Its year-end financial statements for 2012 (with comparatives for 2011) included the following relevant details:

	2012	2012	2011	2011
	£	£	£	£
Revenue		1 936 000		1 877 200
Cost of sales				
Opening inventory	145 550		136 200	
Add: purchases	1 042 255		1 025 666	
	1 187 805		1 161 866	
Less: closing inventory	(160 370)		(145 550)	
		(1 027 435)		(1 016 316)
Gross profit		908 565		860 884
Inventory		160 370		145 550
Trade receivables		226 485		209 063
Trade payables		160 479		151 742

Required: calculate the following ratios for both 2012 and 2011:

i) inventory turnover in days

ii) trade receivables turnover in days

iii) trade payables turnover in days.

Comment briefly on the significance of the changes in the ratios.

The following information about Worsley Bacup plc, a quoted company, is relevant to questions 9.33 – 9.36 inclusive.

Extracts from Worsley Bacup's accounts for the year ending 30 September 2012 include the following useful information:

	£000
Operating profit	986.7
Finance costs	(106.0)
Profit before tax	880.7
Tax	(240.0)
Profit after tax	640.7

The company has 2 200 000 shares in issue. The shares have a nominal value of 25p each. During the financial year ended 30 September 2012 a dividend of £250 800 was paid to the company's shareholders. The market price at 30 September 2012 of a share in the company was £7.66.

9.33 What is the dividend per share?

a) 45.6p
b) 11.4p
c) 25.0p
d) 29.1p.

9.34 What is the dividend cover ratio?

a) 3.51
b) 1.55
c) 3.93
d) 2.55.

9.35 What is the earnings per share (in pence)?

a) 17.72p
b) 29.12p
c) 116.49p
d) 70.89p.

9.36 What was Worsley Bacup plc's market capitalization at 30 September 2012?

9.37 Watkinson Chapel plc is a listed company with a market capitalization of £3 430 000 at 31 August 2012. It has in issue 1 000 000 £1 ordinary shares, and profits attributable to ordinary shareholders for the year ending 31 August 2012 were £243 700. What was the company's P/E ratio at 31 August 2012?

a) 21.4
b) 4.1
c) 3.4
d) 14.1.

9.38 Better Belter Limited had the following capital structure at 31 October 2012:

	£
Ordinary share capital (£1 shares)	80 000
Retained earnings	696 400
Long-term borrowings (8% interest rate)	300 000

Profit before interest and tax for the year ending 31 October 2012 was £35 000, and finance costs were £24 000.

Required: calculate the following ratios:

i) gearing (on the basis of debt/equity)

ii) interest cover.

9.39 Refer back to question 9.20 which examined extracts from the financial information of Tesco plc in its 2009 Annual Report. By the time this book is published, Tesco will have produced subsequent Annual Reports. Using those subsequent reports (available from www.tescoplc.com) produce a table showing the key figures over a period of years. Conduct an analysis of the figures, calculating all relevant accounting ratios. Because you will have several years worth of accounting information, you are also able to produce a horizontal analysis (see Chapter 8).

Write a brief report that summarizes your analysis.

(For obvious reasons, there is no model answer to this question.)

ANSWERS TO SELF-TEST QUESTIONS

CHAPTER 11

Answer to self-test question 1.1

a) Setting up a partnership does not involve any particular legal considerations. FALSE
b) A sole trader is liable personally for all losses made by the business. TRUE
c) A director of a company cannot hold shares in that same company. FALSE
d) Partners are responsible in law for the consequences of each other's actions. TRUE

Answer to self-test question 1.2

The correct answer is c. An issue of shares is not an appropriate source of finance for a sole trader.

Answer to self-test question 1.3

The correct answer is a. The profit on the sale of the building is taxed as a capital gain.

Answer to self-test question 1.4

Sole traders, partnerships and smaller limited companies are not required by law to have an audit. Only larger companies have an absolute legal requirement to have their financial statements audited. However, there is nothing to prevent smaller businesses from having an audit.

CHAPTER 12

Answer to self-test question 20.1

i) The principal advantage of grant finance is that it does not normally require repayment. Also, unlike borrowings, there is no interest charge. However, there are usually quite stringent conditions attached to grant finance. If conditions are breached, the grant may even become repayable. Once the grant is given, a period of careful monitoring often follows during which the business is under scrutiny.
ii) The principal advantage of obtaining finance from family or friends is its availability. If other potential sources of finance have proven to be unfruitful, this type of finance may be the only feasible way to start the business. It may be interest-free and with no fixed repayment date. However, there may be significant drawbacks, too. If the business fails, the unhappy entrepreneur may not be able to repay amounts borrowed, and relationships are likely to suffer as a result.

Answer to self-test question 20.2

Venture capital financing is typically provided for growing businesses, usually for the medium- to long-term (periods of, say, 5 to 10 years). The venture capital firm, funded by institutional investors and wealthy individuals, provides finance and takes an equity stake in the business. Usually, there is some element of active involvement in management of the business. At the end of the agreed period of financing, the venture capital firm will sell its stake in the business. If the arrangement has been successful, the sale will be at a substantial profit.

Answer to self-test question 20.3

1 All takeover bids are hostile bids – FALSE
2 A rights issue is an offer to sell shares to existing shareholders in proportion to their existing holdings – TRUE
3 An offer for sale of shares is limited to a few major financial institutions – FALSE
4 The London stock exchange trades in corporate bonds, as well as shares – TRUE

CHAPTER 13

Answer to self-test question 8.1

Horizontal trend analysis: Jamal's sales 2004 – 2012

Year	£	Percentage increase (decrease) on previous year
2004	250 031	–
2005	347 266	38.9
2006	441 179	27.0
2007	531 150	20.4
2008	523 622	(1.4)
2009	545 331	4.1
2010	590 942	8.4
2011	679 244	14.9
2012	771 485	13.6

Since the start of the business sales have increased each year, apart from 2008 when there was a small drop. Jared claimed at interview that he would be able to increase sales by 15% each year, but it is only in 2011 and 2012 that the increase has approached 15%. The early years of the business were characterized by very rapid sales growth, but this had clearly stopped by the time Jared was appointed. It is possible that Jared has made a major contribution to the improvements in sales, but the figures alone do not prove this conclusively.

Jamal's decision on Jared's salary increase will depend on the answers to some of the following:

- To what extent has Jared been responsible for the recent improvements in sales trends?
- Are there other market factors at work (for example, has demand in the market for pre-packaged foods strengthened)?
- Has Jamal set performance targets for Jared, and have these been met?

Answer to self-test question 8.2

a) the increase in the revenue figures for the companies are:

$$\text{Barnes \& Jack Limited} = \frac{(2\,044\,032 - 1\,743\,906)}{1\,743\,906} \times 100 = 17.2\%$$

$$\text{Carleen Baker Limited} = \frac{(1\,850\,490 - 1\,564\,774)}{1\,564\,774} \times 100 = 18.3\%$$

Carleen Baker's revenue growth is slightly higher.

b) The additional information allows for a more detailed breakdown of Barnes & Jack Limited's revenue, as follows:

Barnes & Jack Limited

	2012	2011	Percentage change
	£	£	%
Domestic and shop market	1 555 725	1 293 106	20.3
Zoos	488 307	450 800	8.3
	2 044 032	1 743 906	17.2

From this analysis, it appears that Barnes & Jack Limited have done slightly better in terms of revenue growth than Carleen Baker Limited, in the areas of their business that are directly comparable.

CHAPTER 14

Answer to self-test question 3.1

Jules

Trading account for the month ended 31 December 2012

Revenue: 66 bags @ £23	1 518
Cost of sales: 66 bags @ £14.50	957
Gross profit	561

Note: the heading specifying the name of the business and the period covered by the trading account is essential information and must not be omitted.

Answer to self-test question 3.2

Jules (continued)

Jules: Inventory movement account for January 2013

	Units	£
Opening inventory: 36 bags @ £14.50	36	522
Add purchases: 68 bags @ £14.50	68	986
Less: items of inventory sold: 42 bags @ £14.50	(42)	(609)
Closing inventory: 62 bags @ £14.50	62	899

Note that this account is part of Jules's business records. It is not shown in his financial statements.

Jules: Trading account for the month ended 31 January 2013

	Units	£	£
Revenue			
42 bags @ £23	42		966
Cost of sales			
Opening inventory: 36 bags @ £14.50	36	522	
Add: purchases: 68 bags @ £14.50	68	986	
	104	1 508	
Less: closing inventory: 62 bags @ £14.50	(62)	(899)	
Cost of sales: 42 bags @ £14.50	42		609
Gross profit for month*			357

*Check: each bag sold gives a gross profit of £23 − £14.50 = £8.50. If Jules sells 42 bags he expects to make a profit of 42 × £8.50 = £357.

CHAPTER 15

Answer to self-test question 2.1

George

Bank overdraft = Liability
Computer and printers used to keep the administrative records of the business = Asset
Plates and cups in the stockroom = Asset
Cash float kept in the till – £100 in various notes and coins = Asset
Loan of £20 000 from George's brother = Liability

Answer to self-test question 2.2

1 The total of assets in Saqib's business is £30 000 (Non-current assets) + £5000 (Inventory) + £4000 (Trade receivables) + £3000 (Cash held in business bank account) = £42 000.
2 There is only one category of liability in the business: trade payables of £6000. Therefore total liabilities are £6000.
3 Saqib's capital is stated in the question as £36 000.
4 Applying the accounting equation to Saqib's business: Assets (£42 000) = Capital (£36 000) + Liabilities (£6000).

Answer to self-test question 2.3

Assets – Liabilities = Capital
Therefore, Amy's capital can be calculated as: £58 000 – £30 000 = £28 000.

CHAPTER 16

Answer to self-test question 6.1

Transaction	Impact on cash	Impact on profits
Purchase of inventory for cash for £1800.	Cash is immediately reduced by £1800.	No immediate effect on profit. A sale of the inventory items will probably take place in due course. When that happens the cost of inventory sold is set off against revenue in the form of cost of sales.
Sale of old delivery van for £360.	Cash is immediately increased by £360.	A profit or loss on sale (see Chapter 5) will be calculated by setting off the proceeds of sale (£360) against the carrying amount of the asset. The effect on profit would be an increase of £360 only if the carrying amount of the asset at the date of sale was nil.
Long-term loan from brother of £5000.	Cash and long-term liabilities are both immediately increased by £5000.	The loan itself has no effect on profit. Any interest paid on the loan will reduce profits.

Transaction	Impact on cash	Impact on profits
Payment of interest of £150 on bank overdraft.	Cash is reduced by £150 (or, more likely, the overdraft is increased by £150).	The interest paid reduces profits.

Amortization charge of £8000 relating to patent rights.	No effect on cash.	Profits are reduced by £8000.

Answer to self-test question 6.2

	Income statement	Non-cash item - depreciation	Non-cash items - trade receivables and trade payables	Cash outflow - Inventory purchase	Total cash inflow (outflow)
	£	£	£	£	£
Revenue	89 300		(8 500)		80 800
Operating costs*	(78 800)	4 500	9 000	(6 900)	(72 200
Operating profit/cash flow	10 500	4 500	500	(6 900)	8 600
Interest paid	(1 000)				(1 000)
Net profit/cash flow	9 500	4 500	500	(6 900)	7 600

*Operating costs = cost of sales (£56 200) + operating costs (£22 600) = £78 800.

Amy Binyon: Statement of cash flows for the year ended 31 December 2012

	£	£
Cash flows from operating activities		
Operating profit		10 500
Depreciation		4 500
		15 000
Less: increase in inventory	(6 900)	
Less: increase in trade receivables	(8 500)	
Add: increase in trade payables	9 000	
		(6 400)
Cash generated from operations		8 600
Interest paid		(1 000)
Net cash inflow from operating activities		7 600

Answer to self-test question 6.3

	Income statement	Non-cash items - depreciation	Non-cash items - trade receivables and trade payables	Cash outflow - Inventory purchase	Total cash inflow (outflow)
	£	£	£	£	£
Revenue	109 300		(200)		109 100
Operating costs total*	(86 500)	5 000	700	(700)	(81 500)
Operating profit/cash flow	22 800	5 000	500	(700)	27 600

*operating costs total = cost of sales + operating expenses (£62 700 + 23 800 = £86 500)

Inventory: there has been an increase in inventory between the two year-ends: £7600 − 6900 = £700. This difference is the total additional cash outflow for the accounting period.

Trade receivables: the amount of cash received in respect of sales revenue in the period is:

	£
Opening trade receivables	8 500
Revenue	109 300
Less: closing trade receivables	(8 700)
Cash received	109 100

The adjustment for non-cash items is the difference between the closing and opening balances: £8700 − 8500 = £200, i.e. an increase in trade receivables.

Trade payables: The amount of cash paid in respect of operating costs and expenses in the period is:

	£
Opening trade payables	9 000
Operating costs total	86 500
Less: closing trade payables	(9 700)
	85 800

The adjustment for non-cash items is the difference between the closing and opening balances: £9700 − 9000 = £700, i.e. an increase in trade payables.

Amy Binyon: Statement of cash flows for the year ended 31 December 2013

	£	£
Cash flows from operating activities		
Operating profit		22 800
Depreciation		5 000
		27 800
Less: increase in inventory	(700)	
Less: increase in trade receivables	(200)	
Add: increase in trade payables	700	
		(200)
Cash generated from operations		27 600

CHAPTER 17

Answer to self-test question 7.1

Since 2005 all listed companies in the European Union are obliged to comply with international accounting standards; this, of course, includes UK listed companies. The Companies Act 2006 allows other companies (unlisted) a choice between setting out their financial statements in a UK format (and by implication complying with UK accounting standards) or using international accounting formats and standards.

Answer to self-test question 7.2

Workings

1 Selling and distribution costs

	£
Selling costs	63 477
Distribution costs	54 460
	117 937

2 Tangible non-current assets: property, plant and equipment

Premises at carrying amount	65 700
Vehicles at carrying amount	44 430
Fixtures and fittings at carrying amount	17 260
	127 390

Uppingham Telephones Limited: Draft income statement for the year ending 31 March 2012

	£
Revenue	717 216
Cost of sales	(509 582)
Gross profit	207 634
Selling and distribution costs (working 1)	(117 937)
Administrative expenses	(24 512)
Profit before tax	65 185
Tax on profit	(19 500)
Profit for the year	45 685

Uppingham Telephones Limited: Draft statement of changes in equity for the year ended 31 March 2012

	Share capital £	Retained earnings £	Total equity £
At 1 April 2011	20 000	161 479	181 479
Profit for the year		45 685	45 685
Dividend		(5 000)	(5 000)
At 31 March 2012	20 000	202 164	222 164

Uppingham Telephones Limited: Draft statement of financial position at 31 March 2012

ASSETS		
Non-current assets		
Intangible assets		30 866
Property, plant and equipment		127 390
		158 256
Current assets		
Inventories	42 370	
Trade receivables	82 026	
Cash at bank	13 222	
		137 618
		295 874

CAPITAL AND LIABILITIES		
Equity		
Share capital		20 000
Retained earnings		202 164
		222 164
Long-term liabilities		
Loan		15 000
Current liabilities		
Trade payables	39 210	
Other payables: taxation	19 500	
		58 710
		295 874

CHAPTER 18

Answer to self-test question 9.1

Augustus Algernon Limited

$$\text{Pre-tax ROE (return on equity)} = \frac{\text{Profit before taxation and after interest}}{\text{Equity (i.e. share capital and retained earnings)}}$$
$$= \frac{162}{120 + 1\,000} \times 100$$
$$= \underline{14.46\%}$$

$$\text{Post-tax ROE (return on equity)} = \frac{\text{Profit after taxation}}{\text{Equity}}$$
$$= \frac{114}{120 + 1\,000} \times 100$$
$$= \underline{10.18\%}$$

$$\text{ROCE (return on total capital invested)} = \frac{\text{Profit before interest and tax}}{\text{Equity} + \text{long-term borrowings}}$$
$$= \frac{186}{120 + 1\,000 + 480} \times 100$$
$$= \underline{11.63\%}$$

Answer to self-test question 9.2

Arbus Nugent Limited

$$\text{Current ratio} = \frac{\text{Current assets}}{\text{Current liabilities}}$$

$$\text{Quick ratio} = \frac{\text{Current assets} - \text{inventory}}{\text{Current liabilities}}$$

For Arbus Nugent Limited for 2012 and 2011:

	2012	2011
Current ratio	$\frac{87\ 620}{31\ 450}:1 = 2.8:1$	$\frac{74\ 850}{32\ 970}:1 = 2.3:1$
Quick ratio	$\frac{87\ 620 - 34\ 300}{31\ 450}:1 = 1.7.1$	$\frac{74\ 850 - 31\ 600}{32\ 970}:1 = 1.3:1$

Both the current ratio and the quick ratio have improved.

Answer to self-test question 9.3

Armitage Horobin Limited

	2012	2011
Non-current asset turnover	$\frac{\text{Revenue}}{\text{Non-current assets}}$	
	$\frac{283.4}{289.2} = 0.98$	$\frac{271.1}{275.3} = 0.98$
Inventory turnover	a) $\frac{\text{Cost of sales}}{\text{Average inventory}}$	
	Average inventory = $\frac{23.7 + 25.9}{2} = 24.8$	Average inventory = $\frac{21.2 + 23.7}{2} = 22.5$
	$\frac{\text{Cost of sales}}{\text{Average inventory}}$	
	$\frac{182.6}{24.8} = 7.36$	$\frac{175.0}{22.5} = 7.77$
	b) Inventory turnover in days = $\frac{\text{Average inventory}}{\text{Cost of sales}} \times 365$	
	$\frac{24.8}{182.6} \times 365 = 49.6$ days	$\frac{22.5}{175.0} \times 365 = 46.9$ days
Trade receivables turnover	$\frac{\text{Trade receivables}}{\text{Sales on credit}} \times 365$	
	$\frac{33.0}{283.4} \times 365 = 42.5$ days	$\frac{28.2}{271.1} \times 365 = 38.0$ days
Trade payables turnover	$\frac{\text{Trade payables}}{\text{Purchases}} \times 365$	
	$\frac{24.5}{184.8} \times 365 = 48.4$ days	$\frac{20.6}{177.5} \times 365 = 42.4$ days

Non-current assets turnover has hardly changed. Inventory turnover has worsened, in that inventory is now held on the premises for an average of 49.6 days compared with 46.9 days in the previous year. Trade receivables turnover has worsened in that it is now taking trade receivables, on average, 42.5 days to pay, compared with 38 days in the previous year. Trade payables turnover has improved, in that Armitage Horobin is taking advantage of the interest free credit offered by trade payables to a greater extent than in the previous year. However, 48.4 days may be regarded as too long a period to wait, on average, for payment, and there may be a loss of goodwill on the part of trade payables towards the company.

Tutorial note: average inventory has been used in the calculations because there was sufficient data available. In the case of trade receivables and trade payables there was insufficient data, and so closing trade receivables and trade payables have been used in the calculations. Although, ideally, averages should be used in the calculations it is often not possible to obtain them.

Answer to self-test question 9.4

Armley Regina Limited

$$\text{Dividend per share} = \frac{220\,000}{1\,000\,000} = 22\text{p per share}$$

$$\text{Dividend cover} = \frac{680\,000}{220\,000} = 3.09 \text{ times}$$

$$\text{Earnings per share (eps)} = \frac{680\,000}{1\,000\,000} = 68\text{p per share}$$

$$\text{Price/earnings (P/E) ratio} = \frac{508\text{p}}{68\text{p}} = 7.5$$

Market capitalization = £5.08 × 1 000 000 shares = £5 080 000

ANSWERS TO EXERCISES

CHAPTER 11

1.1 The only correct statement is c): the sole trader is entirely responsible for the management of the business.

1.2 The only correct statement is d): partners are personally liable for the debts of the business.

1.3 The only correct statement is a): a limited company is a separate person in law.

1.4 The most appropriate form of finance for purchasing a new office building, out of those listed, is a 10 year mortgage loan. The correct answer, therefore, is a).

1.5 The most appropriate form of finance for the new office photocopier, out of those listed, is a lease. The correct answer, therefore, is c).

1.6 Advice to Arnold Tapwood

It is not difficult to set up in partnership. By contrast with the establishment of a limited company, there is no requirement to submit information to the authorities. However, the partners would be well advised to consider drawing up a partnership agreement, for which they would require legal advice. Although the provisions of the Partnership Act 1890 apply where there is no partnership agreement, in most circumstances it is preferable to have a formal agreement. This would cover areas such as profit sharing and arrangements in the event of a dispute between the partners.

1.7 Geoffrey will probably find it difficult to finance this business start-up because of its risky nature. He appears to be quite sure that lots of people will want to pay a subscription to his website, but he appears to have nothing but optimism to support this view. It is highly unlikely that a bank would be at all interested in making a loan in the circumstances.

Geoffrey has no existing resources to draw upon and his family have refused to put money into the business. It is remotely possible that grant finance might be available from a specialist organization, and Geoffrey should explore every remote possibility for grant aid.

Another possibility is to join forces in partnership with another dangerous sports enthusiast who does have some resources to draw upon.

This appears to be a business proposition which will be very difficult to finance. If Geoffrey cannot find a business partner who is prepared to put some money into the venture, he may have to shelve the idea for the time being. If he gets a job, pays off his debts and saves some cash he might be able to finance the start-up himself at some point in the future.

1.8 The only correct statement is d): a sole trader must submit a tax return annually.

1.9 The only correct statement is b): partnerships must prepare annual financial statements as the basis for the calculation of tax.

1.10 The only correct statement is b): a limited company must send annual accounts to all of its shareholders.

1.11 Podgorny & Weaver Limited

List of amounts owed by retail businesses: the directors would be able to see if any of the retailers owed very large amounts. If the list also contained details of the length of time the amounts had been outstanding, the directors would also be able to see if the amounts owing were significantly overdue for payment.

Summary of the value of goods held in inventory: it is important for a fashion goods business not to carry excessive inventories of goods which may be about to go out of fashion. The business will lose money if the inventory cannot be sold. The directors need this statement to assess the risk of having excess inventories.

Summary of the value of orders received in the last month: the directors need to assess whether the orders received meet their expectations. If the value of orders received is less than expected, the directors need to take action to address the problem.

Income statement for the last month: the directors will be able to assess the performance of the business compared to their expectations, and perhaps, compared to the same month in the previous financial year.

1.12 Burnip Chemicals plc

The activist group would probably be looking for the following type of information:

i) details about the amounts of emissions
ii) details of the amounts which the company has paid in fines
iii) details of plans for improvements to the factory which will minimize the emission of toxic waste.

A company's financial statements principally contain information about the financial performance and condition of the business. Details about the amounts of emissions during the year are not financial items, and it is quite possible that the company would make no reference to the matter.

The amount of fines paid might be evident from the financial statements. However, the expenses listed in the income statement are summarized information (it would not be feasible to list each individual payment), and the amount paid in fines might well not be evident.

Details of planned improvements, similarly, may not be evident from the financial statements.

Although annual financial statements can be of interest to activist groups, they do not necessarily provide a full picture.

Tutorial note: some companies voluntarily publish information about their environmental policies and performance in addition to their financial statements, but they are not obliged by law to do this.

CHAPTER 12

20.1 Erika

The main points for the business plan, and the related questions, are as follows:

Description of the service to be offered

Is the service highly specialized, or is it a more general design service? For example, the design services offered may be principally focused on, say, company identity and logo designs, or alternatively upon graphic design input into advertising material. Or, Erika may be planning to cover a broad range of services, depending upon her talents and interests.

Market for the service

- Who will be the principal customers for the services offered?
- Has Erika investigated the market by carrying out any market research?
- Who are the principal competitors? Are they well established?
- How difficult will it be to break into the market for design services?

Profile of Erika

This will include training and education, relevant experience, age, an analysis of personal strengths and weaknesses, and a current portfolio of her best work.

- Does Erika have the appropriate profile of experience for the work she is planning to do?
- Is her portfolio up to date and does it contain examples of the type of work she will be undertaking to provide as a self-employed designer?

Initial investment required

This will be a particularly important section if Erika is planning to borrow money. Has she prepared a plan of her expenditure and income in the first year to 18 months following her business start-up? Relevant expenditure will probably include the following:

- office rental and business rates
- utitlities bills (water, electricity, telephone)
- advertising and marketing
- office equipment and computer
- insurance.

Also, how will Erika support herself in the early months of her new business? In this type of business, Erika will need to find the work, do it, submit it and then invoice the client. Under normal commercial arrangements payment will follow about a month later. So, there is a time lag of up to several months between initially being commissioned for the work and finally receiving payment. In the meantime, Erika needs to live off something, and this element must be built into her initial plans.

Detailed financial projections

If Erika is looking for business start-up finance she will need to prepare detailed financial projections in the form of a budget, showing the projected profit (or loss) and cash flow in the business. Once the business starts she will need to keep business accounting records and submit tax returns. She may need to register for VAT.

- Does Erika have financial management or accountancy skills?
- Will she need an accountant to provide accountancy and tax advice?

Other issues

Will any other professional services be required in the first year or so of the business? For example, Erika may need legal advice in negotiating a lease on the office. Is Erika planning to employ any staff?

20.2 Ben

There are several risks attached to Ben's business start up plan:

Risk of not obtaining work

Although Ben has a good contact list, all his contacts have been made through Amis & Lovett, his employers. Much will depend on whether or not any of Amis & Lovett's existing clients will give their work to Ben's agency. If their relationship with Amis & Lovett is good, and they are satisfied with the work, they may be quite happy to stay with the larger agency. Ben is taking a big risk.

Risk of running out of money

Even if the work does follow Ben, the nature of the type of service he offers means that he will not start receiving payment for his work for quite some time. He has £45 000 which sounds like a lot, but this may not keep him going for very long. If he has not already done so, he needs to make a realistic plan so that he can budget for the first year or so of his new business.

Risk of employing people

Ben is taking a risk by employing people straight away. He may not have enough work to justify employing anybody in the early months of the business. His employees will expect to be paid at the end of the month, whether or not Ben has much work. He would probably be well advised to get the work first, and only then employ staff.

20.3 Nancy

As regards costs, because there is sufficient space for another person to work on the premises, there will be no significant incremental cost involved. There will be a small additional cost in consumables such as hair products and electricity, but the main cost will be in paying the salary of the new stylist, plus any additional administrative costs. Nancy already employs one person, so presumably she or her accountant already operates a payroll system that makes sure that the employee and HMRC are paid the correct amount. There are two main risks:

1. That there will not be sufficient business to keep the new stylist busy. Employing another person does not make financial sense unless the new employee can generate enough additional business to cover the costs of employing him or her.
2. That the new stylist will prove to be unsatisfactory in some way. Perhaps there will be personality clashes with Nancy or the customers, or perhaps he or she will not produce work of sufficient competence. An employee who turns up late, or not at all, or who is unpleasant to clients will create problems.

There could be two additional benefits for Nancy and her business:

1. Additional profits could be generated that would increase Nancy's wealth. She could either draw down more money from the business or could invest the profits in further expansion, perhaps by moving to larger premises and employing more staff.
2. The range of services offered could be expanded and improved.

20.4 Oleander Enterprises Limited

i) Advantages and drawbacks of buying into another business

Buying into another company may be advantageous because Libby and Lisa will be buying up an established business with employees who have knowledge of holiday operations in Turkey. They will not need to start from scratch in finding out about a new country. However, Oxus Orlando is, essentially, a service business which is very dependent upon the quality of its employees. Loretta, the main director, plans to retire, so her expertise will be lost. If the key employees also choose to leave, there may not be much value left in the company, and Libby and Lisa may find that they have paid too much for the investment.

ii) Information needed.

Libby and Lisa need to know:

- The price of the investment in Oxus Orlando, which Lorretta wishes to sell.
- What they would get in exchange for the investment (for example, does the business own its own premises)?
- How profitable Oxus Orlando is (they will be able to ascertain this information from the business's annual financial statements).

- Details about the employees of the business. How much are they paid, how long have they been in their current jobs and how likely is it that they will stay if the company changes ownership?

20.5 Ashton Longton

The company has 8 000 000 shares in issue, each valued at £3.85. Market capitalization is 8 000 000 × £3.85 = £30 800 000.

20.6 The correct answer is a. The Alternative Investment Market is a market for companies that do not currently wish to proceed to full listing.

20.7 Warminster Toys

The rights issue give the holder of 50 000 shares the right to buy 50 000/5 shares = 10 000 shares. Each new share costs £5.42, so the total amount payable to take up the rights is: 10 000 × £5.42 = £54 200. The correct answer is c.

20.8 Brighton Bestwines plc

Potential drawbacks of listing on the Alternative Investment Market include:

1. Additional regulation applies to listed companies, for example, they have to produce additional financial reports. The additional compliance often requires the employment of more staff.
2. There will be legal and other professional fees incurred in listing. These are likely to be around 10% or more of the total amount raised, which means that for every share sold at the target price of £2.50, at least 25p will be spent on fees.
3. Many directors are uncomfortable with the additional attention paid to listed companies by the media. They may incur additional costs in obtaining professional public relations advice.
4. The company's share price may fluctuate for reasons that are unconnected to the fortunes of the company.
5. There is a potential drawback in allowing other parties to buy shares in that the company may lay itself open to takeover bids. However, in this case the shares issued for sale will amount to only one-third of the total, so the company will be safe from the threat of takeover.

20.9 Speke Septima Limited

The principal drawback in the proposed arrangement is the risk that the relationship between the venture capital firm will not work out well. Much will depend upon the person who is appointed to the board by the venture capital firm. If he or she brings the right mix of skills and personality to the business, the arrangement could be very successful, but the relationship could turn out to be problematic. A related problem is that the existing directors may resent the loss of complete control over the activities of the business.

CHAPTER 13

8.1 Ronald's percentage increase in revenue:

$$\frac{110\,450 - 95\,544}{95\,544} \times 100 = 15.6\%$$

His increase in revenue is, therefore, higher than average.
Ronald's percentage increase in gross profit:

$$\frac{38\,392 - 33\,469}{33\,469} \times 100 = 14.7\%$$

His increase in gross profit is, therefore, lower than average.
The correct answer, therefore, is a)

8.2 Horizontal analysis of Rory's income statement data shows the following percentage changes:
Percentage increases over previous year:

	2012	2011	2010
	%	%	%
Revenue	4.2	3.6	3.0
Gross profit	3.3	3.4	3.5

Revenue growth percentage is gradually increasing.
Gross profit growth percentage is gradually decreasing.
The correct answer, therefore, is c)

8.3 Horizontal analysis of selected items from Larsen Locations Limited's income statement 2010 to 2012

	2012	2011	2010
	%	%	%
Sales of services	0.5	5.4	0.1
Administrative expenses	20.1	8.5	0.9
Operating profit	(10.1)	5.8	1.0

Larsen Locations has experienced more volatile change in revenue, administrative expenses and operating profit than The Wilton Group plc. Sales in 2011 increased by a greater amount than Wilton's sales, but there was a negligible rate of sales growth in 2010 and 2012. However, the most obvious difference is in the greatly increased level of administrative expenses in Larsen Locations 2012 accounts. Presumably this increase arises because of the move to larger premises and taking on more staff. The increase in costs in 2012 does not appear, as yet, to have produced a similar level of increase in sales. The higher costs appear to have resulted in a lower level of operating profit – a 10.1% decrease in 2012 compared to the previous year.

8.4 **Vertical analysis: Chapter Protection Limited's income statement for the year ending 31 December 2012**

	£	%
Revenue	188 703	100.0
Cost of sales	(115 863)	(61.4)
Gross profit	72 840	38.6
Administrative expenses	(14 260)	(7.6)
Distribution and selling costs	(20 180)	(10.7)
Operating profit	38 400	20.3
Finance costs	(1 200)	(0.6)
Profit before tax	37 200	19.7
Tax	(7 450)	(3.9)
Profit after tax	29 750	15.8

8.5 Causeway Ferguson plc: horizontal trend analysis of income statements – 2008 –2012

Percentage changes over previous year

	2012	2011	2010	2009
	%	%	%	%
Revenue	(2.6)	(0.3)	9.4	3.6
Cost of sales	(2.5)	–	11.0	4.5
Gross profit	(2.8)	(0.8)	7.2	2.3
Administrative expenses	4.0	0.2	4.3	1.8
Selling and distribution costs	4.2	1.2	0.3	1.1
Profit before tax	(25.8)	(5.6)	25.6	5.5
Tax	(25.7)	(5.6)	25.8	5.4
Profit after tax	(25.8)	(5.5)	25.5	5.6

Causeway Ferguson plc: common size analysis of income statements – 2008 – 2012

	2012	2011	2010	2009	2008
	%	%	%	%	%
Revenue	100.0	100.0	100.0	100.0	100.0
Cost of sales	(60.7)	(60.6)	(60.4)	(59.5)	(59.0)
Gross profit	39.3	39.4	39.6	40.5	41.0
Administrative expenses	(16.5)	(15.5)	(15.4)	(16.2)	(16.4)
Selling and distribution costs	(15.8)	(14.7)	(14.5)	(15.9)	(16.3)
Profit before tax	7.0	9.2	9.7	8.4	8.3
Tax	(2.1)	(2.8)	(2.9)	(2.5)	(2.5)
Profit after tax	4.9	6.4	6.8	5.9	5.8

Commentary

The following key features emerge from the horizontal and the common size analysis:

1. In each of the 5 years from 2008 to 2012 there has been a fall in the gross profit percentage. The falls from year to year are not dramatic but decline gradually.
2. There was some growth in revenue until 2010. The last 2 years show decreases. The decline in revenue together with the steady decline in gross profit margin suggest that the company has some problems to address.
3. Administrative expenses and selling and distribution costs have increased each year. Usually the increases are small, but they represent significant amounts over a 5 year period. In 2012 both categories of cost increased by over 4%, and contribute significantly to the overall substantial drop in operating profit for the year.

4 While it might be premature to announce the 'withering away' of the company, some aspects of its performance would cause concern to a shareholder. The fact that there are new competitors in the market would explain the declining revenue performance of the last 2 years. The gradual decline in gross margin, however, goes right back to the beginning of the 5 year period and could not be completely attributable to competitive effects if the competitors have emerged only recently.

8.6 Report on Marks & Spencer plc's 5 year trading record extracts – 2005 to 2009

The business has achieved very good sales growth, especially in the international sector, except for the UK retail sector in 2009 where there has been a small drop in revenue between 2008 and 2009. This is almost certainly attributable to difficult trading conditions during the recession. However, strong revenue growth internationally has meant that, overall, there was a slight increase in revenue for the 2009 financial year compared to 2008.

Although international sales account for a relatively small part of overall revenue, the proportion has been growing since 2005, and by 2009 international revenue accounted for almost 10% of the business. As this sector tends to be more profitable, further increases in international revenue in the future could be very beneficial to the business.

Turning to operating profit as a percentage of revenue, we can see that there was a very significant downturn in profitability in 2009. Although revenue fell by only a small percentage in the UK (1.7%) the decrease in profitability (31.1%) was much higher, which may indicate that the business had to cut prices in order to maintain market share. Profitability had grown strongly in the years 2005 to 2008, and it may be that the 2009 drop was a temporary effect of the recession in the UK.

Appendix

Percentages of total: UK retail and international retail

	2009	2008	2007	2006	2005
	%	%	%	%	%
Revenue:					
UK retail	90.1	92.1	92.9	93.3	93.9
International retail	9.9	7.9	7.1	6.7	6.1
Total	100.0	100.0	100.0	100.0	100.0
Operating profit					
UK retail	86.7	90.5	91.5	92.3	88.3
International retail	13.3	9.5	8.5	7.7	11.7
Total	100.0	100.0	100.0	100.0	100.0

Operating profit as a percentage of revenue

	2009	2008	2007	2006	2005
	%	%	%	%	%
UK retail	9.2	13.2	12.0	10.8	7.5
International retail	12.9	16.2	14.6	12.6	15.4
Total	9.6	13.4	12.2	10.9	8.0

Percentage increase (decrease) from previous year

	2009	2008	2007	2006
	%	%	%	%
Revenue				
UK retail	(1.7)	4.2	9.7	3.4
International retail	25.9	16.8	16.8	14.7
Total	0.4	5.1	10.1	4.1
Operating profit				
UK retail	(31.1)	14.6	22.0	48.6
International retail	0	29.4	36.0	(6.4)
Total	(28.1)	15.8	23.0	42.1

CHAPTER 14

3.1 i) Jackie has purchased 47 sets during June (i.e. answer b)
Explanation:

	No of sets
Opening inventory	30
Add: purchases (missing figure)	X
Less: closing inventory	(42)
= Sets sold in June	35

The missing figure is 47

ii) Jackie's cost of sales is £2625 (i.e. answer c)
Explanation:

	No of sets	£
Cost of sales:		
Opening inventory at 1 June 2012	30	2 250
Add: purchases during month	47	3 525
	77	5 775
Less: closing inventory at 30 June 2012	(42)	(3 150)
	35	2 625

An even easier calculation is to take the number of sets sold (35) and multiply by the cost price (£75). This gives the answer of £2625.

iii) Jackie's gross profit for the month of June is £1995 (i.e. answer d)
Explanation:

	£
Revenue (£132 × 35 sets)	4 620
Less: cost of sales (see answer 7.1 ii)	2 625
Gross profit	1 995

Another way of calculating this is to work out the gross profit on one set (£132 − £75 = £57) and multiply it by the number of sets sold (£57 × 35 = £1 995)

3.2 The revenue raised through selling the special purchase trainers is as follows:

	£
750 pairs @ £15.50 per pair	11 625
200 pairs @ £12.50 per pair	2 500
50 pairs @ £5 per pair	250
Total revenue	14 375

The cost of sales was the purchase price of £8 500. There is no opening or closing inventory. Gross profit is therefore: £14 375 − £8 500 = £5 875.
If Jay had managed to sell 1 000 pairs at £15.50 the revenue would have been £15 500.
£15 500 less the cost of sales figure of £8 500 = £7 000.

3.3 We can construct Jake's trading account and use it to find the value of the missing figure of opening inventory.

First we put in the total value for revenue, and for gross profit. The difference between these two is cost of sales, i.e. £340 000 − £140 000 = £200 000.

Then we can work in reverse order through the cost of sales calculation. Because closing inventory is £17 400 the total value of opening inventory + purchases must be £217 400 (i.e. we deduct closing inventory of £17 400 to get cost of sales of £200 000).

If the total value of opening inventory + purchases is £217 400 and we know that purchases for the year = £197 300, then opening inventory is the difference between these two figures:

£217 400 − £197 300 = £20 100.

The missing figure (x) is £20 100.

Jake: Trading account for the year

	£	£
Revenue: 8000 units @ £42.50		340 000
Cost of sales:		
Opening inventory – missing figure	20 100	
Add: purchases	197 300	
	217 400	
Less: closing inventory	(17 400)	
		(200 000)
Gross profit: 8000 units @ £17.50		140 000

3.4 **Jethro: Trading accounts for October, November and December 2012**

	October	November	December
	£	£	£
Revenue	39 370	48 998	56 306
Cost of sales:			
Opening inventory	30 863	43 258	53 190
Add: purchases	37 085	40 830	6 250
Less: Closing inventory	(43 258)	(53 190)	(23 980)
	24 690	30 898	35 460
Gross profit	14 680	18 100	20 846

3.5 Leon's trading results are as follows for the 2 years under review:

	2012	2011
	£	£
Revenue	295 993	287 300
Cost of sales	(242 085)	(235 920)
Gross profit	53 908	51 380

i) Gross profit margin in 2012 $= \frac{£53\,908}{£295\,993} \times 100 = 18.2\%$

Gross profit margin in 2011 $= \frac{£51\,380}{£287\,300} \times 100 = 17.9\%$

ii) The amount of the increase in revenue is £295 993 – £287 300 = £8 693

iii) The percentage increase in revenue is: $\frac{£8\,693}{£287\,300} \times 100 = 3\%$

iv) The amount of the increase in gross profit is £53 908 – £51 380 = £2 528

v) The percentage increase in gross profit is: $\frac{£2\,528}{£51\,380} \times 100 = 4.9\%$

3.6 The table shows the gross and net profit margins for Louis's business for 3 years:

	2012	2011	2010
	£	£	£
Gross profit margin	$\frac{£77\,402}{£291\,318} \times 100$ = **26.6%**	$\frac{£75\,980}{£282\,400} \times 100$ = **26.9%**	$\frac{£73\,269}{£269\,340} \times 100$ = **27.2%**
Net profit margin	$\frac{£25\,008}{£291\,318} \times 100$ = **8.6%**	$\frac{£24\,260}{£282\,400} \times 100$ = **8.6%**	$\frac{£23\,999}{£269\,340} \times 100$ = **8.9%**

Louis's revenue figures have increased in each of the 3 years, as have gross profit and net profit. However, the gross and net profit margins have fallen. Gross profit margin has declined from 27.2% in 2010 to 26.6% in 2012. Net profit margin is stable in the latest 2 years, but has declined from 8.9% in 2010.

3.7 **Madigan & Co: Income statement for the year ending 31 March 2012**

	£	£
Fees from clients		95 311
Expenses		
Salaries: assistant	19 300	
Secretary	11 150	
Office rental	10 310	
Office service charge	3 790	
Insurance	794	

	£	£
PII	1 250	
Subscriptions etc	952	
Business travel	1 863	
Entertainment	342	
Telephone	1 103	
Other administration expenses	1 575	
Stationery	761	
Sundry expenses	715	
Charitable donations	120	
		(54 025)
Net profit		41 286

3.8 Norbert

Working: categorising the items

	£	Category
Delivery vehicle	5 020	Statement of financial position: non-current assets
Revenue for the year	351 777	Trading account
Staff costs: storeman's wages	12 090	Income statement
Electricity	2 821	Income statement
Cash at bank	3 444	Statement of financial position: current assets
Capital at 1 April 2011	18 011	Statement of financial position: capital
Administrative costs	3 810	Income statement
Opening inventory at 1 April 2011	20 762	Trading account
Non-current assets in warehouse and office	3 900	Statement of financial position: non-current assets
Drawings	25 219	Statement of financial position: capital
Sundry expenses	1 406	Income statement
Warehouse and office rental	10 509	Income statement
Insurance	3 909	Income statement
Trade receivables	36 623	Statement of financial position: current assets
Water rates	1 226	Income statement
Security services charge	2 937	Income statement
Purchases	255 255	Trading account
Bank charges	398	Income statement
Trade payables	31 950	Statement of financial position: current liabilities
Delivery expenses	8 630	Income statement
Part-time admin assistant's wages	3 779	Income statement
Closing inventory	22 446	Trading account AND statement of financial position: current assets

Norbert: Income statement for the year ending 31 March 2012

	£	£
Revenue		351 777
Less: cost of sales		
Opening inventory	20 762	
Add: purchases	255 255	
	276 017	
Less: closing inventory	(22 446)	
		(253 571)
Gross profit		98 206
Expenses		
Staff costs: storeman's wages	12 090	
Warehouse and office rental	10 509	
Insurance	3 909	
Electricity	2 821	
Water rates	1 226	
Security services	2 937	
Delivery expenses	8 630	
Administrative costs	3 810	
Part time admin assistant's wages	3 779	
Sundry expenses	1 406	
Bank charges	398	
		(51 515)
Net profit		46 691

Norbert: Statement of financial position at 31 March 2012

	£	£
ASSETS		
Non-current assets		
Delivery vehicle	5 020	
Non-current assets – warehouse and office	3 900	
		8 920
Current assets		
Inventory	22 446	
Trade receivables	36 623	
Cash	3 444	
		62 513
		71 433
CAPITAL AND LIABILITIES		
Capital		
Opening capital balance 1 April 2011	18 011	
Add: net profit for the year	46 691	
	64 702	
Less: drawings	(25 219)	
Closing capital balance 31 March 2012		39 483
Current liabilities		
Trade payables		31 950
		71 433

3.9 There will be relatively few users of Mary's accounting information. She herself, as the proprietor of the business, is likely to be the principal user. However, if she needs to borrow money at some point in the future, potential lenders are likely to be interested in seeing her financial statements in order to assess the ability of the business to make repayments of loans and to meet regular interest payments.

Tax collecting agencies such as HMRC will be interested in Mary's accounts as a basis for assessing the amount of income tax due on her profits. The only other group of users likely to have an interest in Mary's accounts is the supplier group. If other businesses supply goods to Mary on credit they are likely to be interested in the likelihood of being paid promptly.

3.10 Calculations and comparisons, of course, depend upon the businesses selected. Where there are differences between the businesses, these could be attributable to some of the following reasons:

1. Loss of market share which would reduce revenue but would not necessarily reduce all of the costs, leading to a drop in profit margins.
2. Exceptional costs, such as business reorganization. The narrative sections of the Annual Report may well describe and quantify such costs.
3. Especially good, or bad, performance in one part of the business. The notes to the financial statements in an Annual Report contain 'segment reporting' where a more detailed breakdown of figures such as revenue is given for different segments of the business. It should be possible to identify from this information those segments of the business that are performing particularly well or badly.
4. Information not fully comparable. Taking the example of Sainsbury's again, the revenue and profit information contains figures relating to Sainsbury's Bank. Other supermarket businesses without banking activities are not, therefore, fully comparable.

See if you can identify other reasons for differences between the figures from different businesses.

3.11 There is no standard answer to this question, because it all depends upon the company selected.

CHAPTER 15

2.1 Alexander

Cash kept in a tin in the factory office	ASSET
Oven	ASSET
Bank loan, repayable over 5 years	LIABILITY
Plastic packaging for biscuits	ASSET
Flour and sugar	ASSET
Amounts payable to supplier of dried fruit	LIABILITY

2.2 Amir

Value Added Tax (VAT) payable to HMRC	CURRENT LIABILITY
Office computer	NON- CURRENT ASSET
Amount due from Lomax plc for consultancy work carried out by Amir	CURRENT ASSET

Bank overdraft*	CURRENT LIABILITY
Bank loan to be repaid in 3 years' time	NON-CURRENT LIABILITY
Amount payable to stationery supplier	CURRENT LIABILITY

*Tutorial note: some businesses have an almost permanent bank overdraft, which they effectively use as long-term finance. However, a bank overdraft is technically 'repayable on demand' – that means that the bank is entitled to demand repayment at any time. Because of this, bank overdrafts are always classified as current liabilities in the business statement of financial position.

The accounting equation is:

ASSETS = CAPITAL + LIABILITIES

Applying the equation to the information given in the questions:

2.3

	£
ASSETS	83 000
LIABILITIES	36 500
CAPITAL (missing figure)	46 500
	83 000

Brian's capital is £46 500

2.4 In this case we turn the accounting equation around to find liabilities:

ASSETS – CAPITAL = LIABILITIES

	£
ASSETS	188 365
Less CAPITAL	(43 650)
= LIABILITIES	144 715

The liabilities in Basil's business total £144 715

2.5 In this question assets are split into non-current and current assets. However, the basic principle remains the same: total ASSETS = CAPITAL + LIABILITIES.

	£
Non-current assets	12 000
Plus Current assets	8 500
= ASSETS	20 500
LIABILITIES	17 300
CAPITAL (missing figure)	3 200
	20 500

Brenda's capital is £3200

2.6 In this question four pieces of information are given. However, the basic accounting equation still holds good.

Total assets = £27 000 (non-current assets) + £16 000 (current assets) = £43 000
Total liabilities = £12 000 (current liabilities) + £10 000 (non-current liabilities) = £22 000.
Brigitte's capital in the business is ASSETS – LIABILITIES, i.e. £43 000 – £22 000 = £21 000.

2.7 Bryony's capital is £34 340 (i.e. answer d).
Explanation:

Total assets = £35 840 (non-current assets) + £16 500 (current assets) = £52 340
Total liabilities = £12 000 (current liabilities) + £6 000 (non-current liabilities) = £18 000
Bryony's capital in the business is ASSETS – LIABILITIES, i.e. £52 340 – £18 000 = £34 340

2.8 Reminder: the accounting equation (ASSETS = CAPITAL + LIABILITIES) can be expressed as

ASSETS – LIABILITIES = CAPITAL
or
ASSETS – CAPITAL = LIABILITIES

ASSETS = £39 497 (Non-current assets) + £26 004 (Current assets) = £65 501
CAPITAL = £33 058

Total LIABILITIES therefore = £65 501 – £33 058 = £32 443
Total LIABILITIES = Current liabilities + Non-current liabilities
therefore:
£32 443 = £16 777 + Non-current liabilities.
Non-current liabilities therefore = £15 666

2.9 The missing figure for long-term liabilities is £9 276 (i.e. answer b)
Explanation:

Total ASSETS = £36 609 (Non-current assets) + £38 444 (Current assets) = £75 053
CAPITAL = £39 477
therefore:
Total LIABILITIES = £35 576 (£75 053 – £39 477)
Current liabilities are £26 300, therefore non-current liabilities = £9 276 (£35 576 – £26 300)

2.10 a) Total ASSETS = £18 337 (Non-current assets) + £12 018 (Inventory) + £365 (Trade receivables) + £63 (Cash) = £30 783
b) Total Current Assets = £12 018 (Inventory) + £365 (Trade receivables) + £63 (Cash) = £12 446
c) Total LIABILITIES = £3 686 (Bank overdraft) + £2 999 (Creditors) = £6 685
d) Callum's capital can be found by using the accounting equation:

£30 783 (Total ASSETS) – £6 685 (Total LIABILITIES) = £24 098.

2.11 Ciera's business: Statement of financial position at 31 December 2012

	£	£
ASSETS		
Non-current assets: Premises		39 000
Current assets		
Inventory	18 600	
Trade receivables	6 500	
Bank	13 000	
		38 100
		77 100
CAPITAL AND LIABILITIES		
Capital		29 600
Non-current liabilities		
Long-term loan		20 000
Current liabilities		
Trade payables	23 700	
Amounts owed to HMRC	3 800	
		27 500
		77 100

2.12 Explanation:

In transaction 1, Dan is using up £1500 of the amount in the business bank account, but at the same time is increasing non-current assets.

Increase non-current assets by £1500
Decrease bank account by £1500

In transaction 2, Dan is using up £3000 of the amount in the business bank account, but at the same time is decreasing trade payables.

Decrease trade payables by £3000
Decrease bank account by £3000

Dan's business: Statement of financial position at 3 May 2012

	£	£
ASSETS		
Non-current assets (30 000 + 1 500)		31 500
Current assets		
Inventory	15 000	
Trade payables	5 000	
Bank account (18 000 – 1 500 – 3 000)	13 500	
		33 500
		65 000
CAPITAL AND LIABILITIES		
Capital		52 000
Current liabilities		
Trade payables (16 000 – 3000)		13 000
Net assets		65 000

Note that the capital in the business has not changed at all between 1 and 3 May.

2.13 Ernest's business: Statement of financial position at 31 December

	£	£
ASSETS		
Non-current assets		
Gallery premises		68 000
Office equipment		2 260
		70 260
Current assets: cash at bank		18 600
		88 860
CAPITAL AND LIABILITIES		
Capital		70 700
Current liabilities		
Payable to artists	16 560	
Payable to printers	1 600	
		18 160
		88 860

Once Ernest has paid the artists and the printers (and, presumably, he will have to in the very near future) he will be left with only £440 in the bank. This will not leave him with enough money to pay the costs which are estimated at £4000 of the exhibition in January.

He may be able to obtain the goods and services needed to put on the exhibition on credit (that is, he will not pay for them straight away), but he would be taking the risk that the exhibition is a failure. If it produces no money, or less than the £4000 or so needed to cover essential costs, then Ernest will be in a very difficult position.

He may be able to borrow some money to put the business on a better footing. The only substantial asset the business owns is the art gallery premises. It may be possible to secure a mortgage loan on the property so as to obtain some much needed cash.

2.14 The business entity concept expresses the idea that the business exists separately from the person or people who have contributed capital to it. They are treated as separate entities, and the capital contribution made by the owner is treated as an obligation that the business owes.

2.15 The correct answer is b.

CHAPTER 16

6.1 Impact of transactions on Fergus's business:

	Impact on cash etc.	**Impact on profits**
Introduction of additional capital of £10 000 in cash.	Cash and capital are both increased by £10 000.	No impact on profits.
Purchase on credit of goods for resale for £8000.	Inventory and trade payables are both increased by £8000. There is no immediate impact on cash, but there will be an outflow of cash when the goods are paid for.	No immediate impact on profits. When the goods are sold, they will form part of cost of sales.

	Impact on cash etc.	**Impact on profits**
Payment received from customer for £1800.	The asset of trade receivables is reduced by £1800 and there is a corresponding increase (inflow of cash) in cash of £1800.	No impact on profits. The sale to which the trade receivable relates would already have been recorded.
Purchase of a new machine for use in the business.	There is an outflow of cash of £12 000 and non-current assets are increased by £12 000.	No immediate impact on profits, but there will be an additional depreciation charge for the year of £1200 (i.e. £12 000 over 10 years).
Sales returns of £1000 in exchange for a cash refund.	There is an outflow of cash of £1000.	Sales returns are increased by £1000. Sales returns are deducted from revenue in the income statement, and thus, reduce profit.
Drawings of £1300.	Cash and capital are both reduced by £1300.	There is no impact on profit. Effectively, Fergus is taking £1300 of his own capital out of the business.

6.2 Gilbert

	£
Non-current asset at cost	20 700
Less: accumulated depreciation	(18 210)
Carrying amount	2 490

The asset is sold for £1300; that is less than it is recorded at in the accounts. A loss is thus incurred on sale of £2490 – 1300 = £1190.

Profits are reduced by £1190 (statement no. 2), cash is increased by £1300 (statement no. 3) and non-current assets are reduced by £2490 (statement no. 5).

The correct answer, therefore, is b.

6.3 Gaston

The net cash inflow from operating activities in Gaston's business for the year ending 31 December 2012 is calculated as follows:

	£	£
Operating profit (36 790 – 763)		36 027
Add back: depreciation		4 585
		40 612
Less: Increase in inventory (37 669 – 31 470)	(6 199)	
Less: Increase in trade receivables (21 777 – 19 303)	(2 474)	
Add: Increase in trade payables (18 250 – 16 264)	1 986	
		(6 687)
Net cash flow from operating activities		33 925

The correct answer, therefore, is c.

6.4 **Spicer & Co: Statement of cash flows for the year ending 31 March 2012**

	£	£
Operating profit		76 496
Add back: depreciation		12 471
		88 967
Increase in inventory (40 747 – 36 600)	(4 147)	
Increase in trade receivables (50 661 – 48 730)	(1 931)	
Increase in trade payables (36 644 – 35 191)	1 453	
		(4 625)
Cash generated from operations		84 342
Interest paid		(230)
Net cash inflow from operating activities		84 112
Cash flows from investing activities		
Purchase of non-current assets (£175 630 – 128 547)	(47 083)	
Net cash outflow from investing activities		(47 083)
Cash flows from financing activities		
Capital returned to owner (drawings)	(45 800)	
Net cash inflow from financing activities		(45 800)
Net decrease in cash		(8 771)
Cash at beginning of period		7 423
Cash at end of period – overdraft		(1 348)

CHAPTER 17

7.1 It is true that directors take complete responsibility for the preparation of accounts, but they do not have to actually prepare the accounts themselves. They may delegate the preparation to others, but the directors take ultimate responsibility for ensuring that the accounts present a true and fair view, and that they are filed on time. It is not a criminal offence to produce accounts that fail to present a true and fair view. However, directors can be subject to criminal sanctions for failing to prepare and file accounts, and they may be guilty of a criminal offence if it can be proven that they have deliberately defrauded creditors.

Statements 2 and 4 are, therefore, correct, so the answer is b)

7.2 Bayliss Chandler Limited has 40 000 shares in issue (£20 000/50p). Ambrose owns 10% of the issued capital, i.e. 4000 shares. He is entitled to a dividend of 6p per share:

4000 × 6p = £240.

The correct answer, therefore, is c.

7.3 A holding of 8000 shares in Peachey plc is equivalent to a nominal value of 8000 × 25p = £2000. The total dividend payable for the year is 10% of nominal value, therefore the holder of 8000 shares will receive 10% × £2000 = £200, half on 31 March 2012 and half on 30 September 2012.

At 31 March 2012 Carina owns all 8000 shares and will receive £100 in dividend.

At 30 September 2012 Carina owns 4000 of the shares and her sister Cathy owns 4000. Therefore, they share the dividend, receiving £50 each.

In total for the year, Carina receives £150 in dividend and Cathy receives £50.

The correct answer, therefore, is d.

7.4 Butterthwaite plc

80 000 ordinary shares × 5p per share =	£4 000
Preference dividend for 2012:	
£20 000 × 6%	1 200
Arrears of preference dividend for 2011	1 200
Total	£6 400

The correct answer, therefore, is c.

7.5 Solar Bubble plc

Workings

1 Cost of sales

Opening inventory	51 240
Add: purchases	603 493
	654 733
Less: closing inventory	(57 210)
Cost of sales	£597 523

2 Selling and distribution costs

As stated in the list of balances	80 714
Add: accrued commission	6 000
	£86 714

3 Administrative expenses

As stated in the list of balances	73 959
Less: prepaid insurance	(1 270)
	£72 689

4 Finance costs

Interest payable as stated in list of balances	1 977
Preference dividend (£10 000 × 8%)	8 000
	£9 977

Solar Bubble plc: Draft income statement for the year ending 31 January 2013

	£
Revenue	975 420
Cost of sales (working 1)	(597 523)
Gross profit	377 897
Selling and distribution costs (working 2)	(86 714)
Administrative expenses (working 3)	(72 689)
	218 494
Finance costs (working 4)	(9 977)
Profit before tax	208 517
Tax on profit	(60 625)
Profit for the year	147 892

7.6 Brighton Magnets Limited

Workings

1 Administrative expenses

	£
Secretarial costs	51 498
Electricity (admin. office)	12 491
Office rental	42 704
Administration office – telephone charges	6 964
Depreciation of office computer equipment	8 390
Office manager's salary	21 704
Directors' remuneration	59 200
Other administrative expenses	36 075
	239 026

2 Selling and distribution costs

	£
Salespersons' salaries	64 299
Delivery van depreciation	12 000
Other selling and distribution costs	5 911
Salespersons' commission	12 270
Delivery van expenses	24 470
	118 950

Note: it is often a matter of judgement as to how expenses are allocated between selling and distribution cost and administrative expenses.

3 Tangible non-current assets: property, plant and equipment

	£
Factory and plant at carrying amount	2 518 000
Delivery vans at carrying amount	120 000
Office equipment at carrying amount	151 020
	2 789 020

4 Other payables

	£
Taxation	216 470

Brighton Magnets Limited: Income statement for the year ending 31 August 2012

	£
Revenue	3 796 842
Cost of sales	(2 712 350)
Gross profit	1 084 492
Selling and distribution costs (working 2)	(118 950)
Administrative expenses (working 1)	(239 026)
Other operating income	12 900
Operating profit	739 416
Interest receivable and similar income	644
Interest payable and similar charges	(1 207)
	£
Profit before tax	738 853
Tax on profit	(216 470)
Profit for the year	522 383

Note: this income statement contains an extra line, for the sub-total of operating profit. This line does not appear in IAS 1 *Presentation of financial statements*, but it is quite often found in practice. It is quite permissible to provide additional information in financial statements, over and above the information that is absolutely required by law or by regulations such as international standards.

Brighton Magnets Limited: Statement of changes in equity for the year ended 31 August 2012

	Share capital	Retained earnings	Total equity
	£	£	£
At 1 September 2011	800 000	1 597 172	2 397 172
Profit for the year		522 383	522 383
Dividend		(40 000)	(40 000)
At 31 August 2012	800 000	2 079 555	2 879 555

Brighton Magnets Limited: Statement of financial position at 31 August 2012

ASSETS

Non-current assets

Property, plant and equipment (working 4)	2 789 020

Current assets		
Inventories	186 420	
Trade receivables	321 706	
Cash at bank	18 290	
		526 416
		3 315 436
CAPITAL AND LIABILITIES		
Equity		
Share capital		800 000
Retained earnings		2 079 555
		2 879 555
Current liabilities		
Trade payables	219 411	
Other payables: taxation	216 470	
		435 881
		3 315 436

7.7 Statement 1 is false: listed companies are not obliged to produce a social responsibility report as part of their annual report
Statement 2 is true: consolidated financial statements do bring together the results and the assets and liabilities of all group companies

Statement 3 is true: compliance with the Combined Code is compulsory for all listed companies.
Statement 4 is false: listed company regulation is handled by the Financial Services Authority (although until recently it was handled by the London Stock Exchange)

Statements 2 and 3 are correct, therefore the correct answer is b.

7.8 Many people think that essentially there has been no change to the duties of directors as a result of CA 2006. However, the Act does contain one provision (section 172) which requires that directors should act in a way that they consider would be most likely to promote the success of the company for the benefit of its shareholders, but also having regard to the interests of other groups such as employees, customers and suppliers. This change to the law was controversial with some people claiming that it meant that directors' duties were significantly extended. However, others say that if directors comply with the guidance in the list of duties then they will have fulfilled their responsibility to shareholders and to other groups.

Opinions vary about whether or not the role of directors should be broader, and whether their responsibility should be only to shareholders or also to other groups of people. Those who think directors should take a broader responsibility point to the fact that large companies such as the FTSE 100 and/or multinational businesses have an enormous influence on the economies in which they operate. Therefore it is only reasonable to expect directors to take a wide range of stakeholders into account when making decisions. Others would argue that a company's only responsibility is to make money for the people and organizations who invest in it. Any broader social responsibilities belong to other bodies such as governments and charities.

7.9 UK accounting standards are gradually losing their importance in the UK as more companies adopt international accounting standards. Since 2005 listed companies have been obliged to use international accounting standards. Unlisted companies can choose which set of standards to use – both conventions are acceptable in company law (CA 2006).

CHAPTER 18

9.1 Pre-tax return on equity:

$$\frac{\text{Profit after interest and before tax}}{\text{Equity}} = \frac{267.8}{2\ 290}$$
$$= 11.7\%$$

The correct answer, therefore, is d)

9.2 Post-tax return on equity:

$$\frac{\text{Profit after interest and tax}}{\text{Equity}} = \frac{189.8}{2\ 290}$$
$$= 8.2\%$$

The correct answer, therefore, is b.

9.3 Return on capital employed:

$$\frac{\text{Profit before interest and tax}}{\text{Equity} + \text{long-term borrowings}} = \frac{302.8}{2\ 290 + 350}$$
$$= 11.5\%$$

The correct answer, therefore, is b.

9.4 The pre-tax return on shareholders' funds is calculated as:

$$\frac{\text{Profit before tax and after interest}}{\text{Equity}}$$

For each company:

Ambit Limited	**Bolsover Limited**	**Carcan Limited**	**Delphic Limited**
$\frac{803.6}{80.0 + 4550.0} \times 100$	$\frac{540.8}{95.0 + 3881.0} \times 100$	$\frac{575.8}{86.0 + 3928.0} \times 100$	$\frac{855.4}{60.0 + 7000.0} \times 100$
= 17.4%	= 13.6%	= 14.3%	= 12.1%

The company with the highest return is Ambit Limited, and so the correct answer, therefore, is a.

9.5 Trixie Stores Limited

Total current assets = 18 370 + 24 100 + 70 = £42 540
Total current liabilities = 15 450 + 6 400 = £21 850

$$\text{Current ratio} = \text{Current ratio} = \frac{\text{Current assets}}{\text{Current liabilities}}$$
$$= \frac{42\ 540}{21\ 850} = 1.95:1$$

The correct answer, therefore, is a.

9.6 Trimester Tinker Limited

Current assets = 108 770 + 94 300 + 1 600 = £204 670
'Quick' assets = 94 300 + 1 600 = 95 900
Current liabilities = 110 650

$$\text{Current ratio} = \frac{204\ 670}{110\ 650} = 1.85{:}1$$

$$\text{Quick ratio} = \frac{95\ 900}{110\ 650} = 0.87{:}1$$

Trimester Tinker's current ratio of 1.85:1 is higher than the industry average of 1.62:1
Trimester Tinker's quick ratio of 0.87:1 is lower than the industry average of 0.93:1
The correct answer, therefore, is b.

9.7 Upwood Sickert Limited
Non-current asset turnover is calculated as follows:

$$\frac{\text{Revenue}}{\text{Non-current assets}}$$

The correct figure to take for non-current assets is carrying amount, i.e. £170 000 + 59 985 = £229 985.

$$\frac{686\ 430}{229\ 985} = 2.98$$

The correct answer, therefore, is d.

9.8 Sole trader

Opening inventory	405 000
Closing inventory	405 000 + 10% = 445 500

$$\text{Average inventory for the year: } \frac{£405\ 000 + 445\ 500}{2} = £425\ 250$$

Inventory turnover in days:

$$\frac{425\ 250}{1\ 506\ 700} \times 365 \text{ days} = 103.0 \text{ days.}$$

9.9 Only credit sales are taken into account when calculating the trade receivables turnover ratio.

Credit sales for the year: £1 703 698 × 70%= £1 192 589

Trade receivables turnover ratio:

$$\frac{218\ 603}{1\ 703\ 698} \times 365 \text{ days} = 46.8 \text{ days}$$

The correct answer, therefore, is a.

9.10 Winger Whalley Limited

1 The absence of the credit controller on sick leave is likely to result in a slowing up of trade receivables recovery. Many trade receivables will be paid on time as a matter of routine, but some always need chasing. Unless a credit controller is chasing this latter group for payment, they will delay or defer settling their debts. This is a valid reason.
2 An increase of 4% in revenue is not likely to make any difference to the collection of debts. A very large increase might put pressure on administrative systems, but 4% is not likely to matter.

3 Early settlement discounts should have the opposite effect: trade receivables should pay up more quickly in order to take advantage of the settlement discount.
4 It is important to state the company's terms on the invoice stationery. If this is not done new and occasional customers will simply not know the terms of trade, and may be inclined to take longer to pay. Other customers may use the absence of stated terms as an excuse to take longer to pay.

Reasons 1 and 4 could be valid explanations. The correct answer, therefore, is c.

9.11 The calculation of the trade payables turnover period ratio should include only purchases made on credit.

Purchases made on credit = 90% × £1 952 278 = £1 757 050

Trade payables turnover in days:

$$\frac{206\ 460}{1\ 757\ 050} \times 365 \text{ days} = 42.9 \text{ days}$$

The correct answer, therefore, is a.

9.12 Waldo Wolff – dividend per share

$$\frac{\text{Dividend}}{\text{Number of shares in issue}} = \frac{300\ 000}{6\ 000\ 000}$$
$$= 5\text{p per share}$$

The correct answer, therefore, is b.

9.13 Dividend cover ratio

$$\frac{\text{Earnings after tax attributable to ordinary shareholders}}{\text{Dividend}}$$
$$= \frac{1\ 131\ 400}{300\ 000} = 3.77$$

The correct answer, therefore, is a.

9.14 Earnings per share

$$\frac{\text{Earnings after tax attributable to ordinary shareholders}}{\text{Number of shares in issue}}$$
$$= \frac{1\ 131\ 400}{600\ 000} = 18.86\text{p per share}$$

The correct answer, therefore, is a.

9.15 Market capitalization is the share price × the number of shares in issue.

£3.11 × 6 000 000 = £18 660 000

9.16 Wilson Streep plc

First, calculate earnings per share:

$$\frac{\text{Earnings attributable to ordinary shareholders}}{\text{Number of shares in issue}}$$
$$= \frac{750\ 090}{3\ 300\ 000} = 22.73\text{p}$$

P/E ratio = price divided by earnings per share:

$$\text{Price per share} = \frac{\text{market capitalization}}{\text{number of shares}} = \frac{6\ 303\ 000}{3\ 300\ 000} = £1.91$$

$$\frac{\text{Price}}{\text{Earnings per share}} = \frac{191\text{p}}{22.73\text{p}} = 8.4$$

The correct answer, therefore, is c.

9.17 Brazier Barkiss Limited

i) Gearing ratio

$$\frac{\text{Debt}}{\text{Equity}} = \frac{2\ 000\ 000}{3\ 739\ 400} = 53.4\%$$

ii) Interest cover

$$\frac{\text{Profit before interest and tax}}{\text{Interest}}$$

$$= \frac{646\ 750}{200\ 000}$$

$$= 3.23 \text{ times.}$$

9.18 **Report to the directors of The Cuttlefish Biscuit Corporation Limited**

Gross profit margin for Cuttlefish is better than the industry average, but net profit margin is worse. This suggests that the business is incurring higher costs on average, such as administration, selling and marketing costs, than its competitors. There may be good reasons in the short-term why this should be so, but if business costs continue at a relatively high level the directors may wish to consider a range of possible cost reductions. In the meantime, it would be helpful to examine costs in detail to identify areas where savings are possible.

The trade receivables turnover ratio shows that Cuttlefish collects its receivables more quickly than average in the industry. Given that most businesses will automatically take 30 days credit, 36 days is very good. There may be room for some improvement, however, and the directors may wish to consider, for example, introducing discounts for early settlement if they have not already done so.

Inventory turnover is slightly worse than the industry average. It may be advisable to look more closely at the level of inventory held in the business and look for ways of managing inventory more efficiently.

On average the industry takes a lot longer to pay trade payables than Cuttlefish. 31.4 days would usually be considered a low turnover ratio where the industry trading terms are settlement within 30 days. The directors might consider extending this period by a few days; it would release some cash into the operating cycle, and could probably be done without endangering relationships with suppliers.

Cuttlefish's gearing ratio is low, compared to others. No particular action is recommended on this point, but if directors are looking for long-term finance for business expansion, they should bear in mind that the business is not currently regarded as highly geared. Further long-term loans, within reasonable limits, would therefore be an option for consideration.

Generally, Cuttlefish appears to be doing well compared to industry averages.

9.19 Confidential report to the board of Cryer Roussillon Limited

Executive summary:

The implementation of the range of new strategies has been very successful. The company is now more profitable than it was a year ago, and its statement of financial position is healthy. The company should now concentrate on consolidating its position, and should seek to expand revenue volume.

Note: The appendix to this report sets out a set of relevant ratio calculations.

Detailed report:

The company's revenue has dropped by almost 2% since last year. However, gross profit has improved by almost 24%, and the gross profit margin is now 41.3% compared to only 32.7% in 2011. The company's strategy of pursuing higher margin revenue appears to have paid off. It should now concentrate on increasing revenue volume in those higher margin products. Operating expenses appear to be well under control; some effective cost-cutting appears to have taken place in 2012.

The company has made a major investment in non-current assets: carrying amount has increased by 88% in the year. It is possible that the benefits to be obtained from these assets have not fed through into revenue volumes and profits yet. The non-current asset efficiency ratio is notably poorer in 2012 but could be expected to improve in 2013 as the assets are utilized throughout the whole year.

Liquidity is not a problem. Liquidity ratios in both 2011 and 2012 are good, and the amount of cash at bank has increased very substantially. The directors' decision not to propose a dividend has helped, and means that spare cash is now available for extra investment.

Inventory turnover has worsened to 43 days (from 37.5 in 2011). The company must ensure that it is not building up too much inventory, and controls in this area may need further attention. Trade receivables, on the other hand, appear to be better controlled in 2012: trade receivables turnover has reduced, and appears to be at a quite satisfactory level.

The company has taken on long-term debt resulting in a relatively modest level of gearing. The level of gearing does not appear to be a cause for any concern at the moment.

Appendix

	2012	**2011**
Performance		
Gross profit margin	$\frac{85\ 272}{206\ 470} \times 100 = 41.3\%$	$\frac{68\ 830}{210\ 619} \times 100 = 32.7\%$
Operating profit margin	$\frac{43\ 813}{206\ 470} \times 100 = 21.2\%$	$\frac{21\ 220}{210\ 619} \times 100 = 10.1\%$
Return on shareholders' funds	$\frac{40\ 813}{129\ 783} \times 100 = 31.4\%$	$\frac{21\ 220}{97\ 070} \times 100 = 21.8\%$
Liquidity		
Current ratio	$\frac{45\ 763}{15\ 470} = 2.96$	$\frac{44\ 610}{16\ 290} = 2.74$
Quick ratio	$\frac{20\ 693 + 10\ 792}{15\ 470} = 2.04$	$\frac{29\ 420 + 640}{16\ 290} = 1.85$
Efficiency		
Non-current assets turnover	$\frac{206\ 470}{129\ 490} = 1.59$	$\frac{210\ 619}{68\ 750} = 3.06$

Inventory turnover (days)	$\frac{14\ 278}{121\ 198} \times 365 = 43.0$	$\frac{14\ 550}{141\ 789} \times 365 = 37.5$
Trade receivables turnover (days)	$\frac{20\ 693}{206\ 470} \times 365 = 36.6$	$\frac{29\ 420}{210\ 619} \times 365 = 50.1$
Gearing		
Debt/equity	$\frac{30\ 000}{129\ 783} = 23.1\%$	Nil

9.20 *Tesco plc*

Report on the performance of Tesco plc in 2009

Between 2008 and 2009 Tesco increased its revenue, gross profit and operating profit by double figure percentages, a very impressive performance. Profit before and after tax also increased, although the increases were less impressive at this level, suggesting perhaps that there has been a relatively large increase in finance costs. Examination of the actual income statement, rather than the extracts given, would help to confirm this suggestion.

Gross profit margin has increased slightly, but operating profit margin is the same, and both pre-tax and post-tax net profit margins have fallen. The figures suggest that operating costs are firmly under control. It would be interesting to know whether revenue increases had occurred because of increased prices, or increases in the volume of goods sold, or expansion into new stores (or a combination of all of these factors). Further examination of the Annual Report would provide relevant information.

Earnings per share has increased, which is likely to please shareholders.

In summary, Tesco has produced a very strong performance in 2009.

Appendix: accounting ratio calculations

	2009	2008
Gross profit margin	7.76%	7.67%
Operating profit margin	5.90%	5.90%
Net profit margin (before tax)	5.43%	5.93%
Net profit margin (after tax)	3.99%	4.5%
Percentage increases over previous year:		
Revenue	14.86%	
Gross profit	16.20%	
Operating profit	14.87%	
Profit before tax	5.39%	
Profit after tax	1.69%	
Earnings per share	2.04%	

GLOSSARY

APPENDIX – GLOSSARY OF INTERNATIONAL ACCOUNTING TERMINOLOGY AND THE UK EQUIVALENT

International	UK
Statement of financial position	Balance sheet
Income statement	Profit and loss account
Revenue	Sales (or turnover)
Finance costs	Interest
Non-current assets	Fixed assets
Property	Land and buildings
Inventory (or inventories)	Stock
Trade receivables	Debtors
Trade payables	Creditors

Note: although, as listed above, there are some significant differences in terminology, many terms are identical, for example, current assets, current liabilities, cost of sales.

INDEX